Dynamics in the History of Religions between Asia and Europe

Dynamics in the History of Religions

VOLUME 1

Dynamics in the History of Religions between Asia and Europe

Encounters, Notions, and Comparative Perspectives

Edited by

Volkhard Krech
Marion Steinicke

BRILL

LEIDEN • BOSTON
2012

This book is printed on acid-free paper.

ISSN 1878-8106
ISBN 978 90 04 18500 5 (hardback)
ISBN 978 90 04 22535 0 (e-book)

FSC www.fsc.org MIX Paper from responsible sources FSC® C004472

PRINTED BY DRUKKERIJ WILCO B.V. - AMERSFOORT, THE NETHERLANDS

CONTENTS

PART TWO

CONTACTS BETWEEN THE MAJOR RELIGIOUS TRADITIONS DURING THEIR EXPANSION

PART THREE

THE NOTION OF RELIGION AND RELIGIOUS SEMANTICS IN A CROSS-CULTURAL PERSPECTIVE

PART FOUR

RELIGION IN THE AGE OF GLOBALIZATION

MULTI-MEDIA PERFORMANCE

INTRODUCTION

Marion Steinicke

This volume documents the opening conference of the Interdisciplinary Consortium for Research in the Humanities "Dynamics in the History of Religions between Asia and Europe", which took place from 15 to 17 October 2008 in the Ruhr University Bochum's conference centre. The Bochum consortium is the result of an initiative by Prof. Dr Volkhard Krech, who submitted a corresponding bid to the German Federal Ministry of Education and Research. This bid was approved in November 2007. By April 2008 the consortium was already able to start work. It is thus one of the first of the now ten consortia of this funding format, which is designed to create a "free space" for outstanding scholars specifically for their interdisciplinary research by exempting them from other university commitments. Overall, the funding from the Federal Ministry of Education and Research aims to intensify the work in humanities disciplines and raise the profile of their achievements nationally and internationally. Thanks to interdisciplinary topics, whose study provides a sound theoretical basis and at the same time is empirically and analytically differentiated, the consortia are intended to bolster interdisciplinary cooperation at universities and thus contribute to the further development of methodology in the humanities. To support this initiative, up to ten visiting scholars from around the world can be invited annually to take part in a one-year research stay. Beyond this, the project has the medium and long-term aim of fostering an intense exchange and sustained cooperation with foreign research institutions.

In honour of the late philologist, literature scholar and philosopher Käte Hamburger, who passed away in 1992, the Interdisciplinary Consortia for Research in the Humanities were renamed the "Käte Hamburger" Consortia in 2010. Käte Hamburger is one of the most significant 20th century German scholars in the humanities. Her work "Die Logik der Dichtung" (The Logic of Literature), published in 1957, is considered a standard reference work for interdisciplinary narratology. During her lifetime, the author examined overarching questions of philosophy, aesthetics and the history of literature, notably the relationships between literature and ethics, development trends in contemporary theatre and the new medium of film and – at a time in which this was considered reprehensible rather than desirable in academic circles – always went beyond the confines of the individual specialist disciplines. As a staunch humanist and child of the Enlightenment, she countered the dehumanisation of Western culture and a political mystification of the "German fate" – popular for a long time as a way of relieving the burden of the past – with objective, historically backed and at the same time sophisticated analyses. Due to anti-Semitic tendencies and gender-specific scepticism before and after the Second World War, which Käte Hamburger spent in Swedish exile, the Jewess born in Germany was never able to establish herself at a German University. She nonetheless untiringly continued her research. Her name reminds us that excellent research was often only possible outside of institutional and political sponsorship, and perhaps even still is, but that we should all strive to prevent scholarship in the humanities being pushed to the margins of society where the necessary space and room for critical questions can be bought only at the price of endangering one's livelihood.

***

The Käte Hamburger Consortium "Dynamics in the History of Religions between Asia and Europe" firmly sees itself as a community of learning in which different knowledge and subject cultures develop innovative approaches for culturally comparative research on religion through exchange and confrontation. Thanks to broad and enthusiastic interest at the Ruhr University, a multitude of disciplines are represented in the Bochum consortium; alongside religious studies and sociology of religion, this includes European history disciplines, classical philology, Protestant and Catholic theology, Jewish studies, Islamic studies, Chinese studies, Korean studies and Japanese studies. The work of the consortium is divided into four 'research fields', each of which focus on one aspect of religious dynamics and reflect upon their synchronic and diachronic mutations through the exchange with the three other working groups. The research fields serve as organisational units for the consortium's work and also determined the structure of the sections of the opening conference as well as how the contributions in this publication are arranged. The four sections of the volume – "The Formation of the Major Religious Traditions through Inter-Religious Contact", "Contacts between the Major Religious Traditions during their Expansion", "The Notion of Religion and Religious Semantics in a Cross-Cultural Perspective" and "Religion in the Age of Globalization" – are conceived as a temporary framework; in a type of comparative test arrangement, they also form grid squares, into which the respective different data, material findings and text analyses, but especially the diachronic and synchronic phenomenon of religious contacts prominent in this context would then have to be entered as temporal and spatial coordinates, in order to verify the usefulness of the methodological framework and potentially modify it in line with the research findings.

Like the work of the consortium as a whole, the discussion at the opening conference focussed on investigations into dynamics in the history of religions specifically between Asia and Europe, with particular accent on the "between". The preposition, which separates, connects, delimits and includes equally, indeed was and is at the heart of our research interest as an indicator of key synchronic and diachronic relationships. From this perspective the "History of Religions" emerges primarily as a history of this "between". The research interest thus lies less in the history – or the histories – of the individual religions, for instance of the so-called world religions, from the point of view of their identity as perceived by themselves or others – their dogmatics, their religious practices, their social linkages – and instead in their politico-geographical, cultural and discursive contacts and conflicts with other religious traditions, these being seen not as marginal but rather central factors in their formation and canonisation processes. Whilst still bearing in mind the known and scientifically widespread specificities of the world religions, the consortium's interest lies mainly in these inter and intra-religious cross-over areas of reciprocal perception and denial, delimitation and inclusion, tolerance and rejection. This also, and not least, means cross-over areas in religious studies sub-disciplines, issues and methodological approaches. The subtitle "Encounters, Notions, and Comparative Perspectives" has a two-fold meaning. The encounters, notions and comparisons figure on the one hand in relation to the objects of inquiry, the different networks of religious traditions, and, on the other hand, in relation to their varying scientific perception, handling and systematisation. This also addresses the methodologically diverging forms of approximation and reflection upon religion and religious semantics in religious studies themselves.

With the expectation of provoking different and possibly controversial reactions, positions and answers, the opening conference of the new research consortium put forward for discussion the central question of areas of contact and conflict of religious networks of tradition as the nucleus and corrective mechanism of their processes of emergence, development and transformation. This question sets the tone for the entire work programme of the consortium. The contributions, material findings and deliberations on the dynamics of religious contacts presented at the conference repeatedly addressed the further question of impetuses and resistances, of the alternating processes of attraction and repulsion within the contact and conflict areas of religious networks of tradition. For this reason, the annual conferences 2010 and 2011, building on the consortium's opening conference, will above all deal with the modalities and models of religious attraction and repulsion.

***

In his "Preliminary Considerations on Aspects of a Research Programme", Volkhard Krech developed the central theme of the consortium – the *dynamics* in the history of religions – in a multi-dimensional scenario, which first confronts past and present transformations in the religious field with synchronic and diachronic perspectives of their exploration, and second, archaic and current religious phenomena with issues relating to how they are observed and described. Actions and actors of the religious field, which become visible as specific objects of inquiry through changing illumination against the backdrop of the broad panorama of religious traditions, appear to be inextricably linked to one another in this relational network and in turn dependent on one another. In Krech's history of science retrospective, central problems faced by religious studies are redefined as tasks. This includes the re-evaluation and reassessment of various hermeneutic approaches and the possibility of further developing them into hermeneutics specific to religious studies, which on the one hand could contribute to a special understanding of religious contacts and their role in the emergence and dissemination of religious traditions, and on the other hand should prove useful as a set of instruments for finding methodology: to clarify the understanding of religious semantics and religious practice, of labelling of self and other, of object language and metalanguage. In this context, it would be important at the same time – with reference to linguistic, visual and media sciences – to develop interpretative procedures which could help to perceive and interpret different religious manifestations and their specific semiotics – liturgy, ritual, iconography, narrative – especially in terms of their reciprocal relationship. The foundation of such interdisciplinary religious studies research is the closest possible linking of material research, systematisation, theory building and critical self-reflection of scientific notions, positions and perspectives. The innovative interest in relational aspects, in dynamics, emergences, factors of fascination and attractors therefore does not mean replacing traditional research interests or subjects, but first and foremost expanding our field of vision, and furthermore, an additional complementary focus on factors which to date have received little attention but could be significant in the formation of religious traditions. The intention is thus for religious studies research to engage in a self-contemplation and re-contemplation of its own methods and aims which complement those of the social and cultural sciences, whilst at the same time differing from them. What Volkhard Krech describes in his prolegomenon is literally intended to be a work in progress: not a list of results targets which must be achieved sooner or later, but elements of a preliminary structure, building blocks on the threshold of an expansive restructuring which can only be tested, accepted or rejected in practice itself and thus in the course of the deconstruction and reconstruction, to consequently be used as a cornerstone or completely refashioned.

The opening conference "Dynamics in the History of Religions between Asia and Europe" was the equivalent to laying the foundation stone. The identical title shared by the consortium and the conference – and these proceedings – can certainly be understood as a declaration of the central theme of our work. The conference intended to present the principal ideas, the thematic spectrum, the key aims and intentions of the consortium to a broad academic audience and to discuss them with select specialist colleagues from a wide range of disciplines. The aim was to collect critical, controversial and constructive opinions; it was an invitation to engage in an initial as well as future exchange of ideas, and in a continuing and long-term collaboration with the consortium. The concept behind the conference was experimental in line with the consortium's work itself. The aim was to present the open and unbiased research of the consortium *in actu* through a debate between top scholars which was as controversial as possible; the contrasting and complementary alternation between presentation and response seemed to be the best way here to encourage a lively and manifold discussion. In four sections corresponding to the "research fields" and thus the four focal areas of the consortium's work, and in this publication introduced by the respective coordinator for the research field in question, the intention was for important representatives of the different disciplines from all over the world to have the opportunity to take the floor so as to initiate the consortium's future internal and external discussion with the largest possible range of religious studies research areas and approaches. A special lecture by Jan Assmann and a thematic multi-media performance by Heinz Georg Held with the support of actors Sarah Franke, Marieke Kregel and Andreas Potulski as well as a round table on "Studying Dynamics in the History of Religions: Convergences and Divergences", which reflected the spontaneous and definitely contradictory impressions left by the conference, provided the frame to the opening conference.

Irrespective of the diverging approaches and the specialist choice of subject of the different speakers or the various different examples cited and methodological deliberations, as this volume documents, it was and is possible to observe interesting correlations. In Section I, *The Formation of the Major Religious Traditions through Inter-Religious Contact,* there was general consensus supporting the thesis that at least the religious traditions widely referred to as "world religions" as a result of their dogmatic sustainability and their historically persistent forces of initial and long-term attraction, emerge from a host of different religious impetuses, trends and reactions and develop largely in contact and through constant confrontation with other religious networks. Victor H. Mair – *Religious Formations and Intercultural Contacts in Early China* – for instance, is of the opinion that just like the three "major doctrines", which are seen as the specifically Chinese product (Confucianism), as an import (Buddhism) and as the combination of indigenous and exogenous elements (Taoism), the religious field of the prehistoric and early-classical period is also characterised in the Chinese cultural area by a heterogeneous ensemble of Sinitic and non-Sinitic elements, and was later to condense into a "core segment of the Sinitic value system". Heiner Roetz – *A Comment on Victor H. Mair's "Religious Formations and Intercultural Contacts in Early China"* – also reaffirms this opinion in his response, but at the same time underlines the difficulty in pinpointing the different influences and areas of contact, which in this case would encompass the whole of Central Asia. In his attempt to sketch the most important line of religious development in Ancient India as a web of religious traditions, Patrick Olivelle – *Kings, Ascetics, and Brahmins: The Socio-Political*

Context of Ancient Indian Religions – emphasises that "the dynamic nature of all human realities, including religion, is often hidden behind (…) essentialized designations", as they exist for instance in the – for religious studies – questionable categories of "Hinduism" or "Buddhism", and thus calls for methodology to be rethought in order for the complex processes of religious development to be able to be properly identified and described. Adding to this in his response, *Did the Buddha Emerge from a Brahmanic Environment?*, Jens Schlieter goes on to discuss the question as to whether and to what extent the early development phase of Buddhism should largely be understood as a dynamic process of the confrontation with, and delimitation from, Brahmanic traditions. In the historical review of the emergence and development of religious studies, *The History of Religions as a Subversive Discipline: Comparing Judaism, Christianity and Islam* by Guy Stroumsa, who backdates "the first non-theological attempts to think comparatively about Christianity, Judaism, and Islam" as "a new science" in "the Age of Reason", methodological reflections again loom largest. The proposal is an exemplary process, in which above all the "transformative moments of religions" would be analysed. Following on from this, Sarah Stroumsa – *Whirlpool Effects and Religious Studies. A Response to Guy G. Stroumsa* – highlights above all the dynamic aspects of the preceding deliberations on how best to approach religions, which at the same time need to be understood as "living structures"; the "whirlpool-effect of the flows of religious ideas" in her opinion requires a "multifocal approach".

In relation to the *Contacts between the Major Religious Traditions during their Expansion* in Section II, there was broad agreement that specific dynamics emerge from the different religious contacts, which furthermore need to be defined or typologised more precisely, and make a significant contribution to the formation and expansion, the dogmatics and ritual practices, to the political and historical self-understanding of religious networks of tradition. Michael Lecker's contribution, *The Jewish Reaction to the Islamic Conquests*, which first recalls the influence of Jewish converts on the early development of Islam, outlines the living conditions of the Jews from cultural and religious perspectives after the Islamic conquests had subjugated the majority of the Jewish world. In addition to repressive aspects, he highlights the new possibility which then arose for Judaism to spread religious or religious-philosophical ideas in Arabic: "Intellectuals continuing a time-old tradition of learning used the Arabic language in Hebrew script to create some of the cornerstones of the Jewish library for all time". Building on this, in his response, *Christian Reactions to Muslim Conquests (1st–3rd Centuries AH; 7th–9th Centuries AD)*, John Tolan underlines the new-found equality of the Christian communities previously oppressed by the orthodoxy (Nestorians, Jacobites, Copts, Melkites). In his view, the interpretation in the theology of history of Arab rule being seen as the realm of the Antichrist and thus as a sign of the last days, is typical. Eun-jeung Lee, in her contribution, *Intercultural Encounter in the History of Political Thought. Christian Wolff, Chŏng Yag-yong and Matteo Ricci,* explains the thesis of a reciprocal influence between Europe and Eastern Asia in the age of the Enlightenment and not just in the area of philosophy but also in the religious field or in that admittedly not uncontroversial border area between philosophy and religion, which is paraphrased using the term "Confucianism". At the centre of her presentation is the role of cultural and religious mediator played by the Jesuits, which in his *Jesuit Mission in Korean Studies. A Response to Eun-jeung Lee*, Michael Lackner also emphasises, though qualifying it too: it is "evident that the Jesuits' cultural transfer of Chinese ideas was restricted to political ideas and to principles of moral philosophy, leaving aside any dangerous religious contamination". Stephen C. Berkwitz – *The Expansion of Buddhism in South and Southeast Asia* – points to the intra-religious diversity of Buddhism itself, whose "expansion was not the movement of a single tradition from a single source (…), it comprised different streams that flowed into a larger current (…) that assumed distinctive features in different locations", though the respective local traditions can also be expected to have played a role. Accordingly, in his response, Sven Bretfeld underlines the prevalence of internal confrontations and the formation of diverging schools during the formative phase of Buddhism in Sri Lanka and South-East Asia.

The problem discussed in Section III, *The Notion of Religion and Religious Semantics in a Cross-Cultural Perspective,* of a non-uniform, not clearly defined or definable notion of religion, which partly reflects the diversity of the religious traditions itself, was generally seen less as an obstacle and more as a reciprocal impetus for the comparative exploration of religious dynamics. In his introductory lecture, *World Religions and the Theory of the Axial Age*, Jan Assmann had developed fundamental deliberations on the way in which the so-called world religions are observed historically. Building on Karl Jaspers' controversial concept of the "Axial Age" and with reference to history of precisely this idea of a radical turning point in history which can be traced back all the way into antiquity; the question arises as to what extent the metaphor of the Axial and the attempts to put world history data into concrete form with the help of a network can be helpful in grasping religious concepts, in describing religious dynamics and for a more precise concept of the notion of religion itself. The suggestion of considering not one, but several axial ages, which could be profiled more accurately within certain cultural spaces in their specific dynamics and interactions, was combined by Assmann with a deterritorial view of world religions, which differentiates these from "traditional cult religions such as ancient Egypt" axially through the textualisation of their traditions: "World religions are disembedded from any territorial, political, ethnical and cultural frames, they (…) found a new kind of transnational and transcultural identity by forming a new form of memory which is canonised scripture".

The controversial nature for the religious studies discourse of the notion of religion developed from the occidental tradition of scripture itself seems beyond doubt amongst the authors of the proceedings, but is evaluated differently. Robert Ford Campany – *Chinese History and Writing about "Religion(s)": Reflections at a Crossroads* – cites the example of Western Chinese studies to illustrate the interaction between the notion of religion and cultural perception. In the description of "some ways in which the modern Western notion of 'religion' shapes our writing of Chinese history and some ways in which Chinese history might impact our use of the notion of 'religion'", it also becomes clear how we perceive another culture, and the way it is handled in discourse can permanently influence both it and the culture of the observer. In his critical *Response to Robert Campany's "Chinese History and Writing about 'Religion(s)'"*, Russell T. McCutcheon puts forward taxonomic analysis itself for discussion, whilst underlining, however, the interrelatedness of the methodological instruments and of the cultural dispositions of the historical scholar, and consequently the inevitable interdependence between observer, methods and heuristics: "The tools that we use to name and thereby divide up and organize the world (such tools as the categories of "the past", "the nation", "tradition", "meaning", and "religion") are our tools and are thus no less a part of the world of human doings than the subjects we study by using them". Tim H. Barrett and Francesca Tarocco, whose contribution *Terminology and Religious Identity: Buddhism and the Genealogy of the Term 'Zongjiao'* investigates the common present-day attempts to translate into Chinese the Western concept of religion as *zongjiao*, notably in "the discourse of policies and of academic analyses" and in particular with regard to Buddhism, also seem to recognise in the lack of a corresponding term for "religion" in the Chinese cultural area, or in the terminological shift which becomes apparent as a result, above all a task for scholarship and thus a key opportunity, namely to learn a fundamentally different religious logic and to understand it in its own relationality: "unless we understand the subtly different ways in which speakers of other languages see the world, rather than imagine that they have inadequately assimilated a normative discourse embodied in European languages, we will not have advanced the academic cause of studying what we term religion very far at all". Ronald M. Davidson – *Canon and Identity in Indian Esoteric Buddhism as the Confluence of Culture* – points once again to the connection between the notion of religion and canon building and emphasises in this the – in contrast for instance to Judaism and Christianity – fundamentally open nature of the religious body of texts in Indian Buddhism, which thus has opened up for itself the opportunity "to appropriate materials from others so that the canon would be continuously renewed by influences from subcultures within India and, eventually, outside of it". Adding to this, Markus Zehnder – *The Christian Canon in a Comparative Perspective. A Response to Ronald M. Davidson* – investigates the dynamic negotiation process which characterises the emergence of the Christian canon – and thus at the same time the Christian concept of a religious canon – both in the formation phase and the further development of Christianity, for instance with regard to its denominational splitting, in which "the inclusion or exclusion of some apocryphical texts in the canon of the Old Testament" plays a prominent role. The contribution by Muhammad Aslam Syed, entitled *The Christian-Muslim Encounters on the Question of Jihad*, deals with a highly controversial issue of religious terms, which "has been one of the most debated in the polemical as well as academic discourses between Muslims and Christians" and is characterised by historical misunderstandings and political abuse on both sides. The notion Jihad and the problems defining it, which, as the author underscores, given its charged nature historically and currently, requires above all a philologically exact analysis as well as inter-religious hermeneutics, can serve as an example that in the context of religious fields of contact and conflict, it is far less a question of unearthing an equivalent in another language and far more of processes of understanding and comparing, of distorting and denying, of reflection, negotiation and agreement with regard to the ideas and concepts associated with the term.

Common ground was also found in Section IV, *Religion in the Age of Globalization*, at least with regard to the double thesis that – regardless of a continuing secularisation process – the formation of a global religious field can be seen as an indication of the continued significance of religious traditions and thus of the relevance of studies of it both from a historical as well as contemporary perspective. The interplay between religious self-understanding and political self-assertion, on the one hand, between territorial limitation to a particular local field of conflict and a far-reaching global network thanks to diasporas is the subject of the case study by Peter Schalk, *On Resilience and Defiance of the Īḻamtamiḻ Resistance Movement in a Transnational Diaspora*, which puts the religious studies interest once again into concrete terms through a current social and political set of problems; characteristically, here too, the politicisation of religious terms and concepts – which has developed over time – plays a key role. With his thesis that concepts such as "religion" and "globalisation" are direct components of the very constructs of reality that they describe, Peter Beyer – *Observing Religion in a Globalized World: Late Twentieth-Century Transformations* – returns once again to the prior discussion of the notion of religion: "What is perhaps most characteristic is that the old search for unity in matters religious is almost entirely gone, and that, if anything the diversity becomes so self-evident as to dissolve the object of inquiry". In this context, too, the role-play between the observer and the act of observing is seen in its historical and cultural dependency as an integral part of the development termed "globalization" and thus as a relational process. On the current premise of a comparative "global view", Ian Reader – *Religion in a Globalized World: Comments and Responses* – speaks in favour of concentrating on the direct observation of contemporary religious practice and thus on placing more weight on research "centred on the contemporary era and on social scientific methods of study" compared to the philological examination of religious texts and the reconstruction of traditions derived from this, as "dynamics of the history of religion" are only imaginable through the linking of historic hermeneutics and sociological methodology, of text analyses and case studies on religion in practice. The call not to use the term "secularisation" as an element of an overarching heuristic explanatory model is picked up by José Casanova in *Religion, Secularization, and Sacralization* and modified into an appeal for doing away with the dichotomy "religious-secular" in the sense of a constant grid of definable opposites, which given new "global" developments, he believes, have to be transferred to flexible constellations: "It is an open empirical question, which should be the central focus of a comparative-historical sociology of religion, how these three ongoing global processes of secularisation, sacralisation, and religious denominationalism are mutually interrelated in different civilizations, sometimes symbiotically as in the fusions of religious nationalisms, or in the religious defence of human rights, but often antagonistically as in the violent conflicts between the sacred secular immanent norms (of individual life and freedom) and transcendent theistic norms".

***

Research into inter-religious and intra-religious dynamics means interdisciplinary zones of contact and conflict should also receive particular attention: both with regard to the mediation processes between religious and other cultural fields as well as with regard to the media which play a crucial role in them, and which, last but not least, in a methodological exchange could enable new and, to date, untested modalities of approximation, description and realisation. A multi-media performance devised by Heinz Georg Held was designed to illustrate this connection at the start of the opening conference through a revue of religiously encoded iconographies, architectures and visual works as well as texts and musical examples, and appears here as an epilogue. The thematic focus was a contact and conflict zone exemplary of the work of the consortium, described as the "Near" or "Middle East" or simply as the "Orient", depending on how its position is defined spatially or politically. From different points of view and with the help of various types of media, the performance simultaneously made reference to the history of interactive East-West (self) perceptions, their fascination, their heuristic energies and their intellectual dynamics. The contribution in this volume, entitled *Reflecting Religious Dynamics. Echoes from Ancient East-West Encounters*, is an abridged version of the manuscript which – for obvious reasons – contains only sporadic visual and musical stage directions.

On behalf of all members of the consortium I would like to thank the German Federal Ministry of Education and Research and in particular the foster fathers and mothers of the funding format of the

"Käte Hamburger Kolleg" for establishing and funding this "free space for the humanities" which made the work of the consortium and in turn also this conference and its publication possible.

The proceedings of the conference are being published by the Brill Verlag as the start of a series of publications which will be devoted to the multi-faceted aspects of "Dynamics in the History of Religions" in individual studies and anthologies under the Bochum consortium's programme title. In my capacity as co-editor of the series, I would like to thank Maarten Frieswijk and Wendy Shamir from Brill Verlag as well as the members of the advisory board for their support in developing the concept and setting up the series as well as for their patience whilst "taking our first steps".

Many have contributed to the success of this volume. Kate Waldie took on the translation and linguistic editing of several contributions which were not written by English native speakers with her typical professionalism and dependability. My express thanks go to her here for the good collaboration which began with the opening conference in 2008 and continues to this day.

Jan Wenke took great care in typesetting this volume. Amongst the student assistants, who are indispensable for the smooth running of the consortium in general, the three "S"s – Sung-yeon Cho, Sandra Frühauf and Sarah Kayß – in particular deserve praise for their struggle with the many diacritics involved in the formatting, completion of bibliographical data and compilation of index lists for the individual essays; Florian Pölking and Yu-jin Lee continued this difficult task, bringing it to a successful conclusion. Thomas Jurczyk contributed to the layout of the cover with his designs, whilst Sami Abu Rayyan successfully saved the hard drives from collapse. I thank them all for their committed support.

It is the quality of the contributions that make a conference. The collection of texts in this volume, which are introduced and acknowledged by the respective research field coordinators – Marion Eggert, Nikolas Jaspert, Lucian Hölscher and Peter Wick – brought crucial new impetus to the consortium's work and stimulated further thought. On behalf of the whole Bochum research consortium my thanks therefore go above all to the authors who were open to joining us in the experiment of a "dynamic history of religions".

DYNAMICS IN THE HISTORY OF RELIGIONS – PRELIMINARY CONSIDERATIONS ON ASPECTS OF A RESEARCH PROGRAMME[1]

Volkhard Krech

A. Introduction

Interdisciplinary research on religion has been facing a host of challenges for some time now; let me name the following examples explicitly:

- First, deconstructivist insights have now made it clear that it is not possible to speak of religious traditions such as "Christianity" or "Buddhism" as single, clearly-defined entities. The difficulty of clearly separating different traditions from each other is one that research on religion shares with cultural studies in general. Just as it is difficult to define individual, distinct formations, there is also the issue of how one can describe and analyse cultural transfer in general and religious transfer in particular.
- Second, research on religion, whether from a historical or present-day perspective, has lost sight of its subject due to epistemological considerations as well as post-colonial studies. If one does not wish to advocate scientism and only adopt a Western-modern perspective, it is difficult to identify "religion" in empiricism.
- Third, it is true that there has been reflection on the concept of religion for a long time in the field of religious studies. However the question of "the" history of religion – of its unity within the different processes taking place individually at different times – i. e. the question of what constitutes the religious field (in the meaning of

[1] Many colleagues contributed to these considerations. I would like to thank them all, in particular Jörg Plassen and Knut Martin Stünkel for their comments and observations and Kathryn Waldie for the English translation.

Pierre Bourdieu[2]) in time and space and what holds it together in its innermost core, is condemned to the margins. Admittedly, there is no lack of grand "history of religions" blueprints. But they tend to lag behind the state of research in cultural studies empirically and methodically. The approaches of *cultural flow* and those of a *global history* should be mentioned in particular here.

The task of providing contributions to a global history of religions from comparative cultural perspectives is what the "International Consortium for Research in the Humanities" has been tackling since April 2008 on the topic of "Dynamics in the History of Religions between Asia and Europe", funded by the German Federal Ministry of Education and Research at the Ruhr-Universität Bochum. The following text presents some of the aspects of the research programme and a report of the work in progress.

1. *Scholarly Deconstructivism and Essentialism in the History of Religions*

Now that deconstructivist paradigms have become second nature in the humanities and social sciences, it is clear that neither individual religions and their traditions nor the religious field as a whole can be understood as substantially defined units. The deconstructivist perspective is expressed in the works of Talal Asad, for example, who states: "My argument is that there cannot be a universal definition of religion, not only because its constituent elements and relationships are historically specific, but because that definition is itself the historical product of discursive processes."[3]

With deconstructivist perspectives, however, the subject risks being blurred or even disappearing (for example as the dissolution of religion in "culture"[4]). Furthermore, with an exaggerated deconstructivism it is not possible to fully understand why religious traditions – though

[2] Cf. Pierre Bourdieu, *Das religiöse Feld: Texte zur Ökonomie des Heilsgeschehens*, Konstanz: Universitätsverlag Konstanz 2000. Translated from French by Andreas Pfeuffer.

[3] Talal Asad, "The Construction of Religion as an Anthropological Category", in: Michael Lambek (ed.), *A Reader in the Anthropology of Religion*, Malden: Wiley-Blackwell 2001, 114–132, here: 116.

[4] Cf. Hans G. Kippenberg/Kocku von Stuckrad, *Einführung in die Religionswissenschaft: Gegenstände und Begriffe*, München: Beck 2003, and Russell T. McCutcheon, *Studying Religion: An Introduction*, London et al.: Equinox Publishing 2007.

construed – in practice are nonetheless perceived as distinct entities; on the level of object language one repeatedly sees essentialism in the history of religions. Consequently, I assume that both the individual religious traditions and the religious field as a whole are not merely something invented by scholars, but that the scientific attributions made are based at least in some way on religious practice. What we call religion is not just a purely academic invention (as, for example, MacCutcheon concluded[5]), although the academic perspective is involved in the formation of its subject. Religion has its own dynamics and at the same time is involved with and related to other circumstances. As a result, it is important to look for correspondences between the object-linguistic labelling of Self and Other as well as the metalinguistic reconstruction. From this starting point, one can explore the question of how traditions arise and condense and how a transfer between traditions occurs.

2. *Structuralism and Hermeneutics/Form and Process*

The issue of identifying cultural units in general and religious ones in particular also entails the need to communicate structuralist with hermeneutic perspectives. In the social and natural sciences the duality of structure and process has been a subject of discussion for some time now. Of course, practice does not just consist of processes nor can everything be broken down scientifically into processes. On the other hand, structures should be understood as "slices of time" representing the transition from one state to another. They refer back to past states and contain predispositions for changed states. And finally, a glance at structures also entails hermeneutic questions as to how structures are to be identified. The complex relationship between structure and process is exactly what a research programme on "Dynamics in the History of Religions" must take into account.

B. Dynamics of Religions and the History of Religious Studies

It is not down to chance that the majority of the theories on the history of religions with a view to a global history date from the end of

[5] Cf. Russell T. McCutcheon, *Manufacturing Religion: The Discourse of "sui generis" Religion and the Politics of nostalgia*, New York: Oxford University Press 1997.

the 19th and beginning of the 20th century. The 19th century was not only a century of transformation, but also one of increased reflection about this transformation. Granted, there have been societal and cultural changes at all times and in all cultures. However, as a result of the technical and industrial progress and the huge increase in knowledge, the change in the 19th century accelerated in the Western societies to a then unprecedented degree. This dynamic led people to a heightened realisation of the contingency of their own situation and thus created the need for orientation.

The acceleration of societal development had consequences for both the mode and subject of scholarship. First, with the transition to the 19th century one sees an empiricalisation of science.[6] Due to the wealth of material in philological and historical knowledge, the spatially conceived classification systems were abandoned in favour of the temporalisation of complex stocks of information.[7] Second, the scientific subjects themselves were historicised, and this interest in history resulted *inter alia* in historicism and its specific problems.[8] History was not relevant merely as a reservoir of historical facts. People wondered about the historical reasons for their own situation, and that is why history had to be able to provide information on the circumstances of emergence and development.

Research on religion reacted to the wealth of material which had accumulated within a short space of time and to the increase in reflection on societal and cultural change first by constructing stages in the history of religions – from pre-animism to animism to the development of myths ("heroic age") and polytheistic systems to the formation of monotheistic religions. In doing so, it was influenced by the theory of evolution, which, however, was often extended to include teleological aspects. Second, the temporal classification led to the invention of so-called world religions.[9] Third, the intention was to identify "the elementary forms of religious life" – as the title of Émile

---

[6] Cf. Wolf Lepenies, *Das Ende der Naturgeschichte: Wandel kultureller Selbstverständlichkeiten in den Wissenschaften des 18. und 19. Jahrhunderts*, Frankfurt a. M.: Hanser 1978, 16ff, and Herbert Schnädelbach, *Philosophie in Deutschland 1831–1933*, Frankfurt a. M.: suhrkamp 1983, 114ff.

[7] Cf. Lepenies, *Das Ende der Naturgeschichte*, 18f.

[8] Cf. Friedrich Jaeger/Jörn Rüsen, *Geschichte des Historismus*, München: C. H. Beck 1992.

[9] Cf. Tomoko Masuzawa, *The Invention of World Religions: Or, How European Universalism was Preserved in the Language of Pluralism*, Chicago: University of Chicago Press 2005.

Durkheim's later principal work on religion as a social phenomenon reads. In addition to the sacred, the taboo, and the totem, the ritual became the most prominent "nucleus" of the religious (analogous, so to speak, to the cell in biology).

One of the consequences was the strange circumstance that the history of religions was divided into separate, elementary parts and arranged temporally, without however doing away with the idea of unified major religious systems ("world religions"). Granted, there was no lack of detailed studies, but from a paradigmatic point of view, the gaping hole was not filled. One of the few exceptions to this is the *Religionsgeschichtliche Schule.* Its members identified separate motifs and motif complexes in the history of religions and reconstructed their transfer. The concept of syncretism was indeed based on false premises – apart from its normative connotations and implications – to the extent that it assumes the homogeneity of what is combined. The research by the *Religionsgeschichtliche Schule* does however go in the right direction. The formation of religious systems is always connected with the amalgamation of elements from different traditions. This process is the general rule; purification and homogenisation are secondary phenomena. This point of view is adopted increasingly in more recent religious historiography[10], and the research programme intends to actively promote this by synthesising different approaches.

C. Conceptional Considerations

The starting premise is that the religious field is formed and reproduced by actors who develop an awareness of what is called religion. Following on from Pierre Bourdieu, we do not have a material, essentialist understanding of the concept "religious field". Rather, one of the constituents of the religious field is the intra and inter-religious controversy surrounding its content and boundaries. The possibilities for scientific meta-language to come into play within object-language can be found wherever actors perceive each other through contact and are stimulated to reflect to a greater degree. Research on religion can

[10] Cf. the seminal article by Wilfred Cantwell Smith, "Traditions in contact and change: towards a history of religion in the singular", in: Peter J. B. Slater/Donald Wiebe (eds.), *Traditions in Contact and Change: Selected Proceedings of the XIVth Congress of the International Association for the History of Religions*, Waterloo (Ontario): International Association for the History of Religions 1983, 1–23.

pick up on this reflection, admittedly without neglecting the categorical difference between the inner and outer perspective. In order to generate connections between object and meta-language, we are proceeding pragmatically, that is abductively, alternating between deduction and induction. Here, research on religion is required to make use of the division of labour – whilst the social sciences and philosophy tend to be responsible for the formation of hypotheses, the historical sciences and philologies have the task of testing proposed hypotheses against the matter of enquiry to determine if they are true or false. The hypotheses developed are carefully held up against the material to be proven or disproved. If proven false, the hypotheses are modified or formulated anew and held up against the material yet again to be proven either false or true and so on and so forth.

When alternating between deduction and induction, we do however face the much discussed problem of the hermeneutic circle. How can we identify concepts (and the compressed semantics and social circumstances expressed within them) as "religious", without presupposing and imposing a universal concept of religion? Conversely, if we were to apply a (for instance, modern and Western) concept of religion to historical material in different religious cultures, we would already know what was supposed to have developed differently diachronically and interculturally, and a process with an open research outcome would be undermined.[11] This hermeneutic circle is also, *inter alia*, the background for the tension between material research and systematisation. According to Immanuel Kant, the following is true: Notions and concepts without empiricism are empty, empiricism without concepts is blind. The circle cannot be broken in principle (and presumably never once and for all), but only unfolded procedurally. In the best case scenario, it can be converted into an realisation spiral, in which we gain increasing or better insight, as we gradually revise our own suppositions for a better grasp of the material or prove them to be true by testing them against it.

In the research programme on "Dynamics in the History of Religions", the following three areas of tension form the basis for which a balance must be struck:

[11] This is perhaps one of the unique characteristics of intercultural research on religion. By contrast, an economic anthropologist, for example, has no problem with classifying both the trade in goods on the basis of cowrie shells and the use of credit cards as economic activities.

- First, we work in abductive alternation between the formation of hypotheses and the study of material.
- Second, we place importance on the sociology of knowledge connection between semantics and social structures.
- Third, we look for correspondences between object language in the history of religions and scientific metalanguage.

With regard to the relationship between object and metalanguage, the research programme is based on the following hypotheses:

1. Metalanguage can best correspond with religious-historical material and avoid a sterile scientism when it links in with the reflection abductively identified as religious, in which an object-linguistic awareness of the religious arises and is actively promoted.
2. The inner-religious reflection is always heightened when
   a) handed-down traditions become thematic, so compiled, reformed or rejected (diachronically stimulated religious reflection),
   b) condensed or condensing religious networks of traditions come into contact with others (synchronically stimulated religious reflection).

1. *Working Hypotheses for the Characterisation and Definition of Religion*

In order to avoid creating too many, possibly misleading, axiomatic presuppositions in the abductive alternation between deduction and induction, the research programme is based on the following, as formal and general possible assumptions. What is today described as religion arises and takes effect in the four fundamental dimensions of the dialectic processes between the psychological and the social:

- in knowledge, which provides orientation,
- in experiences, which generate evidence,
- in actions, which serve the planning, regulation and attainment of aims,
- in handling the relatedness to matter, which co-determine psychic and social developments.[12]

[12] The dimensions "knowledge", "experience", "materiality" and "actions" are to be conceptually developed in future work.

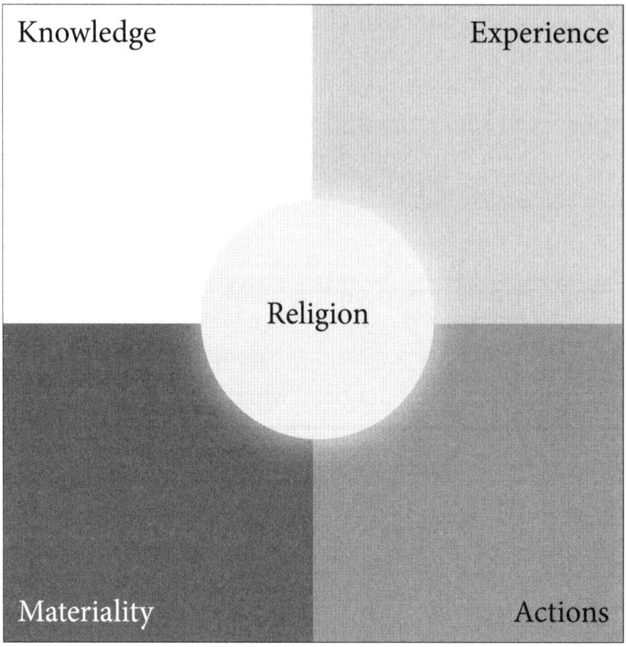

Fig. 1: The four dimensions of religion

In specific religious circumstances all four dimensions always have a bearing simultaneously. For example, actions can only take place on the basis of the knowledge available, and experiences generate knowledge. However, it makes sense analytically to examine the relationship of religion to each of these dimensions, in order to better grasp developments in each of the dimensions and thus, ultimately, to better understand how they interact.

Religion provides the dimensions of the dialectic processes between the psychological and the social – knowledge, experience, actions and the relationship to the material (also already coded and psychologically represented in social communication) – with a specific transcendental meaning and thus is a special form of dealing with contingency. A surplus value is thus attached to social and cultural circumstances, which they otherwise do not enjoy in other forms of treatment. The way in which the transcendental sense is specifically symbolised (temporally, spatially, materially, in terms of shaping actions and cognitions) depends on cultural conditions and is defined *in distinction* from other rationalities.

In order to identify (candidates for) basic religious concepts, from which a concept of religion can be abstracted, reflections on a hypothetical definition of religion are unavoidable. The following considerations are necessary in order to achieve a hypothetical and pragmatic (so not purely axiomatic) definition of religion which would need to be tested and proven or modified in an abductive process. In the course of the history of civilisations, different legitimisation and reassurance strategies are developed beyond biological, physical and practical evidence – for instance, bureaucratic procedures, in politics in the form of turning arbitrary power into rule or in economics in the form of the regulation of the satisfaction of needs through relations of production and trade etc. The legitimisation and reassurance method that I hypothetically identify as religion has to do with *reassurances by the ultimate authority*; with an *understanding on how to deal with what is considered unavailable and inescapable.* Religion establishes different ways of dealing with the unavailable.

To be able to identify religious communication, i. e. to distinguish it from other forms of communication, we must examine what makes it unique. This includes, first of all, the analytically reconstructed (or imposed) distinction between immanence and transcendence. Formally speaking, this distinction is at work in culture in general and in religion in particular – as transcendence of the second order. Both culture and religion are a matter of transcendence – not just, and indeed with regard to the history of religions mostly not at all in the sense of the "Christian-Western" (temporal and spatial) symbolisation of transcendence, but in a universal, modal and theory-of-experience sense, notably by indicating something which is not in the here and now of everyday consciousness, and also something which is not experienced as a genuine part of the Self. This corresponds more or less to what philosophical anthropology (especially Helmuth Plessner), social phenomenology (Alfred Schütz, Peter L. Berger and Thomas Luckmann) and the pragmatic theory of religion (Hans Joas) understand by "transcendence". On the basis of this understanding, many types of transcendence exist: in addition to religion, there is also history, sociality, (the awareness of alter ego), visions of ideal orders, future, dreams, surprising experiences and events, art as a whole etc. If one does not distinguish between the principle of transcendence as such and its religious forms, then everything outside of the direct experience of the here and now would be religious and all cats would be grey by night.[13]

I suggest therefore, that we distinguish the type of transcendental relationship we hypothetically call religion from other types as follows: religion has to do with the problem of how one can describe the transcendence *that cannot be represented in everyday experience* with immanent means, so how one can transform the unavailable into the available or the unsayable into the sayable.[14] This is of course a paradox and as such, cannot be sustained long term (this is something "mysticism", for instance, points out time and again). Accordingly, religion would have to completely evaporate, with the result that – at least as a social fact – it would no longer exist. Religion must, therefore, represent transcendence with immanent signs and in this way keep it in social communication.

It is out of this task that the necessarily tropical character of religious communication arises. It is founded, essentially, in the fact that the 'trans cendental' (the 'absent' – in whatever content form it may take) that religious communication is based on, itself cannot be communicated and therefore must be described using 'immanent' (known, 'present') means. In religious communication, circumstances (for instance, subjective experiences, which cannot not be communicated with established schemes of experience) which are considered new and different are made communicable by referring back to the familiar, so by translating the unfamiliar/unknown into something familiar/known.

Religious communication is characterised, furthermore, by its own typical alternation between "expansion and restriction".[15] On the one hand, religious communication generates sensory overloads due to its tropical character, which transcend the sense of everyday language and in doing so are largely stripped of defence and control through sensory perception and practical requirements. In order, however, to be communicable, understandable and acceptable, to function as a means of legitimisation and reassurance and thus be considered a 'social fact', its sensory overloads must be restricted. This happens

---

[13] This is the case, for example, with Luckmann's concept of "invisible religion"; however to an even greater extent in the adaptation of this theory.

[14] Cf., for example, the theological differentiation between apophatic and kataphatic.

[15] Niklas Luhmann, "Die Ausdifferenzierung der Religion", in: *Gesellschaftsstruktur und Semantik: Studien zur Wissenssoziologie der modernen Gesellschaft, Bd.* 3, *Niklas Luhmann*, Frankfurt a. M.: suhrkamp 1993, 259–357, here: 271ff.

- in socially regulated divination practices, through which certain situations (events, for instance), objects, times and places qualify as 'sacred',
- by fixing certain signs and how these are dealt with,
- by developing set language patterns (such as set phrases and language genres), myths, texts and compilations thereof (for instance, the Talmud, the Bible, and the Qur'an), ritual acts and religious ethics,
- and by addressing topics of everyday communication close to religious communication (such as biographical and collective situations of crisis and their resolution; the subject close to religion *par excellence* is death).

These types of restrictions to the sensory overloads of religious communication, through which a memory and traditions are formed at the same time, are a form of institutionalisation and can condense over the course of time. Paradoxically, these forms of restriction of religious communication, which are supposed to help deal with contingency, also allow contingency to become visible – other religious traditions do things differently, as becomes particularly clear in the contact between religions. Moreover, the restrictions are connected to a particular context and lead to set semantic rigidity, which at some stage or another is no longer compatible with societal and cultural developments and changed conditions of reception. For these reasons – and not least due to diachronic and synchronic religious contact – there are always semantic extensions of the sensory overloads with new (or amalgamated) signs, language patterns, visualisations and texts being formed. This extension can generate de-institutionalisation processes, but can also transform existing social forms or bring forth new ones (for instance, currents, groups, schools and movements [perceived as heterodox or heretical]).

2. *Distinction between Religious Communication and Sacralisation*

We cannot assume that at all times and in all places a state of social differentiation exists in which religion is a clearly distinguished sphere alongside others. Nonetheless, to open up possibilities for comparison, I suggest distinguishing between religious communication and sacralisation. Whatever is sacralised is already defined by another rationality (for instance, by political rule or the economic desire to own possessions), which, however, (for whatever reasons and which would need to be investigated in each individual case) is not sufficient or felt to be sufficient; therefore the politically, economically or however else it may happen to be defined object (for instance, an enthronement or a party convention) is additionally enriched with an aura of the unavailable and inescapable (ruler figures, for example, are considered legitimated by a god or charismatically inspired or even themselves divine). In religious communication, by contrast, which sets itself apart from other forms of communication, non-religious matters may be negotiated, but not in order to additionally *enrich* them with religious sense, but to *fill* them completely with religious sense. A political or economic rationality is converted into a religious one in this case. The religious unification of the distinction between transcendence and immanence is transcendence which must be described using immanent means. The unification of the distinction between transcendence and immanence in sacralisation processes, on the other hand, is immanence, which is made unavailable by referring to transcendence; in this respect one can describe sacralisation as immanent transcendence.

With regard to societal differentiation, sacralisation processes historically precede religious communication where an independent religious field has not (yet) formed, yet sacralisation and religious development run parallel – to this very day. Sacralisation is also always possible within religious communication. In the extreme case of religious communication, notably wherever instead of a reference structure the identity of transcendence and immanence is asserted,[16] a religious ideology can claim the oneness of the physical world and the Absolute (for instance: saṃsāra is nirvaṇā). The sacralised is related to religion in the same way that aesthetics are to art. The sacral is thus the blurred frontier and interface between religion and other spheres of society. This must be taken in to account historically and interculturally and has the advantage of not having to proceed schematically, but instead makes it possible to consider the categorical and the blurred (and their respective specific "negotiation" in space and time) equal-

[16] "Das Sakrale kondensiert gewissermaßen an der Grenze, die die Einheit der Unterscheidung von transzendent und immanent darstellt" (The sacred condenses to a certain extent at the nexus representing the unification of the distinction between transcendental and immanent) (Niklas Luhmann, *Die Religion der Gesellschaft*, Frankfurt a. M.: suhrkamp 2000, 82). Although meant differently, this situation is occasionally referred to in aesthetic literature as a "Realsymbol" (real or genuine symbol), cf. George Steiner, *Von realer Gegenwart: Hat unser Sprechen Inhalt?*, München et al.: Hanser 1990.

ly.[17] There is no gradual lineal, and certainly no teleological connection between the societal differentiation of religion and the process of sacralisation which would allow us to say that religion develops out of sacralisations. Alternating cycles are a far more plausible assumption.

Against the backdrop of these considerations, religion can be defined as follows as a working hypothesis: religion applies the two-valued distinction between transcendence and immanence (in which the positive value is either transcendence or immanence), and with this distinction it addresses how to deal with what is in principal seen as unavailable and inescapable in contrast to the available and disposable. The distinction between transcendence and immanence is presumed to be stable, but the specific content that the distinction between transcendence and immanence takes on varies diachronically and in intercultural comparison. These variations form the core of religious dynamics (diachronically and synchronically, inter-religiously and intra-religiously) and should be highlighted through empirical research.

3. *Interplay between Religious Semantics, Forms of Institutionalisation and Societal Structures*

At the beginning there was the history of religions. At least this is what the pansacrality thesis of the 19th century claims, according to which the starting point for social and cultural development was religion. This thesis continues to have an impact to this very day, but is increasingly problematic. Whatever one's position on the question of the "origin" of society and culture, from today's perspective at any rate, the history of religions cannot be examined in isolation and with regard only for the internal dynamics of religious ideas, as, for instance, religious studies did in their religious-phenomenological form.[18] The fact that religion is also determined in no small part by society is something that has been known since classical antiquity. The social and political function is stressed, for instance, in the presocratic "Fragment of the Critias"[19], by Polybios in his *Historiae*[20], by

---

[17] See also the comments on family resemblances on this.

[18] Cf., for instance, also Günter Lanczkowski, *Einführung in die Religionswissenschaft*, Darmstadt: Wissenschaftliche Buchgesellschaft 1980, 77, who sees religion as "ein unableitbares Urphänomen, eine Größe sui generis" (an underivable primary phenomenon, a sui generis factor).

[19] Diels/Kranz B25.

[20] *Historiae* VI, 56.6–12.

Cicero in *De natura deorum*[21] and by Livius in his treatise *Ab Urbe Condita.*[22] In the 17th and 18th century, a discourse critical towards religion then deliberately referred back to these texts seeking to legitimise a philosophical atheism using the argumentation figures of the antiquity.[23] Religion was exposed as an "instrument of domination". In this context, the theory of priest deception was popular, which traces go back to Herbert of Cherbury (1583–1648), the founder of the concept of *natural religion*.

One must distinguish between these critical discourses on religion and the scientific exploration of religious developments from socio-historical perspectives. Around the turn of the 20th century, Émile Durkheim, Max Weber, Ernst Troeltsch and Georg Simmel, referring back to various previous texts, began in a big way to look at the history of religions in relation to socio-historic developments. Today it is a banal fact that religious ideas do not appear out of thin air or "fall from the heavens".

The history of religions as well as social and societal history must therefore be seen in relation to each other and can only be differentiated analytically for heuristic purposes. The relationship between the history of religions and social history is not a one-way street, however. Historical materialism seems to have seen this in somewhat too simple a light. Its after-effects – admittedly stripped of its political verve – can still be observed to this day in the social sciences. All too often, religion is still seen as a merely ideological superstructure which conceals the political and economic interests as the "actual" historical force or, at least, is determined by these. The aforementioned classics in the sociology of religion saw things differently. To use the words of Georg Simmel, their aim was to build a floor under historic materialism. If one is to do justice to the complexity of socio-cultural reality, religious and social history must be seen in their reciprocal relationship: "Ohne das Verständnis des religiösen Wandels in der modernen Gesellschaft ist … eine verläßliche Sozialgeschichte nicht möglich" (without the

[21] *De natura deorum* I, 118.

[22] *Ab Urbe Condita* I, 19.4.

[23] Winfried Schröder meticulously incorporated existing clandestine literature produced in this context; cf. Winfried Schröder, *Ursprünge des Atheismus. Untersuchungen zur Metaphysik- und Religionskritik des 17. und 18. Jahrhunderts*, Stuttgart-Bad Cannstatt: Fromman Holzboog 1998. This radical criticism of religion was in turn given a positive spin by the positions listed in the following; cf. in this regard Jan Assmann, *Monotheismus als politische Theologie*, unpublished manuscript, Heidelberg 2001.

understanding of religious transformation in modern society … reliable social history is not possible).[24] For Max Weber, the relationship between ideas and interests was such that the latter were the actual historically effective powers, though the former set the course for successfully asserting interests;[25] in research, both can be either the dependent variable on one occasion or the independent variable the next. Just as the history of religions is shaped by socio-historical developments, social history is also determined by factors in the history of religion.

But beyond the interaction between religious and social history, there is a history of semantics with inner and extra-religious parts. In the study of history, approaches such as the history of ideas, concepts and meaning and discourse analysis have established themselves for this dimension.[26] With the Berlin religious philosopher Klaus Heinrich, one can add the history of fascination to the methodical arsenal as well. An analysis from the historical semantic perspective takes into account that semantics and condensed concepts change and in doing so are an expression of social and societal circumstances and shape them at the same time. When applied to the history of religions this means that religion and related concepts such as religiosity, piety, faith, mysticism, ritual and so on are thus part of a continuous process of reflection – both from outside with regard to the religious field and within religious self-description.

In terms of the practice of reflection as a whole, in the modern age, the sciences have taken over a large part of self-description in society. Our world views are significantly shaped by them, and this process is not without consequences for the history of religions either. Yet, like for the relationship between religious and social history, things are

---

[24] Wolfgang Schieder, "Religion in der Sozialgeschichte", in: Wolfgang Schieder/Volker Sellin (eds.), *Sozialgeschichte in Deutschland. Entwicklungen und Perspektiven im internationalen Zusammenhang*. Vol. III: *Soziales Verhalten und soziale Aktionsformen in der Geschichte*, Göttingen: Vandenhoeck & Ruprecht 1987, 9–31, here: 25.

[25] Cf. the following section in *Gesammelte Aufsätze zur Religionssoziologie*, vol. 1, Tübingen: Mohr Siebeck 1920, 252 (MWG I/19, p. 101): "Interessen (materielle und ideelle) nicht: Ideen, beherrschen unmittelbar das Handeln der Menschen. Aber: die 'Weltbilder', welche durch 'Ideen' geschaffen werden, haben sehr oft als Weichensteller die Bahnen bestimmt, in denen die Dynamik der Interessen das Handeln fortbewegte." (Not interests (material and ideal) but ideas directly dominate the actions of humans. But the "world views" which are created by "ideas" have, very often, as moving forces, defined the channels in which the dynamics of the interests pushed forward action)

[26] Cf., for instance, Hans Erich Bödeker (ed.), *Begriffsgeschichte, Diskursgeschichte, Metapherngeschichte*, Göttingen: Wallstein 2002.

not that straightforward here either. A considerable part of modern reflective practice and its condensed concepts is stimulated by the history of religions, and in terms of the history of motifs, in part even significantly shaped by religious topoi. In the case of the relationship of religious and general semantic history, differentiated for analytical purposes, we are also consequently dealing with interaction and interplay.

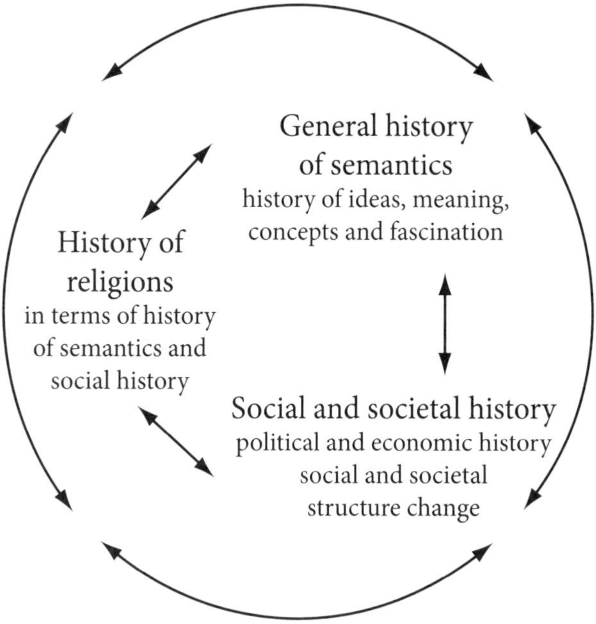

Fig. 2: The cycle of the history of religions, semantics, and society

In religious history, (both in terms of the history of semantics and social history), the general history of semantics and in social and societal history, we are dealing with three types of scientific perspectives on empiricism. With the approaches of Karl Mannheim, Ludwik Fleck, Robert Merton, Thomas Luckmann, Niklas Luhmann and others, we have a tool at our disposal to analyse these dependencies and thus even overcome them – the tool of the sociology of knowledge. In its most general form, it states that semantics (ideas, concepts, topoi) and the socio-cultural situations of what "carries" them (including interests and passion) are in a relationship of interdependence.[27] Against this backdrop, the relationship between the three scientific perspectives of the history of religions (both semantic and social history), general semantic history and social and societal history can be described in relation to the sociology of knowledge: religious semantics and reflection processes on the one hand and social and societal structural developments on the other are connected in a way in which they mutually influence each other. In sociology the question of the chronological sequence of semantic and societal-structural developments is currently a topic of discussion.[28] This debate is, as it were, the continuation of the dispute over the alternative of idealistic and materialistic perspectives. I believe this theoretical question, as my formulation "mutual influence" already indicates, to be futile, it is after all akin to the famous question of whether the chicken or the egg came first. Here, as always, what matters is in-depth empirical studies.

Furthermore, the relationship between two of the three perspectives can of course be communicated by the third, i. e. the relationship between religious and semantic history through social history, the relationship between social and semantic history through religious history as well as the relationship between religious and social history through the history of concepts as a condensation of semantic history. As the diagram above intends to illustrate, we are dealing with a dual-direction cycle.

Three – very rough – examples from the history of Christianity may serve to highlight the interplay between semantic and social history, in which the dynamics of religious history can be described:

[27] This correlation is already based on the analyses of Max Weber; cf. the following section in *Gesammelte Aufsätze zur Religionssoziologie*, cf. FN 3, p. 252 (MWG I/19, p. 101): "Interessen (materielle und ideelle) nicht: Ideen beherrschen unmittelbar das Handeln der Menschen. Aber: die 'Weltbilder', welche durch 'Ideen' geschaffen werden, haben sehr oft als Weichensteller die Bahnen bestimmt, in denen die Dynamik der Interessen das Handeln fortbewegte." (Not interests (material and ideal) but ideas directly dominate the actions of humans. But the "world views" which are created by "ideas" have, very often, as moving forces, defined the channels in which the dynamics of the interests pushed forward action.)

[28] Cf. e. g. Urs Stäheli, "Die Nachträglichkeit der Semantik – Zum Verhältnis von Sozialstruktur und Semantik", in: *Soziale Systeme* 4 (1998) H.2, 315–340.

Table 1: The interplay between semantic and social history

	Religious Semantic	Social and Societal Structure
Person	Divine vessel or tool	Individual as a social attributive category
Social form	Body of Christ	Church organisation or sects (in the meaning of Max Weber and Ernst Troeltsch)
Society	The rule of Christ as the Lord	Political, economic and cultural processes

4. *Dynamics in the History of Religions*

Often it is small stimuli that are at the beginning of momentous religious-historical processes, which trigger far-reaching effects. This leads to constructive and destructive impacts – which either accelerate or inhibit developments – and thus in turn to dynamics in the history of religions. Whatever the term dynamic means in the different sciences that make use of it, in the programme "Dynamics in the History of Religions" it is understood first of all as a description of the *occasionally self-escalating* interplay of production, reproduction and change of semantics and social structures. The term dynamics indicates an (inwardly and outwardly occurring) *intensified* development and change of semantics and social structures in the history of religions. In the process of the formation of social and societal structures, semantics become institutionally condensed. Conversely, established structures are continually relaxed, reshaped and occasionally dissolved by circulating semantics. With dynamics, the main focus is therefore on the interplay between structural condensation and diffusion under the conditions of cultural contact. The formation, reproduction, reform or renewal and transfer of traditions are special examples of this process.

The impacts include different configurations of traditions – such as their densification or diffusion caused by the way they refer to one another. Which direction the developments take and which configurations and re-figurations arise depend on the interplay of religious semantics, the carrier strata, individual actors, institutional frames, the communication media used and environmental conditions. The developments are given their directionality in the interplay of the respective inner logic of religious knowledge, religious experience, religious practices and the religious handling of material relatedness with the interests of the actors.

The currently most advanced approaches in modelling condensation and diffusion come from chaos theory, which investigates structure formation by identifying attractors.[29] Attractor models are now also being applied in social sciences.[30] Building on chaos research, we intend to investigate dynamics in the history of religions using attractors and how they interact in the contact between religions. The innovative aspect of using attractors lies in turning our focus towards endogenous factors within religious-historical dynamics. Granted, the focus on centripetal forces does not rule out an examination of exogenous (for instance political and economic) factors. But, while research on religion increasingly concentrates on socio-historical aspects of religious-historical development, the research programme "Dynamics in the History of Religions" examines the interdependencies between endogenous and exogenous factors as well as centrifugal and centripetal forces. The absorption of elements of a religion and amalgamation processes are usually just as much of an extra-religious as religious nature,[31] and religious ideas can just as equally be stimulated by political or economic developments as, vice-versa, political and economic structures by religious ideas. The analytical distinction between religious and historically endogenous and exogenous factors must also be protected against the danger of the reification of "religion" by paying attention to correspondences between the religious object-language and the scientific metalanguage. What is attributed categorically as religious depends on the degree of development of a religious consciousness identified in empirics which emerges in contrast to other societal rationalities.

In chaos theory and the theory of dynamic systems different sorts of attractors and their interplay have been identified; and this might be useful to be applied to the history of religions. Geometrically, an attractor can be a point, a curve, a manifold, or even a complex set

---

[29] Cf. Edward N. Lorenz, *The Essence of Chaos*, Seattle: CRC Press 2005.

[30] Cf., for example Ben Tamari, Conservation and Symmetry Laws and Stabilization Programs in Economics, Jerusalem: ecometry 1997.

[31] The formulation by Christoph Auffarth, that it is "nicht religiöse Bedürfnisse, die zur Übernahme einer Religion führen" (not religious needs that lead to the absorption of a religion), seems to be only one side of the story (cf. Christoph Auffarth, "Religio Migrans: Die 'Orientalischen Religionen' im Kontext antiker Religion. Ein theoretisches Modell", in: *Mediterranea* vol. IV (2007), 333–363, here: 334).

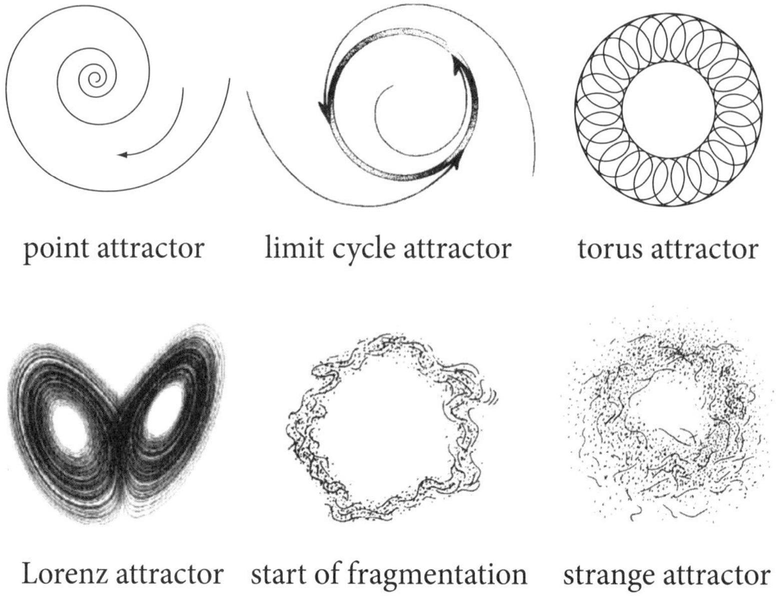

Fig. 3: Types of attractors

with a fractal structure known as a strange attractor. The most important types of attractors may be transferred to the history of religions so as to identify ways of attraction in the dynamics arising from religious contacts. The point attractor is structured by the process of punctualisation. Theoretically, any entity such as currents, groups, organizations, individuals, places, concepts, texts, images and other cultural artefacts might become an attractor in which other entities are strongly attached to each other. However, even an entity that functions as an attractor is situated in a broader process of attraction. This broader process might be described as a limit cycle attractor where two or more points construct a cycle, around which densification processes occur. If the directed circulation of a cycle attractor is slightly influenced by other forces, we might speak of a torus attractor in which the trajectories constitute a torus. If two limit cycle or torus attractors get in contact, we get the constellation of a so called Lorenz attractor. This constellation may lead to diffusion and then to a so called strange attractor – or to a torus respective a limit cycle or even a point attractor again. The direction depends on the proportion between centrifugal and centripetal forces. Thanks to the different attractor types and constellations used for heuristic purposes, religious tradition and identity formation processes can be investigated in the antagonistic field of densification, amalgamation, and diffusion. The heuristic advantage of the model-like transposition of attractor types onto dynamics in the history of religions is the ability to identify centrifugal and centripetal forces in the contact between religions.

As specific case studies for potential attractor constellations, the international consortium is currently discussing mystery and purity. The topic "mystery" starts with ancient mystery cults and extends the research on the religious-historical significance of "mystery" diachronically and interculturally, for instance to the history of hermetism and esotericism up to the present day. With the topic of "purity" we can assume that purity and the opposite concept of impurity are important categories in the history of religions which act as tools to order and categorize the world and, not least, to set one's own religious tradition apart from others. In the meantime, the research consortium has distinguished between a physical, cultic, social, moral and a cognitive dimension in purity concepts, whose mutual dependence on one another in being investigated comparatively.

Religious contacts are being reconstructed on the basis of the attractor types outlined above, with regard to attraction, diffusion and repulsion. As possible attractors, we have started discussing and materially testing the following:

- the constitution of cult communities and practices; here the formation of *rituals* plays a central role, which the physical incorporation and expression of religious ideas is connected to. "Classic" cases here are the comunities and practices of sacrifice and communion, but also, for instance, circumcision and prayer rituals. In connection with ritual acts there is the question of how "holy places" and "holy times" (calender, Sabbath, feasts, etc.) form and act as attractors. The topic of ritual acts is not exactly new, but in the context of looking at attractors in the densification process of religious networks of traditions could be hiding something innovative, it could, for instance, clarify how commitment and communitisation are generated as an important mode of the physical expression and incorporation of the condensation of traditions;
- the implementation of particularly condensed *signs* (Menorah, Cross, Crescent, etc.);

- the development of narratives which pool different semantic motifs, set phrases and *dogmas* (monotheism, messianism, creed, etc.);
- social forms (group, order, monastery or convent, school, lineage, church, etc.);
- ethics governing the conduct of life;
- religious "services" (such as charity work).

With the question of the relationship between the different attractors, we can assume that the route from one attractor to another is by no means (only) that – as usually assumed – of cult practices via texts finally arriving at doctrines and dogmas. Text rituals, for example, are an illustration of the opposite path (this question addresses the debates on the relationship between ritual and myth – from Robertson Smith via the Cambridge School to Sigmund Mowinckel).

Then we started relating the attractor types to each other by analysing the different ways of using signs. To this end, we applied semiotic deliberations borrowing first and foremost from Charles Sanders Peirce. With this approach, I assume that forms of expression are just as bound to perception as to particular contexts of expression. The relationship between signified and signifier is threefold, as the interpretant attributes (thirdness) a quality (firstness) to an object (secondness). For the issue of attractiveness, this means that: x is attractive for y under the conditions or perspectives of z. In contrast to Saussure and structuralism, Peirce therefore distinguishes between various possibilities of semiotic formation of meaning: *icons* as signs which express something through their quality, *indices* as signs which are in a spatial-temporal relationship to their object and *symbols* as conventional signs.

In order to construct a typology of attractors I suggest working with different criteria, namely the anthropological and the sensual dimension, aspects of sign usage (according to Charles Sanders Pierce) and different media:

- Anthropological Dimension:
  - acting;
  - experience, subjectivity;
  - handling of material relatedness;
  - knowledge: Identity through reflection and interpretation.

- Sensual Dimension:
  - haptic and sensorimotor dimension;
  - visual dimension;
  - auditory dimension;
  - olfactory dimension.
- Aspects of sign usage (according to the semiotics of Charles Sanders Peirce):
  - indexicality (external reference to space and time);
  - iconicity (quality of signs, perception);
  - symbolicity (combination of perception and external reference).
- Media:
  - action;
  - images;
  - texts;
  - music;
  - architecture.

On the basis of the combination of these (and further) criteria, a typology of attractors can be constructed.

Table 2: A Typology of attractors

Attractor Types	Anthropological and Social Dimension	Aspects of Sign Usage	Medium
Rituals and ethics	Acting Sensomotoric dimension	Indexicality (external reference to space and time)	Actions
Condensed signs	Experience, subjectivity Visual dimension	Iconicity (quality of signs, perception)	Pictograms, images
Narratives, set phrases, dogmas	Identity through reflection and interpretation Cognitive dimension	Symbolicity (combination of perception and external reference)	Texts and text corpora

Rituals and ethics are part of the anthropological dimension of acting including the sensomotoric dimension; it emphasizes the indexicality of signs, i. e., the external reference in space and time including the body and a social community. The medium of the ritual is actions.

Condensed signs are part of the anthropological dimension of the experience and subjectivity including the visual dimension, but also point to links to the dimension of identity. From a semiotic point of view, they accentuate the iconicity, i. e. the quality of the signs and their perception. Their medium is pictograms and images.

Narratives, set phrases and dogmas are part of the anthropological dimension of identity which results from reflection and interpretation and relates primarily to the cognitive dimension. In semiotic terms, they accentuate symbolicity, i. e. the combination of perception and external reference. Their preferred medium is texts and text corpora.

We should also consider the social dimension, that is the question of who is the carrier of certain attractors and who is attracted by them as well as their circumstances, because attraction is a three-fold concept[32]: x is attractive to y under z conditions. This corresponds to the triadic relation of using signs: the interpretant (the product of an interpretative process) ascribes (that is thirdness) a quality (that is firstness) to an object (that is secondness).

As already stated, this is a sample classification in order to indicate the direction in which we are working in the focus group "attractiveness". Other combinations and models are possible, and furthermore, the criteria are only analytically differentiated for heuristic purposes and go hand in hand on the empirical level. The heuristic advantage of a typological comparison of attractors lies in the ability to identify different types of the densification of a religious tradition (for instance cultification, dogmatisation [synods] and ethicalisation), which in turn dispose different dimensions of the contact.

5. *Temporal Caesuras and Systematic Perspectives*

If one looks at *densification* processes of religious network of traditions, then it is not (yet and so much) a matter of processes of expansion, but – technically speaking – processes of condensation, aggregation or crystallisation of different elements of traditions as well as the transformative and catalytic function of densification processes as an important factor of dynamics in the history of religions. One thesis

[32] An aspect that has been stressed by the fellow Matthias Jung in adopting pragmatic semiotics.

to be tested in exploring the condensation of traditions is that with traditions, the more condensed they are, the more they give a clear sense of identity within the religious field in the sense of helping set themselves apart from others.[33] But even if the special case of explicit identity-generation through densification processes does not occur, the condensation is nonetheless *scientifically* identifiable.

If one takes a look at the *consolidation* and *spread and expansion* of the condensed networks of religious traditions, their preservation, but also their diffusion play a role from temporal and spatial points of view. From a temporal (diachronic) point of view, transmission techniques and media are significant. From a spatial point of view, it is necessary to investigate techniques of inculturation and the semantics of space. Here, geographical constellations and spatial metaphors play a particular role, for instance: zones and nodes of religious transfer, but also islands (diaspora).

When looking at the *reform or renewal* of condensed networks of religious traditions, the question of how traditions are reinvented is of significance, without the factor of the renewal having to be deliberate or thematic. In the reform of traditions back towards what is "original" and "authentic", the new usually remains latent. On the other hand, the adaptation to temporal and spatial circumstances can also take place explicitly and transparently as a renewal. This gives rise to the question of how evidence and social acceptance for the new elements are produced.

Finally, one must observe the *reflections* in the religious field which have a conceptual impact and take place in all three analytically differentiated phases alternating between densification, diffusion, reform or renewal. This applies both to basic religious notions and the concept of religion itself.

The structure of the international consortium is designed with these four factors in mind: in the first research field the formation of the major religious traditions through cultural contact, both diachronically and synchronically, is being analysed based on exemplary studies. The second research field covers case studies on religious contacts within the periods of the institutionalisation, spread and diversification of the major religious traditions. In the third research field, the

[33] In the interplay between communitisation and individualisation as an attributive and appropriation process and at the same time as a way to enable latitude though which the traditions can, in turn, be interpreted anew.

development of the collective singular "religion" as well as the formation and development of basic religious concepts are to be studied. The focal point of the fourth research field is religious encounter, the development of a global religious field and its reflection in the context of colonialism and globalisation.

When systematising processes, one must admittedly first take into the account that with the change from densification, consolidation, expansion, reform and renewal as well as reflection we are not dealing with a uni-lineal development, but only with certain aspects of complex processes. For instance, formation is not limited to the emergence phase of a religious network of traditions, but continually reoccurs as the reproduction of traditions. Second, the transitions should be seen as threshold and ellipse-like (in the meaning of Hans Blumenberg's epoch concept[34]). Third, with contact between religious traditions one must always expect the unsimultaneous to happen simultaneously: whilst one of the religions participating in the contact is already in the consolidation phase, the other can still be in the state of formation.

D. *Methodological Consequences and Working Steps*

In order to investigate religious transfer, the following tasks emerge against the backdrop of the conceptional considerations regarding methodology: first, the processes of tradition formation, reproduction and transformation and the transfer of tradition must be investigated. Second, basic religious concepts used in self-descriptions and descriptions of others must be identified.

1. *Tradition Formation, Reproduction and Transformation*

The intention to research processes of densification, diffusion and delimitation of networks of traditions includes dealing with the formation, reproduction and transformation of traditions. Only if we know how a tradition arises and its inner and outer limits are formed can we explain the processes of transfer and circulation. In the cultural and social sciences, however, a great deal of uncertainty prevails on the question of what defines a tradition. In the research programme

[34] Blumenberg emphasises the threshhold character; cf. Hans Blumenberg, *Die Legitimität der Neuzeit*. Part 4: *Aspekte der Epochenschwelle: Cusaner und Nolaner*, Frankfurt a. M.: suhrkamp 1976.

outlined here, we cannot, admittedly, present a theory of tradition, but can only address a few of the deliberations on the formation and transfer of traditions.

1.1. *Tradition Formation and Reproduction*

A tradition is, first of all, the result of densification processes and – from the perspective of a scientific analysis – a retrospective construction: a tradition is designed to trace back one's own position to "authentic" sources. Tradition means attributing continuity, and is not necessarily an objective condensation. In general, the reason behind the formation of a tradition is the size of a religious movement, due to which internal and external differences require regulating.

Tradition formation includes semantic and socio-structural aspects. So what is condensed in a tradition is particular content-related and socio-structural cultural goods. Cultural goods can be material objects, images, texts, institutional arrangements or actions. The process of densification of individual cultural goods relates to the intensification of content, the density of interaction between the carriers of traditions and the duration of interaction. Densification is thus based on a factual, social and temporal circumstance. The factual circumstances concern the content of cultural goods, the social circumstances are related to the carrier strata as well as the social context of use, and the temporal circumstances concern the transmission process.

In order to avert the danger of seeing traditions as static entities with clear boundaries they must be regarded as social constructions, as communicatively generated entities with relatively clear contours related to a certain context of communication. Against a communication-theory background, cultural goods comprise the following dimensions:

- the semantic and material specifications and constraints of the good, which provide scope for interpretation and use, but also constrain these,
- the reference attributed to the good in the context of production,
- and the reference attributed to the good in the context of reception.

It is important to distinguish between the inner semantic specifications and constraints on the one hand and the attributed reference as two elements of the meaning of a good on the other hand, in order, for example, to be able to identify endogenous and exogenous factors in the continuity of or change in a tradition as well as changes in the transfer of traditions.[35] A content-related motif can, for example, be changed both for inner rationalisation reasons – that would concern the semantic specifications and constraints – and through the particular circumstances of reception – that would concern the attributed reference. Furthermore, every cultural good is simultaneously a carrier of meaning and a product of meaning. By taking into account the double dimension of meaning, the assumption of an essential meaning is avoided. It is always the product of a communication process of information, expression, and understanding.

The reference of a good is reproduced, varied or transformed with its reception. Accordingly, the following forms of reception should be at the fore. Contextual factors which influence the reference attributed in the reception process are, in particular:

- language;
- world view, forms of knowledge;
- experiences and how they are handled;
- ethos (norms, habitus, the conduct of life);
- political history of events;
- social reference units (such as group, association, ethnicity, society, nation, humanity).

From the chain of the production and reception of cultural goods the scheme shown in Fig. 4 (p. 43) can be developed for the purposes of modelling. The producer 1 of the good 1 is also the recipient of antecedent goods, and good 4 is received and reproduced further. In this sense, the model is but an excerpt from a complex chain of reception and production. As neither the beginning nor the end of this chain can be identified, it is impossible to reconstruct an original source and, as a result, innovation must be interpreted as a radical transformation (in the sense of a completely different way of doing and looking at things). Old and new can each only be understood as links of a difference.

[35] Cf. Edward Shils, *Tradition*, Chicago: University of Chicago Press 1981, 213ff, who distinguishes between endogenous and exogenous factors of the transformation of traditions. Terminologically different, but substantially the same cf. also Ulrich Berner, *Untersuchungen zur Verwendung des Synkretismus-Begriffs*, Wiesbaden: Harrassowitz 1982, 95; religious contacts recorded here are exegenous triggers of systematising changes in the religious systems in question.

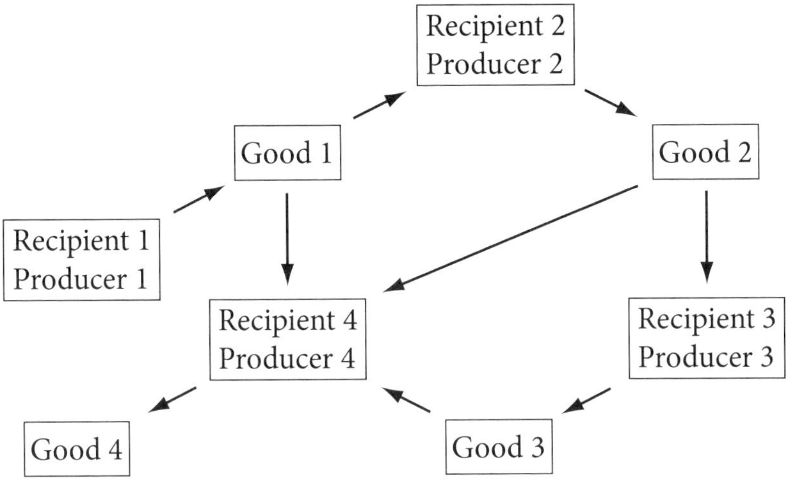

Fig. 4: Relations between producers, recipients, and transferred goods

The good 1 can be the imitation, interpretative appropriation, variation or transformation of antecedent goods. Good 1 has internal semantic constraints and a reference, which depend on the context of the producer 1. A reference is however created just as much by the context of the recipient 2 of the good 1 and can in turn be the imitation, interpretative appropriation, variation or transformation of the sense of the good 1 and the reference stipulated by producer 1. The reception of the good 1 by the recipient 2 is the basis of the production of good 2, which in turn is given a reference by recipient 3 and so on.

The question now is how the references of the goods 1–4 behave towards one another. For example, with good 2, in terms of the form, the internal semantic constrains and the attributed reference, we may be dealing with an extensive imitation of the good 1, whilst good 3 is a variation of goods 1 and 2. The variation can be based on the form or the content, but also by being expanded by a further element that is not contained in the goods 1 and 2. The production of the good 4 is based, according the model, on the reception of the goods 1–3. Let us assume that although it processes the elements contained in the goods 1–3, is does however arrange them in a new pattern and assigns them a different meaning reference and therefore represents the process of transformation. Whilst consequently we are dealing with a unit of tradition in the production and reception of the goods 1–3, good 4 is a deviation that goes beyond the variation. Whether it is part of an existing other tradition or part of an emerging new tradition, or whether it continues to exist as a mere and isolated deviation depends on the rest of the production and reception chain, so the social connections.

The prerequisite for the formation and reproduction of traditions is the following criteria:

- There is a certain aggregate state and a state of competition caused by internal or external differences which makes the formation of a tradition necessary or at least would encourage it.
- There is a recipient chain of individual or of a collection of cultural goods.
- Representatives of the tradition to be established postulate that there is a recognisable pattern amongst the goods 1–n, that the references of the goods in question are similar and relate to one another.
- The use of all motifs takes place in a standardised semantic and pragmatic context of reference or forms this context; i. e. there must be a more or less pronounced awareness of a production and reception community. There are semantic indicators, such as "Christian", "Jewish", "Buddhist" and so on for this. The more encompassing and more general such indicators are, the less defined their socially shared content is.
- The standardised semantic and pragmatic general context is separated from other reference contexts. The extent to which an awareness of the difference must exist outwardly is a research question which has yet to be answered.

The outer limits of a tradition are not always easy to determine. They are defined by both its followers and its content.[36] However, both defining features are only loosely related to each other. For example, a follower does not have to be (and usually cannot be) familiar with all the content of a tradition and all its elements. Identifying with a particular tradition always means highlighting special elements of it. "Varying emphases and idiosyncratic 'slants' are the common fate of intellectual traditions in the course of their transmissions, receptions, and possessions."[37] With regard to the outer limits, one must also dis-

[36] Cf. Shils, *Tradition*, 262.
[37] Shils, *Tradition*, 265.

tinguish between a specific tradition as a "cluster of elements", a "comprehensive tradition" and a "family of traditions".[38]

In spite of the difficulties in determining the outer limits, networks of traditions can be identified using the criteria listed and separated from each other without seeing them as essential entities or having to follow the object-linguistic normative differentiations, for instance between orthodox, heterodox and heretic.[39] Instead both strong and weak boundaries and attachments can be identified. Additionally, it is possible to distinguish less condensed networks of traditions, whose elements are only loosely connected, from more condensed networks of traditions, as the following diagram intends to illustrate.

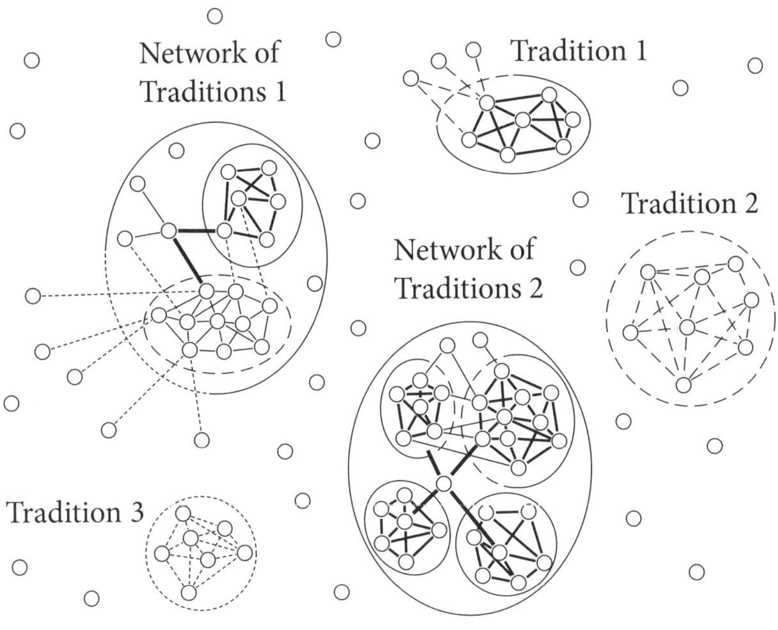

Fig. 5: Figurations of traditions

[38] Cf. here Shils, *Tradition*, 269ff.

[39] An observer might see "the orthodox as the member of a family of traditions, which the orthodox deny even more vehemently than the heterodox" (Shils, *Tradition*, 267).

1.2. *Transfer of Tradition Elements*
The preceding – very schematic – considerations hopefully serve to better understand the process of cultural transfer and thus also of religious transfer. One can speak of a transfer when a good is received from one condensed network of traditions in another.

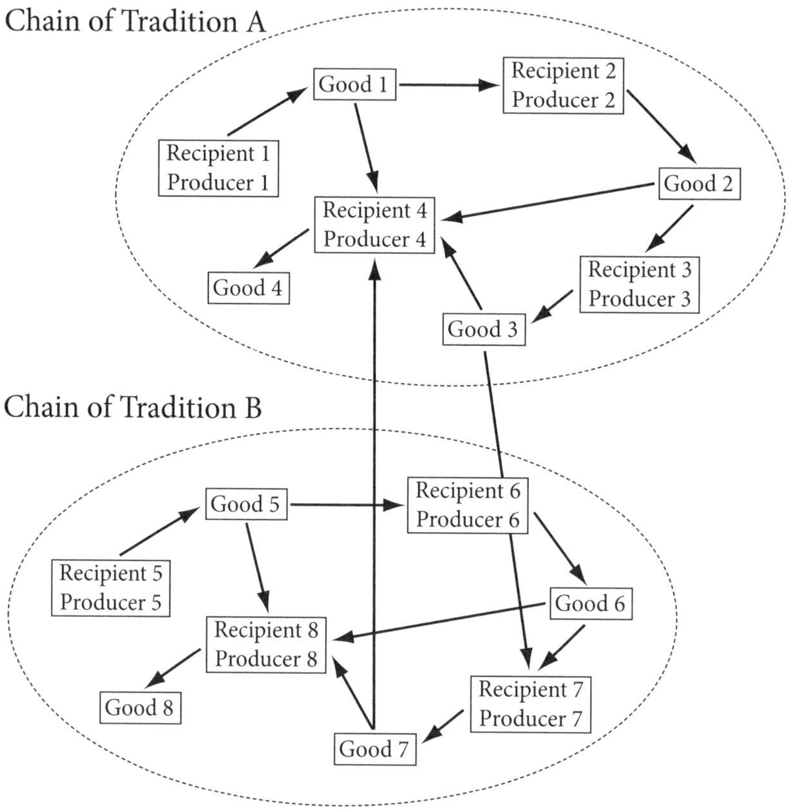

Fig. 6: Relation between two chains of traditions

In this example, the good 3 as an element of a tradition A is adopted by the recipient 7 as part of the chain of tradition B. The way in which it is processed depends, for example, on the absorbed content motif's formative power in relation on the one hand to the context factors, which influence the reference of the motif, and on the other hand on the degree of consistency of tradition B; above all though, it depends on reference strategies. The elements to be appropriated must generally either be believed to already be in possession or be lacking a carrier (for instance as a past, cast-off tradition); otherwise the transfer takes place unconsciously. A situation in which goods are consciously adopted from another tradition with identified carriers is probably the exception.

If we are dealing with an extensive imitation in the form of the good 7, and its reception then feeds into the production and further reception of good 8, the tradition B is permanently changed by the transfer. Conversely, good 3 will be varied or transformed in the event that it is largely adapted to the reception context 7. Third, it is possible that recipient 7 has knowledge of good 3, but rejects it and the production of the good 7 takes place in such a way as to distance itself from good 3. In this case, it is not a transfer but differentiation from good 3 or perhaps even from the entire tradition A. If the processing of a motif of the tradition A in the tradition B impacts back on a recipient of the tradition, then it is a case of reciprocal influence.

In a cultural transfer it is usually only the inner specifications and constraints that are received and appropriated, so the sense of a good. The external reference assigned in the appropriation process can vary considerably. The physical basis and the form and shape of material artefacts, images, universally shared topoi, phrases, words and chains of words (texts) and genres, patterns of action and socio-structural arrangements can all be transferred. Whilst the transferable parts of goods are not without significance due to the semantic stipulations and constraints, they are also polysemous. A clarifying reference is ascribed to the transferred goods during reception. Cultural goods only receive an external reference in the process of localisation, so in their specific context of use.

As an example, I would cite the figure of Heracles/Hercules, which was wider-spread in the Hellenistic hemisphere: the inner specifications and constraints are stipulated, for example, by his attributes: the fur of the Nemean lion, club, bow and quivers; the club cannot be turned into a feather. The attributed reference can vary however.

Often, if not as a general rule, a good from a condensed network of traditions is not received directly in another condensed network of traditions, but via the intermediary of transmitters.[40] This circum-

[40] Cf. Christoph Ulf, "Rethinking Cultural Contacts", in: *Ancient West & East* 8 (2009), 81–132.

stance facilitates reception because the received good is no longer or at least not strongly bound to a carrier or sponsor thanks to the intermediary of transmitter agents but instead culturally sedimented or free-floating. Cultural exchange often does not take place in direct contact between producer and recipient, but as "long distance transmission" (Erik Zürcher) with very different features: "contact is incidental and intermittent; communications are difficult, and there is no feed-back. The transmission is defective and can easily take the form of an unsystematic borrowing of elements that are largely detached from their original context, and therefore easily are changed beyond recognition in their new cultural environment."[41]

2. *The Emergence of Regional Religious Fields and a Global Religious Field*

Aside from the fact that we cannot assume that at all times and in all cultural areas there has been or there is an independent religious field, the identification of a religious field depends on the perspective of the actors and also on the outside perspective (for instance on political and economic processes, or – in line with the abductive procedure – the scientific perspective). Building on different theory traditions, I assume that the identity of individual religious traditions, of the religious field as a whole as well as its relationships to other spheres of society, creates itself through the interaction of semantics, cultural artefacts, institutional frameworks and interactions between actors, for example, through how they categorise themselves and how they are categorised by others. The defining features are thus not substantially determined, but instead exist in the (intra, inter or extra-religious) discursive alternation between the accepted and disputed nature of a religious tradition and of the religious field overall and in the negotiation processes at the "centre", "periphery" and boundaries. What defines "the" "one" Christianity, is the reversion to identified, but often – in their interpretation – controversial elements of tradition, which actors define as Christian in discourses (for instance, it is undisputed that Jesus Christ is the Son of God, however the concept of incarnation is strongly contested).

[41] Erik Zürcher, "Han Buddhism and the Western Region", in: Wilt L. Idema/Erik Zürcher (eds.), *Thought and law in Qin and Han China: Studies dedicated to Anthony Hulsewé on the Occasion of his Eightieth Birthday*, Leiden: Brill 1990, 158–182, here: 182.

From this perspective, the religious field as a whole is not an essential unit either, but instead produces its cohesion and limits through negotiation processes and dynamics of attraction. As a result, both movements *in* the religious field and movements *of* the religious field as a whole can be examined. In this version, religion is not a *sui generis* category beyond the stated elements of a working-hypothesis definition, but can be defined only in interaction with other societal rationalities and fields. Furthermore, in this way it is possible to establish correspondences between religious practice and its scientific reconstruction and thus avoid scientism. The balancing of the empirical lack of clarity of the subject "religion" (in its extension) and its definition (in its intension) is thus systematically taken into account. Against this backdrop it is a matter of investigating the emergence processes inside the religious field and the tendential metalinguistic emergence of a "religious field" with outer boundaries, which in turn have impacts on religious practice.

2.1. *Internal Formation of the Religious Field*

With the formation of the religious field through internal processes, we can assume that, historically, first of all regionally restricted religious fields originate, which in the sense of a continued conceptual abstraction of "religion" then tend – above all under the influence of colonisation and globalisation – to grow together into a global religious field. We presume that local religious fields form through the labelling of Self and Other.

As an example of a figuration, I would mention the discursive field "Sanjiao" that has formed in China (see Fig. 7, p. 50).

Other discursive fields are described with object-linguistic concepts such as religio (and the words derived thereof in the Romance languages and in German), dhamma, sâsana (Pali), dharma (Sanskrit), śaśin (Mongolian[42]), dāt (Hebrew), dīn (Arabic) and shūkyō (Japanese). One can assume that first regionally-bound fields emerge, which with increasingly overarching resonances from modern times onwards (above all through colonialism and globalisation) begin to join to form a global religious field. The research progamme should allow us to historically substantiate Peter Beyer's thesis of the formation of a global religious field.[43]

[42] Cf. Karénina Kollmar-Paulenz, *Zur Ausdifferenzierung eines autonomen Bereichs Religion in asiatischen Gesellschaften des 17. und 18. Jahrhunderts: Das Beispiel der Mongolen*, Akademievorträge, Number XVI, Bern 2007.

[43] Cf. Peter Beyer, *Religions in Global Society*, New York: Routledge 2006.

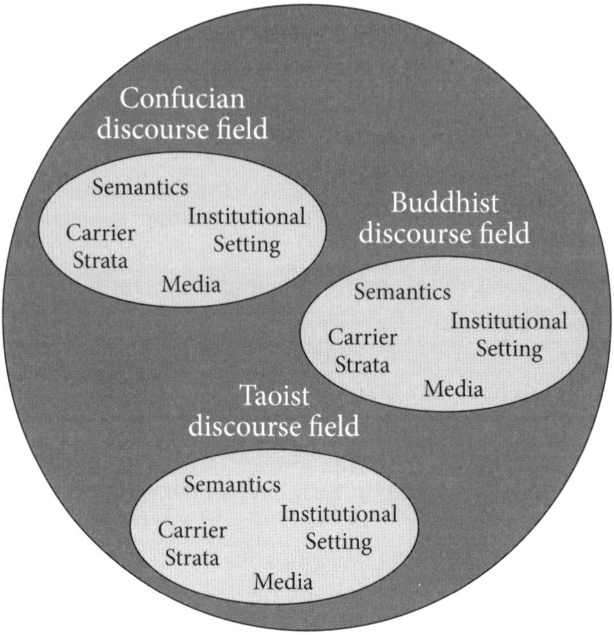

Fig. 7: Discourse field "Sanjiao"

Within the religious field, religious diversity and religious contacts enabled as a result thereof are *key conditions* for triggering dynamics in the history of religions. A plural situation can arise or actively be promoted either through the import and export of religious traditions, for instance, as part of trade relations, during imperial expansion, or through religious innovation and reformation from the inside outwards. Religious contacts challenge religious traditions to differentiate themselves, position themselves and establish an identity and thus promote the controversy of the religious field inwardly and outwardly as well as the demarcation of boundaries. But equally, religious contacts can also lead to explicit or creeping amalgamation of elements of various traditions.

Dynamics in the history of religions are *expressed* in different ways which encompass situations as varied as imitation and new interpretations, more or less institutionalised dialogues and apologetics, chance encounters, exploratory movements, media-generated contacts and violent inter-religious conflicts or intra-religious persecution of "deviants".

Possible *consequences* of contacts between religions in the religious field can be the adaptation and amalgamation as well as the eradication of religious opponents internally or externally, mystical sublimation and salvation religiosity as well as inner-worldly radicalisation and (missionary or charitable) activism.

When examining developments in the religious field it might be helpful to distinguish between intra-religious and inter-religious relationships. This distinction may appear fragile at first glance because it assumes a by no means always clear difference between the internal and external limits of religious traditions. It is however reasonable to assume that as a result of the contact between religions, the variable outer and inner borders do take on clearer contours. Furthermore, research on the formation and reformation of the major condensed networks of religious traditions can perhaps contribute to a better understanding of their internal and external boundaries. For example, outward delimitation can make it possible to attempt to homogenise inwardly. In other cases, the reference to outside opponents can serve to marginalise internal opponents with the argument that they are like the adversaries. Inner and outer boundaries make mutual reference to each other. Examples of inter-religious descriptions are religio vera and falsa and ahl-ul-kitāb (People of the Book). An example of intra-religious delimitation is the object-linguistic distinction between orthodoxy, heterodoxy and heresy. Granted, the object-linguistic distinction between inter and intra-religious can also vary; as we see in the example of John of Damascus and other early Christian authors, who describe Islam as ecclesia Sarracenorum – later, Nicholas of Cues sees Islam as a heretical Christian sect – or Japanese authors who regarded Christianity as a Buddhist sect.

In order to research the internal way in which a or the religious field came into being, I propose, methodologically, to proceed by using family resemblances when looking for basic religious concepts in which religious semantics are compressed. Ludwig Wittgenstein describes family resemblances in his *Philosophical Investigations* as characteristics of concepts which cannot be sufficiently grasped with a hierarchical and categorical system, as concepts have blurred boundaries and tend to be able to escape the categorical. The family resemblance is – logically speaking – a category-forming relationship of equivalence: it is reflexive (so we cannot match different concepts with one another one or subsume them categorically), symmetrical (we must however identify similarities) and transitive (the establishment of a relationship or translation is directional and aligns). The procedure of family resemblances moves in some respects between categorisation and typification. The thesis being that in a contact situation, in which a representative of a cultural entity who does *not* have a semantically clearly (categorically) identifiable awareness of it as a "religion" takes on this concept and due to the contact with a representative of a cultural entity who *does* have a semantically clearly (categorically) identifiable awareness of it as "religion" is prepared to describe something that he does, thinks or feels as a "religion" in the sense of family resemblance (for whatever reasons – to be identified more closely – and in whichever contact situation – for instance under imperial and colonial conditions – these may be).[44] Conversely, it may be that the representative with an awareness of "religion" adapts the concept to the concept taken on by the other representative and the way it is used. In the first case, we are looking at a prototypical concept of religion (prototype in the meaning of the US cognition psychologist Eleanor Rosch, who works with family resemblances[45]), and in the second case a gradual inclusion into the category "religion". It is important to pick up on these object-linguistic processes in order to arrive at metalinguistic concepts which are in resonance with religious-historical object-language.

Several projects are working on the lines of family resemblances, for instance those of my colleagues Heiner Roetz, Wolfgang Ommerborn, and Hans Martin Krämer. They have compiled a set of terms, related to what we call religion, such as

- the Chinese term *wu* in the Shang and Zhou period, which we translate as Shamanism,
- the Chinese term tian or the Japanese ten, which is translated as sky or heaven,
- the Chinese word shen or Japanese shin or kami, translated as "deity",
- the Chinese concept jiao or Japanese kyô/oshie, translated as "teachings" or "doctrine",

[44] Building on the work of the member of the research consortium Knut Martin Stünkel.

[45] Cf. Eleanor Rosch, "Cognitive Representations of Semantic Categories", in: *Journal of Experimental Psychology: General* Vol.104 No. 3 (1975) 192–233.

- the Chinese term li or Japanese rei, translated as "cult", "rite", or "ritual",
- the Chinese concept sanjao and the Japanese concept shûkyô, and so on.

In the European context, the following Latin-based terms can be considered for family resemblances: religio pietas, fides, lex and their derivatives in the European languages. In Arabic, family resemblances between dīn and fak are possible. In the contact between cultures, family resemblances can be created at an object-language level between two or more different word groups, so that in translations, for instance, shûkyô is rendered as religion.

By further investigating concepts of difference and family resemblances we hope to gain insight into how what one can from the perspective of object-language material call a religious self-awareness develops in the contact between religious traditions. A better understanding of these processes will make it possible to examine questions relating to the (constant and long-term, but also lacking) emergence of the religious. Whilst the concepts demonstrating difference can be seen as indicators of the distinction between a religious and non-religious interpretation of the world, family resemblances can shed light on the semantic fringe of meaning of the religious for specific temporal and spatial constellations respectively.

The results of a workshop on the subject of "Labeling Self and Other in Historical Contacts Between Religious Groups" provide an example of the way we work.[46] The table 3 (p. 54) compiled by Hans Martin Krämer show the authors researched and the use of religious-related concepts for labelling the Self and Other.

[46] Cf. Hans Martin Krämer/Jenny Oesterle/Ulrike Vordermark (eds.), *Labeling the Religious Self and Others: Reciprocal Perceptions of Christians, Muslims, Hindus, Buddhists, and Confucians in Medieval and Early Modern Times*, Special Edition of *Comparativ – Zeitschrift für Globalgeschichte und vergleichende Gesellschaftsforschung* 4/20 (2010).

Table 3: Religious concepts used by authors investigated

			Christian Authors		
	WORD(S)	CHRISTIANITY	ISLAM	JUDAISM	REMARKS
13C: RAMON MARTÍ	*pius, fides*	yes	yes	yes	did not use *religio*
16C: MARTIN LUTHER	*fides*	yes			
	religio	yes			
	lex	–	yes		
17C: GERMAN TRAVELERS TO INDIA	*Glaube*	yes	yes	yes	
	Lehre	–	yes	–	
	Gesetz	–	yes	yes	
	Religion	yes	yes	yes	
			Islamic Authors		
	WORD	CHRISTIANITY	ISLAM	JUDAISM	REMARKS
13C: RUMI	*haqq*	yes	yes	yes	Not used for other teachings
PRE-15C WRITERS	*dīn*	–	yes	–	
15C WRITERS	*dīn*	yes	yes	–	direct comparison between Islam and Christianity
			East Asian Authors		
	WORD	CONFUCIANISM	BUDDHISM	DAOISM	CHRISTIANITY
PRE-16C CHINA	*jiao* 教	yes	yes	yes	–
	fa 法	–	yes	(rarely)	–
	dao 道	yes	yes	yes	–
17C JAPAN	*hō* 法	(rarely)	yes	–	yes
	shū 宗	–	yes	–	yes
16–19C CHINA	*jiao* 教	yes (prototype)	yes	yes	yes
19C CHINA	*jiao* 教	yes	yes	yes	yes (prototype)

The following conclusions were drawn in the closing discussion of the workshop:

First of all a general pattern with the following three steps was identified:

1. The alien religious tradition is partly or completely related to the own religion, for instance, as a sub-sect.
2. The foreignness or newness of the other religion is acknowledged, although the terminology used by the own religious tradition is kept.
3. The alien religious tradition becomes an other tradition; in this case, it is categorised into the own terminological system, but labelled as being different.

Examples of the first step are:

- John of Damascus and other earlier observers of Islam ("ecclesia Sarracenorum"), later Islam as a heretical Christian sect (for instance by Nicholas of Cues)
- Indian religions as Christian denominations in descriptions of Christians travelling to India
- in China: Buddhism as a variation of Daoism
- in Japan: Christianity as a sub-sect of Buddhism

These forms of interpretation of Self and Other can perhaps through translation also be examples of the possibility of inscription in the sense of family resemblances.

2.2. *Outward Demarcation of the Religious Field*

The contours of regional religious fields and, tendentially, of a global religious field do not just depend on internal developments but also on outside factors. Here, political, legal, economic, and philosophical circumstances which force religious currents to position themselves should be mentioned first and foremost. Examples of developments in which political factors play a significant role are, for example, the Maccabee uprising, the formation of Western Christianity as the official Imperial religion and the development of Islamic traditions under the caliphates. In the modern age, colonisation and globalisation also come into play, which together with the modern-day Christian mission are considerably involved in the development of a global religious field. Of course, the distinction between factors internal and external to religions in the formation of a or the religious field is also one which was made for analytical purposes; what is accentuated in each case depends on the scientific perspective.

In order to reconstruct the trend towards differentiation of the religious and distinction from other societal spheres, I recommend the methodological approach of developing concepts of semantic differences. By this I mean identifying spectrums of concepts whose meaning on the one hand is closely related, but on the other hand contain specific semantic differences which point to a specific religious meaning, for instance:

- certainty, certitude, wisdom, knowledge, faith;
- superstition, heresy, error, insanity;
- looking (Schauen), seeing, recognising;
- rite, liturgy, routine, habit;
- prophecy, prognosis;
- providence, fate, law, order.

In all of this it is important to take into account the context of such concepts, in order to grasp any semantic differences or polysemies which may exist within one and the same concept. It is also a result if, after in-depth philological examination, it transpires that concept pairs of the named type or semantic differences of the same concept pointing to a differentiated religious area are not present for particular times and cultural areas. For then it would possible to say that in these cases there is no differentiation of the religious (according to Western patterns). Then we would have to examine whether it is possible to identify concepts which bear witness to states of sacralisation, so attributively charging cultural, political and other situations with religious interpretations without it being possible to distinguish conceptually between the religious and the secular as its opposite.

3. *Towards a Typology of Religious Contact*

The research programme "Dynamics in the History of Religions" aims to contribute to a theory of religious transfer and thus to the historiography of a general and tendentially global history of religion; at the same time we also expect the results to produce new ideas for theories of general cultural transfer and comprehension-oriented hermeneutics. The path towards this leads from the search for suitable *tertia comparationis* and on to a typology of religious contacts, which is being developed using individual case studies. For hypothetical purposes, the following considerations are of interest, which certainly will have to be put to the empirical test.

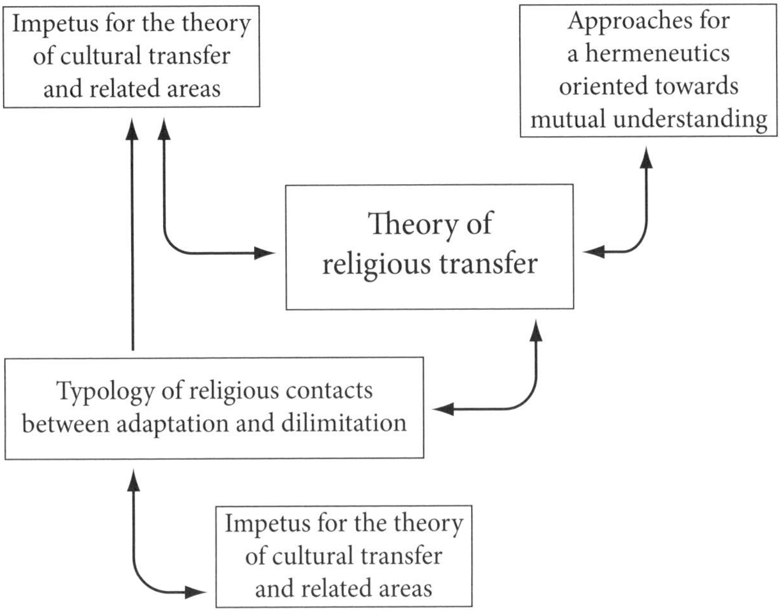

Fig. 8: Research steps

For a complex typology of the contact between religions, a multitude of criteria must be taken into account. First of all, we make a rough distinction between the following *tertia comparationis* in order to arrive at types of religious contact (see Fig. 9, p. 58). Of course, the distinction between endogenous and exogenous is an analytical one for heuristic purposes because we cannot assume there is a distinct religious field at all times and in every cultural area. And even where it is possible to identify one, it is in constant interaction with its social and cultural surroundings. Moreover, the conditions change into consequences and vice-versa at another given time. The model only records a particular section of time.

Other criteria for a typology of religious contact can be the direction, type, scale and duration of the influence arising from contact, the relationship between the religious traditions in contact with each

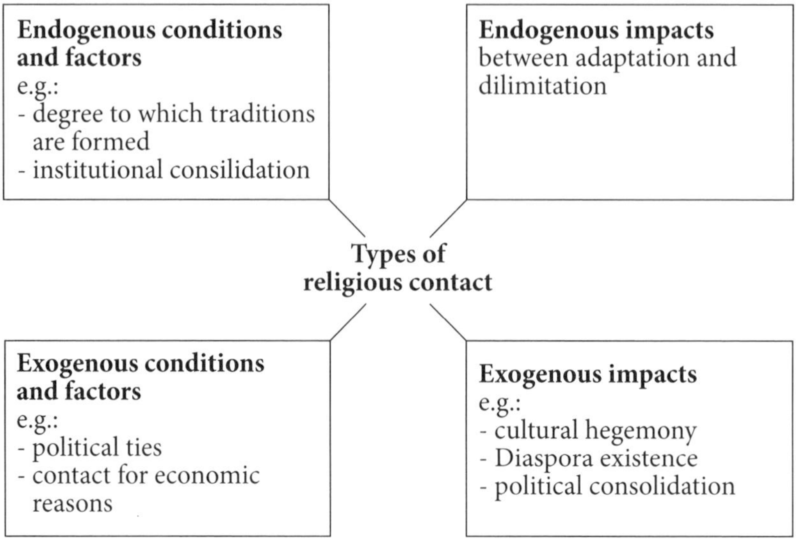

Fig. 9: Conditions and consequences of religious contact

other (such as an established and a circulating religious tradition), media of religious contact (for instance texts, images, material artefacts, architecture, cult practices), transmitting agents and the distinction between diachronic and synchronic as well as between intra and inter-religious contacts.

The following have been discussed and in part tested as *tertia comparationis* in the consortium.

Table 4: Examples of tertia comparationis

Frame of Reference	Examples of Tertia Comparationis
Religious semantics	• Binary distinctions and their symbolisation • Cosmological and anthropological concepts • Conceptions of truth and universalisms
Religious forms of action	• Formation and transfer of cults and rituals • Ethicalisation and influence on how people lead their lives • Sequential and occasional forms of action
Religious social forms	• Religious experts/"laypersons" • Organisational forms (orders, schools, etc.) • Sponsors and interests

Table 4 *(cont.)*

Frame of Reference	Examples of Tertia Comparationis
Discourses and terminologies	• Forms of dialogue (e. g. debates between scholars) • Appropriating interpretations (Interpretatio Christiana, etc.) • Exclusive and inclusive/comparative concepts of religion
Use of signs and media	• Iconography • Narrative literature • Travel accounts • Canon and commentaries
Politico-historical background	• Political ties, expansion and mission • Migration • Imperialism, colonialism, globalisation

In the comments to follow I will, however, limit myself to synchronic contacts and thereby focus on the religious impacts of inter-religious contacts.

3.1. *Synchronic Intra-Religious Contact*

Synchronic intra-religious contacts, which I will only deal with briefly, include first of all processes, usually described as *schisms, the formation of confessions, sects and schools* as well as *the differentiation between orthodoxy, heterodoxy and heresy.* However, these object-linguistic terms must carefully be transformed into the scientific metalanguage. For example, the expansion of the reformatory movements during the early modern age and the popularity that can currently be seen world-wide of the pentecostal-charismatic movements within a largely Christian-shaped culture lead to intra-religious contacts which give dynamism to the rest of the Christian complex of traditions through the reinterpretation and enrichment of Christian traditions. The consortium intends to investigate social closure mechanisms by means of an intercultural comparative analysis and in their interaction with the corresponding semantics to determine their different conditions and impacts.

Second, intra-religious plurality includes *distinguishing between different carrier strata.* The distinction between *official and popular reli-*

gion or intellectual and popular religiosity[47] may be out of date, but does at least indicate a direction of intra-religious plurality which takes into account the different supporting layers. By popular religiosity I mean "verschiedene Vorstellungen und Praktiken [...], die sich infolge einer Monopolisierung der Definition von und Verfügung über 'Heilsgüter' bzw. über das 'religiöse Kapital' bei den von der Definition von und Verfügung über diese Heilsgüter Ausgeschlossenen herausbilden" (different ideas and practices which emerge as a result of a monopolisation of the definition of and command over the 'holy goods' or 'religious capital' of those who are excluded from the definition of and command over these holy goods).[48]

Third, intra-religious plurality encompasses the *differentiation between different strata* within a religious tradition. Perhaps the distinction introduced with regard to this by Theo Sundermeier and further developed by Jan Assmann between primary and secondary religions will prove itself.[49] Elements of primary religions continue to exist in secondary religions in the meaning of Edward Tylor's *survivals.*

The intra-religious contact also includes internal mission. The Muslim mission (in Arabic da'wa) in the 20th century, for example, is not aimed first and foremost at converting non-believers, but far more at its own brothers and sisters in faith who – influenced by Western secularism and materialism – have lost their way (this is the position of Hasan al-Bannâ, the founder of the Muslim Brotherhood, for example). And, not least, the *Innere Mission* (internal mission) propagated by Johann Hinrich Wichern combines social welfare work with (re-) evangelisation initiatives.

Fourth, the encounter of geographically separated factions of the same religious tradition embedded in different cultural contexts can trigger forms of intra-religious contact. This was the case, for example, when the Theravada-Buddhist movement of laypersons' meditation was imported from Burma to Sri Lanka, causing not just an upsurge

[47] Cf. Pieter H. Vrijhof/Jean Jacques Waardenburg (eds.), *Official and Popular Religion: Analysis of a Theme for Religious Studies*, The Hague: Walter de Gruyter 1979.

[48] Michael N. Ebertz/Franz Schultheis, "Einleitung: populare Religiosität", in: *Volksfrömmigkeit in Europa: Beiträge zur Soziologie popularer Religiosität aus 14 Ländern*, München: Chr. Kaiser 1986, 11–52, here: 25.

[49] To compare, and for its use in Near-Eastern religious history, cf. Andreas Wagner (ed.), *Primäre und sekundäre Religion als Kategorie der Religionsgeschichte des Alten Testaments*, Berlin: de Gruyter 2006.

in spiritualised religiosity, but also disconcertedness and radical rejection there.[50]

In addition to schisms and the formation of schools etc., non-exclusive co-existence is also possible in the form of a division of tasks, a variety of offerings or "free cult associations".[51] An example of this would be the accumulative initiations in text-practice complexes in Tibetan Buddhism whereby a cluster of people around a "guardian of tradition", usually institutionalised locally, administers and allocates initiations and instructions in set tantric cycles. The clientele (occasional customers as oppose to the members of the cluster) travels from one centre/master to the next and collects these initiations. We can assume that this form of intra-religious contact leads to particularly intense processes of exchange.

3.2. *Synchronic Inter-Religious Contact*

In the following section I will consider only constellations of synchronic religious contact involving two identifiable networks of religious traditions identifying themselves as such. Aspects such as the simultaneous occurrence of the unsimultaneous – for example through the presence of prior religious history in the remembering tradition – as well as institutional asymmetries between the religious traditions participating in the contact will not be examined.[52]

The following typology therefore is still of a provisional and largely unsystematic nature. Moreover, it concentrates solely on the inner-

[50] We owe this example to Sven Bretfeld.

[51] This consideration is based on input from Sven Bretfeld.

[52] In order to rule in the latter, it might perhaps be possible to distinguish between potential consequences of religious contact for the established religion which is confronted with elements of another religion, and consequences for the circulating religion which introduces new elements into an alien context or enriches itself with alien elements in the formative (or a transformative) phase. The distinction between establishedness and circulation does not necessarily have something to do with majority or minority relationships or balances of power. What is deci sive here is instead the temporal circumstance, the degree of institutional consolidation of a religion and the direction of the religious contact. By the latter criteria I mean the fact that religious contacts often arise through cultural, political or economic movements. Consequently, elements of a religion are "exported" into alien territory and "imported" by the religious culture absorbing them, or indeed, rejected. Additionally, in this process it is important to see whether it is a case of condensation processes in the sense of tradition formation and compressing during the formative phase of a religious tradition or of condensation or diffusion processes in the sense of outward demarcation during expansion. The state of circulation can therefore refer to the formation or to the spatial spread and substantive expansion of a religion.

religious impacts of the contact and takes into account neither the media of the religious contact (such as texts, images, material artefacts, architecture, cult practices) and modes of transmission, nor extra-religious conditions and consequences. It sees itself merely as a probing impetus for material religious-historical research which builds on previous investigations into religious contacts.[53] As this probing is headed towards a typology of religious contacts, the religious-historical examples listed are not intended to form a theory, but instead serve purely illustrative purposes in the development of hypotheses.

1. Identifying one's own religious tradition completely with that of another

It is probably unlikely to see this consequence of religious contact in pure form, as it would lead to the contours of one's own religion dissolving away in favour of diffuse and abstract religious contents.

2. Identifying alien elements with elements of one's own religion

As an illustration, let me cite the following example from Isrealite religious history: "So wurde El, der mit den Sippengöttern gleichgesetzte Gott, als eine in der Vergangenheit geschehene Offenbarung des Gottes gedacht, der sich später als Jahwe zu erkennen gegeben hat. Damit war der Weg dafür geebnet, das Jahwe mancherlei von El übernahm." (El, the god equated with the clan gods, was thus conceived as a prior revelation of the god who later made himself known as Yahweh. The way was thus paved for Yahweh to take over much from El).[54]

As another example of this consequence of religious contact, let me cite the process in which in Greek religion "der Himmelsgott der Erbe vieler Berggötter geworden [ist]" (the god of heaven became the heir

[53] The following typological deliberations are thanks to ideas from Erik Zürcher, *The Buddhist Conquest of China. The Spread and Adaptation of Buddhism in Early Medieval China* (Sinica Leidensia: 11), Leiden: Brill 2007, Ulrich Berner, *Untersuchungen zur Verwendung des Synkretismus-Begriffes* (Göttinger Orientforschungen: Reihe Grundlagen und Ergebnisse, Band 2), Wiesbaden: Harrassowitz 1982, and Günter Lanczkowski, *Begegnung und Wandel der Religionen*, Düsseldorf: Diederichs 1971, which, admittedly, are based on different material and systemise according to different points of view. For instance, Zuercher's systematisations are limited to the case of the integration of Buddhism into Chinese religious culture, and so only take into account one direction of the religious contact. The examples listed in each case are based on sporadic reading and discussions with members of the consortium.

[54] Georg Fohrer, *Geschichte der israelitischen Religion*, Berlin: de Gruyter 1969, 95 (quoted according to Berner, *Untersuchungen*, 103).

of many mountain gods).[55] If the Indo-Germanic god of heaven Zeus does indeed drive out a mountain god from the native religion and takes on one of his characteristics and functions, then this is a case of identifying absorption.[56]

3. Incorporation of alien elements with remaining visibility
This consequence of religious contact, too, is unlikely to occur in its pure form because alien elements continue to have an impact on innovations even in the event of a keen willingness to absorb the new religion. One example, however, is perhaps the religion of the Mani (216–276 or 277 CE), which feeds off Christian, Zoroastrian and Buddhist elements.

4. Adaptive, but transformative use of alien elements in one's own religious tradition
This consequence of the contact between religions can be found, for example, in the situation that Adolf Deissmann dubbed polemic parallelism. He shows this using the historical example of the position of Christianity in the ruler cult of the Late Antiquity: the young Christian community stubbornly refuses to recognise any divinity in the Emperor. But it did start to use titles of reverence for Christ from the terminology of the Imperial cult.[57] Polemic parallelism also exists where terms which were once part of the most original possessions of Christianity come together with similar or homonymous terms of ruler worship. In this case, Christ and the sacred ruler are both given the titles *kýrios, pantokrátor* and *sotér.*

One reason for the adaptive transformation can be the quest to gain power for one's own religious tradition and reduce the power of other religious traditions. This is the case, for instance, in the Roman evocation of a divinity from an enemy town and its inclusion, under a

[55] O. Kern, *Die Religion der Griechen*, Vol. 1, Berlin: Weidmann 1926, 189.
[56] Cf. Berner, *Untersuchungen*, 101.
[57] Cf. Adolf Deissmann, *Licht vom Osten*, Tübingen: J.C.B. Mohr 1923, 289: "So entsteht ein polemischer Parallelismus zwischen Kaiserkult und Christuskult, der auch da empfunden wird, wo der vom Christuskult bereits mitgebrachten Urworte aus den Schatzkammern der Septuagintabibel und des Evangeliums mit ähnlich oder gleich klingenden solennen Begriffen des Kaiserkults zusammentreffen." (Thus arises a polemic parallelism between the Imperial cult and the cult of Christ, which is also felt where original words brought from the cult of Christ and from the treasure chambers of the Septuagint Bible and the Gospel meet with similar or same-sounding solemn terms from the Imperial cult.)

new name, in the Roman pantheon. Livius (V 21, 3.5) teaches that in the year 396 BCE the Roman commander Camillus called upon Uni of Veii, before the final charge on this Etruscan town, by *evocatio*, to leave her temple and her previous worshippers and to turn her attention to Rome. There, she entered the pantheon as Juno Regina.

Another reason for this consequence of religious contact can be the recognition of the "higher quality" or, pragmatically speaking, the more efficient impact of an alien religion or individual elements thereof. This attitude is characteristic, for instance, of the period of the predominance of Buddhism in Japan between the 6th and the 16th centuries (552–1549), especially for the Nara period in the 8th century (710–794). It led to Buddhism's influence on Shintō. Its Gods achieved a status that matched those of Buddhism, the *devas*. They became guardians of Buddha's law that they rejoice in and whose salvation they long for. In the cult area, this meant that holy texts of the Buddhists were read out in the Shintō shrines and that even Buddhist temples were erected in the shrine districts.[58]

A further example is modern reformatory Hinduism, which has absorbed Christian influences. These are shown in a clear turn towards monotheism, as first seen with the Bengali Brahma Rām Mohan Roy (Ray) and his "Community of Believers", Brāhma Samāj, founded in 1828 in Calcutta, and in an ethicalisation of Hinduism with Christian elements, which Gandhi became best known for.

Furthermore, a religious claim to universality can lead to religions becoming open to the influences of another tradition. Alien elements can be absorbed in order to raise the standing of one's own religion and to cement its position. Ambrose of Milan, for example, introduced stoic ethics into the Christian Church. The use of state insignia, developed by the monarchic representation of the Roman Empire in pagan times and under the defining influence of Near-Eastern role models, served to emphasise episcopal authority. At least three episcopal insignia, pallium, stole and pontifical sandals, go back to the insignia of the state dignitaries.

Not least, and actually even very often, transformative adaptations were brought about by accommodations made by missionaries, leading to the conservation of phenomena of an alien or lost religion, to their

[58] Cf. Ichiro Hori, "On the Concept of Hijiri (Holy Man)", in: Paul Williams (ed.), *Buddhism: Critical Concepts in Religious Studies*, New York: Routledge 2005, 184–235 (esp. 193).

survivals (in the meaning of Edward Tylor). They can fit meaningfully into the hegemonic religion, but can also continue to exist whilst being instrumentalised or stripped of their meaning. There are numerous examples I could cite here. I limit myself to that of the Ethiopian veneration of the Virgin Mary in trees: even today, the Abyssinians claim that the Virgin Mary lives in every mulberry-fig.

5. Innovative use of alien elements in the established religion (consciously or unconsciously[59])

The innovative use of alien elements in one's own tradition has a mimetic character in terms of its outer form. The meaning and function of the elements used however vary a great deal from the original context. Let me give the following example: "Während die Christen in Jerusalem alljährlich die Karwoche mit großer Feierlichkeit begehen, feiern zur gleichen Zeit die Muslime daselbst ein großes Fest zu Ehren des Propheten Moses, um neben das christliche Osterfest eine gleichwertige islamische Feier stellen zu können." (Whilst the Christians in Jerusalem observe the Holy Week with great ceremony every year, at the same time, the Muslims themselves hold a great celebration in honour of the Prophet Moses, in order to place an equal Islamic celebration alongside the Christian Easter celebrations.)[60] The thesis presented by Peter Schäfer that the emphasis on Shekhina as the feminine aspect of god in the Kabbala since the Bahir (Provence, 12th century) is connected to an examination of the Christian concept of Mary can also be seen as part of this area.[61]

6. Selection of alien elements and changed attention in the absorbing religion

Impacts of the selection of alien elements due to a changed attention in the absorbing religion might be, for example, the attention to certain dimensions of the religious such as cult practice or the emotional-aesthetic dimension. This kind of impact of religious contact can be

[59] Berner, *Untersuchungen*, 103, distinguishes between conscious and unconscious reinterpretation. To my mind, however, it is difficult to identify this difference empirically. The examples cited by him do not provide any information on this.

[60] Peter Kawerau, *Das Christentum des Ostens*, Stuttgart: Kohlhammer 1972, 199 (as cited by Berner, *Untersuchungen*, 105).

[61] Cf. Peter Schäfer, *Mirror of His Beauty. Feminine Images of God from the Bible to the Early Kabbala*, Princeton: Princeton University Press 2002. I owe this example and the source reference to Elisabeth Hollender.

observed, for example, in the relationship between Christianity as it establishes itself and the Mystery religions: on the one hand, cultification is encouraged in Christianity through the contact with the Mystery religions, but on the other hand, ethicalisation is also driven forward for the purposes of differentiation.

7. Institutional restructuring of a religious tradition through the influence of another

This type of contact is connected with what is described as institutional isomorphism in the social sciences and can be observed, for example, in the Japanese policy on religion around 1900. The criteria for recognising religious communities are developed on the basis of the model of the Christian churches. Islamic currents in present-day Europe, too, are undergoing a "structural churchification process", by organising themselves at least in the form of associations and clubs and – in the case of Germany – are hoping to achieve the status of a public body in order to meet representation criteria.

8. Coexistence (of elements) of one religious tradition with another

The fact that an Indian King must be enthroned according to Brahman ceremonial protocol may be helpful in illustrating this type of contact. Many other matters of the royal court require Vedic ritual acts. Even at the Buddhist royal court of Sri Lanka, court ceremony was organised vedically. Consequently, there was always a Brahman "high priest" *(purohita)* at the service of the King. Numerous sources report that this priest often served as an advisor and exerted a strong political influence.[62]

9. Amalgamation of elements of different religious traditions

One would assume that this type of contact must be one of the most common in the history of religions. Here, I would like to highlight just one example from Indian religious history. For extended periods, the Buddhist Tantrism in India can be seen as an amalgamation of Buddhist and Shivaistic traditions. As the "erotic ascetic", Shiva is the prototype of the wandering yogi smeared with the ash of the dead who seeks to appropriate the powers of enlightenment through controlled sexual practices. For the early Buddhist tantric practitioners, being a

---

[62] M. B. Ariyapala, *Society in Medieval Ceylon*, Colombo: K. V. G. deSilva 1997, 97f. I owe this example and the source reference to Sven Bretfeld.

Buddhist must have been largely irrelevant to their religious identity. The tantric deities *(devatā)* are (from a historical point of view) in many ways mixtures of Buddhas/Bodhisattvas and Hindu deities or aspects/apparitions thereof.[63]

10. Stimulated development triggered by alien elements
Here, with reference to Günter Lanczkowski, one should mention *affinities, eclectic elective affinities and idealised projections.* I will draw examples of these from the European history of ideas:

The *Renaissance* and the *classical period* are characterised by their affinity to antiquity, its gods and myths. But neither epoch reinstated paganism. They remained Christian for all intents and purposes.[64]

The European *Enlightenment* first showed extremely strong affinities to Confucian China. They were based on what was learnt from Jesuit missionaries to China who were deeply impressed by Confucian morals. I can mention Leibniz here, for example, but also Christian Wolff, whose idealisation of Confucius was famously later to become his undoing.[65]

By contrast, the reaction against the Enlightenment, the romantic period, found great enthusiasm for India. For the young romantics, India was the country of longing *par excellence*, the cradle of humanity where the oldest divine revelations waited to be discovered and harnessed.[66]

These examples of the European history of ideas, therefore, at least *prima facie*, can be subsumed under the contact type of affinities, eclectic elective affinities and idealised projections because here elements from other religious traditions are circulating without having any farther-reaching consequences for the worship and the lifestyles of entire groups or even only individuals. For instance, Schopenhauer, the enthusiast of the Upanishads, would hardly have been prepared to live the philosophy of the Upanishad sages and in old age "to leave the home to enter into homelessness" as a homeless ascetic.

It seems, instead, in these examples to be a question of complementary or contrasting enrichment of the world views of people's own tra-

[63] Adelheid Herrmann-Pfandt, *Dākinīs: Zur Stellung und Symbolik des Weiblichen im tantrischen Buddhismus*, Bonn: Indica et Tibetica 1992, 66ff. I owe this example and the source reference to Sven Bretfeld.

[64] Paul Wernle, *Renaissance und Reformation*, Tübingen: J. C. B. Mohr 1912, 66.

[65] Cf. Heiner Roetz, Konfuzius, 3rd rev. ed., München: Beck 2006, 107.

[66] Cf. Christopher Dawson, *Religion and culture*, London: Ams Pr. Inc. 1936.

ditions. How deep such *discursive* inculturation processes go and what motives underlie them is something that would have to be investigated in greater detail.

11. Rejection of circulating elements by the established religion for the purpose of enhancing its own standing

For instance, up until 1938 one could recognise orthodox synagogues in Germany by the "lack" of the organ which had slowly found its way into liberal synagogues since 1830, although there were discussions in liberal circles too as to whether the organ was a "Christian element".[67] In general, this type of contact stands for the fact that differentiation is also part of the modes and impacts of religious contact, because the refusal to accept alien elements does change the existing religion. Even if it is a matter of preserving the old, tried and trusted, the contact between religions forces the traditional religion to confront alternatives and to portray itself in a way – for example by highlighting and cementing certain elements of the tradition – which would not be necessary without the religious contact.[68] The Tibetan Bön religion, for example, did not just hone its profile but probably actually first established its own identity through the discussion of itself based on differentiating itself from Buddhism. Buddhist teachings, divinities and practices were radically rejected; the heroes of Tibetan Buddhist historiography are the anti-heroes, the enemies of the Good in Bön historiography. However, the general influence of the Buddhists was so large that in nearly all areas of religious life and thought, the differences between both religions are marginal. Their literature is full of accusations of plagiarism against each other. In past research, the Bön religion has even occasionally been described bluntly as a variety of Buddhism.[69]

---

[67] On the organ in Jewish religious services cf. Tina Frühauf, *Orgeln und Orgelmusik in deutsch-jüdischer Kultur* (Netiva: Wege deutsch-jüdischer Geschichte und Kultur 6), Hildesheim: Georg Olms 2005 (English edition 2009 entitled *The organ and its music in German-Jewish culture*, New York: Oxford University Press 2008). I owe this example and the reference to Elisabeth Hollender.

[68] On the example of Neo-Hinduism cf. Christoph Auffarth, "'Weltreligion' als ein Leitbegriff der Religionswissenschaft im Imperialismus, in Mission und Macht im Wandel politischer Orientierungen: Europäische Missionsgesellschaften in politischen Spannungsfeldern in Afrika und Asien zwischen 1800 und 1945", in: *Missionsgeschichtliches Archiv* vol. X (2007) 17–36.

[69] Cf. David Snellgrove, *Indo-Tibetan Buddhism*, London: Shambhala 1987.

12. Complete obliteration and replacement (of elements) of one religious tradition by another

This consequence of the contact between religions is presumably rather rare because the impact at least of elements of an existing religious tradition, even in the event of strong cultural hegemony, continue to exist through the forming, spreading or substantively expanding religion. Even in the case of the interpretatio Romana as the key constituent of Roman religion or in the case of the integration of indigenous elements by Catholicism, local cults continue to have an impact. One can see the suppression of "Shamanism" by Lamaism in Mongolia as an example of the substitution of one religious tradition by another (in this case, an expanding one). According to Walther Heissig the Shamans were subject to bloody persecution there during the expansion of Lamaism, yet their functions were taken over by the Diyance-Lamas or Gurtum-Lamas as well as by Tantrism.[70]

E. *Paradigmatic Conclusions*

The statements made in this text, as mentioned at the outset, do not as yet claim to be systematic and are of a provisional nature. They should be seen as methodological building blocks for exploring dynamics in the history of religions from the point of view of religious contact. During the consortium's work it has become clear that we will have to lay greater store by the hermeneutic aspects of religious research. For instance, we must learn methodological lessons from the question of how object-language labeling of the Self and Other can be linked to scientific metalanguage. The question of whether and, if so, how religion can be scientifically identified must be separated from the question of the importance of religious phenomena for people's and collectives' identities. At the same time, we must, of course, also establish links between identifiability and identity.

A second hermeneutic issue relates to the question of how religious contacts can be understood without falling prey to essentialisms. It is true that the cultural sciences talk in general of cultural flows, trans-

[70] Cf. Walther Heissig, "Die Religionen der Mongolei", in: Giuseppe Tucci/Walther Heissig, *Die Religionen Tibets und der Mongolei*, Stuttgart et al.: Kohlhammer 1970, 296–427, here: 342f.

fer processes and hybrid structures. However, the problem of how to understand exchange processes without presupposing set cultural units has yet to be sufficiently resolved. This also applies to research on religious contacts. Instead of speaking of transfer processes and cultural flows, it would appear to make more sense to see contact as a constitutive process in which cultural units in general and religious formations in particular form. To better understand these contexts, the consortium is working on a corresponding approach entitled "Relational Religion", which amongst other things, relates the scientific observation perspective to perceptions and descriptions within the history of religions.

PART ONE

THE FORMATION OF THE MAJOR RELIGIOUS TRADITIONS THROUGH INTER-RELIGIOUS CONTACT

DYNAMIC APPROACHES TO ANTIQUE RELIGIONS IN THE EAST AND WEST. BEYOND CENTRES AND BOUNDARIES

Peter Wick

Down to the present day a great deal of historical research concentrates on the "highlights" of history. New Testament scholarship, for example, privileges research on the theology of Paul. Its reconstruction is based on Paul's letters to the different communities with a preference for Romans and Galatians, which due to their doctrine of justification played an important role during the Reformation and which have influenced protestant scholarship ever after. The theology of Paul is conceived as a closed entity. Sometimes such a view is supplemented by a more dynamic approach, in which the development of Pauline thoughts and beliefs, beginning with his earliest letter to the Thessalonians (approximately 50 CE) and ending with his last letter to the Romans (around 56 CE; respectively to the Philippians; around 60 CE), is taken into consideration. Reconstructing the development of Pauline thought in turn often leads to the Romans and Galatians as the climax and the purest form of Christian theology. With caution one poses the question, as to what degree Paul was influenced by Early Christianity. Even more caution reigns concerning the influence of Paul's "prechristian" life and "Hellenistic" Tarsus as his place of origin.

Such an approach sometimes leads to a very differentiated picture of Pauline theology: biographic and intellectual aspects bring to light, how "the" theology of Paul came into being. The analysis of the different stages that led to the final and purest state of Paul's theology serves to underline its uniqueness. By themselves, the stages of development are of no further interest. Thus, even though the history of development is taken into consideration in this approach, descriptions of Paul's theology analyse this "highlight" of early Christian belief as a static entity. The static of a systematic picture is complemented by dynamic elements, which point out earlier developments regarding the potential of the static entity. Ultimately the dynamic elements serve the static description of the subject in question in the moment at which it has reached its climax. In our case, this is the theology of Paul narrowed down to the letter to the Romans (and Galatians). At best, the dynamic elements are ancillary to the static result. The theology of Paul is understood as an "ideal type". In this way Pauline theology becomes an essentialized and monolithic category.

The approach outlined above seems to be the traditional matrix of historical research: accordingly, the nature and the character of Early Judaism were analyzed in a similar way. Research on the different stages of its development served to understand the entity as a whole. Thus, by defining the nature of Early Judaism prior to the destruction of the second temple in 70 CE, the difference to Judaism after 70 CE and Early Christianity came to light. In addition it was also possible to contrast Early Judaism and Hellenism. The definition of different entities (Judaism, Christianity, and Hellenism) provided the basis for New Testament scholarship to distinguish or derive Early Christianity from this or that background. The different stages of development were only of interest if they helped to clarify the "highlight" in question. Dynamic elements served the sole purpose of describing the formation of a static entity. Thus Early Christianity after 70 CE was understood as an answer to and in dissociation from Rabbinic Judaism, which was considered to be in direct continuance of the Pharisees.

Such an approach is or was characteristic of many other disciplines: Early Buddhism, for example, was derived from the older Vedic religion by distinguishing the new from the old entity. As Patrick Olivelle – with reference to Albert Schweitzer and Max Weber – points out in his paper, the older Brahmanical Hindu religion was conceived as an ideal type: "An ideal type becomes an objective reality, and a constructed category becomes a historical religion." According to Olivelle this pattern of defining religions is not totally absent in contemporary scholarly discourse. Olivelle shows that the formation of Buddhism and Janism and their success resulted in the adaption of the dharma concept by the older tradition of the Vedic and Brahmins. Jens Schlieter points out that the formation of Buddhism was even less influenced by Brahmanic tradition. If "religion" isn't conceived as an essentialized and monolithic category, different dynamic factors influence the formation of new and old. A scientific approach that takes these dynamics into consideration becomes dynamic itself, insofar as each dynamic has its own say and doesn't serve to illustrate an ideal type.

The pattern described above is also present in the research on Early Islam, which is contrasted with contemporary Christianity, Judaism and the tribal religions. Ultimately a comparative approach also looks for "ideal" identities. Guy Stroumsa claims in his paper that the need to define Christianity, Judaism and Islam as closed entities is a precondition to be able to compare them: "In order to compare these religions, one must posit them (at least implicitly) as individual, well delimited entities." Sarah Stroumsa responds by saying that a comparative and phenomenological approach ultimately focuses on the static instead of the dynamic aspects of religions.

This scientific paradigm is deeply rooted in the world-view of the 19th century that found one of its expressions in nationalism. In nationalism, the true nature of a nation is of primary importance. The explanation of the developments that influenced the formation of such an ideal nature serves to lay it open and to conserve it. Such definitions have the function of drawing boundaries in respect to other nations or entities, whose nature had been defined beforehand.

In recent decades many alternative models have been proposed and implemented. In some disciplines they have become part of the methodical canon, in others they still play a minor role. In New Testament scholarship, James D. G. Dunn discovered Paul as "the apostle of Christian diversity". Even Paul's theology can, therefore, be understood as flexible and highly dynamic: Paul reacts to different, changing situations. As he tries to persuade his addressees of the gospel as he understands it, the situations in turn shape his thoughts and beliefs. To put it bluntly: Paul did not try to impose a cluster of fixed ideas or beliefs – his theology – on his addressees no matter what their situation, but rather the different situations also influenced and respectively shaped his ideas and beliefs.[1] This dynamic understanding of Paul and his way of thinking has still to make its way into New Testament scholarship.

In contrast, the research on rabbinic Judaism has made much more progress. Rabbinic Judaism is no longer conceived as the continuation of Pharisaic Judaism after the destruction of the Second Temple. In order to explain its formation, not only its roots in Second Temple period Judaism, but also its highly dynamic conflicts with emerging Christianity are taken into account: the dynamics of interaction,

[1] James D. G. Dunn, "Diversity in Paul", in: Dan Cohn-Sherbok/John M. Court (eds.), *Religious Diversity in the Graeco-Roman World* (BiSe 79), Sheffield 2001, 107–123, here 123.

of demarcating boundaries, of competition and of adaptation had a major influence on the formation of Rabbinic Judaism.[2]

As we have already seen, the old scientific paradigm focused on the moment in which a religion – conceived as a closed entity – reached its climax and in turn revealed its true nature. The climatic moment itself, that is the time the purest form of the subject in question emerged, was of course hotly disputed. No matter which moment was considered as the climatic moment, compared with the climax, all the other stages of development faded into the background as less important. As in NT scholarship the theology of Paul was conceived as the climax of early Christian theology which was followed by a history of decadence already present in the New Testament itself, Roman history was interpreted in the same manner: Augustus as the climax of Roman history was succeeded by decline. In NT scholarship Ferdinand Christian Baur is perhaps the best example of such a perspective, since his matrix influenced the historical interpretation of the NT up until the 20th century. In Baur's eyes, Paul overcame the particularistic roots of Judaism, and after Paul with "early Catholicism" a period of decline that was characterised by the resumption of particularistic Jewish values began.[3]

On the basis of this matrix, the timeline was divided into superior and inferior moments respectively and – since the moments of these highlights of history could be variable – epochs. Periods of cultural, political and religious hybridity were considered inferior. In the history of arts this classification is still present: the time after 480 B.C.E is defined as the "classical period", in which the Greek arts came into full bloom. The great oriental influence prior to the classical epoch was conceived as a necessary precondition, Hellenism as decline.

However, it was not just the temporal axis (time) that was analytically reconstructed according to different sequences of epochs, the same also happened to the local axis (space) within this approach to history and to the world in general. Likewise, the world was divided into centres of development which are of central importance for research, as well as into peripheries which are marginal not only with respect to geography but also in terms of their significance. Rome is of

---

[2] Daniel Boyarin, *Border Lines: The Partition of Judaeo-Christianity*, Philadelphia 2004.

[3] Ferdinand Christian Baur, *Geschichte der christlichen Kirche, vol. 1: Kirchengeschichte der drei ersten Jahrhunderte*, Tübingen 3rd ed. 1863.

quite a different value for the exploration of Roman history than the provinces. The border zones of the Roman Empire are still in danger of being of marginal interest for current research. The area behind the borders is at best explored by marginal and minor disciplines, even if those areas belonged to the Parthians and their Sassanian successors who ruled as long as the Romans over an empire comparable to that of the Romans.

This type of evaluative approach to history constructs a topography of temporal and geographical climaxes with inferior zones in between. These are the rules:

- border areas are the most primitive regions;
- periods between epochs are underdeveloped or decadent;
- such areas and periods are far away from the centre or the cultural climax;
- this is where there is the greatest danger of hybridity and impurity;
- these are the polluted areas and periods.

This approach of qualitative judgment has also been extended to other areas. For example, the notion of "world religions" has not only been used as a quantitative but also as a qualitative definition. It defined what constitutes the "world religions" in their purest and most characteristic forms and how they are to be differentiated and distanced from inferior and mixed forms of religion. Likewise, "pure" religion was distinguished from "primitive" magic or folk religion. The rules are:

- religion is better than magic;
- "theology" is more important than rituals;
- orthodoxy is better or "higher" than sects;
- central religions are better than peripheral movements;
- the fiction of pure origin is preferred to a bad and later mix, eclecticism
- or hybridity.

These qualitative topographies are part of European traditions whose precursors can be found in antiquity. In the 19th century these traditions were elevated to a leading position that continues to have an effect today. The Greeks differentiated themselves from the "barbarians", the latter being an identity constructed by the Greeks. Hellenism spread this kind of consciousness of cultural superiority. By means of its own culture, Hellenism transported such interpretative patterns that were partly adapted to Hellenistic culture but also adapted against the mainstream of Hellenism. In the same vein, Judeans with similar concepts of interpretation downgraded Samaritans as a neither Jewish nor Gentile group. The Gospel of Matthew, when describing Jesus' ministry in Galilee, characterizes this district purposefully as a debased, hybrid periphery. The starting point of Jesus' ministry is "... Galilee of the gentiles, the people living in darkness ..." (Matth. 4:15–16). This description is an adaptation of a Judean (Jerusalem) view of this Jewish border region. Leading on from this, the book of Acts, while not characterising the Samaritans themselves as Gentiles, gives a negative account of their miraculous ministry as "magic" (Acts 8:4–25).

Of course, there have always been alternative approaches to research. However, time and again the matrix described above has gained the upper hand in interpretations. Depending on the subject, it still partly prevails today, despite many new approaches to research. For this reason, in her contribution, Sarah Stroumsa demands that one not only contemplate foreign influences in a given system, but also that one be careful not to judge such influences as negative. She is critical of modern scholarship where this danger is not seen: "Tracing influences is often frowned upon in modern scholarship. Many feel that 'Quellenforschung', which highlights the separate components of a given system, devaluates the originality of this system and diverts scholarly attention from contents and ideas to the history of their transmission".

In our Consortium and in Research Field I we do not intend merely to demarcate the borders less clearly and give more weight to the border regions. Rather, we want to leave the focus on the static behind and take, figuratively speaking, an ocean of dynamic movement as our starting point. From here, we want to find out whether there is some dry land in spite of all the movement. If this is indeed found, we will need to explore the circumstances that lead to this solidification. The Dynamics in the History of Religions between Asia and Europe in the Early Period and in antiquity need to be investigated against the background of this dynamic paradigm.

The hitherto neglected peripheries of research tend to have to move to the centre of research in order to realise such a dynamic approach to research. However, these peripheries will not become the new centres. Rather, we will avoid any kind of qualitative debasement of the peripheries. At the same time, peripheries are of central importance in the exploration of the dynamics of the history of religions (and history of culture), for if there were dynamics between the old "highlights", these must have been particularly strong in the peripheries. This is true of the temporal transitions between the ages of "highest cultural ascendency" as well as of the regions between the cultural "centres".

Central Asia becomes particularly important for the study of the dynamics of the history of religions between Asia and Europe during the Early Period as well as antiquity. If Central Asia only played a marginal role for historians, the region would be in danger of losing its importance for a scientific synopsis of this period. In this case, the scientific community would not attribute appropriate significance to Central Asia as the most important passageway between South- and East-Asia and the Near East (the latter being connected to the Mediterranean region). Nevertheless, if Central Asia is not the passageway, then there would be no passageway at all, and the different cultures could and would have to be explored as if they existed free from contact to the surrounding environment.

However, it is possible to have a different scientific perspective on this region. This region can be regarded as an independent and highly innovative cultural community which encompasses the geographical region of today's Iran, Afghanistan, Pakistan, Turkmenistan and Uzbekistan, that is, the region from the Zagros Mountains to the Indus and from the Indian Ocean to the border of the Eurasian steppe. The cultural communities that established themselves in this region covered the period from Neolithic times till the Islamic occupation (7th century CE), and was not interrupted by the Islamic time.

Situated between the cultural areas of Mesopotamia, India, Eurasia, China and the ancient Mediterranean region, this region is a passageway for traders (silk road) and military expeditions (Alexander; Scythes), peoples (Indoirans/Arians, Sakai, Kushans, Hephthalites) and religious groups (Manichaeans, Jews, Christians, Buddhists, Zoroastrians). It is also a place of direct contact between settled cultures and nomadic peoples, as well as a gateway for conquerors from the steppe (nomads), from Europe (Greeks) and the Near East. At the same time, it was the starting point of large oriental empires (Elamites, Achaemenians, Parthians, Sassanians), who in turn influenced the surrounding cultures with their culture and religion, thus turning the region into a melting pot of cultures and the gravitational center of religious and cultural dynamics.

As we have already seen, the common approach to this area in the context of universal historiography with its separation of centre and periphery is that of a particular peripheral zone. In terms of European historiography, this approach has been mainly negative. For example, in Germany little money was provided for the exploration of these seemingly peripheral regions. Up to now it has scarcely been possible to pool the few individual research projects because they approach the region from very different disciplines (with the exception of Iranian studies).

It is only possible to determine potential religious-historical and cultural connections between South- and East-Asian regions on the one hand and the Near East and the Mediterranean on the other through a scientific exploration of this cultural region. This would be of great benefit for religious, philosophical and cultural studies. During the inaugural conference of the IKGF "Dynamics in the History of Religions", we had an exhibition of coins influenced by Hellenism that came from this region. The goddess of victory typical for minting under Alexander the Great is still a motif in the Northwest of India three centuries later. Coins with Indian gods marked with Greek inscriptions are placed next to those which legitimise the ruler at the Hindu Kush as a real Macedonian. In the second century (CE), the Kushana depicted Buddha for the first time on coins with Greek transcriptions.

Due to its geographic location, a new definition of this larger region would lead to a new formulation of the concept of the history of the Mediterranean, the Near Eastern and South- and East-Asian region.[4] As long as this region mutates time and again and there are blank spots on the map between Europe/the Near East and Asia (apart from some individual studies), the results of research that build on the high permeability of this region will find it hard to achieve general acceptance. As one of the many examples, we can point to the teaching of the transmigration of souls of the Greeks. In 1990 Walter Burkert cites a remark by Kurt v. Fritz in a book review with cautious agreement: "The teaching of the transmigration of souls appears much more out of place among the contemporary religious conceptions of 6th/5th century Greece than the formation of religious associations. Nonetheless, there is sufficient unambiguous early evidence for its existence within Pythagoras, so that there is no room for doubt that it was taught by Pythagoras. For a long time it has been an open question how Pythagoras acquired this teaching because a direct

---

[4] This short description of the Central-Asian cultural community and its significance mainly goes back to Sylvia Winkelmann (IKGF Fellow) and Sven Bretfeld (IKGF Colleague).

link to India appeared impossible. However, in recent times new evidence suggests that Indian religion and philosophy had already spread to Persia at the time of Pythagoras or even before. It thus no longer seems impossible that Pythagoras came into contact with this teaching in this way. In Pythagoras, this teaching took on a different, more Greek form than was common in India. However, India was also the classical country of religious associations."[5] This text describes the phenomenon outlined above. Von Fritz writes: "There is something true in the conception that every epoch has its own style which finds its expression in various different realms. This conception emerged in the 19th century and was often made absolute in our century." However, with the above example he warns of the danger of denying the "most obvious facts", in order to maintain the "absolute unity of the style".[6]

Once the Central-Asian region gains significance in research, it will obviously become the real axis between the cultural regions that have up to now been believed to be central. In his paper Victor H. Mair offers a number of examples which show the transfer of cultural elements from the West to China in the Early Period. For instance, China has religious specialists who were originally called *mag*. A *mag* thus had the same name as a religious specialist from Iran: the Persian *magus*. Apparently such specialists came from the West to China. In the Christmas story of the Gospel of Matthew such wise men from the East come from the opposite direction. They are designated with a word from the same stem, *magoi* (Matth. 2:1). Accordingly, in antiquity the term *magus* links the Mediterranean and China via Central Asia and Iran.

If not only the thin threads of the silk road but also the entire region becomes the new axis, this will shed new light on the Axial Age Theory provided by Karl Jaspers. This theory states that between 800 BCE and 200 CE a new type of thinking appeared in China, India and the Occident, all of them having a lot of strong parallels and similarities with each other. However, there were no signs of ideational transmission between these different regions. It is postulated that there is no proof of any extensive intercommunication between Ancient Greece,

[5] Walter Burkert, *Antike Mysterien: Funktionen und Gehalt*, München 1990, 74, citing Kurt von Fritz, "Review of J. A. Philip: Pythagoras and Early Pythagoreanism, Toronto 1966", in: *Gnomon* 40 (1968), 6–13, here 8–9. Von Fritz refers to Friedrich Cornelius, *Indogermanische Religionsgeschichte*, München 1942, and mentions oral information from Cornelius about Brahminical influence in Persia.

[6] Kurt von Fritz, 9.

the Middle East, India and China. These new movements are Hinduism, Buddhism, Daoism, Confucianism, Early Judaism and Greek Philosophy.

Here is a potential solution to this riddle: the axial age is an age of real/physical axes. The 19th and 20th century views on Central Asia and Iran could not perceive this, because they only saw a peripheral region of impure origin, a later mixture of styles, a region full of hybridity and border areas with no cultural importance.

In Research Field I we have consciously changed our approach. Hybridity, diffusion into all directions and syncretism become the norm. Dynamic processes become the rule. What is solid and has a separate profile becomes something special. If it can be observed it needs special explanation. For instance, early Judaism gains its distinctive image through strategies of demarcation from Hellenism although it is nonetheless part of the latter. The same is true for early Christianity that demarcated itself from both Judaism and Hellenism, which led to densification.

In this way, in Research Field I, we are examining the formation of the "world religions" in a framework of religious dynamics. Our main questions are: how do common traditions change by intellectual contact with and/or through physical transfer to a different world or region or group? Are there any patterns of (trans)formations and changes? Important concepts in our research are: diffusion, absorption, adoption, re-evaluation of traditions due to contact with others, demarcation, densification, consolidation or retraction.

In summary we can say that our aim is not only to explore the dynamics between religions and cultures, but that the latter should themselves be regarded as dynamic entities. However, if everything changes it is something special when an entity within this movement solidifies. Along these lines, the advance of a culture based on written traditions is something special, and it can be regarded as a significant factor for the phenomena that has been called "Achsenzeit" or axial age (cf. Jan Assmann). Likewise, the stronger orientation towards the transcendental could be comprehended as the attempt to fathom the divine as that which is unmovable, that which can be removed from the dynamics of human experience.

Will such a change in the matrix of scientific research also have an effect on classical topics of research such as the theology of Paul? The change in the matrix changes everything. In this vein, Paul will, in the future, surely be seen much more as a man of constant movement (apostle). His geographic movements significantly influenced his thinking. The fact that in spite of the short time his work lasted we are left with a fair amount of epistles is something special because in it we can grasp something solid, something that endures. Only the static form of writing allows us to reconstruct his thinking as an entity of its own. However, this thinking is not just a static theology, but dynamically applied to the very different situations of his addressees. It is also intermeshed with the great movements of history and thought in the middle of the first century CE. Tradition-history will return to being important, but no longer as an attempt to distil the influences on Paul in order to differentiate his thinking as a (static) product of these influences more clearly. Rather, the aim is to comprehend Paul as a distinctive part of his environment and to better understand his dynamic integration in his surroundings.[7]

As a New Testament researcher I have used Paul here merely as an example for what is already happening or could happen in the future in many areas of historical and philological research. A more dynamic matrix will lead to more dynamic results. The static will become an exception which will need special explanation.

[7] Excellent examples in Troels Engberg-Pedersen (ed.), *Paul beyond the Judaism/Hellenism divide*, Louisville (Ky.) 2001.

RELIGIOUS FORMATIONS AND INTERCULTURAL CONTACTS IN EARLY CHINA

Victor H. Mair

1. *Abstract*

Of the three major doctrines (San Jiao 三教) of China – Confucianism, Buddhism, and Taoism – the first is fundamentally a native product, the second is mainly a foreign importation, and the third is a fusion of indigenous and alien elements. As established doctrines or religions, the San Jiao evolved chiefly during the late classical period through the early medieval period, roughly the 2nd c. BC through the 6th c. AD. Thus it is evident that the study of the history of religion in late classical and early medieval China cannot ignore the interfusion of Sinitic and non-Sinitic elements and influences. The thesis of this paper is that the same is true for the early classical and prehistoric periods. Evidence of pre-imperial xeno-Sinitic religious exchange is presented here under four rubrics: lamb of goodness, goat of justice; magi from the west; heavenly horses; heavenly questions.

2. *Introduction*

Scholarly understanding of the history of religion in China, like that of so many other aspects of Chinese history, tends to be disturbingly schizophrenic: on one hand, the uniqueness and insularity of Chinese religion is stressed; on the other hand, the foreign origins of Buddhism, Islam, Christianity, Manichaeism, Zoroastrianism, and Judaism are reluctantly admitted. All of the religions just mentioned came to China and took root there during the medieval period – basically from the Eastern Han (25–220 AD) through the Tang (618–907 AD).[1] In this chapter, I wish to develop a model of cultural interfusion for

[1] Foltz, Richard C., *Religions of the Silk Road: Overland Trade and Cultural Exchange from Antiquity to the Fifteenth Century*, New York: St. Martin's 1999.

the period of early China – before the Qin (221–206 BC) and the Western Han (206 BC–23 AD) dynasties and moving backward in time through the Iron Age to the Bronze Age and beyond. This is the time of "China before China," to adopt the fine phrase turned by Fiskesjö and Chen.[2]

The picture that I would like to paint in this essay is more like a sketch of the main outlines of religious development than a detailed portrayal of all facets of the history of early Chinese religion, which would require book-length treatment. I shall focus on several essential aspects of religious belief and behavior during pre-Qin times that established the foundations for the evolution of organized religion in China. I would be the first to recognize that there were many other religious manifestations in pre-Qin times that are not covered in this treatment. For instance, the elaborate Neolithic goddess worship of the Hongshan Culture in the northeast and the Bronze Age sacrificial pits filled with ivory tusks and peculiar statues at Sanxingdui in the southwest are evidence of vital cults outside of the East Asian Heartland (EAH), and there were many other local and regional traditions. Yet it is difficult to determine the degree to which such traditions contributed to mainstream practice and ideology of later times.

Instead of a comprehensive survey of the evolution of religion within the present territory of China during pre-Qin (i. e., pre-imperial) times, I shall focus on a limited number of phenomena that have remained central to Chinese ideas about ethics, spirituality and sacredness right up to modern times.

3. *Lamb of Goodness, Goat of Justice*

Somewhat surprisingly, the foundations of Chinese ethical and moral precepts are intimately linked to ovicaprids (or caprovines, i. e., sheep and goats). This is surprising in the sense that China is viewed as a typical agricultural society, which means that the modus vivendi of its people was settled, not pastoral or nomadic, as one might expect in light of the high esteem in which ovicaprids were apparently held by the founders of the civilization.

[2] Fiskesjö, Magnus/Chen Xingcan, *China Before China: Johan Gunnar Andersson, Ding Wenjiang, and the Discovery of China's Prehistory*, Stockholm: Museum of Far Eastern Antiquities 2004.

The earliest remains of domesticated sheep and goats in China date to the fourth millennium BC and have been discovered to the north and northwest (i. e., north[west]) of the EAH, especially in Gansu Province. It is significant that the earliest ovicaprid remains in China are to be found in the distant north(west), since this location fits perfectly with a trajectory of introduction from the west. Goats were first domesticated in the region of Anatolia and Kurdistan during the 8th millennium BC, while sheep were domesticated in Iran and Iraq around the same time or slightly later than the goat. Domesticated sheep and goats did not occur in the middle and lower Yellow River Valley until the early Longshan period, represented by goat remains *(Capra hircus)* found at the site of Miaodigou in Sanmenxia, western Henan Province, which are dated to around 2800 BC.[3]

Presented here as a mere list without extensive discussion, the following ethical, moral, and esthetic concepts are all manifestly linked to ovicaprids, as can be seen by the *yang* 羊 signific (note the two horns at the top) which all the characters used to write them contain:

yi 義	("justice, righteousness")
shan 善	("good[ness]")
xiang 祥	("felicitous, auspicious")
yang 養	("raise, nourish, nurture, rear, take care of in old age")
mei 美	("beauty")
xiu 羞	("shame")
you 羑	("to guide to goodness/right/reason")
xian 羡	("admire; be fond of")
xian 鮮	("fresh; delicious food, delicacy; good and kind"– an obvious merging of ovicaprid and piscine qualities)[4]

The fact that so many basic values are linked to ovicaprids could not be a mere accident, but must embody an inescapable truth about the deep psychology of the Chinese mind. This psychological makeup,

[3] Liu, Li, *The Chinese Neolithic: Trajectories to Early States*, Cambridge: Cambridge University Press 2004, 59; Mair, Victor H., "The Horse in Late Prehistoric China: Wresting Culture and Control from the 'Barbarians.'", in: Marsha Levine/Colin Renfrew/Katie Boyle (eds.), *Prehistoric steppe adaptation and the horse*, McDonald Institute Monographs, Cambridge: McDonald Institute for Archaeological Research 2003, 181ab of 163–187.

[4] Mair 2003, 177.

moreover, must have arisen as a result of the mode of existence of the people whom it informed.

Not only did north(west)ern pastoralists and nomads introduce fundamental ethical, moral, and esthetic concepts using presumed attributes of ovicaprids as metaphors for the deepest foundation of morality in the EAH, they also supplied basic components of Sinitic mythology. To give only one example, Fuxi (or Paoxi), who is reckoned to be the father of Chinese civilization and polity, the inventor of the trigrams of the *Yi jing/I-ching* (Classic of Changes), and many other vital components of Chinese civilization besides, was inseparably linked to animal husbandry. Numerous variant writings of his name reveal his perceived association with the sacrificial slaughter and roasting of ovicaprids and bovids (*niu* 牛): 伏/庖 羲/犧/戲/牺.[5] Yet another variant, Paoxi 炮犧, quite literally means "roast sacrificial

[5] As briefly as possible, the *fu* syllable of his name means "prostrate" (a suitable posture for the presentation of sacrificial viands), the variant *pao* is a direct reference to the kitchen or butchering room where the sacrifice is prepared. In the *Book of Changes*, although the name is written as 包牺, the 包 here is pronounced as *pao* (not its usual *bao* meaning "wrap") and means the same thing as 庖, viz., "kitchen". Forms of Fuxi's name beginning with 宓 (usually pronounced *mi* and meaning "tranquil, quiet") instead of Fu or Pao are probably due to regional phonological variation (the Old Sinitic reconstructions of all these orthographical variants of the initial syllable of Fuxi's name are fairly close, with initial bilabials that are aspirated, rounded vowels, and final velars). Be that as it may, in variations of the name Fuxi, the character 宓 is supposed by philologists to be interchangeable with and pronounced the same as *fu* 伏. The *xi* of Fuxi straightforwardly signifies an animal slaughtered for sacrifice or the act of slaughtering such an animal, with ovicaprids as the primary referents, but with the subsequent addition of the semantic indicator for bovids. *Xi* 犧 ("sacrificial animal") is an expanded form of *xi* 羲. When the latter, which originally must have indicated mainly ovicaprid sacrifice, became incorporated into and identified with the names of gods (Fuxi, Xihe 羲和 [the Solar Charioteer]) (Snow, Justine T., "The Spider's Web. Goddesses of Light and Loom: Examining the Evidence for the Indo-European Origins of Two Ancient Chinese Deities", in: *Sino-Platonic Papers* 118 (June) (2002), 1–75, plus 2 plates, 35–37), the bovid signifier was added to it to reemphasize the meaning of "sacrificial victim" (Chang Hsüan張瑄, *Zhongwen changyong san qian zi xing yi shi*中文常用三千字形義釋 (the Etymologies of 3,000 Chinese Characters in Common Use [original English title → Explanation of the Shapes and Sounds of 3,000 Commonly Used Chinese Characters]), Hong Kong: Hong Kong University Press 1968, 496). The addition of the bovid signific by no means meant that the newly formed character could apply only to the sacrifice of cattle, since we have such expressions as *xiyang* 犧羊 ("sacrifice an ovicaprid") as well as *xiniu* 犧牛 ("sacrifice a bovid"). Furthermore, that the addition of the bovid signific served to extend the basic meaning of *xi* 犧 to a wider sacrificial framework beyond primarily ovicaprids may be deduced from the expression *xiquan* 犧牷, where the *quan* is a complex character that is similarly formed from a basic character, *quan* 全 ("complete, whole"), whose meaning is extended to refer to sacrificial animals that are presented to the gods in their entirety or that are entirely of one color (preferably white). Despite the fact that it carries the bovid signific, *quan*

animal" (HDC 7: 55a). Thus, it is to be expected that Fuxi would be credited by mythicizers with teaching people how to eat the meat of domesticated, herded animals.

Just as the Sinitic notion of justice was intimately bound up with ideals based upon ovicaprid imagery, so was the concept of law inextricably linked to a most peculiar type of goat. The character that has been used to write this important word – *fa* 法 – is actually an old simplified form that came into use with "seal style" writing, which was popular about 2,300 years ago. Before then, another very complicated, but also highly revealing, character was used to write *fa*, which at that time would have sounded something like **pjwap*. In the process of simplification, several important elements were omitted, leaving behind an eight stroke character (the original form had twenty-one

---

牷 does not refer only to cattle, but to ovicaprids and occasionally other domesticated animals as well.

Ideally, the animal to be sacrificed *(xi)* should be "pure" (*chun* 純), i.e., all of one color, with white being the most highly desired hue. (The rarer variant for the *xi* syllable ostensibly means "play", which might conceivably have to do with the ritual aspects of the slaughter, although this is rather unlikely. Hence, philologists customarily explain this *xi* simply as being a phonological equivalent of the *xi* meaning "sacrificial animal"). But there is a linkage of interchangeability among 羲 (the second syllable of Fuxi's name), 犧 (variant of the second syllable of Fuxi's name; "sacrificial animal"), 戲 (variant of the second syllable of Fuxi's name, "play"), and 獻 (*xian*; "offer sacrifice of a domesticated animal"), all within the semantic field of the sacrifice of domesticated animals (*HDC* 5.252a). The sole exception to this nexus of the sacrifice of domesticated animals among the more than a dozen known variants of the name Fuxi/Paoxi/Mixi → Fuxi is to be found on the controversial Chu silk manuscript, said to have been stolen in 1942 in the eastern suburbs of Changsha, Hunan, and supposedly dating to the late WS period, ca. 300 BC (Wilkinson, Endymion, *Chinese History: A Manual*. Harvard-Yenching Institute Monograph Series 52, Cambridge: Harvard University Asia Center 2000, 463). Although exposure to the light has darkened the Chu silk manuscript and left it illegibile, on copies that were made while it could still be read Fuxi's name is written as Baoxi 雹戲 (literally, "hail play"), but the graphs are in an archaic, regional orthography. Like the *mi* → *fu* of Mixi → Fuxi discussed above, the *bao* of Baoxi on the Chu silk manuscript is doubtless a regional phonological variant of Fuxi. The second character of Baoxi is apparently the same as one of the orthographical variants of the name Fuxi/Paoxi already discussed above. In any case, the totality of the written forms of the name Fuxi/Paoxi/Mixi → Fuxi (Baoxi is clearly an anomaly) are unmistakably related to the ritual sacrifice of domesticated animals.

Sheep-goats and cattle were the characteristic herded animals of the steppe peoples who must have furnished the symbolism for the invention of the mythological figure known as Fuxi or Paoxi. Even if it be asserted that Fuxi (Paoxi) is essentially the phonetic transcription of a bisyllabic name, the semantic implications of the constituent graphs cannot be dismissed out of hand as being entirely inoperative, since they are consistent among the numerous variants and carefully chosen to convey the meanings discussed above. Indeed, Fuxi was so closely identified with sacrificial slaughter that the syllable *xi* alone could refer to him.

strokes 灋) consisting of two elements, a water radical on the left and a phonophore ("sound carrier") pronounced *qu* (meaning "go") on the right, which – by itself – is totally mystifying and makes sense neither semantically nor phonologically. When we carefully analyze the full, complicated form of the original graph, however, even the simplified form can be explained more or less satisfactorily.

The original form of the graph for *fa* consisted of three components, one of which can be further broken down into two components. At different times and different places, the positions of the three main components could be shifted around virtually at random, although they eventually stabilized as follows: on the left was a schematized stream signifying water. To the right, at the top, was a pictograph of a one-horned goat-like creature and beneath that on the right was a man coming out from the opening of a cave.

How could such a strange configuration possibly signify a notion as exalted as "law"? Let us first dispose of the two-part component at the bottom. A man coming out of a cave is "going" somewhere, so that part of the graph implies "go (away), depart".[6] The water on the left signifies "level," hence "equitable". The most perplexing part, of course, is the one-horned caprine creature on the top right. We actually know the name of this supernatural animal; it is the *xiezhi* 解/獬 廌/豸. This is *not* the fabled *qilin* 麒麟 (Japanese *kirin*), which is often (erroneously) referred to as a unicorn, but that is an entirely different story that needs to be taken up separately. The function of the *xiezhi* was to butt the guilty party in a lawsuit.[7] Pictures or stat-

---

[6] Whether the component being discussed actually depicts a man departing from a cave (the usual explanation of the graphic form, but there are others [e.g., Karlgren, Bernhard, *Grammata Serica Recensa*, Stockholm: Museum of Far Eastern Antiquities 1972, 170, no. 642a–b]), hence "depart", is immaterial. Whatever this component depicts, we do know that it means "leave, depart, go".

[7] Because of its propensity for butting those who are guilty, I shall refer to the *zhi* or *xiezhi* as "goat-like" or "caprine". However, since the *(xie)zhi* is, after all, a mythical or supernatural animal, we should not get bogged down in issues of whether it is actually a goat, a deer, or something else. As a matter of fact, both the shape of the character used to write *zhi* (the predominant operative morpheme of the word *xiezhi*, *xie* being auxiliary in nature) and textual explanations of its nature developed through time. As with other fantastic creatures in early China, different authors offered diverse descriptions of what it looked like, often resulting in a composite being possessing characteristics of various animals known in real life. Suffice it for present purposes to make the following drastically abbreviated remarks: 1. the character for *fa* does not occur in the first stage of the Chinese writing system, that of the OSBIs circa 1200 BC; 2. the first appearance of the character for *fa* is in the second stage of the Chinese writing system, that of the early Zhou bronze inscriptions, roughly around 1000 BC

ues of the *xiezhi* were actually posted in ancient Chinese courtrooms, and several powerful wooden and bronze representations of the *xiezhi* have recently been archeologically recovered from the far northwest (N. B.) of China.[8] A large, correctly labeled, modern, bronze statue of the *xiezhi* may be seen in the center of the lobby of the University of Pennsylvania Law School, should anyone be interested in seeing one for him/herself (albeit with the horn pointing backward in the wrong direction!).

It may sound far-fetched for a one-horned goat to be looked upon as the dispenser of justice, but there is actually a long, well-documented Eurasian tradition of trial by animal ordeal behind this seemingly bizarre belief.[9] There can be little doubt that these old ideas were brought to the EAH along with the importation of domesticated ovicaprids (sheep and goats) during the third and second millennia BC.

(Karlgren 1972, 171, no. 642m); 3. *zhi* does occur by itself (not as an element in *fa*) on the OSBIs; 4. alone on the OSBIs and as a component of *fa* on the bronze inscriptions, *zhi* – judging from its two horns, placement of its legs, and other attributes – is neither *lu* (cervid) nor *yang* (ovicaprid), though it is closer to the latter; 5. in the subsequent stages of its development, the character for *zhi* – both alone and as part of *fa* – retained two horns like an ovicaprid or bovid (but stylistically more like the former, and never developing branched antlers like a cervid [this is a crucial point]), but with a head somewhat resembling the graphic representation of an equid; 6. some rare instances among early forms have one horn exaggerated to an extent that it almost looks like a unicorn is being portrayed; 7. some late variants of *zhi*, whether alone or as part of *fa*, develop the stylized feet of cervids; 8. all early pictorial and plastic representations of the *zhi* that have survived show it with only a single horn, not antlers, and with cleft hooves more nearly resembling an ovicaprid than the even-toed hoofs of a deer (see below Figs. 1–3).

[8] Watt, James C. (ed.), *China: Dawn of a Golden Age, 200–750 AD*, New York: The Metropolitan Museum of Art; New Haven and London: Yale University Press 2004, 177–178 nos. 81 and 82, where they are misidentified as *qilin*; see Figs. 1–3 at the end of this chapter. The Later Han (ca. 100 AD) reconstruction of *xiezhi* is gɛ-ḍɛ. (Schuessler, Axel, *ABC Etymological Dictionary of Old Chinese*, Honolulu: University of Hawai'i Press 2007, 620.) Linguistic, archeological, and cultural evidence indicate that the word "goat" (< **ghaidos*) is a northwestern regionalism in Germanic (Mallory, J. P./Adams, D. Q. (eds.) *Encyclopedia of Indo-European Culture*, London and Chicago: Fitzroy Dearborn 1997, 510b–512a). For many years I have been intending to write a detailed philological study on *fa* ("law"), *xiezhi* ("one-horned goat of justice"), and trial by animal ordeal among Eurasian peoples. Now that I have given this scaled-down account, the chances that I shall present a longer version in the not-too-distant future have improved.

[9] Meserve, Ruth I., "History in the Search for Precedent: 'Animal Judgments.'", in: *Altaica* (Moscow) 5 (2001), 90–97; Meserve, Ruth I., "Public Ridicule.", in: Alice Sárközi/Attila Rákos (eds.), *Altaica Budapestinensia, MMII*. Proceedings of the 45th Permanent International Altaistic Conference (PIAC). Budapest, Hungary, June 23–28, 2002, Budapest: Research Group for Altaic Studies, Hungarian Academy of Sciences; Department of Inner Asian Studies, Eötvös Loránd University 2003, 225–233.

To summarize, in the earliest form of the graph for writing the word *fa*, we have a one-horned caprine-like imaginary animal (the *xiezhi*) equitably (like level water) butting the guilty party away (from the notion of "go"). After simplification more than two thousand years ago, only the "water" and the "go" were left, the one-horned caprine having been lost in the shuffle.

When Buddhism came to China during the Eastern Han period (25 BC–220AD), *fa* was used to translate the word *dharma*, whereupon it took on all of the dozens of meanings of the Sanskrit word. Long before that, however, already by the time of the Warring States (hereafter WS; 475–221 BC), *fa* had evolved from its primitive meaning of meting out justice through increasing stages of abstraction and generalization to mean "law," "method," and "model" (both noun and verb).[10]

Even the Chinese idea of "community group" was based on an ovicaprid metaphor, that of the flock. In a celebrated passage extolling the superiority of human beings over animals, the late WS thinker, Xun Zi (c. 298–238 BC), subconsciously alludes to ovicaprid behavior as a model for social organization:

> Water and fire possess material energy but lack life. Grasses and trees possess life but lack sentience. Birds and beasts possess sentience but lack justice. Human beings possess material energy, life, sentience, and also justice; therefore, they are the noblest of all under heaven. Their strength is not comparable to that of bovines, they do not run as fast as horses, yet how is it that horses and bovines are used by them? One may answer, "It is because human beings can form communities, but those other creatures cannot do so." (*Xun Zi*, 9, "Wang zhi" [Kingly Regulations])

The chief irony of this passage is that the word for "form communities/groups" is derived from a caprovine term meaning "(to) flock" (*qun* 群), not to mention that the moral excellence of human beings, as noted above, is also based on a caprovine metaphor *(yi)*. Furthermore, the whole tenor of Xun Zi's discussion is framed by multiple comparisons with domesticated animals brought from western Eurasia via the steppe.

---

[10] Mair, Victor H., "*Soldierly Methods*: Vade Mecum for an Iconoclastic Translation of *Sun Zi bingfa*." With a complete transcription and word-for-word glosses of the Manchu translation by H. T. Toh, in: *Sino-Platonic Papers* 178 (February), 2008, i–xvi, 1–195. Web publication.

Given that animal husbandry played a minor role in traditional Chinese agriculture, with meat (and that mainly the flesh of pigs and dogs) contributing only a small share of the diet,[11] it is illuminating to observe how images and practices drawn from pastoral and nomadic lifestyles dominated ethics and ritual from the very beginning of Sinitic civilization.

Pastoral and nomadic peoples from the north and northwest, with the main avenues of access being the Gansu Corridor and the Ordos Plateau, have had an enormous impact on the political and cultural fortunes of the EAH for the past five millennia. It is no wonder that they have left their imprint on the ethical conceptions and religious life of the inhabitants of what would later become China, including the Extended East Asian Heartland (EEAH) far to the south.[12]

4. *Magi from the West*

If we seek to identify the single most important characteristic of indigenous Chinese religion, nothing can compete with ancestor worship.[13] Indeed, from the very first historically verifiable dynasty, the Shang (from around 1600 to the middle of the 11th c. BC), rituals dedicated to the ancestors were essential to the well-being of the state and its rulers:[14]

[11] Sterckx, Roel, *The Animal and the Daemon in Early China*, Albany: State University of New York Press 2002, 28 and passim.

[12] Mair, Victor H., "The North(west)ern Peoples and the Recurrent Origins of the 'Chinese' State.", in: Joshua A. Fogel (ed.), *The Teleology of the Modern Nation-State: Japan and China*, Philadelphia: University of Pennsylvania Press 2005, 46–84, 205–217.

[13] Eno, Robert, "Shang State Religion and the Pantheon of the Oracle Texts.", in: John Lagerwey/Marc Kalinowski (eds.), *Early Chinese Religion. Part One: Shang through Han (1250 BC – 220 AD)*, Leiden: Brill. 2008, 41–102; Smith, D. Howard, "Chinese Religion in the Shang Dynasty.", in: *Numen*, 8.2 (July) (1961), 142–150.

[14] Naturally, as befits an agricultural people, concern for fertility – symbolized by an altar to the god of the earth (*she* 社) – was also prominent, but can not compare with the constant attention paid to the altar for the ancestors (*zu* 祖), the archaic form of the character for which depicted a phallus. Desiderata such as *shou* 壽 ("longevity", first seen in the bronze inscriptions) and *xian* 仙 < 僊 (customarily translated as "immortal", but more accurately rendered as "transcendent"; first encountered in the seal script in the late WS period), although assiduously sought after by respectively the Chinese populace at large and religious practitioners in particular during historical times, arose much later than the core ethical, moral, spiritual and esthetic concepts discussed above.

> Shang religion was inextricably involved in the genesis and legitimation of the Shang state. It was believed that Ti [Di], the high god, conferred fruitful harvest and divine assistance in battle, that the king's ancestors were able to intercede with Ti, and that the king could communicate with his ancestors. Worship of the Shang ancestors, therefore, provided powerful psychological and ideological support for the political dominance of the Shang kings. The king's ability to determine through divination, and influence through prayer and sacrifice, the will of the ancestral spirits legitimized the concentration of political power in his person. All power emanated from the theocrat because he was the channel, "the one man," who could appeal for the ancestral blessings, or dissipate the ancestral curses, which affected the commonality. It was the king who made fruitful harvest and victories possible by the sacrifices he offered, the rituals he performed, and the divinations he made. If, as seems likely, the divinations involved some degree of magic making, of spell casting, the king's ability to actually create a good harvest or a victory by divining about it rendered him still more potent politically.[15]

The Shang state was thus, in essence, a theocracy, with the king, for all intents and purposes, a reigning theocrat.

What we know about the religion of the Shang is basically what might be called Royal Religion. We have very little idea of what the religion of the people, daily or otherwise, must have been.[16] If we wish to delineate the religion of the Shang, what we can discern on the basis of the Oracle Shell and Bone Inscriptions (OSBIs) may be outlined as follows. It was: 1. premised upon the authority of Shangdi (the high god), 2. circumscribed by the court of Di 帝 (heavenly god[s], i.e., deified ancestors) and his/their officials, 3. attentive to the spirits of wind and rain, 4. concentrated on questions concerning Di, 5. solicitous of the spirits of the earth, 6. mindful of the rivers and mountains, 7. focused on sacrificial rituals for rain.[17]

---

[15] Keightley, David N., "The Religious Commitment: Shang Theology and the Genesis of Chinese Political Culture.", in: *History of Religions* 17.3–4 (1978), 212–213 of 211–225.

[16] Keightley, David N., "The Shang: China's First Historical Dynasty", in: Michael Loewe/Edward L. Shaughnessy (eds.), *The Cambridge History of Ancient China: From the Origins of Civilization to 221 BC*, Cambridge: Cambridge University Press 1999, 232–291.

[17] Chen Mengjia 陳夢家, *Yinxu buci zongshu* 殷虛卜辭綜述 [Summary of Oracle Inscriptions from the Wastes of Yin], Beijing: Kexue Chubanshe 1956, 561–603; Chang, Tsung-tung, *Der Kult der Shang-Dynastie im Spiegel der Orakelinschriften: Eine paläographische Studie zur Religion im archaischen China*, Wiesbaden: Otto Harrassowitz 1970, 224–226; Li Chi, *Anyang*, Seattle: University of Washington Press 1977.

OSBIs pertain to such matters as the following: sacrificial rituals, military campaigns, hunting expeditions, comings-and-goings of the king and other members of the royal family, well-being during the next day, night, or ten-day period (*xún* 旬), weather, harvest, sickness, life or death, the birth of a child, dreams, building, and so forth.[18] In their purpose and manner of production, Shang divinations and the written inscriptions resulting therefrom are religious and ritual in nature. Judging from the OSBIs and from the entire archeological record, religious ritual pervaded Shang royal life.[19]

The individuals charged with divination concerning such questions and interpreting the responses from the gods were called *wu* 巫, who were also healers.[20] The usual translations given for *wu* are "shaman, sorcerer, wizard, witch, magician." Although it is the most common rendering, "shaman" is not really appropriate, since it signifies a type of Tungusic medium whose activities are altogether different from those of the *wu*. The term "sorcerer" is even less suitable for *wu*, inasmuch as it signifies the use of supernatural power over others through the assistance of evil spirits. "Wizard" and "witch" are also poor matches for *wu* because they cast spells and are thought to have dealings with the devil, hardly the types of concerns displayed by the *wu*. "Magician" is slightly preferable to the other four translations, but its modern English connotations of "illusionist" and "prestidigitator" are likewise inapposite for *wu*. However, as we shall soon discover, "magician" in its ancient, etymological sense offers a much better fit than any of the other customary renderings of *wu*.[21]

---

[18] Chang, Kwang-chih, *Shang Civilization*, New Haven/London: Yale University Press 1980, 34.

[19] Chang 1980, passim.

[20] It is noteworthy that a variant of the graph for "doctor", *yi* 醫, which has the signific "alcohol" (used in treating illnesses) at the bottom, is 毉, replacing "alcohol" with "mage". Texts of the classical period corroborate fairly well the activities of the *wu* recorded in the OSBIs. According to these texts, the *wu* were said to undertake sacrifices and deliver prayers, perform ritual dances, serve as healers, be in communication with the spirits, undertake divination, and interpret dreams (Chen Mengjia 陳夢家, "Shang dai de shenhua yu wushu" 商代的神話與巫術 (Myths and witchcraft during the Shang period [original English title: Myths and Magianism of the Shang Period]), in: *Yanjing xuebao* 燕京學報 (Yenching Journal of Chinese Studies), 20 (December) (1936), 533–544).

[21] As Eno (2008/9: 93) has correctly pointed out, scholars too often confuse Shang and early Zhou *wu* with the classical type of shamanism as described in Western anthropological literature or the *wu* as described in Chinese texts of much later date. The same problem exists with scholars who apply the term *wu* or *wu*ism to archeologically attested ritual behavior dating to the Neolithic or even Paleolithic, and per-

The king himself was a *wu*; indeed, he was the chief of the *wu*. On the OSBIs, the king is often said personally to divine about various vital matters (*wang bu* 王卜, *wang zhen* 王貞, *wang zhan* 王占) such as the weather (especially the wind and the rain), sacrifices, military expeditions and campaigns, excursions, disaster, good fortune (auspiciousness), and dreams. The king also supplicated (*wang zhu* 王祝) to the ancestors and to the spirits of nature. And he performed ritual dances, primarily for rain, but also for other purposes.[22]

Just who were these mighty magi *(wu)*? Two small heads carved from mollusk shell and discovered in the autumn of 1980 within the precincts of the Zhou royal palace at Fufeng in Shaanxi Province provide valuable clues to the identity of the *wu*. Dating to the early 8th century BC, the tiny (about 2.85 centimeters in height) figures clearly depict the features of Caucasoid or Europoid individuals. What is more, one of the heads has carved on its top the archaic character for *wu* 巫, unmistakably identifying him as such a religious specialist (see Fig. 4). Still more astonishing are the facts that the Old Sinitic reconstruction of *wu* is roughly **m^(y)a(g)*,[23] that the archaic character for *wu* *(*m^(y)a[g])* is identical with the ancient sign of magicians (in the old, primary sense) in the West, and that the duties and abilities of the *wu* were roughly the same as those of early Iranian magi.

A mage or magus (from Persian *maguš*) signifies someone who has power or who is able, from the Indo-European root √**magh-* ("be

taining to locations far removed from the late Shang and early Zhou capitals – which are the only places that merit the designation of centers of late 2nd-millennium early 1st-millennium BC divination, supplications, sacrifices, and rituals presided over by *wu*. All other applications of the terms *wu* and *wu*ism are either anachronistic or signify spirit mediums and other types of religious specialists who engage in practices that are quite dissimilar to those of the archetypal Shang *wu*.

[22] I disagree with those OSBI specialists who assert that *wu1* 巫 = *wu3* 舞, since these two morphemes ("mage" and "dance" respectively) had separate representations in the OSBI script and separate etymons: *wu1* is written with 巫, the cross potent (an attribute of powerful diviners), whereas *wu3* clearly depicts a dancing figure holding cattle tails in his or her hands 舞.

[23] Recent phonological reconstructions of *wu1* generally lack the final velar, but the reconstructions of Dong Tonghe and Zhou Fagao both retain it (Chou Fa-Kao 周法高 (chief ed.), 漢字古今音彙 (A Pronouncing Dictionary of Chinese Characters in Archaic & Ancient Chinese, Mandarin & Cantonese), Hong Kong: The Chinese University of Hong Kong 1973, 81). It should be noted that the reconstruction of Old Sinitic is still at a very primitive stage compared to that of Proto-Indo-European. In any event, no Old Sinitic reconstructions should be taken as giving actual pronunciation values for particular characters. Rather, they should be understood as schematic representations of phonological relationships within an overall system of writing.

able").[24] The magi were members of the Zoroastrian priestly caste who possessed special knowledge of astrology. They represent the "old" religion, and *magu* is a western Iranian term for priest (the comparable term in Avestan was *athravan* and in Sanskrit it was *atharvan*) that was still in use into Sasanian times (by then modified to *mog*). Originally, it seems to have conveyed an ethnic designation, as Herodotus describes the *magoi* as one of the Median tribes (and Media is in western Iran). They appear at first to have been involved with polytheism, but by or in Achaemenid times they associated themselves with the worship of Ahura Mazda and consequently came into the Zoroastrian "fold." Their presence was thought to be essential for the success of sacrificial rites. Like their *wu* (*$m^{(y)}a[g]$) cousins in the EAH, the West Asian magi specialized in taking omens, interpreting dreams, and carrying out ritual sacrifices, and they were experts in cosmogony, cosmology, astronomy, and astrology.[25]

5. *Heavenly Horses*

When the Zhou Dynasty replaced the Shang around the year 1046 BC, they also replaced the supreme deity of the latter, Di 帝, with their own overarching godhead, Tian 天 ("heaven").[26] Tian subsequently

---

[24] Mallory/Adams 1997, 3a.

[25] Mair, Victor H., "Old Sinitic *$m^{y}ag$, Old Persian *maguš*, and English 'Magician.'", in: *Early China*, 15 (1990a), 27–47. Chinese translation by Qu Xutong 瞿旭彤 as "Gu Hanyu wu (*$m^{y}ag$), Gu Bosiyu *Maguš* he Yingyu *Magician*" 古汉语巫(*$m^{y}ag$), 古波斯语 *Maguš*, 和英语*Magician*, in: Xia Hanyi 夏含夷 (ed.), *Yuanfang de shixi <Gudai Zhongguo> jingxuan ji* 远方的时习《古代中国》 精选集, Shanghai: Shanghai Guji Chubanshe, 2008, 55–86; Jao Tsung-i, "Questions on the Origins of Writing Raised by the Silk Road", in: *Sino-Platonic Papers*, 26 (September) (1991), 1–10, Jao Tsung-i, "New Light on Wu", 1990; Boyce, Mary, *A History of Zoroastrianism*. Vol. 1: *The Early Period*, Leiden, Köln: Brill 1975; Boyce, Mary, *Zoroastrians: Their Religious Beliefs and Practices*, London: Routledge and Kegan 1979 [passim, but especially 98]; Boyce, Mary, *A History of Zoroastrianism*. Vol. 2: *Under the Achaemenians*, Leiden, Köln: Brill 1982 [passim, but especially 67, 165, 167–168, 180, 183, 215]; Boyce, Mary/Grenet, Frantz, *A History of Zoroastrianism*. Vol. 3: *Zoroastrianism under Macedonian and Roman Rule*, Leiden, Köln: Brill 1991.

[26] So similar are *di* and *tian* in meaning and function, and so close do they resemble each other in pronunciation that one suspects they may hide the same word as spoken in two different languages or topolects. This is not the place to make a full-dress case that ultimately both *di* (OSM **têkh*) and *tian* (OSM **thîn*) are cognate with IE **deiw-* ("to shine," and in many derivatives "sky, heaven, god" [Zeus, Deus, Tiwaz, Tiw, Tig, Tyr, deity, Sanskrit *deva*, divine, etc.) and also with Sumerian *dingir* ("heaven, god, deity"). The near identity of meaning and the close resemblance should be enough to give pause and cause for consideration. It is, moreover, not merely a matter of curiosity that the

became an epithet of anything that was viewed as divine or celestial. Among the most enduringly fascinating of "heavenly" cultural marvels was the *tianma* 天馬 ("heavenly horse"). This was particularly the case from the time of the Western Han Dynasty, after the official opening of the Silk Road by Emperor Wu Di (140–87), when the Chinese became acquainted with the fabulous "blood-sweating," "thousand-tricent"[27] horses of Ferghana.[28]

---

written forms of *dingir* (original star-shaped ideogram ✳; early cuneiform ✻; classic Assyrian 𒀭 – perhaps originally an emblem of the sky) resemble those for OSBI *di* (帝, 帝 – said to be the depiction of an altar supported on sticks [legs] bound together at the centre; if there is any visual resemblance and any sort of connection between the Sumero-Assyrian ideogram and the archaic Sinogram, a process of reinterpretation must have occurred between the creation of the former and the borrowing of the latter*). A note of caution should be entered, however, that the resemblance of the Old Sinitic word for *tian* and Turkic *tängri*, Mongolian *tengri* (both "sky, heaven, heavenly deity") can not be due to borrowing from "Altaic" into Sinitic, since Turkic and Mongolian are both much younger languages that are historically, linguistically, and textually attestable only about two thousand years after Sinitic (Shaughnessy, Edward L., "Western Cultural Innovations in China, 1200 B.C.", in: *Sino-Platonic Papers*, 11 (July) (1989), 1–8). Rather, the resemblance – if they are actually related – must ultimately be due to the fact that both Sinitic and "Altaic" borrowed *tian* and *tängri/tengri* from West Eurasian languages. Minimal Old Sinitic (OSM) reconstructions are taken from Schuessler (2007).

Yet another Old Sinitic word for "sky, heaven" is also likely related to an IE source: *qilian* 祁 連 or *kunlun* 昆侖< Tocharian *kaelum*, cf. Latin *caelum* ("sky, heaven"). (Lin Meicun, "Qilian and Kunlun – The Earliest Tokharian Loan-words in Ancient Chinese.", in: Victor H. Mair (ed.), *The Bronze Age and Early Iron Age Peoples of Eastern Central Asia*. 2 vols. Washington: The Institute for the Study of Man; Philadelphia: The University of Pennsylvania Museum Publications. Vol. 1, 1998, 476–482) Considering the recent and well-received Old Sinitic reconstructions of Zhengzhang Shangfang (Zhengzhang Shangfang 郑张尚芳, *Shanggu yinxi* 上古音系 (Old Chinese Phonology), Shanghai: Shanghai Jiaoyu Chubanshe 2003), it is possible that *di (*teegs)*, *tian (*qhl'iin//t-hiin)*, and *qilian* all derive from the same IE etymon for "sky, heaven, god" (Zhou Jixu, "Old Chinese '*tees' and Proto-Indo-European '*deus': Similarity in Religious Ideas and a Common Source in Linguistics.", in: *Sino-Platonic Papers* 167 (December) (2005), 1–17). Two years after this chapter was completed, John C. Didier published his monumental In and Outside the Square: The Sky and the Power of Belief in Ancient China and the World, c. 4500 BC – AD 200 in 3 vols. as Sino-Platonic Papers, 192 (January, 2010). Didier's magnum opus calls for a thorough reassessment of the old graph di in its relationship to astronomical configurations, especially in connection with a polar quadrangle.

[27] A "tricent" (*li* 里) consists of 300 paces, roughly a third of a mile. A "thousand-tricent horse" supposedly could run that far in a day, i. e., around 333 miles.

[28] Waley, Arthur, "The heavenly horses of Ferghana: a new view.", in: *History Today*, 5 (1955), 95–103; Mallory, J. P./Mair, Victor H., *The Tarim Mummies: Ancient China and the Mystery of the Earliest Peoples from the West*, London: Thames and Hudson 2000, 92–93. Yoshizawa Satoru, et al. (ed.), *Tenba – Shiriku Rodo o kakeru yume no uma/Pegasus and the Heavenly Horses: Thundering Hoofs of the Silk Road*, Nara: Nara National Museum 2008.

In truth, the horse was a source of wonderment to the Chinese long before the Western Han Dynasty. Indeed, from their very first acquaintance with the domesticated horse toward the end of the second millennium BC, the peoples of the EAH were both fascinated and terrified by this speedy, spirited creature.[29] By the time the horse arrived in the EAH, the indigenes had already seen the advent of domesticated ovicaprids (as described in the first section above) and cattle (not discussed in this paper) by the third millennium BC.[30] Although the inhabitants of the EAH never fully mastered the horse, always relying on the steppe peoples for their main supplies of warhorses and ceremonial steeds, they had a keen appreciation of the power and swiftness of the animal.[31] While the Chinese never elaborated a cult of the horse, as happened among the Indo-Europeans, the Japanese, and the Mongols, the horse was looked upon as the most prestigious animal victim for sacrificial purposes. For routine sacrifices, indigenous animals (pig, chicken, dog) were considered adequate. For more important sacrifices, sheep, goat, and cattle (which had been introduced from western Eurasia) were thought more desirable. Horses, in contrast, were reserved for the most solemn occasions, such as the death of a ruler.

During both the Shang and the Zhou dynasties, when a ruler died a lavish burial was provided for him, reflecting a profound concern for life beyond death. Royal tombs were outfitted with the sort of items that were thought essential for post-mortem existence. Deposited in the royal tombs were carriages, utensils, sacrificial vessels, and weapons. The latter two classes of burial goods were particularly numerous since war and sacrifice were the two most vital royal enterprises of Shang and Zhou times.[32] In addition, many victims, including persons and horses, were buried with the king. The larger tombs of the Shang

[29] A major breakthrough in research on the domestication of the horse occurred just as the final draft of this chapter was being completed. Archeologists and biomolecular scientists have determined that 5,500-year-old pottery fragments from the site of Botai, Kazakhstan bear the isotopic signature of mare's milk ("Trail of Mare's Milk Leads To First Tamed Horese", *Science* 322 (October 17) (2008), 368). This could only have come about if horses were domesticated by that time, because no one would dare milk a wild horse. The discovery of mare's mild residue on Botai pottery cements earlier evidence for horse domestication that includes signs of corrals and bit wear marks on horse teeth.

[30] Mair 2003, 166–167.

[31] Mair, Victor H., "Kinesis versus Stasis, Interaction versus Independent Invention.", in: Victor H. Mair (ed.), *Contact and Exchange in the Ancient World*, Honolulu: University of Hawai'i Press 2006b, 1–2.

[32] Smith 1961, 148.

Royal burial grounds at Anyang, for instance, each contained around four hundred human victims.[33] And one local Zhou ruler in horse-poor Shandong had the stupendous number of more than 600 horses deposited in a pit 200 meters long to accompany him in death.[34] In general, the similarities between the burial of a Shang or Zhou ruler and that of a Scythian, Wusun, or other steppe group leader are striking, especially with regard to the sacrifice of horses.[35] Recent archeological research has demonstrated clearly the key role of the Iranian peoples (the leading pre-Turkic and pre-Mongolic denizens of the steppe) in the transmission of horse culture – including chariots, fighting styles, head-and-hoof rituals, art motifs, and myths – from west to east during the Bronze Age and the Iron Age.[36]

6. *Heavenly Questions*

An Iranian-style mage and an Indian-like *ṛṣi* ("seer") appear together in a memorable passage from the *Zhuang Zi*, a Taoist philosophical text dating to around the latter half of the 4th c. BC. This is the story of the contest of spiritual powers between Ji Xian and Master Hu (7.5). The former, a mage, also appears in 14.1 playing the role of dispenser of cosmic wisdom who can answer riddles that would stump even an ancient Chinese sage. The puzzles that mage Xian solves have an even broader, trans-Eurasian resonance since they take the form of an extended series of riddles uncannily like those posed by early Indo-European seers and priests.[37]

The Indo-European quality of such riddles appears even more clearly in one of the most unusual and baffling texts in the whole of

[33] Guo Moruo 郭沫若, *Nuli zhi shidai* 奴隸制時代 [The Age of Slavery], Shanghai: Xin Wenyi Chubanshe 1952, 68–69, 73–74.
[34] Mair, Victor H., "Horse Sacrifices and Sacred Groves among the North(west) ern Peoples of East Asia.", in: *Ouya xuekan* 欧亚学刊 (Eurasian Studies), 6, Beijing: Zhonghua Shuju 2007b, 22–53: 41n2; see Fig. 5 below.
[35] Mair 2003, 2007b.
[36] Kuzmina, Elena E., *The Prehistory of the Silk Road*, in: Victor H. Mair (ed.), Philadelphia: University of Pennsylvania Press 2008; Kuzmina, Elena E., *The Origin of the Indo-Iranians*, in: J. P. Mallory (ed.), Leiden: Brill 2007.
[37] Mair, Victor H. (tr. and intro.), *Wandering on the Way. Early Taoist Tales and Parables of Chuang Tzu*, New York: Bantam 1994; Honolulu: University of Hawaii Press, 1998: xliv, 68, 14.1; Chen Guying 陳鼓應 (ed. and tr.), *Zhuang Zi jin zhu jin yi* 莊子今注今譯 [A Modern Annotation and Translation of the Chuang Zi], Beijing: Zhonghua 1983; a slightly revised reprinting of the edition published in 2 vols. by Taiwan Commercial Press in 1975, 220–221, 360–361.

Chinese literature, "Heavenly Questions" (*Tian wen* 天問).[38] Attributed to the first Chinese poet known by name and about whom we have a modicum of biographical information, Qu Yuan (340?–278 BCE), "Heavenly Questions" forms a part of the celebrated southern anthology known as the *Chu ci* 楚辭 (Elegies of Chu). Qu Yuan was a member of the royal family of Chu and a loyal official to two of its rulers.

"Heavenly Questions" consists entirely of a long series of mysterious and essentially unanswered queries concerning the origin and nature of the universe, the founding of civilization by various semidivine beings, and the complicated affairs of the rulers of the legendary and historical kingdoms right up to the time of the poet himself. Most of the questions are of such maddening obscurity that they are extremely difficult to interpret, let alone answer. If, however, we treat "Heavenly Questions" as part of the Indo-European tradition of riddle texts, it becomes perfectly intelligible as a well-known type of catechism for imparting wisdom.

The authors of the ancient Vedic hymns, the earliest of which date to roughly the beginning of the first millennium BC, were often deliberately cryptic (e. g., *Ṛg Veda*, I.164). The subject matter of their riddles is, furthermore, virtually the same as that of the "Heavenly Questions" (e. g., *Atharva Veda*, X.7–8). The *Upaniṣads,* which followed the *Veda*s, are even more similar to the "Heavenly Questions." The *Śvetāśvatara Upaniṣad* begins with a series of comparable questions, and the *Praśna Upaniṣad* (literally, the "*Upaniṣads* [Secret Session] of Questions") consists entirely of all sorts of difficult and profound questions that are put to a *ṛṣi.* Elsewhere in the *Upaniṣads* and in the *Brāhmana*s as well, there are series of questions concerning cosmology and mythology that are quite like the "Heavenly Questions."

In the ancient Iranian *Zend-Avesta*, doctrine is presented in a series of questions and answers between the prophet Zarathustra (i. e., Zoroaster ["possessing old camels"]) and the creator-deity Ahura Mazda (i. e., O[h]rmazd, Ormuzd ["wise spirit/lord"]). In "Yasna" 44, for example, the questions posed by Zarathustra are astonishingly reminiscent of those in the opening portion of the "Heavenly Questions": "Who is it that supported the earth below and the sky above so that

[38] For a complete, annotated translation of "Heavenly Questions," see Mair, Victor H., *The Columbia Anthology of Traditional Chinese Literature*, New York: Columbia University Press 1994, 371–386.

they do not fall?" "Who is it that joined speed with wind and welkin?" "Who is it that created blessed light and the darkness?" Even at the far northwestern end of the Indo-European range, the same types of riddles persist in some of the earliest of the poetic *Edda*. In "Vafthrudnismāl," questions between Gangrath (Wodan) and Wabedrut focus on the origins of heaven and earth. Similar questions abound in "Fiölvinnsmāl," "Alvissmāl," and other songs in the *Edda*.

In chapter VI ("Playing and Knowing") of his classic *Homo Ludens*, Johan Huizinga[39] has analyzed such question series as related to cult indoctrination and sacrifices. The tradition of imparting and testing knowledge through a series of riddles is prominent throughout the ancient Indo-European tradition, especially its Indo-Iranian and Germanic branches. The texts consisting of questions cited above (and many others like them) may thus be viewed as vestiges of ancient riddle-solving contests, the participants in which were rewarded or punished (sometimes with their lives), depending upon their performance in responding to the questions. The emphasis on cattle in the "Heavenly Questions" also indicates an Indo-European, steppe connection.

7. *Conclusion*

Veneration of the ancestors (*zu* 祖) was the consuetudinary foundation upon which the superstructure of traditional Chinese religion was erected. A corollary of ancestor worship was filial piety (*xiao* 孝), respect for one's elders. The obligatory duties of ancestor worship and filial piety lasted throughout the entirety of traditional Chinese history and were premised upon the observances of settled, agricultural society. Added to these elements of Chinese religion that derived from the autochthonous agricultural patterns of the denizens of the EAH were two major waves of influence from abroad: 1. values and practices brought by Bronze Age and Early Iron Age pastoralists and nomads arriving from the north(west), 2. organized religions transmitted by monks, merchants, and missionaries, chiefly during the medieval period, but continuing through the early modern period and right up to the present day. The enormous complexity of Chinese religion is

[39] Huizinga, Johan, *Homo Ludens: A Study of the Play-Element in Culture*, Boston: Beacon 1955. tr. from the German ed. of 1944, 105–118.

the result of all these diverse components being combined into a multifaceted whole.

In this chapter, I have concentrated chiefly on early steppe influences from the north and northwest, and these have been primarily of Iranian affiliation. It might also have been possible to emphasize more heavily pre-Buddhist Indian religious elements in early Chinese culture.[40] However, the further back in time one goes, the division between the Indic and the Iranian branches of the Indo-Iranian group becomes less and less sharp until, by the 3rd millennium BC, they are virtually indistinguishable (or, to state the matter differently, they have not yet diverged).[41]

Although I have emphasized the difference between the steppe and the sown, the distinction was by no means absolute. Archeologists often find traces of agropastoralism on the steppe, and the settled peoples obviously interacted with and absorbed elements of animal husbandry and secondary products utilization.[42] The interconnectedness of Bronze Age Eurasian civilizations is evident from a distinctive custom concerning the first plowing of spring that was observed from Greece to China and from Scandinavia to India. Namely, the ruler himself would plow the first three furrows, no less and no more. (*Li ji* 禮記 [Record of Rituals], "Yue ling" 月令 [Monthly Ordinances], 6.7.[43] There were also significant cultural influences from the south in the evolution of Chinese myth and religion, but they are neither as pervasive nor as formative as those from the north(west).[44] In any

[40] Mair, Victor H. (tr. and intro.), *Tao Te Ching: The Classic Book of Integrity and the Way*, New York: Bantam 1990b, 140–148, 155–161.

[41] Mair, Victor H., "The Beginnings of Sino-Indian Cultural Contact.", in: *Journal of Asian History* 38.2 (2004), 81–95.

[42] Sherratt, Andrew G., "The Secondary Exploitation of Animals in the Old World.", in: *World Archaeology,* 15.1 (1983), 90–104.

[43] Lau, D. C./Chen Fong Ching (ed.), *A Concordance to the Liji*. Chinese University of Hong Kong, Institute for Chinese Studies. The Ancient Chinese Text Concordance Series. Hong Kong: Commercial Press 1992, 39; Glob, P. V., *The Mound People: Danish Bronze-Age Man Preserved* (Joan Bulman tr.), Ithaca: Cornell University Press 1974, 148–150; see Fig. 6.

[44] Mair, Victor H., "Southern Bottle-Gourd (*hu-lu* 葫蘆) Myths in China and Their Appropriation by Taoism.", in: *Zhongguo shenhua yu chuanshuo xueshu yantaohui lunwen ji* 中國神話與傳說學術研究討會論文集 (Proceedings of the Conference on Chinese Myth and Legend). Hanxue yanjiu zhongxin congkan 漢學研j究中心叢刊 (Center for Chinese Studies Research Series), No. 5, Taipei: Hanxue yanjiu zhongxin 1996; vol. 1, 185–228; Mair, Victor H., "The Rediscovery and Complete Excavation of Ördek's Necropolis.", in: *The Journal of Indo-European Studies* 34.3–4 (Fall/Winter) (2006a.), 275–318.

event, fuller treatment of southern elements in Chinese religion must wait for another day.

To conclude, we have seen that moral metaphors based upon sheep and goats are so deeply embedded in the Chinese ethical consciousness that I would not hesitate to coin a term, ovicaprolatry, to describe a major component of the religion of the third and second millennium BC fathers of Chinese civilization. Certainly, a core segment of the Sinitic value system was premised upon a pastoral, nomadic lifestyle, not a settled, agricultural mode of existence. The next layer of Chinese religion was laid down when Shang ancestor worship underwent a fusion with magianism. This established the lineaments and solemnities of orthopraxis for divination and sacrifice already from before the time of Confucius to the conclusion of the empire in 1911. After that came the advent of more theological and cosmological concerns centered on the "heavenly" – Tian, as introduced by the northwestern Zhou people. Moral, ethical, and esthetic values, ancestor worship, divination, sacrifice, theology, cosmology: these constituents formed the basis of Sinitic religious life and behavior throughout imperial times. The massive overlay of organized religions during the medieval and early modern periods did not alter the fundamental nature of Sinitic religion that had long ago been determined by the Late Neolithic, Bronze Age, and Early Iron Age fusion of Western and Eastern elements described above. These "new" religions, however, significantly reshaped the religious landscape of China, modifying its art, architecture, music, thought, literature, and institutions, making the study of Chinese religions extraordinarily demanding, but also tremendously fulfilling.

If this investigation has shown anything, it is that the diverse early cultures of Eurasia were integrated, not isolated. Neither were the individual cultures of Eurasia isolated from each other, nor were the religions, technologies, arts, and other components that they shared transmitted separately. Cultures are integral packages. Thus, for example, when late Neolithic pastoralists brought their sheep and goats eastward, they also brought their sacrificial practices and moral precepts with them; when early Iron Age metallurgists introduced their new weapons and tools to the EAH, they perforce injected new ideas about war, death, and the cosmologies within which they smelted their iron and fought their battles.[45] Later, when papermaking, printing, the compass, and gunpowder were transmitted westward, the individuals who brought them also introduced more ethereal and spiritual ideas related to alchemy, the body, and the mind. The free sharing of cultural attributes, however, does not necessarily imply their total acceptance as is. Societies, when they borrow elements of culture from each other, pick, choose, and transform, and they meld what they acquire into what they already have. This is what might be called the combinatorial calculus of cultural convergence. The result is neither merely what they began with nor simply what they absorbed from outside. Rather, it is something new that is more (or less) than the sum of its parts. Thus do cultures, and the religions that inform them, progress – and sometimes wane.

8. *Acknowledgements*

It is my pleasure to acknowledge assistance from Robert Eno concerning Shang religion; from Donald Harper, Xing Wen, Constance Cook, Robin Yates, and John Major regarding the orthography of the Chu Silk Manuscript; from David Branner on the phonology of Fuxi and related names; from Denis Mair on the mythology of Fuxi; from Gianni Wan on ovicaprid terms; from Melinda Takeuchi with regard to heavenly (and other magnificent) horses; from Judith Lerner concerning Zoroastrianism; from John V. Day regarding spring plowing; and from Heiner Roetz with regard to typesetting.

[45] Mair, Victor H. (tr. and intro.), *The Art of War: Sun Zi's Military Methods*, Columbia: Columbia University Press 2007a, 37–46; Chang, Tsung-tung, "Indo-European Vocabulary in Old Chinese: A New Thesis on the Emergence of Chinese Language and Civilization in the Late Neolithic Age.", in: *Sino-Platonic Papers* 7 (January) (1988), 35–39; Eliade, Mircea, *The Forge and the Crucible*, Stephen Corrin, tr. from the French *Forgerons et alchimistes*, New York: Harper and Row 1971; 2nd ed., University of Chicago Press, 1978.

9. *Abbreviations*

EAH	East Asian Heartland
HDC	*Hanyu da cidian* 漢語大詞典 [Unabridged Dictionary of Sinitic]
IE	Indo-European
OSBI	Oracle Shell and Bone Inscription(s)
OSM	Minimal Old Sinitic

10. *Figures*

Fig. 1: (Xie)zhi from a Han Dynasty wall-painting in a Han Dynasty tomb near Kröran *(Loulan)*. Xinjiang Uyghur Autonomous Region. Photo courtesy of Xinjiang Institute of Archeology.

Fig. 2: Eastern Han Dynasty *(25–220)* wooden sculpture of a (xie)zhi from Mouzuizi, Wuwei, Gansu Province. Photo courtesy of the Metropolitan Museum of Art, New York.

Fig. 3: Eastern Han Dynasty bronze sculpture of (xie)zhi from Xiaheqing, Jiuquan, Gansu Province. Photo courtesy of the Metropolitan Museum of Art, New York.

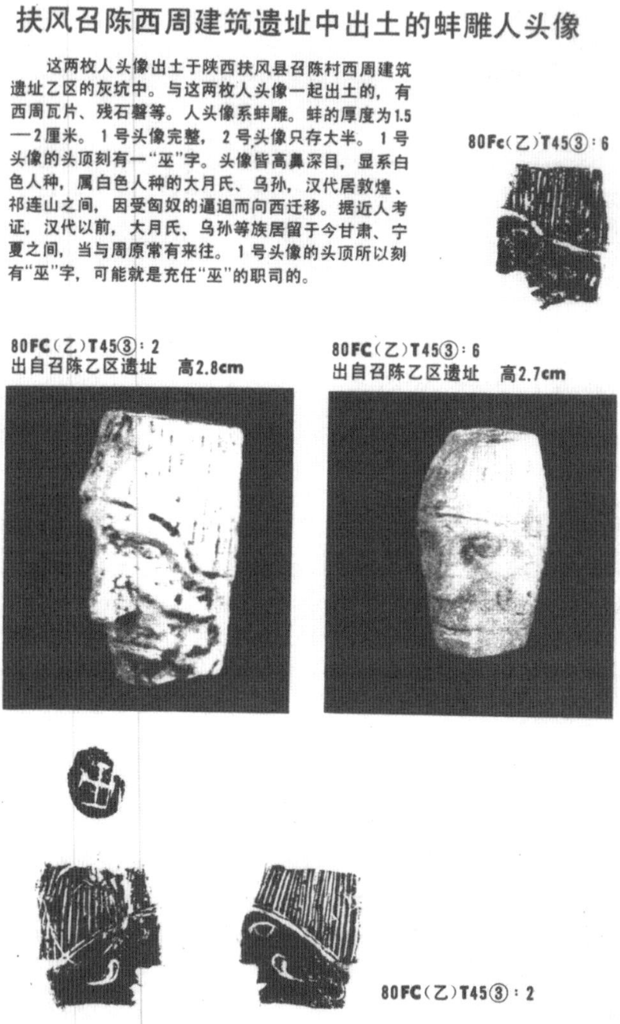

扶风召陈西周建筑遗址中出土的蚌雕人头像

这两枚人头像出土于陕西扶风县召陈村西周建筑遗址乙区的灰坑中。与这两枚人头像一起出土的，有西周瓦片、残石磬等。人头像系蚌雕。蚌的厚度为1.5—2厘米。1号头像完整，2号头像只存大半。1号头像的头顶刻有一"巫"字。头像皆高鼻深目，显系白色人种，属白色人种的大月氏、乌孙，汉代居敦煌、祁连山之间，因受匈奴的逼迫而向西迁移。据近人考证，汉代以前，大月氏、乌孙等族居留于今甘肃、宁夏之间，当与周原常有来往。1号头像的头顶所以刻有"巫"字，可能就是充任"巫"的职司的。

80Fc（乙）T45③：6

80FC（乙）T45③：2
出自召陈乙区遗址　高2.8cm

80FC（乙）T45③：6
出自召陈乙区遗址　高2.7cm

80FC（乙）T45③：2

Fig. 4: Two heads carved from mollusk shell. Circa 800 BC. Found in the precincts of the Western Zhou royal palace. Fufeng County, Shaanxi Province. Photo courtesy of Victor Mair.

Fig. 5: Sacrificial horse pit near the tomb of Lord Jing of Qi. Heyatou, Linzi, Shandong Province. After Chang, Kwang-chih/Xu Pingfang, The Formation of Chinese Civilization: An Archaeological Perspective. The Culture and Civilization of China, New Haven and London: Yale University Press 2005, 233, Fig. 7. Photo courtesy of New World Press.

Fig. 6: Ithyphallic plowman beginning a third furrow. Bronze Age petroglyph at Litsleby in Bohuslän, Sweden. After P. V. Glob, The mound people: Danish bronze-age man preserved, London: Faber, 1974, 149. Photo courtesy of Faber & Faber.

A COMMENT ON VICTOR H. MAIR'S "RELIGIOUS FORMATIONS AND INTERCULTURAL CONTACTS IN EARLY CHINA"

Heiner Roetz

While intellectual transfer to China from outside the "East Asian Heartland" after the Qin dynasty is beyond doubt and well-documented, pre-imperial imports are much less easy to identify. Victor Mair is one of the most prominent authors to argue for significant very early intercultural contacts. He not only maintains that such contacts existed to a considerable extent, but that they shaped Chinese "mainstream practice and ideology" and determined the "fundamental nature of Sinitic religion". In his essay, he focuses only on a selection of phenomena due to influences from the northwest of primarily "Iranian affiliation". However, he regards these to be examples of a much broader variety of impacts from the surrounding world that substantially contributed to the making of China. For arguments regarding India, the reader can refer to the passages on "Parallels between Taoism and Yoga" in Mair's famous translation of the Mawangdui manuscripts of the Laozi, with the thesis that this text was not only the product of "internal sociopolitical conditions" but also of "radically new religious and philosophical stimuli from without".[1]

I share Victor Mair's conviction that Chinese culture – like any culture – has been the constantly changing result of a confluence of knowledge and experience from quite different sources from its very beginnings – any nucleus theory has proven untenable. Many of these influences were met with unspectacular acceptance while others have vanished, and some of them have brought about far reaching change. Yet, this has not forestalled essentialist theories contending a unity of "Chineseness" to the present day. Victor Mair is right in opposing this one-dimensional view. The view of a "culture" as a closed unit with the center of gravity in itself, as was brought forward by Johann Gottfried Herder (1744–1803), and, in recent times, revived by Samuel Huntington, has never been plausible and should be a thing of the past.

[1] Victor Mair, *Tao Te Ching. The Classic Book of Integrity and the Way*, New York: Bantam Books, 1990, 140–148, here: 145.

Still, as Victor Mair himself admits, the development of China has not only been instigated from abroad but has also been the outcome of internal experiences, conflicts, crises, and learning processes. In general, and not only in the case of China, it is often hard to decide whether a given phenomenon is of indigenous or of foreign origin. Given all of the commonalities of the mental and physical apparatus of the human being, of the course of human life, of natural phenomena and social structures in general, manifold parallel developments without one-sided dependence also have to be expected. And if there has been a transfer of knowledge and ideas, they have not necessarily been taken over in a passive manner, but productively transformed into something new by the receiving side. Galton's argument against Tylor, that data gathered from different cultures is not a secure comparative basis for inferences with regard to general cultural evolution unless one has shown the compared items to be genetically unrelated ("Galton's problem") can be reversed: one cannot make secure inferences with regard to the existence of transfer unless the respective data is shown to be really genetically related. In many cases, there are clear indications of cultural "borrowings", above all the peculiarity and perhaps unexpectedness of a phenomenon, provided that the specific intercultural contacts and means of communication are given. On the other hand, Victor Mair would agree that one is well advised to avoid a diffusionism that overstates its case.

Such caution seems especially apposite if one looks for influences not only on the level of material goods but also on the level of more complex social phenomena, let alone comprehensive world-views that might have been transported together with the material borrowings. Victor Mair's argument with regard to the Chinese "wu" 巫 (conventionally but, according to Mair, wrongly translated as "shamans") is perhaps a rather unproblematic case: here he convincingly combines a linguistic reconstruction – provisional, as it can only be – with archeological evidence to argue for an Iranian origin not only of the term but also of the corresponding religious practice. Mair's other examples are less persuasive to this commentator.

As to horses and ovicaprids, it is most probably uncontroversial that they were brought to China via inner Asia, with a key role played by Iranian peoples. But does this mean that along with them pastoralist and nomadic "fundamental ethical, moral, and esthetic concepts", as the author puts it, were also introduced to China? I do not find corroboration for this far-reaching thesis in Mair's article. It is difficult to see more than an instrumental role for these animals as sacrificial offerings in religious ritual. What is, indeed, astonishing, is the appearance of the *yang* 羊 (sheep/goat) element in a number of characters denoting "good" things or acts. But this is perhaps only at first glance of the importance that the author attributes to it. In fact, the nine appearances which he mentions can be reduced to only one phenomenon: the connotation "good" of the element *yang* itself, the original rationale for which is a matter of speculation – it may simply have been due to the fact that mutton was a commodity of special value. In any case, we would not only have to explain why the *yang* element appears in characters for words with a positive connotation, but also why it appears in some others with a negative meaning like 痒 (yǎng, to itch; yáng, disease) and 佯 (yáng, to pretend, to deceive, false), and what impact this fact might have on the "deep psychology of the Chinese mind". One possible explanation is that *yang* 羊 does not serve as a "signific" (V. Mair) in the first place but primarily as a phonophore. Moreover, *yang* 羊 is not an all too conspicuous item if we consider the bulk of the normative vocabulary of ancient China (like rén 仁, lǐ 禮, zhōng 忠, xìn 信, xiào 孝, shèng 聖, hǎo 好, dào 道, jìng 敬, gōng 恭, hé 和, ài 愛, dé 德 etc.), which is not written with characters containing this element. What is more important, however, is that it is hard to detect any foreign "pastoral" impact when it comes to the content of the specific ethical theorems which use, among other things, the "caprovine" terms or characters. The usage of "to flock" (*qun* 群) as the word for "community" in the passage from *Xunzi* 9 is no exception. For Xunzi society is something that human beings are capable of forming *in distinction* from animals. I do not see any parallel between humans and sheep or goats and an indication of a "nomadic lifestyle" that "dominates ethics" in the quoted passage. This remains true also if we take other appearances of *yang* terminology into account.[2]

To my mind, one comes to no other conclusion with regard to what Victor Mair calls the "concept of law". The character for the word *fa*, "law", has an early form 灋 which adds the element *zhi* 廌 to the elements "water" (*shui* 水) and "remove" (*qu* 去) that constitute the shorter form 法. *Zhi* is interpreted as a magic animal that butts the one who is guilty in a lawsuit with its horn. According to Victor Mair,

[2] More examples are discussed in Ulrich Lau, "Vom Schaf zur Gerechtigkeit" [From the sheep to justice], in: Christiane Hammer/Bernhard Führer, (eds.), *Tradition und Moderne. Religion, Philosophie und Literatur in China*, Dortmund: project, 1997, 37–48.

the character is reminiscent of an animal ordeal of possibly Eurasian decent. Be that as it may, the theory has its blemish: to my knowledge, this explanation of the character 灋 appears only in the late 1st Century AD in Wang Chong's 王充[3] *Lun Heng* 論橫 from where it was included in Xu Shen's 許慎 etymological dictionary *Shuowen jiezi* 說文解字.[4] It is reminiscent of an account given in the *Mozi* of a lawsuit in Qi taking place in the 8th Century. In order to come to a decision, both parties agreed to swear an oath of blood at the earth altar, for which a sheep was sacrificed. When the case of the guilty party was read, the sheep arose and butted him, breaking his leg.[5] Whether or not this story has influenced the aforementioned later reading of the character 灋, the reading itself is speculative (like, in fact, nearly all character etymology) and dubious. Ulrich Lau has suggested that 灋 might be a combination of *pei* 沛 (marsh) and *qu* 去 (remove), meaning "to clear woodland", which explains why it is used for *fei* 廢 (remove) in bronze inscriptions.[6] In any case, we are not forced to accept the Han explanation in order to make sense of the character. Its short form 法 does not appear to be "totally mystifying" without the butting animal allegedly represented by the element *zhi* 廌 – one can easily imagine that the "water" radical 氵 symbolizes justice and *qu* 去 stands for "removing" a culprit – if we can give a plausible explanation in the first place. However, what is more important, again, is that steppe influences should not only be identified in characters but in the thought and the practices expressed by the corresponding words. Ordeal was certainly not a salient characteristic of the Chinese juridical system. So I would hesitate to subscribe to Victor Mair's conclusion that "the Sinitic notion of justice was intimately bound with ideals based upon ovicaprid imagery".

As to the similarities between the *Tianwen* and Indian, Iranian and even Scandinavian riddle literature, it remains open whether we are dealing with borrowings from a common (in this case indo-European) source or with independent phenomena. It is not only possible but to be expected that people from different cultures will ask the same basic questions (Why does the sky not fall down? Who causes light and

---

[3] Wang Chong, *Lunheng*, *Zhuzi jicheng* edition, Hongkong: Zhonghua, 1978, vol. 7, 173.

[4] *Shuowen jiezi* 10a, Hong Kong: Zhonghua, 1977, 202.

[5] Mozi, *Zhuzi jicheng* edition, Hongkong: Zhonghua, 1978, vol. 4, 144.

[6] Lau, loc. cit., 41.

darkness? etc.) out of their own experiences, learning processes and wonderment over the world without necessarily being inspired from outside. There are, for example, statements in philosophical Greek and Chinese texts that sound like they are being copied in one direction or the other. Yet, it is very unlikely that they are, and borrowing is not a necessary assumption in order to explain their appearance.

To conclude, it is not my intention to question Victor Mair's basic hypothesis that all kinds of influences from inner Asia have to be taken into account in order to understand the development of the "East Asian Heartland" long before the textually unequivocal and well-documented post-Qin cases. China's links with her neighbors may well have been far more intimate, long lasting and important than has often been acknowledged. It is another matter, however, to make plausible that and how "pastoral" culture has in fact dominated a "core segment of the Sinitic value system". To corroborate this thesis would require more evidence.

KINGS, ASCETICS, AND BRAHMINS: THE SOCIO-POLITICAL CONTEXT OF ANCIENT INDIAN RELIGIONS

Patrick Olivelle

This paper is partly substantive – I want to explore the major contours of the history of religions in ancient India – and partly methodological – I want to argue for a particular way to study this period of Indian history and especially to argue against some ways in which that history has been studied in the past by some scholars. I want to examine how we should research this period, how we should teach this period to our students, and how we should encourage the educated public to envisage this period of ancient Indian history.

When we deal with the religions of ancient India we have first of all to deal with the problem of labels. What do we call them? Two easy terms have become current: Hinduism and Buddhism. But such labels are not without their problems. They reflect to varying degrees modern and often scholarly classifications. Projecting them into the distant historical past, especially in reified form, can cause historical distortions and anachronistic conclusions. The dynamic nature of all human realities, including religion, is often hidden behind these essentialized designations.

The categories "Hindu" and "Hinduism" are, of course, extremely problematic. In their current usage with regard to the majority religion in India, they are categories invented within the colonial context with the need felt by colonial powers to classify the people they ruled. The term "Hindu"or a parallel indigenous category is absent in pre-colonial India. Some scholars have thrown up their hands in despair and advised us against using the term at all. But that is not feasible, given the ubiquity of this category not only in scholarship but also as a term of self-reference among millions of contemporary Hindus, and the practical need for a short-hand term. The term has also become part of Indian constitutional law, which defines "Hindu" negatively – anyone who is not a Moslem, Christian, Jew, or Parsi is a Hindu by definition, or rather by exclusion, thus making Sikhs, Buddhists, and Jains legally Hindus.[1] The fact that a colonial and scholarly term has become an emic term of self-reference should not blind us to the problems inherent in such a category. Once we go beyond the 19th century, the category "Hinduism" poses great difficulties, even though we continue to use it in scholarship as an umbrella concept or a shorthand. But it is clearly unwise to use this category as a tool of analysis for the period under discussion in this paper. People talk, for example, about the Buddha being a Hindu before he became a Buddhist!! Or say that the Buddha preached against Hinduism!! These statements make no historical sense. The problem with such a label is that it makes us assume that a sociologically and demographically identifiable group answering to that label existed at that time, an assumption that is clearly untenable. Such a category makes sense only within the mind of the scholar who looks at a large spectrum of data, demarcates some of them, and then gives them a label. Such category formation is quite legitimate as a scholarly enterprise, but the danger is that we often think that those categories were actual historical realities. Today we have a demography within India and the Indian diaspora that answers to the identification "Hindu". But it did not exist even four hundred years ago, let alone two thousand.

"Buddhism" may seem a less problematic category, especially because it is what can be called a "founded religion", and we are used to dealing with such religions that we think have definite historical contours and identities. Yet, if we are attempting to describe, much less analyze, the religious landscape of northern India in the middle of the first millennium BCE, we would be hard pressed to find "Buddhism" there in the way we conceive it as a category today. There were ascetics, often living in communities, who professed faith in the preachings of Siddhārtha Gautama; there may have been even some public monuments associated with him, and lay individuals who showed partiality toward this ascetic sect. But it was one among many ascetic groups vying for influence and patronage among rich and politically influential people. "Buddhism" has to be understood and analyzed within its on-the-ground historical context and its multi-faceted interactions with other religious and societal groups.

[1] See The Constitution of India, Part III, Article 25: "the reference to Hindus shall be construed as including a reference to persons professing the Sikh, Jaina, or Buddhist religion". See also The Hindu Adoption and Maintenance Act, 1956.

If we could for a moment give up grasping, as the Buddha would say, grasping at labels as a vehicle for understanding, then perhaps we can more fully understand the variegated tapestry that Indian society and religion was. I want to focus here on the intersection between the realms of the socio-political and the religious with the strong implication of the dynamic nature of this interaction and of the intimate connection between religion, society, and political formations. I want to lay special emphasis on the dynamic and changing nature of ancient Indian religions and to counter the implicit, and sometimes explicit, assumption of a "changeless India" fostered by colonial and orientalist discourse.

As we look today at the ascetic and world-renouncing ideologies at the heart of the religious reformations in northern India in the middle of the first millennium BCE, it is well to take note of the kinds of rhetoric on this topic we have heard from modern scholars and to not fall into the same trap. The convenient category Hinduism has often been used as a reality out there rather than as a category for organizing our own thoughts; it has often been reified and essentialized so as to make it immune to change and diversity. It has been made a-historical. We need to put history back into Hinduism. History implies change, change that is not natural or automatic but created by human agency. Unfortunately, this is the type of change that is far too often either explicitly or implicitly denied to India with the projected image of the "changeless India". It has been exacerbated by the western image, often absorbed by Indians themselves, of a mystical east in contrast to the materialist west. The mystical is timeless and eternal and transcends history and historical vicissitudes. This attitude is typified in Albert Schweitzer's book *Indian Thought and its Development*. He writes about the "world negating" thought of India which he believed was at the heart of Indian religions: "When Hellenistic thought turns towards world and life negation, it is because in the end it begins to have misgivings about the world and life affirmation which for centuries had seemed a matter of course … In the thought of India, on the other hand, world and life negation does not originate in a similar experience. It is there from the very beginning, self-originated, born as it were in a cloudless sky:"[2] nice poetry, but historically inaccurate. This sort of rhetoric is infrequent, although not totally absent, in con-

[2] Schweitzer, Albert, *Indian Thought and its Development*, New York: Beacon Press 1960 (1936), 19.

temporary scholarly discourse; yet attitudes underlying Schweitzer's statement are discernible even among serious scholars.

We may excuse this sort of exaggeration and essentialism in a Christian theologian like Schweitzer, but surely we have a right to expect better from the pre-eminent sociologist of the 20th century, Max Weber. But that is not the case. The category he uses is "Buddhism". In his excellent recent book on religious nationalism in Sri Lanka, the Sri Lankan anthropologist H. L. Seneviratne[3] has drawn our attention to the insidious propensity of Max Weber to slide down the slippery slope from his "ideal-type" to historical reality in the context of Buddhism.

> Weber's "ancient Buddhism" was more an extrapolation from an essentialized Buddhist doctrine than an abstract of monastic life as it was actually lived … His typology of world religions needed an "other worldly mysticism", and he invented one in his conception of "ancient Buddhism". In Weber's work, "ancient Buddhism", logically meant to be an ideal type, expresses itself as an empirical reality. This indeed is the general problem with the ideal type as an analytical construct: those who work with ideal types sometimes proceed as if they were real.

This is a problem similar to the one I mentioned about the category of "Hinduism" - once you have constructed a category, even with appropriate caveats, it is a slippery slope to considering it as something out there. An ideal type becomes an objective reality, and a constructed category becomes a historical religion.

Coming to contemporary times, the well-known anthropologist McKim Marriott[4] edited a widely read and cited volume *India through Hindu Categories* with the assumption that there is out there within a three-thousand-year history in a vast subcontinent a set of "Hindu categories" that can be recovered. "Hindu" here is an essentialized and monolithic category, resistant to change and enduring unchanged through the centuries.[5] Another anthropologist, R. S. Khare[6], in many

---

[3] Seneviratne, H. L., *The Work of Kings: The New Buddhism in Sri Lanka,* Chicago: University of Chicago Press 1999, 1–2.

[4] Marriott, McKim, *India through Hindu Categories. Contributions to Indian Sociology,* Occasional Studies, 5. New Delhi: Sage 1990.

[5] Olivelle, Patrick, "Caste and Purity: A Study in the Language of the Dharma Literature", in: *Contributions to Indian Sociology* 32 (1998) 190–216.

[6] Khare, R. S., *The Hindu Hearth and Home: Culinary Systems Old and New in North India,* Delhi: Vikas Publishing House 1976; Khare, R. S., *Culture and Reality: Essays on the Hindu System of Managing Foods,* Simla: Indian Institute of Advanced Study 1976;

of his fine writings on food speaks of the "Hindu ideology of food" as if such an ideology remained intact from the Upaniṣadic writings several centuries before the common era to the comments of a modern taxi driver in Delhi.[7] The very influential book *Homo Hierarchicus* by the French social-anthropologist Louis Dumont[8], likewise, assumes an unchanging caste structure based on an immutable ideology of purity throughout the millennia of Indian history.[9]

Interestingly and ironically, this view of an eternal and unchanging religion is taken straight out of the Brahmanical play book. Mīmāṃsā, the dominant tradition of exegesis within Brahmanism, sees the Veda not only as eternal but also as without an author, human or divine *(apauruṣeya)*. It sees all other authoritative texts, such as the Mahābhārata, the texts on Dharma, and the Purāṇas – all the texts comprehended in the amorphous category called *smṛti* – as deriving their authority from the Veda in so far as they reflect the memory of Vedic injunctions now lost but recalled by the sages who composed the *smṛti* texts. Thus the entire Vedic tradition can be presented as eternal, agentless, and outside human history. The complex of doctrines, duties, rites, and practices comprehended under the term *dharma* also participates in this eternality; *dharma* is found in the Veda. The Veda thus stands as the mythical font – unchanging and eternal – of the tradition, every change and every new doctrine or institution being "discovered" within it through laboriously elaborated techniques of interpretation. It is unfortunate that modern scholarship that should deconstruct these theological constructs have instead often adopted the same strategies.

1. *Ideology of Varṇa and the Vedic Value System*

I now turn to the historical development of the religious traditions of ancient India. Given the constraints of space, I will select one significant element of the ancient Indian world as seen through Brahmanical eyes for

Khare, R. S. (ed.), *The Eternal Food: Gastronomic Ideas and Experiences of Hindus and Buddhists*, Albany, NY: State University of New York Press 1992.

[7] See my review: "Food in India: A Review Essay", in: *Journal of Indian Philosophy* 23, 367–380.

[8] Dumont, Louis, *Homo Hierarchicus: The Caste System and Its Implications.* Revised Edition. Tr. M. Sainsbury, Chicago: University of Chicago Press 1980 (1966).

[9] See my critique: "Caste and Purity: A Study in the Language of the Dharma Literature", in: *Contributions to Indian Sociology* 32, 190–216.

comment and analysis, along with the values underlying it and the entire Brahmanical world view. And that is the system of *varṇa*, the classification of human society into four groups: Brāhmaṇa, Kṣatriya, Vaiśya, and Śūdra. Even though this classification is presented in ancient Brahmanical texts, including the oldest, the Ṛgveda, as a descriptive formulation – that is, as a faithful depiction of ancient Indian social stratification – we must not be deceived; behind the descriptive and disinterested rhetoric lies hidden a prescriptive ideology based on the supremacy of the Brāhmaṇa within a hierarchical arrangement of society. The famous Purṣua Hymn of the Ṛgveda (10.90) presents the four *varṇas* as originating at the very moment of creation from different parts of the primeval Man sacrificed and dismembered:

> His mouth was the Brāhmaṇa his arms were made into the Rājanya; his thighs were made into the Vaiśya; and from his feet the Śūdra was born.

These four social classes of human beings are presented as different species, distinguished by their very origin within the creative process. They are as distinct from each other as horse and cow, and sun and moon, which also originated through the same process:

> From it horses were born … The cows were born from it … From his mind was born the moon; from his eye the sun was born.

Here we find a clear example of the process of "naturalization" whereby contingent humanly created categories are presented as natural and therefore unchangeable realities.

Whenever the specter of *varṇa* is raised, or whenever in the Dharmaśāstras – the books of religious and civil law authored by Brahmins – the duty to uphold the *varṇadharma* is enunciated, we can see the Brahmanical ideology of hierarchy at work. This is especially evident in the middle and late Vedic texts, the Brāhmaṇa and Upaniṣads, in which the ideology of the *brahma-kṣatra* alliance – between the priestly power and the political power – is formulated. This relationship, at once fraught with danger and contestation, was yet presented as beneficial to both; the two flourish only when allied to each other and wither when separated. The *Bṛhadāraṇyaka Upaniṣad* (1.4.11) locates this complicated yet intimate relationship between the two once again within the very creative moment:

> In the beginning this world was only *brahman*, only one. Because it was only one, *brahman* had not fully developed. It then created the ruling

> power, a form superior to and surpassing itself, that is, the ruling powers among the gods – Indra, Varuṇa, Soma, Rudra, Parjanya, Yama, Mṛtyu, and Īśāna. Hence there is nothing higher than the ruling power. Accordingly, at a royal anointing a Brahmin pays homage to a Kṣatriya by prostrating himself. He extends this honor only to the ruling power. Now, the priestly power *(brahman)* is the womb of the ruling power. Therefore, even if a king should rise to the summit of power, it is to the priestly power that he returns in the end as to his own womb. So, one who hurts the latter harms his own womb and becomes so much the worse for harming someone better than him.

Here the Kṣatriya is presented as arising from the Brāhmaṇa, who is the womb and mother of the Kṣatriya. It is the special duty of the Kṣatriya to protect the Brāhmaṇa, as pointed out in the *Aitareya Brāhmaṇa* (8.17) significantly within the rite for anointing a new king:

> Do ye proclaim him, O men, as overlord and overlordship, as paramount ruler and father of paramount rulers, as self ruler and self rule, as sovereign and sovereignty, as supreme lord and supreme lordship, as king and father of kings. The *kṣatra* (royal power) has been born, the *kṣatriya* has been born, the suzerain of all creation has been born, the eater of the commoners (*viś*) has been born, the slayer of foes has been born, the guardian of *Brāhmaṇas* has been born, the guardian of *dharma* has been born. (Tr. Keith with modification)

As Brian Smith[10] has shown, the metaphor of food and eater is commonly used in Brahmanical texts to show the relationship of power and dominion among the upper and the lower *varṇas*. The *Brāhmaṇas* and Kṣatriyas together represent the eaters and the Vaiśyas (and by extension the Śūdras) the food.

The value system underlying this Brahmanical world view is one centered on the married householder and is expressed in the theology of debts articulated in several texts from this period. The *Taittirīya Saṃhitā* (6.3.10.5) says that a Brāhmaṇa at his very birth is born with three debts to the seers, the gods, and the ancestors. He is freed from these debts by studying the Vedas during his Vedic studentship *(brahmacarya)*, by performing sacrifices, and by procreating offspring to continue the family line.

---

[10] Smith, Brian K., "Eaters, Food, and Social Hierarchy in Ancient India: A Dietary Guide to a Revolution in Values", in: *Journal of the American Academy of Religion* 58 (1990) 177–205.

At the center of these obligations stands the married householder who is the only person entitled to perform a Vedic sacrifice, which requires the participation of the wife, and to beget offspring. Going back to an old conception of the son as the father's immortality, the *Aitareya Brāhmaṇa* (7.13) proclaims:

> A debt he pays in him
> And immortality he gains,
> The father who sees the face
> Of his son born and alive.

The married householder thus represents the ideal religious life within the Vedic world. He is the *homo religiosus.*

Both these ideological cornerstones of the Brahmanical world – the supremacy of the Brāhmaṇa articulated in the *varṇa* system and the centrality of the married householder enunciated in the theology of debts, which are precisely the kind of "world and life affirmation" that Albert Schweitzer would deny in the case of India – will be challenged by the new religions and the new political formations arising in the eastern regions of the Ganges valley in the subsequent centuries.

2. *Shifting Geography of Power: Magadha*

Between the 5th and 3rd centuries BCE we see an important geographical shift in socio-political and religious formations from the north-central region of the Ganges-Yamuna Doab, the area of the old Kuru-Pañcālas (today's Uttar Pradesh), farther east to an area centered on what came to be known as Magadha (today's Bihar). We already see this shift in the *Bṛhadāraṇyaka Upaniṣad* that presents the philosopher-king Janaka and his favorite Brāhmaṇa priest-theologian Yājñavalkya, both located in the region of Videha in north-eastern India. It is this region that gave birth to the major ascetical religions of Buddhism, Jainism, and the Ājīvika sect. The recent book by Johannes Bronkhorst[11], appropriately entitled *Greater Magadha*, argues for the dominant role played by this region in the religious, philosophical, and political developments in India during the middle of the first millennium BCE. Without repeating Bronkhorst's detailed account, I

[11] Bronkhorst, Johannes, *Greater Magadha: Studies in the Culture of Early India*, Leiden: Brill 2007.

want here simply to enumerate some of the major innovations that occurred during this period in the north-eastern region of India, innovations that at one level challenged the western Brahmanical ideology and at another contributed some of the best known features of ancient Indian religion and culture.

These include the major features of the emerging ascetic culture centered around the wandering mendicant to which we will turn shortly. The ascetic culture of Magadha presented a value system that was in stark contrast to the core values of the Brahmanical religion. Ascetic values included the following: celibacy with the attendant rejection of the centrality of marriage, family, and procreation; mendicancy implying poverty and abstention from economic activities; itinerant mode of life, rejecting stability of domicile and social structures including caste; abandonment of fire and ritual activities that were central to the Brahmanical religion; distinct ochre-colored garments or even total nudity; and the cultivation of mystical knowledge through various techniques of physical and mental training.

On the ideological side, we see the rise of novel doctrines that were to characterize later Indian religion and civilization. These include the following: belief in rebirth and the ethicization of the rebirth process through the doctrine of *karma* and karmic retribution; the doctrine of *saṃsāra* that saw rebirth as an essentially negative condition defined as suffering and bondage; and finally the belief in the possibility of escape from the bondage of *saṃsāra* into a state of absolute freedom (*mokṣa* or *nirvāṇa*) through techniques of moral, physical, and mental discipline, yogic techniques that came to define the ascetic cultures and much of later Indian religions.

On the sociological side, we see the development of urban centers, formation of complex and large monarchical states, economic development, facility of travel and trade, and the rise of what we would call today an affluent middle class. The surplus economy permitted a class of economically unproductive people including religious mendicants.

3. *The Rise of New Religions: Buddhism and Jainism*

What happened in Magadha during the middle of the first millennium BCE was seminal and changed the future course of Indian religious history. The most visible way in which this period was to mark the rest of Indian history was the emergence of new religious movements, two of which, Buddhism and Jainism, were to become major Indian and world religions.

What distinguished these two religions, especially Buddhism, was the institutionalization of asceticism into monastic orders, especially the Buddhist *saṅgha*. This permitted the development of religious institutions and monumental buildings, the creation of a literary corpus of sacred texts that paralleled the older Vedic canon, and in a special way the flow of patronage both economic and political into the new religions. In all these areas the new religions were able to challenge effectively the Vedic religion and the Brahmanical religious monopoly on many fronts. We also see the emergence of language politics, with the new religions rejecting the sacred language Sanskrit in favor of the vernaculars in their preaching and textual composition. For the first time in India, we have multiple scriptural traditions, the Vedic being no longer unique, and multiple kinds of religious virtuosi, Brahmins being no longer unique.

Although each of these ascetic traditions developed monastic rules and doctrinal tenets that were distinct, it is clear that both inherited the general ascetic culture and many of the ascetic practices discussed above. Yet each presented in novel ways the uniqueness of its own founder, Siddhārtha Gautama, the Buddha, and Mahāvīra, the Jina. They were clearly charismatic personalities who drew large ascetic followings. In opposition to the practice of the Vedic tradition, however, these religions ascribed to their founders unique and absolute authority with respect to doctrines, morals, and the path to liberation they discovered. For the first time in Indian theological history, a single person was invested with absolute authority with respect to truth. In Buddhist exegetical theology, for example, the doctrine of *buddhavacana*, the word of the Buddha, prevailed as the litmus test for the authenticity of any scriptural passage.

One way in which the founders and their doctrines were exalted was the use of royal or imperial symbols and vocabulary with respect to them. The founders of these ascetic groups were called *jina*, "conquerer"; they were called *cakravartin*, "roller of the wheels" or universal emperor. The Buddha's doctrine was compared to a wheel, a metonym for the war chariot and conquest; and his first sermon is the *dharmacakrapravartanasūtra*, "the Sūtra that set the wheel of *Dharma* rolling". The Buddha's teaching is *śāsana*, the counterpart of a royal edict. These are all clearly royal symbols used, deliberately I think, to define new ascetic groups and new religious ideologies as better suited for a new royal age. Siddhārtha Gautama and Mahāvīra are, of course, given royal pedigrees. The strategy is obvious: the new religions are presented as the ones best suited to the new age of royal power, large states, an affluent mercantile community, and urban centers.

Why these two traditions, the Buddhist and the Jain, among the many ascetic sects that existed at that time, succeeded in surviving and even flourishing until contemporary times, while other ascetic groups either never organized themselves to an extent that permitted them to become historically identifiable traditions or, like the Ājīvikas[12], withered over time, cannot be answered with any degree of certainty. One factor in their development, however, was their success in attracting patronage, especially political patronage, an issue to which I will turn shortly.

There are indications in the Buddhist Vinaya, the corpus of Buddhist monastic rules, itself that the Buddha or the formulators of these rules were keenly aware of the importance of public perceptions; it contains elements that we would today call PR. Many of the occasions for the Buddha promulgating particular rules are the negative reaction of the lay public to the behavior of some of the Buddhist monks. The Buddha is depicted as reacting to this negative perception and forbidding that behavior. The Buddha's "middle path", the desire to avoid extremes, also plays into this public perception. The reasons why the Buddha or the early Buddhist community wanted to cater to public sensibilities remain unstated; but at least one of these reasons was without doubt the need for public support and patronage, especially the support of the urbanized upper and middle classes, for the community of Buddhist monks.

4. *Aśoka: Religious Reforms and Imperial Formation*

Unfortunately, apart from Buddhist and other religious texts, whose dates are at best uncertain, we do not have independent evidence of state formations, political ideologies, or royal patronage of religious communities prior to the edicts and inscriptions of Aśoka in the middle of the 3rd century BCE. The invasion by Alexander the Great of the far north-western region of the Indian subcontinent in 327–324 BCE was followed by the rapid rise of the Maurya empire located in the

[12] Basham, A. L., *History and Doctrines of the Ājīvikas*, London: Luzac 1951.

eastern region of Magadha, to which we have already referred, with Pāṭaliputra (modern Patna) as its capital. Aśoka's grandfather, Candragupta, founded the empire in 320 BCE, which was greatly expanded and consolidated by Aśoka (268–233 BCE).

Aśoka left us the first extant writings of India in the extensive edicts recorded on rocks and pillars. These are the first firmly datable and localizable texts from ancient India. Their language, like that of the early Buddhist writings, is also a kind of vernacular *koine* (Prakrit) and not Sanskrit. In these edicts we find clear indications of royal interest and patronage of various religious traditions. The seventh Pillar Edict, for example, mentions that his Dharma-Mahāmātras, the Ministers of Dharma, were to look into the affairs of Brāhmaṇas, Ājīvakas, and Nirgranthas (Jains), as well as other ascetic communities. We know from other inscriptions that Aśoka considered himself a Buddhist and actually endowed several sites sacred to Buddhists. The inscriptions in the Barābar and Nāgārjunī Caves show that they were constructed and donated for the use of Ājīvakas ascetics.[13]

The major Aśokan reform that reverberated down the centuries, however, was the elimination from his imperial ideology the concept of "Brahmanical exceptionalism" most evident in the ideology of *varṇa* and of the *brahma-kṣatra* alliance that was central to the Brahmanical conception of society and kingship. To what extent the ideology of Brahmanical exceptionalism was adopted on the ground by early rulers is impossible to tell; but later Brahmanical reflections on the abandonment of this ideology by kings during the subsequent centuries clearly indicate that Aśokan reforms marked a turning point in the intersection between the political and the religious in ancient Indian society. The challenge to Brahmanical exceptionalism is most succinctly enunciated in the oft-repeated phrase in Aśokan inscriptions: *śramaṇa-brāhmaṇa*, ascetics and Brāhmaṇas, as two classes of religious people worthy of respect and support. The Brāhmaṇa is now put on a par with the ascetic; they are mentioned, so to speak, in the same breath.

Aśoka's adoption of the ethics of *ahiṃsā* – not killing, not injuring living beings – also undercut one of the major factors underpinning Brahmanical exceptionalism and the special relationship between the Brahmin and the king. The Vedic sacrifice, which was at the heart

[13] Basham 1951.

of what made the Brahmin exceptional and of indispensable service to the royal power, often involved the immolation of animals, especially the horse sacrifice *(aśvamedha)* where a horse was immolated to enhance royal power and prestige. The use by Aśoka of the technical term *prahotavya* in prohibiting the killing of animals in Rock Edit 1, a term used specifically with regard to the killing of animals within the context of sacrifices, is a clear indication of imperial displeasure at animal sacrifice. The recent work of Harry Falk[14] indicates that many of the Aśokan edicts were placed strategically near sites that had local religious significance and where animal sacrifices may have been carried out.

The Aśokan inscriptions also opens a new window into the society and religion of that period. A remarkable feature in these documents is that they do not mention the central tenet of early Brahmanical view of society, the system of *varṇas*. The term itself does not occurs in the inscriptions, and nowhere is the division of society into four classes mentioned. Even the Brahmin is presented not as a social class but as a religious group paralleling the ascetic groups collectively called *śramaṇa*. This is a salutary warning to us not to see Brahmanical presentations of social reality as descriptive, but to see them as prescriptive and as ideologically driven.

The Aśokan reforms had broken the link between *brahma* and *kṣatra*, between priest and king. New religious formations were emerging requiring imperial attention and patronage. New ideologies were emerging with different conceptions of human life, morality, and society. This was the complex social, political, and religious dynamic in the period I have called "Between the Empires", between the Aśokan empire of the 3rd century BCE and the Gupta empire of the 4th century CE.[15]

The period is vast and its history too complex to review within the compass of this presentation. As a way of getting a handle on this period and to highlight the centrality of the interaction between religion and politics, let me take up for comment undoubtedly the most central term and concept in the whole of Indian civilization. That term is Dharma.

---

[14] Falk, Harry, *Aśokan Sites and Artefacts: A Source-Book with Bibliography*, Mainz am Rhein: Philipp von Zabern 2006.

[15] Olivelle 2006.

5. *The Emperor and the Ascetic: Political History of Dharma*

Because I have written several articles on the history of the term Dharma,[16] and edited a volume containing studies by 18 scholars on the semantic history of this term[17], I will only present here a synopsis of those findings. Briefly, then, the term emerges as a neologism (it is not found in cognate Indo-European languages, including Avestan) in the *Ṛgveda*, where it is used 68 times with a somewhat wide semantic range: foundation, institute, moral order.[18]

One would have expected that this term, which made such a promising start in the *Ṛgveda*, would grow in significance and centrality in the vocabulary of the middle and late Vedic periods to become the central concept it became in later Indian history. And this is precisely how it is presented in most studies of Indian religions. This, however, was not to be the case. Except for changing its gender from the neuter *dhárman* to the masculine *dharmaḥ*, it became a marginal term in the later Vedic lexicon. Indeed, its use within the other Vedic Saṃhitās, the Brāhmaṇa, and even the Upaniṣads, which together form an enormous corpus of literature, is infrequent. Parallel to its relative infrequency, we can detect also a semantic restriction of the term. It is used most frequently with reference to Varuṇa, the heavenly king par excellence, and to his earthly counterpart. If we exclude verses cited from the *Ṛgveda* and repetitions, all the Yajurvedic Saṃhitās combined use it 28 times; in the enormous corpus of the Brāhmaṇas, it occurs just 13 times; and in the four ancient prose Upaniṣads, it is found in only 9 passages.

[16] Olivelle, Patrick, "The Semantic History of Dharma. The Middle and Late Vedic Periods", in: Patrick Olivelle (ed.), *Dharma: Studies in Its Semantic, Cultural, and Religious History*. Special issue of *Journal of Indian Philosophy* 32 (2004) 491–511; Olivelle, Patrick, "Power of Words: The Ascetic Appropriation and the Semantic Evolution of dharma", in: Patrick Olivelle, *Language, Texts, and Society: Explorations in Ancient Indian Culture and Religion*, Florence: University of Florence Press 2006; Olivelle, Patrick, "Explorations in the Early History of Dharmaśāstra", in: Patrick Olivelle (ed.), *Between the Empires: Society in India 300 BCE to 400 CE*, Oxford University Press, New York 2006, 169–190.

[17] Olivelle 2004.

[18] For a discussion of the semantics of *dharma* in the Ṛgveda, see Horsch, Paul, "From Creation Myth to World Law: The Early History of *Dharma*", in: Patrick Olivelle (ed.), *Dharma: Studies in Its Semantic, Cultural, and Religious History*, Motilal Banarsidass, Delhi 2005, 1–26. English translation of 1967 German article; and Brereton, Joel, "*Dhárman* in the *Ṛgveda*", in: Olivelle 2005, 27–67.

A startling statistical fact emerges from this: the term Dharma occurs 68 times within the relatively short *Ṛgveda*, whereas it is used in just 51 independent passages in the vast literature of the middle and late Vedic periods. The semantic range of Dharma is by and large restricted to the sphere of the king, occurring most frequently within the context of the consecration of the king *(rāūjasūya)*. The term is clearly not central to the theology and ritual exegesis of these Vedic texts. I think we need to rethink our assumptions regarding the centrality of Dharma within the cultural history of India. The term is also conspicuous by its marginality in the post-Vedic ritual literature of the Śrauta and the Gṛhya Sūtras.

By contrast we see that Dharma is employed by Aśoka as the pivotal concept in a new imperial ideology articulated in his brief edicts, where term is used over 100 separate times (excluding copies of the same edict given in different locations). I believe that Aśoka used Dharma as the central concept to construct an imperial ideology – one may even call it an imperial theology – that gave legitimacy to his rule and a religious/moral foundation to his empire. I think one can justifiably present Aśoka's activities as an attempt to institute a civil religion to which not only all the citizens of his empire, but also people living in other parts of the world, could subscribe. The central concept in this new civil religion is Dharma.

Unlike the Vedic texts, however, Aśoka gives us quite a clear picture of what he meant by Dharma. In Rock Edict 3 he instructs his ministers to teach the Dharma in the following words: "Obedience to mother and father is good *(sādhu)*. Giving *(dāna)* to friends, acquaintances, and relatives, and to Brāhmaṇas and Śramaṇas is good. Not killing is good. Spending little and possessing little is good." Other lists add the proper treatment of slaves and servants. Similar sentiments are expressed frequently in the edicts, which he frequently refers to as "*dharmalipi*" – "inscriptions relating to *dharma*", or perhaps "dharmic inscriptions". In the long Pillar Edict 7, which was to be his last and where he uses *dharma* 30 times, he defines the practice of Dharma as consisting of compassion, liberality, truthfulness, purity, gentleness, and goodness. For Aśoka, then, Dharma was an essentially moral concept; and teaching Dharma, which Aśoka looked upon as one of his major imperial obligations, meant teaching his subject how to lead a good and moral life. For the first time we even have the translation of this term into Greek and Aramaic in Aśoka's bi-lingual Minor Rock Edict IV of Kandahar, where the Greek *eusebeia*, meaning something like piety, and the Aramaic *qsyt*, with a meaning related to truth, are used as equivalents of Dharma.

The semantic development of Dharma within the middle and late Vedic period that saw it closely associated with kingship made it a likely candidate for adoption by an ancient Indian emperor. But how did a term that had a restricted semantic compass, referring to social order and laws, become a broad ethical concept in the Aśokan inscriptions. I think for this we must look at the ascetic communities, especially Buddhism, that predated Aśoka.

This semantic transformation and the central position he accorded to Dharma, I believe, suggest that Aśoka's use of Dharma was mediated by its appropriation sometime before Aśoka by the emerging ascetic communities. This appropriation was probably part of the broader adoption of royal symbols and vocabulary by ascetic leaders and communities that I discussed above; remember that Dharma had become part of the royal vocabulary especially in the context of the royal consecration.

Within the historical religion of Buddhism, Dharma stands at the very heart of its theology, defining the very essence of what the Buddha, the Universal Emperor *(cakravartin)* of a new moral universe, is thought to have discovered. Dharma here defined the truth discovered by the Buddha, the truth that conferred authority on him. It forms part of the Triple Gem *(triratna)* that defined the core of Buddhism: Buddha, Dharma, and Saṇgha. In this transfer from king to ascetic, however, Dharma came to be redefined in terms of doctrine, especially moral doctrine, and it was given a centrality within religious discourse that it lacked in the Vedic lexicon. Especially in its use with regard to the non-monastic life of the Buddhist laity, one can see how Dharma came to acquire an essentially moral meaning, as in the five *śīlas*, or moral precepts, that they were expected to follow.

The term and the concept of Dharma acquired such a prominence and centrality through both Buddhism and the Aśokan imperial ideology and civil religion that it was impossible even for the Brahmanical tradition to ignore it. My hypothesis is that the emergence of the Dharmaśāstric literature, a genre of technical texts devoted to the concept of Dharma, first in the form of prose *sūtras* and then in metrical treatises beginning with Manu, was a direct consequence of Buddhist and Aśokan reforms. That a *śāstra*, an expert tradition of knowledge, be devoted to *dharma* would seem improbable from its marginal use within the theologies expressed in the middle and late

Vedic texts. Since the time of Aśokan Dharma came to define the very essence of the Brahmanical religion, and the term *varṇâśramadharma*, the Dharma of social classes and orders of life, became a synonym for this tradition.

We have come a full circle. A brand new term invented by ancient Brahmanical poets of the Ṛgveda has become the central and defining term for the Brahmanical religion and way of life with considerable help from their rivals for religious authority and influence, the ascetic communities, and from an emperor with dreams of conquering the world through and for Dharma.

6. *Foreign Emperors and the Resurgence of Brahmanism*

The Maurya empire rapidly disintegrated after the death of Aśoka, and it came to an end in 185 BCE with the assassination of the last Maurya emperor, Bṛhadratha. Numerous political formations followed in northern India, but the ones that most influenced the religious and cultural history of the period were the kingdoms established by foreigners. There were, of course, the Greco-Bactrian kingdoms in the far north west resulting from Alexander's military expeditions. But in the centuries immediately before and after the beginning of the common era we have invasions by people from central Asia who established kingdoms in the western and central parts of north India; these were the Śakas and the Kushanas.

Kushana rulers became Buddhists and strong patrons of Buddhist institutions. We find this especially in the public visual presence of Buddhism in the architecture of the Kushana period, a time when few Hindu/Brahmanical structures were present. Foreign rule and Buddhist rule represented by the Kushanas, including the in-your-face challenge of Buddhist public monuments, were a double challenge to the Brahmanical conception of society, kingship, and the place of the Brahmin community within society.

It is within the context of the historical memory of the Maurya reforms, always recreated and re-imagined, and the contemporary reality of foreign rulers with strong Buddhist leanings that we much consider the major Brahmanical literary monuments of the period, especially the two Epics, the *Mahābhārata* and the *Rāmāyaṇa*, and the major Dharmaśāstric texts such as that of Manu. Recent scholarship represented by Madeline Biardeau[19], Alf Hiltebeitel[20], and James Fitzgerald[21] has seen the Brahmanical epics as implicit answers to the challenges posed by Maurya and other political reforms, as well as by Buddhism. I have argued that the legal text of Manu should also be seen as a Brahmanical response to this challenge.[22]

This Brahmanical resurgence was directed especially at the ruling class to teach the proper way of being a king and to reestablish the old *brahma-kṣatra* alliance with the concept of Dharma now formulated in terms of *varṇa*, the ideological classification of society, and *āśrama*, the new theological formulation that accommodates asceticism within a scheme where the married householder still occupies the center stage. The recent study by Sheldon Pollock[23] on what he terms the "Sanskrit cosmopolis" where Sanskrit was adopted as the court language both in inscriptions and in court poetry *(kāvya)* also points in the direction of Brahmanical influence within new state formations. One question that Pollock does not ask or answer is why at this particular juncture in history the rulers found it necessary or advantageous to use a language that had until then been principally a language of liturgy and scholarship. One possible answer is that this may have been part of the Brahmanical resurgence represented by the Sanskrit epics; use of Sanskrit would clearly have given them greater access to and influence in the ruling courts. How they convinced the rulers that adopting Sanskrit was a good imperial strategy to consolidate power remains unclear. But the Brahmanical influence in this Sanskritization of court culture is unquestionable.

It is broadly within this period also that the recasting of the major ancient text of political science and statecraft, the *Arthaśāstra* ascribed to Kauṭilya, was carried out. As Mark McClish in his recent doctoral dissertation has shown, the ancient core of the *Arthaśāstra,* the so-called Prakaraṇa text, was devoid of the ideology of Brahmanical exceptionalism. It was the Brahmanical redaction of the work carried

---

[19] Biardeau, Madeleine, *Le Mahābhārata: Un récit fondateur du brahmanisme et son interprétation*, Paris: Seuil 2002.

[20] Hiltebeitel, Alf, *Rethinking the Mahābhārata: A Reader's Guide to the Education of the Dharma King*, Chicago: University of Chicago Press 2001.

[21] Fitzgerald, James, *The Mahābhārata: 11. The Book of the Women, 12. The Book of Peace*, Chicago: University of Chicago Press 2004.

[22] Olivelle, Patrick, *Manu's Code of Law: A Critical Edition and Translation of the Mānava-Dharmaśāstra*, New York: Oxford University Press 2005, 37–41.

[23] Pollock, Sheldon, *The Language of the Gods in the World of Men: Sanskrit, Culture, and Power in Premodern India*, Berkeley: University of California Press 2006.

out in the early centuries of the common era that saw both the division of the text into Adhyāyas (chapters) and the insertion of passages espousing Brahmanical exceptionalism.

What happened in northern India around the turn of the millennium from BCE to CE was historic in nature. Sheldon Pollock[25] refers to the rupture in cultural time that occurred as the birth of what he calls the Sanskrit Cosmopolis that would within a few centuries stretch from today's Pakistan and Kashmir in the west to Cambodia and Indonesia in the east, from Nepal in the north to Sri Lanka in the south, a cosmopolis that was much larger than any the world has seen in pre-modern times, a cosmopolis united not by political power but by the power of a language, Sanskrit, and a culture carried by it.

Quite counter-intuitively, this entry of Sanskrit from the religious to the public sphere was caused or at least facilitated by foreign rulers: the Śaka and Kushana rulers, who came from central Asia within a couple of centuries on either side of the turn of the millennium to put down Indian roots.

The Brahmanical resurgence was complete when the next major empire in ancient India, that of the Gupta dynasty, arose in 320 CE. Often called the Golden Age of ancient India, the Gupta Empire was not only rich but also the driving force in various areas of cultural and religious expression, including art, architecture, poetry, and law. In all these areas we see a strong Brahmanical imprint. In an interesting way we have come a full circle with Brāhmaṇas at the center of kingly power, directing and controlling it through ministerial appointments and acting as judges in courts of law. The *brahma-kṣatra* alliance has been re-instituted once again.

I will end this tour of the cultural landscape of ancient India with where I began. I have argued for a particular way to study this period of Indian history and against some ways in which that history has been studied in the past by some scholars. I hope these somewhat scattered thoughts will help us rethink how we should research this period, how we should teach this period to our students, and how we should encourage the educated public to envisage this period of ancient Indian history.

DID THE BUDDHA EMERGE FROM A BRAHMANIC ENVIRONMENT? THE EARLY BUDDHIST EVALUATION OF "NOBLE BRAHMINS" AND THE "IDEOLOGICAL SYSTEM" OF BRAHMANISM

Jens Schlieter

In the following paper – a response to Patrick Olivelle's rich presentation of the religious dynamics of Brahmanism and other traditions in early India[1] – I will focus on the general conviction, shared, as it seems, by Olivelle, that early Buddhism can be seen as an answer to Brahmanism. More or less, early Buddhism is widely conceived of as an ascetic, ethically rigorous reformist movement in a Brahmanic environment. Although there seems to be sufficient evidence that (at least a certain number of) Brahmins were present in the early Buddhist environment, it was perhaps not the case that Brahmanism formed the major background tradition for the historical Buddha and the early Buddhist communities.[2] Actually, for more than a century now Buddhologists and Indologists have been puzzled by the fact that there are no close links between the teachings of the Vedas, and especially of those Upaniṣads acknowledged to be pre-Buddhist, and Buddhist teachings.[3] Étienne Lamotte observed that Magadha, one "kingdom", or area, which counts as one of the central territories which the Buddha peregrinated and in which he taught, "was not completely ary-

[1] "Dynamics in the History of Religions between Asia and Europe. Encounters, Notions, and Comparative Perspectives" (Conference of the IKGF "Dynamics in the History of Religions", Bochum, Oct. 15–17, 2008), see this volume above p. 117.

[2] The knowledge of the life and teachings of the Buddha is, more or less exclusively, conveyed through Buddhist texts. However, some sources are older than others. Without touching upon the difficult question of the authenticity of the "teachings of the Buddha", I will refer – in a simplified manner – to this older stratum of sources as "early Buddhist teachings".

[3] Hermann Oldenberg already characterized the situation with the following words: "Was der Erforscher dieser Gedankenentwicklungen besonders lebhaft vermisst, wäre als ein Sichzusammenordnen der der brahmanischen und buddhistischen Traditionen [...] in einem gemeinsamen Rahmen zu beschreiben, als Vorhandensein einer Kontinuität datierbarer Verbindungsglieder [...]. Wo der Buddhismus in die Erscheinung tritt, hebt sich unvermittelt gleichsam ein Vorhang an einer Stelle, die früher ausserhalb des Gesichtskreises lag" (Oldenberg, Hermann, *Die Lehre der Upanishaden und die Anfänge des Buddhismus,* Göttingen: Vandenhoek & Ruprecht 1915, 289).

anized, but simply crossed by bands of renegate Āryans named *vrātya* who did not follow the vedic rites".[4] Despite the fact that the degree of prevalence of Brahmins and Brahmanic teachings at the time of the Buddha might be open for discussion, most scholars of Buddhism are convinced that Brahmins were an important impact factor for the Buddha and his teachings. The evidence for this claim seems to be quite obvious, because, as Buddhist sources narrate, Brahmins crossed the Buddha's way quite frequently and formed, again according to the sources, a large group among his converted followers. Yet, one may ask – as a thought experiment – how early Buddhist accounts of Brahmins and their cosmological and philosophical teachings, their social status, ritual procedures etc. will have to be re-evaluated if Brahmins were at that time *not* a predominant cultural force. As Buddhist texts were transmitted orally for at least 150 years, and the canonical scriptures were finalized even later, a significant amount of the Buddhist depictions of Brahmins and the 'ideological system of Brahmanism' might have been conceptualized and inserted at a much later date. These descriptions may, therefore, reflect a situational change of Brahmanic predominance that evolved in the meantime. One may be tempted to argue that this kind of 'polemical' literature is the result of a – possibly inferior? – discourse position of Buddhists that became true in the subsequent historical period.

Even if one may not be able to prove sufficiently that this dynamic and complex scenario is, on the whole, a plausible reconstruction, it may nevertheless be useful. It could help to shed some new light on certain – more or less odd – facts of early Buddhist accounts of Brahmins and Brahmanism.

Most interestingly, the current conception of the Brahmanic background of early Buddhism, and the largely polemical encounter between Buddhists and Brahmins, seems to be primarily informed by Buddhist dogmatic, historiographic and hagiographic literature. If, as we assume, the strong opposition to Brahmanic ideas were dated back (or "retrojected") to the time of the Buddha and his early followers, one should take into account that Buddhist discourse was largely

[4] Lamotte, Étienne, *History of Indian Buddhism. From the Origins to the Śaka Era*, Louvain-la-Neuve 1988 [= orig.: *Histoire du Bouddhisme Indien*, Louvain 1958], 5; compare Erdosy, George, "The Prelude to Urbanisation: Ethnicity and the Rise of Late Vedic Chiefdoms", in: Frank Raymond Allchin, *The Archealogy of Early Historic South Asia. The Emergence of Cities and States*, Cambridge: Cambridge University Press 1995, 91.

borne by monastic specialists (and not individual ascetic adepts or lay followers). Monks, as seems obvious, have certain social and political interests, because their maintenance by lay followers[5] is always immediately in danger if political circumstances change. As a matter of fact, the earliest Buddhist textual sources we can get hold of reach back into an era where monastic communities were already firmly established. The formation of Buddhism as a tradition should not only be regarded as a process of an initial separation, followed by an inner differentiation in schools (that is, of course, what Buddhist historiography, e. g., of the schisms, and doxographical literature would like to suggest). In addition, it seemed to be a bundle of processes consisting of special arrangements with leading elites of political power, ongoing contacts with Brahmanic thought and practices, and the assimilation of various local folk traditions, respectively.

1. *The Localisation of the "Āryan Range" as an Indicator for the Prevalence of "Brahmanic Culture" in Magadha*

Patrick Olivelle marks two ideological cornerstones of the Vedic world: "the supremacy of the *Brāhmaṇa* articulated in the *varṇa* system and the centrality of the married householder". These cornerstones were challenged by wandering ascetics of Buddhism, Jainism and others – rejecting family and procreation, abandonment of Vedic ritual activities; generating new teachings of *karma*, suffering, and absolute freedom.

For sure, there seems to be abundant evidence that these mendicants formed the earliest stage of Buddhist followers – the Buddha, Gautama Siddhārtha, being one of them.

But was the Vedic culture at large, relying on oral, and later written Sanskrit sources, the culture that was predominant in the greater region of Magadha at the time of the Buddha (4th c. BCE)? Let me now turn to Bronkhorst's recent observations.[6] As is well known, it is still very difficult to get an overview of early Indian history. Historical dates of events, dynasties and texts are still subject to endless debates and speculation. Anyhow, it seems to be more or less clear

[5] Compare Chakravarti, Uma, *The Social Dimension of Early Buddhism*, Delhi/Oxford: Oxford University Press 1987, 69–84.

[6] Bronkhorst, Johannes, *Greater Magadha. Studies in the Culture of Early India*, Leiden/Boston: Brill 2007.

that Vedic-Sanskritic culture is connected to Indo-Aryan invaders to North-West India. It seems that they were not able to dominate the Indian sub-continent at once, but were, in the first millennium BC, slowly progressing to the East. In several texts from the respective time frame, the last three to four hundred years of the pre-Christian era, a word is given for the "living sphere"; the "range of the habitat" of the Aryas, the *"āryāvarta"* (i.e. *āryāṇâm āvartaḥ*).

The Āryas are clearly depicted as the high-ranking, noble followers of the Vedic-Brahmanic Sanskrit-Culture; *"ārya"*, in other words, are "distinguished by a set of ideas"[7] and a certain language, but not by ethnicity.[8] Some sources allude that the territory of the *"āryāvarta"* had an Eastern limit; it did not extend beyond the confluence (prayāga) of the rivers Gaṅgā and Yamunā.[9] Patañjali's *Mahābhāṣya*, an important commentary to the oldest extant Indian grammar, states: "Which is the land of the Āryas? It is the region to the east where the Sarasvatī disappears (ādarśa), west of the Kālaka forest, south of the Himalayas, and north of the Pāriyātra mountains".[10] Bronkhorst concludes his analysis: "According to the passages [...] the region east of the confluence of the Gaṅgā and the Yamunā was not considered Brahmanical territory at the time of Patañjali".[11] Indeed, "[t]he fact that ‚easterners' *(prācyas)* in general, and Magadhans in particular, were regarded with disapproval by Late Vedic seers shows that the spread of new values had not transcended the Ganga-Yamuna Doab in the 6th century BC".[12]

In later sources of the second or third century CE, however, things seem to have changed, and Brahmins incorporated the region of (Greater) Magadha in the *"āryāvarta"* or *"madhyadeśa"*-region; they looked at it now "as *their* land".[13] If we concede that all the single steps of this conclusion are correct, then it may imply that in the second century BCE Brahmanic Sanskrit culture (as a "cultural category" in the sense of Erdosy) was not dominant in the region of Magadha. If this assumption is correct, it will most likely be the case for the preceding centuries (6th to 2nd century BCE). So, one may assume that

[7] Erdosy 1995, 90.

[8] Lopez, Donald S. Jr., *Buddhism and Science. A Guide for the Perplexed*, Chicago: University of Chicago Press 2008, 78–83.

[9] Today Ganges and Yumna; the *prayāg* – one of the ancient pilgrimage sites of India – is located near the modern city of Allahabad in Uttar Pradesh.

[10] Mahā-bh I. 475 1. 3; III. 174. 1. 7–8; cited in Bronkhorst 2007, 1.

[11] Bronkhorst 2007, 2.

[12] Erdosy 1995, 91.

[13] Bronkhorst 2007, 2.

Brahmanic culture was not widely spread in (Greater) Magadha at the time the Buddha and his early followers stayed there (4th c. BCE).

Interestingly, some Buddhist texts display a certain difference between "āryan" and "non-āryan" language[14]: "It is important to note, however, that the Buddha appears also to accept the widely held connotation of āryan as referring to those who have language, or at least proper language."[15] This characterisation of different languages and respective cultures seems to be an essential feature of the Jina Mahāvāra and the early Jaina tradition, too. As the Jain sources describe, Mahāvāra, who spoke *Ardhamagadhī*, taught to "Non-Aryans" *(anārya)* and to "Aryans", speaking automatically in their mother-tongue.[16]

To substantiate his observation about the "range of the Ārya", Bronkhorst refers to a second category of information, namely, the political history of the Ganges valley east of the confluence with the Yamunā. More precisely of interest in our context is information on the religious groups or teachers that were supported by the local rulers in the respective area. The early kings of Magadha, Bimbisāra and Ajātaśatru seem to have supported the Jaina and the Buddhists. Then the Nanda, on the other hand (ruled around 360–320 BCE), supported exclusively the Jaina; the preceding Maurya emperors, Candragupta Maurya and his son Bindusāra (ca. 293–268 BCE), again the Jaina, and the Ājīvika, the "materialists". Aśoka, again, supported mainly the Buddhists. An eminent shift can be noted in the following dynasty of emperors, the Śuṅga: "It is only with the Śuṅgas, who were Brahmins themselves, that Brahmins may have begun to occupy the place in society which they thought was rightfully theirs. This happened around 185 BCE".[17]

---

[14] Deshpande, Madhav M., "What to do with the *Anāryas*: Dharmic Discourses of Inclusion and Exclusion", in: Bronkhorst, Johannes/Deshpande, Madhav M. (eds.), *Aryan and Non-Aryan in South Asia: Evidence, Interpretation and Ideology*, Cambridge: Harvard Oriental Series 1999, 121 [with references].

[15] Lopez 2008, 83.

[16] Compare Deshpande 1999, 116.

[17] Bronkhorst 2007, 3. Because the historical circumstances will be of some importance, a quotation from Robert DeCaroli may be added: "Although the brahmans were also heavily involved in the acculturation of remote people, unlike the Buddhists they posed a political threat. This potential political rivalry from the brahmans was actualized in the emergence of the Śunga Dynasty (185–173 BCE), who were low-ranking brahmans by caste [Reference given: *Thapar, Romila; A History of India.* Vol. 1 of 2. Baltimore: Penguin Books 1966, 151–153]. Although the date of this political shift is subject to debate the sequence of events is established. And, given the probable caste affiliations of the Śunga kings, it is not surprising that Puśyamitra, the first of the Śunga

This observation fits perfectly well with the other findings. If we additionally take into consideration that according to the revised, "short" chronology of the Buddha he may have died in the 4th century, we may be able to conclude that a Brahmanic preponderance in the Eastern Ganges plain, where the Buddha taught, was not very significant (a closer look to the sources, which is not possible to undertake here, might provide the result that the North- and South-Eastern Mahājanapadas ["great realms", i. e. countries or regional kingdoms] of Kosala, Sakiya, and Kāsī with its capital Bārāṇasī, modern Benares, were more advanced in the process of "brahmanization" than the Mahājanapadas of Magadha, Vajjī and Malla).

To emphasize this point: If this holds true, the early Buddhist movement cannot be regarded as a "protest movement" against a Vedic-Brahmanic source culture. Early Buddhism could not be construed as essentially a counter-reaction against a Brahmanist system, simply because at that time Brahmanism – as an organized system – was not there.

Since Bronkhorst is mainly interested in the origin of the doctrine of rebirth and karmic retribution, his over-all conclusion pertains to the religious background of pre-Buddhist, and even pre-Jainist "Greater Magadha". The ideology of rebirth and a moral interpretation of *karma*, may form an even elder tradition that predated Jainism, Buddhism, and Brahmanism in that area alike. According to his assumption the idea of karma and rebirth was invented by this unknown tradition that did not survive as an independent strand but merged into the three other traditions. A second conclusion is drawn in respect to the relative chronology of the late Vedic texts, namely, the Upaniṣads. If the Buddha did not adopt the ideas of *karma* and rebirth from Upaniṣadic sources, because these, as part of the Brahmanic-sanskritic discourse, were not known to him, it should be safe to conclude that these sources do not predate the Buddha, but are dependent on him, that is, later.

---

rulers, focused his religious patronage almost exclusively on Vedic sacrifices. The Buddhist texts attribute harsh and fanatical persecutions to Puśyamitra, whom they claim sought to destroy Buddhism. It is possible, however, that he simply ignored the saṃgha and that contemporary monks saw this withdrawal of long-standing royal support as the death knell of the order" (DeCaroli, Robert, *Haunting the Buddha. Indian Popular Religions and the Formation of Buddhism*, Oxford: Oxford University Press 2004, 33).

2. *Single Brahmins and the "Brahmanic System": Two Different Categories in the Buddhist Accounts?*

However, Bronkhorst did not expand the implications that these findings may have in regard to the history of early Buddhist accounts of Brahmanism. I will try to highlight in just a few words some of the possible implications and will thereafter return to the question of the dynamics of inter-religious contacts. To repeat – and extend – the hypothesis: (a) there is quite good evidence that in the early parts of Buddhist canonical sources, such as the Sutra-collections, only few religious ideas or practices are mentioned that can be traced to Vedic origin.[18] If (b) the intensive encounter of Buddhism and Brahmanic society happened to take place some centuries later, many of those passages in the Buddhist texts that consist of elaborate descriptions of Brahmins, their rites and myths, their ideology and philosophy, might be – in terms of text transmission – of secondary nature. The motive for these amendments may (c) consist of a deliberate or even non-intentional move to inscribe the recent conflict into the traditional accounts that were passed on to them. Even the intimate connection between the Buddha and the "warrior-caste" *(khattiya)*, as well as the astoundingly high esteem of the Khattiyas displayed in early Buddhist sources, and possibly the local construction of a "khattiya-caste" as such may be part of a reaction against the Brahmins depiction of themselves as first in rank.

The full-fledged "Brahmanic system" may tentatively be defined by the following elements: (1) the vision of a hierarchical stratified society, (2) Brahmins as the supreme hereditary caste/class in the system; (3) the ideology of a graded system of (im)purities restricting class transgression; (4) the centrality of sacrifice for the well-being of the individual and, more important, the social community (cf. A I.155); (5) Brahmins as the exclusive media for the transmission of the sacred Vedic (lingual) tradition.

Due to the fact that Buddhist texts were initially composed and transmitted orally, the time frame of the beginning of their written fixation – around the first century BCE – might coincide with the assumed "aryanization" and "sanskritization". If those descriptions reflect a later constellation of Buddhists and Brahmins, the Buddhist

[18] Compare Bronkhorst 2007, 207–218.

depiction of the "Brahmanic system" might, consequently, be construed as a reaction against an invading Brahmanic tradition that had – only recently – began challenging the established position of Buddhists in society. Moreover, if at the time of the encounter Buddhists were already organized in larger monastic communities *(saṅghas)*, supported with food and financed by a wealthy lay community, the recent spread of the "Brahma-kṣatra alliance"[19] challenge might have been envisioned by the Buddhists as a danger to their subsistence: especially in a situation where the Brahmins would successfully proceed to establish strong relationships with the royal powers.

To speculate, however, a little further, one could even imagine that monastic Buddhists not only construed the "bad" – i. e., the greedy Brahmin striving for power – but also the "good" Brahmin, i. e. those Brahmins who already lived in Magadha in earlier times – but only in small numbers and far from the cities and royal centres. Those Brahmins were "good" and "noble" exactly because they lived in consonance with ascetic ideals and, furthermore, were far from being able to form royal alliances against the Buddhists. It is highly significant that many passages in the early texts try to show that the Buddhist worldview far better suits royal purposes than the Brahmanic worldview (e. g., the uselessness and costs of Brahmanic sacrifices), while the same texts express that the ruling emperors have the highest regard for the Buddhist view, if they are not Buddhists themselves. Moreover, Buddhist texts protest against the idea of the (bloody) Brahmanic sacrifice. For those Brahmins, however, who wish to sacrifice and want to gain a real return from sacrifice, Buddhist texts offer the recommendation of donating directly to true ascetics, i. e. Buddhist monks (see, for example, Sn 462 ff.).

But can we indeed produce sufficient evidence for the claim that early Buddhist sources display two different depictions of Aryans and Brahmins? Certainly, Buddhist accounts of Brahmins, and the Buddhist use of the Sanskrit term "*ārya*" (Pāli: ariya), show a significant polarity between the "good Brahmins", who possess self-control and a restrained mind (e. g. Sn 284), the "samaṇa-brāhmaṇa", "ascetics and Brahmins", i. e. those Brahmins who live as ascetics and teachers, and the "bad Brahmins", i. e. those living "today" – greedy, worldly, hypocritical, enmeshed in passion, sense pleasures, etc. The affirmative

[19] Olivelle 2010, see this volume above p. 117.

Buddhist usage of the compound "samaṇa-brāhmaṇa" clearly points to a "continuity and symbiotic co-ordination or complementary"[20] between the two. However, in the *Samaññaphala-Sutta* the term *samaṇa-brāhmaṇa* is applied to the six 'heretical teachers', too.[21] In this context, it seems to denote ascetics in general, and the Buddha, the "*samaṇa* Gotama", being an accomplished example of those ascetic mendicants. In almost the same positive sense the term "*ariya*" is used in Buddhist texts as a general qualification of nobleness, goodness and moral pureness: the Buddhist truth, the way to liberation, the anthropological quality of advanced practitioners and so on are likewise qualified as "*ariya*".

Yet, according to Deshpande, the Buddhists were "clearly aware of the different associations of terms like 'Ārya'".[22] The Brahmin's claim to be 'Aryan' by birth – in a superior class – is heavily criticised in Buddhist texts (e.g., in the *Assalāyanasutta*, M II.147 ff.).[23] Here, "*ariya*" as well as "brāhmaṇa" denotes the systematic legitimization of the members belonging – in their own view – to the highest, superior caste. Buddhist texts, which place the warrior-caste (of the *khattiya*) on top of the scale,[24] criticise this claim – Brahmins created the caste system (four *varṇa*) for their own purpose, i.e. to legitimize the supremacy of the Brahmins in a hierarchical society (to be found, e.g., in the "Puruṣa hymn", Ṛg-Veda 10.90).[25] Further points of criticism of the "Brahmanic system" include the position of Brahmins held in society should not be based upon the accidental fact of being born as Brahmin, but on moral excellence (Skt. *brahmacārya*); to perform bloody sacrifices is useless, unethical, and a waste of expensive and

---

[20] Ruegg, David Seyfort, *The Symbiosis of Buddhism with Brahmanism, Hinduism in South Asia and of Buddhism with 'Local Cults' in Tibet and the Himalayan Region*, Wien: Verlag der Österreichischen Akademie der Wissenschaften 2008, 5.

[21] See additionally Franke, Otto, *Dīghanikāya. Das Buch der Langen Texte des Buddhistischen Kanons. In Auswahl übersetzt*, Göttingen 1913, 304 ff.; Ruegg 2008, 5 f.

[22] Deshpande 1999, 119.

[23] Pāli sources are indicated according to the abbreviation system of the Pali Text Society (PTS).

[24] Buddhist texts know of a second – and unique – classification system of castes, which is threefold: *khattiya*, *brāhmaṇa*, and *gahapati* (householder) (compare Chakravarti 1987, 98 f.); significantly, however, the fourfold division "is associated most often with situations in which the Buddha converses with a *brāhmaṇa*," (ibid.).

[25] Interestingly, in Buddhist accounts the Brahmin is born from the mouth of Brahmā, whereas in the Puruṣa-hymn the Brahmin is born form the mouth of the primordial giant Puruṣa (compare Bronkhorst 2007, 213). This – as well as other slight differences between Vedic and Buddhist sources – may add further plausibility to the hypothesis presented here.

important resources (see below); the Brahmins in former times possessed no wealth, but nowadays are owners of chariots, horses, cattle etc.; the gods *(deva)* of the Vedic-Brahmanic pantheon do not possess the qualities ascribed to them, for instance, the ability to create the world; the succession row of tradition bears no guarantee for truth ("simile of blind Brahmins"), and so on.

To provide an example in order to illustrate this interpretation, we may turn to the Suttanipāta, parts of which belong to the oldest stratum of Pāli Buddhist texts. One small text therein, the "Good conduct of the Brahmin", or "Brahmanical Lore", *Brāhmaṇa-dhammika-Sutta* (I.7, Sn 284–315; = K I. 311–314), relates the following event. One day some old Brahmins were approaching the Buddha and asked him if the Brahmins today would still live up to their high moral standards. The Buddha replies that the sages today no longer stick to their former duties. The text continues:

> [284] 'The seers of old had fully restrained selves, (and) were austere. [T] hey practiced for their own welfare.
>
> [285] The brahmans had no cattle, no gold, no wealth. They had study as their wealth and grain. [...]
>
> [295] Having asked for rice, a bed, clothes, and butter and oil, having collected them properly, from that they performed the sacrifice. [T]hey did not kill cows. [...]
>
> [298] [...] As long as (the lore) existed in the world, this race prospered in happiness.
>
> [299] (But) there was a change in them. Seeing little by little the splendour of the king, and women adorned,
>
> [300] and chariots yoked to thoroughbreds, well-made, with variegated coverings, dwellings and houses evenly proportioned and (well) laid-out,
>
> [301] (and) great human wealth, surrounded by herds of cows, [...] the brahmans coveted this.
>
> [302] Having composed hymns for this purpose, they then went up to Okkāka.[26] 'You have much wealth and grain. Sacrifice, (for) your property is much. [...]
>
> [303] And then the king, lord of warriors, induced by the brahmans, having performed these sacrifices, the *assamedha*, the *purisamedha*, the *sammāpsa*, the *vācapeyya*, (and) the *niraggaḷa*, gave wealth to the brahmans:

[26] Okkāka = a mythical king; eventually of the Śākya-dynasty, the clan of the Buddha. Compare Tsuchida, Ryutaro, "Die Genealogie des Buddha und seiner Vorfahren", in: Bechert, Heinz (ed.), *The Dating of the Historical Buddha 1,* Göttingen: Vandenhoek & Ruprecht 1991, 121.

> [304] cows, and a bed, and clothes, and adorned women, and chariots [...].
> [305] [...] and dwellings [...]
> [306] And they, receiving wealth there, found pleasure in hoarding it up. Overcome by desire, their craving increased the more. Having composed hymns for this purpose, they then went up to Okkāka again. [...]
> [308] And then the king, the lord of warriors, induced by the brahmans, had many hundreds of thousands of cows killed in a sacrifice.
> [309] Not by their feet, [...] nor by anything (else) had the cows harmed (anyone). [...]
> [310] And then the devas, and the fathers, Inda, asuras and rakkhasas cried out: "(This) is injustice", when the knife fell on the cows (Translation by Norman).[27]

In this account a strong opposition between the Brahmins of former times and those of today is drawn.[28] The main criterion for the difference is possession of wealth, or, more precisely, interest in the possession of wealth.[29] Those who lived as non-wealthy ascetics were not interested in the accumulation of wealth. The text portrays the encounter of Brahmins with rich kings of the "warrior"-caste (Pāli: *khattiya*) as the initial situation in which the Brahmins became interested in prosperity. To achieve this, they invented the ideology of sacrificial duties and put into practice the performance of bloody sacrifices to fulfil the newly generated "need" of others. Namely, the king and the upper classes had to pay for the sacrifice-services offered by organized Brahmins. In effect, only thereafter did the promoted, wealthy Brahmins move to houses in the city and documented their new status by various means.[30] Finally, according to this account further consequences arose from the major alteration in Brahmins: the falling apart of justice and morals, a split of the castes, origin of diseases, etc. (Sn 311–315). Judged on the passage above, the theory of a division between "good" Brahmins who lived quite ascetically and non-organized – and, most relevantly – posed no threat to the emerging Buddhist monastic institutions, and "bad" Brahmins finds further support. However, according to this text the "original sin" of Brah-

[27] Norman, Kenneth Roy, *The Group of Discourses (Sutta-Nipâta)*, Vol. I, London, Boston: Pali Text Society 1984, 49–51.

[28] Compare the fivefold scheme of Brahmins in *Doṇabrāhmaṇa* Sutta, A III.223 ff.

[29] Compare Norman, 1984, Sn 620; Sn 628–630.

[30] Accordingly, Buddhist texts describe that Brahmins themselves, e.g. Vassakara, an "important official of Magadha" (Chakravarti 1987, 40), praised a householder's skill in business (see ibid.).

mins happened as early as the time of the mythical ancestor Okkāka. But this follows the logic of the context, because in some Suttas of the cited work, the Suttanipāta, the Buddha himself is already portrayed as a critic of the ambient "Brahmanic system". Therefore, the establishment of the "Brahmanic system" must predate the Buddha.

3. *Conclusion*

Given that the interpretation outlined above bears some plausibility: What does it say about the dynamics of religious encounters and the formation of religious traditions? First, religious traditions in a formative phase, where neutral interaction slowly changes toward competition and political as well as economic rivalry, will seldom produce reliable descriptions of those phases. In the first formative phase a "new" tradition may be composed entirely of hybrid identities (or "converts"); its actors are part of both "traditions" – their ancestral background *and* the new one. Substantial criticism, in such a situation, is neither seen from the Buddhist, nor the Brahmins side. But economic progress, religious institutionalization, and the origination (or creation) of a supportive laity are certainly effective incentives for professional religious actors. Now, in this phase, they may feel obliged to display dissent. And, as a consequent move in this phase, they work out details of a polemic critique, like the anti-Brahmanist cited above. In the eyes of his followers, however, this critique must have been already part of the Buddha's teaching, according to the general logic of religious traditions that "if a particular idea had become accepted, one could scarcely imagine that it had not been preached by the Buddha himself".[31] This critique will be even more persuasive if the roots of the other's degeneration (an "obvious fact" of the Buddhist author's recent environment) can be identified in a distant past. Only then it is highly plausible that proponents of the other tradition will not be able to improve by the following day – an important, albeit "discursive", reinsurance for organized monastic Buddhists who had become used to living with continuous economic and political support.

[31] Vetter, Tilmann, *The Ideas and Meditative Practices of Early Buddhism*, Leiden, New York: Brill 1988, viii.

THE HISTORY OF RELIGIONS AS A SUBVERSIVE DISCIPLINE: COMPARING JUDAISM, CHRISTIANITY AND ISLAM

Guy G. Stroumsa

Until recently, the scholarly study of religions, variously called Comparative Religion, *histoire des religions*, or *Religionswissenschaft*, seemed to be a branch of scholarship that had passed its prime. After the naïve confidence of late-nineteenth-century historicism, which sought to reconstruct religious history beyond the affirmations of orthodoxies, the pretensions of religious phenomenology, before and after the Second World War, claimed to identify a perennial *homo religiosus* beyond the various historical and cultural conditions. Intellectual discomfort with both the explicit vagueness and implicit dangers of this phenomenological inclusivism grew, and seemed for a while to sound the dirge of ambitious, comparative studies of religious phenomena, past and present. In our generation, historians of religions have increasingly become historians of, at most, one religion. Gone are the days of encompassing theories and of daring comparative studies. The more one invokes interdisciplinary studies, the less one seems to practice that dangerous sport. Safe scholarship, with clearly defined boundaries, not to be trespassed, and with no threat of unexpected results, has become the name of the game. But the new, or newly perceived, immediate challenges compel us to renounce this epistemological timidity. We must urgently find new tools to understand religion, if only in order to confront its current threats to our societies.

Such new tools are probably not easy to fashion, but this is no reason for not trying. Various ways are open to us, and collective intellectual effort should eventually prove fruitful. In a forthcoming book, entitled *A New Science: the Discovery of Religion in the Age of Reason*, I search for the historical roots of our discipline, and seek to show that they are to be found in early modernity rather than in the second half of the nineteenth century, when Chairs were first established in Western European universities.[1] One of my claims is that the modern, comparative study of religious phenomena was first developed,

[1] This book will be published by Harvard University Press.

rather than by followers of the radical Enlightenment, by "enlightened Christians" who did not systematically oppose religion. This fact is of major importance, as these scholars, both Catholics and Protestants, attempted in different ways to find a common denominator to religious practices and beliefs throughout the earth. This "new science" was a direct consequence of three major historical phenomena: the great discoveries in America and Asia, the Renaissance interest in philology, and the Wars of Religion, which shook the conscience of ethically sensitive Christians, forcing them to admit that the followers of other religions, such as Islam, might show some traits of human decency absent from contemporary Christian societies. It is in this context that we should see early Hebraists, Arabists and Orientalists, and the first non-theological attempts to think comparatively about Christianity, Judaism and Islam.

To be sure, these early attempts were not always quite convincing, and one is often tempted to look at them with a condescending smile. We would be wrong to do so, however, as one must remember that, *pace* Max Weber, there can be no *wertfrei* stand in the Humanities, and certainly not in the study of religion. Scholars are the product of their time and of their background. And if one can try, and perhaps succeed to a certain extent, to extirpate herself or himself from traditional prejudices about other religions than her or his own, neutralizing inbred emotions and instinctive reactions is a much more difficult task.

We should seek to avoid perceiving religions as monolithic entities, and rather look for the constant dynamic between religious attitudes and beliefs, a dynamic through which religious patterns of *theoria* and *praxis* are perpetually evolving. The best way to look for the common denominator to a series of related phenomena is to look at them from outside. It is hard, if not impossible, "to see ourselves as others see us" – in Robert Burns' words. This creates a particular difficulty for the comparative study of Judaism, Christianity and Islam, a study which is now an obvious and urgent desideratum.[2] I have had the opportunity to meet the Dalai Lama in Jerusalem, but to my regret did not dare to ask him how he perceived the differences and similarities between Jews, Christians and Muslims.

[2] For the most serious and encompassing effort so far, see F. E. Peters, *The Monotheists: Jews, Christians, and Muslims in Conflict and Competition*, Princeton, London: Princeton University Press, 2003, two vols.

For better or worse, the comparative study of religions was born in Christian Europe, and developed mainly in culturally Christian countries. In this sense, Israel or Japan are perhaps oddities, or special cases, but not quite. Spiritually, we may all be Semites, as noted by Pius XI (in dark times, in 1938), in an emotional rejection of growing anti-Semitism. But culturally, we are all Christians, also in Israel, as I used to point out to my students, adding that in the study of religion, we should be methodological atheists, as we must treat religions as social facts, and approach them with the same criteria. In other words, we should study other people's religions as if they were our own, and our own religion as if it were those of other people. Similarly, we should study dead religions as if they were alive, and living religions as if they were dead.

More than in other fields of the Humanities, the study of religion requires a constant move, to and fro, between emic and etic approaches. Dilthey's famous *Verstehen*, which distinguishes the *Geisteswissenschaften* from the *Naturwissenschaften* is only true when combined with the no less necessary demand for neutralization of any feeling of closeness, of sympathy. The emic ability to understand a religious phenomenon from within must be combined with an etic ability to distance oneself from it, to look at it with a cold, analytic eye. Such a double attitude, if not impossible, at least represents a rare feat of intellectual elasticity.

The title of this paper presents the comparative history of religion as a subversive science.[3] There is subversion enough in the demand for distancing oneself from one's own religious tradition, and for endearing other people's religions as one's own. But there is even more. How are we to conceive Judaism, Christianity and Islam, and why is the demand to compare them at once so obvious to conceive and so difficult to obey? Throughout the twentieth century, "the Judeo-Christian tradition" emerged as a new concept, intended to underline the deep connections between Judaism and Christianity. In various contexts, and in particular in the USA, "the Christian tradition" was now more and more often replaced (and the movement sped up after the Second World War) with another one, insisting on the fundamental common points between contemporary Jews and Christians. In the last decades, this term, in its turn, is often replaced by "the Abrahamic traditions", (or faiths) in order to include Muslims. The Queen or King

[3] For another "subversive" approach to the discipline, see B. Lincoln, "Theses on Method", in: *Method and Theory in the Study of Religion* 8 (1996), 225–227.

of England, as we know, is traditionally Defender of the Faith. Prince Charles, feeling that the times demanded bold, new approaches, has suggested transforming the genitive singular into a plural, expressing willingness to be called one day "Defender of the Faiths," a simple 's' incorporating the faring of Judaism and Islam, at least, into the Crown's responsibility. The ongoing ethnic and religious transformation of Europe, and the fast-growing presence of Muslims, as was the case until the battle of Vienna in 1683, demands from us a willingness to think of the three great monotheistic religions as of three aspects of a central phenomenon.

A major danger stems from the public demand, or at least expectation, that we insist on the similarities between the three religions. They may look different, but these differences are only epiphenomena, while their true kernel is one (the mystics are often considered, mistakenly, to have always known the essential unity of the different religious traditions). Such a recognition, it is held (implicitly or explicitly) should offer a major buffer against religious prejudices of all kinds. The historian of religions should resist such temptations (this does not mean, of course, that he is against the extirpation of prejudices in his own society!). As citizens of their respective societies, historians must take a stand on important questions of the times, but should not offer to put their scholarship at the service of political goals. "The scholars' treason *(la trahison des clercs)*" to use the title of Julien Benda's famous pamphlet from 1927, often comes from good intentions. But despite appearances, there is not much in common between interfaith discourse and comparative religion. The first insists on similarities, the second on differences. *Qua* historians, historians of religions must always retain critical powers. This is the way in which they are asked to play a role in society.

There is a more complex problem in comparing Judaism, Christianity and Islam, which stems from the very hypostasis of those three entities. In order to compare these religions, one must posit them (at least implicitly) as individual, well-delimited entities. When we think Judaism, Christianity and Islam, the danger is to forget, at once, the various polytheistic milieus within which they grew, and also the multiple trends vying between them, which become "heresies" as soon as they lose the battle for (spiritual) power. Assuming that "Judaism", for instance, is an entity similar *(mutatis mutandis)* to "Christianity" and to "Islam", and that the comparative study between these three entities is more significant than the study, in any given situation, of its *Umwelt*, is a fallacy, as obvious as it is often affirmed, or at least implicitly accepted.

A more subtle danger in the comparison is that which I propose to call the "theology of comparative religion". Traces of the Christian origins of the comparative study of religion can easily be detected in the work of the late Wilfred Cantwell Smith, who sought to overcome Christian theology, but searched for a common denominator among the "faith" expressed by other "world religions". Smith, with whom I studied at Harvard, had an interesting mind, and was deeply involved in his attempt to reach the religious core of "other men".[4] Yet, I always retained an impression of "déjà vu" at his analysis of the great religious traditions. Despite his sincere efforts, the questions he put to the different traditions seemed to me to retain a distinctly Protestant color. I am sure that a similar feeling of uneasiness could be detected in the approach of other distinguished scholars of "world religions", a concept and a field which is the last avatar of missiology: world religions, like the G-7 or the G-20 all belong into a club of the "big ones", the "universal" religions, jealously keeping its gates. (One wonders why Judaism is often included as a member of this club. Is it mainly because of its genetic relationship with Christianity, or as a kind of atonement, as it were, for the sad fate of European Jews? In any case, neither numbers nor theology would by themselves warrant such a membership.) It is worth noting that Smith had nothing to say about either religions of antiquity or those of aborigines. When asked, he would argue that he did not have any friends who believed in the Greek gods, or who lived in the Australian or Amazonian hinterland, and could therefore not develop the inter-subjective trust needed in order to pierce through the wall between cultures. This may remind one of Buber's argument, in *Ich und Du,* about the specificity of human contact, but also sounds a bit disingenuous. In any case, any serious comparative study of religious phenomena should take dead religions into equal account. In the field of religion like elsewhere, as we learned from Durkheim, small, like black, is beautiful. Smith spoke of "history of religion" in the singular, in order to stress that the various historical developments, throughout the world, all reflected, in

[4] Among his books, see in particular *The Faith of Other Men*, New York: Harper and Row, 1963; *Faith and Belief*, Princeton: Princeton University Press, 1979; *Towards a World Theology: Faith and the Comparative History of Religion*, London: Macmillan, 1981.

highly different ways, the progressive evolution of one single, universal concept of religion. Such an approach smacks of late, almost bastardized Hegelianism.

In the delicate balance between emic and etic approaches, one may say that Smith's approach leans too much on the emic side. In other, irreverent words, one might say that it suffers from an overdose of reverence. The scholar of religion does not need to have practitioner friends of a given religion in order to understand it. Discovering the hidden mechanisms of a given religious situation, managing to get an X-ray of it, has nothing to do with the possibility of dialoguing with "believers of another religious tradition". I would surmise, moreover, that the historian of religions should seek to understand better than the insider how a religious system functions.

What has all this to do with "Judaism, Christianity and Islam"? If the point of comparison is to identify and analyze the main differences between terms, any attempt insisting on similarities, and seeking to show that such similarities, even when hidden, are more significant than "superficial" differences, is condemned to lead us into the wrong direction. Too often, the comparative study of Judaism, Christianity and Islam seems today to search for the "spiritual roots of Europe." Neither the Jews, nor the Muslims, should be perceived as "orientals", inherently and irremediably foreign to a Western, Christian Europe, as has too often been the case.[5] The attempt to fashion a new, broader, more inclusive European identity is certainly a worthy cause. It is certainly true that the radical opposition between Athens and Jerusalem, standard from Tertullian to Chestov, might advantageously be replaced by a long axis, from Baghdad to Toledo, through Mecca, Jerusalem, Athens and Rome. It is along this axis that the complex interface between languages, religions and cultures, throughout the centuries, would eventually forge what we call European cultural identity. Rather than roots, it would be much more judicious to speak of heritage. "Roots" entails looking back to an identity coiled around itself, while "heritage" points to the future of a culture as much as it refers to its past. Such an approach is certainly a legitimate, even an

[5] See for instance the demonstration of D. Müller, about two case studies, *Staatsbürger auf Widerruf: Juden und Muslime als Alteritätspartner im rumänischen und serbischen Nationscode: Ethnonationale Staatsbürgerschaftskonzepte 1878–1941*, Wiesbaden: Harrasowitz, 2005.

urgent task, but it is not quite identical to a comparative and historical study of Judaism, Christianity and Islam.

How, then, should we approach the comparative study of "the three monotheistic religions"? First of all, it seems to me, we should seek to dismantle this concept. There may be certain common characteristics to these three systems, but are they always the same, in the various historical and cultural contexts, and are they exclusive of these three religions, and absent from others, genetically related to these religions, such as the Samaritan, Manichaean, Druze, Bahai or Mormon religions? And what about the religion of Plotinus? To the impartial observer, Plotinus is more of a monotheist than Origen. In this regard, dualism seems to be a special, radical case of monotheism. I once chaired a panel, at a conference in Jerusalem, in which both the Zoroastrian High Priest and the President of the Parsi community in Mumbai participated. While the latter spoke with pride of the dualistic system of his religion, the former argued that it was nonsense to claim that Zoroastrianism was anything but a monotheism.

Similar problems will immediately surge if we seek to highlight, rather than the one God of the Abrahamic religions, the bookish character of their respective revelations. Other religious systems, not only those belonging to the monotheistic family, highlight a book, or a series of books, as holy, as a direct reflection of the Divinity. On the other hand, speaking of "religions of the book" is not always a convincing way of describing, for instance, Christianity, while Judaism underwent a "retreat into the oral" in late antiquity, precisely at the time identified by W.C. Smith as that of "the scriptural movement" that led from the collection of the New Testament (and of the Mishnah) to that of the Qu'ran.

Again, will prophecy prove heuristically more useful than monotheism or holy books, as a category specific to Judaism, Christianity and Islam? Obviously not, as it is to be found in various other religions, from that of ancient Greece and the ancient Near East, not to speak of Zoroastrianism, Manichaeism, and all the religions which grew on monotheistic soil. Even the dominant status of ethics in religion, which seems to single out Judaism in the ancient world (and which is directly linked to the central role of prophecy in biblical Israel) may not have appeared so clearly to contemporary observers. Does not the Emperor Julian state that "there is no difference between the religion of Israel and our own (i. e., the Hellenic tradition), except for the fact that the Hebrews have only one God"?[6]

The different but closely related phenomena of religious violence and intolerance are often perceived as directly linked to monotheism. Indeed, the idea of a single, jealous God appears to be tantamount to the rejection, by all possible means, of all other claims to divinity by masquerading idols, falsely pretending to be gods. Such an intolerant stance is traditionally seen in contradistinction to the pluralism inherent to polytheistic systems. This approach clearly reflects a drastic simplification of reality. While it is obvious that the total rejection of idols does not leave much space for tolerance, even the most cursory observation of the religious scene, anywhere, at any time, will reveal the universality of intolerance toward the religious other, and also the ubiquity of violent means to counter manifestations of religious otherness. Contemporary Hindu devotees and even Buddhist monks can be as violent as late antique bands of fanatic Christian monks. The uniqueness of God can thus be a powerful motor of intolerance, but it is by no means the only one. After the destruction of the Jerusalem Temple, universal religious ambitions disappeared from among the Jews. Such ambitions, ever present in Christianity and in Islam, are to my mind a more effective fuel of religious intolerance than monotheism, which, if reality demands it, can learn to accept the existence of other religions, even when they worship idols.

So far, we are thus left with very little, in terms of a common denominator of our three religions (and only of them). I propose, therefore, to down-grade our quest and to look only for what Wittgenstein called "family resemblances" between phenomena. We will find various such "family resemblances" between Christianity and Islam (universalist claims), between Judaism and Christianity, between Christianity and Islam, and between Judaism and Islam. To give some obvious examples: Judaism and Christianity share the Hebrew Bible, or Old Testament, and often follow similar patterns of biblical interpretation, while Judaism and Islam have rather parallel ways of dealing with religious law. *Halakha* and *Shari'a* rule the community of believers in rather similar ways, and there is nothing really similar among Christian communities, not even in the East. Both Jewish and Muslim thinkers always thought that the similar patterns according to which their communities

[6] *Against the Galileans*, Fragment 72.

were run reflected true monotheism, while the lack of a rigid religious law among Christians reflected their less than rigorous monotheism.

The obvious disadvantage of the proposed "light" method, searching for "family resemblances", lies in the fact that it gives up on the search for a grand, inclusive theory. The no less obvious advantage is that it permits multiple forays, focusing each time on a different "knot", as it were, or overlapping of different sets. Rather than offering a general history of religion – or of the "three monotheistic religions" – such an approach proposes to focus on specific moments of particular interest. Such moments occur when the contact between two or more different sets generates a new dynamic between them and the creation of fresh patterns of interaction – as well as the creation of new entities. The proposed method of analysis of religious phenomena has another advantage: one does not have to restrain oneself to the study of the three monotheistic religions. What happens in the *Auseinandersetzung* between Christianity and Manichaeism in late antiquity, or between Gnostic and non-Gnostic forms of early Christianity, or the passage from *Jahiliya* or Zoroastrianism to Islam, or else the survival and transformations of Christianity in Communist societies, are all as interesting and as significant, even for comparative purposes, as direct comparisons between the three religions.

In order for such an approach to be successful, the crucial element is to make sure that the analysis deals with *transformative* moments, search for those particular moments in the history of a social phenomenon when it undergoes a radical evolution, or mutation. Religions are structures, and structures are usually rigid, and can sometimes appear to be frozen. Yet, as social facts, they are living structures, i. e., they constantly evolve, sometimes in drastic ways; they also are born at some point, and die at another. Comparative studies have a natural tendency to crystallize things, to take a snapshot, as it were, where elements appear frozen, and where movement and constant change in the relationship between the individual subjects cannot be guessed. As an experiment reconstituting the conditions of life and transformation of religions cannot be done, our goal should be to search for the mechanisms of transformation, and to focus on particularly rich moments, in order to reconstitute these mechanisms. In other words, we should look for the life of structures in history, that is, for those moments when they are destabilized, rather than crystallized.

There are as many choices as there are scholars, and it makes no sense to decide *ex cathedra*, and for others, what phenomena, which moments to study. There is no reason to believe that one particular choice is in itself more fruitful than others. I can here only speak for myself, and reflect on the field that I have decided, long ago, to toil upon. My doctoral dissertation focused on the origins of Gnostic mythology, and further work brought me to Manichaeism and early Christian mysticism in late antiquity. In other words, I consistently look for the religious *limen*, for those elements of transformation at the margins of broad social and religious phenomena. In this respect, late antiquity strikes me as being particularly rich, as in the Roman world religions were in constant contact, in a flowing process of transformation. Moreover, as I have argued in a recent book, late antiquity represents a key period in the history of religions in the Mediterranean and in the Near East. Indeed, the religious structures that emerged of this period (broadly, medieval Christianity, Islam and Judaism) reflect much more than the victory of the single God (and its heavenly court) over the pantheons of antiquity: they show the transformation of the very idea of religion.[7]

I started by emphasizing the subversive character of our discipline. I hope that by now, what I mean by this adjective is a bit clearer. The comparative study of religion does not need to take a stand on the question of the existence of the gods, or of the single God, and on that of his revelation. The student of "the three monotheisms" must not necessarily share the view of the pamphlet circulating (under the name of Spinoza) in the eighteenth century: *De tribus impostoribus* (i.e., Moses, Jesus and Muhammad). The scholar can, and perhaps must practice what Husserl called the *Epoche*. In that sense, we are all phenomenologists, and should not touch the ultimate question of truth. And yet, the very practice of our discipline represents a powerful rebuke to the pretension of orthodoxies to be the sole keepers of truth. Historians of Judaism, Christianity or Islam, or at least those who happen to be inheritors of the civilizations forged by those religions, must behave like readers of Lessing's *Nathan der Weise*: they cannot know which of the three identical rings is the true one.[8]

[7] *The End of Sacrifice: Religious Transformations of Late Antiquity*, Chicago: Chicago University Press, 2009. The book was first published in French as *La fin du sacrifice: les mutations religieuses de l'antiquité tardive*, Paris: Odile Jacob, 2005.

[8] On the possible connections between the legend of the three rings and the traditions about the three impostors, see F. Niewöhner, *Veritas sive Varietas: Lessings Toleranzparabel und das Buch von den drei Betrügern*, Heidelberg: Schneider, 1888.

WHIRLPOOL EFFECTS AND RELIGIOUS STUDIES. A RESPONSE TO GUY G. STROUMSA

Sarah Stroumsa

A respondent, trailing behind the lecturer, has basically two options: the docile option, to uphold the views of the lecturer, or the mean option, to criticize him. The approach suggested by Guy opens for me as a respondent a third way, that of adopting a subversive attitude to the lecture, that is to say: accepting the main thesis of the lecture, but taking it somewhere else. Guy focused mainly on the comparative and phenomenological side of the study of religion, which is, at any given moment, a static study. My response will focus on the dynamic aspects the study of the history of religion, which is, in fact, one aspect of intellectual history.

Professor Jaspert has asked me at first to present, in my response the perspective of Islam, but I have asked to speak more broadly on the medieval world of Islam (in which Jews and Christians were also active participants). Indeed, the intellectual history of the medieval world of Islam seems to be a perfect case study for the approach of this conference, and for the dynamic aspect of the history of religion. In the domains of theology and of polemics, this dynamism has been depicted by the metaphor of a marketplace, where the same coins change hands. This metaphor, however, is misleading, since in the fiscal transaction the coins remain intact and unchanging (except for the usual wear by continuous use). In the medieval intellectual marketplace, on the other hand, ideas and motifs moved from one religious or theological system to another, slightly modifying the system into which they were adopted, and, in the process, undergoing some transformation themselves. Like colored drops falling into a whirlpool, new ideas were immediately carried away by the stream, coloring the whole body of water while changing their own color in the process. In the swift flow of ideas that characterized the Islamic world, it is rarely possible to follow neat trajectories of "influences" or "impacts" that allow us to isolate the source of the influence and to accurately measure the force of its impact. Moreover, when such trajectories are occasionally traced, this may satisfy our detective curiosity, but it does not necessarily reveal the balance of the full picture. To give just one example: Medieval Jewish discussions of the divine attributes (written in Judaeo-Arabic) bear the marks of medieval Muslim thought. They struggle with the same questions (such as the antinomies of free will or the relations between God's essence and His attributes), expressed in the same Arabic formulae. A correct analysis of the evidence, however, will necessary take into account the direct influence of pre-Islamic Christian thought, as well as the indirect influence of this same Christian thought, which, filtered through Muslim thought, reached Jewish thinkers through Muslim channels. The inherent complexity of the picture cannot be over-emphasized, and it would be a mistake to simplify it.[1]

Another example is the widespread apologetic genre of "signs of prophecy" which appears in Arabic writings of Muslims, Christians and Jews. The prophecy of Muhammad was the main point of contention between Muslims and their Jewish and Christian neighbors, and it can therefore be argued that it was the Muslims who started this genre, and that the others developed their own version of it in response to the Muslims. But in the texts themselves, this neat schema – Muslims first, then Jews and Christian – is impossible to show. The first extant Theological *Summa* in Arabic (from the first half of the ninth century) happens to be written not by a Muslim but by a Jew, who had been a convert to Christianity. His "signs of prophecy" list bears unmistakable marks of his Christian education, such as typical Christian formulas and terminology. These Christian characteristics, in their turn, seem to have already been transformed by the contact with Islam: the terminology is in Arabic, the formulas reflect familiarity with the Koran.

Tracing influences is often frowned upon in modern scholarship. Many feel that *Quellenforschung*, which highlights the separate components of a given system, devaluates the originality of this system and diverts scholarly attention from contents and ideas to the history of their transmission. When the previous life of ideas must be recognized, scholars nowadays prefer to concentrate on the mechanisms of their appropriation, and the word "influence" is often placed, with a

[1] For a fuller exposition of the issues discussed here, see S. Stroumsa, "The Muslim Context of Medieval Jewish Philosophy", in: S. Nadler/T. Rudavsky (eds.), *The Cambridge History of Jewish Philosophy: From Antiquity throught the Seventeenth Century* (Cambridge: Cambridge University Press 2009), 39–59; Eadem, *Maimonides in his World: Portrait of a Mediterranean Thinker* (Princeton: Princeton University Press, 2009), Preface.

skeptical grin, between inverted commas. But the detection of hitherto unrecognized direct influences is, I believe, an indispensable tool for the historian of ideas and of mentalities. The identification of influences is critical in our attempt to gauge the depth of a thinker's attachment to his milieu. It enables us to transform this milieu from a scenic background into the pulsating world in which the thinker lived. Far from obfuscating the originality of religious thinkers, the identification of influences allows us to flesh out the person, his way of thinking, and his creative genius in recognizing the potential of the available crude material and in using it.

I should like to underline in the capital importance of the multifocal approach to the study of this world. An examination which focuses on the output of only one religious community, with an occasional dutiful nod to the rest of the religious puzzle, is similar to examining it with a single eye, and is likely to produce a flat, two-dimensional picture. Reading Jewish and Muslim intellectual history together is a *sine qua non* condition if we strive to achieve a correct, well-rounded picture of this history. One should emphasize that, for a correct application of the multifocal approach, a parallel but separate study of the different communities will not suffice. If one were to close successively one eye, then the other, one would still obtain only a flat two-dimensional picture. Furthermore, in this complex intellectual world the ideas flow into each other, brazenly oblivious to communal barriers. The flow of ideas was never unilateral or linear, but rather went back and forth, creating what I proposed to call a "whirlpool effect". In order to follow the course of these ideas, and to see how a particular thinker contributed to their flow, a full picture must be obtained.

This whirlpool metaphor may also convey some of the difficulties involved in our approach. It is much easier to trace the course of neatly-divided currents and trends than to reconstruct the way in which they contributed to the whirlpool. Of course, this understanding does not free us from the need to try and detect direct contacts, proximate channels, and influences.

I should like to take the opportunity to present a new project which aims at bringing this dynamic approach to the cyber world of scholarship. There are many websites dedicated to Islamic thought, but they are exclusively geared towards presenting the cultural legacy of a particular community. None of the available websites addresses the multi-cultural nature of this legacy in anything that can pass for more than lip-service. Such presentations or analyses of the intellectual tradition of one community which do not take into account the constant fertilization by others are bound to produce distorted pictures. The project, called “intellectual encounters”, is directed by an international academic committee, and its purpose is to establish a website that will present the philosophical and scientific heritage of the medieval world of Islam in a way that will do justice to its tightly interwoven intellectual tissue, and to its inter-confessional, multicultural character.

It has been suggested that the source of Lessing’s *Nathan der Weise* goes back to a Christian Arabic text from the eight-century source *(Apology of Timothy)*. Lessing, like Timothy, point to the inability to choose the true ring from its perfect two imitations. In fact, the arena has more than three sides to it; and it is all one ring, which rolls and rolls, sliding material from one religion to the other.

PART TWO

CONTACTS BETWEEN THE MAJOR RELIGIOUS TRADITIONS DURING THEIR EXPANSION

CONTACTS BETWEEN THE MAJOR RELIGIOUS TRADITIONS DURING THEIR EXPANSION. AN INTRODUCTION

Nikolas Jaspert

At first glance, the contributions assembled in the second section of these proceedings might appear to be a chronological continuation of the first section's papers. But closer scrutiny should reveal that the articles not only advance in time, but also treat other issues than those dealt with in section one. Research in this block – and in the corresponding research field within the Käte-Hamburger Consortium "Dynamics in the History of Religions between Asia and Europe" – is geared towards observing and comparing phenomena within the religious field that are affected by processes of expansion or that themselves have an impact upon such processes. The term expansion is hereby understood in the widest sense of the word, thus not only comprising political and military, but also economic or cognitive processes. Peaceful and antagonistic forms of interaction can and often do occur simultaneously, and developments are neither teleological nor as clear-cut as hindsight might suggest. Military, economic or intellectual expansion could and more often than not did have an effect on religious traditions: mission could bring about religious expansion; contact with hitherto unknown religions could lead to religious transfer. All such developments represented challenges to existing religious traditions, challenges which could meet with a diversity of responses: the consolidation of canonical texts, the establishment of orthodoxy, the emergence of deviance and heresy, of hermetical or popular religion. Such reactions, diversifications or condensations are the subject of the analyses that follow.

The papers assembled here have a wide geographical and chronological spectrum: the subjects addressed range from the ancient Near and Middle East to the medieval Mediterranean all the way to early modern Far East Asia. They study the impact expansionistic movements had in a series of fields: the first block concentrates on the social and intellectual effects of military expansion, the second on the consequences that economic expansion could have on the intellectual field of political philosophy; and finally, our third block will be closely centred on the religious field, more precisely on monastic history. In different ways and to different degrees, all these articles touch upon aspects of religious transfer and expansion that the researchers cooperating in Bochum believe to be of central relevance. Six such "sets of questions", they could also be termed "transversal issues" or even "denominators of religious expansion", have been identified and elaborated during the first two years of the consortium's work.[1] Evidently, these sets of questions have fuzzy borders and overlap to a certain degree, but such an attempt to categorize the analysis of religious expansion may prove to be a helpful heuristic instrument. Indeed, the articles that comprise the following section of these proceedings have proven to be an effective test as to these denominators' validity and value.

1. *Six Fields of Research into Religious Expansion*

A first major issue in the study of religious expansion and transfer appears to be the relationship between expansion and governance. To what degree did the expansion of religious traditions depend on the existence of political power, are proximity and distance to power relevant criteria for the study of the expansion of religious ideas? German scholarship, particularly medievalism, has extensively elaborated the concept of "Herrschaftsnähe" and "Herrschaftsferne" – proximity to power versus distance to power – over the past decades,[2] though its implications for the religious field have not been sufficiently accentuated. To what extent did the activity of governing influence religious transfer, and under which conditions could shifts of religious semantics for their part affect political settings? More importantly still: were such shifts the result of inter-religious contact and transfer? And finally: under which conditions and with the help of which media did religions expand below the level of stately or political structures? This transversal issue is notably historical by nature; it lies at the interface between comparative religious studies and historical studies.

---

[1] My thanks go to all members of research field 2 within the consortium "Dynamics in the History of Religions between Asia and Europe", particularly Christian Frevel, Reinhold Glei, Jason Neelis, Jörg Plassen and Amy Remensnyder, whose thoughts and comments I have attempted to incorporate into this summary.

[2] On the concept of "Herrschernähe" and "Herrscherferne" cf. the pertinent studies by Peter Moraw, *Über König und Reich. Aufsätze zur deutschen Verfassungsgeschichte des späten Mittelalters*, Sigmaringen 1995.

A second understanding of religious expansion deals with the phenomenon from the perspective of alterity and xenology by studying both the perception and the treatment of the alien and unknown. The questions and themes raised through this field of research have been widely formulated in recent studies and are in no way reduced to processes of othering and restriction, but also include forms of adaptation and modification.[3] It is well known that the spectrum of possible dealings with the alien ranges from inclusion und accommodation to assimilation und exclusion right up to segregation und extermination. The same holds true for the religiously "other". This perspective can easily be extended by picking up on "theories of recognition"[4] and analysing the relationship between religious contact and recognition, or by studying the interdependencies between religious contacts and ethical identity. It might also be extended by analysing the practical operating level of religious expansion, which implies studying such phenomena as mission and conversion.

Considering expansion's inherently spatial dimension it is hardly surprising that a third set of questions is strongly marked by concepts of space. Geographical areas can be defined locally, but they can also be seen as transit zones of encounter and transfer from a wider perspective. Here, interface zones such as borderlands become particularly important. As recent historical research into medieval frontiers has shown, these were by no means barriers alone, but also functioned as areas of intensified exchange.[5] In fact, areas deemed peripheral from a political perspective were often very central from the viewpoint of religious transfer processes. This insight is activated by the research consortium "Dynamics in the History of Religions between Asia and Europe" in order to better understand and analyse processes of religious transfer. In extension of the frontier zones, one might also ana-

---

[3] Cf. Herbers, Klaus/Jaspert, Nikolas (eds.) *Eigenes und Fremdes in den deutsch-spanischen Beziehungen des späten Mittelalters* (Geschichte und Kultur der Iberischen Welt 1), Münster - Berlin 2004; Grammars of Identity/Alterity: A Structural Approach, ed. Gerd Baumann/Andre Gingrich (The EASA series 3), New York 2004 (with references to the scientific debate).

[4] Honneth, Axel, *Kampf um Anerkennung: zur moralischen Grammatik sozialer Konflikte*, Frankfurt am Main 1992; Honneth, Axel, *Verdinglichung: eine anerkennungstheoretische Studie*, Frankfurt am Main 2005.

[5] The discussion is synthesized in: Power, Daniel/Standen, Naomi, Houndmills [et al.] (eds.), *Frontiers in question: Eurasian borderlands 700–1700,* 1999; Herbers, Klaus/Jaspert, Nikolas (eds.), *Grenzräume und Grenzüberschreitungen im Vergleich. Der Osten und der Westen des mittelalterlichen Lateineuropa* (Europa im Mittelalter, Abhandlungen und Beiträge zur historischen Komparatistik 9), Berlin 2007.

lyse the functioning and the effects of inter-religious networks. The network concept effectively complements the frontier paradigm as it does not concentrate on extended surface areas of contact but rather considers focal points and their position within larger communication systems.[6] Despite the undeniable heuristic value of frontier and network studies for the analysis of religious expansion, any study of spaces of religious transfer cannot limit its attention to the literal meaning of the word, that is to the investigation of geographic areas in a physical sense alone. It must also take into consideration the cognitive dimension that religious concepts of space can possess. Consequently, the degree to which physical space could and can be symbolically charged deserves particular attention, for shifts and changes such symbolic focal points underwent due to processes of expansion could trigger wide societal reactions in the religious field. To give an example: the notion of the Holy Land or the Holy City played a major role for Judaism, Islam and Christianity alike, and the fall of such symbolically charged places could have an enormous impact in theology and philosophy, liturgy and ritual, literature and the arts.

A fourth denominator enquires about the concrete settings and processes of religious transfer, that is, we ask which models of contact and exchange are observable when religious traditions enter into contact due to processes of expansion. The interplay between the institutions and semantics of religious traditions is of great relevance to this set of questions. That means one must focus on forms in which religious semantics and their practical specificities interacted or interact. This not only implies describing the many forms of selection and adaptation of religious knowledge and practices discernable – ranging from complete rejection to assimilation and finally hybridization –, but also uncovering the reciprocal relationship between religious semantics and religious institutionalization. As such processes of institutionalization are always set in a wider context, it is important to consider exogenous catalysts such as the economy, science, violence, culture and learning, all of which could both promote or impede inter-religious transfer. Such a wider understanding of the factors influencing religious transfer – including antagonistic forms of religious interaction – is necessary, not least in order to counteract a tendency inherent to the study of cultural transfer in general, that is the tendency to affirm the com-

[6] Vásquez, Manuel A., "Studying Religion in Motion: A Networks Approach", in: *Method and Theory in the Study of Religion* 20 (2008), 151–184.

municative and ultimately harmonious aspects of interfaith relations while setting aside phenomena of inequality and resistance.

Processes of religious systematization form the fifth transversal issue, for after their constitutional phase, religious traditions tend not only to define themselves, but also to define others. This occurs particularly often in the wake of expansionistic movements and the interfaith contacts these entail. Such processes of systematization can be brought about in several ways: intra-religiously by normative texts, jurisdiction and canon, inter-religiously by categorization, apologetics and polemics. Learned religious experts and religious institutions contributed substantially to such attempts to systematize one's own as well as alien belief-systems. But systematization is not only a phenomenon related to othering and demarcation, but also marks processes of adaptation and hybridization, of transplantation, transmission and transformation. First, alien attempts at systematization can lead to a reflection and redefinition of one's own perspective, as inter-textual relationships illustrate. Second, processes of adaptation and hybridization within religious traditions can trigger fresh attempts to understand and define these novel developments within one's own belief-system. Systematization is thus an ongoing process which must consequently be studied diachronically.

The field of systematization lies at the interface between inter and intra-religious transfer. The latter is important for the sixth and last denominator I would like to present. It deals with institutions created as a result of reform initiatives and heterodox movements, for phases of expansion often went hand in hand with deviance and reform. The emergence of new forms of religious, regular life (for example the foundation of new religious orders), or the development of mechanisms to define and persecute practices considered aberrant are examples of such developments. In both cases we are dealing with phenomena that did not mark the constitutional phase of religious traditions as much as later periods characterized by consolidation and expansion. More often than not, such processes of institutionalization were the result of prior, more fluid phenomena such as changes in devotional practice or flows of ideas and semantics; both such underlying currents and their consolidation in the form of specific institutions require our attention. The analysis of intra-religious institutionalization consequently considers both horizontal forms of contacts between major religious traditions as well as vertical forms of intra-faith relations.

A fundamental axiom of the six set of questions expounded above is the conviction that endogenous and exogenous vectors of religious transfer are interdependent. Consequently any research into transfer processes must take both semantic and institutional aspects, both religious thought and religious practice into account – without losing sight of the societal conditions into which the religious field is embedded.

2. *Dynamic Nodes and Push-Factors*

On a functional level, one of the major issues to address in order to comprehend the relationship between expansion and transfer of religious ideas is to understand exactly how and through which channels religious ideas tend to spread. The picture of gradual diffusion based on the assumption that religious ideas expanded owing to point to point contact has recently been criticized, among others by Erik Zürcher and Jason Neelis.[7] Neelis claims that the expansion of religions resulted from a more complex process of transplantation, transmission and transformation based on nodes of interaction that were interconnected by capillary routes. Such dynamic nodes – or "hubs" – in which religious traditions meet, interact and mutually influence each other deserve special attention.

The concept of hubs which initially pertains to the field of logistics and communication technologies has recently been applied to network theory and could also prove to be fruitful for research on religious transfer.[8] A differentiation has been proposed between "passive hubs" that simply serve as a conduit for transfer, and "intelligent" or "manageable hubs" that monitor the traffic passing through them. Applied to our field of studies and understood in a general sense, such nodes could and can take differing forms: places, institutions, individuals and groups, but also intellectual currents or literary genres can be termed hubs in such a functional sense. For needless to say, these spatial met-

---

[7] Zürcher, Erik: "Buddhism Across Boundaries: The Foreign Input", in: *Buddhism Across Boundaries – Chinese Buddhism and the Western Regions: Collection of Essays 1993,* ed. John McRae/Jan Nattier, Tapei 1999, 1–59; Zürcher, Erik: *The Buddhist Conquest of China: The Spread and Adaptation of Buddhism in Early Medieval China,* 3rd ed. (Sinica Leidensia 11), Leiden 2007; cf. Neelis, Jason, *Early Buddhist Transmission and Trade Networks: Mobility and Exchange within and beyound the Nortwestern Borderlands of South Asia,* Leiden, Boston: Brill 2011.

[8] Examples of modern applications: Taylor, Philip: *Goddess on the Rise: Pilgrimage and Popular Religion in Vietnam,* Honolulu 2004; Gopin, Marc: *To Make the Earth Whole: Citizen Diplomacy in the Age of Religious Militancy,* Lanham 2009.

aphors are not only geared towards describing physical, but also to describing intellectual and semantic space.

Focusing on the religious expansion from a historical perspective, the wide range of hubs of religious transfer can be divided into four groups. Basically, one can distinguish nodes of power such as courts etc., nodes of learning and knowledge such as universities, madrasas etc., nodes of economy, such as trading emporia, major trading towns etc., and nodes of worship such as centres of pilgrimage, cemeteries, monasteries etc. What all these dynamic centres of interaction have in common is that they often served as points of religious transfer. Certainly, several nodes or hubs evade classification and belong to different types at once. But then again, such an attempt at classification might improve the concept as an analytical tool.

While religious expansion was undoubtedly facilitated by nodes and hubs, it was also actively advanced by driving forces. The role that pull-factors such as the attraction of religious traditions played for the latter's consolidation has been dealt upon elsewhere in this publication and within the consortium.[9] But expansion of religious traditions was by no means due to pull-factors alone: push-factors also played a part that need not be underestimated. Such push-factors could take manifold forms, the most notable of which being mission. As is well known, mission is a much debated issue, claims being that it has historically led to acculturation, westernization, cultural destruction etc., but without a doubt, attempts to proselytize individuals or entire peoples was one – and historically not the least important – way of expanding religious traditions. Modern missiology has underlined that processes of conversion are both active and passive: the mindsets of those missionized were situated in a wide spectrum ranging from acceptance, adaptation and modification to repulsion. Furthermore, one should bear in mind that territorial expansion does not necessarily go hand in hand with mission, as the mediaeval Crusader States or the Iberian Peninsular in the Middle Ages demonstrate. This is not the place to determine under which conditions expansion and mission coincide or to define the relation between push- and pull-factors during such processes. Instead, I would like to turn to a second example in order to

[9] Cf. Peter Wick's contribution above in this volume p. 73.

illustrate the importance of push-factors for the expansion of religious ideas: the relocation of sacred places.[10]

From a comparative, historical perspective, the basic condition for expanding religions does not seem to be local stability, but spatial dynamics. Apparently religions have the inherent tendency not only to transcend local borders while maintaining a cultic epicentre, but also to dis- and translocate the very centre itself. Examples of this phenomenon are multiple and range from the relocation of the Trojan cult of the Penates to Italy by Aeneas, to the Exodus or the Babylonian exile in the case of Judaism all the way to Muhammad's migration from Mecca to Medina and the Prophet's night trip to Jerusalem. Equally, the transfer of the imperial residence from Rome to Byzantium (and later to Moscow), actually a *translatio imperii*, must also be understood as a *translatio religionis*. Apart from such major translocations, the countless minor ones must also be taken into account, for instance the translocation of relics in the Christian Middle Ages, which could turn previously unimportant places into centres of pilgrimages. Changes of sacred place may in retrospect thus often be understood as a trigger for internal leaps within the history of religious traditions. Last but not least, the fictional translocation of holy places should also be considered: the list ranges from the Islands of the Blessed to Atlantis to the Heavenly Jerusalem.

To sum up, both dynamic nodes of religious transfer such as monasteries, courts or centres of education and push-factors such as mission or the translocation of sacred places facilitated and enhanced the expansion of religious ideas both within and between Europe and Asia.

3. *Six Articles in a Grid*

The set of questions expounded above are the result of collaborative work within the research field 2 of the consortium "Dynamics in the History of Religions between Asia and Europe". The articles that follow provide an opportunity to test their validity. Indeed, every contribution touches on some or even all of the issues elaborated in the course of our work, as a brief overview should suffice to illustrate.

[10] The following paragraph summarizes thoughts developed and expounded by Reinhold Glei in November 2009 during meetings of Research Field 2: Contacts between the major religious traditions during their expansion.

Our first set of questions on the relationship between governance and religious expansion plays a pivotal role in several articles. Michael Lecker deals with expansion in its most concrete and physical form: military conquest. He underlines the importance exogenous factors such as war had upon religious groups by describing the immediate social impact that the change from Christian to Muslim rule as a result of the Islamic expansion had upon the Jewish populace of the Near East. For subdued Jews, "Herrschaftsnähe" is shown to have been important in a very elementary sense. Stephen Berkwitz, in contrast, uses the example of Sri Lanka and South Asia to show that the success of Theravāda Buddhism in these regions depended to an absolutely essential degree on royal power and patronage, an analysis very much corroborated by Sven Bretfeld through his study of Buddhist expansion in Tibet. "The Theravāda ideology of righteous kings whose great merit is evidenced by their royal position and reinforced by the patronage of orthodox Buddhist institutions made this form of Buddhism appealing to Burmese and Thai monarchs" (Berkwitz). Finally, Eun-jeung Lee uses the reception of Confucianism by some Western thinkers to illustrate how new theories of governance could be formulated as a result of intercultural contact.

How the religiously "other" was dealt with in concrete terms is touched upon in Michael Lecker's and John Tolan's contributions, which both deal with the religious push-factor conversion and the effect it had upon Jewish and Christian communities during the early Middle Ages. Fear of conversion had an important impact on some learned Christian authors' views of Islam and also had a retroactive effect upon the understanding of their own religion, thus causing reactions not only in the social and juridical, but also in the intellectual and theological fields. Stephen Berkwitz in turn underlines, "that Buddhism originated in Gangetic Plains of India and spread across Asia as arguably the world's first missionary religion" and illustrates this through the example of Mahinda's activities in Sri Lanka, which included large-scale preaching.

The spatial dimension of religious expansion, or more concretely, the importance of political borderlands as transit zones and that of religious hubs as dynamic nodes of transfer comes to the fore in many papers. The success of Buddhism in Sri Lanka was facilitated by the fact that the island was geographically divided from the heartlands of Brahmanism. John Tolan's examples illustrate that intellectual grappling with Islam on the part of Christian scholars occurred at the periphery of the Dār al-Islām, and Michael Lecker's example of Jewish garrisons left in newly conquered frontier zones as the sole representatives of Islam helps put simplistic notions of clearly divided religious entities into proper perspective. Eun-jeung Lee's contribution is an enlightening study into the repercussions inter-religious contact at the periphery had within the heartlands of European Christianity, whereas Michael Lackner underlines the fact that according to a sinocentric understanding of East Asia, China was the centre and Korea the periphery of the civilized world, which in turn had effects on the acceptance of western religions in Asia. Professor Lackner also points to the fact that the distance between Asia and Europe resulted in filtering tactics within Jesuit writings about Asia and the beliefs of its peoples.

The respective settings and processes of religious transfer are described by Michael Lecker, John Tolan, Sven Bretfeld and Eun-jeung Lee. Michael Lecker's paper raises the question of whether slavery can be seen as a vector for religious dynamics, as it necessarily produced contact situations on the micro-level of society. John Tolan's rendering of Christian thinkers' attitudes toward Islam shows perfectly how contemporary phenomena such as political expansion were fitted into theological views of the past and the future. The scholars conveyed religious knowledge and prejudice to co-religionists by selecting, adapting and more often than not distorting Islamic beliefs. Institutional settings and push factors such as economic pressure (taxes etc.) triggered fear of conversion, which in turn led to religious apologetics and ultimately to a new understanding of one's own religion. In the case of Sri Lanka, the competition between different transmission lineages of Buddhism in turn led to a condensation of this religious tradition on the island. And the tributary status of Chŏson versus China and the state of Chŏson society in general lay at the heart of Chŏng Yag-yong's egalitarian understanding of religious rites (Lee).

Processes of systematization were the basis of several contributions. The condensation of varying forms of Buddhism into a Theravāda ideology in Sri Lanka can be seen in this light, just as the standardization of canonical texts by Mahāvihārin monks (Stephen Berkwitz), and even more so the translations and the creation of a particular genre of writing in Tibet as described by Sven Bretfeld. This "three-vow" literature was an attempt to systematize divergences between Tibetan Buddhist transmissions and effectively not only helped consolidate Buddhism within Tibet, but also served as a starting point for the expansion of

Buddhism to Mongolia and China. Eun-jeung Lee's rendering of Chŏng Yag-yong's reception of Western science illustrates the way in which different schools of learning attempted to systematize and homologate Western religion and Confucian thought. In turn, John Tolan's article is itself no less than a systematization of historical attempts to systematize religions. His four overlapping phases of Christian intellectual reactions to Muslim expansion are based on polemic or apologetic texts that more often than not are examples of systematic demarcation and a reflection of the authors' own beliefs.

Intra-religious reform is dealt with extensively by Stephen Berkwitz and to a lesser degree by John Tolan and Eun-jeung Lee. The rise of rival orders and reform movements had a major impact on Lankan Buddhism and ultimately led to its condensation (Berkwitz). Inner-Christian deviance and its persecution provided the backdrop for an interpretation of Islam as a heretical strain of Christianity, as John Tolan lays out. Finally, Eun-jeung Lee presents a particularly intriguing case of Chŏng Yag-yong's missionary zeal clothed in the garb of alleged inner-Chinese reform. But on a comparative level, the authors of this volume take an intra-religious perspective to a much lesser degree than an inter-religious viewpoint, which very much correlates with the work of the entire consortium.

Let us turn from our set of questions to our two examples for means and agents of religious transfers, that is hubs and push-factors. Stephen Berkwitz's and Sven Bretfeld's contributions underline the importance of monastic hubs for the expansion of religious ideas in Asia. Buddhism expanded to Sri Lanka not through point-to-point diffusion as a gradual spread, but rather punctually via monasteries. In very much the same way, Sri Lanka and Tibet served as a point of acceleration for the expansion of Buddhism in South and South East Asia. Sven Bretfeld uses the term "cultural relay" to describe this phenomenon and underlines that such relays could act as cultural filters by monitoring and changing the traffic passing through them, thus effectively functioning as "intelligent hubs". In Sri Lanka, for example, Buddhism was condensed into one understanding of this religious tradition, whereas Tibet on the contrary acted as an "intelligent hub" by conveying a decidedly diversified notion of Buddhism and by systematizing it. On a less spatial and more cognitive level, John Tolan presents an important literary hub in the form of apologetic texts of the early and High Middle Ages. This genre not only condensed religious knowledge and prejudice, but also accelerated their diffusion among scholarly elites and less learned groups of society.

The relationship between push-factors and pull-factors is nicely exemplified by an extract from Theodore Abû Qurrah's writings on Islam presented by John Tolan. Abû Qurrah ascribed the expansion of Islam to the military and political power of its adherents and thus to push-factors alone, whereas Christianity allegedly spread far and wide thanks to pull-factors, namely due to its religionists' desire for God and for extra-worldly merit. Sven Bretfeld, in turn, outlines the "meritorious surplus" that acceptance of foreign understandings of Buddhism entailed in Tibet, thus illustrating the reciprocal nature of push and pull factors. Eun-jeung Lee and Michael Lackner deal with examples of the ways in which Asian terms and concepts were adapted by Matteo Ricci and Chŏng Yag-yong in order to further Christian expansion. As for the translocation of sacred places, such processes are discerned in the Middle East, in South and in East Asia. Michael Lecker uses his close reading of Jewish capitulation treaties in order to demonstrate the mechanisms behind the appropriation of sacred places on the part of Muslim invaders. Stephen Berkwitz describes how promoters of Buddhism appropriated and de-centred local spirits and their cults, and Theravāda Buddhism later strengthened its authority both by appropriation of local sites and via the transmission of relics throughout South East Asia. By the same token, the localization of Buddhism in Sri Lanka can also be seen as a particular form of translocation, namely as an attempt to tie a tradition to its immediate social and cultural environment.

The articles assembled in this section thus help illustrate the imbrications between exogenous and endogenous factors of religious expansion. They highlight the concrete settings that accelerated or impeded such forms of transfer – be it patronage, institutional consolidation or active propagation – and define the effect such movements had upon different religious traditions – for example in the form of systematization or adaptation. Further research within the consortium "Dynamics in the History of Religions between Asia and Europe" will strive to pinpoint more precisely this intricate interdependency between context and contents of religious transfer processes.

THE JEWISH REACTION TO THE ISLAMIC CONQUESTS

Michael Lecker

1. *Early Jewish Converts to Islam*

Muḥammad's Companion Mu'ādh ibn Jabal who was probably a former Jew[1] officiated towards the death of the Prophet Muḥammad as the governor of Janad in central Yemen. At that time most of the inhabitants of Janad and of the rest of the Yemen were Jewish. Mu'ādh led a mass conversion of Jews at the mosque of Janad on the first Friday of Rajab (the seventh month of the Islamic year) which was later commemorated by an annual visit to that mosque.[2] Muḥammad's own success among the members of the Jewish tribes of Medina was far less spectacular, since only a handful of them embraced Islam. We probably know about these converts because those who embraced Islam from among "the people of a sacred book" *(ahl al-kitāb)* play a role in anti-Jewish and anti-Christian polemics by providing "proofs that Muḥammad was a true prophet". Such a role is played, for example, by 'Abdallāh ibn Salām who was the most famous Jewish convert at the time of Muḥammad.[3] The latter reportedly expressed his resigna-

[1] Michael Lecker, "Zayd b. Thābit, 'a Jew with two sidelocks': Judaism and literacy in pre-Islamic Medina (Yathrib)", *JNES* 56 (1997), 259–273, at 269, no. 17; cf. Josef van Ess, "Die Pest von Emmaus: Theologie und Geschichte in der Frühzeit des Islams", *Oriens* 36 (2001), 248–267, at 264.

[2] Mu'ādh brought a letter from Muḥammad to the dominant group among the Sakāsik tribe, the Banū l-Aswad, who were the inhabitabts of the Janad region. His sermon on the first Friday of Rajab was attended by former Jews from this tribe who had already converted to Islam before his arrival. Among them there was a group of Jews who questioned him about the keys of Paradise. He not only gave them the right answer, but also told them that Muḥammad had anticipated their question, and hence they converted to Islam. Miraculously every year it rains on that Friday or on the Thursday that precedes is; Muḥammad ibn Yūsuf al-Janadī, *al-Sulūk fī ṭabaqāt al-'ulamā' wa-l-mulūk*, ed. Muḥammad ibn 'Alī ibn al-Ḥusayn al-Akwa' al-Ḥiwālī, Ṣan'ā': Maktabat al-Irshād, 1414/1993–1416/1995, 2 vols., I, 81–82; M. Lecker, "Judaism among Kinda and the *ridda* of Kinda", *JAOS* 115 (1995), 635–650, at 638–639.

[3] His tribal affiliation and the time of his conversion were disputed and regarding both we should opt for the less flattering version: he did not belong to the main Jewish tribe Qaynuqā' but to the marginal tribe Zaydallāt; and he embraced Islam some

tion with regard to the small number of converts from among the Jews of Medina: "Had ten Jews followed me, every single Jew on earth would have followed me", he said.[4] In another version of his utterance the ten Jews that should serve as an example for the rest of the Jews are learned men *(aḥbār)* rather than ordinary people.[5] Muḥammad and the Jews whom he encountered in Medina were on a collision course from the outset. The war against them ended with Muḥammad's total victory, but it still haunts Jewish-Muslim relations due to the image of the Jewish "enemies of Allāh" as it comes through in Muḥammad's biography.

2. *The Trials and Tribulations of the Conquests*

Rape, enslavement and corvée usually accompany conquests, and the Islamic Conquests of the 7th century were no exception. Some comparative evidence can be found in connection with an internal Muslim war that took place some half a century after Muḥammad's death, namely the conquest of Medina by the Umayyad army following the

two years before Muḥammad's death, not around the time of the *hijra;* M. Lecker, *The 'Constitution of Medina: Muḥammad's First Legal Document*, Princeton: Darwin Press, 2004, 63–66. I have recently realized that many years ago Joseph Horovitz had arrived at more or less the same conclusions; see the entries about the famous convert in the *Encyclopaedia Judaica*, online edition (where Horovitz argues that his family was under the protection of the Zaydallāt), and in the *Encyclopaedia of Islam*, second edition (where he argues that the version regarding the later conversion date "is worthy of more credence").

[4] See Suhaylī, *al-Rawḍ al-unuf*, ed. 'Abd al-Raḥmān al-Wakīl, Cairo: Dār al-Kutub al-Ḥadītha, 1387/1967–1390/1970, 7 vols., IV, 409–410 *(islām 'Abdillāh ibn Salām)*, who claims that only two Jews converted to Islam at the time of Muḥammad *(lawi ttaba'anī 'ashara mina l-yahūd lam yabqa fī l-arḍ yahūdī illā ttaba'anī)*. The Jewish convert Ka'b al-Aḥbār claimed (on the basis of Qur'ān 5,12) that the required number of Jewish converts was twelve, which brought about a harmonizing version: both claims are correct, Muḥammad meant ten converts in addition to the above mentioned two.

[5] Aḥmad ibn Ḥanbal, *Musnad*, Cairo: al-Maṭba'a al-Maymaniyya, 1313/1895, reprint Beirut, 6 vols., II, 346, l. 12 *(law āmana bī 'ashara min aḥbāri l-yahūd la-āmana bī kull yahūdī 'alā wajhi l-arḍ)*. The word *aḥbār* is part of the nickname of the above mentioned convert Ka'b al-Aḥbār who converted to Islam at the time of the second caliph 'Umar ibn al-Khaṭṭāb; see e. g. his entry in *Encyclopaedia Judaica*. In Sarah Stroumsa, "On Jewish intellectual converts to Islam in the early middle ages", *Peamim* 42 (1990), 61–75, at 63 (Hebrew); and in: idem, "On Jewish intellectuals who converted in the early middle ages", in: Daniel Frank (ed.), *The Jews of Medieval Islam: Community, Society and Identity: Proceedings of an International Conference held by the Institute of Jewish Studies*, University College, London, 1992, Leiden: Brill, 1995, 179–197, at 182, his name is misprinted as Ka'b al-Akhbār; he was not the first Jew who converted to Islam.

Battle of the Ḥarra in 683 CE. Nine months later "the children of the Ḥarra" were born to raped Muslim women of Muḥammad's own tribe, Quraysh, and of the Anṣār, or the Arab tribes of Medina.[6] The reports about the atrocities committed by the Umayyad army are undeniably anti-Umayyad[7] and probably exaggerated, but they give one an idea of what conquests were like at that time. One assumes that for an unknown number of years or perhaps decades following the Conquests non-Muslim local communities of all denominations were in a precarious situation, especially where their rights were not safeguarded by capitulation treaties.

Enslavement was a major threat. Men – often belonging to the higher levels of society – were captured and sent to agricultural estates in Arabia and elsewhere. In the intertribal wars before Islam and at the time of Muḥammad the victors were often selective and only took captive those deemed likely to be ransomed by their relatives. Since many of the foreign slaves were not born into slavery, assassinations of Muslim slave owners by their slaves were not uncommon.[8] Enormous deals regarding the sale of slaves were concluded between members of the Qurashī elite. For example, two prominent Qurashīs bought slaves from the second caliph ʿUmar ibn al-Khaṭṭāb (r. 634–644) in a trans-

[6] The battle received its name from the *ḥarra* or volcanic hill east of Medina. See Laura Veccia Vaglieri, s. v. "al-Ḥarra", *Encyclopaedia of Islam*, Second Edition; Meir Jacob Kister, "The battle of the Ḥarra", in: Myriam Rosen-Ayalon (ed.), *Studies in Memory of Gaston Wiet*, Jerusalem: Institute of Asian and African Studies, 1977, 33–49. For *awlād al-Ḥarra* see al-Samhūdī, *Wafāʾ al-wafā*, ed. Qāsim al-Sāmarrāʾī, London-Jedda: al-Fur-qān, 1422/2001, 5 vols., I, 257. Reportedly the raped women that gave birth to children numbered one thousand; ibid, 259; or eight hundred; Yāqūt al-Ḥamawī, *Muʿjam al-buldān*, Beirut: Dār Ṣādir-Dār Bayrūt, 1957, 5 vols., s. v. Ḥarrat Wāqim, II, 249.

[7] A woman of Quraysh who was circumambulating the Kaʿba suddenly hugged and kissed a black man whom she met. She explained to a shocked onlooker that it was her son: she had been raped by his father during the Battle of the Ḥarra; Samhūdī, *Wafāʾ al-wafā*, I, 260.

[8] For example, Saʿīd the son of the third caliph ʿUthmān ibn ʿAffān conquered Samarqand and was governor of Khurāsān under the caliph Muʿāwiya. After Muʿāwiya's death he returned to Medina and was murdered by his Soghdian slaves; Ibn ʿAsākir, *Taʾrīkh madīnat Dimashq* (henceforward *TMD*), ed. al-ʿAmrawī, Beirut: Dār al-Fikr, 1415/1995–1419/1998, 80 vols., XXI, 227. Elsewhere we read that having been dismissed by Muʿāwiya from the governorship of Khurāsān, Saʿīd brought with him to Medina young Soghdian hostages *(min awlād al-Ṣughd)* whom he assigned to an estate as agricultural labourers. One day they closed the estate's gate, murdered him and committed suicide as the pursuit after them was taking place; Ibn Qutayba, *al-Maʿārif*, ed. Tharwat ʿUkāsha, Cairo: Dār al-Maʿārif, 1969, 202 (*fa-alqāhum fī arḍ yaʿmalūna lahu fīhā bi-l-masāḥī*, "he assigned them to an estate to work for him with shovels"). They may well have belonged to aristocratic families.

action that may well have included thousands of slaves.[9] The fourth caliph ʿAlī ibn Abī Ṭālib (r. 656–661) manumitted slaves on condition that they work on his estate for six years.[10] During ʿAlī's caliphate Muḥammad's Companion Abū Ayyūb had demanded from the governor of Baṣra, Ibn ʿAbbās, eight slaves to cultivate his land and received many more.[11] The Umayyad caliph ʿAbd al-Malik (r. 685–705) sent Byzantine slaves to his estates in Yamāma (near presentday Riyadh). They rebelled and were killed by local tribesmen.[12] References to slaves employed on estates, for example in digging underground irrigation aqueducts, could easily be multiplied. One thing is certain: many thousands of non-Arab slaves captured during the Conquests worked on agricultural estates and elsewhere. Small communities of Jews, Christians and others could have been depleted of all their young men.

Women and children of male slaves and of those killed in the Conquests were sold into slavery. When Caesarea was conquered, four thousand slaves (or "heads", as they are sometimes referred to) were captured. They had been sent to the caliph ʿUmar in Medina and alighted in the Jurf plain northwest of Medina before being distributed by the caliph among orphans of the Anṣār. Other slaves from the same shipment – presumably young literate boys – were employed as clerks in the emerging state apparatus.[13] Figures are notoriously inaccurate; but the fact that the slaves alighted at the Jurf plain suggests that they

[9] M. Lecker, "Biographical notes on Abū ʿUbayda Maʿmar b. al-Muthannā", *Studia Islamica* 81 (1995), 71–100, at 78–79.

[10] Ibn Shabba, *Akhbār al-Madīna*, ed. Dandal and Bayān, Beirut: Dār al-Kutub al-ʿIlmiyya, 1417/1996, 2 vols., I, 141.

[11] He received forty or, according to another version, twenty; Ibn ʿAsākir, *TMD*, XVI, 54–55.

[12] Namely, the Banū Qays ibn Ḥanẓala of the Tamīm; Meir Jacob Kister, "The social and political implications of three traditions in the Kitab al-Kharādj of Yahya b. Adam", *JESHO* 3 (1960), 326–334, at 334, quoting Balādhurī, *Ansāb al-ashrāf*, VII, i, ed. Ramzi Baalbaki, Beirut: al-Sharika al-Muttaḥida li-l-Tawzīʿ, 1417/1997, 9. Kister also adduces evidence regarding the employment of black slaves on estates belonging to two prominent Qurashīs, ʿAbdallāh ibn ʿĀmir and ʿAbdallāh ibn al-Zubayr. He discusses a tradition according to which Muḥammad preferred dates from trees watered by rainfall to ones from trees that were irrigated, because the former were grown without causing suffering to hungry and naked slaves.

[13] Balādhurī, *Futūḥ al-buldān*, ed. Michael Jan de Goeje, Leiden: Brill, 1863–1866, 142 *(wa-ja ʿala baʿḍahum fī l-kitāb wa-l-aʿmāl li-l-muslimīna)*. In the early days of Islam there was an acute shortage in literate people, and hence non-Muslim scribes were even employed in preparing copies of the Qur'ān. A Christian from Ḥīra charged ʿAbd al-Raḥmān ibn Abī Laylā (d. 83/702) 70 *dirham* for a copy of the Qur'ān. The Christians of Ḥīra, or the *ʿIbād*, were first hired by the Muslims to prepare copies of the Qur'ān, and later they copied Qur'āns and sold them at their own initiative; they

were numerous, since the plain was used by troops setting out from Medina before proceeding to the battlefields.[14] A slave's life did not agree with everyone: 'Umar's predecessor Abū Bakr (r. 632–634) had given two slave girls from an earlier shipment to the daughters of a prominent Companion of Muḥammad, but both slave girls died. 'Umar replaced them with slave girls from the Caesarea shipment.[15]

Several accounts link the above mentioned Jewish convert, 'Abdallāh ibn Salām, to the ransoming of Jewish female captives by the Exilarch, or the head of the Jews in exile. Polemics, rather than an interest in the Exilarchate, are behind the preservation of the following accounts in Muslim sources. 'Abdallāh reportedly paid 700 *dirham* for an old female *('ajūz)* Jewish slave from Balanjar, the then capital city of the Khazars in the northern Caucasus; the wording of the account that tells us about it suggests that he was there with the Muslim army. On his way back he met the Exilarch who was prepared to pay for the old woman 1,400 *dirham*, while 'Abdallāh demanded 4,000. The Exilarch only paid the full amount after 'Abdallāh had whispered in his ear a verse of the Torah that reportedly made it incumbent upon Jews to release prisoners. Finally 'Abdallāh only took 2,000 *dirham* and returned the remaining 2,000 to the Exilarch.[16] The polemical anti-Jewish point is slightly disguised in this account. A succinct account along the same lines has it that the Exilarch only ransomed Jewish female slaves who had not been raped by the Arabs. The Exilarch had to be reminded of the Torah command that all the female captives should be ransomed *(fa-fādūhunna kullahunna)*. When the Exilarch intended to deviate from the sacred law of the Torah regarding the

---

were the first to trade in Qur'āns; Ibn Abī Dāwūd al-Sijistānī, *Kitāb al-maṣāḥif*, ed. A. Jeffery, Leiden: Brill, 1937, 171.

[14] Ibn 'Asākir, *TMD*, II, 31; Ibn Sa'd, *al-Ṭabaqāt al-kubrā*, Beirut: Dār Ṣādir-Dār Bayrūt, 1380/1960–1388/1968, 8 vols., II, 248–249.

[15] Balādhurī, *Futūḥ*, 142. The Companion in question was Abū Umāma As'ad ibn Zurāra from the Khazraj/Najjār who had made Muḥammad a custodian of his daughters. The deceased slavegirls (singular: *khādim*) were captured in 'Ayn al-Tamr.

[16] Ibn Abī Ḥātim al-Rāzī, *Tafsīr*, ed. Aḥmad Fatḥī 'Abd al-Raḥmān Ḥijāzī, Beirut: Dār al-Kutub al-'Ilmiyya, 1427/2006, 7 vols., I, 146, no. 865. The supposed Torah verse says: "Every slave of the Children of Israel you should buy and manumit [what follows in bold face belongs to Qur'ān 2,85] *And if they come to you as captives, ransom them since it is forbidden for you to banish them*" *(innaka lā tajidu mamlūkan fī banī isrā'īl illā shtaraytahu fa-a'taqtaqhu* wa-in ya'tūkum usārā tufādūhum wa-huwa muḥarramun 'alaykum ikhrājuhum*)*. The relevance of the anecdote to the Qur'ān and its interpretation is questionable; but the Jewish captive from Balanjar and the meeting between the famous convert from Medina and the Exilarch may be historical.

ransoming of captives, ʿAbdallāh ibn Salām who was well versed in the Torah guided him to the truth. The implication is clear: the Jews also turned their backs on the Torah's command that they follow the future prophet Muḥammad when he is sent to mankind. Another account on the same topic is a philologist's feast because of its wealth of detail. It is doubtful that the anecdote it describes is historical; but the preference given to the ransoming of Jewish women who had not been raped – a background detail – must be historical. This account has it that after the Muslim conquest of Nihāwand the Exilarch ransomed Jewish female slaves. A Muslim who had captured a young attractive Jewess asked ʿAbdallāh ibn Salām to broker for him a good deal with the Exilarch. The latter inquired the girl through an interpreter (who probably translated from Aramaic to Persian) whether her captor had raped her. ʿAbdallāh who understood the Exilarch's words objected, claiming that according to the Exilarch's sacred book [i. e. the Torah] such a question was forbidden. Following an angry exchange with the Exilarch (ʿAbdallāh argued that he knew the Exilarch's book better than the Exilarch himself), ʿAbdallāh accepted the latter's invitation to visit him, hoping to convert him to Islam. For three days ʿAbdallāh was reciting the Torah to the Exilarch, while the latter kept weeping: "How shall I deal with the Jews", he asked. In other words, he was worried about the Jews' reaction if he converted to Islam. Finally "he was overcome by misery", i. e. he remained Jewish.[17] The polemical point is evident; still we gain a glimpse of the state of many women (and small children) in the conquered towns and villages.

As to corvée, the Muslims were following time-old practices.[18] Local people were employed as guides and led the Muslims from their own town to the next one.[19] They also served as manual workers, building and maintaining roads and bridges.[20]

[17] Ibn Ḥajar al-ʿAsqalānī, *al-Maṭālib al-ʿāliya bi-zawāʾid al-masānīd al-thamāniya*, ed. Ḥabīb al-Raḥmān al-Aʿẓamī, Beirut: Dār al-Maʿrifa, 1407/1987, 5 vols., IV, 31–32.

[18] The Byzantines would capture foreigners that arrived at their towns and employ them in the reconstruction of churches; Isaac Hasson, "Le chef judhāmite Rawḥ ibn Zinbāʿ", *Studia Islamica* 77 (1993), 95–122, at 101, n. 23.

[19] ʿAbd al-Razzāq, *Muṣannaf*, ed. Ḥabīb al-Raḥmān al-Aʿẓamī, Beirut: al-Majlis al-ʿIlmī, 1390/1970–1392/1972, 11 vols., V, 279 *(hal kuntum tusakhkhirūna l-ʿajam? qāla: kunnā nusakhkhiruhum min qarya ilā qarya yadullūnā [ʿalā] l-ṭarīq thumma nukhallīhim).*

[20] See for example the capitulation treaty of Edessa (al-Ruhā, modern Şanlıurfa); Balādhurī, *Futūḥ*, 174 *(wa-ʿalaykum irshādu l-ḍāll wa-iṣlāḥu l-jusūr wa-l-ṭuruq).* See also Jørgen Bæk Simonsen, *Studies in the Genesis and Early Development of the Caliphal Taxation System*, Copenhagen: Akademisk Forlag, 1988, 127: "Conscripted labour was

Rape, enslavement and corvée belong to the period that immediately followed the Conquests. But the inferior legal status of the *dhimmī*, or the "protected person", shared by Jews, Christians and Zoroastrians was permanent. Qur'anic law prescribed that the payment of tax (*jizya* in this context usually means poll-tax) be carried out in a fashion that was humiliating for the payer.[21] Humiliation had nothing to do with the treasury; it was ideological, and hence not subject to pragmatism or tolerance. In the Islamic state non-Muslims were constitutionally humiliated regardless of their wealth or social status.[22] The *dhimmīs* are comparable to the clients or protected neighbours of pre-Islamic tribal society, since even a rich and otherwise respectable client was legally inferior to any full-fledged member of the tribe.[23] Some claimed that the humiliation also extended to the land tax paid by non-Muslims. A Muslim who bought land from a *dhimmī* and undertook to pay the tax *(jizya)* due from it was inflicted by the humiliation *(dhull, ṣaghār)* attached to it.

3. *Competition and Urbanization*

The foreign slaves employed on Muslim estates were but one aspect of a major early Islamic trend of investment in agriculture that posed

rapidly introduced to provide canals, roads, ships for the new Arab fleet, and for the building of mosques, palaces, etc."; idem, "Muhammad's letters", in: Kjeld von Folsach et alii (eds.), *From Handaxe to Khan: Essays Presented to Peder Mortensen on the Occasion of his 70th Birthday*, Aarhus: Aarhus Univesity Press, 2004, 215–223, at 220.

[21] Uri Rubin, "Qur'ān and poetry: more data concerning the Qur'ānic *jizya* verse *('an yadin)*", *Jerusalem Studies in Arabic and Islam* 31 (2006), 139–146. See e.g. the capitulation treaty of Tbilisi *(... 'alā iqrār bi-l-ṣaghār wa-l-jizya)*; Balādhurī, *Futūḥ*, 201. Ṭabarī, *Ta'rīkh al-rusul wa-l-mulūk*, ed. Michael Jan de Goeje et alii, Leiden 1879–1901, 15 vols., I, 2675, has a slightly different version of this expression *('alā l-iqrār bi-ṣaghāri l-jizya)*. Cf. *The History of al-Ṭabarī*, XIV, trans. G. Rex-Smith, New York: State University of New York Press, 1994, 46: "with the imposition of a small tribute". But *ṣaghār* in this context refers to the humiliation which is the permanent condition of the *dhimmī*; see Paul L. Heck, "Poll tax", *Encyclopaedia of the Qur'ān*, IV, 151.

[22] According to Shī'ite experts on Islamic law, there is nothing wrong in looking at women from "the people of a sacred book" *(ahl al-kitāb)* and at their hair because their status is that of slavegirls *(imā')*; however, this permission excludes suspicious aims or pleasure; al-Baḥrānī, *al-Ḥadā'iq al-nāḍira fī aḥkām al-'itra al-ṭāhira*, Beirut: Dār al-Aḍwā', 1405/1985–1414/1993, 26 vols., XXIII, 58–59.

[23] Akhnas ibn Sharīq who was a client of Quraysh could not grant security that was binding for the Qurashīs "of pure lineage"; M. Lecker, *The 'Constitution of Medina'*, 116.

a serious threat to the very livelihood of *dhimmī* farmers, be they Jewish, Christian or Zoroastrian. Members of the Quraysh tribe had been involved in agricultural projects outside Mecca before the advent of Islam, and their intensive activity in this field in the early Islamic period was an extension of their pre-Islamic endeavours. The Prophet Muḥammad and the four so-called "Rightly-Guided" caliphs *(rāshidūn)* owned large estates in Medina and elsewhere in northern Arabia that yielded huge revenues. The same is true of many prominent members of early Islamic society. The creation of estates continued under the Umayyads, and it can be shown that land ownership was sometimes taken into account in the appointment of governors to certain provinces. It is true that the purchase of *dhimmī* land by Muslims was frowned upon by both the doctors of Islamic law and the treasury, since the tax paid for Muslim land was much lower than that paid for *dhimmī* land. However, while the doctors of law engaged in legal disputes, large tracts of arable hands changed hands in Iraq and elsewhere. The difference in taxation between *dhimmī* land and Muslim land meant that the *dhimmī* farmers suffered from disadvantage when competing with the Muslim land owners.

The pricing of agricultural produce was but one aspect of a presumed marketing problem encountered by *dhimmī* farmers. Their access to markets controlled by Muslims could have been restricted when they competed with a governor or another influential figure who wanted to sell his own produce first. Suffice it to mention that one of Muḥammad's Companions, al-Zubayr ibn al-ʿAwwām, owned in Baṣra not only a market but also agricultural lands allotted to him by the state *(khiṭaṭ)*.[24]

4. *Assistance to the Conquest Army Put in Context*

The sad outcome of the first encounter between Judaism and Islam at the time of Muḥammad and the expulsion of many Jews from Arabia, most notably from Khaybar in northern Arabia, by the second caliph ʿUmar (that actually took place after the Conquests had begun) were

[24] Yaʿqūbī, *Mushākalat al-nās li-zamānihim*, 13 *(fa-banā l-Zubayr ibn al-ʿAwwām dārahu l-mashhūra bi-l-Baṣra wa-fīhā l-aswāq wa-l-tijārāt ... wa-taraka ... wa-khiṭaṭan bi-Miṣr wa-l-Iskandariyya wa-l-Kūfa wa-l-Baṣra)*. Cf. *Encyclopaedia of Islam*, second edition, s. v. khiṭṭa ("a term used of the lands allotted to tribal groups and individuals in the garrison cities founded by the Arabs at the time of the conquests").

no secret for the Jews who lived in Palestine, Iraq and elsewhere. But for all their sympathy for the fate of their Arabian brothers, life went on and events in Arabia could not have had a lasting effect on their attitude to the advancing conquest army. Besides, one must take into account that for many Jews living in Palestine and Syria, the Conquests, for all the trials and tribulations that accompanied them, brought an end to terrible Byzantine oppression, not to mention the disruption of the Byzantine-Sassanian wars.[25] Hence it is not unreasonable to expect that Jews would assist the conquest army. Intelligence, for example, can be a decisive factor in the takeover of a besieged town or in finding a convenient ford across a river.[26] It is impossible to obtain an accurate picture of the Jewish military contribution during the Conquests and immediately after them. Still it is noteworthy that upon the conquest of Tripoli (Lebanon) the then governor of Syria, Muʿāwiya, stationed in its citadel a Jewish troop.[27] The members of this troop that came from the Urdunn province are supposed to have been Tripoli's only inhabitants for several decades.[28] In other words, for several decades they were the only representatives of the Muslim state in Tripoli (that was also inhabited by Byzantines and others). It can be said that the

[25] For Jewish eschatology in the context of the Conquests ("the secrets that were revealed to R. Shimʿon bar Yoḥai when he was hiding in a cave") cf. Bernard Lewis, "An apocalyptic vision of Islamic history", *BSOAS* 13 (1950), 308–338; Robert G. Hoyland, *Seeing Islam as Others Saw it: A Survey and Evaluation of Christian, Jewish, and Zoroastrian Writings on Early Islam*, Princeton: Darwin Press, 1997, 308–312.

[26] Regarding the possible Jewish participation in the Arab armies see also Robert G. Hoyland, *Seeing Islam*, 528–529; Stefan Leder, "The attitude of the population, especially the Jews, towards the Arab-Islamic conquest of Bilād al-Shām and the question of their role therein", *Die Welt des Orients* 18 (1987) 64–71.

[27] Qudāma ibn Jaʿfar, *Kitāb al-kharāj wa-ṣināʿat al-kitāba*, ed. Muḥammad Ḥusayn al-Zabīdī, Baghdad: Dār al-Rashīd, 1981, 296 *(jamāʿa mina l-yahūd)*. Balādhurī, *Futūh.*, 127, has at this point "a large troop" *(jamāʿa kaībra)*.

[28] Ibn ʿAsākir, *TMD*, XXI, 356. The Muslims trusted the Jews since the latter were unlikely to betray them and cooperate with the Byzantine enemies. See also Moshe Gil, *A History of Palestine, 634–1099*, translated by Ethel Broido, Cambridge: Cambridge University Press, 1992, 58: "... Muʿāwiya then placed a large number of Jews from al-Urdunn, that is, the north of Palestine, in the city's citadel"; but clearly a troop is meant here rather than civilians. Fred McGraw Donner, *The Early Islamic Conquests*, Princeton: Princeton University Press, 1981, 247, has it that Muʿāwiya settled Tripoli with Jews, [p]erhaps because Jews were excluded from other Syrian towns, e. g. Jerusalem". But the Jews in question formed a non-Arab unit employed as a garrison force. The emerging Muslim Imperial army included, among others, many Persians. Regarding the stationing of Persian garrisons by the caliph Muʿāwiya see e. g. Balādhurī, *Futūḥ*, 117 (again the term *jamāʿa*, or troop, is used; the Persians included *asāwira*, or heavy cavalry, from Baṣra and Kūfa; and one of their *quwwād*, or commanders, is mentioned by name).

role of Jews as garrisons in Spanish towns after the Muslim conquest of Spain[29] had a prominent precedent in Tripoli.

It should be taken into account that the evidence regarding the assistance of the local population to the Muslim conquest army was not preserved only to educate later generations, but also to legitimize the purchase of land from members of communities that provided assistance in one form or another. These communities were granted capitulation treaties which secured for them an improved legal status compared to that of communities that were conquered without such treaties. The former had the right to sell their land to Muslims, while the land of the latter was to remain an asset of future Muslim generations. Farsighted statesmen refrained from dividing the land of the latter category as spoils, and it is sometimes put on a par with *waqf*, or charitable endowment, that cannot be sold or given away as a gift.[30]

However, the sale of *dhimmī* land to Muslims, be they owners of large estates or small farmers, no doubt took place regardless of the status of the land and new realities were constantly created on the ground. Some proponents of *jihād* wished all the Arabs to remain warriors and were probably opposed to each and every land transaction; but in general the purchase of land from *dhimmīs* who had capitulation treaties was deemed legitimate. The need to legitimize the purchase of land from these *dhimmīs* is sometimes behind the preservation of evidence regarding their assistance to the conquest army.

5. *Religious Edifices*

Symbolic value was attached to the takeover of places of worship belonging to defeated communities, be they sites of idol worship in Arabia, or churches and synagogues outside Arabia. Central edifices, especially those located in prominent places such as hilltops or town centres, were more at risk than marginal ones for both ideological and practical reasons.

---

[29] Norman A. Stillman, *The Jews of Arab Lands: a History and Source Book*, Philadelphia: Jewish Publication Society of America, 1979, 23–24; Norman Roth, "The Jews and the Muslim conquest of Spain", *Jewish Social Studies* 38 (1976), 145–158.

[30] The person who was in charge of the *kharāj* or land tax in the Urdunn province at the time of 'Umar ibn 'Abd al-'Azīz asked the caliph about land of *Ahl al-dhimma* found in the hands of Muslims (in other words, land purchased by the latter from the former). He was ordered to prevent such transactions because the land was considered *waqf* or charitable endowment; Ibn 'Asākir, *TMD*, II, 199.

A case in point is the central church of Damascus or *kanīsat Yūḥannā* for which we have detailed evidence. Fifteen Damascene churches and synagogues, among them *kanīsat al-yahūd*, or the synagogue of the Jews – out of dozens of churches and synagogues that existed in Damascus at that time – remained Christian or Jewish property through their listing in the capitulation treaty of Damascus[31]that later served as a point of reference. When the Christians brought a dispute with an Arab dignitary over the ownership of a church before the caliph ʿUmar ibn ʿAbd al-ʿAzīz (ʿUmar II, r. 717–720), the caliph told the dignitary that if the church was one of the fifteen churches included in the treaty, he had no right to it.[32] ʿUmar II was also involved in the dispute over another church, "the church of Banū Naṣr" who had received it from the caliph Muʿawiya. ʿUmar II expelled the Banū Naṣr from it and returned it to the Christians. However, as was the case with other reforms of ʿUmar II, when Yazīd ibn ʿAbd al-Malik (r. 720–724) ascended the throne, he returned it to the Banū Naṣr.[33]

Beside the synagogue near al-Ḥayr that was included in the capitulation treaty, the Damascene Jews had another synagogue in Darb al-Balāgha that was not included in it, and hence became a mosque.[34] As to the central church *kanīsat Yūḥannā*, half of it was included in the treaty and remained in Christian hands, while the other half became the central, or Friday Mosque of Damascus. However, several decades later the caliph al-Walīd ibn ʿAbd al-Malik (r. 705–715) demolished the church and joined it to the Friday mosque.[35]

It is noteworthy that the task of demolishing the Christian half was given to the Jews – the Umayyads were probably interested in strain-

[31] Ibn ʿAsākir, *TMD*, II, 353–357.

[32] Ibn ʿAsākir, *TMD*, II, 354. The dignitary in question was Ḥassān ibn Mālik al-Kalbī who was the governor of Filasṭīn under the caliphs Muʿāwiya and Yazīd ibn Muʿāwiya.

[33] Ibid (printed *kanīsat ibn Naṣr*; but the variant reading *kanīsat ibn Naṣr* is better).

[34] Ibn ʿAsākir, *TMD*, II, 357 *(wa-kanīsatu l-yahūd ʿinda l-Khayr* [read: al-Ḥayr] *bāqiya wa-qad kānat lahum kanīsa ukhrā fī Darbi l-Balāgha lā dhikra lahā fī kitābi l-ṣulḥ juʿilat masjidan)*. For the place name al-Ḥayr see Ibn ʿAsākir, *TMD*, XL, 468. See also Ibn ʿAsākir, *TMD*, II, 297; Ibn Kathīr, *al-Bidāya wa-l-nihāya*, Beirut: Dar Iḥyāʾ al-Turāth al-ʿArabī, 1412/1992–1413/1993, 8 vols., VII, 27 (who reports about the destruction in 717/1317–1318 of a synagogue built in the Islamic period).

[35] Abū ʿUbayd al-Qāsim ibn Sallām (d. 224/839) was shown the place of the church of Damascus before it was demolished and included in the mosque; see his *al-Nāsikh wa-l-mansūkh fī l-qurʾān al-ʿazīz*, ed. Muḥammad ibn Ṣāliḥ al-Mudayfir, Riyadh: Maktabat al-Rushd, 1411/1990, 287–288, no. 525, who also reports that the above mentioned Jewish convert Kaʿb al-Aḥbār anticipated (in an eschatological context) the destruction of the chuch of Damascus and the building of a mosque on its site.

ing the relations between the Jewish and Christian communities. The official who enlisted the Jews for this task was the one in charge of land tax *(kharāj)*, which indicates that the demolition was imposed on the Jews as a kind of corvée labour.[36] It appears that 'Umar II's returning of churches to their original owners was part of a bigger scheme: when the Christians complained to 'Umar II about al-Walīd's confiscation of their church, 'Umar ordered that this wrong be remedied. But the Muslims of Damascus, including prominent jurisprudents *(fuqahā')*, protested and struck a deal with the Christians: all the churches of the Ghūṭa, or the Damascus hinterland, that had been taken from them forcibly *('anwa)* would be returned to them in return for the dropping of their claim to the church of Yūḥannā, or their half of the Friday mosque. 'Umar II ratified the deal.[37] The churches that were taken from them forcibly were those listed in the capitulation treaty. As we have just seen, 'Umar II returned two of them to their legitimate owners. However, his time in office was short.

In sum, during the Conquests many Damascene churches and synagogues became Muslim property. But even those included in the capitulation treaty were not immune from confiscation.[38]

6. *Leaders and State Officials*

Two specific *dhimmī* groups were spared the hardships of the Conquests due to the pragmatic and realistic policy of the new regime. First, the leaders of the religious communities preserved their status. The Arabs could not and would not intervene in the daily life of the non-Muslim communities that kept their autonomy and leadership. Through the existing leadership the communities were controlled

[36] Ibn 'Asākir, *TMD*, LXV, 134 (he was Yazīd ibn Tamīm ibn Ḥujr al-Sulamī, the *mawlā* or freedman of the secretarty *[kātib]* 'Ubaydallāh ibn Naṣr ibn al-Ḥajjāj ibn 'Ilāṭ al-Sulamī). See also Balādhurī, *Futūḥ*, 125 (where the identity of the labourers and the demolition experts *[al-fa'ala wa-l-naqqāḍīna]* employed by al-Walīd is not specified).

[37] Balādhurī, *Futūḥ*, 125–126.

[38] It is noteworthy that new churches (and probably new synagogues) were built after the Conquests. The Christian Sarja or Sarjūn (Sergius) who was a secretary *(kātib)* under Mu'āwiya and later caliphs had a church built for him after the Muslim conquest of Damascus. Later Mu'wiya "received his conversion to Islam", but the church remained; Ibn 'Asākir, *TMD*, XX, 161. His conversion at the hands of Mu'āwiya made him a *mawlā islām* of Mu'āwiya rather than his freedman. About Sarjūn see also Robert G. Hoyland, *Seeing Islam*, Index. One assumes that the church served relatives of his who remained Christians.

effectively.[39] Second, *dhimmī* state officials kept their posts. The Muslims preserved the taxation systems of the Sassanians and Byzantines in their respective original languages, and hence the members of the former administrations remained in their employ, be they Jewish, Christian or Zoroastrian. The conquerors were a minority in the new territories, and there was of course the language barrier. The heyday of the *dhimmī* clerks continued to the Arabization of the state apparatus under the caliph ʿAbd al-Malik, but one assumes that even after that time these clerks remained the backbone of the administration.[40] The several decades that elapsed since the Conquests allowed them to acquire whatever Arabic proficiency that was needed to run a taxation ledger.

In any case, *dhimmīs* from all communities were only tolerated as long as they knew their place in the hierarchy of power and had no political or military aspirations.

***

The Conquests brought most of the world Jewry under the rule of Islam. Jewish farmers struggling for their livelihood were pushed to the new garrison cities. However, urbanization opened new horizons for two Jewish elites: the international traders and the intellectuals. Custom dues paid by *dhimmīs* were much higher than those paid by Muslims, but few restrictions were imposed on their trade and the Conquests created for them a huge market. Intellectuals continuing a time-old

[39] Jørgen Bæk Simonsen, "Mecca and Medina. Arab city-states or Arab caravan-cities", in: Mogens Herman Hansen (ed.), *A Comparative Study of Thirty City-State Cultures: An Investigation*, Copenhagen: Kgl. Danske Videnskabernes Selskab, 2000, 241–250, at 246, argues that the policy of non-intervention was an old Arabian tradition: in Muḥammad's agreements with tribes and cities in Arabia one notices "a complete lack of political control *vis-à-vis* the tribes and cities on the peninsula on the part of Medina. In this way Medina continued the policy of its predecessor Mecca. The same policy was followed when Medina organised the conquests after Muhammad's death in 632. The expansion was successful, but the administrative system established in the conquered areas was founded solely on the experience of the caravan-city. Medina never tried to control the conquered areas directly. In Syria, Iraq and Egypt the administration was left to the local upper class, and their autonomy was extensive. In the early caliphate the central administration never interfered with local administration. If the tax-demands were met, the caliphate left matters entirely to the local administration". See also idem, *Studies in the Genesis*, 127.

[40] One must bear in mind that it was easier for the governor to discipline or even put to death a non-Arab clerk who did not have the backing of a tribe.

tradition of learning used the Arabic language in Hebrew script to create some of the cornerstones of the Jewish library for all time.

CHRISTIAN REACTIONS TO MUSLIM CONQUESTS (1ST–3RD CENTURIES AH; 7TH–9TH CENTURIES AD)

John Tolan

Michael Lecker has described varying Jewish reactions to the Muslim conquests; I will make a brief survey of how *Christians* reacted to the conquests and to finding themselves thrust into the role of *dhimmi*. This is a brief summary of a subject I have treated in greater length elsewhere, in particular in two books, *Saracens* and *Sons of Ishmael*.[1]

At first glance, of course, the position of the Christians was very different than that of Jews, both before and after the conquests: they were a ruling majority before the conquests (except in Persia) and they remained a numerical majority for several centuries after the conquest. Whereas the Jews had already a long experience of minority status under the Roman/Byzantine rule, Christians had none since the adoption of Christianity as the state religion in the late 4th century. Many Jews may have welcomed the change from Christian to Muslim rule: Jews had long been banned from living in Jerusalem and had been objects of punitive persecution for their purported role in helping the Persian invaders in the early 7th century.

Christians, one might think, could only lament the passage from dominant state religion to tolerated subservient one. Yet that depends on which Christians one asks. Miaphysites (Jacobites in Syria and Copts in Egypt) had long faced intermittent persecution from Constantinople; the Nestorians had faced harsher persecution – most of them had emigrated to Sassanian Persia. Under Muslim rule, each of these Christian communities was allowed its religious freedom and legal semi-autonomy, just as were the Greek Orthodox (Melkites).

So we in fact find a great diversity of reactions to Muslim expansion from Christian authors, depending on their particular circumstances and point of view: the Christian community they belong to, the status of *dhimmi* in Muslim-ruled lands or on the contrary inhabitant

[1] John Tolan, *Saracens: Islam in the Medieval European Imagination*, New York: Columbia University Press, 2002; *Sons of Ishmael: Muslims through European Eyes in the Middle Ages*, Gainesville: University Press of Florida, 2008.

of Byzantium or Latin Europe, and various other circumstances. But on the whole, we can roughly distinguish four overlapping phases in Christian reactions to Muslim conquest (phases we see both in Syria/Shams and, a century later, in Spain):

1. Saracen invaders portrayed as a divine scourge (seen as yet another military invader, but not as a threat spiritually or culturally)
2. Saracens painted as precursors to Antichrist (this reflected Church leaders' real fears of growing conversions to Islam)
3. Muslims as heretics with Muḥammad as a heresiarch
4. Christianity defended in the language of Muslim theology.

1. *Saracen Invaders as a Divine Scourge*

On Christmas Day, 634, the Christians of Jerusalem, unable to go to recently-conquered Bethlehem for the traditional Christmas Mass, stayed in Jerusalem and heard a sermon by their patriarch, Sophronios. He spoke of the invasions and of the fear that they struck into the hearts of Jerusalem's Christians: this was punishment for "countless sins and very serious faults."[2] Just as Adam and Eve were banished from the earthly paradise by the angel's flaming sword (Gen. 3:24), Sophronios says, so are we Christians prevented by the sword of the Saracens from approaching Bethlehem on Christmas. Just as the pagan gentile "slime" had once prevented King David from reaching Bethlehem so the "godless Saracens" now keep the Christians away.[3]

The invaders, for Sophronios, present a formidable military threat, but a negligible spiritual menace: he does not bother to find out what their religious beliefs and practices are. Rather, the invaders represent the Scourge of God so familiar to readers of the Old Testament: God, angry with His people, punishes them by sending godless barbarians to conquer them. The path to victory, as always, is repentance:

> Therefore I call on and I command and I beg you for the love of Christ the Lord, in so far as it is in our power, let us correct ourselves, let us shine forth with repentance, let us be purified by conversion and let us curb our performance of acts which are hateful to God. If we constrain

[2] Sophronius, *Christmas Sermon;* trans. Walter Kaegi, "Initial Byzantine Reactions to the Arab Conquest", *Church History* 38 (1969), 139–149.

[3] This refers to the Philistine occupation of Bethlehem in 1 Chronicles 11:16–19; 2 Samuel 23:14–17.

> ourselves, as friendly and beloved of God, we should laugh at the fall of our Saracen adversaries and we would view their not distant death, and we would see their final destruction.[4]

Sophronios looks forward to the imminent destruction of the Saracens, whose role in the divine scheme of history he limits to a brief cameo appearance as divine chastisement, an unpleasant but necessary interlude in the reign of the Christian Roman Empire.[5] Other church leaders took a similarly dim view of their new overlords. Maximus the Confessor, in a letter written from Alexandria between 634 and 640, bemoaned the losses incurred to the barbarian invaders:

> What could be direr than the present evils now encompassing the civilized world? To see a barbarous nation of the desert overrunning another land as if it were their own, to see our civilization laid waste by wild and untamed beasts who have merely the shape of a human form.[6]

These "beasts", for Maximus, are *Jews* and followers of Antichrist; this is all he tells us about their religious orientation. Repentance by Christians is what is needed to repulse the invaders.

Yet to other Christians the situation did not look so bleak. If the Melkite church (i.e., the duophysite "orthodox" church now under Muslim dominion) saw its power and prestige diminished by the Arab conquests, adherents of rival churches on the other hand seemed to breathe a collective sigh of relief. No longer subjected to pressure (and intermittent persecution) from Constantinople, they were granted broader religious freedoms by their new Muslim rulers. Sebeos, an Armenian Miaphysite, wrote in 661 that Muḥammad was learned in the law of Moses, taught the knowledge of God of Abraham to Arabs, who "abandoning the reverence of vain things, ... turned toward the living God, who had appeared to their father Abraham."[7] God granted to Arabs the lands He had promised to Abraham, and gave them victory over the impious Byzantines. Other seventh-century chroniclers

---

[4] Sophronius, *Christmas Sermon;* trans. Kaegi, *Initial Byzatine Reactions*, 141.

[5] He gives a similar view of the invasions as chastisement for Christians' sins in his *Synodal letter* (PG 87:3146–3200, at 3197D); see Christoph von Schönborn, *Sophrone* de Jerusalem: vie monastique et confession dogmatique, Paris: Beauchesne, 1972, 89–90. 100.

[6] Translation by John Lamoreaux, "Early Eastern Christian Responses to Islam", in: John Tolan (ed.), *Medieval Christian Perceptions of Islam: A Book of Essays*, New York: Garland, 1996, 3–31 (here 14–15), from PG 91:540.

[7] Quoted by Lamoreaux, *Early Eastern Christian Responses to Islam*, 19; see also Alain Ducellier, *Chrétiens d'Orient et Islam au Moyen Age*, Paris: Armand Colin 1996, 27–35.

also painted Islam in positive terms. One, having described how Abraham constructed a shrine to God in the desert, asserts: "the Arabs do nothing new when they adore God in this place, but continue the ancient usage, as is proper for people who honor the ancestor of their race."[8] Sebeos created a niche in history for the Muslim conquerors by using Daniel's four-empire scheme; contemporary Jewish authors did the same.[9] But for Sebeos the "Ishmaelites" represented not one of the horns of the beast, but the fourth beast itself, in other words, the last great world empire, an honor generally reserved for Rome.

Various Latin chronicles, written in Spain and elsewhere in Europe, portrayed the Muslim conquests and raids of the 8th and 9th centuries, in similar ways, as a divine scourge, at times presenting the loss of Spain as punishment for the sins (political infighting, sexual crimes) of the Visigothic kings and nobility.[10] Boniface, in a letter to King Ethelbald of Murcia, portrayed the Saracens invasions as punishments against the Christians of Spain and Provence for the sin of fornication.[11] Yet the Saracens were not the only such scourge: Zacharias wrote to Boniface of the "tribulation" wrought by "Saracens, Saxons, and Frisians."[12] No effort is made to distinguish the religious beliefs or practices of these groups.

2. *Saracens as Precursors to Antichrist*

In the midst of the rising tide of conversion and Arabization, a new, darker vision of God's plan was forged: the anonymous Syriac author of the *Apocalypse of Pseudo-Methodius* (c.692) presented the Muslim

[8] I am quoting this Nestorian chronicler of c.670 as translated in Claude Cahen, "Note sur l'accueil des chrétiens d'Orient à l'Islam", *Revue de l'histoire des religions* 166 (1964), 51–58 (quotation at 52–53).

[9] Norman Roth, *Jews, Visigoths and Muslims in Medieval Spain*, Leiden: Brill, 1994, 206.

[10] Tolan, *Saracens*, ch. 4.

[11] "Sicut aliis gentibus Hispaniae et Provinciae et Burgundionum populis contigit; quae sic a Deo recedentes fornicatae sunt, donec iudex omnipotens talium criminum ultrices poenas per ignorantiam legis Dei et per Sarracenos venire et saevire permisit." MGH epp. Sel 1:151. See Ekkehart Rotter, *Abendland und Sarazenen: das okzidentale Araberbild und seine Entstehung im Frühmittelalter,* Berlin: Walter de Gruyter, 1986, 230.257–258.

[12] "tribulatio … Saracinorum, Saxonum et Fresonum" Zacharias, *Epistola ad Bonifatium* MGH epp. Sel 1:123; Rotter, *Abendland und Sarazenen*, 258.

domination as part of the drama of the last days.[13] The work bears the title *Apocalypse of Pseudo-Methodius* because it purports to be the work of Methodius, Bishop of Olympas (d. c. 311). God had supposedly revealed the course of military and political history to Methodius, from Adam to the world's end. In this vision, the Muslim invasions become both the punishment God metes out to sinful Christians and the "testing furnace" meant to try the true Christians before the ultimate Christian victory. By attributing the *Apocalypse* to the respected Church father Methodius and by placing it in the fourth century, the anonymous author passes off his *descriptions* of the Muslim invasions as authoritative, divinely-inspired *predictions* of the invasions and hopes in turn to lend credibility to his predictions of imminent Christian victory over the "pagan" Ishmaelites.

The author's major preoccupation is to explain Muslim hegemony and the conversion of Christians to Islam in Christian terms. Just as God gave the Holy Land to the Jews to punish the sins of its previous inhabitants, "So too with the sons of Ishmael, it is not because God loves them that He allows them to enter into the kingdom of the Christians, the like of which has never been done in any of the former generations."[14] What are the unprecedented sins being punished? For this author, they are not Christological but sexual, described in lurid detail: men dress in drag as harlots in the market place and fornicate with each other; men take their sons and brothers to whore-houses to share the same prostitutes, men fornicate with men and women with women, etc. The punishment is described in detail as well: Methodius "predicts" the scope and magnitude of the conquests of the Ishmaelites, couching them in terms of apocalyptic destruction: rape and pillage, fire and tempered steel, and – worst of all – tribute and taxes!

Even the mass conversions of Christians to Islam is "predicted" by Methodius, as part of this "furnace of trial." Paul himself had predicted "that in the latter times some shall depart from the faith, giving heed to seducing spirits and doctrines of devils".[15] These "latter times", the

[13] *Apocalypse of Pseudo-Methodius*, Francisco J. Martinez, ed. & trans., in: *Eastern Christian Apocalyptic in the Early Muslim Period: Pseudo-Methodius and Pseudo-Athanasius* (Dissertation, Catholic University of America, 1985), 58–201; Gemit J. Reinink, "Pseudo-Methodius: A Concept of History in Response to the Rise of Islam", in: Averil Cameron/Lawrence Conrad (eds.), *The Byzantine and Early Islamic Near East* 1, Princeton: Princeton University Press, 1992, 149–187.

[14] *Apocalypse of Pseudo-Methodius*, § XI, 140.

[15] 1Timothy 4:1.

world's final days, have come; the mass, voluntary apostasy of Christians is proof of it. During this period, the *Apocalypse* makes clear, the good Christian who perseveres will suffer more persecution than the bad Christian who apostatizes. Why?

> It is so that they might be tested, and the faithful might be separated from the unfaithful, and the tares and those who are rejected from the choice wheat, because that time will be a furnace of trial. And God will be patient while His worshipers are persecuted, so that by means of the chastisement the sons might be made known, as the Apostle proclaimed beforehand, "if we are without chastisement, whereof all are partakers, then ye are bastards, and not sons".[16] This period of punishment and trial, a rod that a loving father uses to discipline his children, was almost over: God had declared that the Ishmaelites' dominion would last "ten weeks of years" – in other words, seventy years.[17] It is unclear what the author considered the beginning of the seventy-year dominion: perhaps the invasions of Syria in 634–636. The message to Christians of 692 (the probable date of composition) is clear: hang on for a few more years, patiently enduring the "furnace of trial", and you will see vindication and revenge.

A similar apocalyptic vision is given by Cordoban Paulus Alvarus, in his *Indiculus luminosus* (written in the 850s). Alvarus, writing to defend the voluntary martyrs of the Cordova martyr movement, weaves an elaborate exegetical argument to identify Muḥammad as the Antichrist, or rather as a *praecursor Antichristi*, since he affirms (in the conservative tradition of Augustine) that there are many Antichrists. In a series long and intricate exegetical calculations, he identifies Muḥammad with the eleventh king in the Prophet Daniel's description of the beast. Like Pseudo-Methodius, Alvarus seeks to convince his Christian readers that Muslims are following Antichrist, that their religion has no legitimacy; the goal is to justify the strident opposition of the voluntary martyrs as the only true Christian response to a pernicious enemy.[18] Yet the apocalyptic fear-mongering of these authors did little or nothing to stem the conversion of Christian *dhimmi* to Islam; other churchmen tried other strategies.

---

[16] *Apocalypse of Pseudo-Methodius*, § XIII, 147–148; Heb. 12:8.
[17] *Apocalypse of Pseudo-Methodius*, § V, 130; § X, 139.
[18] Tolan, *Saracens*, ch. 4.

3. *Muslims as Heretics, Muḥammad as Heresiarch*

It is in this context that John of Damascus completed, in 743, his *On the Heresies,* a erudite tract of polemics meant to describe and refute 100 heresies that have plagued Christianity since the days of the Apostles. Islam is heresy no. 100: the latest in a long line of deviant strains of Christianity. John presents Muḥammad is a false prophet and heresiarch, schooled by an Arian monk, who then concocted his own ridiculous doctrine which he set down in writing.

What is absurd and risible in Islam, for John, is its rejection of the divinity of Christ, of the crucifixion, and of other fundamental Christian doctrines. Here John turns and interrogates a hypothetical Muslim adversary, asking him to produce witnesses to prove the legitimacy of the prophet's revelation. He contrasts Muḥammad to Moses, who received the law on Mount Sinai in full view of the people. Your law requires witnesses for weddings, land sales, and other transactions; why do you not ask for witnesses to prove that the Koran is truly revealed by God? Such arguments are unlikely to convince a real Muslim, who could retort that Christians accept the Gospels and the books of the Hebrew Prophets without any witnesses. The very lack of theological sophistication in this argument shows that this is not so much *polemical* (i. e., an offensive attack on Islam) as *apologetical* (a defensive strategy designed to slow down the defection of Christians to the Muslim camp). John seems to be furnishing arguments that could be deployed by Christians wishing to defend their faith to Muslim interlocutors and is certainly not offering an attack which Muslim thinkers could take seriously. He needs to convince his reader of the efficacy and irrefutability of his arguments, in response to which, he asserts, his Muslim opponents were "surprised and at a loss"; "they remain silent because of shame".[19] The practical, defensive nature of his apologetics becomes even clearer in the two sections that follow, offering aggressive counter-arguments against two common Muslim objections to Christianity. "They call us *associators*, because, they say, we introduce beside God an associate to Him by saying that Christ

---

[19] John of Damascus, *Liber de haeresibus*, in: P. Bonifatius Kotter (ed.), *Die Schriften des Johannes von Damaskos* (5 vols.; Berlin, 1969–1981), 4:62; english translation by Daniel Sahas, *John of Damascus on Islam: The "Heresy of the Ishmaelites"*, Leiden: Brill, 1972, 134–135.

is the Son of God and God".[20] John responds with two arguments, defensive and offensive. First, the defensive argument: the prophets announced Christ's coming and the Gospels confirmed it; if we are wrong, they are wrong. Second, the offensive argument:

> Again we respond to them: "Since you say the Christ is Word and Spirit of God, how do you scold us as *associators*? For the Word and the Spirit is inseparable each from the one in whom this has the origin; if, therefore, the Word is in God it is obvious that he is God as well. If, on the other hand, this is outside of God, then God, according to you, is without word and without spirit. Thus, trying to avoid making associates to God you have mutilated Him ... Therefore, by accusing us falsely, you call us *associators;* we, however, call you *mutilators* (κσπτας) of God".[21]

In other words, by depriving the divinity of the Word and the Spirit, Muslim "mutilators" deprive God of his key attributes. Such Trinitarian arguments, based on triads of divine attributes, are to become standard fare in Christian polemic against Islam. Here John gives a simplified version of such an argument, primarily, it seems, to provide the Christian with a handy insult word to bandy back against any Muslim who accuses him of being an associator.

For Byzantine chronicler Theophanes, Muḥammad is "the leader and false prophet of the Saracens".[22] Theophanes claims that the Jews had first flocked to Muḥammad, thinking he was their long-awaited Messiah; when they saw him eating camel (a forbidden food), they realized their error, yet some of them stayed with him out of fear "and taught him illicit things directed against us, Christians".[23] Theophanes describes Muḥammad's marriage to Khadîja and his travels in Palestine where he sought out the writings of Jews and Christians. Muḥammad had an epileptic seizure, and at this Khadîja became distressed; he soothed her by telling her: "I keep seeing a vision of a certain angel called Gabriel, and being unable to bear his sight, I faint

[20] John of Damascus, *Liber de haeresibus*, in: *Die Schriften des Johannes von Damaskos* 4:63; Sahas, *John of Damascus*, 134–139.

[21] John of Damascus, *Liber de haeresibus*, in: *Die Schriften des Johannes von Damaskos* 4:63–64; Sahas, *John of Damascus*, 136–137.

[22] Theophanes, *Chronographia* 333–334; Theophanes. English translation by Cyril Mango/Roger Scott, *The Chonicle of Theophanes the Confessor,* Oxford: Clarendon Press, 1997, 464–465. It is unclear what Theophanes' sources of information about Muḥammad; see Anne Proudfoot, "The Sources of Theophanes for the Heraclian Period", *Byzantion* 44 (1974), 367–439; esp. 386.

[23] Theophanes, *Chronographia* 333; Mango/Scott trans., 464.

and fall down".[24] Khadîja sought the advice of "a certain monk living there, a friend of hers (who had been exiled for his depraved doctrine)"; this heretical monk seems to be based on the Muslim legends around Waraqa and Bahira.[25] The monk told Khadîja that Muḥammad was indeed a prophet to whom the Angel Gabriel came in visions. With such beginnings, his "heresy" soon was spread by force. Theophanes recounts that Muḥammad promised to all who fell fighting the enemy a paradise full of sensual delights: eating, drinking, and sex. He said "many other things full of profligacy and stupidity"[26] Eulogius of Cordova, like his ninth-century contemporary Alvarus, was an apologist for the Cordovan martyr movement (and martyr himself in 859). He again shows that categories of heresiarch and Antichrist overlap. In 850, Eulogius travels to Navarra; in the monastery of Leyre, he discovers a brief biography of Muḥammad in a Latin manuscript. He copies it and includes it in his *Liber apologeticus martyrum*. This short text shows some knowledge of Islam: it describes Muḥammad's marriage with Khadîja, the role of Gabriel in the revelation of the Qur'an, the titles of various Qur'anic Suras, and Muḥammad's marriage to Zaynab. All of these events, however, are presented in the worst possible light, twisted almost beyond recognition by the hostile pen of the author. Muḥammad's death is described in a manner which has nothing to do with Muslim tradition, but comes straight out of Christian traditions about Antichrist: before dying, Muḥammad predicts that the third day after his death the archangel Gabriel will come to bring him back from the dead. This is course fails to happen; his disciples decide finally to abandon his cadaver; dogs, not angels come.[27]

4. *Christianity Defended in the Language of Muslim Theology*

Other churchmen, however, sought less to stem the tide of conversion than to justify and defend their own role as *dhimmi* in Muslim soci-

---

[24] Theophanes, *Chronographia* 334; Mango/Scott trans., 464. Theophanes is the first author to charge Muḥammad of being an epileptic, an accusation that will be repeated by many later polemicists; see Astérios Argyriou, "Éléments biographiques concernant le prophète Muḥammad dans la littérature grecque des trois premiers siècles de l'Hégire", in: Toufic Fahd (ed.), *La vie du prophète Mahomet: Colloque de Strasbourg (octobre 1980)*, Paris, 1983, 160–182, esp. 168; Ducellier, *Chrétiens d'Orient*, 127.

[25] See Tolan, *Saracens*, ch. 2.

[26] Theophanes, *Chronographia* 334; Mango/Scott trans., 464–465.

[27] See Tolan, *Saracens*, ch. 4; Tolan, *Sons of Ishmael*, ch. 1.

ety. They sought less to attack Islam through polemics than to defend Christianity through apologetics. While John of Damascus portrayed Muslim doctrine from a Greek Christian perspective as a Christological heresy, Theodore Abû Qurrah (d. c. 820) attempted to justify Christianity in the terms of Muslim theology. Some of Abû Qurrah's works show a practical, apologetic aim: he denies that Islam had supplanted or abrogated Christianity in God's favor just as Christianity had supplanted Judaism[28] he defends Christian veneration of images against the charge of Idolatry.[29] He wrote his *Refutation of Outsiders*, he says, because when he came out of the Church of the Holy Sepulcher in Jerusalem with some friends, a group of Muslims accosted them and began questioning them about their faith. Theodore's *On True Religion* is much more ambitious: it purports to prove the superiority of Christianity over other religions through rational, objective criteria.[30]

Abû Qurrah starts with a philosophical proof of the creation of the universe and of the existence of a creator, God. His point of departure is a Neoplatonic view of the universe: the effects of God as creator are evident in the order and harmony among the elements of the universe. He concludes that God as cause must be greater than his effects: he must be eternal, unchanging, good, wise, etc.: here he provides a long list of the divine attributes commonly accorded to God by Muslim thinkers. Having established certain truths about God from a rational, non-sectarian perspective, he then asks which religion is true: he briefly describes each of nine prominent religions. Only one of these religions can be true, he says, but how are we to tell which one? He imagines a man from a remote mountainous region coming down into a city, seeing that people have different religions, and trying to determine which one he should choose. He proposes to compare the scriptural tenets of each of these religions with the philosophical truths about God enumerated in the beginning of his treatise. Unsurprisingly, he will conclude that only Christianity is consistent with what an objective, philosophically-minded person can ascertain about God.

[28] Sahas, *John of Damascus*, 157–159; on the common charge of abrogation *(naskh)* see c35–41.

[29] Griffith, "Theodore Abû Qurrah's Arabic Tract on the Christian Practice of Venerating Images", *Journal of the American Oriental Society* 105 (1985), 66–67.

[30] On this text, see Sydney Griffith, "Faith and Reason in Christian Kalâm: Theodore Abû Qurrah on Discerning the True Religion", in: Samir Khalil Samir/Jørgen S. Nielsen (eds.), *Christian Arabic Apologetics during the Abbasid Period (750–1258)*, Leiden: Brill, 1994, 1–43.

His arguments are both apologetical (in defense of the Trinity, for example) and polemical: he criticizes Islam for condoning violence and for promising sensual rewards in this life and the next. Islam, like most other religions, spread with the military and political power of its adherents; base, worldly reasons (political ambition, greed, etc.) play a prominent role in encouraging conversions to Islam. Not so for Christianity, says Abû Qurrah: it spread far and wide despite the best efforts of the Romans to extinguish it; this shows that its adherents are inspired only by a desire for God and for the rewards of the world to come, not by earthly ambitions.[31]

Abû Qurrah's *On True Religion* rejects Islam's spiritual claims directly and unequivocally. Yet it does so in a very different way from the other texts we have examined. Abû Qurrah places himself in a (fictional) non-sectarian viewpoint and attempts to prove the superiority of Christianity in rational, objective terms. While John of Damascus portrayed Islam in Melkite terms as a Christological heresy, Abû Qurrah attempts to justify Christianity through the vocabulary and ideas of the *mutakallimûn* of 'Abassid Baghdad. He calmly accepts the existence of Islam on the political and social level: we are all seekers of truth, he seems to be saying to Muslims; you just happen to be wrong. Abû Qurrah, like the anonymous Christian who wrote the first Arab apology for Christianity a few years earlier, was an Arab who thought and wrote using the vocabulary of the Koran and the intellectual categories of his Muslim contemporaries.[32] The Muslim intellectuals of Baghdad are not the horrible barbarians of Sophronios or Pseudo-Methodius; they are his companions. Yet they are companions who have erroneously picked the wrong religion for understandable but insufficient reasons. Islam is the religion of enjoyment of this world; Christianity is the religion of the next. In this way, it seems, Abû Qurrah hopes to persuade his Christian readers to remain faithful to Christianity while at the same time explain to them the success of Islam.

In ninth-century Spain, Paulus Alvarus had fulminated against Christian youths who preferred Arabic poetry to Latin letters; his own son, it seems, composed Arabic poems. Hafs ibn Albar, according to

---

[31] This same line of argumentation is taken by the anonymous author of an earlier Arabic apology for Christanity; see Samir Khalil Samir, "The Earliest Arab Apology for Christianity (c. 750)", in: Samir Khalil Samir/Jørgen S. Nielsen (eds.), *Christian Arabic Apologetics during the Abbasid Period (750–1258)*, Leiden: Brill, 1994, 103.

[32] Samir, *The Earliest Arab Apology for Christianity.*

one of his Muslim contemporaries, was the most intelligent and most arabized of the Andalusian Christians. af translated the Psalms from Latin into Arabic verse. He also composed a *Book of Fifty-Seven Questions*, an Arabic apology of Christianity which (although it is now lost) seems to have been much less virulent than his father's.[33] Rather than vilifying Islam, as had his father, he crafted apologetical works which aimed to defend and justify Christianity in the eyes of both Christians and Muslims.[34] Mozarab Christians had found the spirit of polite apologetical dialogue familiar to oriental Christians.

We hence see roughly the same range of reactions to Muslim conquest and dominion in Christian Spain in the eighth and ninth centuries that we saw in the East in the seventh and eighth. The Muslims are initially portrayed above all as a scourge sent by God to punish wayward Christians, subsequently as a player in the drama of the eschaton, then as heretical followers of the heresiarch Muḥammad. Finally, minority dhimmi Christians seek to defend their place in Muslim society through apologetics.

---

[33] Fragments of *Book of Fifty-Seven Questions* survive in al-Qurtubî's *al-I'lâm*, a thirteenth-century work of anti-Christian polemic. On Hafs' ibn Albar, see van Koningsveld, "Christian Arabic Literature from Medieval Spain: an Attempt at Periodization", in: Samir/Nielsen (eds.), *Christian Arabic Apologetics*, 203–204, esp. 206–212; Hafs' Ibn Albar, *Le Psautier mozarabe de Hafs le Goth*, Marie-Thérèse Urvoy, ed. & trans., Toulouse: Presses Universitaires du Mirail, 1994; D. Dunlop, "Hafs' ibn Albar, the Last of the Goths?", *Journal of the Royal Asiatic Society* (1954), 136–151; idem, "Sobre af ibn Albar al-Qûtî Al-Qurtubî," *Al-Andalus* 20 (1955), 211–213. On al-Qurtubî's use of af ibn Albar, see Burman, *Religious Polemic*, 158–160.

[34] This distinction between polemics and apologetics corresponds to the one drawn by Millet-Gérard between "polémique fermée" and "polémique ouverte" (*Chrétiens mozarabes,* 173).

INTERCULTURAL ENCOUNTER IN THE HISTORY OF POLITICAL THOUGHT CHRISTIAN WOLFF, CHŎNG YAG-YONG AND MATTEO RICCI

Eun-jeung Lee

1. *Encounter between Catholicism and Confucianism*

Even before East Asia came under the sway of European imperialism, an important exchange of ideas and culture had taken place between Europe and East Asia. To give an example, Chinese porcelain and styles became very fashionable in Europe during the 17th and 18th century. This fascination with China became known in the history of art and culture as Chinoiserie, yet it also had an impact in the fields of philosophy, religion and political thought.[1] In fact, it also had a remarkable impact on East Asia. H. G. Creel, a well-known sinologist, holds that this was the beginning of modernity in China.[2] This might be somewhat exaggerated, but there is little doubt that Western thought had a strong impact on the philosophy and religion of East Asia. Thus, the encounter between Europe and East Asia that began during the European Enlightenment left its mark in Europe as well as in East Asia. In this paper, I will exemplify this encounter in the thought of two thinkers, namely Christian Wolff (1679–1754) und Chŏng Yag-yong (1762–1836).

Christian Wolff together with Gottfried Wilhelm Leibniz was a key figure in Europe's philosophical encounter with Confucianism. His speech on the "Practical Philosophy of the Chinese" in 1721 was a heyday in the positive reception of Confucianism in Germany. Chŏng Yag-yong, on the other hand, was a Korean thinker and philosopher

---

[1] Lee, Eun-jeung: *"Anti-Europa". Die Geschichte der Rezeption von Konfuzianismus und der konfuzianischen Gesellschaft in Europa seit der frühen Aufklärung,* Münster: Lit Verlag, 2003.

[2] Creel, Herrlee G.: *Confucius, the Man and the Myth*, Seoul: Hangilsa, 1949 (Korean Edition from 1983), 290.

and is considered a pioneer of Korean modernity. He was the first scholar in Korea to adopt the Catholic faith.

The most important link in the encounter between East Asia and Europe was Matteo Ricci. He was the founder of the Jesuit mission in China. Through his method of accommodation, his aim was to harmonise the spiritual bases of Chinese and European philosophy.[3]

Both Christian Wolff and Chŏng Yag-yong were greatly impressed by Matteo Ricci's writings on China, Confucianism and, respectively, on European religion, philosophy and science. It is not the purpose of this paper to corroborate a direct line of causality between the ways of thinking of these scholars, nor to present a comprehensive analysis of the impacts and effects of each case. Instead, I will focus on the contexts within which imported ideas were articulated with the thought of Wolff and Chŏng. This is not a matter of discussing whether the interpretations of these two authors were right or wrong, which, at least in the case of Confucianism, is practically impossible, as Confucianism, because of its discursive character, allows for many interpretations. Instead, I will try to determine the place and function of alien concepts in the thought of these two thinkers.

2. *Discursive Properties of Confucianism and Matteo Ricci*

In his treatise "The True Meaning of the Lord of Heaven" *(Tianzhu shiyi)*, published in 1595, Ricci makes frequent references to Chinese classics and distinguishes between the original thought of Confucius and the materialism of the then dominant Neo-Confucian school of Zhu Xi, also called Xingli School, which, in his opinion, had been influenced by Buddhism.

Ricci criticises Chu Hsi by means of Aristotelian metaphysics and Thomist logic in the sense that the founding principle *li* could not be identical to the creator of the world order, as it did not even have any substance itself, but and merely was an element dependent on things (Dinge).[4] He maintains that Zhu Xi's thought not only was completely alien to Christian thought, but that furthermore, the former did not even have a basis in the Confucian classics. Based on this discrepancy,

[3] Widmaier, Rita: "Nachwort zum Buch", in: id. (ed.): *Leibniz korrespondiert mit China. Der Briefwechsel mit den Jesuitenmissionaren (1689–1714)*, Frankfurt a. M.: Klostermann 1990, 271.

[4] Ricci 1999, chap. 2–8, 87–89.

Ricci works out a compromise, or to be more precise, a harmonious relationship between Christian and Confucian thought. In this effort, he uses extrinsic elements of both bodies of thought and articulates them as intrinsic moments of a discursive construction.[5] Without hesitation he uses the terms "*shangdi*" (the Supreme God) and "*tian*" (heaven) of Chinese classic texts for the Christian God he was promulgating himself. He requests the Chinese to return to the classic texts of Confucius and Mencius, which, in his view, had expressed monotheism with great clarity.[6]

Matteo Ricci acts in the discursive field of the Chinese Confucian scholars of his time.[7] He introduces new, alien elements into this field and articulates them with his religious-missionary ambitions. The early successes of the Jesuit missionaries to no small extent were due to Ricci's extraordinary ability to present his arguments in such a way that the scholarly Confucian elite was attracted to his mission. Besides, when Ricci arrived in China in 1583, the country was involved in a period of profound political and intellectual debate and change.

It is well within the spiritual needs of the time that Ricci accused Buddhism of having spoiled the old Chinese tradition and placed emphasis on moral strengths and scientific knowledge. The polemic against the political influence of Buddhism became the constitutive outside for the articulation of Christian and Confucian elements in a novel type of discourse. The resonance Ricci found among the Chinese literati was due to this specific insertion into the contemporary discourses in China. He understood the discursive field of the Chinese State and in fact had become an actor within this field. The same can be said of Chŏng Yag-yong who acted in the discursive field of Chosŏn/Korea of his time.

When Christian Wolff studied the Jesuit texts on Confucianism and China, he did not know the discursive field of the Jesuits in China. As could not be otherwise, his reception of Ricci's writings took place within the European context only. Knowingly or not, he extricated

[5] Ricci, cf. Wiesinger, Liselotte: "Die Anfänge der Jesuitenmission und die Anpassungsmethode des Matteo Ricci", in: *China und Europa.* Catalogue for the exhibition from 16.9. to 11.11. 1973 in Schloß Charlottenburg, Berlin: Verwaltung der Staatlichen Schlösser und Gärten 1973, 12–17, here 15.

[6] Ricci 1999, chap. 4-1, 154–159.

[7] Bourdieu's concept of "field" is a multidimensional space of social relations, within which specific field effects occur. Within them conflicts occur; they are places for permanent change with open outcomes (cf. Rüdiger, Axel: *Staatslehre und Staatsbildung*, Tübingen: Niemeyer, 2005, 25).

these texts from their original discursive field and transferred them into the European and German field of political thought and eruditeness. Confucianism became articulated in a specific manner in the European/German context. It was transformed into something different and gained a new cultural significance. Because the constitutive conditions of discursive fields diverge, it is futile to ask whether Wolff's interpretation of Confucianism is correct or not.

3. *Confucianism and Political Reform*

3.1. *Christian Wolff's Reception of Confucianism in the Context of Enlightened Absolutism*

According to Wolff himself, the books of Father Noël, a Jesuit who had been sent to China[8], aroused his interest in China. Wolff tries to understand, order and evaluate the basic notions of Confucianism within the frame of his philosophical and political thought.[9] The result is an interesting symbiosis of Confucian and his own political philosophy, which was to exercise considerable influence on the German and European reception of Confucianism.[10]

Unlike Thomas Morus and Campanella, Wolff did not construct a utopian state, which could have served as a point of reference for the appraisal of existing states.[11] Instead, his endeavour was to design an ideal State, which could serve as a practical model for the existing real states of his time. The Chinese State based on Confucian philosophy, as he had perceived it in the writings of Noël, appeared to be an exem-

[8] Cf. Ching, Julia/Oxtoby, Willard G.: *Moral Enlightenment: Leibniz and Wolff on China*, Nettetal: Steyler, 1992, 15.

[9] Because of the affinity of Wolff's philosophy and Chinese thought, Wolff believed that he had a better grasp of the Chinese texts than the Jesuit interpreters (cf. Albrecht, Michael: *Einleitung zu Wolffs Oratio de Sinarum philosophia practica (1721)*, Hamburg: Meiner Felix Verlag, 1985, IX–XXXIX, here XVII.

[10] Lee 2003, 637.

[11] Political utopias flourished in Europe for more than two centuries. Humanist dreams were cast into "wonderful new worlds", for example by Thomas More (*Utopia*, 1516), Tommaso Campanella (*Civitas solis*, 1633), Francis Bacon (*The New Atlantis*, 1627), James Harrington (*Oceana*, 1656), Cyrano de Bergerac (*Voyage dans la lune*, 1657), François de Salignac de la Mothe Fénelon (*Télémaque*, 1699), Jean-Jacques Rousseau (*La Nouvelle Héloise*, 1761), Denis Diderot (*Supplément au Voyage de Bougainville*, 1772), Louis Sébastien Mercier (*L'an deux mille quatre cent quarante*, 1770). Cf. Saage, Richard: *Politische Utopie der Neuzeit*, Darmstadt: Wissenschaftliche Buchgesellschaft, 1990.

plary embodiment of an ideal State. What Wolff therefore did was to integrate the example of the Chinese State as a model of an ideal state into his political philosophy.

For Wolff, monarchy was the best possible and most readily realisable form of the state for his time and age. As a result, he is often accused of having blind faith in the authority of the state, which supposedly is an outgrowth of his sinophilism. As I have shown elsewhere, such views of Wolff need to be corrected, as they miss the kernel of Wolff's state theory and of his admiration for China.

What Wolff articulates in his theory of the state is by no means a plea for despotism, but an invitation to political reform, which, if it had been realised, would have involved dramatic changes in the political and social conditions of his time. For him the decisive lever was not the specific forms of political representation of political authority (monarchy, aristocratic rule, democracy), but questions of the practical organisation of government and public administration. This does not exclude in his view a strong monarchic sovereign, as long as he promotes the necessary reforms of the State. The reformist potential of Wolff becomes very apparent when he writes about the thoroughly rational administrative system in China. With all his sympathy, he endorses the Chinese practice of assigning public offices according to personal merits, yet not by birth and descent. Such practice, he writes, is in complete accordance with natural law.[12]

Wolff vehemently rejects German feudal society. In his opinion, prerogatives based on descent were not in accordance with natural law. For the same reason he rejected rules limiting marriage to people within the same social class.

Wolff's enthusiasm was not limited to the Chinese model of a meritocratic government, but included his admiration for the Chinese educational system. The influence of philosophy as a form of political knowledge depends, as Plato had argued in his Dialogues, on the importance of an educational system for the reproduction of political power.

For Wolff, in China school is a place where a certain form of political knowledge is generated. While the successful acquisition of this knowledge forms the basis for the advancement into the political class, it too is related to the common good. Wolff calls this knowledge in

[12] Wolff 1972, §. 212.

the tradition of Plato "philosophy". It invokes canonised texts and can relieve philosophy from its subordinated status with respect to the dominating classes and to other bodies of knowledge like theology. Wolff notes the emancipation of philosophy in China from the status of an odd and unbefitting servant of theology, jurisprudence and medicine to the only legitimate representation of the common good. Through education and certificates of education, the citizen can rise into the administrative and political class. Similarly, the educational system does not only foster abstract knowledge, but also a certain political attitude and a certain political habitus. It brings about a political structure, in which philosophical education determines the rank of a person. It opens the way for the idea of the enlightened state, in which the educated *"State nobility"* (Pierre Bourdieu) occupies positions of responsibility; a state that creates the possibility of the rational representation of the common good through the sovereign. Wolff demonstrates how in China the "*State nobility*" is not recruited by birth and descent, but through state examinations open to any intellectually gifted person. Hence, for Wolff the primacy of the educational principle and of governance by the citizens' Amtsadel had become reality in China. Wolff, himself a member of the rising literate bourgeoisie in Germany, admires and lauds China for this achievement of having realised in a practical manner an ideal state.

For Wolff it is a matter of course that the authority and power of the sovereign are structured in direct analogy to private households. He invokes Confucius who taught that in order to govern a state one only has to follow the well-proven principles individuals and families apply in everyday life. The state is nothing more than a large family, and the King is no more than the head of this family.[13]

One might say that the combination of the enlightened philosophical discourse on education and of the patriarchal model of the household is an articulation of rationalism with sovereign patrimonialism into a type of "enlightened absolutism".

Neither in Wolff's nor in Confucian state philosophy can the authority of the sovereign be legitimised by mere recourse to the patriarchal relationship. The sovereign cannot determine the norms of behaviour. This is something the Law of Nature does in Wolff's and the *Dao* in Confucius' thinking.

---

[13] Wolff 1983, §. 6.

In the final analysis, it is the Law of Nature, which according to Wolff allows human beings to practice virtue and to avoid vice. This requires that human beings are able to recognise this law and to rely on the "doctrine of nature".[14] For Wolff, the Chinese have provided proof that this is possible. The Chinese did not have a notion of the "creator of the world" nor "testimonies of divine revelation." Therefore, "they could only rely on the doctrine of nature". And "they used this doctrine – as a part of the inheritance of the likeness of God – most successfully and distinguish themselves through the fame of their virtue and wisdom".[15]

Pietistic theologians ventured against Wolff's rational substantiation of the Law of Nature, because for him it could exist even in the absence of god. They therefore accused him of atheism. As a result, on November 8 1723, the king issued a cabinet decree, which ordered Wolff to leave the country within 48 hours, or face the gallows. In this way, the battle between the primacy of ontology and that of epistemology was decided, at least for the time being.

When feudalism in Germany had not yet vanished and the bourgeoisie was economically still weak and without political influence, Christian Wolff believed that the sovereigns could be convinced of the need for reforms. In this context, Confucian China was a welcome and positive example supporting his proposals for the reform of the state and administration. Yet, as the unwillingness of the sovereigns to engage in reforms as conceived by Wolff, who was a very popular and widely read author at that time, was demonstrated over and over again, the resentment towards the feudal order grew. As a result, not only the power of the sovereign, but also the political theory which wanted to reform it from within, became the focus of popular discontent. The Confucian philosophy, as part of Wolff's theory, thus fell under the verdict of the changing times. Thereafter China came to symbolise the Orient, taking the former position of Turkey as the counter image of European modernity.

---

[14] Wolff 1985, 33.
[15] Wolff 1985, 33.

3.2. *Chŏng Yag-yong's Reception of "Western Science" and the Hopes for a Reform King*

Chŏng Yag-yong learned about the culture of the West, in particular its religion *(sŏgyo)* and its science *(sŏhak)* through China.[16] Translations of European academic books into Chinese had been known in Chosŏn/Korea since the early 17th century. In the 18th century, a large number of Western books on philosophy and natural sciences had become available in Korea.[17]

The knowledge about Western religion *(sŏgyo)* was so widespread that scholars belonging to Yi Yik's (1682–1764) so-called *Sŏngho School*, could engage in a fervid debate on the Catholic concept of god.[18] Matteo Ricci had postulated that the Catholic god, *chŏnju* in Korean, was identical with the Confucian lord of heaven, *shangje*. Some members of this school, among them Sin Hu-dam (1702–1761) and An Chŏng-bok (1712–1791), rejected such claims. Their point of departure was the traditional *hua-i* distinction. It readily allowed them to formulate a critique of Western religion based on Confucian thought. On the other hand, scholars around Kwŏn Ch'ŏl-sin (1731–1801) of the so-called *Left Sŏngho School* went to such lengths as to form the first of Catholic community in Korea. Chŏng Yag-yong was a member of this group.

While Chŏng Yag-yong was writing his treatise Chungyung *(Chungyong kangŭi)* in 1784, he was involved in extensive discussions with Yi Byŏk (1754–1786). The core of this thinking is shaped by a

[16] *Sŏhak* did not have a precise meaning. Sometimes it stands for all Western science, including religion, sometimes a separate term is used for the Catholic faith *(sŏgyo)*.

[17] Between 1591, the year Matteo Ricci arrived in China, and 1773, the year the Jesuit order was disbanded, the missionaries had translated a total of 437 books from the West into Chinese. Of these, 251 books dealt with matters of religion, 55 with the humanities and 131 with natural sciences. According to Ro T'ae-hwan, approximately 100 books on the humanities and natural sciences became known in Chosŏn/Korea (Ro, T'ae-hwan: "Chŏngjo sidae sŏgi suyong nonŭi-wa sŏhak chŏngch'aek" [Debate on the Reception of Western Technique and on Policies toward Western science during the reign of of King Chŏngjo], in: Chŏng, Ok-cha et al. (eds.): *Chŏngjo sidae sasang-gwa munhwa [Philosphy and Culture during the Reign of King Chŏngjo]*, Seoul: Tolbaegae, 1999, 201–245, here 208.

[18] This debate began with a review of Ricci's book *Tienzhu shiyi* by Yi Yik. He wrote: "His science serves alone *chŏnju*. Although *Chŏnju* is the god *shangje* of Confuzianism, the way *chŏnju* is revered and served, instills fears and is believed in, is similar to Shakyamuni in Buddhism." (Yi Yik, *Chŏnjubalŭisilmun*, in: Matteo Ricci, *Tienzhu shiyi*, translated by Song Yŏng-bae, Seoul et al.: Seoul National University Press 2006, 435–448, here 435–436).

critique of the Neo-Confucian idea of the "unity of man and heaven" *(ch'ŏnin habil)* and by the concepts of *li* and *qi (yigiron)*. On this basis, he developed a specific worldview and a practical morality and ethics.

Chŏng Yag-yong's point of departure is the same as that of Matteo Ricci, that is, the concept of soul of Aristotle.[19] He distinguishes between human beings, who are able to feel, perceive and make rational judgements, and animals, which are able to perceive the world, yet are unable to think, and finally plants, which merely are able to grow.[20] While Ricci used this argument in order to promote his missionary interests, Chŏng Yag-yong, in particular through his egalitarianism, puts it forward as a fundamental challenge to orthodox Neo-Confucianism.

Just like Ricci, Chŏng Yag-yong criticises the Neo-Confucian theory of the unity of the nature of all things, including mankind *(inmulsŏngdongron)*.[21] In terms of Zhu Xi's Neo-Confucianism, all men and all things are equal with respect to the principle *(li)*, while differences arise merely in terms of their material condition *(qi)*. Chŏng Yag-yong cannot quite agree with this. If Zhu Xi's enunciation is to be understood in the sense that the only difference between man and things lies in *qi*, while both receive the same *li* from heaven, then this distinction could not be found in original Confucian thought. Instead, it could only be an emanation from Buddhism, as the latter postulates the homogeneity of all things and preaches reincarnation.[22]

Comparing the approach of Chŏng Yag-yong with that of Ricci, it is readily apparent that both base their arguments on Neo-Confucianism and Buddhism as a "constitutive outside", while the thrust of their arguments is quite different.

Chŏng Yag-yong argues that the Neo-Confucian scholars, who believe that virtue and non-virtue are both a gift from heaven, would just sit in front of a wall and expect their minds to be enlightened by

---

[19] Ricci, *Tienzhu shiyi*, Vol. 1, Ch. 3, Dialogue 3–3: "The souls of this world fall into 3 categories. … The highest one is the human soul." (Ricci 2006, 124).

[20] Chŏng Yag-yong, Yŏyudang chŏnsŏ [Yŏyudang Schriftensammlung], II, Nonŏ kogŭmju, Vol. 9, 338: "Among all ephemeral beings of this world there are 3 categories: 1) Plants have the faculty of growth, yet do not have the faculty of cognition; 2) animals have the faculty of cognition, yet do not have the faculty of reason; 3) human beings have the faculty of growth, cognition and reason."

[21] M. Ricci, *Tianzhu shiyi*, Vol. 1, Ch. 4, Dialogue 4–5, 4–6 (Ricci 2006, 175–184).

[22] Cf. Chŏng Yag-yong, Yŏyudang chŏnsŏ, II, Chungyong Kangŭibo Vol. 1, 83; Nonŏ kogŭmju, Vol. 9, 339.

li (*kŏgyŏng kungli:* to sit in front of a wall and ponder about the true principle).

It is useful to consider the social and cultural significance of *kŏgyŏng kungli.* This is in reality a highly intellectual act. Its pursuit requires a solid economic basis and plenty of time. Therefore, *kŏgyŏng kungli* simply was far beyond the possibilities of normal people struggling to survive. Precisely for this reason, the Confucian predilection for reflections on the nature of man and virtue was the monopoly of a tiny elite. Chŏng Yag-yong's critique is aimed at this implicit elitism of Zhu Xi and of Neo-Confucianism in general.[23]

Chŏng Yag-yong's own egalitarian approach is clearly discernable from his thinking on virtue. In principle, human beings possess reason and a free will. Therefore, they can commit good deeds as well as bad ones. Chŏng Yag-yong, just like Matteo Ricci, believes that virtue only exists in human beings and not in animals and plants.

As human beings tend to commit bad deeds from time to time and as it is difficult to do good deeds all the time, it necessary to have a personified god, *shangje*, who through his authority and wisdom can supervise human behaviour. Because of the mere existence of god, Chŏng Yag-yong says, human beings cannot do anything bad because they are aware that god observes them even during darkness.[24] Chŏng Yag-yong's concept of god has one revolutionary connotation that cannot be found in Ricci: he undermines the Sino-centrism underlying Neo-Confucian thought of the Chŏson Dynasty.

When Chŏng Yag-yong says that all human beings are responsible towards god, *shangje*, for their deeds, he also means that all human beings are existentially able to communicate with god. This is possible because all human beings have the intellectual capacity to think rationally. These human beings serve god by means of rituals, come to know him through time, accompany him and live according to the principles of heavenly virtue.[25] Therefore, Chŏng says in his moral philosophy that all human beings are obliged to adhere to the rites for

[23] Cf. Ch'a, Sŏng-hwan: *Kŭllobŏl sidae Chŏng Yag-yong segyegwan-ŭi kanŭngsŏng-gwa han'gye* [Global Age and the Thought of Chŏng Yag-yong. Potentials and Limitations], Seoul: Chimmundang, 2002, 133.

[24] Chŏng Yag-yong, Yŏyudang chŏnsŏ, II, Chungyongjagam, Vol. 3, Korean Edition 1, 206.

[25] Chŏng Yag-yong, Yŏyudang chŏnsŏ, II, Chungyongjagam Vol. 3, Korean Edition 1, 202.204.224–225.227.

shangje. Precisely at this point, he negates one of the basic pillars of the neo-Confucian philosophy of the Chŏson Dynasty.

In Chŏson, not everybody was allowed to perform rites. This was a privilege of the king and of the *yangban* (those with the highest status by birth in society). Even the right to perform the rites for ancestors was restricted. Performing the rites for heaven was the prerogative of the Chinese king. The kings of China's tributary states (Chŏson was one of them) were not allowed to perform these rites. Under such an order of things, Chŏng Yag-yong spoke of a god, which every human being should serve and obey, a god, which everyone could approach. In the context of Chŏson's Neo-Confucian society, this was a revolutionary proposal, because it called into question the legitimacy of Sino-centrism and the prevalent social order.

Chŏng Yag-yong writes: "Heaven does not ask whether someone is a public official or a commoner"[26] and emphasises that all men and women are equal in the face of god.[27] He wishes that all men and women of the country would become *yangban* – which obviously would be the end of the *yangban* class.[28]

The writings of Matteo Ricci were of fundamental importance for the development of the views of the young Chŏng Yag-yong on man and society. Western science and religion helped him to discover new veins of thought in the context of changing Chŏson society. In this sense, the role of Western science and religion in Chŏng Yag-yong thinking played a similar role to the one of Confucianism in Christian Wolff's thought. In contrast to Wolff, Chŏng Yag-yong did not make any explicit references to sources that had inspired him. This is due to the seclusiveness of philosophical discourse in Korea at that time. Whenever somebody wrote something contrary to the perceived tradition of Neo-Confucianism, they were considered sectarian and in all likelihood would be ostracised. In spite of these pressures and dangers, Chŏng Yag-yong cultivated a marked interest for Western science and

[26] Chŏng Yag-yong, Yŏyudang chŏnsŏ, II, Maengjayoŭi, Vol. 1, (Kŭm, Chang-t'ae: *Chosŏn hugi sŏgyo-wa sŏhak* [Western Religion and Western Science in late Chosŏn], Seoul: Seoul National University Press, 2005, 130).

[27] Chŏng Yag-yong, Yŏyudang chŏnsŏ, II, Maengjayoŭi, Vol. 22, 2: "Above there is heaven, below there are the people".

[28] Chŏng Yag-yong, Yŏyudang chŏnsŏ, I, Simunjip, Vol. 14, Munjip, 306: "If all people become yangban, then there can be no more yangban in the country. Only because the young exist, the existence of the old becomes visible. In the same way, the existence of the yangban becomes visible only through the existence of common people. When all are yangban, then there are no more yangban."

used it to criticise orthodox Neo-Confucianism. The deeper reason for this pursuit was the rise of poignant contradictions in society and political order and the detrimental effects they had.

In 1809 Chŏng Yag-yong commented on the exasperating state of Chŏson society. The dissatisfaction of the farming population was so enormous and widespread that it was about to explode. There was a danger of rebellion. Without any consideration for their fate, the state bureaucracy continued to put an ever-heavier burden on the people.[29] His recommendations are downright revolutionary. He looks at the king as an institution. Initially, people lived without any leaders. Only when conflicts among them became to frequent and too difficult to solve, did they give themselves leaders. The responsibility of leadership was to make life easier for the people. This was just as valid for the king. Therefore, in principle, a king could be demoted, if he did not comply with his responsibilities.[30]

Hence, Chŏng Yag-yong's view is that the relation between king, officials and subjects is not an immutable hierarchical relationship. Instead, taking the equality of man as his starting point, he perceives the state as an organic community within which king and subject comply with their respective obligations and thus complement each other.[31] In a sense, he sees the state as an apparatus with interlocking parts. Here there is a parallel between the political thought of Christian Wolff und Chŏng Yag-yong. Furthermore, both are in favour of abolishing the privileges of noble birth. In principle, all people must have the right to participate in state examinations and become officials.[32]

Notwithstanding these radical proposals, Chŏng Yag-yong does not reject monarchy or argue in favour of the creation of an entirely new, least of all utopian political system. His thought aimed at reforms which could be implemented in practise. He believed that the authority of the king was desirable and even necessary for the realisation of his reform proposals. In fact, King Chŏngjo (1752–1800, reg. 1777–1800), the so-called reform king, was quite sympathetic to his ideas.

King Chŏngjo protected Chŏng Yag-yong against his political enemies. Yet, after the king's death, the enemies of Chŏng, accusing him

[29] Chŏng Yag-yong, Yŏyudang chŏnsŏ, I, Vol. 19, Letter to Kim Gong-hu.
[30] Chŏng Yag-yong, Yŏyudang chŏnsŏ, I, Vol. 10, Wŏnmok, 213.
[31] Chŏng Yag-yong, Yŏyudang chŏnsŏ, V, Kyŏngseyupyo, Vol. 6, chŏnje 5, 217.
[32] Chŏng Yag-yong, Yŏyudang chŏnsŏ, V, Kyŏngseyupyo, Vol. 13, 500–501.

of being a Catholic, ostracised him for many years. Therefore, all possibilities for the realisation of his proposals for reforming the Choson monarchy vanished. Yet, the legacy of his theory of the monarchic state lives on in the history of political ideas in East Asia.

4. *Conclusion*

There is no need to emphasise the importance of Matteo Ricci, Christian Wolff and Chŏng Yag-yong in the intercultural history of political ideas. What is striking is that both Wolff and Chŏng used certain elements of an alien corpus of theory and articulated them with their discursive strategies within the socio-symbolic field of operation of their respective political discourses. Through this, they gained a voice in the debates of their time and could even set their agenda. In the end, they were not terribly successful with their proposals for reform, but this was due to certain historical contingencies and does not invalidate their efforts.

To gain a hegemonic position in the socio-symbolic field of operations was a competitive process. Their opponents perceived the body of thought of both Wolff and Chŏng Yag-yong as dangerous and eventually managed to ostracise them. Chŏng suffered this fate several times, the last time for 18 years. Christian Wolff, too, had to leave Halle in 1723; otherwise, he would have been hanged. When he returned to Halle 18 years later, he continued to challenge ontology and the hegemony of theology. In a similar vein, from 1784 onwards, Chŏng Yag-yong promoted a theory of man and state that involved a direct critique of the hegemony of established neo-Confucian/ontological thought.

Both Wolff and Chŏng Yag-yong placed emphasis on self-cultivation as a way toward the perfection of morality, yet they did not resort to any predetermined essentialism. Their non-essentialist view of man, which was based on the autonomous ability of man to reason, ultimately turned out to be the main problem in the controversy, on the one hand, between Wolff and the Pietists in Germany and, on the other hand, between Chŏng Yag-yong and the orthodox Neo-Confucians in Chŏson. Yet, Wolff and Chŏng were not attacked because of their political-philosophical conceptualisations, but because of their alleged lack of faith in the dogmatic beliefs of their opponents.

Matteo Ricci was the bridge which facilitated the encounter between both cultures and provided both Wolff and Chŏng with the elements they used in their respective discursive fields. Unlike these two thinkers, Matteo Ricci did not get into any political or other difficulties because of his writings. This is due to his method of accommodation, with which he interlaced two different discursive fields, i. e. that of Confucianism and Catholicism; yet without calling into question the authority of the Chinese emperor. Not until the Vatican prohibited this approach to proselytising in 1704 was the platform for the interlacing of these two discursive fields destroyed. It was replaced by confrontation – a confrontation that was to characterise the efforts of subsequent generations to deal with Confucianism.

5. *Primary Sources*

Chŏng, Yag-yong, Yŏyudang chŏnsŏ [Collected writings of Yŏyudang], Seoul: Minjok munhwa ch'ujinhoe 2001.

Ricci, Matteo: Ch'ŏnju sillŭi [Tianzhu shiyi – Die wahre Bedeutung des Herrn des Himmels], Seoul: Seoul National University Press. 1999.

Song Si-yŏl, Songjadaejŏn [Collected writings of Song], Seoul: Minjok munhwa ch'ujinhoe 1993.

Wolff, Christian: De Rege philosophante et Philosopho regnante, in: Christian Wolff, Gesammelte Werke, II. p, vol. 34.2, Hildesheim-New York-Zürich 1983, 563–632.

Wolff, Christian: Oeconomica Methodo Scientifica Pertractata, in: Christian Wolff, Gesammelte Werke II. p. vol. 27, Hildesheim-New York 1972.

Wolff, Christian: Oratio de Sinarum philosophia practica. Rede über die praktische Philosophie der Chinesen, translated by M. Albrecht, Hamburg 1985.

Yi, Yik: Chŏnjubalŭisilmun, in: Matteo Ricci, Ch'ŏnju sillŭi, Seoul: Seoul National University Press 1999, 435–448.

Zhu Xi: Chujadaejŏn [Zhuzi daquan – Collected Works of Zhu Xi], Seoul: Kyŏngmunsa 1977.

Zhu Xi: Chujaŏryu [Zhuzi ulei – Gespräch von Zhu Xi] (ancient copy from Korea).

JESUIT MISSION IN KOREAN STUDIES. A RESPONSE TO EUN-JEUNG LEE

Michael Lackner

Let me first apologize for some possible shortcomings in my discussion of Eun-jeung Lee's highly interesting paper. I have made some contributions to Chinese studies, and even more specifically, to the Jesuit mission in China, but I am far from being a specialist in Korean Studies. However, it is precisely this lacuna that might make me somewhat more sensitive to the innovative ideas in Eun-jeung's contribution. Many scholars have made inquiries into the texts written by the Jesuits in China (including all types of publications, the ones written directly for a Chinese audience, the translations for the Chinese audience, as well as the treatises, reports, and translations for a European audience), and in recent years, numerous studies have shed new light on the religious practices of the Jesuits and the question of inculturation of Christian religion in large parts of the Chinese population. In contrast to the claim Jacques Gernet made in his pioneer study "Chine et Christianisme", that being Chinese on the one side and being Christian on the other was mutually exclusive, we now know much more about the specific responses to Christianity in different social strata of Chinese society. In addition, research works on European responses to the Jesuits' reports on China also have a long tradition. But, as far as I know, a comparison between a specific kind of European reception of these reports on the one hand, and a Korean Confucianist's reaction to the ideas promulgated by the Jesuit missionaries in China has not been undertaken so far. By introducing the 18th century Korean literatus Chŏng Yag-yong into the complex game of religious, political and cultural interaction that took place with the Jesuit mission, Professor Lee has indeed added a new dimension, quite in the vein of the "tertium comparationis" Professor Krech and his International Research consortium are looking for. Christian Wolff and Chŏng Yag-yong represent a kind of meeting of minds far away from the scene of the actual encounter.

Professor Lee's approach is inspired by the idea that the Jesuits were precursors of the Enlightenment. Notwithstanding the fact that they count among the first victims of Enlightenment once it came to political power, the Jesuits no doubt had laid the foundations for the perception of Reason (with a capital R) as the guiding principle of the Chinese Empire and thus, a possible alternative to contemporaneous Western ways of governance. Christian Wolff sees Reason embodied by the Chinese meritocracy, which in turn is brought upon by a secular view of the Law of Nature. Meritocracy was based on the Civil Service Examinations system, and gave no priority to the right of birth and descent. We now know that this perception was reflecting more an ideal than a reality, since it was the Manchus who had reintroduced aristocratic principles into the society of the Empire, moreover, venality of offices was an ever increasing practice in late imperial China; but we may also add that, as early as in 1583, in his description of India, Japan, and China, Alessandro Valignano, the Jesuit Superior of the Indian Provinces had drawn a comparison between the meritocratic principles of organisation of the Jesuit order and the government of the Chinese Empire. In Valignano's view, what the Chinese lacked was not Reason but the final touch of Christianity; on the other hand, the Europeans to some extent still lacked reason, which only the Jesuits would be able to bring upon. Wolff's basic innovation consists in depriving the Law of Nature of its religious – or perhaps better: transcendent – foundations. (Wolff's China is a paradise of egalitarianism.)

In a similar vein, Chŏng Yag-yong makes use of the subversive egalitarian potential of Christianity. In a rather pessimistic statement, Montesquieu had once remarked that Christianity would never succeed in China, because in China, no man was another man's equal. It is very characteristic for an East Asian thinker to choose the field of ritual for his interpretation of Christianity. In China as well as in Korea, rituals were the mirror of political and social hierarchies which they were meant to enact. To state that each human being is equal in the face of God and that, consequently, the ritual devotional performance for the Supreme Being cannot be restricted to the ruler, is indeed a revolutionary message in this context. Early in 1616, the first anti-Christian persecution instigated by Shen Que had been legitimized by the suspicion that the Christians, as a heterodox subversive movement, were preaching and practicing an egalitarianism akin to the teachings of universal love represented by the philosopher Mozi. Given the orthodox interpretation of the so-called Neo-Confucian teachings prevailing in his time, it is no wonder that Chŏng Yag-yong also rejects theories of a different endowment – conferred by Heaven – that distinguishes human beings according to the material conditions received by birth, the *qi*. When attacking these interpretations, Matteo Ricci met with an intellectual climate in China that was rather open for rethinking the assumptions of orthodoxy, and it would be interesting to elaborate on the respective conditions in Korea. Was 18th century Confucianism devoid of any creative potential or were there still some remainders of the innovative approach that characterized Korean scholars of the 16th century, like Yi Toeg'ye and Cho Sik?

I deliberately chose the term "interpretations of Neo-Confucianism", because the basic theories of Zhu Xi regarding the relationship between Man's Nature and the Will of Heaven are somewhat more complex than their subsequent orthodox readings.

Professor Lee also points out that in the context of the East Asian political sphere, this message implies a denial of yet another superiority – the one that has China as the center and Korea at the periphery of the civilized world. It is interesting to note that the ideal of a monarchic state depicted by Chŏng Yag-yong in many ways corresponds to what the Jesuits, facing their Western audience, had described as the Chinese reality: he perceives "the state as an organic community within which king and subject comply with their respective obligations and thus complement each other". This may be called one of the ironies of cultural transfer. Let me now come to some more general comments and questions. First, the issue of the texts and their addressees: in fact, Wolff and Chŏng did not read the same texts. Wolff was inspired by the writings of François Noel. Noel counts among the so-called "figurists", a faction of French Jesuits mostly from Normandy (de Prémare, Bouvet, Foucquet) who were convinced that the truths of Christian revelation were contained in the Chinese Classics, albeit in a cryptic form that they had to decipher. Earlier on, Matteo Ricci had made some allusions to this primordial knowledge, but it is still not clear to what extent he believed in the veracity of this argument, whereas the figurists definitely did. Leibniz had read Noel's translation of the Zhongyong ("The Invariable Mean"), one of the Four Books canonized by Neo-Confucianism, but later turned to the even more rationalistic translation by Philippe Couplet and 10 other Jesuits published in 1689. Although large parts of the Zhongyong can be qualified as mysticism, most of the translations of the Zhongyong are entitled "Scientia politico-moralis", and it is evident that the Jesuits' cultural transfer of Chinese ideas was restricted to political ideas and to principles of moral philosophy, leaving aside any dangerous religious contamination.

But even if we leave the question of factionalism within the Jesuit order aside, we still have to acknowledge that all the Jesuit writings in European languages were destined to address a European audience. Filtering tactics were the order of the day, and the deliberate exclusion of the religious elements in Confucian theory and practice, as well as the silence over the less agreeable sides of Chinese *Lebenswelt* were most common phenomena. This holds even more true for the figurists than for any other member of the Jesuit mission. (Remember that even the original version of Ricci's account on his experiences in China was purified, later on, by Father Trigault's Latin translation "De Christiana expeditione apud Sinas"). The figurists were not interested in depicting the presence of religious practices in China, their task was to unearth similarities between the prophecies of the Hebraic Bible and the Chinese Classics. Later on, during the famous Rites Controversy the Jesuits would firmly reject the religious character of most of the ceremonies of the Chinese state religion. So Wolff perceived something that was perhaps close to our modern understanding of "Zivilreligion", but certainly not the ubiquitous presence of religion in China.

On the other hand, if Matteo Ricci's "Tianzhu shiyi" (The True Meaning of the Lord of Heaven) was one of the main sources for Chŏng Yag-yong, we are dealing with a work exclusively written for a Chinese audience. True, this work is inspired by the mixture of Aristotelian logic and Catholic scholasticism so characteristic for the Jesuits; it is more based on persuasion through the power of argument than by an appeal to miracles or devotional practices – but, nevertheless, it is meant for a Chinese context, which implies the use of a considerable amount of filtering tactics.

Later on, the problem of the double audience of the Jesuits will become more evident with publications like the "Zhifang waiji" (Report on the countries outside the tributary system) by the Jesuit Giulio Aleni where Aleni describes a peaceful and orderly Western world under one king (the Pope) without any quarrels and with a high sense of moral behaviour.

It would be interesting to know whether Chŏng Yag-yong had some kind of perception of the truly religious – and less philosophical – implications of Christianity. As a neophyte, he must at least have been familiar with the reality of Catholic religious practices (we know that the first high-ranking Chinese Christian, Xu Guangqi, was led to conversion by both the useful aspects of Christian teaching *and* his devotion to the Virgin Mary). Professor Lee's paper is mainly dealing with the intercultural transfer of political ideas, but we should not forget that a religious agency was at the origin of this transfer and that religious issues were at stake in both cases. It was only in China that the process of interlacing of two different discursive fields took place.

Nevertheless, if we compare the different sources of Wolff and Chŏng, we might perhaps come to the conclusion that Chŏng's source was more authentic – in the sense that the Christian dogma was more authentically contained in Ricci's "Tianzhu shiyi" than the Chinese systems of belief in the writings of authors of the same provenance as Ricci. The fact that their information provided the foundations for emancipatory thought on the two opposite sides of the Eurasian continent is in itself rather amazing, if we take into consideration the somehow dramatic difference between the materials that reached Europe and the ones that came to China. So it will be worthwhile to take a closer look at the informants themselves. Whether the Jesuits were aware of it or not, there must have been something in their agenda that encouraged Enlightenment.

THE EXPANSION OF BUDDHISM IN SOUTH AND SOUTHEAST ASIA

Stephen C. Berkwitz

Although we know that Buddhism originated in the Gangetic Plains of India and spread across Asia as arguably the world's first missionary religion, its expansion involved many different forms of Buddhism, as distinctive monastic orders and various schools. Once we abandon the notion that Buddhism was a singular entity, the notion of its expansion is made more complex. The focus on Southern Asia, moreover, invites an effort to reconsider and dispel one of the foundational myths of Theravāda Buddhism, which has been the dominant form of the religion (although not always referred to as such) in Sri Lanka and peninsular Southeast Asia for many centuries. One of the main myths of Theravāda Buddhism states that a singular, distinctive tradition spread from Sri Lanka across Southeast Asia in a uniform and unidirectional manner. Instead, the establishment of Buddhism around the Indian Ocean took place over many centuries, with periodic restorations and reforms demonstrating that there was no decisive moment wherein one Buddhist tradition was established once and for all without subsequent changes or reversals in fortune. Nevertheless, it may be helpful to reflect on some larger processes whereby Buddhism was introduced into various territories beyond India. The scope of this study is large, and thus I will only offer a preliminary analysis of the modes of appropriation, legitimation, and localization that facilitated the spread of a diverse array of texts, practices, and monastic lineages, which were eventually subsumed under the category of "Theravāda".

The subject of this essay requires that a distinction be made between the history of the expansion of Buddhism in South and Southeast Asia and the narration of that history in Buddhist sources. Any examination of this subject must reckon with questions concerning the often teleological nature of histories of the Buddha's *sāsana* (Dispensation), which comprises his Teachings and the institutions he founded to sustain and disseminate them. Thus, for example, local histories in Sri Lanka and Southeast Asia have been known to connect the establishment of Buddhism in their territories with a prophecy of the Buddha and with efforts by King Aśoka to expand Buddhism beyond his Indian empire in the third century BCE. In other words, we often find narrative accounts that present the expansion of the Buddha's *sāsana* in mythic terms as a predestined event. According to Buddhist authors, the establishment of Buddhism around the Indian Ocean was not a chance occurrence. It occurred because great and righteous persons willed it to happen. The very notion of the *sāsana* suggests that the expansion of Buddhism was the result of the Buddha's efforts to proclaim a universal path for liberation from worldly suffering. Admonishing his monastic followers to go out and preach for the good of the many, for the welfare of the many, and for the happiness of the many, the Buddha is depicted as having instructed them to travel in different directions and to proclaim the life of a renunciant.[1] The expansion of Buddhism is modeled after this early injunction to spread the Buddha's Dharma to all beings, since all beings are otherwise subject to suffering and repeated existence in the cycle of birth and death.

In as much as the spread of Buddhism thus appears as a purposeful act, historical accounts are liable to portray it in heroic, even triumphalist terms. However, it is likely that the expansion of Buddhism was actually a more uncertain enterprise. The territory of Lanka and the kingdoms in peninsular Southeast Asia lacked the Brahmanical hegemony found elsewhere in much of the Indian subcontinent, but Hindu influences were still strong in these lands and could challenge Buddhism for influence. In addition, there were indigenous religious cults centered on local deities that received popular support. And among Buddhists themselves, rival monastic orders and schools each sought to acquire the support necessary to be established and to occupy a favored position among the ruling elites and general public. These various factors meant that the expansion of Buddhism was neither a steady nor inexorable development. Instead, the proponents of Buddhism had to negotiate multi-religious landscapes wherein people's religious aspirations and loyalties were often directed toward more than one religious system.

[1] Hermann Oldenberg (ed.), *The Vinaya Piṭakaṃ*, vol. 1, Oxford: Pali Text Society, 1997, 21.

1. *The Buddhist Expansion in Sri Lanka*

History suggests that Buddhism was formally established in the island of Sri Lanka by the third century BCE when King Devānāṃpiyatissa accepted and promoted the religion that was introduced by the monk Mahinda. The textual sources, most of which postdate this event by a period of several centuries, are not wholly reliable. Inscriptions, however, afford us with the means to date the period and the method for the expansion of Buddhism in Sri Lanka. Numerous inscriptions in old Sinhala and written in Brāhmī script have been found above the entrances of caves donated to the universal Sangha by ancient kings and lay supporters.[2] The textual and archaeological evidence combined suggests that the expansion of Buddhism in Sri Lanka was largely facilitated by the patronage of kings. Also, there appears to be little sign of a strong presence of Hindu Brahmins or Jains in the island prior to the third century BCE. Thus while Sri Lanka appears to have been close enough to India to receive Buddhist monks at an early date, its location across the straits may have allowed it to evade the heavy influence of Brahmin priests. Instead local cults dedicated to mundane spirits in the form of *yakṣas* and *nāgas* appear to have comprised the main form of religious practice at this time.

When King Devānāṃpiyatissa accepted the Dharma from Ven. Mahinda, his support for the religion went a long way toward establishing Buddhism as the dominant tradition in the island. There is no sign of a vigorous challenge from an established Hindu community at this early date. Instead, those persons who promoted the Buddha's *sāsana* in Lanka simply had to appropriate and de-center local spirits and their cults. The chanting of protective *paritta* verses from Pāli *suttas* and offerings made to spirits enabled Buddhist agents to pacify and subdue local spirits, techniques that Buddhists replicated and expanded on in different areas across Asia.[3] To reiterate, we might characterize the first steps in the expansion of Buddhism in Sri Lanka in terms of seeking royal patronage and displacing local cults. In both cases, the support of kings and the appropriation of local supernatu-

---

[2] Lakshman S. Perera, *The Institutions of Ancient Ceylon From Inscriptions*, vol. 1, Kandy: International Centre for Ethnic Studies, 2001, 2–3.

[3] See, for example, Robert De Caroli, *Haunting the Buddha: Indian Popular Religions and the Formation of Buddhism*, Oxford: Oxford University Press, 2004, and Bernard Faure, "Space and Place in Chinese Religious Traditions", in: *History of Religions* 26, no. 4, 1987, 337–356.

ral forces paved the way for the larger public to adopt the Buddha's religion.

Buddhist narratives from the *vaṃsa* or "chronicle" literature describes how Ven. Mahinda and his fellow monastics from India preached to large crowds around the ancient capital of Anurādhapura, and began to ordain local men, and later women, into the Sangha. Ritual settings wherein monks preached the Dharma, and laypeople in turn gave them alms, established a relationship of mutual dependence between the Sangha and society in Sri Lanka. The island's proximity to the Indian mainland allowed for a steady influx of monks as teachers – and later as pupils, as Lanka's reputation for Buddhist learning grew. And near the beginning of the Common Era, steps were taken to secure and consolidate the growth of Buddhism in the island. Around two decades before the Common Era, a group of monks at Aluvihare monastery began to rehearse and write down the oral teachings of the Buddha. The formation of a Buddhist Canon in the Pāli language was ostensibly undertaken to preserve the Buddha's words from possible loss, but it also may have been an effort toward authorizing the local monastic order associated with the Mahāvihāra (or Great Monastery) as the possessors of the Buddha's Dharma.[4] Added to this were efforts by Mahāvihārin monks to write down and standardize commentaries on canonical texts, as well as to develop a coherent historiographical tradition in the form of *vaṃsa* texts.[5]

The move to define and authorize a local monastic order was prompted by the rise of a rival order called the Abhayagiri-vihāra in the first century BCE. The formation of this order resulted from royal patronage received by a particular monk who broke away from the Mahāvihāra to form a new order. These two orders would remain the two largest monastic communities up through the tenth century BCE. Whereas the Mahāvihāra moved to enforce a conservative vision of the tradition, the Abhayagiri monks embraced a wide variety of teachings, including but not strictly limited to the mainstream, pre-Mahāyāna texts. Although the evidence is limited, Abhayagiri monks appear to have adopted certain Mahāyāna and Tantric teachings during its history. Both major orders periodically enjoyed more patronage and sup-

[4] E. W. Adikaram, *Early History of Buddhism in Ceylon,* reprint, Dehiwala, Sri Lanka: Buddhist Cultural Centre, 1994, 79–94.

[5] Steven Collins, "On the Very Idea of the Pali Canon", in: *Journal of the Pali Text Society* 15, 1990, 101–102.

port than the other, and both of them maintained large networks of affiliated monasteries and shrines throughout much of the island. In the north of the island, moreover, Tamil-speaking Buddhists may have practiced a form or forms of the religion adopted from monks from various locations in the Deccan peninsula.[6]

Rivalries for patronage and alms between orders in Sri Lanka led to the next major step in the expansion of Buddhism in the region. Buddhist agents sought to obtain legitimation for their particular practices and interpretations of the religion. Legitimation amounted to the recognition that one's order represented the heirs to the actual teachings and monastic ordination lineage that derive from the Buddha and his band of immediate disciples. Given the Buddha's status as the Awakened One who discovered and taught the means to put an end to suffering and to obtain the transcendent goal of *nirvāṇa*, it was in the interest of all successive monks to claim fidelity to the Buddha's teachings. The literary work of the Mahāvihāra represented efforts toward this goal. And their fifth-seventh century commentaries include references to themselves as belonging to the ordination lineage founded by the Buddha's disciple Upāli centuries earlier.[7] This monastic tradition associated with the Mahāvihāra monks would in time claim the title of Theravāda, or the "The Teachings of the Elder-Monks," to indicate their claims to be the legitimate inheritors of the Buddha's *sāsana*.

Following successive waves of invasions by South Indian armies, the different monastic orders in Sri Lanka grew closer in terms of cooperation and the shared desire to survive the tumultuous times. King Parākramabāhu I is said to have initiated a large-scale reform of the Sangha in the twelfth century. This king imitated the model defined by King Aśoka in ancient India, who likewise is thought to have intervened in the Sangha to purify it of corrupt and immoral influences. Although Parākramabāhu's initiative is often thought to have resulted in the unification of the different orders under the auspices of the Mahāvihāra, monks from every order were examined and disciplined for any deviation from the orthodox tradition, as defined

---

[6] A. Veluppillai, "History of Tamil Buddhism in Śri Lankā", in: R. S. Murthy/M. S. Nagarajan (eds.), *Buddhism in Tamil Nadu: Collected Papers*, Chennai: Institute of Asian Studies, 1998, 46–47.

[7] N. A. Jayawickrama (ed. and trans.), *The Inception of Discipline and the Vinaya Nidāna*, London: Pali Text Society, 1986, 55–64.

by forest-dwelling Mahāvihāra monks.[8] A monk's unfailing adherence to the Vinaya monastic code was seen as evidence of his commitment to the true Dharma. Efforts to reform the Sangha often served to focus administrative power and to legitimate moral authority. Despite the persistence of some Abhayagiri institutions for several more generations, the Mahāvihāra interpretation of the Buddha's Dharma and the Mahāvihāra corpus of texts and institutional identity became the sole marker for Buddhist orthodoxy in Sri Lanka from the late medieval period onward. Nevertheless, unification also allowed the Mahāvihāra to adopt certain Mahāyānist elements from the Abhayagiri including the *bodhisattva* cult.[9]

It is worth noting that the processes of legitimation in turn gave rise to localization – the next step in the expansion of Buddhism in Sri Lanka. From around the twelfth century onwards, Buddhism ceased to have a significant presence in India. Sri Lankan Buddhists, encouraged by ancient narratives that portrayed the island as a refuge for the Dharma, began to strengthen local forms of Buddhism. From this point on, the majority of texts composed were written in a literary version of the vernacular Sinhala language. Such texts thus became more accessible to laypersons, as they could be read or understood when read aloud. Some medieval Sinhala Buddhist texts dealt with technical subjects, but the majority of the early prose works re-tell stories about the Buddha and his previous lives, as well as stories about his relics that came to be deposited in shrines in Sri Lanka. These narratives often drew upon local idioms and a local geography of sites that were familiar to many in their audiences.[10] Localization, or attempts to ground a tradition in its immediate social and cultural environments, also reflected an expansion of Buddhism. Localization entails deepening and broadening knowledge of the *sāsana* among the populace.

The development of an indigenous monastic organization in the medieval period was also part of this process. The older *nikāyas*, or sects, of Sri Lankan Buddhism had become divided into different local fraternities or *mūlas* by around the eleventh century. Defined by local monastic lineages and possessions, these *mūlas* were later incor-

---

[8] R. A. L. H. Gunawardana, *Robe and Plough: Monasticism and Economic Interest in Early Medieval Sri Lanka*, Tucson: University of Arizona Press, 1979, 333–334.

[9] See John Clifford Holt, *Buddha in the Crown: Avalokiteśvara in the Buddhist Traditions of Sri Lanka*, Oxford: Oxford University Press, 1991.

[10] Stephen C. Berkwitz, *Buddhist History in the Vernacular: The Power of the Past in Late Medieval Sri Lanka*, Leiden: Brill, 2004, 109–111.

porated into an organizational system divided into village-dwelling and forest-dwelling monks.[11] And during the thirteenth century, one of the results *of* a series of monastic reforms was the establishment of the office of the *sangharāja*, the so-called "King of the Sangha," who was invested with the authority of overseeing the affairs of the entire Sangha in Sri Lanka. These reforms also typically issued books of monastic laws called *katikāvatas* to formalize and codify acceptable norms for monastic practice. In sum, monastic organization, administration, and purifications were all revised and established in accordance with local interests and powers.

The trend towards localization in medieval Sri Lankan Buddhism did not mean, however, that Sri Lankans remained isolated from other communities abroad. There is evidence of pockets of Buddhist communities along the Tamil Nadu coast up to about the sixteenth century. And Sinhala-speaking Buddhists strengthened their ties with Buddhists in Southeast Asia after most Indian Buddhist communities declined and disappeared. Notably, in the eleventh century, the Sri Lankan king petitioned monks in Burmese lands to come to Sri Lanka and purify the local Sangha that had been weakened during the Coḷa invasions and reigns. These monks, likely either Mons from Ramañña or perhaps Sinhalas who had earlier fled the island, are thought to have reintroduced the higher ordination lineage to the local Sangha.[12] The ties between monks in Sri Lanka and in Southeast Asia became increasingly important thereafter.

2. *The Buddhist Expansion in Southeast Asia*

The expansion of Buddhism in peninsular Southeast Asia shares some parallels with the Sri Lankan case, despite the fact that the peninsula was home to larger and more diverse ethnic communities with influ-

[11] Gunawardana, *Robe and Plough*, 329–333.

[12] Keyes suggests that these monks were Mons. See Charles F. Keyes, *The Golden Peninsula: Culture and Adaptation in Mainland Southeast Asia*, reprint, Honolulu: University of Hawaii Press, 1995, 80. On the other hand, Gunawardana agrees with Senarath Paranavitana's theory that the monks who reintroduced the ordination lineage were Sinhala expatriate monks who fled the Coḷa invasions. To support this theory, he notes how Burmese annals do not refer to their monks purifying the Sinhala Sangha, and how this restoration did not result in a community named after Burma, as happened later on when foreign monks were brought to initiate similar ceremonies. See Gunawardana, *Robe and Plough*, 273.

ences from China as well as India. In Southeast Asia we see similar processes of appropriation, legitimation, and localization taking place. These eventually resulted in the establishment of a dominant form of Theravāda Buddhism, which was modeled largely after the Mahāvihāra in Sri Lanka, in the lands known today as Burma, Thailand, Cambodia, and Laos. Theravāda became ascendant in peninsular Southeast Asia from around the thirteenth century, although the Mons in southern Burma appear to have practiced a form of Pāli Buddhism even earlier.

The Southeast Asian kingdoms that emerged in the latter part of the first millennium were affected by both Buddhist and Hindu cultural forms. Indian models of kingship wherein kings, who were served by Hindu Brahmin priests, ruled over what Stanley Tambiah has called "galactic polities". These polities are defined by shifting territorial control and by pulsating alliances with client kings located around a centralized royal authority.[13] Various Burmese, Khmer, and Thai kings looked alternatively to Hindu Brahmins and Buddhist monks to legitimate their authority and to stabilize their rule. Indigenous cults dominated at the village level, leading to a highly syncretic religious culture across much of peninsular Southeast Asia up to the thirteenth century.[14] The rise of kingdoms in Pagan and Angkor depended in part upon the cultural capital that Hinduism and Buddhism afforded their respective kings. The rulers of expansive kingdoms laid claims to the universal powers attributed to deities and bodhisattvas to strengthen and consolidate their own power. Up through the twelfth century, the galactic polities of Southeast Asia looked to Hinduism, Buddhism, and local deities to support their territorial ambitions.

Beginning with the thirteenth century, however, powerful kings began to express a stronger preference for the power and stability offered by Buddhism as practiced by the monks in so-called "Theravāda" lineage, which associated itself with the transmission of texts and ordinations dating back to the Buddha's original disciples. Kings in Pagan built monuments and assumed ownership of Buddha relics, which became visible signs of their righteousness and fitness to rule. The power wielded by the twelfth-century king Parākramabāhu I in Sri Lanka apparently left a strong impression in Southeast Asian

---

[13] Stanley J. Tambiah, *World Conqueror and World Renouncer: A Study of Buddhism and Polity in Thailand against a Historical Backdrop*, Cambridge: Cambridge University Press, 1976, 122–123.

[14] Keyes, *The Golden Peninsula*, 68.

kingdoms, helped no doubt by his imperial designs and the visits of monks from Burma to the island. Having encountered a reformed and revived form of Theravāda in Sri Lanka, those Burmese monks returned home in 1190 to establish a Sinhala form of Theravāda, which continued to spread across the peninsula.[15] As the new Sīhaḷa Nikāya found a firm footing in the peninsula, the Tai people began to break away from the galactic power of the Khmer court. The establishment of an independent Thai kingdom at Sukhodaya was complemented by royal support for the Buddhism of the Sinhala sects. The Theravāda of Sri Lanka regarded the king as the lay head of Buddhism and the virtuous protector of the Sangha.[16] Bolstered by the virtue and authority of being the chief lay supporter of the Sangha, and receiving much merit and power from the Buddha relics kept in one's kingdom, Burmese and Thai kings strengthened their respective positions as world-conquerors, or rulers with imperial ambitions.

These new monarchies sought to appropriate the power and prestige associated with the Theravāda tradition from Sri Lanka. The Theravāda ideology of righteous kings whose great merit is evidenced by their royal position and reinforced by the patronage of orthodox Buddhist institutions made this form of Buddhism appealing to Burmese and Thai monarchs. Moreover, Sinhala Theravāda Buddhism offered both continuity with Mon Pāli Buddhist traditions and the means for the Burmese and the Thais to assert religio-cultural dominance over the latter traditions in their respective kingdoms.[17] Thus, whereas Buddhism in Southeast Asia was previously a rather diverse and heterogeneous collection of traditions, new monarchies in Burma and Thailand threw their support to the Sīhaḷa tradition from Sri Lanka in efforts both to purify and unify the Sangha in their realms. The ordination of some Mon monks in the Mahāvihāra lineage in Sri Lanka set the stage whereby many Burmese monks were re-ordained in this particular Theravāda lineage, eventually leading to a rise in the status of Sinhala Buddhism over the older Mon and Mahāyāna traditions in Southeast Asia.[18] The embrace of Sinhala Theravāda traditions did not

[15] Keyes, ibid, 81.
[16] Tambiah, *World Conqueror and World Renouncer*, 96.
[17] Donald K. Swearer, "Buddhism: Buddhism in Southeast Asia", in: Lindsey Jones (ed.), *Encyclopedia of Religion*, vol. 2, 2nd ed., Detroit: Macmillan Reference USA, 2005, 1137–1138.
[18] Swearer, ibid, 1136–1137.

wholly displace other Buddhist forms, but rather provided a new rubric within which to adopt and legitimate many existing local traditions.

Meanwhile, the Khmer kingdom in Cambodia gradually moved toward expressing a preference for the Theravāda of Sri Lanka. While the earlier Angkor period was dominated by a Hindu-Buddhist syncretism, with more attention given to Mahāyāna notions and figures, the later Angkor rulers replaced the cult of the *devarāja*, or the divine king imagined as the apotheosis of Hindu deities, with that of the *buddharāja*, or the king portrayed as a righteous *bodhisattva* or future Buddha. Khmer kings starting with Jayavarman VII (1181–1220) mostly supported and promoted Theravāda Buddhism, which showed their desire to reach out diplomatically and spiritually to other influential kingdoms where Theravāda was found.[19] The moral authority and spiritual power available to *bodhisattva*-kings increased the appeal for the Sinhala style of Theravāda throughout Southeast Asia. And further, the tradition's conservative discipline and renowned historical roots added to the impressions of its authority among the laity. In time, extant religious sites that earlier were connected to Hindu or Mahāyāna Buddhist institutions in Cambodia became transformed into Theravāda sites starting in the sixteenth century onward.[20] The appropriation of local sites with historical religious significance only strengthened the position of Theravāda among the Khmers.

In this way, we see that from the thirteenth century, Southeast Asian kingdoms began to favor monks who associated with Sri Lankan Theravāda traditions of monastic ordination and textual transmission. Local monks who traveled to Sri Lanka to receive ordination could return with the enhanced prestige of having been trained within a tradition that was renowned for its discipline and antiquity. Pāli texts were brought back to Southeast Asia, and these in turn became the foundations for additional literary activity for composing local vernacular texts. In other words, once the Theravāda lineages from Sri Lanka were established in Southeast Asia, Buddhists strived to make them more "local" by composing vernacular language texts and by subsuming cults of local deities into the ideological superstructure of the Buddhist religion. The adoption of Theravāda by religious and political elites required its domestication and popularization to earn the sup-

[19] Ian Harris, *Cambodian Buddhism: History and Practice*, Honolulu: University of Hawai'i Press, 2005, 23–24.

[20] Harris, ibid, 36.

port of the wider society. The writing of texts dealing with edifying narratives, doctrine, and local histories in a language accessible to the public paved the way for the broad adherence to Buddhism in Southeast Asian communities by the fifteenth century. Mundane tutelary deities from local landscapes were appropriated by Buddhist agents and functioned to incorporate Buddhist ideas and values into popular local cults.[21] It must be said that in many ways, the idea of the Sīhaḷa Sangha functioned mainly as a rhetorical device, since there were other sources from which Buddhism was re-made in Southeast Asia in the late medieval period. Southeast Asian Buddhism developed as much from local, indigenous Buddhist traditions as from Sri Lankan ones.[22] The traditions of the Mons and other Mahāyāna elements exerted considerable influence over the emerging Theravāda Buddhist orthodoxy in Southeast Asia both prior to the fourteenth century and afterwards. Distinctive, non-Sri Lankan traditions associated with local cults to the *arhat* Upagupta and other figures demonstrate that Southeast Asian Buddhist traditions have retained their adaptations of Sanskritic North Indian forms of Buddhism as well.

3. *Conclusions*

The broad schematics that this paper draws are meant to be suggestive of large-scale processes that guided the expansion of Buddhism in South and Southeast Asia. This expansion was not the movement of a single tradition from a single source. Instead, it comprised different streams that flowed into a larger current – a current that assumed distinctive features in different locations. Although these regions were marked by Indian Brahmanical influence, their societies were not as thoroughly permeated by Hindu traditions and institutions as was the case in much of the Indian subcontinent. As a result, the establishment of Buddhism in these lands depended mainly on the support given by local elites and on the success of appropriating local religious forms into the structures of Buddhist thought and practice. Religious and political ties forged across the Bay of Bengal meant that the models of the Sangha and the righteous Buddhist king in Sri Lanka were quickly

[21] Harris, ibid, 52–53.

[22] Peter Skilling, "The Advent of Theravāda Buddhism to Mainland Southeast Asia", in: *Journal of the International Association of Buddhist Studies* 20, 1997, 103.

adopted in peninsular Southeast Asia after the thirteenth century. The Theravāda in Sri Lanka self-consciously chose to emphasize its authority through claiming ancient ties to the Buddha through his relics and to the early Indian Sangha through a shared monastic lineage. The tradition's social and political utility ensured a close relationship with local kings, in spite of the fact that at times some rulers were openly hostile with the Sangha as their sole rival to power and authority. In general, however, Theravāda afforded local rulers with a system that served to unify their subjects within a network of moral relations and righteous giving.

If this impressionistic sketch of the history of Buddhism in South and Southeast Asia teaches us anything, it is that the religion was spread by different sources and various efforts. Monks and kings possessed the most influence over the establishment of Theravāda in medieval South and Southeast Asia. The transmission of texts, relics, and ordination lineages served to establish the foundations for Theravāda's development and regional identity. At the same time, the proponents of Theravāda were tactical in their efforts alternatively to differentiate their tradition from other systems, and to subsume aspects of local cults within their own religion. They relied on inter- and intra-regional ties to establish and reestablish their monastic institutions, and yet they also took concrete steps to lend Theravāda distinctively local characteristics wherever it was established. Long before Theravāda became a meaningful and broadly familiar designation for a particular type of Buddhism, a shared and overlapping collection of texts and institutions came to be established in Sri Lanka and Southeast Asia between the twelfth and fifteenth centuries. And the sum total of these religious activities and political efforts paved the way for Theravāda to become an inclusive religious identity that is commonly applied to monks and laypersons in Sri Lanka, Burma, Thailand, Cambodia, and Laos in the present day. Al-though in retrospect the expansion of Buddhism in these regions often assumes mythic perspectives, the adoption of Theravāda traditions that are variously related but still distinct suggests that the spread of the idea of Theravāda did not preclude the establishment of heterogeneous, local Buddhist communities. Our use of terms such as "expansion" and "spread" in religious history should not obscure the complex processes at work when religious traditions are variously imagined, adopted, and transformed in new cultural settings.

RESPONSE: THE EXPANSION OF BUDDHISM IN SOUTH AND SOUTHEAST ASIA

Sven Bretfeld

So far in this section we have heard about contacts *between* the great religious traditions in the process of their expansion. This is different for the tradition that we use to call Theravāda Buddhism. Although there were influences from Hindu and other religions when Buddhism became a dominant religion in Sri Lanka and Southeast Asia, the major religious contacts that engaged Buddhist actors and provoked religious transformations seem to have been the contacts between different transmission lineages, interpretations and powerful institutions of Buddhism itself. So, Theravāda Buddhism gives us the opportunity to study a special kind of religious dynamics, namely the transformations deriving from intra-religious struggles which followed relocation and subsequent localization processes.

Stephen Berkwitz has introduced us to this topic very well. I would like to take the opportunity to emphasize some of his points again from a global perspective.

As we have seen, the Theravāda traditions of Burma, Thailand, Laos and Cambodia are dependent on intercultural contacts with Sri Lanka. Sri Lanka functions – as I would like to name it – as a 'cultural relay' for the expansion of Buddhism into Southeast Asia. So far, this is nothing special. A culture receives a religion or religious and cultural elements and, in turn relays them further on to other cultures or even back to the original culture in a modified form. This is a quite normal process of cultural flows. But the case of Sri Lanka shows that something special happens, if a society *reflects* its function as a 'cultural relay'. In this case, it is likely that transmission activities will become rationalized as a religiopolitical program. Let's have a closer look at the Sri Lankan case.

Stephen Berkwitz has shown that some decades before Buddhism was exported from Sri Lanka to the regions of present-day Myanmar and Thailand in the 12th century, there was a major reform of the monastic communities. In this act of censorship, the Sri Lankan king Parākramabāhu I excluded a great number of members of the Buddhist orders. These persons either had to return to lay-life or had to be ordained again according to the ritual precepts of the reformist community. As it were, the king's choice of who had to be expelled was influenced by a certain group of eminent monks belonging to one of three competing networks *(niākya)* of Buddhist monastic institutions. These three networks had struggled against each other for social prestige and political influence for more than a millennium of Sri Lankan history.[1] Seemingly these three disagreed in their interpretations of the Buddhist teachings and applied divergent patterns of religious practice to a certain degree, however, their differing transmission lineages were the main factors of their group-identity. When Parākramabāhu executed his reform, he implicitly or intentionally put an end to the internal diversity of Sri Lankan Buddhism, since after the reform, two of the three lineages gradually died out, and less than a handful of their literary works have been preserved to the present day. No matter which constellations of political and religious power led to this king's decision, the effect of his reform can be described as a 'condensation' of Buddhism in Sri Lanka. One tradition – the Mahāvihāra-vāsin – prevailed and dominated the further developments in the religious field, almost unchallenged by concurring religious institutions, at least not by collective actors opperating on the same level of institutionalization. Now in the position of the victor, this tradition could distribute the story of their own history as a master narrative showing how the true inheritors of the Buddha's doctrine have prevailed over the aberrations that had appeared in the past.[2] The literature of this tradition indicates that the notion of having inherited true Buddhism was used as a rationale in a power-knowledge complex that propagated the duty to protect and propagate this heritage as the moral responsibility of Sri Lankan society.[3]

---

[1] Cf. the still very instructive work by Adikaram, E. W., *Early History of Buddhism in Ceylon.* Migoda: D. S. Puswella, 1953.

[2] Appart from references in the great Pāli chronicles, the history of the schisms and deviations within the Saṃgha of Sri Lanka is treated in detail from the perspective of the Mahāvihāra-vāsin in the important, but less well-known 14th century Sinhala work *Niākyasaṃgrahaya* by Jayabāhu Dharmakīrti (cf. Godakumbura, C. E., *Sinhalese Literature.* Colombo: The Colombo Apothecaries, 1955, 122 and passim).

[3] Cf. Bechert, H., *Buddhismus, Staat und Gesellschaft in den Ländern des Theravāda-Buddhismus.* 1: *Grundlagen, Ceylon (Sri Lanka).* 2nd ed. Schriften des Instituts für Asienkunde in Hamburg 5. Frankfurt: Alfred Metzner Verlag, 1966; Bechert, H., "Zum Ursprung der Geschichtsschreibung im indischen Kulturbereich", in: *Nachrichten der Akademie der Wissenschaften in Göttingen, philologisch-historische Klasse* 1.2. (1969), 35–58; Bretfeld, S., "Zur Institutionalisierung des Buddhismus und der Suspendierung

If we investigate the subsequent export of Sri Lankan Buddhism to Burma and Thailand, we have to ask why Sri Lankan-style Buddhism was attractive for these societies that were already deeply rooted in their own traditions of Buddhist religion. Stephen Berkwitz plausibly suggested that the power wielded by king Parākramabāhu of Sri Lanka left a strong impression in Southeast Asian kingdoms. This can be explicated if we take into consideration that the political situation of the Thai people was in a state of upheaval at that time. When the Thai emancipated themselves from the Khmer hegemony and erected the independent Thai kingdom of Sukhodaya, the royal patronization of a newly imported variant of an already implemented religion could well have served as a powerful means to break up established sociopolitical structures. Sri Lankan Buddhism was then perceived as a cleaned-up foreign variant of the Thai people's own religion – a variant that had recently reaffirmed its roots of authenticity and, therefore, could be promoted as a superior access to authentic and well ordered religious knowledge and power.

To sum up. Sri Lanka, as a 'cultural relay' for the expansion of Buddhism in Southeast Asia, served as a 'cultural filter' that handed on a condensed form of Buddhism to its neighbouring countries. Local discourses and corresponding political action produced and consolidated a self-imagination of the religious elites to be the possessors of a cultural treasure that was no longer available elsewhere in the known world. This ideology, in turn, shaped social interaction in two directions:

1. It lay base to the notion of a collective social mission to preserve true Buddhism for the welfare of the world. Thereby, Sri Lankan culture could be repositioned as the source of authentic religious knowledge bridging the gaps of time and space between old India at the time of the Buddha and the present world outside of Sri Lanka, where the teaching of the Buddha was already in an advanced state of decay.
2. This cultural capital seems to have been a major appeal for Southeast Asian cultures that intended to refresh their own Buddhist traditions. The import of Sri Lankan Buddhism to Southeast Asian countries usually was initiated by official requests from a king to the

der ethischen Norm der Gewaltlosigkeit in Sri Lanka", in: *Zeitschrift für Religionswissenschaft* 11 (2003), 149–165.

head of a Sri Lankan monastery humbly appealing to send educated monks and books.

We can find similar structures in other cases of religious contact. To stay in the Buddhist world, I will briefly compare the case of Tibet.

Almost simultaneously in the 12th century at the opposite gateway of Asian intercultural contacts, Tibetans reacted to the collapse of Indian Buddhism with the development of a self-image representing Tibet as the legitimate successor of Indian Buddhist culture. In contrast to Sri Lanka, the neo-conservative Buddhist movement that rose to power in 12th century Tibet[4] did not claim to have inherited the one and only true interpretation of the word of the Buddha. Rather, the diversity of the various transmission lineages represented by the scattered Buddhist communities all over Tibet was embraced by a superstructure consisting of the notion that the Tibetans had inherited the entire multi-facetted wealth of the teachings and practices that were once available in India. The development of this notion is reflected in a large amount of historiographical, practological and philosophical literature that endeavors to approve the authenticity of the divergent Tibetan Buddhist transmissions. A special genre, the *sdom-gsum* ("three vow") literature, deals with the determination of the mutual relationship between the Hīnayāna, Mahāyāna and Vajrayāna variants of Buddhist religion and prescribes how all three could be practiced simultaneously by one and the same individual.[5] The vast collection of Tibetan translations of Buddhist texts, the so-called Tibetan canon, consisting of translations of the Buddha's words *(bka'-'gyur)* and of the works by the great Indian Buddhist masters *(bstan-'gyur)*, that was produced in the 13th century with the financial support of the Mongol empire, can be seen as a material expression of the Tibetan Buddhist self-image as the inheritors of the Buddhist dharma in all its complexity and variation. This self-image was further reinforced by the symbolic transformation of Tibet into a worldly representation of the spiritual world

---

[4] Cf. Davidson, R. M., *Tibetan Renaissance. Tantric Buddhism in the Rebirth of Tibetan Culture and the Rise of Sakya.* New York: Columbia University Press, 2005.

[5] Cf. Sobisch, J.-U., *Three Vow Theories in Tibetan Buddhism. A Comparative Study of Major Traditions from the Twelfth through Nineteenth Centuries.* Contributions to Tibetan Studies, 1. Wiesbaden: Dr. Ludwig Reichert Verlag, 2002; Rhoton, J. D., *A Clear Differentiation of the Three Codes. Essential Distinctions among the Individual Liberation, Great Vehicle, and Tantric Systems. The sDom gsum rab dbye and Six Letters.* Suny Series in Buddhist Studies. New York: State University of New York Press, 2002.

of the Bodhisattva Avalokiteśvara which was the political program realized by the 5th Dalai Lama and his regent Saṅs-rgyas-rgya-mtsho in the 17th century.[6] From the 13th century onwards Tibet served as a 'cultural relay' for the spread of Buddhism in Mongolia and also China in certain periods of history. Like in Sri Lanka this function was reflected and idealized in discourses that presented Tibet as the new center of the Buddhist world. Filtering effects of these intercultural contacts can be determined, for example, when the Yüan emperors played off the Tibetan variants of Buddhism against the Buddhist traditions that already had a long standing in China. The main attraction of this ideology is evident and still working today: this image of Tibet as the treasure chamber of spiritual knowledge forms the base of the so-called "Mythos Tibet" that shapes the common perception of Tibetan culture up to the present.[7]

I suppose that similar structures can be perceived in other cases where a culture sees itself as an idealized heir of a parent culture. For instance, I'm thinking of Rome or Europe in general as the successor of Hellenist culture or, later, as the center of the Christian church.[8] Comparisons between these cases promise a better understanding of religious contacts, especially when a shifting of religious centers is reflected in religiopolitical ideologies.

[6] Cf. Ishihama, Y., "On the Dissemination of the Belief in the Dalai Lama as a Manifestation of the Bodhisattva Avalokiteœvara", in: *Acta Asiatica* 64 (1993), 38–56; Pommaret, F. (ed.), *Lhasa in the 17th Century. The Capital of the Dalai Lamas*. Brill's Tibetan Studies Library, 3. Leiden: Brill, 2003.

[7] Cf. Dodin, T./Räther, H. (eds.), *Mythos Tibet. Wahrnehmungen, Projektionen, Phantasien*. Köln: DuMont, 1997; Lopez, D. S., *Prisoners of Shangri-la. Tibetan Buddhism and the West*. Chicago: University of Chicago Press, 1999.

[8] For a theoretical reflexion in this direction cf. Brague, R., *Europa. Eine exzentrische Identität*. Vol. 13. Edition Pandora. Frankfurt, New York: Campus Verlag, 1992. Translated from French by G. Ghirardelli.

PART THREE

THE NOTION OF RELIGION AND RELIGIOUS SEMANTICS IN A CROSS-CULTURAL PERSPECTIVE

RELIGION TO THE POWER OF THREE

Lucian Hölscher

1. *Doing Conceptual History of Religion in a Global Context*

In its 3rd research field the Interdisciplinary Research Consortium "Dynamics in the History of Religion between Asia and Europe" explores the history of religious concepts, especially the history of the concept of 'religion' itself.[1] The contributions collected in this volume open a discussion on comparative religious history, which will go on in the Consortium for the next years. They deal with three major issues: the *theory of the axial age* (Assmann), interreligious quarrels about the *concept of holy war* (Syed), the *concept of religion in China* (Barrett/Tarocco, Ford Campany, McCutcheon) and the *concept of canonisation* (Davidson, Zehnder). Of course, these can be but exemplary studies, intending to open broad perspectives on the history of religion between Asia and Europe and a scientific practice of self-reflection, which is necessary in order to bridge such huge spaces and periods of time as the Consortium is going to do. In the following opening remarks I should like to focus some problems, which have to be observed and solved, if we want to succeed with our efforts.

1.1. *Concepts as Structures of Society*

Religious concepts cannot be considered as belonging to the concept of religion in a way comparable to pieces within a container. Each of them has its own structure deciding what is included and what excluded, and this structure may well change over time and space. Looking closer to the pragmatic usage made of them over time we find, that many of these structural distinctions run different from the distinction of "the religious" and "the non-religious": A term like 'piety' for instance may refer to a religious but also to a secular virtue,

---

[1] Cf. Project description on the homepage of the Käte-Hamburger-Kolleg: http://khk.ceres.rub.de.

hence 'impious' may be called as much an atheist as a mean man who has no honour.[2] To give another example: 'confession' may be called a religious act, but also an act in civil court procedures; hence to deny a confession may refer either to the opposition to a religious believe system or to deny an accusation at court. Depending on its present usage different things are included resp. excluded. It is not easy to define a religious language separate from secular language.

But what most terms considered in the work of the consortium have in common is, that in the European languages they were built up to concepts in early modern times. So far they all belong to a historical wave of European concept building, which centred between the 16th and 18th century owing much to the reception of Hebrew, Greek and Latin scholarly traditions. This is also true for the term 'religio'/'religion' which despite of its long lasting tradition in medieval writings became a wide spread term only in the 16th and a key concept of European societies only in the 18th and 19th centuries. Pushing other terms like 'law' or 'teaching' or 'sect' aside the term was broadly accepted for the worship of god by a social group of believers, pointing as much to the variety of different practices in the world as to the assumed general readiness of people to worship some kind of god at all.[3]

It is not the place here to go deeper into this historical process of establishing 'religion' as the general linguistic reference point of all mental and social activities, which may be covered by this term today. I should rather focus on some problems connected with the ambition to extend the methods of conceptual history first to religious concepts in general, and second to religious items in non-European cultures:

---

[2] Cf. "Pious", in: *The Oxford English Dictionary*, vol. 7, Oxford: Oxford University Press, 1961, 892.

[3] Cf. Michel Despland, *La religion en occident. Évolution des idées et du vécu,* Montréal: Fides 1979; Ernst Feil, *Religio. Die Geschichte eines neuzeitlichen Grundbegriffs vom Frühchristentum bis zur Reformation*, 4 vols., Göttingen: Vandenhoeck & Ruprecht 1986–2007; Hans-Michael Haußig, *Der Religionsbegriff in den Religionen. Studien zum Selbst- und Religionsverständnis in Hinduismus, Buddhismus, Judentum und Islam*, Berlin: Philo 1999; Mathias Hildebrandt/Manfred Brocker (eds.), *Der Begriff der Religion. Interdisziplinäre Perspektiven*, Wiesbaden: VS Verlag 2008; Wilfred Cantwell Smith, *The meaning and end of religion*, Minneapolis: Fortress Press 1991; Falk Wagner, *Was ist Religion? Studien zu ihrem Begriff und Thema in Geschichte und Gegenwart*, Gütersloh: G. Mohn 1986.

1.2. *Words and Objects*

Conceptual history in the German tradition of the "*Geschichtliche Grundbegriffe*"[4] is based on the theoretical assumption that words and historical objects are linked together in the actual meaning of a word within a given context, but that they have to be considered apart from one another in looking to their historical change.[5] Historical objects like the industrial revolution may have occurred long before the concept 'industrial revolution' labelling it today was invented, or their realisation may be anticipated as in the case of 'communism'.[6] This is important for taking into account that historical objects are constituted not only by the contemporaries, but also by later or foreign observers like historians or anthropologists. There is no "nominalistic" link between language and reality in general, but only in the presence of a given speech act.[7]

This theory of conceptual history works quite well with social and political objects, which can be studied independently from the contemporary conceptualisation. By comparison and new findings we indeed may know much more about historical objects such as premodern "states" or "markets" today than the contemporaries were able to express. But this cannot be said in the same way of religious objects: Their reality depends much more on the objectification of contemporary practices, naming them is an essential part of their identification. Today for instance it is fashionable to write a "biography" of the Christian God,[8] but of course this is nothing but following the changing reports about God in the Bible or its reception and commentaries. To think religious objects like God or a future world after death independent from man's imagination and worship may be called a theological necessity (as Karl Barth and others did), but such a statement is bound to the practice of believers to take them as being independent.

---

[4] Otto Brunner/Werner Conze/Reinhart Koselleck (eds.), *Geschichtliche Grundbegriffe. Historisches Lexikon zur politisch-sozialen Sprache in Deutschland*, 8 vols., Stuttgart: Klett 1972–1998.

[5] Cf. Reinhart Koselleck, *Begriffsgeschichten*, Frankfurt am Main: Suhrkamp 2006.

[6] Cf. Lucian Hölscher "Industrie", in: Otto Brunner/Werner Conze/Reinhart Koselleck (eds.), *Geschichtliche Grundbegriffe*, vol. 3, Stuttgart: Klett 1982, 296–297; Wolfgang Schieder, "Kommunismus", in: Otto Brunner/Werner Conze/Reinhart Koselleck (eds.), *Geschichtliche Grundbegriffe*, vol. 3, Stuttgart: Klett 1982, 455–457.

[7] Cf. Lucian Hölscher, "The Concept of Conceptual History (Begriffsgeschichte) and the 'Geschichtliche Grundbegriffe'", in: Hallym Academy of Sciences (ed.), *Concept and Communication*, vol. 1, no. 2, Seoul: Hallym University Press 2008, 179–198.

[8] Jack Miles, *God: A Biography*, New York: Vintage Books, 1996.

1.3. *Contested Concepts in Religious History*

All key concepts in highly developed societies are basically contested.[9] Different groups in society take them in a different understanding or they even deny their usage. In this sense to be "contested" may be called an essential feature of concepts used in daily life.[10] But religious concepts are contested in an even more radical sense: In modern societies of the West there are often intellectual, political and social tensions to be found between those who believe in the real existence of what theses concepts refer to, and those who challenge it. Hence in modern Western societies, which rely on the coexistence of these groups, it is impossible to define religious objects as such: Scientific research may deal with 'gods' or 'sacred places', but it can never prove that these 'gods' exist outside the mind of those who believe in them, or that certain places *are* sacred. Scientific research can only ascertain that they are *seen* and *treated* by some people as being sacred.

That's why studies on the history of religious concepts depend so much more on the concepts of the contemporaries than studies on the history of political and social objects as such: They avouch and stand for the existence of what they point to. This also accounts for the great number and high diversity of definitions, what 'religion' is. There is no general agreement on a scientific usage of the concept 'religion'. Many scholars even argue that there can be no agreement at all, because each concept privileges a certain religious tradition excluding others from the status of being a religion.[11] The impression prevails that religion in terms of scientific definition is a pure construction, despite its reality as social and mental practice.

This also makes clear the special character of modern Western religiosity compared to that of other regions of the world: Religion in modern societies of the West, at least in the Christian tradition, is always defined from within, i. e. the believers, *and* from without, i. e. the non-

---

[9] Cf. Walter Bryce Gallie, "Essentially Contested Concepts", in: *Proceedings of the Aristotelian Society* 56 (1956), 167–198, and the following debate.

[10] Cf. Wikipedia, "essentially contested concepts" http://en.wikipedia.org/wiki/Essentially_contested_concept (last modified on 24 October 2010); Michael Freeden, *Ideologies and Political Theory – A Conceptual Approach*, Oxford: Oxford University Press 1998.

[11] Among many others cf. Lucian Hölscher, "Religion im Wandel. Von Begriffen des religiösen Wandels zum Wandel religiöser Begriffe", in: Wilhelm Gräb (ed.), *Religion als Thema der Theologie. Geschichte, Standpunkte und Perspektiven theologischer Religionskritik und Religionsbegründung*, Gütersloh: Gütersloher Verlagshaus 1999, 45–62.

believers. The critique of religion (taken in the form of theories, which deny the outside existence of religious objects) plays an essential role in defining what religion is. This can easily be proved by looking to religious concepts such as 'the transcendent', a 'future life' after death, or to concepts such as 'God', 'devil' or the 'angels'. But it is true for other concepts, too, concepts such as 'piety' or 'fate' or 'contingency'. Those who do not believe in the religious content of these concepts nevertheless have put their stamp on their socially excepted meaning.

1.4. *Translating Religious Concepts*

This cannot be said to the same extent for societies outside Christian Europe and even not for Christian Europe in pre-modern times. The European "Sonderweg"[12] probably is the outcome of various factors which still have to be explored more carefully: a special structure of the religious system in Christian societies, which tended to draw sharp lines between believers and non-believers; another type or intensity of social communication, which bound both groups together in defining the proper place of religion in society; and behind all these factors may be even the European co-existence of many different religious groups such as Christians, Moslems and Jews in medieval and modern times, which derived from the same religious and cultural sources in antiquity, had its impact.

All these factors may account for the difficulty to translate the European concepts to the languages of other regions of the world resp. to find equivalent concepts there. Nevertheless they were translated and established as indigenous concepts in almost all non-European societies by the end of the 19th century. This demonstrates above all that translation of concepts is not so much a question of adequacy between "real" objects in different languages, but rather an act of making them equal resp. different. Conceptual history has to be done in a pragmatic way in order to follow these processes of translation.

But it also shows that at least for a long period of reception conceptual history and conceptual policy in these countries are concerned with other disputes than in Western societies: Instead of being contested and disputed among believers and non-believers, as in modern Christian societies of the West, in non-Western resp. non-Christian

[12] Cf. Hartmut Lehmann, *Säkularisierung. Der europäische Sonderweg in Sachen Religion*, Göttingen: Wallstein Verlag 2004.

societies these concepts are contested between those, who support or oppose Western societies. This mental structure may be overwritten by the religious/non-religious-pattern as in the case of communist China, but in any case it makes disputes about religions in these countries more complex and more-dimensional.

2. *Religion to the Power of Two and Three*

2.1. *The Discovery of Religion*

How old is religion? We do not know. But we know that the question itself is almost as old as the concept of religion itself. In the intellectual history of modern Europe it has passed many forms and stages from the early esoteric literature of Georgios Gemistos and Marsilio Ficino in 15th century Italy through the enigmatic speculations of 18th century freemasonry and the well known sketches of Lessing, Herder and Hegel in the German philosophy of history up to the more scientific theories of Saint-Simon, Wundt, Durkheim, Weber and many other authors of the 19th and early 20th century, demonstrating a historical development from pre-religious animism through the religions of revelation to modern science and rationality.

But in all these attempts to historisize religion there was little concern for dating the origin of religion. It was Karl Jaspers' theory of the axial age, which first tried to do this. According to Karl Jaspers between 800 and 200 BCE religious systems developed, independent from one another, in four regions of the Eurasian continent: Daoism and Confucianism in China, Hinduism and Buddhism in India, Zoroastrianism and Judaism in the Near and Middle East, Greek cults and philosophy in Europe.[13] The theory of axial age, further elaborated in the writings of Shmuel N. Eisenstadt and many others from the 1970s onwards[14], did much for the discussion of religion in comparative and historical terms. Nowadays to take religion as a historical phenomenon is a common practice in all religious studies. History is a major reference point in defining the reality of religion all over the world. To underline this is important even when we concede that religion is a cultural or anthropological concept, which in itself includes various

---

[13] Karl Jaspers, *Vom Ursprung und Ziel der Geschichte*, München, Zürich: Artemis-Verlag, 1949.

[14] Cf. the contribution of Jan Assmann in this volume.

concepts of history: There is constant pressure on comparative studies of religious concepts to relate them to one another in terms of historical chronology.

2.2. *The Discovery of the Discovery of Religion*

In dating the discovery of religion religious studies usually go back to antiquity or to pre-historic times. But taking into consideration that the concept of 'religion' was developed much later, we enter a second level of reflection and historical dating: "religion to the power of two", so to speak. Here the semantic patterns of religion are considered, which were established only in modern times. Hence the discovery of the discovery of religion is something, which has to be discussed on another level of scientific research.

Already in the European encyclopedias of the 19th century articles on religion usually started with relating the history of religion back to the history of the concept 'religion' itself. By doing so these articles made clear that the history of religion as a historical object is closely linked to the rise of the concept. Instead of being told as a historical narrative about changing believe-systems, institutions and practices, the history of religion was situated on the meta-level of language. That's why even in the 20th century the articles on 'Religionsgeschichte' (history of religion) in the German encyclopedia "Religion in Geschichte und Gegenwart"[15] never comprised a historical narrative about the various religious cultures in the world, but only reports about the development of the discipline "Religionsgeschichte".

However, under the conditions of 19th century epistemology, language and history were taken as but two sides of the same medal: According to this epistemology the linguistic roots of the word 'religion' pointed to the roots of religion themselves. There was no distinction made between the history of the term 'religion' and the history of what that term referred to. Only by the late 19th century, when in the new disciplines of religious studies and sociology of religion systematic approaches to religious history were developed, the exploration of etymology and of religious objects in the past could be taken apart. Now investigations on the history of religion were based on systematic

---

[15] *Die Religion in Geschichte und Gegenwart,* 1st edition 1909–1913, 2nd edition 1927–1931, 3rd edition 1957–1964.

definitions of religion, which were designed to cover as many "religious" objects as possible all over space and time.

By doing so the field of historical and comparative research could be extended far beyond the limits of Christian Europe. Of course, in the age of colonialism and imperialism Christianity, where the concept of 'religion' was at home, still was taken as the paradigm and hidden agenda of all these efforts. But this was either not apparent or not questioned; in the contrary, by being extended to other religious cultures the study of religion seemed to get a broader and more solid conceptual framework: Concepts such as 'rite' and 'symbol', 'the sacred' and 'the transcendent', 'magic' and 'animism' were taken as universal categories applicable to all religions wherever. But in the course of time, towards the middle of the 20th century this turned out to be an illusion. It became clear that the categories of religious studies were heavily biased: They described ancient and foreign religions in modern categories of Christian Europe and didn't care much for the immanent logic and structure of their real existence.[16]

Hence language came in again, but in a different way. In the early stage of religious studies before and after 1900 terms of those who lived with the religious objects, terms like 'totem' or 'karma', were introduced to scientific descriptions. Suggesting that there was something in reality corresponding to them, they were taken as adequate scientific terms, in a way as existentials. Later it became obvious that such an identification of terms with objects was problematic. But since the religious object was difficult to be described without reference to the label, which the users put on them, the pragmatic usage of indigenous concepts and of the external concepts of foreign observers became more and more important. Religious history began to include a semantic dimension by the second half of the 20th century. Today it cannot be dismissed any more.

On this level of a self-reflective study of religion it makes sense to prefer another concept of religious history: To distinguish between the semantics of the contemporary users and the semantics of external observers doesn't mean any more that only contemporary semantics are adequate to describe religious objects. But to underline the external perspective on religious objects takes into account that they imply a

[16] Cf. Hans G. Kippenberg/Jörg Rüpke/Kocku von Stuckrad (eds.), *Europäische Religionsgeschichte. Ein mehrfacher Pluralismus*, Göttingen: Vandenhoeck & Ruprecht 2009.

religious practice and structure, which is different from the practice and structure of the indigenous users.

Hence it is possible to explain the new dimension of religious studies in the following way: In the axial age theory the discovery of the transcendent was dated to the first millennium BC, but the discovery of the semantic patterns of this discovery belongs to the second half of the 20th century. The same is true of many other historical relations between objects and meta-language: The discovery of monotheism for instance may be ascribed to the time of the Egyptian pharaoh Echnaton and the Jewish prophet Mose, as Jan Assmann does.[17] But the conceptualisation of monotheism has been accomplished only in early modern Europe. Hence it makes sense to assign the origin of monotheism to the age of European enlightenment.

2.3. *The Discovery of the Discovery of the Discovery of Religion?*

Historicising the historisation of religious concepts raises the question, what stands behind such an activity: What is the perspective we make use of in historising religious concepts? Under which historically specific conditions seems such a historisation evident for many people? Or to put in another way: What is the epistemological status of conceptual history in the 20th century? In order to find an answer to such questions we may start with the hypothesis, that historising general concepts as much as theories is a way to come to terms with contradictory claims and definitions. Arguing that a concept or a theory is appropriate to a certain period of time or region in the world, is a way to assign a limited truth to them. By doing so the contradiction of claiming universal applicability for concepts, which are not compatible with one another, is solved without deciding which is right and which is wrong.

But any historisation implies a perspective on history, some hypothesis about the origin and the end of historical development. Hans Joas in a recent article has argued that for Reinhart Koselleck, the leading conceptual historian in 20th century Germany, an implicit idea of secularisation (which owed much to the concept of Karl Löwith) was the driving force for doing conceptual history.[18] According to Koselleck,

---

[17] Cf. Jan Assmann, *Die Mosaische Unterscheidung oder Der Preis des Monotheismus*, München: Carl Hanser 2003.

[18] Cf. Hans Joas, "Die Kontingenz der Säkularisierung – Überlegungen zum Problem der Säkularisierung im Werk Reinhart Kosellecks", in: Hans Joas/Peter Vogt (eds.),

Joas argues, in the "Sattelzeit", the century between the middle of the 18th and of the 19th centuries, religious concepts were steadily replaced by secular concepts. Taken this to be the case one may argue, that for Koselleck from the 18th century onwards religious concepts lost more and more of their former persuasive power; but that today Koselleck's perspective begins to lose evidence itself, because secularisation seems to be not so evident for many people.

It may be left open, whether this is a fair description of the Koselleckian concept of conceptual history. We also could argue with Koselleck, that in doing conceptual history we cannot historizies all categories at the same time. We have to fix some conceptual reference points in order to define a historical perspective resp. a hypothesis for the story we want to elaborate. And since we have to organise evidence for such a story (which in any case is more than summing up empirical data from the past), every conceptual history is open to be questioned and revised.

In doing so we enter a third level of historical reflection: "religion to the power of three", so to speak. But what do we discover here? At first glance it seems a never ending regress to observe the observer of an observation … But looking closer it seems to me that such an activity doesn't lead us to higher levels of historisation, but rather to a kind of de-historization of religious history. It doesn't make sense to construct a new master-narrative of the historical development of religion on the 3rd level, because all historical master-narratives are based on past facts and mentalities, i. e. on the 1st and 2nd level.

It is true, every master-narrative has its time and loses evidence under changing conditions in the changing past. But what remains is but a strong version of those concepts of the past, which have succeeded to set their stamp on a limited space of historical reality. Something of past narratives survives, when the narrative itself loses its evidence. In late Roman historiography for instance the death of Caesar was part of the basic myth of the Roman empire. But even, when this master-narrative lost its evidence in modern historiography, it opened a new epoch of world history. The myth of the Roman Empire was implanted into modern historiography in the way that

---

Begriffene Geschichte. Beiträge zum Werk Reinhart Kosellecks, Frankfurt am Main: Suhrkamp 2010, 309–338, here 327ff.

it was reduced to a "strong" fact, a turning point of world history.[19] The same is true of all narratives in religious history: They may reflect the conditions under which older narratives have been born and have died, but they nevertheless are narratives on the 2nd level. Hence there is a necessary perspective on religion from the sociology of science, but no "religious history to the power of three".

Taking all this together we may sum up our efforts in three points: First, it is necessary to consider religious concepts not only as tools for understanding religious culture all over the world, but also as social practices. Second, we have to take into account the different strategies of concept building in various religious cultures in order to define the dimension of their social and scientific "exploitation". And last, but not least we have to reflect the religious concepts, which we make use of in scientific research, as much in their historical context as our historical findings in relation to systematic concepts. Religious history should not be done any more without a dimension of conceptional self-reflection, i. e. as "religion to the power of two and three".

---

[19] Cf. Lucian Hölscher, "The New Annalistic. A Sketch of a Theory of History", in: *History and Theory* 36 (1997), 317–335; Lucian Hölscher, *Neue Annalistik. Umrisse einer Theorie der Geschichte*, Göttingen: Wallstein 2003.

WORLD RELIGIONS AND THE THEORY OF THE AXIAL AGE

Jan Assmann

The theory of the axial age as put forward by Karl Jaspers in 1949 and elaborated since then especially by Shmuel Eisenstadt and his circle[1] is centred on the following principal assumptions: there is but One Truth and One Mankind.[2] At a given point in its moral, spiritual and intellectual evolution, mankind 'broke through' to a much clearer apprehension of this Truth. This happened independently in several places at approximately the same time around 500 BCE. The main characteristics of this break-through may be summarized as universalisation and distanciation. *Universalisation* is concerned with the recognition of absolute Truths, valid for all times and all peoples; this implies features such as reflexivity, abstraction, second order thinking, theory, systematisation etc. *Distanciation* is concerned with introducing ontological and epistemological distinctions, such as the eternal and the temporal world, being and appearance, spirit and matter, critique of the 'given' in view of the true, etc., in short: the invention of transcendence and the construction of two-world theories.

The Axial Age is generally understood as an evolutionary achievement of the highest order, a kind of mutation through which, in Jaspers' words, "entstand der Mensch, mit dem wir bis heute leben"[3] – man as we know him today came into being, *homo sapiens axialis*, so to

---

[1] Karl Jaspers, *Vom Ursprung und Ziel der Geschichte*, Munich: Piper 1949. The debate on the "Axial Age" was continued in the 70s in the American journal *Daedalus* whose most important issue appeared in 1975 under the beautiful title "The Age of Transcendence". Since then, Shmuel N. Eisenstadt has organized a series of conferences published in Shmuel N. Eisenstadt (ed.), *The Origin and Diversity of Axial Civilizations*, SUNY Press: Albany 1986; id., *Kulturen der Achsenzeit. Ihre Ursprünge und ihre Vielfalt*, 2 vols., Suhrkamp: Frankfurt 1987; id., *Kulturen der Achsenzeit II. Ihre institutionelle und kulturelle Dynamik*, 3 vols., Suhrkamp: Frankfurt 1992, and Johann P. Arnason/ Shmuel N. Eisenstadt/Björn Wittrock (eds.), *Axial Civilizations and World History*, Jerusalem Studies in Religion and Culture 4, Brill: Leiden–Cologne 2005. Cf. also W. Schluchter, *Religion und Lebensführung*, 2 vols., Suhrkamp: Frankfurt 1988.

[2] Aleida Assmann calls this the "Zentralperspektive in der Geschichte", see "Jaspers, Achsenzeit, oder: Schwierigkeiten mit der Zentralperspektive in der Geschichte", in: Dietrich Harth (ed.), *Karl Jaspers – Denken zwischen Wissenschaft, Politik und Philosophie*, Metzler: Stuttgart, 1988, 187–205.

[3] Jaspers 1949, 19.

speak. “Das Menschsein im Ganzen tut einen Sprung”[4], humanity in its entirety performs a leap. Eric Voegelin speaks of a “leap in being” with regard to the axial event.[5] The term “axis” refers to a point – the “axial moment” as Robert Bellah calls it – that divides the stream of time into “before” and “after” in the manner of the birth of Christ. Jaspers’ opposition of the axial and the pre-axial worlds indeed appears to me in many respects like a secularized version of the Christian opposition of true religion and paganism or *historia sacra* and *historia profana*. The Biblical (both Jewish and Christian) concept of history implies radical changes, sharp discontinuities, a spiritual “mutation”, the emergence of a new man. The Axial Age narrative has the structure of such a retrospective construction that dramatizes a tendency, a development, a process of emergence in the form of a revolutionary break and personifies it in the figure of a great individual. Almost all of the “axial” features apply to the rise of monotheism or, to use Theo Sundermeier’s more general term[6], of “secondary religion”, which may therefore be recognized not only as the most typical and most distinctive but also even as the quint-essential axial event.

With regard to the agents that brought about this “great transformation” (Karen Armstrong’s word for “Axial Age”[7]), there is still much controversy. Jaspers subscribed to Alfred Weber’s theory on the “Reitervölker”, equestrian tribes or peoples, who by means of their new technology of horse-riding and chariot-driving were able to overrun the ancient world and to spread new ideas.[8] It is, however, more than unclear how these migrations, invasions and conquests could be related to intellectual and spiritual breakthroughs of the kind Weber and Jaspers are reclaiming for the Axial Age. The displacement of people or the expansion of empires does not lead to the conception of

[4] Jaspers 1949, 23.

[5] Eric Voegelin, *Order and History I, Israel and Revelation*, Louisiana: University Press/Baton Rouge 1956, passim.

[6] For the concepts of ‘primary’ and ‘secondary’ religion see Andreas Wagner (ed.), *Primäre und sekundäre Religion als Kategorie der Religionsgeschichte des Alten Testaments*, Berlin, New York: de Gruyter 2006.

[7] Karen Armstrong, *The Great Transformation: The Beginning of Our Religious Traditions*, New York: Knopf 2006. This book appeared in German under the title *Die Achsenzeit. Vom Ursprung der Weltreligionen*, Berlin: Siedler 2006. It seems doubtful, however, that Armstrong took notice of the debate on the Axial Age (n.1) in writing this book.

[8] Jaspers 1949, 37–39, see Alfred Weber, *Kultursoziologie*, Amsterdam: A. W. Sijthoff 1935.

universal ideas nor does the migration of these ideas depend on such phenomena.

When identifying agents of change, we have to distinguish between changes on the plane of history and those on the plane of memory, by which I am referring to the media of symbolic storage. On the plane of history, I follow Jaspers in seeing a strong relationship between breakdown and breakthrough.[9] Severe crises such as the collapse of the Old Kingdom in Egypt or the almost contemporaneous collapses of the Sargonid and Neo-Sumerian empires in Mesopotamia brought about considerable cultural changes. The most conspicuous examples of such a crisis leading to a new intellectual and spiritual creation are the Babylonian exile in 587–539 BCE which became the formative period of IInd Temple Judaism and the two catastrophes following the Jewish war and the Bar Kochba revolt leading to the formation of Rabbinic Judaism. It is easy to ascertain similar connections between historical crises and intellectual innovations in India, China and Persia. But this is not my concern here. In this lecture, I am more interested in the changes on the plane of memory. Any intellectual and spiritual innovations would remain inefficient without a means of conveying them to cultural memory. The most efficient and in fact decisive medium of cultural memory is without any doubt the invention and development of writing. As early as 1783, the Jewish philosopher Moses Mendelssohn stated that "the grammatological transformations which occurred in different periods of cultural development had an important impact on the revolutions of human cognition in general and changes in religious concepts in particular."[10] Homo axialis is the man, the symbol-user, who was formed by the very tools he invented. Writing is a technology that (a) makes cultural creations possible which would otherwise never exist, and that (b) preserves cultural creations in memory that would otherwise be forgotten and would have van-

[9] See my contribution "Axial 'Breakthroughs and Semantic 'Relocations in Ancient Egypt and Israel", in: Johann P. Arnason/Shmuel N. Eisenstadt/Björn Wittrock (eds.), *Axial Civilizations and World History*, Jerusalem Studies in Religion and Culture 4, Leiden/Cologne 2005, 133–156

[10] "Mich dünkt, die *Veränderung*, die in den verschiedenen Zeiten der Kultur mit den Schriftzeichen vorgegangen, habe von jeher an den Revolutionen der menschlichen Erkenntnis überhaupt und insbesondere an den mannigfachen Abänderungen ihrer Meinungen und Begriffe in Religionssachen sehr wichtigen Anteil" – Moses Mendelssohn, "Jerusalem oder Über religiöse Macht und Judentum", in: Martina Thom (ed.), *Schriften über Religion und Aufklärung*, Berlin: Union Verlag 1989, 422–423.

ished and keeps them accessible for later recourse. Writing, in short, is a factor of cultural creativity and of cultural memory.

In order to clarify these points, I would like to start with some very general remarks. We human beings live in a world of symbolic articulation which we have created ourselves. This world of ours is created through communication. Aristotle's two definitions of man, as *zoon logon echon,* the animal that has language and reason, and as *zoon politikon*, the animal that lives in a community, belong together: we possess language as a function of our dependency on, and capacity for, bonding and we use language and other means of symbolic articulation in order to form social bonds and inhabit the world which we create. This space or world of symbolic articulation borders on the inarticulate which we bear in us as the unconscious and which surrounds our world from without.

It is in this space of symbolic articulation and communication that, 5–6000 years ago, writing emerged at various places on the earth, in very different forms and on a different scale, and also with different cultural and social consequences. By writing, I understand a special kind of symbols that bestow visibility to the invisible, stability to the volatile and wide dissemination to the locally confined. The invention of writing is indeed an event of axial range, dividing the world into literate and oral societies. But it was not the invention as such that led to axial transformations. This was the first step, and I will try to show that it was only a third step in the process of literacy that changed the world.

The first step, the invention of writing, led to what I propose to call "sectorial literacy".[11] At this stage, writing is used exclusively in the sectors of cultural activity for whose needs it had been invented, which in most cases is the economy and administration. The turn from 'sectorial' to 'cultural' literacy occurs when writing penetrates into the central core of culture which we call "cultural memory". This is the second step towards axiality. It occurred in Mesopotamia towards the end of the 3rd millennium BC, when the sagas of the Gilgamesh cycle were first collected into a continuous epic, and in Egypt at the beginning of the 2nd millennium BCE where the first truly literary texts (in the sense of belles-lettres) were composed.

[11] The term corresponds more or less to what Havelock (*A Preface to Plato,* Oxford: Blackwell 1963) calls "craft literacy".

'Cultural memory' is the form of collective memory that enables a society to transmit its central patterns of orientation in time, space, divine and human worlds to future generations and by doing so to continue its identity over the sequence of generations. Cultural memory provides a kind of connective structure in both the social and temporal dimensions. It provides the kind of knowledge which enables an individual to belong, and since human beings need to belong they serve their drive to belong by acquiring the relevant knowledge, which in German is called "Bildung", in Greek *paideia* or *paideusis*, in Hebrew *musar* and in Egyptian *sebaiit*. With these concepts, we associate institutions of reading and writing, book cases, libraries, schools, universities and find it hard to imagine a kind of cultural memory that is not based on writing and literacy.

The contrary, however, is the case. Orality and ritual are the natural media of cultural memory, frequently accompanied by basic methods of notation or pre-writing such as the Australian *tchurungas*, the knotted chords *(quipus)* of the Inkas and similar mnemonic devices. For most of the time, these oral mnemotechniques were found to be much more efficient than the early forms of writing, because the various cultural texts tend to be multi-medial involving, in addition to language, pantomime, music, dance and ritual and may not easily be reduced to the one stratum of symbolic articulation that lends itself to transcription into writing. For this reason, it took the Mesopotamians and Egyptians more than a millennium to take this step. When writing is introduced into this domain, however, there is a high degree of probability that it will lead to drastic transformations.

With the literarisation of significant parts of cultural memory and the production of cultural texts that are *conceptually* literate (requiring writing in order to be composed in the first place and addressing a reader), a writing culture changes from *sectorial* to *cultural* literacy. Only now do the techniques of writing and reading affect the connective structure of a society. One of the typical effects of this transformation is the construction of a glorious, heroic or classical past or "antiquity". The cultural memory becomes two-storied, divided into the new and the old, modernity and antiquity.

An Egyptian wisdom text of the 13th century gives a list of eight 'classics' of the past whose models the pupil should follow in his strive for immortality. These authors achieved immortality, not by building pyramids but by writing books that are still read, learned and quoted because of their ever valid truth and authority:

Is there anyone among us like Hordjedef?
Or someone like Imhotep?
Among our contemporaries, there is none like Neferti
or Kheti, the greatest of them all.
I mention to you only the names of Ptahemdjehuti
and Khakheperreseneb.
Is there another Ptahhotep
or somebody like Kairsu?[12]

I think that it is possible to generalize the Egyptian case. At a certain stage, every literate culture enters the stage of a split culture, divided into the old and the new, and it is writing in the form of cultural literacy that brings this split about. Since this split is dependent on linguistic change and finds its typical expression in the distinction between classical and vernacular language, and since linguistic change is a largely unconscious and uncontrolled process, we may even speak here of evolution. The cultural and social consequences of this split, however, depend on cultural decisions and institutions.

Even the typically Egyptian association of this split with the idea of immortality may, at least to a certain degree, be generalized. In its literate, written form, cultural memory appears as a timeless or at least enduring space of immortality which one may enter by creating a book or work of art of everlasting beauty, truth or significance. This idea of literary or artistic immortality may be considered a first step in the direction of transcendence or transcendental visions (Shmuel Eisenstadt). The use of writing for the fulfilment of the desire to transcend one's life span and to live on in the memory of posterity dates back, in Egypt, to the very beginnings of literate culture, but I would classify this use of writing for tomb inscriptions as sectorial literacy. The step towards cultural literacy is achieved when the tomb monument is topped by the literary work, e. g., in the words of Horace who said with regard to his book of odes:

Exegi monumentum aere perennius
Regalique situ pyramidum altius.

[12] Pap. Chester Beatty IV rto. 2.5–3.11. See my article "Schrift, Tod und Identität. Das Grab als Vorschule der Literatur im alten Ägypten", in: Aleida Assmann/Jan Assmann/Christof Hardmeier, *Schrift und Gedächtnis.* Archäologie der literarischen Kommunikation I, Fink: Munich 1983, 64–93, repr. in: Jan Assmann, *Stein und Zeit. Mensch und Gesellschaft im Alten Ägypten*, Fink: Munich 1991, 169–199.

This motif already appears in the same Egyptian text that contains the canon of classical authors:

> They (the sages of the past) have not created for themselves
> pyramids of ore
> nor stelae of iron;
> they have not contrived to leave heirs in the form of children,
> to keep their names alive.
> But they created themselves books as heirs
> and teachings that they have written.
> They employed the scroll as lector priest
> and the slate as "loving son."
> Teachings are their pyramids,
> the reed their son,
> the polished stone surface their wife.
> Their tomb chapels are forgotten,
> but their names are recalled on their writings, that they
> have created,
> as they endure by virtue of their perfection.
> Their creators are remembered in eternity.[13]

We are not yet dealing with 'real' axiality here because this step of canonisation is still culture-specific and lacks the global claims typical of axial movements. But it is a step in the direction of axiality, and it is a step within the space of writing.

The construction of a classical, heroic or "golden" age, an 'antiquity' as a past to look back to for models of behaviour and literary production means a first step in the direction of canonisation. This cultural split into antiquity and modernity seems to me one of the characteristic prerequisites if not elements of axiality. It introduces into a given culture an element of critical distance and reflexivity. Canonisation, in this first stage, means the collection of cultural texts of the past to form an obligatory syllabus of cultural knowledge, to be learned by heart and to be referred to as authoritative in critical discussions and situations. This canon of a classical tradition provides the touch-stone of truth and value which creates a difference between the norm and the given, between what is and what should be, so typical of what Jaspers claims to be axial thought.

Another sphere of cultural memory which is strongly affected by the use of writing is history. The existence of written sources about the

---

[13] Pap. Chester Beatty IV rto. 2.5–3.11; Dietrich Wildung, *Imhotep und Amenhotep*, Munich: Deutscher Kunstverlag, 25–27.

past makes it possible to draw the distinction not only between the old and the new, but also between myth and history. The use of written records creates history in the sense of a critical discourse, separating mythical tales about the past from reasoned accounts of documented history. In this sense of documented past and critical verifiability, it is writing that produced history and dispelled mythology. Writing caused history to be where myth was, because it documented conditions in which not gods but human kings reigned and humans were responsible for their actions. Writing bestows to historical memory the quality of verifiability and adds a truth value to its accounts about the past which myth, in spite of its truth claims, is lacking.

A third domain of cultural memory where the use of writing leads to dramatic changes is religion. It is here that the second and decisive step towards canonisation is achieved; a step of truly universal significance, which in my opinion forms the very center of Jaspers' concept of the Axial age. In the realm of religion, writing appears with the same critical pathos as in the sphere of history, opposing its superior truth to the invalidated truth claims of myth. Here, its claims to superior truth are based on a revelation which it codifies. All world religions – Judaism, Christianity, Islam, Buddhism, Jainism, the religion of the Sikh, Confucianism, Daoism – are founded on a canon of sacred scripture that codifies the will of their founder and the superior truth of his revelation. This step of canonisation was invented only twice in the world: with the Hebrew canon and the Buddhist canon. All later canons followed these examples.[14] This second step of canonisation changed the world in a truly "axial" way.

The first step of canonisation which we encountered in Egypt and Mesopotamia was connected with a cultural split into antiquity and modernity, drawing a distinction within the culture.[15] Canonisation here means the selection of the timelessly authoritative and exemplary from the plethora of written literature. The second canonisation applies a different criterion: the criterion of absolute and universal truth, drawing a distinction that sets one particular culture or religion including its past off against all other religions, which are then excluded as paganism, idolatry, heresy and error. Some of this pathos of distinc-

[14] See Aleida Assmann/Jan Assmann (eds.), *Kanon und Zensur*, Munich: Fink 1987.

[15] See Dieter Kuhn/Helga Stahl (eds.), *Die Gegenwart des Altertums. Formen und Funktionen des Altertumsbezugs in den Hochkulturen der Alten Welt*, Heidelberg: edition forum 2001.

tion and exclusion still seems present to me in Benjamin Schwartz's definition of the Axial Age as the "age of transcendence" and Shmuel Eisenstadt's concept of "transcendental visions" as the hallmark of axiality. All this is to a large degree a feat of cultural memory and an effect of writing and canonisation. We don't know anything about the transcendental visions of shamans, kings, priests and seers unless they are not only written down but, above all, are received into a canon of sacred scripture. Only then do they become part of cultural memory and religious identity.

If primary canonisation can be partly explained in terms of evolution, dependent, as we have seen, on the truly evolutionary process of linguistic change, secondary canonisation is by no means an evolutionary achievement, but a matter of conscious revolution which in an individual's life could be compared to a conversion. The distinction between evolutionary processes and other forms of change implying conscious interventions and decisions between alternative options seems to me highly important in the study of the axial age.

In the West, the Hebrew canon of sacred scripture is complemented by a Greek and Latin canon of classical literature. The cultural memory of the West rests on these two projects of canonisation which were conducted roughly simultaneously – and probably not quite independently – by specialists in Palestine and Alexandria. The distinctive hallmark of what I call secondary canonisation is the rise of exegesis. In the stage of primary canonisation, the texts selected as classics exist in a form which the Medievalist Paul Zumthor called "mouvance".[16] They were constantly reformulated, amplified or substituted by other texts in order to accommodate the changing conditions of understanding. Their 'surface structure' was sacrificed in order to save at least part of their meaning. This is why even written texts tend to exist over a longer stretch of time in many different versions. The continuous growth of the book of Isaiah, first into Deutero-Isaiah then into Trito-Isaiah is a typical case of how a cultural text changes in what the Assyriologist Leo Oppenheim called "the stream of tradition".[17] The Epic of Gil-

[16] Paul Zumthor, *Introduction à la poesie orale*, Paris: Éd. du seuil 1983, 245–261, cf. also Aleida Assmann, "Schriftliche Folklore. Zur Entstehung und Funktion eines Überlieferungstyps", in: Aleida Assmann/Jan Assmann/Christof Hardmeier (eds.), *Schrift und Gedächtnis*. Archäologie der literarischen Kommunikation I, Munich: Fink 1983, 175–193.

[17] Leo Oppenheim, *Ancient Mesopotamia: Portrait of a Dead Civilization*, Chicago: University of Chicago Press 1968.

gamesh developed over the course of its transmission and redaction from a cycle of sagas into the 'twelve-tablets-composition' as which it appears in the Neoassyrian library of Assurbanipal at Niniveh. In a similar way, the Egyptian Book of the Dead developed from just a pool of unconnected spells, out of which every individual funerary papyrus picked its own specific selection, into a real book with a fixed selection of 167 spells in a fixed order. Written texts, in this 'stream of tradition', share to a certain degree the sort of oral texts.

This flexibility or 'mouvance' is categorically stopped and excluded by the process of secondary canonisation. Secondary canonisation means the combination of a sacralisation of the surface structure typical of sacred texts like hymns, incantations and ritual spells on the one hand, and the preservation of meaning typical of cultural texts in the state of 'mouvance' through the constant adaptation of the text to changing conditions of understanding on the other hand.[18] Sacred texts are not necessarily cultural texts since they may be known only to specialists and withheld from public circulation. Sacred texts are verbal enshrinements of the holy. In sacred texts, not a syllable may be changed in order to ensure the 'magical' power of the words to 'presentify' the divine. In this context, it is not 'understanding' that matters, but rather correctness of pronunciation, ritual purity of the speaker and other requirements concerning proper circumstances of performance. As the case of the Rgveda shows, this principle of non-mouvance and verbatim fixation applies to sacred texts independently of their oral or literate form of transmission.[19] Sacred texts, therefore, are exempt from the pressure to adapt to the hermeneutical conditions of a changing world.

[18] For the concept of 'cultural text' see Andreas Poltermann (ed.), *Literaturkanon – Medienereignis – Kultureller Text. Formen interkultureller Kommunikation und Übersetzung*, Berlin: Erich Schmidt 1995.

[19] The case of India, where the sacred texts were not committed to writing, but memorized by specialists, the Brahmins, seems to contradict this reconstruction because even here, in the context of oral tradition, we meet with secondary canonisation and traditions of exegesis. However, here, the techniques of memorization have been brought to a degree of perfection that human memory could very well fulfil one of the main functions of writing which is stabilizing the text. The decision to withhold the sacred texts from writing seems to have been common to several Indo-European religions such as Zoroastrianism and the Celtic Druids. It is usually explained to avoid the mistakes of copyists but the main motive seems rather to have been the fear of unwanted dissemination which is also one of Plato's arguments against writing. Stabilizing the text can be achieved either by writing or by an elaborate mnemotechnique. The latter requires usually a very strict poetic formalization of the text.

In the process of secondary canonisation, the principle of sacred fixation is applied to *cultural* texts. On the one hand, they are treated like verbal temples enshrining divine presence, but on the other hand, they require understanding and application in order to exert their formative and normative impulses and demands. The solution of this problem is exegesis. Exegesis or hermeneutics is the successor to 'mouvance'. In the 'mouvance' stage of literary transmission, the commentary is being worked into the fabric of the text. This method has been shown by Michael Fishbane to be typical of the biblical texts in their formative phase.[20] These texts are full of glosses, pieces of commentary which later redactors have added to the received text. Only with the closure of the canon is this process stopped and exegesis must now take the form of a commentary that stays outside the text itself.[21]

This distinction between text and commentary typical of secondary canonisation applies not only to the sacred but also to the classical canon. In this respect, the Alexandrinian "philologoi" seem to have led the way. They introduced into their collection of ancient writings the distinction between "hoi prattómenoi" and the rest, meaning by "prattómenoi" literally those to be treated, the classical texts worthy of exegetical treatment, i. e. a commentary.[22] The Latin author Aulus Gellius compared this textual elite to the highest class of Roman text payers called "classici". In the Jewish tradition, this split into, and relationship between, text and commentary typical of secondary canonisation finds its earliest expression in the concept of a 'written' and an 'oral Tora' (*torah she be'al khitav* and *torah she be'al pe*). Here, commentary has to be oral in order not to violate the space of writing which is exclusively reserved for and occupied by sacred scripture. The oral Torah is a collection of oral debates and commentaries on the written Torah that itself became codified in the Talmudic and Midrashic traditions. It is believed to go back via an unbroken chain of "reception" *(shalshelet ha-qabbalah)* to Moses himself.

The oral exegesis of a sacred text accompanying its public recitation seems indeed to correspond to Jewish custom dating back to the

[20] Michael Fishbane, *Biblical Interpretation in Ancient Israel,* Oxford: Clarendon 1986.

[21] Cf. Jan Assmann/Burghard Gladigow (eds.), *Text und Kommentar,* Munich: Fink 1995.

[22] Cf. Ernst A. Schmidt, "Historische Typologie der Orientierungsfunktionen von Kanon in der griechischen und römischen Literatur", in: Aleida Assmann/Jan Assmann (eds.), *Kanon und Zensur*, Munich: Fink 1987, 246–258.

beginnings of canonisation. Nehemiah reports of a public reading of the Torah, where Ezra read the text and several of the Levites gave a commentary:

> And Ezra opened the book in the sight of all the people, for he was above all the people, and as he opened it all the people stood. And Ezra blessed the LORD, the great God, and all the people answered, "Amen, Amen," lifting up their hands. And they bowed their heads and worshiped the LORD with their faces to the ground.
>
> Also Jeshua, Bani, Sherebiah, Jamin, Akkub, Shabbethai, Hodiah, Maaseiah, Kelita, Azariah, Jozabad, Hanan, Pelaiah, the Levites, helped the people to understand the Law, while the people remained in their places. They read from the book, from the Law of God, clearly, and they gave the sense, so that the people understood the reading. (Neh 8:5–8)

Some centuries later, the Jewish historian Flavius Josephus testifies to the same custom, when he contrasts Jewish and Greek religion:

> Can any government be more holy than this? or any Religion better adapted to the nature of the Deity? Where, in any place but in this, are the whole People, *by the special diligence of the Priests, to whom the care of public instruction is committed, accurately taught* the principles of true piety? So that the body-politic seems, as it were, one great Assembly, constantly kept together, for the celebration of some sacred Mysteries. For those things which the Gentiles keep up for a few days only that is, during those solemnities they call Mysteries and Initiations, we, with vast delight, and a plenitude of knowledge, which admits of no error, fully enjoy, and perpetually contemplate through the whole course of our lives.[23]

It is obvious, that Josephus, in this polemical passage, does not do full justice to the Greek organisation of cultural memory. He ignores the classical canon, the traditions of scientific discourse and the various forms of exegesis practiced in the schools of philosophy, medicine and other branches of knowledge. He focusses only on religion and compares the Jewish institutions of religious instruction and the Greek mystery cults. As arbitrary and highly selective as this comparison may be, it illustrates a very important distinction: the distinction between ritual and textual continuity.[24]

---

[23] Josephus Flavius, *Contra Apionem* cap. 22 trans. William Warburton, *The Divine Legation of Moses*, London: F. Gyles 1738–41, I 192f.

[24] For this distinction see my book, *Das kulturelle Gedächtnis*, Munich: Beck 1992, 87–103.

In spite of their extensive use of writing, Egyptian and other "pagan" religions still relied on ritual continuity. In the world of ritual continuity, the public must indeed wait for the next performance in order to gain access to the sacred texts of cultural memory. Textual continuity is only achieved when institutions of learning and exegesis are established that keep the ancient texts constantly present and semantically transparent. The transition from ritual to textual continuity means a complete reorganisation of cultural memory in the same way as the transition from the ethnically and culturally determined religions of the Ancient world to the new type of transcultural and transnational world religions meant a totally new construction of identity. The canon, in a way, functioned as a new transethnical homeland and as a new trans-cultural instrument of formation and education.

A strong alliance between revelation, transcendence and secondary canonisation seems to exist. The codification of revelation leads to an expatriation of the holy from the worldly immanence into transcendence and into scripture. The pagan or pre-axial cult-religions presuppose the immanence of the holy in images, trees, mountains, springs, rivers, heavenly bodies, animals, human beings and stones. All this is denounced as idolatry by the new scripture-based world religions. Scripture requires a total reorientation of religious attention – attention which was formerly directed towards the forms of divine immanence and is then instead directed towards scripture and its exegesis. Secondary canonisation means an exodus both of the holy and of religious attention from the cosmos into scripture. The textual character of his revelation corresponds to the extra-mundane nature of God. To be sure, these remarks concern only the sacred canon such as the Tanakh, the Christian Bible and the Qur,an, and not the canon of Greek and Latin classics. The structure of the classical canon is different in that it is open and allows for constant modifications around an unquestionable core, whereas the sacred canon is closed. This distinction between closed and open canons applies, however, only to the West. Eastern, especially Buddhist canons have a different, less strict structure. Common to all corpora of secondary canonisation, however, is the existence of a fully-fledged culture of exegesis and the strict distinction between text and commentary.

Seen as an agent of change, we may ask to which aspect of axiality literacy at the stage of secondary canonisation makes the most decisive contribution. In my opinion, this is precisely the aspect that has been shown to function as a common denominator of most of the axial features discussed above: distanciation and disembedding. Writing is a technology that restructures not only thought[25] but also, under certain cultural circumstances, the whole network of relations between human beings, man and society, man and cosmos, man and god, and god and cosmos. The meaning of distanciation and disembedment as 'axial, moves, however, can only be properly understood if we achieve a better understanding of what embedment and integration mean.

In the evolutionary framework of the axial narrative, embeddedness appears as the 'not-yet' of the axial achievement of distanciation and disembedding. What disappears in this perspective is the positive aspect of embedding. Embedding man in a social, political and conceptual or ideological network of meaning and coherence and embedding the divine in a cosmic network whose meaning and coherence is modelled on the same basic ideas of order, truth and harmony, should first of all be recognized in its own right as a major civilizational achievement. There is perhaps no society on earth that went so far as the ancient Egyptians in articulating, elaborating and also institutionalizing their vision of socio-cosmic coherence, which they called Ma'at.[26] There is no reason not to call this conceptualization a "transcendental vision". We cannot point to a "great individual" to have first formulated it, since no institutionalization of this first 'vision' has been preserved, but the Egyptians themselves would have pointed to Imhotep, the first of their celebrated sages, who worked as a vizir under king Djoser (2750 BCE) and was divinized for his great invention, the art of building in stone and the erection of the first pyramid, the step pyramid at Saqqara. His frequently cited 'instruction' is lost to us, but the transcendental character of the idea of Ma'at is obvious. Ma'at is what Kant would have called a 'regulative idea'.

Ma'at, however, works in the opposite direction of distanciation and disembedment. It is the very principle of embedment, of creating connectivity in the social, temporal and cosmic dimensions, establishing social bonds between humans and temporal connections between yesterday, today and tomorrow ensuring memory, success, stability and even immortality. He who lives in and by Ma'at, such is the great

---

[25] See Walter J. Ong's important essay "Writing is a Technology that Restructures Thought", in: Gerd Baumann (ed.), *The Written Word: Literacy in Transition*, Oxford: Clarendon Press 1986, 23–50.

[26] See my book *Ma'at. Gerechtigkeit und Unsterblichkeit im Alten Ägypten*, Munich: Beck 1990.

Egyptian promise, will not perish but pass through the test of the judgment after death to eternal life in the Elysian fields. However, even this concept implies an element of distanciation, which is self-distanciation, renunciation of an immediate fulfilment of one's drives and impulses. The ideals of self-control, discretion, modesty, altruism, beneficence, openness to the needs of others, pity, compassion, empathy are at the core of the Egyptian concept of virtue. Knowing how to listen well is deemed more important than knowing how to speak well. This form of self-distanciation is the prerequisite for self-integration. It may also be described as a way of "standing back and looking beyond"[27]: at standing back from one's own narrow sphere of interests and looking beyond to the whole or at least a broader horizon of community. It is certainly not a mere coincidence that the hero of Egyptian wisdom was both a vizir and an architect. Knowing how to build a pyramid and knowing how to build a state and a society require comparable qualities. Certainly, this is not the kind of state and society we would very probably like to live in and 'Egyptian man', able to perfectly integrate him/herself into this pyramidal socio-political edifice is not the man we know or rather want today, at least after the breakdown of socialist totalitarianism, but even this construction of reality was illumined by transcendental visions, otherwise it would not have persisted for three millennia and more. It was certainly not the "house of serfdom" as it is depicted or rather debunked in the Bible. What the Egyptian example may teach us, is that even the 'pre-axial' world is the result of positive achievements and that the axial break-through is not just the result of discoveries of what was unknown before, but also the result of conscious acts of rejection, abolition and rebellion that cannot be accounted for in an evolutionary perspective.

By adopting Christianity, the Egyptians themselves were able to perform a change in the most radical way. From champions of integration, they turned into champions of isolation. To the ancient Egyptian mind, nothing could perhaps appear less meaningful than total self-disembedding, since social embeddedness was identified with life, virtue and morality. Seth, the god of evil and brutal violence, is the

[27] "If there is some common underlying impulse in all these 'axial' movements, it might be called the strain towards transcendence … a kind of standing back and looking beyond – a kind of critical, reflective questioning of the actual and a new vision of what lies beyond…", wrote Benjamin I. Schwartz, "The Age of Transcendence", in: *Wisdom, Revelation, and Doubt: Daedalus*, (Spring 1975), 3–4.

typical solitary one, and anyone evading social life would be associated with Seth and considered evil.[28] After converting to Christianity, however, the Egyptians became virtuosos of solitude and went to unprecedented extremes in their search for isolation and renunciation. The Egyptian saint Anthony became the patron of Christian hermits, the Egyptian monasteries with their rules as codified by Pachom and Schenute became the models for Christian monasticism. The Egyptians adopted the Christian idea of the kingdom of God as a goal of integration and re-embedment with the same passion and perfection as they previously had the kingdom of Pharaoh who was believed to be a god on earth and the son of the highest god.

The disembedding of man from society and the world corresponds with the disembedding of god from cosmic immanence and a pantheon of co-deities. These two movements of disembedding, i. e. monotheism and the birth of individualism have always been seen in strong connection with each other. The connection becomes only all the more obvious if one realizes that it is towards god that the hermit, and towards man that God turns. The hermit abandons human society in order to draw nearer to God, and God, one could say, renounces divine companionship in favour of the "covenant" he establishes with his chosen people. In the early stages of Biblical monotheism, the texts lay great stress on God's "jealousy" and compare the covenant between God and people, God and man, to the erotic, sexual and matrimonial bonds between man (God) and wife or bride (Israel). God can by no means be alone; what he abhors most and what puts him into fits of fury is to be abandoned by his people. Man in his turn leaves society not out of misanthropy but for the love of God. Both forms of solitariness, God's and man's, are not absolute but rest on a new form of partnership. Within this partnership, man grows individualistic and god grows monotheistic.

It is fascinating to see how important a role writing, literacy and scripture play even in this respect. With monotheism, the case is obvious. No monotheistic religion, in fact no "secondary" religion can do without a canon of sacred scripture. The solitude of God is, one could say, "scripture-aided". Similar statements apply to the solitude of man. Generally speaking, there can be a solitary reader but no solitary lis-

[28] See my article "Literatur und Einsamkeit im alten Ägypten", in: Aleida Assmann/ Jan Assmann (eds.), *Einsamkeit*. Archäologie der literarischen Kommunikation VI, Munich: Beck 2000, 97–112.

tener. Writing and reading create the possibility of communication without interaction. To scripture, however, this concept of interaction-free communication applies in a much more poignant sense. Studying the torah and learning it by heart is the first and foremost requirement of man in the frame of monotheistic religion. Scripture, i. e. the torah is the only mediator between the two solitary partners, god and man. *ger anokhi ba-'aretz* "I am a stranger on earth", the psalmist says in Ps 119:19, adding: *'al-taster mimméni mitswoteýkha* "do not conceal thy commandments from me". We see that man's solitude as well, his alienation on earth, is scripture-aided. God's commandments, which are codified in the torah, offer him a home which he is missing "on earth". This home is what Heine called "ein portatives Vaterland" and what Robert Bellah calls "a portable religion".

This capacity of disembedment is what the prefix 'world' means in the term "world religion". World religions are disembedded from any territorial, political, ethnical and cultural frames, they are transnational, transcultural and transterritorial. They are capable of mission, diaspora and conversion. They can be taught to other peoples speaking different languages and dwelling in different countries, they can be brought along to other cultures observing a different religion and one may convert to them; all this is quite unthinkable for traditional cult religions such as ancient Egyptian and other "pagan" religions. World religions found a new kind of transnational and transcultural identity by forming a new form of memory which is canonised scripture.

CHINESE HISTORY AND WRITING ABOUT 'RELIGION(S)': REFLECTIONS AT A CROSSROAD

Robert Ford Campany

I want to offer some brief reflections on some ways in which the modern Western notion of "religion" shapes our writing of Chinese history and some ways in which Chinese history might impact our use of the notion of "religion".[1] I will not discuss modern (by which I mean post-1900) Chinese usages of the term *zongjiao* 宗教, which, as has long been known, was a neologism adopted around that time from the Japanese term *shūkyō* 宗教 created expressly to translate the generic term "religion", for which both premodern Chinese and Japanese lacked direct equivalents.[2] (Usages of *zongjiao* are more or less precisely equivalent to uses of "religion" in Western languages.) Rather, I will discuss early medieval (roughly ca. 100–600 CE) Chinese usages relevant to our topic. "Western" and "modern" as used here to modify "notion of 'religion'" are of course shorthand for a discourse that may have had Western origins but has now spread worldwide. For better or worse, wielders of the discourse of "religion" are no longer just "Western" people: they include Chinese, Indian, Japanese, Korean, African, and many other people.[3] If "religion" is by origin a Western category then it is one that has now been globalized – certainly in all areas touched by Western educational systems, languages, intellectual taxonomies, media, or missionary activity.

I will do four things below. First I will summarize the points I made in an already-published article concerning the modern Western discourse on "religion*s*" in the plural and the application of this discourse to phenomena in early medieval China. Then, turning to the singu-

[1] Translations from Chinese are my own unless otherwise indicated, even where previous translations are cited for the reader's convenience.

[2] A rather impassioned counterargument to this notion was presented during our symposium, but I did not find it at all convincing; it is possible to turn up a few instances of the compound *zongjiao* in medieval Chinese texts, but the term in those settings is not at all close to the modern, Western-origin, folk or scholarly senses of "religion".

[3] Chidester, David, *Savage Systems: Colonialism and Comparative Religion in Southern Africa*, Charlottesville: University of Virginia Press 1996.

lar term *religion* in its generic sense, that is, "religion" as a realm of concern as opposed to other realms of concern with which it sharply contrasts, I will ask three sets of questions:

1. What conceptual and terminological pitfalls arise when writing about religion in premodern China?
2. How does Chinese religious history invite us to rethink our models and assumptions about religion? Are there ways in which it could or should affect how we think and write about religion at the level of both methodology and, more subtly, of descriptive language?
3. Did the generic notion of "religion" uniquely arise in the West, or are there analogues in (for example) early medieval China? If there are no premodern Chinese analogues, why might that be the case?

1. *Synopsis of "On the Very Idea of Religions (in the Modern West and in Early Medieval China)"*

In this section I summarize an article of mine published a few years ago on recent Western discourse on plural "religions" and on apparent analogues in early medieval China.[4]

The article opens with the following series of points:

- Discourse on religions is first of all a linguistic affair, whatever else it is. We often focus on big concepts, but at the working end of writing about religions much is decided at the more concrete level of descriptive and interpretive language.
- Language is metaphorical in character. Underlying even the most apparently neutral statements about religions will therefore be found powerful metaphoric structures that shape the questions we ask and the assumptions we make.
- Discourse about religions is rooted in Western language communities and histories. Other cultures in other times may and often do lack closely equivalent ways of demarcating phenomena.
- The helpfulness of the category "religions" is not necessarily to be measured by the extent to which people in the culture we are describing would have recognized it as one of their own. It is a sec-

[4] Campany, Robert Ford, "On the Very Idea of Religions (in the Modern West and in Early Medieval China)", in: *History of Religions* 42 (2003).

ond-order concept, ours to define. But use of this category without any regard to whether, for example, medieval Chinese usages work differently may lead to misunderstandings and projections, examples of which are discussed below.
- That a culture such as early medieval China lacked one-for-one equivalents of the category "religions" does not mean that it lacked words and concepts that are *analogous* – ones that *did similar sorts of work in similar sorts of rhetorical and social situations.*

I then presented some common metaphors that structure modern Western discourse on religions: Religions are entities; religions are living organisms; religions are containers of people, ideas, texts; religions are personified agents; religions are marketable commodities; religions are armies and their spread is warfare. Implied is a critique of these: while they may be useful for certain rhetorical, historiographic, etc., purposes, such expressions are strictly and literally false: *religions are not in fact any of these things, including entities in any literal sense.* Turning next to early medieval China, I found a different set of metaphors, but ones employed to do similar work; in other words, I found discourses about certain topics that are clearly *analogous* to Western talk of "religions", ways of speaking that we find in contexts where a Western author would understand the topic to be plural "religions". We find,[5] for example: founder or paragon synecdoche (e.g., what we would term "Buddhism", and not merely "the Buddha", inescapably intended by the way the term *fo* 佛, normally meaning *Buddha*, is used in a certain discursive context); a discourse of various "ways" or "paths" (*dao* 道 and various compounds); and a language of plural "laws", "methods", or "regulations" (*fa* 法). We also find a small set of standard metaphors in which the *relations* among *various* species of these genuses were characterized – for example, "root and branch" (*ben mo* 本末) – and various binary or triadic classification schemes (e.g. left/right, yin/yang, life/death).

Some conclusions I drew from this discussion of Chinese metaphors for things contextually analogous to "religions" were as follows. We

[5] One thing we find very little of in early medieval times is the later-ubiquitous "X *jiao* 教", literally "teachings of or about X", where X is a noun usually denoting a religious founder, sage, teacher, or deity. In modern Chinese this becomes standard usage for every instance of what we would term "religion", and there are ample premodern usages of this term, but in early medieval texts such usage was not yet common.

do find in early medieval Chinese texts some tendency to linguistically reify phenomena that correspond to things called "religions" in Western discourses. It is not as if nothing approaching this idea ever occurred to people in China in the first six centuries of the common era. On the other hand, the standard early medieval Chinese metaphors are different and have different implications. The way in which *dao*s, etc., are spoken of does not imply that they are total, encompassing "systems" or conceptual frameworks, unlike the frequent case in Western writing about religions. Nor do the Chinese metaphors imply the high degree of holistic integration implied by their Western counterparts. (An incidental remark on translation: We are generally much better served by literal translations than by ones that unhesitatingly map Chinese usages onto Western ones without noting any differences. *Fodao* 佛道, for example, is much better rendered as "the way of Buddha[s]" than as "Buddhism".)

Such reification of things corresponding to the Western "religions" arose, as did similar Western usages, in a particular sort of social and historical context. That context was one of religious plurality and difference, of comparison and contrast occasioned by the forced juxtaposition and the jostling for prestige of practitioners with different priorities. The texts employing these metaphors arose at the boundaries between one set of teachings-practices and another. In every case they were written from the point of view of someone who, even when favoring one side or the other, deems it possible to weigh both on the same scale and consider them both as members of a common genus. Such situations naturally involved contestation. It was, then, in the presence of others that communities began naming and defining themselves and each other and it was in the midst of plurality that authors began using nominal forms to denote entities that would be called "religions" in Western languages.[6] Such early medieval Chinese discourses are analogous to the early modern "comparative religion" of the West, but with one big disanalogy: to speak of a "religion" in Western discourse is to imply a strong sense in which it is a "religion" *as opposed to some other type of thing* – some *non-religious* type of thing – as well as to differentiate it from other species in the genus "religion". This was not quite true in early medieval China. There were,

[6] Moerman, Michael (1965, 1967) found that even something as apparently basic as people's ethnic self-identifications varied by situation, interlocutor, and topic of discussion. The same might be even more true of discourse about collective bodies.

naturally genuses of *daos* and of *fas*, but these were not sharply demarcated as realms of concern or power from the non-*dao* or the non-*fa*. I return to this point in section 4 below.

I concluded the article with two proposed alternatives to speaking of religions as things in the world that act and have volition like personified agents, grow (etc.) like plants, spread (etc.) like conquering armies, and so on. Another way of putting this is that I set the metaphors aside to ask what the purported things we call religions *really, non-metaphorically speaking, are* in an ontologically rather literal sense. They are, among other things, (1) repertoires of cultural resources (citing Ann Swidler's excellent work on cultural repertoires[7]) made and used over time by many agents, and (2) imagined communities (citing Benedict Anderson's work on this theme[8]) stretching across time and space. Thinking of them in these ways, rather than as agents, plants, armies, containers, and the like will open up new avenues of research – and will close others that are based on disanalogies, misunderstandings, and faulty projections.

2. *Common Pitfalls in Writing "Religion" in Early Medieval China*

What conceptual and terminological pitfalls arise when authors – whether they are American, European, Chinese, Japanese, or other – write about religion in early medieval China, a culture which, as we will see below, (at least to a very great extent) lacked analogues to our generic sense of "religion" as a kind or area of concern distinct from other? Here I simply want to point out a few common assumptions about religion – assumptions built inexorably into our very vocabulary for talking about and imagining religion as a subject of discourse – that create misunderstanding and falsify our representations of the Chinese religious situations, often profoundly. Many of the difficulties faced by American undergraduate students in understanding the subjects taught by people like me stem from the disjunction between these assumptions and the realia of Chinese religious history.

It is possible, in fact, to be much more specific. As many scholars have noted, Christianity has often served as the implicit model of reli-

[7] Swidler, Ann, *Talk of Love: How Culture Matters*, Chicago: University of Chicago Press 2001.

[8] Anderson, Benedict, *Imagined Communities: Reflections on the Origin and Spread of Nationalism*, 2nd ed. London: Versa 1991.

gion and religions generally, the case *par excellence*. ("'Religion' means 'things like Christianity'"[9]) All of the assumptions about religion that I am about to point out result from the prevalence of the Christianity model in discourse on religion and religions in general.

It is often assumed, for example, that a dichotomy between the natural and the supernatural must be a feature of religion generally, so much so that "supernatural" almost becomes synonymous with "religious" (when describing an event) or "deity" (when describing a being). An early medieval Chinese genre of writing about human encounters with ghosts, nature spirits, celestial gods, animal sprites, near-death experiences, and other religiously tinged anomalies will thus end up being characterized as "supernatural fiction"[10] or as "tales of the supernatural and the fantastic"[11] when, in fact, not only were these writings never intended as "fiction" in the standard sense of that term[12] but the modifier "supernatural" does not fit the subject matter.[13] The lack of fit is not trivial, either. To put it simply, and without lingering over the details of early medieval Chinese notions of spirits, gods, the ordinary dead, and demons, many of these beings were not understood as "supernatural": they were neither non-natural, nor were they metaphysically above nature, nor were they non-material. They were natural in the sense that they were located in this natural world that surrounds us and in which we, too, live; they were material in that they (with the possible exception of a few deities at the very top of the pantheon, so rarefied as to remain non-personified) had bodies made of the same stuff – *qi* 氣 – that composed all other existent phenomena. The overlay of the term "supernatural" onto such phenomena is understandable as a piece of economizing English-language shorthand but it creates a blind alley if the goal is to represent accurately in English the phenomena being described.[14] The assump-

[9] Griffiths, Paul J., "The Very Idea of Religion", in: *First Things* 103 (2000), 32.

[10] Zhao, Xiaohuan, *Classical Chinese Supernatural Fiction: A Morphological History*, Lewiston: Edwin Mellen Press 2005.

[11] Kao, Karl S. Y. (ed.), *Classical Chinese Tales of the Supernatural and the Fantastic*, Bloomington: Indiana University Press 1985.

[12] Campany, Robert Ford, *Strange Writing: Anomaly Accounts in Early Medieval China*, Albany: SUNY Press 1996.

[13] The same usage applied to the same sorts of texts is seen in Kenneth DeWoskin's translation of the title of a famous work of this sort, *Soushen ji* 搜神記, as "In Search of the Supernatural".

[14] It might also be possible to construct a stipulative definition of "supernatural" that would fit the early medieval Chinese religious scene, but this is rarely done and the modifier is simply applied without further discussion.

tion that such phenomena and beings in China are correctly described as "supernatural" is precisely one of the assumptions that instructors must disabuse Anglophone students of. Early medieval Chinese worldviews (like many other worldviews in predominantly animistic, non-monotheistic civilizations) tended not to dichotomize reality along the lines of nature/supernature.

Another cluster of assumptions basic to discourse on religion but misleading when it comes to describing early medieval China centers on fideism. Adopting Western usages, many modern scholars working on early medieval China write as if individuals' "beliefs" were the salient – or even the only – thing linking them to this or that religion, and as if a list-like creed were the heart of any religion. To describe Daoism, then, is to list the beliefs that were essential to it in all its forms and to which all Daoists assented; to describe a person as "a Daoist" is to signal that he or she mentally assented to these beliefs. A concomitant research program is then entailed: we sift through this individual's writings or historical statements about his words or deeds, expecting to find (at least in those records that happen to have survived) the clear signs of his inner beliefs concerning ultimate things. A closely related tendency is to assume a denominational model of religious "belonging" or identification, so that it is seen as making sense to ask, of a known individual, whether he "was" a "Daoist" or something else. The unspoken assumption is that he must have "been" only one at any given time – an assumption again based on a denominational and creed-based model of religious membership.[15] It seems never to have occurred to these writers to ask whether this entire complex of assumptions about religion, religions, and how people relate to them – a complex obviously based on post-sixteenth-century Christianity – is even applicable when describing a culture such as early medieval China.[16]

An article was recently published, for example, in which the author tried to make out whether a noted figure, Tao Qian (365–427), "was" really a "Daoist," a "Confucian", or perhaps even a "Buddhist".[17] First,

[15] Or, perhaps, a membership-based mode of religiosity, as if there were no other kind.

[16] I would argue that it was *perhaps* at least *partially* applicable only when describing two phenomena: the earliest generations of the Celestial Master movement and the taking of Buddhist lay and monastic vows; but the matter is complex and an adequate discussion is impossible here.

[17] Holzman, Donald, "A Dialogue with the Ancients: Tao Qian's Interrogation of Confucius", in: Scott Pearce/Audrey Spiro/Patricia Ebrey (eds.), *Culture and Power in*

then, it has been assumed that this very question makes sense in Tao Qian's time and place, that there is no better (i. e. more empirically accurate) way of imagining and talking about an individual's relationship to "a religion" than this essentializing use of the copula. Next, in what does this "Daoistness" etc. consist? In "belief", of course. And how are Tao's "beliefs" to be ascertained, especially since he left writings that seem to indicate positive interest in more than one "ism"? To answer this question the author takes the extraordinary approach of counting the number of times Tao quotes from or alludes to works identified with one or the other tradition, even referring at one point, without apparent irony, to "the quotation scoreboard".[18] Whichever tradition's works Tao cited most (in his works that happened to have survived the vicissitudes of time) must be the winner![19]

The often-unconscious assumptions about religion(s) made by writers about a culture such as that of early medieval China profoundly shape the questions asked and the research agendas posed. When the lack of fit between those assumptions and the historical phenomena is as severe as it is in the example just discussed, the result is problematic scholarship.

3. *Ways in which Religion in Early Medieval China Invites us to Rethink our Discourse on Religion and Religions*

Here I want to ask what an understanding of the early medieval Chinese religious scene might contribute to the modern, comparative study of religion – that is, to the very terms in which it is carried out. Whether or not we find indigenous analogues to the sort of theorizing we are inclined to do ourselves,[20] are there at least ways in which the Chinese phenomena encourage us to rethink our assumptions? Are

the Reconstitution of the Chinese Realm, 200–600, Cambridge, Mass.: Harvard University Press 2001, 75–98.

[18] Holzman 2001, 85.

[19] For further discussion, and a suggestion of alternative models, see Campany 2003 287–319, and idem, "Two Religious Thinkers of the Early Eastern Jin: Gan Bao and Ge Hong in Multiple Contexts", in: *Asia Major* 3rd ser. 18 (2005), 175–224.

[20] Early on I tried to argue for such indigenous analogues (Campany, Robert Ford, "'Survivals' as Interpretive Strategy: A Sino-Western Comparative Case Study", in: *Method and Theory in the Study of Religion* 2 (1990), 1–26; idem, "Xunzi and Durkheim as Theorists of Ritual Practice," in: Frank Reynolds/David Tracy (eds.), *Discourse and Practice,* Albany: SUNY Press 1992, 197–231.); now I am less confident that the analogies are close or true – that the *very same sort of thing* was being done in both sets of

there even perhaps models that we might appropriate into the discourse on religion?[21] Might it be the case that aspects of early medieval Chinese religious life can teach us new ways of thinking about religion not just in early medieval China but comparatively, at the level of categories? I will briefly sketch five areas in which the answer might be "yes". Further development of these suggestions must await another occasion.

As has already been proposed by Buswell and Gimello[22], the fundamental Buddhist metaphor of "path" (Sanskrit *mārga*, Chinese *dao* 道) suggests a way of envisioning and describing individuals' relations to religions that is an alternative to the discourse of "believing in" this or that and "belonging to" X or simply "being an X-ist". One advantage is that the language of "path" (and its attendant metaphors) takes "belief" off center stage and focuses instead on movement in a certain direction along a series of prescribed, tradition-sanctioned stations or stages, by means of further tradition-sanctioned methods or practices. It understands participating in a religion, or being religious, as movement toward a goal (or progression through a series of goals) by means of things done, rather than as a simple toggle-switch-like assent to doctrinal propositions. Adopting this model in describing not simply Buddhists but others as well would mean that the status of propositions about reality and the role of individuals' assent to them would be reopened for investigation, rather than assumed; but it would also mean that our attention would be broadened beyond beliefs to practices, and to how and why those practices were held to advance practitioners toward the specified goal(s).

A disadvantage of path-based models for religious participation is that, like confessional models based on Christian denominationalism, they are exclusivist: if it is a matter of paths, then by the very logic of the metaphor one can only travel (or backtrack on, or try to leave, etc.) one path at a time, just as, if it is a matter of the affirmation of beliefs, one is presumed to assent to only one church's set of creeds at

---

cases (Xunzi and Durkheim, early medieval Chinese folklore collectors and Tylor and Frazer). To me at least, the question remains open.

[21] "The problem is really that of one-sidedness, a failure of mutuality. Where, for example, are the Hindu categories used to illumine Christianity, the Taoist concepts employed in analyzing Judaism, the shamanic themes applied to Islam?" (Buswell, Robert/Gimello, Robert, *Paths of Liberation. The Marga and its Transformations in Buddhist Thought* [*Studies in East Asian Buddhism series, 7*], Honolulu: University of Hawaii Press 1992, 1).

[22] Buswell/Gimello 1992, 1–17; cf. Campany 2003, 305.

a time. These are disadvantages precisely because, as the example of Tao Qian above shows, we find individuals – not only in early medieval China! – quite often mixing, borrowing, combining, or playing between two or more religions' assertions or idioms, not just leaving one to adopt another but at the same time actively using both at once. Such was the rule, not the exception. So even the path metaphor has its limits when it comes to providing a model that matches the suppleness and complexity of *what people often actually do*. (People have a funny way of not conforming to our models of how they should behave.) That is why I have elsewhere suggested a model of *repertoires of resources* as more empirically accurate for describing how people often relate to religions and how they use elements of their culture.[23] Still, the path metaphor might be more useful than the language of "belief", "belonging to", and "being an X-ist" when it comes at least to describing the normative programs for spiritual advancement, salvation, or perfection taught by religious communities and advocated in their texts.

Second, when we study how people actually related to religious institutions, ideas, groups, and activities in an environment such as early medieval China, we see a much richer array of possibilities than confessional assent or denominational membership – possibilities that also, unlike the confessional/denominational model, include not just an on/off toggle switch (where person P either believes in X-ism or he doesn't, "is" an X-ist or isn't) but a subtler range of scenarios. We see people acting as *patrons* or *sponsors*, for example, of advanced, specialist, virtuoso practitioners of esoteric arts: theirs was a different mode of participation than that of the ones on the path, but it was a mode that was recognized and respected as such and that brought certain rewards in its own right. We also see people *sponsoring* the making of devotional objects or structures by *donating* resources, and again, this was a recognized, even formalized role, with a developed terminology and the careful recording of donors' names for posterity right onto the objects or structures they sponsored. We see individuals *commissioning* the making of scripture copies or images so that the merit gained from this activity could be transferred to their ancestors. Most ubiquitously, but for that very reason often forgotten, we see individuals constituting the *audiences* before whom virtuoso practitioners carried out

[23] Campany 2003, 317–319; Campany 2005, 176–177; based on Swidler 2001.

their esoteric or ascetic disciplines and, often enough, performed their wonders and acted out their strange violations of conventional mores: in short, to be a part of the *witnessing audience* of the performance of a religious adept was itself to play a sort of religious role. It was often only other people's recognition that accounted for his an individual's being deemed a transcendent, a wonder-working monk, etc., and being remembered as such in the written record.[24] Of course, any good historian of religions anywhere – including European Christianity in any period – knows that there was a rich array of roles and modes of participation available to people. But in much writing on religion this richness is forgotten, and the language used is by no means adequate to the complex realities found in the historical record; often a person is said to simply *be* a this rather than a that, as if there were nothing else to say on the matter.

Third, the history of religions in a place and time such as early medieval China suggests different models for understanding religious communities themselves, as well as pointing up the need for such models. Rather than seeing them as congregations or denominations, we might, in any cases, do better to see them as two things: *repertoires of resources* on which individuals drew in shaping ideas, framing texts, and creating rituals and regulations; and *lineages of transmission* through time and across space, such transmission often formalized in rituals that were among the most important in society at the time. That lineages were sometimes fictively and retrospectively constructed does not lessen their importance as a key way in which people in early medieval China thought about and constituted religious communities. Scholars writing in Western languages, particularly in English and recently, often speak of "religious traditions", perhaps because this seems a touch less reifying and essentializing than "religions", but in such discourse the etymological force of *traditions* is often ignored. To take it seriously would mean seeing "religions" as, in part, imagined communities always in the process of being (re)constructed by linguistic and ritual acts of collective memory and the transmission of ideas, values, techniques, and other resources.

Fourth, as already hinted above, studying religion in early medieval China suggests the need for a model of religiosity – an understanding of what it means to "be religious" – that is grounded more in practice

[24] Campany, Robert Ford, *Making Transcendents: Ascetics and Social Memory in Early Medieval China*, Honolulu: University of Hawaii Press 2009.

than in belief per se. Affirmation of lists of beliefs was rarely, in short, the defining marker or shaper of religious identity. If anything did perform this function it was either the performance of certain practices or behaviors, especially ones that conspicuously marked a person as inhabiting a role different from that of ordinary, "default" persons (e. g. shaving the head, wearing a distinctive robe, abstaining from certain foods or from eating at certain times of day, not marrying), or the formal taking of vows to obey certain precepts that similarly marked the vow-taker as different from others. Belief in certain beings, along with trust in one's spiritual superiors and in the teachings of the tradition one was thereby joining, were certainly not irrelevant,[25] but *the sheer fact of belief* in this rather than that was not the centrally defining feature.

Fifth, a few writers in late classical and early medieval China developed reflection on some religious topics that approach the sophistication of "theories" that perhaps bear comparison with modern Western analogues or at least contain ideas worth considering and applying in cross-cultural analysis. Without elaborating further on these, I will simply mention here two such areas: ritual (what it means, how it functions, its effect on performers, how its symbolic code works and why symbolic expression is used, etc.) and the path (Buddhist writers in particular developed a supple discourse that approaches being a "pathology").

4. *Early Medieval Chinese Analogues to Generic "Religion"?*

One Western author recently observed, summing up (and quoting) an argument made late in his career by Wilfred Cantwell Smith: "The modern notion of religion is '*au fond* secularist'; it sets up a dichotomy between religion and what is not religion".[26] Another wrote: "Christianity was rarely, if ever, thought of by Christians as one religion among many: the idea that there is a genus called 'religion' of which there are many species did not gain much currency until the seven-

[25] Case in point: T 2102, 52.82c26–27, "To accept this [the Buddhist teaching of the far-distant results of karma over countless lifetimes] and to be able to believe – is that not difficult?" 取之能信，不亦難乎; cf. Zürcher 1971, 235.

[26] Schüssler Fiorenza, Francis, "Religion: A Contested Site in Theology and the Study of Religion", in: *Harvard Theological Review* 93 (2000), 17.

teenth century. It is, by and large, a modern invention".[27] There were certainly many things going on in early medieval China that anyone familiar with the folk senses of the term would now say were "religious" in nature, and there were phenomena that many would now say constituted "religions" – and to this latter notion there were even, as seen above, at least partial indigenous analogues. But were there any analogues in early medieval China to the putatively uniquely modern, Western notion of "religion" (or its adjective "(the) religious" as opposed to "(the) non-religious" or the secular) in the generic sense? I will argue here – all too briefly and sketchily – that the answer is "almost, but not quite". I will also suggest a reason why such a notion, although briefly approximated in China, failed to persist there.

So far as we know, texts, images, and monks representing the Buddhist religion were first introduced into China by the middle of the first century CE. By the beginning of the fifth century there were beginning to be significant numbers of monks, nuns, temples, and monastic landholdings. Monasteries owned property, taking it out of the tax base and redistributing production based on it. Buddhist devotion also soaked up lay funds for donations and metals for the fashioning of images of Buddhas and bodhisattvas. Furthermore, monks and nuns absented themselves from some of the most basic Chinese social and ideological frameworks: they left their families rather than creating descendants and venerating ancestors through sacrificial ritual; they took the Buddha's surname and renounced their own; they wore distinctive robes that, in the case of monks, left one shoulder bare (which offended the sensibilities of some Chinese), and shaved their heads – the latter gesture seen as another renunciation of the family and of the veneration of ancestors, since, ideologically speaking, one's body was inherited from the family line and one was to carefully preserve it. Politically, too, the Buddhist sangha posed a problem insofar as it set itself up as an authority independent of imperial control – an independence powerfully symbolized by monks' refusal to bow to rulers as a sign of respect. Not surprisingly, objections were soon raised. The first recorded debate on monks' refusal to pay obeisance to rulers took place in 340 CE. Another, more extensive one occurred in 402 CE and it is on this one that I will focus. My aim is not to present anything like a full account of this affair but to examine closely some

[27] Griffiths 2000, 31–32.

of the arguments wielded on both sides of the issue and the language in which they were couched.[28]

Between 401 and 403 CE, during an era of political division and recurrent military conflict, a provincial governor and military general, Huan Xuan 桓玄 (369–404), briefly usurped power and took ill-fated steps to initiate a new dynasty. As he moved to consolidate power, one of his first acts was to attempt to have some prominent Buddhist monks returned to lay status, to impose a government-organized "selection" or winnowing of membership in the sangha, and to assume control over registration of monks and nuns. In this context he also chose to reopen "a great matter of our time" (*yidai zhi dashi* – 代之大事) as he called it,[29] by calling for the carrying out of Yu Bing's former plan (of 340 CE) to require monks to bow before the ruler. This disturbed some of his own followers, most notably an official named Wang Mi 王謐 (360–407), as well as monastic leaders, most notably the monk Huiyuan 慧遠 (334–417). Many documents exchanged in the ensuing debate, all of them written in the spring of 402, have survived. The arguments are complex and rather voluminous. I will focus here only on those most relevant to our topic.

Huan Xuan's most basic argument for monks' obeisance to rulers is that the ruler gives life (*sheng* 生), or at least helps sustain, regulate, circulate, and distribute the stuff that makes life possible. Appealing to chapter 25 of the received text of the famous *Daode jing* 道德經, which numbers the king among the "four greats" (*si da* 四大) which also include the Dao, heaven, and earth,[30] Huan argues that since

---

[28] This matter has been voluminously treated in Western-language scholarship: see epecially Zürcher, Erik, *The Buddhist Conquest of China*, Leiden: E. J. Brill 1972, 231–239 (still the best and clearest account in a Western language); Hurvitz, Leon, "'Render unto Caesar' in Early Chinese Buddhism: Hui-yüan's Treatise on the Exemption of the Buddhist Clergy from the Requirements of Civil Etiquette", in: Kshitis Roy (ed.), *Liebenthal Festschrift*, Santiniketan: Santiniketan Press 1957, 80–114; and Tsukamoto, Zenryū, *A History of Early Chinese Buddhism: From its Introduction to the Death of Hui-yüan*, Tr. Leon Hurvitz. 2 vol. continuously paginated, Tokyo: Kodansha 1985, 828–844. For general discussions of sangha-state relations in China see also Storch, Tanya, "The Past Explains the Present: State Control over Religious Communities in Medieval China", in: *The Medieval History Journal* 3 (2000), 311–335; Yu, Anthony C., *State and Religion in China: Historical and Textual Perspectives*, Chicago: Open Court 2005, 90–134; Weinstein, Stanley, *Buddhism Under the T'ang*, Cambridge: Cambridge University Press (period-specific but detailed coverage) 1987.

[29] T 2102, 80b24.

[30] See Mair, Victor, *Tao Te Ching: The Classic Book of Integrity and the Way*, New York: Bantam 1990, 90. Some early versions of the *Daodejing* replace "king" with "life"; the rude insertion of the king into this series clearly troubled some: see Boltz, William

monks and nuns receive life and depend on it to exist in this world and carry out their practices, they must be required to show respect to the one who is responsible for managing and sustaining the life granted by heaven and earth: the ruler.[31] They may not benefit from life and the conditions of life without paying obeisance to the one who maintains these.

Another, related argument of Huan's that is of great interest for our purposes unfolds in the following terms: Buddhism above all values "things of the spirit", or perhaps we might translate "that which is spiritual" (*shen* 神). But qualities of the spirit, e. g., understanding or the lack thereof, are possessed by individuals according to their "allotted shares" (*fen* 分). All a Buddhist teacher can do is work with his disciples' natural allotment of talents and endowments, just as the craftsman can only work with the raw material that nature provides: he cannot create it but can only modify it once given. "The deepest virtue [in this situation] lies with the initial provision of the material" 深德在於資始; "the subsequent work of polishing and beautifying it is truly only secondary to this" 拂瑩之功實已末焉. The ruler, not the monk, is the one involved in the provision and maintenance of life and its conditions, and life is the source of each individual's "allotted shares"; hence "the way of the ruler" 君道 encompasses 兼, rather than being encompassed by, "the way of the teacher" 師道[32] – all of which amounts to saying that the spiritual work of Buddhist monks presupposes the prior world-ordering, life-sustaining work of rulers and polities. This priority of origin and function entails an obligation on the part of the sangha to acknowledge ritually its dependence on the imperium by bowing to the ruler.

The monk Huiyuan from his monastic retreat on Mount Lu crafted a response to these arguments.[33] His treatise contains a preface that quotes from Huan Xuan's original letter on the subject, followed by five sections; the fifth, on the non-perishing of the soul at death, while fascinating, does not concern us here.

G., "The Religious and Philosophical Significance of the 'Hsiang Erh' *Lao tzu* in the Light of the *Ma-wang-tui* Silk Manuscripts", in: *Bulletin of the School of Oriental and African Studies* 45 (1982), 95–117.113–114.

[31] This argument is most clearly enunciated at T 2102, 80b.

[32] Text at T 2102, 83b; cf. the summary in Zürcher 1972, 234.

[33] Text at T 2102, 29c–32b. This text is introduced and translated in Hurvitz 1957; the translation is a bit outdated and in need of improvement but suffices to give a sense of the arguments.

The first section treats lay Buddhists who remain in the household. Such persons are "people who acquiesce to transformation" 順化之民, where "transformation" (*hua* 化) captures both the inevitable changes that constitute life in this world and the moral transformations rulers seek to inculcate in people through social institutions. Of lay people Huiyan says that "in their traces they accord with that which is within the realm" 迹同方內. He draws here on two tropes that would have been familiar to his readers. One is that of "traces" (literally "tracks" or "footprints"): people who involve themselves in ordinary life leave "traces," whereas hermits, those who withdraw from political affairs, and others who disengage themselves are said to "cut off their traces" or "leave no traces." The other is that of being "within the realm", an expression traceable to the inner chapters of *Zhuangzi* (ca. 320 BCE): those who operate "within the realm" of custom or etiquette abide by social convention, whereas there are others who are "beyond the realm" and whose behavior cannot be judged by conventional standards – or at least that is what users of this language want their readers to believe.[34] Huiyuan asserts in this section that Buddhist householders, properly acquiescent to transformation and leaving traces in the social world, are obliged to bow before their rulers. This provision, he says, "is how the teaching of Buddha honors the provision of life and assists kingly transformation in the way of governance" 斯乃佛教之所以重資生王化於治道者也.

The second section treats "those who have left the household" – Buddhist monks and nuns. These men and women are "guests beyond the realm" 方外之賓 "whose traces are cut off from among [other] beings" 迹絕於物. Because of the teaching they live by, "they understand that woes and entanglements come from having a body [or a self] and that by not maintaining the body [or the self] one extinguishes woe" 達患累緣於有身, 不存身以息患. They further know that "the generation of successive lives comes from undergoing transformation and that it is by not acquiescing to transformation that one seeks the ultimate principle" 生生由於禀化, 不順化以求宗; "the ultimate principle" here connotes nirvana, the cessation of change and of rebirth (as is stated explicitly in the next section). "If extinguishing woe does not depend on maintaining the body/self, then [monks and nuns] do not honor the benefits that foster life" 息患不由於存身, 則不貴厚生之

[34] For a brief discussion of this topos see Campany 2005, 187.

益. Later in this section Huiyuan speaks of monks and nuns as having "crossed to beyond transformation in order to seek the ultimate principle" 超化表以尋宗. So: the ruler governs the realm of change and the processes of transformation; monks and nuns seek to move beyond these, so they are not obliged to bow to the ruler, even though their practice benefits other beings and assists the ruler in his work of transformation.

The third section, titled "Those who seek the ultimate principle do not acquiesce in transformation", works from the dyads established earlier to extend the argument. It opens with a hypothetical interlocutor's objection on the grounds that understanding the ultimate principle must involve "embodying the ultimate" 體極 and that such embodiment must in turn require acquiescence in transformation. (A possible paraphrase of the objection would be: practitioners of your teachings must exist as embodied beings; to the extent that they remain embodied beings they participate in this realm of change, and so they are the ruler's subjects and must pay him obeisance.) Huiyuan responds with another dyad: there are beings that "have feelings concerning transformation" 有情於化 and others that do not. "If one has no feelings concerning transformation, then when transformation ends one's lives cease" 無情於化, 化畢而生盡, whereas if one has feelings concerning transformation one reacts and responds to it, causing ongoing life (i.e. rebirth). Nirvana is the cessation of transformation. So it is by "not encumbering one's life with feelings that one's lives can be extinguished" 不以情累其生, 則生可滅, and "if one does not encumber one's spirit with [repeated] lives, then one's spirit can be made ethereal. An ethereal spirit breaking the bounds: this is what is called nirvana" 不以生累其神, 則神可冥, 冥神絕境, 故謂之泥洹. (The term I here translate as "ethereal", *ming* 冥, was often used to denote the "dark" or "unseen" or "subtle" world of spirits, ghosts, demons, etc., as opposed to the quotidian daylight world.)

The fourth section, which takes up the relationship between Buddhist and indigenous teachings and writings, is less directly relevant for our purposes except insofar as it continues the conceit of distinguishing between matters "within the realm" and those "beyond the realm" and links the latter with things "beyond the six directions" and beyond the senses.

Like a great many arguments in traditional China and elsewhere, then, this one proceeds by setting up an interlinked series of distinctions that function as hierarchical dyads, one side clearly marked as superior to the other:

Table 1: Dyads structuring Huiyuan's argument

+	-
cutting off traces	leaving traces
beyond the realm	within the realm
not acquiescing to transformation	acquiescing to transformation
not involving oneself with life	involving oneself with life
being without feelings	having feelings
not maintaining the body/self	having a body/self
beyond change	within change

In this instance Huiyuan's arguments carried the day; Huan Xuan relented, and monks and nuns retained the prerogative of not bowing before rulers. But this victory would prove short-lived, as will be seen below.

Let us pause to reflect on the terms in which Huiyuan made his case. In positing a state or realm beyond change, beyond rulers' sphere of transformation, and "beyond the realm" of everyday life, a realm further characterized (as Huan Xuan himself also said) by its attention to matters of "spirit", by being "ethereal", and by having as its goal something described as ultimately authoritative and as sharply contrasted with the concerns of ordinary human life as possible, Huiyuan came rather close to positing *a distinct arena of effort and concern that functions analogously to* what would much later come to be designated, beginning in Western European societies, as *"religion"* (as opposed to non-religion) or *"the religious"* (as opposed to the non-religious). The analogy seems even stronger when we consider that Huiyuan had in mind a particular institution – an institution constituted by a human *tradition* of teaching and practice – as the locus in this world where the "cutting off of traces" and the "pursuit of the ultimate principle" were carried out, in contrast to the pursuit of "life" that constituted the default mode of social existence. And, most arrestingly of all, we find this articulation of a distinct sphere precisely at a moment when this institution's authority relative to the imperium was being challenged. A ruler was pushing for ritual obeisance from monks and nuns, whose growing power, status, and wealth he feared; the argument as framed by both sides quickly became a matter of which realm or zone – that of "life" or that of its renunciation, that of "within the realm" or that of "beyond the realm" – was to be recognized as having higher status. For the moment, at least, that argument won which, having posited a distinct realm beyond this one of life and death and change, staked its prestige on that realm and on the extraordinariness and difficulty of reaching it successfully. The parallels to medieval European debates on "temporal" versus "spiritual" power are striking, though I lack space here to explore them further. It is those debates in medieval and early modern Europe that, having carved out "the religious" or "the spiritual" as a zone of power distinct from "the secular", set the stage for the eventual rise of *the generic concept of religion*. It was, I am suggesting, because the Roman Catholic Church successfully claimed a distinct realm of power for itself not subject to the authority of kings, and was able to back up that claim with significant social status and financial and legal power, that *religion as a domain of concern distinct from secular life – religion as a sui generis category of phenomena – became thinkable*, and indeed came to seem so natural that modern scholars registered surprise when they found that many other premodern societies lacked such a category.

But in China, despite the force and temporary success of Huiyuan's argument, the sangha was soon absorbed by the imperial state and was never again – even if it was in Huiyuan's own day, which remains unclear – a truly autonomous body. Monasteries could own land, but such lands were often seized during government crackdowns on monastic wealth and status. In theory the sangha was headed by a monk, but in many eras that monk was appointed by the imperial court and in any case he functioned as an official of the empire, reporting to the central court; and from the Sui dynasty onward even this small degree of autonomy was removed, the office in charge of the sangha being subsumed as one of three bureaus of the Court for State Ceremonials. It was also from the Sui on that government "overseers" (*jian* 監) were placed in every Buddhist monastery and Daoist temple. By the mid-Tang, control of the sangha was solely and powerfully in the hands of the central government, and there it would remain down to the present. And meanwhile, looking at the other side of the coin, the Chinese empire was never, from its inception down to its end in 1911 CE, conceived as anything other than a deeply (in our terms) "religious" system in purpose and in function. Its primary mandate was nothing less than the maintenance of proper relations, primarily through the ritual idiom of sacrifice, between humanity and the forces and divinities of the cosmos. The emperor was a sacred figure; the very term we often render as "emperor" really meant "thearch". So the assumption that the empire should control what we would term "religious" affairs was an old, indigenous assumption in China, and the Buddhist sangha never attained enough power and status to hold for long to any real autonomy. The already-religious nature of the Chinese state never left the sangha (or the Daoist priesthood) much of a separate ground on which to stand.

The shifting nomenclature of the offices charged with oversight of monasteries and temples is of interest for our purposes, as is the shifting placement of these offices in the larger bureaucratic structure of the empire. The details are far too numerous to treat in any detail here, but a few examples will suffice.[35] The term *xuan* 玄 was often used, roughly in the sense of "things beyond ordinary ken, things mysterious", a usage dating back at least to the famous first chapter of the received text of the *Daodejing*: "Mystery of mysteries, the gate of all wonders!"[36] Under the Northern Wei dynasty, for example, the sangha was nominally headed by a single, state-appointed monk; at various times the bureau housing this figure was titled the Office for the Illumination of Mysteries (*zhaoxuan cao* 昭玄曹). The Northern Qi dynasty kept this same nomenclature but raised the office in question to the status of a Court (*si* 寺). Under the Sui this court was downgraded again to the level of a bureau and renamed Bureau for the Veneration of Mysteries (*chongxuan shu* 崇玄署). The Tang seems to have preferred to reserve *xuan* for the titles of Daoist-related offices; special schools for Daoist studies, called *Chongxuan xue* 崇玄學 or Schools for the Veneration of Mysteries, were established within the state university to prepare candidates for an exam on the Daoist canonical scriptures modeled on civil service exams. The old, vaguely metaphysical sense of *xuan*, then, suggested that what was managed under this bureaucratic rubric was somehow importantly *different in kind from* ordinary government affairs.

[35] For a numbingly exhaustive treatment, see Yamazaki Hiroshi 山崎宏, *Shina chūsei Bukkyō no tenkai* 支那中世佛教の展開, Tokyo 1942, 473–516; works by Weinstein, Ch'en, Barrett, the *Cambridge History*, etc., are also useful, although all of these works share the unfortunate habit of examining official treatment of only one religion (Daoism or Buddhism) at a time rather than studying them side by side, making it hard to form a complete picture – a task for future research.

[36] Mair 1990, 59.

But the placement of these offices in the larger bureaucratic system suggested otherwise. Pro-Buddhist (or at least non-anti-Buddhist) rulers tended to subsume them under the Board of Rites, implying that the Buddhist sangha and all that went on there was just another function – and a fully integrated function – of the state, parallel to specifically Confucian rites and to the many kinds of state cults venerating everything from gods of localities and the dynastic ancestors to Heaven and Earth. During the reigns of anti-Buddhist rulers they tended to be placed under the Court for State Ceremonials (*honglu si* 鴻臚寺), the body responsible for receiving foreign emissaries and conducting diplomatic relations, implying that the sangha was seen as not fully integrated and was to be treated as if it were a foreign body. In some cases the location of these offices flip-flopped in the span of a year or two, as rulers changed and ideological winds shifted at court.

Starting in the mid-Tang (the earliest mention dates to 774 CE), a new office with a new name was created to oversee the Buddhist sangha: the Commissioner of Meritorious Works (*gongde shi* 功德使), responsible for merit-making activities such as erecting images, building temples and bridges, and holding vegetarian merit feasts.[37] In 807 Daoist priests and nuns were also placed under this same jurisdiction. To the best of my knowledge, this was the first time in Chinese history that the monastic/priestly institutions of Buddhism and Daoism were placed on a par with one another under the aegis of a common bureaucratic entity. We might be tempted to see here the germ, at least, of the idea of a common genus, of which the things we term "Buddhism" and "Daoism" were both finally being seen as species. Perhaps so. But, unlike "religion(s)", the genus was not a thing separate from ordinary life or the polity: it was an arm of imperial government. And what these two "isms" were being implied to have in common was that they were both systems for the generation of the abstract, moral-theological-cosmological commodity known as "merit". "Merit" was, in turn, the concern not just of private individuals or even families or local communities but also of the state as such. Not only was it a concern of the state: it was a proper function of the state, and so the state oversaw it.

---

[37] For a seminal discussion of the economy of Buddhist merit-making activities, focusing on the practice of bridge-building, see Kieschnick, John, *The Impact of Buddhism on Chinese Material Culture,* Princeton: University Press 2003, 157–219.

I suggest that it was largely due to this aspect of Chinese history that no generic concept or category parallel to our "religion" (in its generic sense) was developed very far. If Huiyuan had conceded that other sorts of practitioners besides Buddhist monks and nuns might be in quest of the "ultimate principle" and thus stand "outside the realm" or "beyond the bounds", if he had imagined his Daoist colleagues on or near Mount Lu to be engaged on a parallel if distinct path, if he had spoken of them too as men and women who were "cutting off their traces" and "not acquiescing in transformation", perhaps he might have been the Chinese progenitor of a category in Chinese history that was closely analogous to "religion" as opposed to "non-religion". But, if he thought in this way, which is highly unlikely, he left no record of it. And after him, there were few or no proposals for a separate sphere of power and activity in the human world, corresponding to a separate level of cosmological or theological reality, that was tolerated by any Chinese dynasty for any length of time.[38] The state itself was – in our terms – among other things a religious institution; it never was thought of as inhabiting a distinct, delimitedly "secular" realm of power, or rather, there was no fundamental distinction between two realms of power and concern, one of them corresponding to what we call "religious" and the other to what we call "secular". The state never ceded these functions to any institutions distinct from itself. Instead, right down to 1911 and beyond, what we would term religious institutions were almost always closely and indeed in many cases very intensely overseen by the state – when tolerated at all – and were conceptualized as branches of government that existed, in part, to serve the state by enhancing its merit and by invoking divine or karmic blessings on it. Without a socially and institutionally distinct space which it might have been created to name, no analogue to the Western generic category "religion" ever emerged indigenously. It was, instead, imported from Western languages by way of Japanese. Now that it has become thoroughly rooted in Chinese discourse, it will remain there, having forever changed the ideological, social, legal, and – as "we" and "they" would both now say – religious landscape of Chinese culture.

[38] One thing that there *were* were periodic debates at court between representatives of Daoism and of Buddhism. One way in which I hope to expand and improve this paper is to study closely the nomenclature and terminology used in records of these debates to see if anything is mentioned that comes close to constituting a genus of which these two great traditions were conceived as species. But this would be a very surprising finding.

A RESPONSE TO ROBERT FORD CAMPANY'S "CHINESE HISTORY AND ITS IMPLICATIONS FOR WRITING 'RELIGION(S)'"

Russell T. McCutcheon

Because I suspect that Prof. Campany and I have some theoretical differences when it comes to the role played by classification in knowledge systems, before I offer my reply let me first briefly illustrate how I understand classification systems to work.

I draw my example from the first U.S. Presidential election debate, held on September 26, 2008; in his opening remarks, the moderator, American journalist Jim Lehrer, set the evening's parameters as follows: "Tonight's [debate] will primarily be about foreign policy and national security, which, by definition, includes the global financial crisis." Now, for anyone following the U.S. news during the last weeks of September, it was obvious what he was talking about, for at the time of the debate a proposal to inject $700 billion tax dollars was being considered by the U.S. Congress, transferring what the press was already calling "toxic debt" from private banks to the government. The two parties' Presidential candidates had, earlier that day, flown to Washington DC, at President Bush's invitation, to participate in meetings intended to create a consensus among the two parties concerning how to address what pretty much everyone was by then calling a crisis. The meetings failed and so, at the time of that evening's debate, the government had arrived at no plan to rescue U.S. banks.

Although that first debate was previously scheduled to be on foreign policy and national security – focusing on topics external to the nation – events internal to the U.S., which already had obvious worldwide consequences, could not be ignored, suggesting that the common distinction between inside and outside was no longer as useful as the Commission on Presidential Debates had previously thought. In fact, the moderator's choice of opening words – calling what was then simply one nation's problem a "global financial crisis" – made evident that, at least when it comes to banking, the day had long past when such classifications as "domestic" and "foreign" could sensibly be used as if they applied to separable things. (A fact made evident as the American banking and insurance crisis began sweeping across the rest of the world.)

I assume it was because he recognized that his viewers' common sense understanding of the world – what a scholar might term their folk classification system – normally distinguished between the domestic and the foreign that the moderator made the linkage explicit when prefacing the debate by saying:

> General Eisenhower said in his 1952 presidential campaign: "We must achieve both security and solvency. In fact, the foundation of military strength is economic strength".[1]

Despite a generation of scholars theorizing this process that we now know as globalization, I'd hazard a guess that most of the debate's viewers assumed that the local is easily distinguishable in some essential way from the global. That this distinction does not necessarily reflect how such things as corporations and banks actually work has become painfully evident to investors around the world.

What I find interesting about this minor episode in classification is that it makes apparent that there are times when the analytic utility of widely used folk taxonomies – that is, conceptual systems that members of social groups use to manage their environment and their place, and the place of Others, within it – can be so diminished as to make their continued use part of the problem. Although there are times when one can unreflectively distinguish between such seemingly different things as, say, military, political, and economic issues and events, or when the usually self-evident boundaries of a nation-state enable one to distinguish, say, an American issue from a French or German situation, the fact of the U.S. waging a war which is currently estimated to cost $12 billion per month[2] while also injecting nearly a trillion dollars into a transnational investment and insurance system[3] – money that

[1] The complete transcript of the debate used can be found at http://www.clipsandcomment.com/2008/09/26/full-transcript-first-presidential-debatebarack-obama-john-mccainoxford-ms-september-26-2008/(accessed September 28, 2008).

[2] See http://abcnews.go.com/International/wireStory?id=4418698 (accessed September 28. 2008). See http://www.cbo.gov/ftpdocs/86xx/doc8690/10-24-CostOfWar_Testimony.pdf for the U.S.'s Congressional Budget Office document from March 24, 2007, which estimates that $604 billion had been spent on the two wars from September 2001 until the end of 2007.

[3] According to the Whitehouse's Office of Management and Budget, the 2008 budget's projected income will total $2.662 trillion (the expenditures will total $2.9 trillion, adding $239 billion to the Federal deficit), making the proposed "bail out"

has to be borrowed from lenders abroad – and doing all of this in the final weeks of a U.S. Presidential election, well, this made apparent that it was in no ones interest to continue to distinguish between the domains formerly known as domestic and foreign.

I open my response to a paper on the place of the category "religion" in writing Chinese history by referencing this example to make the following point, one that I think ought to guide us in our work on the category "religion": for historically-minded scholars – that is, scholars who conceive their object of study, the world of human doings, as a contingent affair with no pristine originary moment and no Hegelian end point to which events are irresistibly moving – the tools that we use to name and thereby divide up and organize the world (such tools as the categories of "the past," "the nation," "tradition," "meaning," and "religion") are our tools and are thus no less a part of the world of human doings than the subjects we study by using them, making our categories not neutral descriptors of stable, self-evident realities but, instead, products of human interests that are used by social actors in specific situations. What's more, should those social actors, their situations, and their interests change, then the tools will need to be retooled, perhaps even discarded entirely – much as the once prominent categories "taboo" and "mana" have long departed from our scholarly, analytic vocabularies. The scholars that I have in mind therefore do their work presuming that there is no god's eye vantage point and thus, as Prof. Campany points out near the opening of his paper's pre-distributed version[4], that there is no neutral language – which I read as recognizing that there is no significance to be found without also evidence of prior systems of signification – themselves historical products. To illustrate the first: despite its inventor's hopes for universality, Esperanto is but one more language among others. To illustrate the second: without prior sets of interests (such as U.S. voters' concern for their retirement savings and their homes'

approximately 38% of 2008's receipts; see http://www.whitehouse.gov/omb/budget/fy2008/summarytables.html (accessed September 28, 2008).

[4] The paper that Prof. Campany delivered at the conference was slightly different from the earlier version which I received and based on which this reply was written. I gather that the final version which he submitted for publication in this volume was another revision. This reply, which was sent to him prior to it being delivered at the conference, is based on the original version of the paper received prior to the conference.

values), there would have been no reason to spend half of that first Presidential debate discussing banks and home mortgages.

With all this in mind, I propose that studying classification systems – such as the longstanding practice of naming a part of the world of human doings as "religion" or "religious" – by examining, as Prof. Campany proposes, which taxonomy better fits the facts on the ground, so to speak, is an unhelpful way to advance our studies, for the positivist facts on the ground can be argued to be a product of the classification systems themselves. To appeal to a biological example, it makes little sense to ask whether a whale really is a fish or a mammal (that is, which category better fits the apparent biological reality of the whale), for in and of itself – whatever that sort of ontological speculation may actually mean – a whale is neither. Instead, what we know as a whale becomes understandable as a fish – that is, can be seen to share a certain number of traits with those other things we call fish – only once we use a specific set of criteria to name, sort, and thereby manage our surroundings. Change our interests and needs, change our criteria, change the way in which we establish relationships of similarity and difference among items we deem significant and worth paying attention to, and the whale ends up being a mammal – a case made abundantly clear in Graham Burnett's recent book, entitled *Trying Leviathan*[5], in which he examines an 1818 New York state court case on this very topic – a case that took place just as once dominant morphological classifications of the biological world were giving way in Europe and North America to taxonomies based on anatomical studies. Should your interests be to exchange barrels of whale oil for profit, without paying what was then a New York state tax on the sale of fish oils, then you might understand what drove the effort to reclassify what was then the commonsense designation of the whale as merely being a big fish.

What I hope is evident from this example is that a close examination of the facts on the ground – whether whales in the sea or people doing supposedly religious things (or, better put, leaving artifacts that we can name as religious) in ancient China – cannot settle such a taxonomic debate; it can only be settled by adjudicating between the competing sets of interests that drive, and the effects that result from, the

[5] Burnett, D. Graham, *Trying Leviathan: The Nineteenth-Century New York Court Case That Put the Whale on Trial and Challenged the Order of Nature.* Princeton, NJ: Princeton University Press 2007.

application of differing systems of classification. And it is this focus on unspoken criteria, and the theories and interests that drive them, that I bring to my reading of Prof. Campany's paper. I will therefore pose six questions in response, questions whose answers may shed some light on what he has described as the "conceptual and terminological pitfalls [that] arise when writing about religion in premodern China".[6]

1

Although it seems to prioritize actual historical data over merely imported theory, I do not believe that Prof. Campany's inversion of his original paper title is all that helpful – such as when he opens by saying, "I will ask, in short, not so much how the modern Western notion of 'religion' shapes our writing of Chinese history as how Chinese history might impact our use of the notion of 'religion'"[7]; for without the prior category religion, defined in a particular sort of way (and more on this below), I am unsure what criteria he employed to narrow down the human doings within that grouping he names as "early medieval Chinese history" to just those that, in his words, "are relevant to our topic".[8] For as I understand discourses on the past, they must employ some mechanism of constraint to enable one to conceptualize anything as constituting this thing we call "the past." I say this because I assume that the archive of human doings that have preceded our own is virtually limitless (even taking into account that this archive only contains those acts which left some sort of empirical trace for us to find). So if we start, as in his inverted paper title, with the so-called historical facts on the ground, to see how well they fit our category – what Prof. Campany elsewhere refers to as "the realia of Chinese religious history"[9] or simply "the historical phenomena"[10] that, as I read him, seem to precede the "often-unconscious assumptions about religion(s) made by writers" – then what system of constraint has he employed to find in that massive archive of long past human doings, all of which, he agrees, predate or at least fall outside the invention of the category

[6] See above the article in this volume Campany, p. 274.
[7] In the here printed version this quotation slightly differs, cfr. p. 273 (the editors).
[8] In the original conference paper Campany speaks about „early medieval Chinese usages" (the editors).
[9] See above the article in this volume Campany, p. 277.
[10] See above the article in this volume Campany, p. 280.

"religion," just those that, to quote again, "are relevant to our topic"? So my first question is: How, without starting with the category "religion," did he select the historical acts discussed in his paper from the many things that constitute early medieval Chinese history? I ask this because all of his data strikes me as remarkably alike those particular beliefs, behaviors, and institutions that would normally be grouped together in a world religion's textbook's chapter as comprising this thing called early medieval Chinese religion. My point? I detect here a methodological problem similar to Max Weber's well known opening claim, in his *The Sociology of Religion*,[11] that religion could only be defined at the end of his study; despite working without a definition, Weber somehow yet knew that his study ought to have chapters on gods, priests, ethics, prophets, congregations, pastoral care, preaching, etc. So my point has to do with the fact that, at least as I see it, we have no choice but to employ imported, so-called alien categories when we, as scholars, confront the world – a point that, I believe, runs contrary to what I suspect is Prof. Campany's phenomenologically-based, historiographically positivist assumption that an external world of historical phenomena precedes our use of theoretical, organizing concepts.

2

Despite how popular it has become to distinguish between the plural noun "religions" and the singular noun "religion," I think that this distinction is terribly misleading. While I understand that many today think that, for example, talking about, "Judaisms" rather than "Judaism" is evidence of a more nuanced approach to social difference – inasmuch as it avoids the sort of essentialism and reification that comes with presuming religions to be monolithic things – such work leaves untheorized just what it is about these many Judaisms that enables us to see them, in the first place, as each constituting a distinct species and, in the second, to see them as members of the same genus. Simply put, I am unsure how one regulates this endlessly plural economy, for, according to this line of thought, would there not be as many Islams as there are Muslims? Or, as I suspect to be the case in such scholarship, are there certain unarticulated, and thus untheorized, differences that

[11] Weber, Max, *The Sociology of Religion*, Talcott Parsons (intro.), Boston: Beacon Press (1922) 1993.

we can obviously overlook, in order to produce such workable generalizations as, for example, "Mainline Protestantism" versus "Evangelical Protestantism"? To press further, do we overlook the differences and accentuate the similarities that group members themselves overlook or focus upon in their effort to form group identities or are we, as scholars, not limited to the participants' folk taxonomies? For, according to my opening illustrations, uncritically reproducing – instead of studying! – local classification systems will lead to us, as scholars, normalizing participant distinctions and the interests that drive them, such as when we, for example, adopt a distinction specific to a group and end up talking about Shi'ites as being obviously different from Sunnis. Sadly, in adopting these participant distinctions we fail to ask: different according to whose criteria? – a question that, once posed, would allow us to examine the mechanisms by which identities are created and contested. Therefore, to my way of approaching these topics, the seemingly progressive move to the plural simply side-steps the tough work of identifying the supposed theme upon which differences are said to play. So let me ask my second question: Of what are these things called religions composed so as to make them all members of a genus that is apparently distinguishable from, say, social and political systems? Depending how this question is answered, the discredited but resilient category of sui generis religion re-enters our field.

3

I am also unsure how looking for "indigenous analogues"[12] for our notion of religion helps us – whether we go looking in China's past or anywhere else, for that matter. I say this because, as every knows, there are more definitions of religion than we know what to do with – back in 1912 the appendix to James Leuba's *A Psychological Study of Religion*[13] famously informed us that there are more than fifty. So, before looking for analogues of our concept religion in ancient China, I think we need to ask my third question: Analogues of what? That is, why did Prof. Campany settle on the prototype that he did as the basis for his cross-cultural comparative work? For when he states that "[t]

[12] See above the article in this volume Campany, p. 280.
[13] Leuba, James H., *A Psychological Study of Religion: Its Origin, Function, and Future.* New York: The MacMillan Co. 1912.

here were certainly many things going on in early medieval China that anyone familiar with the term ['religion'] would now say were 'religious' in nature"[14], I wonder with which use of the term "religion" we must be familiar in order to recognize these things – for will we not see different things, all depending which concept we come armed with? From the data on which he draws – things called Buddhism and Daoism which apparently involve such things as tales about founders, sacrificial ritual, temples, monks and nuns, textual traditions, ancestor veneration, and some sort of distinction between the spiritual and the mundane or this realm and some other – it is obvious that he is not employing either Sigmund Freud's definition of religion as illusory wish-fulfillment or Karl Marx's understanding of religion as a form of bourgeois ideology, let alone Ninian Smart's view of religion as but one among the host of worldviews – for using any of these old but well known models as his prototype would not have limited his cast of historical characters to the usual suspects. So it seems to me that, in looking for analogues to a particular folk conception of religion prominent in our own social group, his paper naturalizes one local, historically specific understanding of the term (an apparently classical, phenomenological sense of the term, though I admit I did not find his definition of religion explicitly stated anywhere in the paper – more than likely because it is simply the popular folk concept operative throughout our own social group and thus one that most readers simply assume from the outset) – something which is less than helpful if scholars wish to historicize the discourse on religion and the interests that are furthered by reproducing the notion that certain human institutions are something other than, or more than, social, political, and economic.

4

After describing the metaphorically loaded nature of discourses on religion – and I recall here my appreciative citation, earlier in this reply, of Prof. Campany's thoughts on the situatedness of language – he suggests, again, in a surprisingly positivist manner, that we proceed by "set[ting] metaphors aside to ask what the purported things we call religions really, non-metaphorically speaking, are in an ontologically

[14] See above the article in this volume Campany, p. 285.

rather literal sense".[15] He concludes that, instead of being what many people take them to be – that is, seeing religions as entities, agents, organisms, or containers, all of which can act in the world and do things for people – they instead ought to be understood as repertoires of cultural resources and imagined communities.[16] Now, I admit that I have some difficulty placing his claim about literal meaning in anything but a contradictory relationship with his earlier claim that "language is metaphorical in character"[17], unless, of course, Prof. Campany's scholarly language is somehow exempt from the limitations of ordinary language – a position I suspect that he is not trying to assert, given that his paper, like my own, is filled with metaphors. Now, as I understand it, meaning-making is, by definition, a metaphoric activity whereby relationships of similarity and difference are established (as opposed to being passively recognized) within systems of constraint (such as a grammar) – systems that are themselves social and historical and thus by no means in any sort of necessary correspondence to the way things really are. It is precisely in this way that we can say that, despite that old saying, apples and oranges are indeed comparable since they both possess sufficient traits that we have identified as belonging to our higher order concept, "fruit." To press the point I could make reference to Prof. Campany's earlier claim that historical phenomena "impact" our theoretical categories (for the word "impact" suggests an attribution of agency and massive solidity that, at least when found in descriptions of religions, he finds problematic) but, instead, consider how moving from saying that a religion is like an agent that grows (a position he finds limiting because it reifies) is any different from saying that religion is like a repertoire of resources that get used. My fourth question, then, is: By what standard can we judge which metaphoric way of talking about the world is any closer either to the literal truth of the situation or the so-called facts on the ground? Moreover, will not our criterion of judgment, used to decide between these options, be metaphoric as well? Why, in other words, should I be persuaded that the Buddhist metaphor, as Prof. Campany identifies

[15] See above the article in this volume Campany, p. 277.

[16] The text passage of the conference paper McCutcheon refers to reads: "They are, among other things, (1) repertoires of cultural resources made and used over time by many agents, and (2) imagined communities stretching across time and space" (the editors).

[17] See above the article in this volume Campany, p. 274.

it, of "path" is any more or less adequate to the study of religion, than is "religion"?

5

I would also like to ask: How can our assumptions about religion be judged to "create misunderstandings and falsify our representations of the Chinese religious situations"[18]? I would like this answered because, without the category of religion up and running, I do not see how Prof. Campany can qualify any Chinese situation as religious – a qualification that, once made, he then uses to judge some modern uses of the category "religion" as inappropriate (I recall how this problematic circularity arises in the second question he sets out to answer in his paper: "How does Chinese religious history invite us to rethink our models and assumptions about religion"[19]) The use of the adjective "religious," here and in many other places throughout his paper, is apparently unproblematic, much as those who seem to be untroubled by the assumption that, although the noun religion is a reifying colonial import, the actual people who are inappropriately grouped by means of this singular noun nonetheless have active and rich religious lives. Only if one assumes a specific view of the individual, a view more than likely limited to post-seventeenth-century Europe, is the adjective, which apparently qualifies the individual, somehow free of the problems of the noun – whether singular or plural.

6

And finally, I am curious what other modern field of intellectual pursuit has the problems that Prof. Campany finds to plague our own. For if, as he argues, "conceptual and terminological pitfalls arise when authors … write about religion in early medieval China, a culture which … lacked analogues to our generic sense of 'religion'"[20], then what about the no less alien, Latin based concept "culture" that he uses in that very sentence, let alone the presumption that the relatively recent nation-state designation, "China," can be pitched backward in

[18] See above the article in this volume Campany, p. 277.
[19] See above the article in this volume Campany, p. 274.
[20] See above the article in this volume Campany, p. 277.

time to unify a few thousand years of history, as well as the imported chronological designation "medieval"? Now, please do not misunderstand me; I am not suggesting that we cannot use local terms to talk about things removed from us in time and space; on the contrary – I think that's all we are able to do. So, my sixth and final question is: Which of our alien imports must be used with caution and which can be used without thinking. For I suspect that Prof. Campany would have no trouble talking about, say, the DNA or the ideology of ancient Chinese people; if so, then why the difficulties with the concept "religion"?

I pose these six questions in hopes of pressing further with our work to historicize the means by which we as scholars name and study the world we inhabit – itself an historically specific practice that I think ought not to involve authorizing certain folk taxonomies that we may come across in our work, as if they adequately describe the very nature of things – even if they be the taxonomies of the groups that we ourselves go home to when we leave the offices and classrooms.

TERMINOLOGY AND RELIGIOUS IDENTITY: BUDDHISM AND THE GENEALOGY OF THE TERM *ZONGJIAO*

Tim H. Barrett and Francesca Tarocco

> There is no doubt that we live on one side of a great divide, where religion is something one thinks about rather than something one does.[1]

In contemporary China and Taiwan, the hegemonic projection of uniformity of the meaning of the word *zongjiao* (宗教) that is used to represent the English term 'religion' in the discourse of policies and of academic analyses and that implies a coherent and exclusive system and a churchlike organisation is still contested and subverted by dissonant voices. Vincent Goossaert notes grassroots use of the term 'superstition' whereby practitioners choose to identify their own activities as belief not in 'religion' but in 'superstition' (*wo bu xin zongjiao, wo xin mixin* 我不信宗教我信迷信).[2] Recent field work in Taiwan highlights the discomfort of regular temple goers with having to identify with any one 'teaching' (*jiao* 教) over one's normal reference to 'paying respect/worshiping gods and buddhas' (*bai shenfo* 拜 神佛)[3] However, the progressive affirmation in China of the notion of an exclusive religious identity based on contrastive conceptions of religious traditions is undeniable.

While research on religious topics has been constantly growing during the last decade, the emergence in the nineteenth century of a novel conception of religion – a notion that was at considerable variance with the ideas and practices of earlier periods – and of the terminology to describe it, are yet to be fully investigated. China, of course, lacked the lexical equivalent of the term 'religion' in its post-Reformation acceptation as a discrete feature of culture and a matter of individual

[1] Charles John Sommerville, *The Secularization of Early Modern England: From Religious Culture to Religious Faith*, New York and Oxford: Oxford University Press, 1992, 9.

[2] Vincent Goossaert "The Concept of Religion in China and the West", in: *Diogenes* 205, 19.

[3] Ester-Maria Guggenmos, personal e-mail communication, 24 November 2008.

belief.[4] The subject of the present short paper discusses the Buddhist bias intrinsic in the choice of the new term *zongjiao* to designate official discourse on religion in the twentieth century.

The work of Talal Asad may have alerted scholars everywhere to the problems involved in using the word 'religion' as if it were a universal category innocent of specifically European connotations.[5] Yet, for the one fourth of humanity who live in East Asia and use forms of writing based on the Chinese script, most scholars still seem content to accept a simplified account of the origins of the modern Japanese word *shûkyô* and Chinese *zongjiao* that glosses over many of the complexities and ambiguities involved in its creation.[6] What is offered here, then, is a step towards a fuller account of the history of the term that gives due weight to the crucial but complex developments in the mid-nineteenth century. We believe that these developments, while they resulted in the adoption by so many contemporary language users, for better or worse, of a term now regarded as their word corresponding to 'religion', may be seen as pointing to a background in earlier discourse on religious topics. A close look at the evidence does not suggest a neologism especially coined to meet the needs of contact with the West, and so conveying no more and no less than the connotations of the word in Europe and America, but something much more nuanced. As we are at pains to point out in our conclusions, we do not see our work as definitive, and we have also striven to be fairly concise in the presentation of our findings, which might at a number of points bear more extended discussion. Even so, it is hoped that this brief communication may serve as a stimulus to further debate, and especially further research.

[4] For the situation in the late nineteenth century see Vincent Goossaert, "1898: The Beginning of the End for Chinese Religion?", in: *The Journal of Asian Studies* 65 no. 2. (May 2006), 307–336. Cfr. Stephan Feuchtwang/Wang Ming-ming "The Politics of Culture or a Contest of Histories: Representation of Chinese Popular Religion", in: *Dialectical Anthropology* 16 (1991), 251–272, for post 1978 official attitudes.

[5] See Talal Asad, *Genealogies of Religion: Discipline and Reasons of Power in Christianity and Islam*, Baltimore: John Hopkins University Press, 1993. Cfr. Ugo Bianchi (ed.), *The Notion of 'Religion' in Comparative Research: Selected Proceedings of the XVIth Congress of the International Association of the History of Religions*, Rome: L'Erma di Bretschneider, 1994; Jordan Paper, *The Spirits are Drunk: Comparative Approaches to Chinese Religion*, Albany: SUNY Press, 1995.

[6] In what follows, we have not considered the origins of the Korean term, since we assume that Korea was not significantly involved in bringing the two components of the term together. This assumption may be incorrect.

To most modern writers on China the matter is simple: the Chinese language had no word for 'religion', and the modern term is simply a borrowing from Japanese.[7] This certainly accounts for the proximate origin of the term in Chinese, and conveniently situates it amongst the many novel combinations of Chinese characters put together to express neologisms drawn from the vocabulary of European languages that first came into use in Japan in the late nineteenth century and were later transmitted to China, as reformers in that country looked to Japan for a model of modernization.[8] If we turn to writers on Japan, however, we find a palpable sense of unease in the use of the word, a sense that somehow its semantic range is surprisingly restricted, together with some attempts at trying to uncover the roots of this phenomenon.[9] One recent investigation would see the conjunction of the two Chinese characters employed in the term as going back rather earlier, to the eighteenth century writings of Tominaga Nakamoto (1715–1746), wherein they are already used to express a notion roughly equivalent to the European one of 'religion', but as the result of independent developments, not borrowing from Europe.[10] Tominaga was certainly a thinker far ahead of his time, and the notion that he was already formulating some sort of disciplined study of religion is a very attractive one.[11] But unfortunately to the extent that this

[7] This contention may be found as early as William Edward Soothill, *The Three Religions of China,* Oxford: Oxford University Press, 1923, 14–15. A short analysis of missionary and Buddhist discourse is found in Francesca Tarocco, "The Making of Religion in Modern China", in: Nile Green/Mary Searle Chatterjie (eds.), *Religion, Language and Power*, New York: Routledge, 42–56.

[8] As we shall see, though Federico Masini has questioned this general narrative up to a point in his pioneering study "The Formation of Modern Chinese Lexicon and its Evolution Towards a National Language: The Period from 1840 to 1898", in: *Journal of Chinese Linguistics*, Monograph Series number 6, 1993, he still sees the word *zongjiao* as having taken the course – hitherto regarded as unproblematic for most of China's modern intellectual vocabulary – from Japanese invention back to China. The earliest occurrence of *zongjiao* in China cited by Masini is the *Ribenguo zhi* (an account of the state of Japan, 1890).

[9] For a good encapsulation of this sense of a problem, see Ian Reader, *Religion in Contemporary Japan,* Basingstoke: Macmillan, 1991, 13–14.

[10] Thus Michael Pye, "What is 'Religion' in East Asia?", in: Ugo Bianchi, (ed.), *The Notion of 'Religion' in Comparative Research: Selected Proceedings of the XVIth Congress of the International Association of the History of Religions*, Rome: L'Erma di Bretschneider, 1994, 115–122.

[11] Note Tim H. Barrett, "Tominaga our Contemporary", in: *Journal of the Royal Asiatic Society,* series 3, 3.1 (July, 1993), 245–252, which attempts to provide a reading of part of Tominaga's work bringing out some of his combination of erudition and critical sense.

argument is based upon this apparent specific innovation in the terminology that he employs in discussing religion, it must be set aside as deriving from nothing more than a mistranslation. Tominaga, in the passage in question, is discussing the range of doctrines that had formerly rivalled Buddhism, in the course of which he refers in passing to the Manichaean heresy. How accurate his knowledge was, and whence he derived it, are interesting questions that cannot be entered into here. But it does certainly appear as though he speaks as if a certain "Futtotan transmitted two religions", using the two Chinese characters meaning 'main line or principle of doctrine' and 'teaching' that go to make up the modern word *zongjiao*.[12]

In fact, research into the history of this famous heresy in China suggests that the apparent name is actually a title and that the reference is not to "two religions", but to the "Teaching of the Two Principles", an important work within the Manichaean tradition well attested in Chinese sources that the dignitary is said to have been the first to transmit to China.[13]

This is not to say that the two characters meaning 'main line/principle' (*zong* 宗) and 'teaching' (*jiao* 教) do not occur in some relation to each other in pre-modern texts, but a full investigation of their relationship takes us back to China rather than Japan and requires a few words on the invention of the religious vocabulary there by Buddhists in early mediaeval times. *Zong* is a slightly tricky term, originally meaning the main ancestral line, and by extension anything else one looked back to and identified with, so that in more abstract contexts it is often translated 'principle'. The move from a kinship term to indicate also an intellectual relationship parallels the same course taken by *jia* (家), originally 'family', but also used variously over time as a label grouping intellectual phenomena, and later *zu* (祖), used in both the literal and religious (specifically Zen) sense of patriarch.[14] The second element, *jiao*, on the other hand, means, more or less, 'teaching'. The two words, to judge by the recapitulation of earlier classifications of

[12] The translation is that of Michael Pye, in: Tominaga Nakamoto, *Emerging from Meditation,* London: Duckworth, 1990, 157.

[13] For the work in question, see Samuel N. C. Lieu, *Manichaeism in Central Asia and China,* Leiden: E. J. Brill, 1998, 114.147–148.162–163 and for the dignitary in question 84.

[14] On the former term, see Mark Csikszentmihàlyi/Michael Nylan, "Constructing Lineages and Inventing Traditions Through Exemplary Figures in Early China", in: *T'oung-pao* 89 (2003), 59–99; on the latter, note Tim H. Barrett "'Kill the Patriarchs!'", in: Tadeusz Skorupski (ed.), *The Buddhist Forum*, I, London: SOAS, 1990, 87–97.

varieties of Buddhism by the great Chinese Buddhist thinker Fazang (642–712), had first been brought together in the sixth century by one or two scholar-monks who differentiated strand in Buddhist thought as different 'principle-teachings', combining the two terms, though other similar terms were also current.[15] This terminology, moreover, did not become established. Fazang himself classified the strands of Buddhist thought into five teachings and ten principles, with the first term covering obvious distinctions and the second the more subtle doctrinal positions, particularly those differentiating the 'teachings' lumped together as outside the scope of developed Mahåyåna Buddhism, but does not conjoin the two terms himself in his own analysis.[16] It seems furthermore unlikely that Fazang's work, a somewhat dense philosophical piece, perpetuated the use of the compound term *zongjiao*, though it was intensively studied after its export to Japan amongst the Buddhist clergy there – more so, it seems, than eventually became the case in China.[17] The combination of *zong* and *jiao* appears to have remained a slightly *ad hoc* one, as is evidenced by the fact that in commentary we sometimes find the collocation *jiaozong* (教宗), or the Japanese equivalent, reversing what to us has become the normal order of the two components.[18] This is true also in a work by one

[15] Fazang seems not to have been the first great master of the Sui-Tang period to allude to these earlier classifications, but his remarks are the most explicit; cf. Mochizuki Shinkô, *Bukkyô Daijiten*, Tokyo: Sekai seiten kankô kyôkai, 1957–68, 2229–2230; Suzuki Norihisa, *Meiji shûkyô shichô no kenkyû*, Tokyo: Daigaku shuppansha, 1979, 14.

[16] Fazang, *Huayan yicheng jiao yi fen qi zhang*, 1, 480c–481b, in the Taishô edition of the Canon, vol. 45, text no. 1866. Later exegetes generally refer to this text by the shorter, unofficial title of *Huayan Wujiao zhang*. For an attempt at conveying its thought in English, see Francis H. Cook, *Hua-yen Buddhism: The Jewel Net of Indra*, University Park: The Pennsylvania State University Press, 1977.

[17] Kamata Shigeo, *Kegongaku kenkyû shiryô shûsei*, Tokyo: Tokyo daigaku Tôyô bunka kenkyûjo, 1983, 247–304, provides a very useful survey of the history of commentary on this text in East Asia. The main text itself was included in the official, government produced imperial canon under late imperial dynasties, including that of the final Manchu dynasty, but by the nineteenth century seems to have been little studied, to judge by the Chinese interest in Japanese editions and commentaries, once contact between fellow Buddhists in these countries had been re-established towards the end of the imperial period: note Chen Jidong, *Shin-matsu Bukkyô no kenkyû*, Tokyo: Sankibô, 2003, 511.514. 538.564.577.

[18] Nakamura Hajime, *Bukkyôgo daijiten*, Tokyo: Tokyo shoseki, 1975, 231c, cites an example of the two elements in reverse order from a medieval Japanese commentary on a work in the same tradition as Fazang by Gyônen (1240–1321); according to Suzuki, *Meiji shûkyô*, 14, this monk also used the elements in the more usual order in one of his other compositions.

of Fazang's later successors in his line of exegetical thought, Zongmi (780–841), which we take to be far more significant to the history of *zongjiao*.[19]

His is an introductory work outlining his overall view of the Zen tradition, to which he also adhered, in relation to other varieties of Buddhism.[20] In two instances, (one from the preface, which is by Zongmi's lay patron), the collocation *jiaozong* seems to be used to indicate a doctrinally distinct strand of Buddhism, or rather a strand distinct from the field of Zen with which the author concerns himself, but in a third passage, *zongjiao* is used for something more inclusive, the teaching of the entire lineage of Zen masters stretching back through Bodhidharma to the Buddha himself, a usage more concrete than in Fazang, and one no doubt prompted by the prominence in Zen of more pseudo-familial terminology than elsewhere.[21] Zongmi's Zen writings, unlike the doctrinal treatises of Fazang, made little headway in Japan, but were immensely influential in Korea and China.[22] In the former country, Chinul (1158–1210) drew on Zongmi in constructing a form of Zen practice that could be harmonized with the doctrinal (i. e., *jiao*) approach of other schools.[23] In the case of China, it is possible to trace the study of Zongmi's *Prolegomenon* down to the nineteenth century, when *zong* and *jiao* first became embroiled with European meanings, since in the early nineteenth century the reformer Gong Zizhen (1792–1841) specifically commends it, and notes the edition currently availa-

[19] On this important figure one may consult the excellent monograph of Peter N. Gregory, *Tsung-mi and the Sinification of Buddhism*, Princeton: Princeton University Press, 1991.

[20] *Chanyuan zhuquanji duxu, Prolegomenon to the Collected Expressions of the Zen Source*, in the translation of Jeff Broughton, who gives a good overview of the traditional and modern scholarship relating to it in "Tsung-mi's *Zen Prolegomenon:* Introduction to an Exemplary Zen Canon", in: Steven Heine/Dale Wright (eds.), *The Zen Canon: Understanding the Classic Texts*, New York: Oxford University Press, 2004, 11–51.

[21] For these references, see respectively Zongmi, *Chanyuan zhuchuanji duxu*, 1, 398b23 (by Zongmi's patron, Pei Xiu); 2, 409a3; and 1, 405b16, in the edition of the Taishô Canon, volume 48, text number 2015. The last type of usage also occurs in another text on Zen by Zongmi, according to Komazawa daijiten hensanjo (ed.), *Zengaku daijiten*, Tokyo: Taishûkan, 1978, 481d. For Zen 'patriarchs', see n. 14 above; the different branches of Zen were also commonly referred to as 'families', *jia*.

[22] For Zongmi in Japan, see Broughton, "Tsung-mi's *Zen Prolegomenon*", 40–41, which draws on work by Kamata Shigeo.

[23] Robert Buswell, *The Collected Works of Chinul*, Honolulu: University of Hawai'i Press, 1983, 25.

ble.[24] This makes the use of Zongmi's terminology by Gong's friend and fellow-reformer Wei Yuan (1794–1856) particularly interesting. Wei contrasts "emphasizing one's own spirit within, concentrating on the perfect and sudden", which he terms *zong-jiao,* with "looking up to the Buddhas without, and using one's spiritual power to trigger their power", which is how he understands the devotional practices subsumed under the name of Pure Land; both of these he declares to be sustained by a further element, the observance of the Buddhist precepts *(vinaya).*[25] In another passage in praise of Pure Land piety, he states that the Buddhist clergy is composed of the two groupings concerned with *zong* and *jiao,* but then commends one great exegete and one great Zen master who combined their approaches with Pure Land practice as well.[26] Since the Zen master in question, Yanshou (904–975), a later admirer of Zongmi, in one of his works also explicitly follows him in using the terms *zong* and *jiao* both together and in apposition to represent respectively the lineage of Bodhidharma and the doctrinal school to which he adhered (again, like Zongmi, that of Fazang), one might suspect that Wei had read Yanshou's remarks too.[27] But though Gong Zizhen was demonstrably at least aware of this work by Yanshou, he does not specifically commend it, so there is less likelihood that Wei Yuan had been encouraged to tackle it.[28] It is indeed hard to judge how readily available the work would have been. However, it must be noted that the Morrison Collection, based on materials gathered at the start of the nineteenth century in the Canton area by China's first Protestant missionary, does include a short work by Yanshou, but not this much more substantial treatise.[29] For even if Wei Yuan had attempted to read it, unlike Yanshou's writings on Zen and Pure Land, the text is unusually voluminous (twenty-five times the bulk of Zongmi's work), with the relevant material over one third

[24] Gong Zizhen, *Gong Zizhen quanji,* Part 6, Shanghai: Shanghai renmin chubanshe, 1975, 405.

[25] Wei Yuan, *Wei Yuan ji,* Beijing; Zhonghua shuju, 1976, 247.

[26] Wei Yuan, *Wei Yuan ji,* 249.

[27] For the passage in question, note Yanshou, *Zongjing lu* 34, 614a13–21, in the edition of the Taishô Canon, no. 2016, vol. 48; note also earlier *Zongjing lu* 29, 588b24. Broughton, "Tsung-mi's *Zen Prolegomenon*", 38, observes that this treatise by Yanshou was also used by Chinul, and briefly had an influence in Japan, though this had waned long before the nineteenth century.

[28] Gong Zizhen, *Gong Zizhen quanji,* 390.

[29] Andrew C. West, *Catalogue of the Morrison Collection,* London: School of Oriental and African Studies, 1998, 195.

of the way through. We hesitate to assume that Wei Yuan read that far, and so had Yanshou's recapitulation of Zongmi in mind as well in the two passages in which he discusses *zong* and *jiao*, though it is of course a distinct possibility.[30] These sections in Wei's writings on Pure Land Buddhism even so may be taken to show that Wei considered the business of clerical Buddhism, beyond the pietism suitable for both clergy and laity, to be summed up in the two terms, which to him appear to indicate the *zong*, or ancestral lineages of the Zen school, and the *jiao*, or doctrines of the other schools. This usage still appears to be somewhat *ad hoc*, suggesting not a regular compound but two terms with semantic affinities that tended to bring them together. But although the two may perhaps have been brought together elsewhere accidentally, in China as in Japan, the precedent of Zongmi's text does appear to be the relevant one in Wei's case. It is, indeed, Zongmi's usage that appears to have engendered the most consistent appearance of the compound bringing together both the elements *zong* and *jiao* in later Zen texts composed during the thousand years separating the two men, as a term (by no means the only one) for the totality of the Zen tradition. At the same time, Zongmi's contrast of the Zen line with other traditions concerned with doctrinal teaching *(jiaozong)* no doubt suggested to readers like Wei the type of combinations and contrasts that are in evidence in Wei's Pure Land writings.[31] We cannot claim that Wei's specific formulations had any consequences in themselves. Though Wei's pioneering works on the geography of the western world were widely circulated, and were especially influential in Japan, his writings on Buddhism, penned in 1854, were initially little known.[32] Rather, his use of terminology is most useful as evidence of how educated Chinese persons who were not Buddhist monks themselves could construe the totality of the Buddhist religious tradition in his time. Specifically, *zong* and *jiao* seem to be used by Wei to cover those activities that were proper to the Buddhist clergy, terms that

[30] For some account of Yanshou on Pure Land covering the type of material that Wei Yuan probably did read, see Heng-ching Shih, *The Syncretism of Ch'an and Pure Land Buddhism*, New York: P. Lang, 1992.

[31] The use of the term *zongjiao* in Zen texts of the Song and Ming periods is readily attested by the works in the Taishô Canon: see volume 47, 937b22.942c5 (text number 1998); volume 48, 1103a16 (text number 2024); cf. also Suzuki, *Meiji shûkyô,* 14.

[32] Wei Yuan's much greater fame as a geographer is covered in Jane Kate Leonard, *Wei Yuan and China's Rediscovery of the Maritime World,* Cambridge, Mass.: Harvard University Press, 1984.

might be brought together to constitute a sort of shorthand summary of the intellectual world of the religious professional.

It is this usage, we believe, that must be kept in mind when we go back to consider the involvement of *zong* and *jiao* in translation from European languages at a slightly earlier point. In 1838, the pioneering missionary Karl Friedrich August Gützlaff (1803–1851) was seeking to convey in his Chinese-language periodical, the *Dong-Xiyang meiyue tongjizhuan*, some elements of European history to a Chinese readership.[33] Faced with the need to characterize the unusual status of the Papal State in the Italy of those days, he chose to describe them, fatefully, as constituting a *jiao-zong* state. This is unlikely to reflect the technical use of the term by Zongmi to indicate a doctrinal lineage, but rather something much more vague, closer to the sort of layperson's characterizations used by Wei Yuan. Perhaps the combination of characters was intended to mean specifically 'clerical' rather than more broadly 'religious', for later on, in an explanation of the rise of the influence of the Catholic Church in European affairs, he speaks of the influence of "persons of *jiao* and *zong*" (教宗者).[34] Some interesting evidence to support this possibility was to emerge over two decades later, and will be considered shortly. By contrast, however, the immediate impact of missionary publications of this sort was in all probability very slight. It is therefore, we believe, inconceivable that Wei Yuan, for example, for all his interests in the West, could have derived his vocabulary in a Buddhist context from this missionary source, and that is why we have preferred to construe his work as evidence of the sort of Buddhist usage that a missionary translator or a convert advising him may have had in mind in writing this passage concerning Italy. But as the First Opium War and other pressures forced the reformers to learn more about the West, another geographer, Xu Jiyu (1795–1873), picked up either from this passage or something like it the epithet in question describing the Papal States, and used it in his

[33] For a brief introduction to this figure and his publishing ventures in China, see Jessie Lutz, "Karl F. A. Gützlaff, Missionary Entrepreneur", in: John K. Fairbank/Suzanne Wilson Barnett (eds.), *Christianity in China: Early Protestant Writings*, Cambridge, Mass.: Harvard University Press, 1985, 61–87. For a more recent assessment, see Thoralf Klein/Reinhard Zöllner (eds.), *Karl Gützlaff (1803–1851) und das Christentum in Ostasien: Ein Missionar zwischen den Kulturen*, Nettetal: Institut Monumenta Serica, Sankt Augustin, Steyler Verlag, 2005.

[34] Aihanzhe (i. e. 'Philosinensis', Karl F. A. Gützlaff) (ed.), *Dong-Xiyang kao meiyue tongjizhuan* 1984.3., 48; as reprinted in Beijing: Zhonghua shuju, 1997, 342.

Yinghuan zhi lue of 1848.[35] In this case, too, as with Wei's writings, the new information was avidly taken up in Japan, where Xu's work was reprinted in 1861.[36] Here, though, we find an additional interlineal gloss, apparently from a *rangakusha*, or Japanese scholar of Dutch, giving also the still standard Dutch equivalent of 'Papal State'.[37] The gloss in Dutch, *kerkelije staat*, might perhaps be rendered into English with an attempt at literalism as 'churchly state', but meanings such as 'ecclesiastical', 'clerical', or maybe even more loosely 'religious' might, we understand, also fit. Dutch studies in Japan, as the main medium through which knowledge of the West entered the country from mid- to late Tokugawa times (eighteenth and early nineteenth centuries), had resulted by this point in a certain tradition of lexicography, though given Japanese sensitivity at this time to Christian influences, religious vocabulary surely lay outside the scope of this tradition, and is unlikely to have been at all fixed.[38] The source of the glossator's knowledge remains therefore mysterious. As far as we are aware, moreover, the history of the compound *jiaozong* in Japan in the next few years is as yet unexplored. But we do know when the same compound in reverse came into use, namely during the course of 1867, as foreign powers sought to secure religious tolerance for their missionaries. At first the meaning of *shûkyô* seems a little unstable, perhaps indicating Christianity as such, and in one case certainly it translates the word 'faith'.

[35] For Xu, see Fred W. Drake, *China Charts the World: Hsü Chi-yü and his Geography of 1848*, Cambridge, Mass.: Harvard University Press, 1975.

[36] For the dissemination of Chinese language works on the West in Japan, including that of Xu, see Masuda Wataru, tr. Joshua Fogel, *Japan and China: Mutual Representations in the Modern Era*, Richmond, Surrey: Curzon, 2000, 16–22.23–27, deal also with the dissemination of Wei Yuan's work.

[37] Xu Jiyu, *Yinghan zhilue* 6.25a, in: Beijing: Zhongguo quanguo tushuguan wenxian suowei fuzhi chongxin, 2000, reprint of 1861 Japanese edition. Note that the *Jin Xiandai Hanyu Xinci Ciyuan Cidian*, Shanghai: Hanyu da cidian chubanshe, 2001, quotes the passage from Gützlaff/Aihanzhe on Italy in the entry on *jiaozong* (p. 127) but is clearly wrong in saying that it means 'Pope' here, even if it does mean that in some other texts, because he uses *jiaohuang* (教 皇) to mean 'Pope' slightly later on the same page. *Jiaozong* may not mean 'religious' exactly, but it must mean, as in the Dutch gloss on this passage as incorporated in the Japanese edition of Xu, 'clerical', 'churchly', or something approaching 'religious'. Note also that the passages on Europe and Italy in the *Haiguo tuzhe* normally have *jiaohuang* for 'pope'. Today, both forms are used but there seems to be a slight preference among Chinese writers for *jiaohuang*. In Vatican sources the term 'encyclical' is rendered as *jiaozong tongyu* (教宗 通 諭).

[38] For a brief survey of this lexicography in the context of the development of Japanese knowledge of Western science, see Masayoshi Sugimoto/David L. Swain, *Science and Culture in Traditional Japan*, Rutland, Vermont and Tokyo: Charles E. Tuttle, 1989, 332–334.

But by the following year the now standard equivalence between the term and 'religion' in English is undeniable.[39] This, then, is the term that is reintroduced to China as *zongjiao* towards the end of the nineteenth century, according to current scholarship.[40]

A quick examination of a few lexicons and dictionaries shows that it took some time for *zongjiao* to become the one and only translation of the term religion. In 1903, the Shanghai Commercial Press *English and Chinese Dictionary* aimed at a Chinese readership used *jiao* to designate various religious traditions ('the religion of Jesus, *jesu jiao*; the religion of the Mohammedans, *huihui jiao*; the religion of the Romanists *tianzhu jiao*; the religion of the literati, *ru jiao*; the religion of Buddha *shi jiao*; the religion of Tau, *dao jiao*; to adopt a religion, *jin jiao*; to follow a religion, *xinjiao*; to propagate a religion, *zhuanjiao*; to forsake a religion, *fanjiao*').[41] In 1910, the lexicon *Technical Terms English and Chinese*, glosses 'religion' as *dao* (道), an interesting choice given that the term is certainly one of the most complex and polysemous in the whole of the Chinese religious vocabulary.[42] Finally, *New Terms for New Ideas: A Study of the Chinese Newspaper* (1917), an anthology of translations of excerpts taken from the Chinese daily press and devoted to 'documenting' the processes of lexical change, has an interesting passage probably written by the public intellectual and Buddhist sympathiser Liang Qichao (1873–1929) that confidently uses *zongjiao* as the translation for 'religion' calling for the creation of a 'new Chinese religion' based on Buddhism.[43]

---

[39] See Suzuki, *Meiji shûkyô*, 15–16.

[40] Masini, *Formation*, 222. Note that Masini writes that the famous translator Yan Fu (1854–1921) 'preferred the Buddhist term *jiaozong*' and quotes Yan's translation of *An Inquiry into the Nature and Causes of the Wealth of Nations* by Adam Smith (*Yuan Fu*, 1901–1902, reprint Shangwu Yinshuguan, Beijing 1981, 2 vols., 649). He cites the *Zhongwen da cidian*, (Zhang Qiyun [ed.], *Zhonguo wenhua janjiu suo,* Taibei, 1973, 10 vols.).

[41] See *Commercial Press English and Chinese Dictionary*, Shanghai: Commercial Press, 1903, 202.

[42] See Committee of the Educational Association of China (eds.), *Technical Terms English and Chinese*, Shanghai: Methodist Publishing House, 1910.

[43] Ada Haven Mateer, *New Terms for New Ideas: A Study of the Chinese Newspaper*, Shanghai: Presbyterian Mission Press, 1917, 49–50. As an example from a widely circulated newspaper, Zhou Xun has pointed out to us that the Shenbao申報 of 10 May 1912 carries a report from Shanghai on Taoist insistence that anti-queue measures then being enforced in the wake of the Qing fall should not impinge on the Taoists' right to their topknots, which formed part of the outward indicators "that distinguished them from persons of other religions" (區別於其他宗教者).

This, provisionally, concludes our short history of 'religion' in its East Asian linguistic garb. We would concede, of course, that further clarification of the origins of the modern word *zongjiao* is possible. Ideally we would wish to know more about the use of its component elements among Chinese lay Buddhists immediately prior to the arrival of the Protestant missionary translators. Given, however, that no one has thought so far to discover anything about Chinese Buddhism at that particular time, we have not attempted to launch an entire new field of research simply in order to uncover a single word. A more systematic search of early Protestant translations, too, might turn up more useful material.

In addition, we feel that though the history of the term *jiaozong* in Japan after the importation of Xu Jiyu's work lies beyond the scope of our own interests, it might repay investigation. We note for example that at this point other compounds were similarly unstable, and sometimes ultimately took a different order in different languages: compare, for example, Japanese *dankai* with Chinese *jieduan*, for a stage or level of development. A fuller consideration of the problem would moreover need to move beyond narrow questions of a single etymology to consider more extensively the language used to represent the identities of the various religious traditions involved in East Asia by the nineteenth century, and the ways in which that language situation shifted to accommodate a new, generic term for 'religion' – we can already point to some preliminary findings in that area.[44] But while conscious of the need for further research, we believe that we have established one or two points beyond question. First, the assertion by some in Japan that the modern term and earlier Buddhist usages are "completely different", implying a radical linguistic discontinuity between the discourse of Buddhist tradition and secular modernity, is in the light of the evidence we have brought forward very difficult to maintain.[45] Secondly, in terms of the type of argument put forward by Talal Asad, we can be fairly sure of the original connotations of the word used in East Asia from 1868 as an equivalent of the word 'religion' in European languages. At the time of its adoption to fit this

[44] For Buddhist attempts at self-definition see Francesca Tarocco, "The Making of Religion in Modern China", in: Nile Green/Mary Searle Chatterjie (eds.), *Religion, Language and Power*, New York: Routledge, 2008, 42–56. For Taoist attempts see Vincent Goossaert, *The Taoists of Peking, 1800–1949: A Social History of Urban Clerics*, Cambridge: Harvard University Asia Center, 2007.

[45] For an assertion of complete difference, see Mochizuki, as cited above, n. 10.

role, it skewed the meaning of 'religion' for the East Asian language speaker very much in the direction of the beliefs of the professional, clerical groups representing such religions as Buddhism and Christianity, rather than the practices of the many. To the extent that the neologism may implicitly have embodied clerical Buddhists' view of their own tradition, it may also have induced reactions from the many, as well. Since a number of lay practices existed beyond the scope of the Buddhist message, the *Buddhadharma*, and belonged in the clerical Buddhist way of thinking to the secular world, some may either have sensed that the new word was covertly imposing distinctions that devalued their own practices, or else set a standard so high as to lack all appeal for them. This may account both for the problems sensed by researchers in Japanese religion to which we have already alluded, and also to other anomalies noted in research on China.[46] To say this is not to deny a certain process of convergence with the European conception of religion, especially amongst the most cosmopolitan – though of course a full understanding of the position of the educated would have to take due account of the prevailing notion of 'superstition' also.[47] Finally, moreover, Talal Asad's main argument is in any case strongly reinforced even by the findings within the strictly circumscribed limits of our present investigation.

Whatever the effects of later developments, the word for 'religion' in East Asia was not invented *ex novo* overnight, as it were, but emerged over the course of a couple of generations of linguistic instability. That phenomenon needs to be grasped accurately in order to construct a reliable 'genealogy of religion' for East Asia. And surely unless we understand the subtly different ways in which speakers of other languages see the world, rather than imagine that they have inadequately assimilated a normative discourse embodied in European languages, we will not have advanced the academic cause of studying what we term religion very far at all.

[46] For an example of a patent anomaly, see the statistics given (with entirely appropriate authorial comments) in Holmes Welch, *The Buddhist Revival in China*, Cambridge, Mass.: Harvard University Press, 1968, 210.

[47] Some interesting material to ponder in this regard is provided by Eileen Chang (1921–1995), as translated by David Pollard, *The Chinese Essay*, London: Hurst and Company, 2000, 283–292, giving her views on the religion *(zongjiao)* of the Chinese. See also Francesca Tarocco, *The Cultural Practices of Modern Chinese Buddhism: Attuning the Dharma*, London: Routledge, 2007, 1–39. The forthcoming book by Rebecca Nedostup, *Superstitious Regimes, Religion and the Politics of Chinese Modernity*, will certainly contribute to our knowledge of these issues.

CANON AND IDENTITY IN INDIAN ESOTERIC BUDDHISM AS THE CONFLUENCE OF CULTURES[1]

Ronald M. Davidson

Canon formation in Indian Buddhism operated along very different lines than canonicity found in the Semitic religions, primarily because the process not only entailed leaving the canon open in some measure, and therefore incomplete, but also because Buddhists resisted all efforts at final closure, long after Buddhist communities had been introduced to such ideas both within India and from abroad. Esoteric or tantric Buddhist representatives from the late seventh century CE forward continued the tradition as they had received it from the early schools and the Mahāyānists who preceded them – and who indeed still surrounded them – but tantric masters emphasized both ritual and charisma to a degree not previously seen. The Buddhist resistance to canonical closure allowed Indians a facility to appropriate materials from others so that the canon would be continuously renewed by influences from subcultures within India and, eventually, outside of it. By the end of the eighth century, we find small esoteric communities formed in proximity to the larger orthodox monasteries but separate from them. Because of the preeminent position of the tantric master in such communities, and because the parameters of the tantric canon were so amorphous and unclear, such tantric communities took the ritual and ideological texts and statements affirmed by the teachers as the focus and defining characteristics of community membership and identity.

1. *Canon as a Contested Category*

The formation of canons of literature, especially religious literature, has been a contentious issue in the West with the formation of the Jewish

[1] I would like to thank Drs. Sven Bretfeld, Volkhard Krech and all members of the Consortium for giving me the opportunity to participate.

and Christian canons in the first few centuries of the common era.[2] For Jews, despite the lengthy history of the *Torah*, the tripartite canon as accepted today (Law, Prophets and Writings) is largely a product of the Rabbinical tradition, especially as developed by Masoretic scholars like Ben Asher (10th cen. CE) in Tiberias, who codified the canon and formulated a pronunciation text that has been widely accepted.[3] For Christians the fourth century proved the watershed in canonical development; although earlier canonical lists had been circulating, Ferguson has argued that the acknowledgement of the twenty-seven books of the *New Testament* by the councils of Hippo (393) and Carthage (397, 419) appeared seemingly an acquiescence to the consensus already fait accompli.[4] Around the canonical texts grew a wealth of referential literature, whether the *Mishnah* and *Talmud* of the Jews or the Apostolic and early Church writings in Christianity.[5] Consequently, the canon became iconic in a manner similar to the way that category structures in natural language are established by iconic or prototypic systems of reference, with both denotative and metaphorical semantic systems developed over time through authoritative voices, popular acceptance, folk sayings and a mutually reinforcing sense of textual charisma.

In the course of canon formation, as has been generally acknowledged, a basic strategy was to limit the range and number of texts.[6] While Josephus argued that the defining characteristic of the Hebrew

[2] Lightstone, Jack N., "The Rabbis' Bible: The Canon of the Hebrew Bible and the Early Rabbinic Guild", in: McDonald, Lee Martin/Sanders, James A. (eds.), *The Canon Debate*, Peabody, MA: Hendrickson Publishers, 2002, 163–184; Lang, B. "The 'Writings': A Hellenistic Literary Canon in the Hebrew Bible", in: van der Kooij, A./van der Toorn, K. (eds.), *Canonization and Decanonization,* Leiden: Brill 1998, 41–66.

[3] Tov, Emanuel, "The Status of the Masoretic Text in Modern Text Editions of the Hebrew Bible: The Relevance of Canon", in: McDonald, Lee Martin/Sanders, James A. (eds.), *The Canon Debate*, Peabody, MA: Hendrickson Publishers 2002, 234–251; Zevit, Z., "The Second-Third Century Canonization of the Hebrew Bible and its Influence on Christian Canonizing", in: van der Kooij, A./van der Toorn, K. (eds.) *Canonization and Decanonization,* Leiden: Brill 1998, 133–160.

[4] Ferguson, Everett, "Factors Leading to the Selection and Closure of the New Testament Canon: A Survey of Some Recent Studies", in: McDonald, Lee Martin/Sanders, James A. (eds.), *The Canon Debate*, Peabody, MA: Hendrickson Publishers 2002, 295–320, especially 320.

[5] The papers collected in: Gregory, Andrew F./Tuckett, Christopher M. (eds.), *The Reception of the New Testament in the Apostolic Fathers*, Oxford and New York: Oxford University Press 2005, detail the Apostolic references in the case of Christianity.

[6] Gnuse, Robert, *The Authority of the Bible: Theories of Inspiration, Revelation and the Canon of Scripture,* New York: Paulist Press 1985, 95–101; Ferguson 2002, 311; the limitation principle has been questioned by Barton, John, "Marcion Revisited", in: McDonald, Lee Martin/Sanders, James A. (eds.), *The Canon Debate*, Peabody, MA:

scriptures was the reliability of prophetic authority, the Christians employed models of divine authority, apostolicity, the rule of faith, anti-quity, inspiration and wide acceptance *(homolegoumena)*, as Eusebius affirms.[7] In this process, prophetic inspiration was understood to have closed for Jews, while the inspirational activity of the Holy Spirit for Christians was understood to have rested with the proclamation in hand *(kerygma)* and emphasized the sacramental and intellectual patterns of the culture bearers of Christianity; there was a general agreement that precluded clear post-second Temple additions to the categories of prophetic utterance and revealed scripture, although an occasional later text like *Revelations* could be excepted.[8]

The method for the limitation of the literary corpus was elegant and straight-forward: a list of titles, initially understood as a catalog *(katalogos)*, but later reframed with the language of the rule of faith *(kanōn)*, the initial meaning of canon. Even granting that different recensions of texts would circulate under the same title, the strategy was remarkable effective. It is clear that several alternative *Torahs*, books of prophets, epistles and gospels circulated in the first few centuries of the common era – the proto-Samaritan *Pentateuch*, the Gnostic gospels, etc. – and most were successfully excluded for a variety of reasons, although both the Jewish and Christian authorities sometimes supported the study of certain of these books as Apocrypha or Pseudepigrapha.[9] In generating the canonical lists, the Semitic religious authorities apparently relied on the idea of a finite universe, and a teleology of election (however understood) coupled with a theology of restricted revelation to or for the elect.

I wanted to review these canonical models of canon for a very simple reason. In any discussion of religious canons, these models have

Hendrickson Publishers 2002, 341–354, especiallly 343, with respect to the difference between Marcion and other church fathers.

[7] Mason, Steve 2002; "Josephus and His twenty-Two Book Canon", in: McDonald, Lee Martin/Sanders, James A. (eds.), *The Canon Debate*, Peabody, MA: Hendrickson Publishers 2002, 110–127; Metzger, Bruce M., *The Canon of the New Testament: Its Origin, Development, and Significance*, Oxford: Clarendon Press 1987, 75–111. 253–254; Patzia, Arthur G., *The Making of the New Testament: Origin, Collection, Text & Canon*, Downers Grove, IL: InterVarsity Press 1995, 102–111.

[8] Blenkinsopp, Joseph, *Prophecy and Canon: a Contribution to the Study of Jewish Origins*, Notre Dame, IN: University of Notre Dame Press 1977, 109–138; Patzia 1995, 102–111. Metzger 1987, 254–257.

[9] Klauck, Hans-Josef, *Apocryphal Gospels: An Introduction*. Trans. Brian McNeil. London & New York: T & T Clark International 2003, reviews much of the apocrypha.

been invariably taken as the base line, against which other canonical strategies have been measured. If I may divert Alfred Korzybski's metaphor from its initial moorings for a minute, the Hebrew and Christian canons have established the map in light of which the territory of other religions must be discovered and against which they will be measured.[10] While it is now acceptable to call many aspects of the investigation of foreign cultures into question – in the case of India because postcolonial studies have appropriated Said's rhetoric of a critique of orientalism – yet it remains the case that the rigorous development of comparative religion has so often labored under its Jesuit or other missionary past, precisely because the Semitic religions were so well explored and formed the basis for category formation and assessment in much of the humanities.

It is therefore illuminating to understand that virtually all fundamental facets of the diverse Christian canonical strategies are violated in the development of the collections known as the Buddhist canon, usually identified as the *Tripiṭaka* or the *Three Baskets*. During the entire history of Buddhism in India, there is no canonical list of titles belonging to these three sections as a group. Not once in the almost two millennia of the history of Buddhism in India do we find a list of specific sūtras or closed list of titles that satisfies all the requisites of a closed canon. We know that certain texts were disputed, certain traditions were looked askance, but in each instance we find Indians wrestling with the question of scriptural authenticity rather than the circumscribed limits of canonical authority.[11] In Metzger's phrasing, Indian Buddhists had a collection of authoritative texts but did not have an authoritative collection of texts.[12]

The enormity of this lapse is most evident when we look at the reception of Buddhist literature outside of South Asia. The Chinese, arguably the most rigorous of all Asian list makers, were the first to compile a list of titles and the earliest of our scriptural lists, that

[10] Korzybski, Alfred, *Science and Sanity: An Introduction to Non-Aristotelian Systems and General Semantics*. Lakeville, Connecticut: International Non-Aristotelian Library Pub. Co. 1933, 55–65, 747–761; his original metaphor was appropriated by Smith, Jonathan Z., *Map is not territory: studies in the history of religions*, Leiden: Brill 1978, who turned the semantic and epistemological functions to his own purpose.

[11] See Davidson, Ronald M., "An Introduction to the Standards of Scriptural Authenticity in Indian Buddhism", in: Buswell, Robert (ed.), *Chinese Buddhist Apocrypha*. Honolulu: University of Hawai'i Press 1990, 291–325, for the standards of scriptural authenticity.

[12] Metzger 1987, 282–288.

attributed to Daoan, was fully integrated into the later canonical list of Sengrui, the *Chusanzang jiji* (T. 2145), and many later canonical lists built on these two.[13] The Tibetan experience was not much different in this regard. Two of the three imperial catalogs survive from the early ninth century, the *Lhan-dkar-ma* and the *'Phang-thang-ma*.[14] As with Daoan's list, Tibetan catalogs posed initially as library shelf lists but actually represented lists of imperially approved translations, and the imperial limitations to such translation activity is reasonably well documented. The surviving lists were composed about the time that the Tibetan Imperium achieved the stability that allowed for multiple libraries and imperially sponsored translation programs, all in some imitation of the process exhibited much earlier among the Chinese. The later Tibetan canonical catalogs – written to describe the sponsored manuscript canons and then expanded with the first printing of the Tibetan canon – divided up the texts differently than the imperial catalogs, but there appears little doubt in anyone's mind about the necessity to list the titles, including the approximate length of each work.

2. *The Indian Canonical Categories*

If we return to India, we may ask ourselves: what were the Indian monks thinking? This question has even greater force when we realize that still, more than a millennium after their exposure to the Chinese initial forays into canonical lists, Indian Buddhists yet produced no canonical list in India. In the face of such evidence, we may easily presume that there were strong symbolic and institutional forces at work that kept the Buddhist canon in a quasi-open condition rather than closed. Indeed, I have argued elsewhere that, in terms of religious literature, one defining characteristic of Indian Buddhism was that it

[13] Nattier, Jan, *A Guide to the Earliest Chinese Buddhist Translations: Texts from the Eastern Han* 東漢 *and Three Kingdoms* 三國 *Periods*. Tokyo: The International Research Institute for Advanced Buddhology, Soka University 2008; Tokuno, Kyoko, "The Evaluation of Indigenous Scriptures in Chinese Buddhist Bibliographical Catalogues", in: Buswell, Robert (ed.), *Chinese Buddhist Apocrypha*. Honolulu: University of Hawai'i Press 1990, 31–74.

[14] Herrmann-Pfandt, Adelheid, *Die lHan kar ma: Ein Früher Katalog der ins Tibetische übersetzten buddhistischen Texte*, Wien: Verlag der Österreichischen Akademie der Wissenschaften 2008; Kawagoe, Eishin (ed.), *dKar chag 'Phang thang ma*. Sendai: Tohoku Society for Indo-Tibetan Studies 2005.

was a culture of scriptural composition. One may even argue that a target culture's appropriation of the entire spectrum of Indian Buddhism – as in China, Tibet, Central Asia and elsewhere – was incomplete unless the missionary culture zones begin to accede to the process of scriptural composition within their own languages. This has been taken as one measure of the vitality of Six Dynasties and Tang Buddhism, fifth to eighth century Tarim Buddhism, and tenth-eleventh century Tibetan Buddhism, for all these evinced a willingness to accept indigenously composed apocryphal works as legitimately Indian texts. In such instances, we begin to find the attribution of "doubtful" texts becoming the focus of polemics and questions of legitimacy.

With respect to the Indian Buddhist canon, most often instead of a list of titles, Indian Buddhists conceived of textual categories. Certainly we see this strategy in other canonical collections as well, with such categories as gospels, epistles, law, prophets, writings, pseudepigrapha, etc., and similar categories are most clearly seen in Eusebius' classification: acceptable, disputed, spurious and ungodly.[15] However, these genre classifications became collection systems – one might say bibliographic typologies – for sections of the lists of approved items. After Eusebius in the West, the list became the most important item, and it is perhaps germane to observe that this strategy was continued in the modern period with the Papal index of disapproved books (*Index Librorum Prohibitorum*, 1529–1966), the diabolic shadow of the canon.

Buddhists first began to articulate their criteria of what was "the teaching of the teacher," *(śāstuḥ śāsanam)* and then to formulate the mythology of revelation: how the Buddha understood such a doctrine, when and to whom it was taught, and how it was recited by the Buddha's cousin Ānanda at the first communal recitation, so that all approved scriptures must retain the formulaic introduction: "Thus have I heard, at one time the Lord was residing in place X, and such-and-such a person came with a question, etc." Scriptures were initially differentiated as to whether they pertained to doctrine/meditation/general praxis, thus being a sūtra (the well-said), or if they pertained to an item of behavior that required a new rule, thus becoming an

[15] Kalin, Everett R., "The New Testament Canon of Eusebius", in: McDonald, Lee Martin/Sanders, James A. (eds.), *The Canon Debate*, Peabody, MA: Hendrickson Publishers 2002, 386–404, especially 391–393, identifies disputed *(antilegomena)* with spurious *(notha)*, rendering three rather than four categories.

item in the *vinaya*, the disciplinary system. Over time, more analytical materials evolved and the new category of *abhidharma* was developed as a third basket, supplementing the materials included in the sūtras and the *vinaya*. Within the basket of the sūtras we see texts classified into other sections – the lengthy texts *(dīrghāgama/dīghanikāya)*, the middling texts *(madhyamāgama/majj-himanikāya)*, texts ordered by number *(ekottarikāgama/aṅguttarani-kāya)*, texts grouped by topic *(saṃyuktāgama/sañyuttanikāya)*, and sometimes we find a miscellaneous collection of "minor" texts, some of which are actually the oldest sūtras *(kṣudrāgama/khuddakanikāya)*, and even a later collection of "great texts" *(mahāsūtras)* in some schools. Similarly, *vinaya* texts may be classified into the "heap" *(skandhaka/khandhaka)* or the explanation of the lists of rules *(vibhaṅga)*, depending in some measure how closely they were associated with the hagiography of the Buddha or the formula for confession *(prātimokṣa)*.

This seemingly clear division, however, is belied by the actual chaos we find when we begin to compare individual examples of these collections. The sūtra collections translated into Chinese do not agree either with each other or in any manner with those in Pali, and we even find minor disagreements between canonical traditions of the Theravāda school as to the inclusion or exclusion of scriptures in their canon. Moreover, neither the Chinese materials nor the Pali agree with the newly discovered collections that are just now being explored from manuscript finds in Central Asia.[16] The situation is even worse with reference to the five substantial *vinaya-piṭakas* preserved in Chinese and Tibetan translation (Mahīśāsaka, Mahāsāṃghika, Dharmaguptaka, Sarvāstivāda, and Mūlasarvāstivāda); not only do they disagree with each other and the Pali *vinaya-piṭaka*, but the longest of the *vinayas*, belonging to the Mūlasarvāstivāda, demonstrates substantial disagreement between three archives: Yijing's 703 CE translation (T. 1442–1458), the early ninth century Tibetan translation of the imperially sponsored translators (To. 1–7), and the surviving Sanskrit fragmentary corpus of the Gilgit and Central Asian manuscripts. Thus while those outside of the fold of Buddhist studies have been blithely lead by

[16] For one such problem see Hartmann, Jens-Uwe, "Further Remarks on the New Manuscript of the Dīrghāgama", in: *Kokusai Bukkyogaku Daigakuin Daigaku kenkyu kiyo* 5: 98–117. For the overall issue of non-correspondence of the *sūtra-piṭakas*, see Lancaster, Lewis (ed.), *The Korean Buddhist Canon: A Descriptive Catalogue*. Berkeley: University of California Press 1979, 212–273.

the Pali Text Society into speaking of *The* Pali Canon, it is better to discuss *A* Pali Canon, and to differentiate it from the other early canons overall.[17] In the case of the *abhidharmapiṭa-ka*, there was hardly any pretense to consensus, but the three surviving lists (Dharmaguptaka, Sarvāstivāda, and Theravāda) are one of the few places where Indian Buddhists at least formulated lists of texts, possibly because *none* of the individual elements were in agreement, as opposed to the other two baskets, where there was some overlap.[18] Even then, the three *abhidharma* schools appear to have agreed that their materials should still somehow adhere to the mythology of realization and revelation by the Buddha, followed by a separate recitation of the *abhidharma* basket at the first mythic recitation of the scriptures after the Buddha's demise.

Eventually, we find that a new typology of scripture emerges, that of the branches, either the nine-branch version employed by several of the early groups, especially the Sthaviravāda and Theravāda schools, or the twelve-branch version maintained by the Sarvāstivāda and its related systems. Yet the relationship between either the nine or twelve-branch systems to the three baskets said to contain the word of the Buddha was seldom well expressed, and the few places where we find such a discussion leaves much to doubt. The fourth-century *Abhidharmasamuccaya*, for example, defines the nine-branch system in the following manner:[19] *Sūtra* is that which is a prose text expressed [by the Buddha] through drawing the audience to the intended goal *(yad abhipretārthaṃ sūcanākāreṇa gadyabhāṣitam). Geya* is that which will be sung through verse at the middle or at the conclusion of the sūtras. Alternatively, it may constitute some indirect point that is expanded (*sūtrāṇāṃ madhye vā ante vā gāthayā yad gīyate | sūtreṣu anirūpito 'rtho vā yad vyākhāyate*). *Vyāka-raṇa* indicates the different prophecies given to the advanced noble disciples in the past about the different births and attainments in various places. Or it may mean the further expansion of a point made in the sūtras, since there is the delineation of

[17] Collins, Steven, "On the Very Idea of the Pali Canon", in: *Journal of the Pali Text Society* 15 (1990), 89–126, explores the ideas around the Pali canon in detail.

[18] For some of the difficulties in the *Abhidharmapiṭaka* lists, see Bareau, André, "Les sectes bouddhiques du Petit Véhicule et leur Abhidharmapiṭaka", in: *Bulletin de l'École française d'Extrême-Orient* 44/1 (1951), 1–11.

[19] *Abhidharmasamuccaya* 78; *Abhidharmasamuccayabhāṣya* 95–96; Lamotte, Étienne, *History of Indian Buddhism: From the Origins to the Śaka Era*. Trans. Sara Webb-Boin. Louvain-Paris: Peeters press, 1988 (1958), 143–191 discusses the traditional scriptural assignments with especially reliance on the Theravāda.

an intention to be unfolded (*tat sthāneṣu samatikrāntānām atītānām āryaśrāvakāṇāṃ prāptyutpattiprabhedavyākaraṇam | api ca sūtreṣu nirūptārthasya sphuṭīkaraṇam | vivṛ-tyābhisandhivyākaraṇāt*). *Gāthā* is demonstrated in the sūtras by association with verse feet, either two, three, four, five or six verse feet (*sūtreṣu pādayogena deśyate | dvipadī tripadī catuṣpadī paṃcapadī ṣaṭpadī vā*). *Udāna* is that pronounced sometimes in the sūtras by the Tathāgata with joy *(sūtreṣu kadācit tathāgatena āttamanaskena yad udāhṛtam). Nidāna* is that which [the Buddha] expressed with an inquiry, whether having to do with origins or for setting forth a teaching (*pṛṣṭena yad bhāṣitam | sotpattikaṃ śikṣāprajñaptikaṃ vā*). *Avadāna* is that expressed [by the Buddha] in the sūtras with an example *(sūtreṣu sadṛṣṭāntakaṃ bhāṣi-tam). Itivṛttaka* is that which teaches the previous worldly behavior of the noble disciples *(yad āryaśrāvakāṇāṃ pūrvalaukikaṃ vṛttaṃ deśay-ati).* Lastly, *Jātaka* is that which teaches the behavior associated with the canonical basket of the bodhisattva's activity *(yad bodhisattvacaritapiṭakasaṃprayuktaṃ vṛttaṃ deśayati).* Here, we notice that only the *Jātaka* is directly identified with even a section of scripture, let alone a specific text.

Had the Indian Buddhists formulated a canonical list of titles, none of the problems of referential ambiguity inherent in their system would be apparent. Instead of proposing this curiously vague description of attributes, they could have placed under each rubric a list of appropriate scriptures. Yet not only is the given system vague, but the definitions provided by the various surviving witnesses do not agree, and we see in the list just mentioned some items even have alternative interpretations, all of which facilitates disputes and sectarian polemics. And as incomprehensible as it might seem, it is indicative of Buddhist values that, even in the midst of such polemics, it is comparatively rare for opponents to cite disputed or apocryphal scriptures by name.

All of this suggests an entirely different conceptualization of the word of the Buddha than that implicated by apostolic revelation or prophetic utterance. Indeed, Mahāyānist statements sometimes, as in the case of the *Adhyāśayasaṃcodana-sūtra*, simply affirm that "all that is well-said is the word of the Buddha" *(yat kiṃcin maitreya subhāṣitaṃ sarvaṃ tad buddhabhāṣitam).*[20] Of course, the scripture goes on to qualify what is well said, but nonetheless we find mutually reinforcing institutional and discourse-related symbolic structures that strongly inhibit canon-

[20] Snellgrove, David L., "Note on the *Adhyāśayasaṃcodanasūtra*", in: *Bulletin of the School of Oriental and African Studies* 21 (1958), 620–623, discusses this text.

ical closure and support continued scriptural composition. We see, for example, that individual orders and, within each order, individual monasteries were authorized to make decisions on their own, with no centralized system of control, supervision, or court of adjudication in the case of canon law. Moreover it has been understood that – during the time of the Buddha – saints, divinities and others could speak for the Buddha, so that their speech becomes Dharma with the approval of the Buddha. Just as effective was the understanding that there was not to be a single scriptural language, for monks were understood to be able to reformulate the Dharma in their own idioms, because monks were to take recourse to meaning, not to the word.[21]

The ambiguity of the Buddhist model would suggest that the consequences of an orally based culture of sacred texts still sat heavily on the Buddhists and that is certainly true, both then and now, for Buddhist monks in South and Central Asia continue to memorize lengthy passages of the canon.[22] In this light, it is instructive to recall that Indians did not accept printing for more than a millennium after the Chinese Buddhists invented xylography to publish the Chinese Buddhist scriptures. Finally, we find in many traditions the idea that no one tradition has successfully preserved the entirety of the Buddha's pronouncement, so that there is the expectation that "lost scriptures" will be again secured from their hidden repository, and we sometimes read of a dharma-treasury *(dharmakośa)* wherein reside the undiscovered scriptures.[23]

In fact, I would argue that the greatest similarity with the Buddhist ideology of scripture and canon is found not within the sacred literature of the Near East, but rather in the Linnaean taxonomy of biological kingdoms, phyla, etc. In each case, we find different opinions about the nature of the categories, a willingness to reassess the membership of a category over time, and a continuing ambiguity as to the definition of some of the levels of categories, such as the notorious problem of the definition of a species, and how it is that all the dogs of the

---

[21] Lamotte, Étienne, "La critique d'interpretation dans le bouddhism", in: *Annuaire de l'Institut de Philologie et d'Histoire Orientales et Slaves* IX (1949), 341–361.

[22] Rocher, Ludo, *Orality and Textuality in the Indian Context.* Sino-Platonic Papers 49, Philadelphia, PA: University of Pennsylvania, Department of East Asian Languages and Civilizations 1994, explores orality and textuality outside of Buddhist practice.

[23] E. g., *Daśabhūmika-sūtra,* 104: sa bhūyasyā mātrayā tathāgatadharmakośaprāpto bhavati; same phrase 145.160: tathāgatadharmakośaṃ ca rakṣati, 162: sa evaṃ pratisaṃvidāṃ jñānābhinirhārakuśalo bho jinaputrā bodhisattvo navamīṃ bodhisattvabhūmim anuprāptas tathāgatadharmakośaprāpto mahādharmabhāṇakatvaṃ kurvāṇaṇ.

world occupy one species, canis lupus, from Chihuahuas to Grand Pyrenees to wolves and other canids. In this typology there are no numerical parameters: there may be as many individuals in the species as are present; there may be as many species in a genus as is necessary; there may be as many genera in a family, families in an order, orders in a class, classes in a phylum, etc. The standards of identification and categorization are continually under dispute in this system, and the precise definition of the various levels, the members of each level, are accepted only with much dissent.[24] In particular, there is the problem of "fuzzy species" in which the populations at the margins of the species are nested into larger taxa populations; yet the empirical sciences must make sense of the data and cannot simply ignore it.[25]

Likewise, a rigorous analysis of religious data requires that we look at formulations that challenge category constructions received from the Semitic religions. In the case of Buddhism, it appears that Indian Buddhists accepted a semi-open canonical architecture, which was the norm in the development of all canons prior to the circumstances that led some religions to decide on closure.[26] In the Buddhist case, monks presumed that there were scriptures of which they were unaware, and had developed me-chanisms for the affirmation of scriptural authenticity, which relied on questions of non-contradiction and similarity of style and content with previously accepted scriptures. The semi-open canonical architecture was supported by an open cosmological and symbolic architecture, in which the universe is beginningless and endless, and the pronouncements of truth are potentially infinite. Consequently, the curriculum of instruction in Indian Buddhism monasteries was often renewed – first to incorporate *abhidharma*, then Mahāyānist scriptures, and then the later epistemological *(pramāṇa)* and skeptical (Madhyamaka) literature – so that the relationship between curriculum and canon was as close in Buddhist India as van der Toorn and others have argued was the case in the Hebrew instance.[27]

---

[24] See Hey, Jody, *Genes, Categories, and Species: The Evolutionary and Cognitive Causes of the Species Problem.* Oxford and New York: Oxford University Press 2001, 45–66 for an interesting analysis of the problem.

[25] Hey 2001, 181–185; Beatty, John, "Classes and Cladists", in: *Systematic Zoology* 31/1 (1982), 25–34, especially 32–33.

[26] The sides to this argument are explicitly found in Ulrich's (canon = closed) and Sanders' (canon as ambiguous) contributions to McDonald, Lee Martin/Sanders, James A., *The Canon Debate*, Peabody, MA: Hendrickson Publishers 2002, 21–35, 252–266.

[27] Van der Toorn, Karel, *Scribal Culture and the Making of the Hebrew Bible,* Cambridge, MA: Harvard University Press, 244–247.

Just as important, Buddhist monks presumed that they had at their command the religious tools that allowed them access to the same transcendental reality discovered by the Buddha, the realization of which afforded him the expressions, teachings and verbal dexterity to teach the scriptures in the first place. Even more, by Buddhist standards, not only was that reality available to the highly motivated, but the entire purpose of the Buddha's dispensation was to provide them the expectation that they not only could, but should, achieve that level of understanding as a soteriological imperative. Moreover, in light of the dogged durability of Buddhist clerical orders, the day-to-day life of many monks were consistently imbued with the sense of responsibility that they should attain this exalted status, whether to be realized in this life or in a future existence. It is difficult to imagine a better system for the support of continued scriptural production.

3. *The Esoteric Canon*

All the above is background to the formulation of the final phase of Indian Buddhism, the vehicle of mantras, often rightly called tantric Buddhism.[28] Tantric Buddhism emerged out of the Mahāyānist method of *dhāraṇīs* in the environment of Post-Gupta India (550–1200 CE). *Dhāraṇīs* are coded linguistic non-linear expressions, much the same as mantras, but in Mahāyānist terms, *dhāraṇīs* could convey soteriological force whereas mantras could be just as representative of apotropaic spells, keeping off snakes, insects, the undead and other undesirables.[29] The socio-political factors were definitive, for this was a time in which the old Buddhist guild-alliances became eclipsed and Buddhists were under political and military pressure in much of India, for there was a marked decline in personal security throughout much of the north subcontinent in the seventh and eighth centuries. In the terminology of Chattopadhyaya, this is a time of *sāmanta*-feudalism, when the trading centers of the Gangetic Valley became reduced in both population and vitality, with culture bearers relocating to new

[28] See Davidson, Ronald, *Indian Esoteric Buddhism: A Social History of the Tantric Movement.* New York: Columbia University Press. 2002, for this material.
[29] Davidson, Ronald: "Studies in Dhāranī Literature I: Revisiting the Meaning of the Term *Dhāranī*," in: *Journal of Indian Philosophy* 37/2 (2009), 97–147.

metropolitan centers among partly Hinduized agrarian or tribal peoples.[30]

The consequences of the new socio-political arrangement were dramatic: Buddhist monasteries, in hopes of securing their own protection, began to assume the trappings of the feudal system that had become the leitmotif of the world around them. We see the decline in women's participation leading to the eclipse of the nuns' orders and a change in monastic syllabi to accommodate the new intellectual climate of epistemology and debate. We also see an increasing emphasis on ritual systems as the currency of social relationships between monks and laity, in some measure displacing the traditional Buddhist emphasis on intellectual, financial, medical and legal services that had been part of the previous symbiosis between mercantile guilds and the monasteries.

Tantric Buddhism first coalesced in the early seventh century, and, as I have argued elsewhere, embodied a central, organizing metaphor: the meditator becoming the *rājādhirāja*, the imperial overlord. The traditio-nal Indian coronation ceremony *(abhiṣeka)* became appropriated as the gateway rite of passage into the tantric system with the meditator becoming invested at the center of a maṇḍala of vassal Buddhas, and authenticated as a mantrin, a word that means both a councilor of state and a ritual specialist.[31] He employed fire ceremonies *(homa)* for a variety of purposes, from the pacific to the destructive, much as these rituals had served surrounding feudal states. Because of the synthetic nature of the tantric system and the contemporary realpolitik that it sacralized, tantric Buddhists became involved in local lore and a host of "little tradition" values espoused by the communities of the new order.

Our historical records are, sadly, not as complete as we would want them, a weakness often seen in early medieval India. However, they are supported by records found in China and Tibet, either as translations from authentic Indian documents or as texts posing as translations, and therein lies the problem of documentary authentication.

[30] Chattopadhyaya, Brajadulal, *The Making of Early Medieval India*, New Delhi: Oxford University Press 1994, 183–222.

[31] On the use of *abhiṣeka* prior to tantric Buddhism, see Davidson, Ronald, "The Place of *Abhiṣeka* Visualization in the Yogalehrbuch and Related Texts", in: Franco, Eli/Zin, Monik (eds.), *From Turfan to Ajanta: A Festschrift for Dieter Schlingloff on the Occasion of his Eightieth Birthday*, 1, 185–198, Lumbini, Nepal: Lumbini International Research Institute, 2010.

As should be clear from the paper so far, Indian Buddhist textual production was highly adaptive. In India, this meant adapting local discourse and genres – in whatever language – to Buddhist scriptural needs. The process did not stop at the borders, however, and I have pointed out that Indian Buddhist missionaries were described as being invited into a foreign locale, ascertaining the local needs according to Indian Buddhist lights, and then working with the indigenous intellectual community to produce a text along Indian lines that would satisfy all parties.[32] As in the case of scriptures produced in the Indian environments, the text authentically represents an Indian perspective, but in the new socio-cultural environment. We can have confidence that some of these texts could not have been produced in India, despite their claims to Indian authenticity, because of the contents found therein. Such texts I have termed *gray*, meaning that they are the fusion of two horizons: Indian and other, whether the other is Chinese, Tibetan, Khotanese or whatever.[33] They are not indigenous texts, because the Chinese or Tibetan monks could not have produced such works on their own. They are not Indian texts, because they embody a horizon of expectations that we do not find elsewhere in Indian Buddhism. Thus they are gray texts, truly formed on the borders of civilizations.

Our discussions of Tantric canons are reflective of this process. The earliest list of a catalog of authoritative texts available to me is a short list found in a medium length work, the *Rite for cultivating the Dharmayoga of the victorious Uṣṇīṣa* (*Uṣṇīṣavijaya-dharma-yoga-bhāvanā-vidhi*, 尊勝佛頂修瑜伽法軌儀, T. 973). In my estimation, the *Uṣṇīṣa* ritual system, which this text reflects, is the threshold tantric system in Buddhism, the first one to bring together the disparate elements and to establish the paradigm of Buddhist tantrism in the first half of the seventh century. The text in question is but one of about two dozen representing this *Uṣṇīṣa* system, only some of which survive in Sanskrit as parts of the received *Mañjuśrīmūlakalpa*, the *Sarvadurgatipariśodhana* and the *Uṣṇīṣavijaya* literature. Like most watershed rites, the *Uṣṇīṣa* system was not to be come iconic but was surpassed by subsequent developments, most particularly the *Vajroṣṇīṣa* practices, whose ter-

[32] Davidson, Ronald, *Tibetan Renaissance: Tantric Buddhism in the Rebirth of Tibetan Culture*, New York: Columbia University Press, 2005, 232–233.

[33] Davidson, Ronald, "*Gsar ma* Apocrypha: The Creation of Orthodoxy, Gray Texts, and the New Revelation", in: Eimer, Helmut/Germano, David (eds.), *The Many Canons of Tibetan Buddhism*, Leiden: Brill 2002, 203–224; Davidson 2005, 148–151.

minology has incorrectly been Sanskritized as Vajraśekhara. The **Uṣṇīṣavijaya* text under discussion was said to have been translated by Śubhakarasiṃha into Chinese during his residence in China in the first half of the eighth century.

His short list of authoritative texts comes at the beginning of the eighth chapter of the work, and it announces that the maṇḍala about to be constructed and the consecration of disciples *(abhiṣeka)* about to be given are synthesized from the following works: the *Vajroṣṇīṣa-mahāvairo-cana-sūtra* translated in 10 rolls (T. 848), the *Susiddhikara* (T. 893), the *Subāhuparipṛcchā* (T. 895), the **Cintāmaṇicakra* (T. 961), the *Cuṇḍīdevī-dhāraṇī* (T. 1078), the *Guhya-tantra* (T. 897), the *Amoghapāśa* (T. 1097, 1092), etc. (今略金剛頂大毘盧遮那經。并釋義十卷。蘇悉地。蘇摩呼。如意輪。七俱胝。瞿醯且怛羅。不空羂索等經).[34] The text then emphasizes that, while this material appears as three varieties (kula?), the maṇḍala rite is really just one ritual and the differences between the forms evident in disparate texts is only appearance. (撰集壇儀舉一法現其三種。唯形色等異)

There is much that is notable about this section of the text. First, it is clear that it is composed by Śubhakara, since it refers to his translation of the *Mahāvairocanābhisambodhi*, translated in 725 CE, but it makes no similar reference to his translations of other texts, like the *Susiddhikara* and *Subāhuparipṛcchā*, said to be translated in 726 CE, so we may surmise this part was composed between these two translation efforts. Second, because this section of the text is seemingly an admonishment about textual authority written by Śubhakara, it would appear that this **Uṣṇīṣavijaya* is a gray text, and it seems constructed from pieces of the *Uṣṇīṣavijaya-dhāraṇī* and pieces of the other texts mentioned above. Finally, we notice that the list of authoritative texts is followed by an "*et cetera*," a common form in Indian textual lists. We have little sense that Śubhakara ever learned written Chinese, and the translation of his documents was really performed by a committee of translators, very common in China. Thus, the list reflects Indian values of textual reference and malleability, faced with Chinese insecurity as to how all these different texts somehow work together. In some very deep sense, the Chinese appeared obsessed with the idea of an underlying unity – whether political or philosophical – whereas Indians continue to be extremely comfortable with distinction, dif-

[34] **Uṣṇīṣavijaya-dharmayoga-bhāvanā-vidhi*, T. 973.19.377c26-29.

ference and cognitive dissonance. In this light, I believe Śubhakara's comments overall reflect the Indian address of Chinese concerns for harmony.

The list is also quite different from the next major list of authoritative texts, the well known *Indications of the Goals of the Eighteen Assemblies of the Yoga of the Vajroṣṇīṣa* (T.869, 金剛頂經瑜伽十八會指歸) said to have been translated by Amoghavajra between 746–774 CE. This list claims that it is an authoritative list of scriptures, these being the eighteen texts of the Vajroṣṇīṣa system. While I have no doubt that the texts were authoritative – we have some of the works otherwise represented, either in Sanskrit originals or in Chinese or Tibetan translation – I doubt that the list is as authoritative as it is presented. We notice, for example, that it is a closed list, and thus its authoritative character. While the number eighteen is commonly used in India, as in the eighteen *mahāpurāṇas* and the eighteen books of the *Mahābhārata*, it is seldom employed this way. Certainly, we have an earlier list of the eighteen *Mahāsūtras* of the Sarvāstivāda found in its *vinaya*, but this list has many irregularities as well, as Skilling has shown.[35] We do see occasional esoteric representatives alluding to the number eighteen, and Jñānamitra, for example, indicates that the number eighteen is important for him, but he simply speaks of the "eighteen tantras of the *Sarvabuddhasamayoga*, etc."[36] In distinction to Śubhakarasiṃha, Amoghavajra was raised in China and knew Chinese civilization well. He would have understood the anxiety that Chinese people had voiced about the unabated flood of scriptures from India, and he had just returned from a trip to India (where he had not been since a child), so that he saw for himself the different textual sensibilities. And in fact, as Giebel has already pointed out, Japanese scholars have argued since the eighteenth century that the list was composed by Amoghavajra in China.[37]

The different senses of canonicity are most acutely visible when we review the testimony of Amoghavajra's Indian contemporary, Bud-

---

[35] Skilling, Peter, *Mahāsūtras: Great Discourses of the Buddha*, vol. II, parts 1 & 2. Oxford: Pali Text Society 1997, 4,20–24.54–55. I may be germane to observe that none of the lists of Mahāsūtras Skilling considers agrees with each other.

[36] *Āryaprajñāpāramitā-nayaśatapañcāśatkā-ṭīkā*, To. 2647 fol. 273a3: sarba buddha sa ma yo ga la sogs pa sde chen po bco brgyad phyag na rdo rje'i byin gyi rlabs kyis za hor gyi yul du gshegs pa.

[37] Giebel, Rolf W., "The *Chin-kang-ting ching yü-ch'ieh shih-pa-hui chih-kuei*: An Annotated Translation", in: *Naritasan Bukkyō Kenkyū kiyō (Journal of Naritasan Institute for Buddhist Studies)* 18 (1995), 107–201, especially 108–109.

dhaguhya. Buddhaguhya, who reputedly corresponded with the late eighth century Tibetan king Khri-srong lde'u-btsan (*Bhoṭasvāmidāsagurulekha* To. 4194), articulated in several works the now familiar genre system of Indian canon. In his various commentaries, he makes a distinction between the kinds of tantras that are oriented toward external ritual *(kriyā)* – whether associated with objective characteristics or associated with deep and sublime realities – and those oriented to internal yoga, and even discusses a third type between.[38] He provides examples of each of these, but for him the examples demonstrate the validity of the argument about individuals predisposed to one or another approach, not the authority of the texts, which he takes as a given. Consequently, Buddhaguhya's argument is fundamentally focused on personality types – a very old Indian and Buddhist concern – and the appropriate skill in means demonstrated by the Buddha to provide a correct ritual environment and correct meditative antidotes for these personality types.

4. *Esoteric Community Identity*

Thus, we are left in India with the idea of a semi-open canon of authoritative texts formulated for fluid communities in need of different approaches. What does this tell use about community identity? First, we should understand that involvement with Buddhism in India was almost always volitional: there are no normative rites of passage for the laity in the Buddhist system. That is, one can be born, obtain a name, reach adulthood, become married, retire and die without ever needing a Buddhist monk to facilitate the passage or ensure its legal status. The corollary to this approach is that Buddhist monks were required to reach out across communities, and to provide services, as mentioned above, to those in need of them. Because the older intellectual and financial service system became threatened after the fall of the Gupta, Buddhists moved with the times to an increased ritualization of social relationships through the expansion of the ritual repertoire, displacing in some mea-sure the sociology of knowledge and author-

[38] **Vairocanābhisambodhi-mahātantra-ṭīkā* To. 2663, fol. 65a4–b6; *Vairocanābhisambodhi-tantra-piṇḍārtha* To. 2662, fol. 3b1–4; *Dhyānottarapaṭala-ṭīkā* To. 2670, fol. 9a4–10a3.

ity of textual/meditative virtuosity that had held together the older paradigm.

As may be surmised, this accelerated ritualization worked in concert with the semi-open, genre-based canonical model to reinforce the need and authority of a preceptor. Certainly preceptors had been accorded authority in some measure before, whether we are speaking of monks as preceptors for the *vinaya* or the preachers *(dharmabhāṇaka)* for the Mahāyānist sūtras. Yet these prior Buddhist institutional systems had moderated the position of the charismatic preceptor, requiring consensus in decision making on a broad range of issues.[39] However, in the medieval proliferation of the Buddhist ritual menu – healing, exorcism, prognostication, rites of material benefit or control, new pilgrimages, to name a few – tantric Buddhism emphasized charismatic spirituality to a degree not seen previously. Consequently, the rise of the new *siddha* (perfected) sociological form in tantric Buddhism and their eventual ritual monopoly over the tantric tradition, combined with the profusion of new tantric scriptures, collectively reinforced the position of the master who adjudicates the validity of a new scripture, its applicability to the individual, and the nature of the ritual program to be employed.

Subsequent to the beginning of tantric Buddhism, all ritual acts were to be mediated through the person of the magus *(vidyādhara)*, who united both religious and political metaphors of dominion in his person. In our earliest surviving tantric document, the 654 CE *Dhāraṇīsaṃgraha* (T. 901) the author/editor Atikūṭa argues in his lengthy ritual appendix exactly the similarity of the tantric master, who has multiple dis-

[39] Good work has been done on medieval and modern Theravāda systems with respect to the moderation of charisma in normative monastic spheres; Friedrich-Silber, Ilana, *Virtuosity, charisma, and social order: a comparative sociological study of monasticism in Theravada Buddhism and medieval Catholicism,* Cambridge: Cambridge University Press 1995; Tambiah, Stanley J., *The Buddhist Saints of the Forest and the Cult of Amulets*, Cambridge: Cambridge University Press 1984; Carrithers, Michael, *The Forest Monks of Sri Lanka: an Anthropological and Historical Study*, Delhi: Oxford University Press 1983; Tiyavanich, Kamala, *Forest Recollections: Wandering Monks in Twentieth-century Thailand.* Honolulu: University of Hawai'i Press 1997; Tiyavanich, Kamala, *The Buddha in the Jungle.* Honolulu: University of Hawai'i Press 2003; Taylor, Jim L. *Forest monks and the nation-state: an anthropological and historical study in northeast Thailand.* Singapore: Institute of Southeast Asian Studies 1993; Dreyfus, George, *The Sound of Two Hands Clapping: the Education of a Tibetan Buddhist Monk.* Berkeley: University of California Press 2003; and Mills Mills, Martin A., *Identity, Ritual and State in Tibetan Buddhism: the Foundations of Authority in Gelukpa Monasticism*, New York: RoutledgeCurzon 2003, from different positions, have furthered the issue with respect to modern Tibetan monasticism.

ciples, with the king in his royal court surrounded by vassals, and the central Buddha in the maṇḍala of vassal divinities, whose subordinate relationship to the central figure is affirmed.[40] Charismatic preceptors could moreover access certain groups in a manner seldom seen before, especially in the cases of village and lower caste groups. Because we have little sense that medieval Buddhists were inhibited by caste prejudices, the centrality of the "perfected" teacher further came to reflect in part the sensibilities of such marginal peoples in the affirmation of vernacular languages and the integration of local deities into the esoteric maṇḍalas.

The charismatic emphasis, however, that relied on textual and ritual flexibility also ensured that the more orthodox institutions would resist the new revelation, and they seem to have done just that. We have no evidence for a widespread acceptance of early-phase tantric Buddhism in the great monasteries of medieval India. Instead, our earliest figures come from regional centers. The earliest document (*Dhāraṇīsaṃgraha* T. 901) comes from three monks – Atikūṭa and his two cohorts Kāśyapa and *Saṅghānandamokṣa – from Vajrāsana (the site of the Buddha's awakening), which then (as now) was a site of multi-national, multi-denominational vitality, but which also had many questionable groups associated with it. Similarly, through most of its history, the majority of our esoteric representatives apparently dwelt in regional sites that had stronger relations with local communities than with the elite monasteries. So we see eighth to eleventh century esoteric enclaves in Kāṇherī (the teacher Balipāda), lower Swat valley (the teachers Vilāsavajra and Indrabhūti), Śrī-śaila (Nāgabodhi), an unnamed center ~25 miles NE of Vajrāsana (Buddhajñānapāda), Kāṅgra (Jālandharapāda), Dakṣiṇā Kośala (Vairocanavajra), Ujjain (Kukuripāda), Phullahari (Nāropā), Devīkoṭa (Kāṇha), etc. While esoterism eventually became part of the ritual syllabus of sections of Vikramaśīla and a few others of the great monasteries, there can be little doubt that the small market towns *(haṭṭa)* and local centers remained the sources of tantric vitality. This is as we should expect, given the wedding of multiple "little tradition" rites and vocabulary – drawn from *nāga*, *yakṣa*, *śaiva*, *vetāla*, tribal and village systems, especially those of the isolated village, the *palli*.

[40] *Dhāraṇīsaṃgraha* T. 901.18.897b10–17.

In these areas, both the mythic and the authentic expanse of the Buddhist canon hovered like a wish-granting tree, one that no one could control. The esoteric preceptors *(vajrācārya)* would have an extensive ritual menu and, if needs be, make reference to great scriptures. Some were clearly imaginary and of exaggerated length, like the half million verse *Hevajra-tantra*, being but one of many such "root scriptures" *(mūla-tantra)* for which the tantra actually available and employed is the "lite tantra" *(laghu-tantra)*, which was considered a part, a chapter or a summation of the "root tantra." In all such instances, the master was the authority, for he had received – perhaps in visions or in dreams, perhaps in real life – the coronation/consecration rite from his master. Thus, the canon as icon became a source of charisma for the teacher in the lineage of reputedly perfected beings. Indeed, some part of the tantric discourse about being unencumbered by conventional morality is simply a reflection of the institutional realities: the small regional Buddhist esoteric centers no longer necessarily abided by the monastic consensus that was still maintained in the great monasteries, a consensus that inhibited charisma and provided institutional oversight adjudicating personal claims to grand spirituality. The identity of the figures in these regional centers was that of the master, in the center of a web of relationships tying together Buddhist history, imagined scriptures, village practices, the remnants of monastic codes, the medieval rites of kingship, cemetery divinities, tribal lore, and vernacular sayings. In terms of literature, it curiously meant the temporary return to some literary systems seen in the earliest Buddhist community: the validation of first person and vernacular poetry, which had been a mainstay of the early Arhat traditions but lost in the Mahāyāna. Now, however, all such systems promoted the omniscient master, whose position became no longer the "son of the Buddha" but, essentially, the Buddha himself.

5. *Conclusion*

The Buddhist canon remains to this day a shifting, somewhat imaginary enterprise, whose boundaries are not structured in the manner of the Semitic religions, but operate in greater concord with the deutero-canons of Hinduism and Taoism – the *smṛti* collections for the former and the *Sandong* (三洞) for the latter, each with multiple authoritative groupings and subcollections – where the authoritative scriptures were also under continual renegotiation. Tantric Buddhism added a body of ritual and yogic material that emphasized and supported the displacement of the community consensus for the charismatic preceptor, who represented both the ideal paradigm of the divine overlord and the problematic reality of human relations. Thus the fluid tantric canon, the rapidly composed tantric texts and the charismatic tantric master became mutually referencing and reinforcing systems of identity for the members of such communities and their networks throughout India.

6. *Abbreviations*

T. *Taishō Shinshū Daizōkyō*. Takakusu Junjirō and Watanabe Kaikyoku, eds. 1924–35. Tokyo: Daizōkyōkai.

To. sDe-dge canon numbers from Ui, Hakuju, et al, eds. 1934. *A Complete Catalogue of the Tibetan Buddhist Canons (BKaḥ-ḥgyur and Bstan-ḥgyur).* Sendai: Tôhoku Imperial University.

7. *Primary Sources*

Abhidharmasamuccaya. Pradhan, Pralhad (ed.), *Abhidharma Samuc-caya of Asanga.* Visva-Bharati Studies 12. Santiniketan: Visva-Bha-rati 1950.

Abhidharmasamuccayabhāṣya. Tatia, Nathmal (ed.), *Abhidharmasa-muccaya-bhāṣyaṃ.* Tibetan Sanskrit Works Series No. 17. Patna: Kashi Prasad Jayaswal Research Institute 1976.

Āryaprajñāpāramitā-nayaśatapañcāśatkā-ṭīkā. To. 2647

Daśabhūmika-sūtra. Kondō, Ryūkō (ed.) 1936. *Daśabhūmīśvaro nāma Mahāyānasūtra ṃ*. Rpt. Kyoto: Rinsen Book Co., 1983.

Dhāraṇīsaṃgraha. 陀羅尼集經. T. 901.

Dhyānottarapaṭala-ṭīkā. To. 2670.

Jingang dingjing yuqie shibahui zhigui. 金剛頂經瑜伽十八會指歸. T. 869. Giebel 1995 trans.

**Uṣṇīṣavijaya a-dharmayoga-bhāvanā-vidhi*. 尊勝佛頂修瑜伽法軌儀. T. 973.

**Vairocanābhisambodhi-mahātantra-ṭīkā*. To. 2663. trans. Hodge, Stephen, *The Mahā-vairocana-abhisa ṃbodhi Tantra, with Buddhagu-hya's Commentary.* London and New York: RoutledgeCurzon 2003.

Vairocanābhisambodhi-tantra-piṇḍārtha. To. 2662. trans. Hodge, Stephen, *The Mahā-vairocana-abhisaṃbodhi Tantra, with Buddhagu-hya's Commentary.* London and New York: RoutledgeCurzon 2003.

THE CHRISTIAN CANON IN A COMPARATIVE PERSPECTIVE. A RESPONSE TO RONALD M. DAVIDSON

Markus Zehnder

1. *Introduction*

The paper presented by Prof. Davidson has given us insights in some very interesting aspects of the concept of canon in the Buddhist tradition.

As a biblical scholar, I am of course not in a position to scrutinize his interpretation of the Buddhist material in any detail. However, this does not interfere with the task we will address in this response, which is to enlarge the picture by shifting our attention to the concept of canon as developed in and applied to the biblical world. I will try to do this from a comparative perspective, taking into consideration some of the characteristics of the Buddhist notion of canon that were mentioned in Prof. Davidson's paper.[1] Within the biblical world, I will look specifically at the Christian notion of canon.[2] The comparative perspective has the positive potential to enhance our understanding of all the traditions considered in the comparison.[3]

In the context of a short paper such as this one it is of course not possible even to name the main issues related to the Christian notion of canon, let alone develop them in some depth. So we have to content

[1] While it seems defensible to speak about a more or less generally shared *notion of canon* in Buddhism, it is somewhat problematic to speak of a *Buddhist canon* in the singular, taking into consideration the enormous differences between the "canons" used by the different branches of Buddhism. It is true that differences in canon delimitation also exist in the Christian tradition; they are, however, of a much more limited extent than the differences found in the Buddhist tradition.

[2] By this phrase the notion of canon that manifests itself historically from about the fourth century CE is meant. It is clear that the movement initiated by Jesus of Nazareth, which ultimately came to be known as "Christianity", did not always have a unified and clearly developed concept of canon.

[3] Cf. Miriam Levering, "Scripture and Its Reception: A Buddhist Case", in: M. Levering (ed.), *Rethinking Scripture*, New York: State University of New York Press, 1989, 58–101, here 59.

ourselves with a modest selection of topics dealt with from a certain historical perspective[4] – a perspective which will not exclusively but predominantly focus on differences rather than on similarities.

As far as the Christian concept of canon is concerned, there is virtually no single aspect that would not presently be exposed to rather intense discussions, discussions that only rarely lead to consensual results. This observation holds true for a whole range of historical questions as well as broader cultural and theological issues.[5]

I do not want to offer solutions to any of the fundamental questions related to the concept of the Christian canon, nor do I pretend to be able to do so. What I will attempt is more modest: to make explicit some of the implications connected with this concept and formulate some questions in a manner that may come across at times as provocative, but that really aims to stimulate the debate.

2. *The Eccentric Nature of the Christian Canon*

Over the course of the second century CE the growing Christian community had already started to become a predominantly "European" entity, at least an entity increasingly detached from its original Judaic background even in its Eastern, Semitic branches in Syria and further east. And yet, the Hebrew Scriptures[6] continued to hold a central position in the life of almost all currents within the emergent Church, even after the increasing use of additional texts in different areas of church life, texts of which some would eventually be dubbed "New Testament". These Hebrew Scriptures were ultimately recognized as forming an integral part of the canon of the Church, designated as the scriptures of the "Old Testament".

---

[4] This perspective could be linked to what I would label "traditional Protestant Christianity" in a rather loose and broad sense of the term.

[5] For an overview of some of the most pertinent questions see Lee Martin McDonald/James A. Sanders, "Introduction", in: L. M. McDonald/J. A. Sanders, *The Canon Debate: On the Origins and Formation of the Bible*, Peabody: Hendrickson Publishers, 2002, 3–17.

[6] The exact delimitation of the corpus that could be summarized under this category was disputed for centuries among various groups within the Jewish and Christian traditions; however, these disputes did in most instances not relate to what is now known as the Hebrew Bible, with the exception of Ezekiel, Song of Songs, Esther and Ecclesiastes. See, e. g., Jonathan Rosenbaum, "Judaism", in: F. M. Denny/R. L. Taylor (eds.), *The Holy Book in Comparative Perspective*, Columbia: University of South Carolina Press, 1985, 10–35, here 16.

At the time of the appearance of more or less official lists delimiting the Christian canon, historically documented from the second half of the fourth century CE onward, the Church's centre of gravitation had clearly come to be located in the Roman-Hellenistic "Western" world. At the same time, the first part of the two-partite canon was wholly "Hebrew", and the second part at least to a high degree, in spite of the Greek language of the documents contained in it. This meant that both the Church and its canon had what I would like to call an eccentric nature, with both a Semitic/Hebrew pole and a Western pole. In the words of Wilfred Cantwell Smith: "Christian scripture is the only instance in world history where one movement explicitly incorporates the scripture of another as such within its own, adding things new but making the old part and parcel".[7]

Its eccentric nature is perhaps one of the most salient features of the Christian canon, defined most importantly by the fact that it incorporates not only texts produced in the Jesus movement's own circles and the emerging church, but also the Jewish Scriptures that came to be designated as the Old Testament, and not just a selection of Jewish scriptures that seemingly would best fit into the new theological system, but all of the 22 or 24 books that were singled out by Jews themselves, at least from the first century CE onward, as ranking highest in authority.

This is of course only seemingly paralleled in the Islamic religious tradition by the Qur'an's recognition of Jews and Christians as people of the book and by the broad recurrence to biblical material in the Qur'anic texts. The fundamental difference in the Qur'anic approach lies in the fact that Old and New Testament scriptures are not acknowledged as canonical as such, but only accepted as divine in a form which – because of the Jews' and the Christians' successful attempts to distort the earlier revelatory documents – does no longer exist and is fully restored only by the Qur'an itself.[8] The Qur'an, therefore, in fact functions not as an addition to the biblical canon, as the New Testament does with respect to the Old, but as its factual replacement.

The eccentric nature of the Christian canon can certainly be compared to other phenomena in the history of religions, for example the

[7] Wilfred Cantwell Smith, "Scripture as Form and Concept: Their Emergence for the Western World", in: M. Levering (ed.), *Rethinking Scripture*, New York: State University of New York Press, 1989, 29–57, here 38.

[8] See, e.g., Rosenbaum, *Judaism* 12.

adaptation of ancient Buddhist traditions in places outside the cradle of India. And yet it seems to me that we are not dealing with exactly the same degree of eccentricity, because the canonical collections in non-Indian Buddhism in varying degrees also include texts actually produced in their own realm, originating for instance in Tibet or China, and, perhaps more importantly, because the canonical texts do not derive their importance so clearly and sweepingly from being related to a specific historical context, which became a real foreign context, as opposed to the situation in the biblical world. On the other hand, the opposition between the Christian and the Buddhist notion of canon is reduced by the fact that the Buddhist canons mainly contain sayings of the Buddha Siddharta Gautama and Indian Buddhas and Bodhisattvas and by the fact that non-Indian traditions rarely appear in unveiled forms.[9]

Is it too daring to assume that the eccentric nature of the Christian canon has contributed considerably, among other factors, to the interest in foreign cultures that according to some scholars is historically more characteristic of Western civilization than of many others?[10]

The Christian canon's eccentric nature is related to what could be called the way-character of revelation in the Christian tradition: Foundational divine revelation in history in this tradition is thought to have taken place over a long period of time, basically from Abraham through the first and possibly second generation of disciples of Jesus, whereas in other traditions the foundational revelation is focused much more on punctual episodes like the enlightenment or awakening of the Buddha Siddharta Gautama or the angelic commission of Allah's words to Mohammad.[11]

---

[9] The bulk of non-Indian material tends to be found in so-called "apocrypha". It must be stressed that the situation in the Buddhist realm is more complicated than can be outlined here. For example, the inclusion or exclusion of local non-Indian traditions in canonical collections would be subject to changes over time, with modern editions being more likely to incorporate local non-Indian material.

[10] For this interest see, e. g., Rémi Brague, *Europa, eine exzentrische Identität*, Frankfurt a. M.: Campus Verlag, 1993.

[11] It is of course possible to describe the religious history of Buddhism in a different way, as focusing on a multitude of Buddha manifestations; however, these manifestations had to be located in what would best be described as a "supra-historical" framework that does not compare with the biblical way-concept of revelation, because the written testimonies of Buddha Siddharta Gautama's and his followers' teachings are testimonies of an ever present Truth or an ever-present possibility of enlightenment; cf. Reginald A. Ray, "Buddhism", in: F. M. Denny/R. L. Taylor (eds.), *The Holy Book in Comparative Perspective*, Columbia: University of South Carolina Press, 1985, 148–180, here 150.

Though the eccentric nature of the Christian canon stands out as something special within the history of religions, I am not suggesting that there are no analogies both in religious and more broadly in cultural history that can somehow and probably usefully be compared to the Christian canon. The relation of Chinese or Tibetan to Indian Buddhism may be such a case in point in spite of the reservations adduced above, or the absorption of Sumerian cultural elements by the Akkadians, or Assyria's religious and cultural orientation towards Babylonia, or Rome's cultural and religious orientation towards Greece. It seems, however, that at least one element of the eccentric nature of the Christian canon is matched in none of the adduced parallels: the two poles of Old and New Testament do not stand on anything like an equal footing, and there is no adoration of the Old Testament as the "higher" element; rather, the old "testament" is acknowledged, integrated and interpreted through the lens of the new "testament", with God's revelation in Jesus understood as the real climax of history.[12] Further investigation of these phenomena and their cross-cultural comparison may well be rewarding in many respects.

3. *History as the Primary Focus of the Christian Canon*

The Christian canon is inseparably related not to the enshrinement of philosophical, soteriological or other types of "timeless" ideas, or even to the enshrinement of *mantras*, as seems to be the case in Buddhism,[13] but instead to history as its primary organisational principle, more specifically to the concept of salvation history:[14] The texts collected in

[12] Cf. Harry Y. Gamble, "Christianity", in: F. M. Denny/R. L. Taylor (eds.), *The Holy Book in Comparative Perspective*, Columbia: University of South Carolina Press, 1985, 36–62, here 38.45–46; McDonald/Sanders, *Introduction* 14.17; Rainer Riesner, "Ansätze zur Kanonbildung innerhalb des Neuen Testaments", in: G. Maier (ed.), *Der Kanon der Bibel*, Giessen: Brunnen Verlag, 1990, 153–164, here 158. An analogy of a very limited kind may be seen in the *p'an-chiao* ("classification of the teachings") schemata of the Buddhist tradition; see, e. g., Peter N. Gregory, "Tsung-mi and the Sinification of Buddhism", in: *Studies in East Asian Buddhism* 16; Honolulu: University of Hawai'i Press, 2002, 93–114.

[13] And similarly in Hinduism (to use a somewhat generalizing term both here and in the remainder of the article), or, to be more precise, in Veda in the narrower sense of the term; see Robert C. Lester, "Hinduism", in: F. M. Denny/R. L. Taylor (eds.), *The Holy Book in Comparative Perspective*, Columbia: University of South Carolina Press, 1985, 126–147, here 126–139. For the Buddhist case see Ray, *Buddhism* 149–150.

[14] Again, the opposition between the Christian and the Buddhist tradition is not a complete one. History does in fact play a role in the Buddhist notion of canon, in

the canon are thought to be those that most faithfully testify to this history and of course to the divine revelation connected with it. This is true for both parts of the Christian canon, the Old Testament and the New Testament.[15] One element to prove this point is the fact that the two parts of the canon are of unequal size, since they cover historical periods of highly uneven length. The period covered in the New Testament is much shorter than the one covered in the Old Testament, because it focuses solely on Christ and the first one or two generations of his followers.

It may be assumed that probably this element of closest possible witness to God's revelation in salvation history is the primary principle at work in the decisions of the early Church taken with respect to establishing or acknowledging the canon, underlying other criteria that are often mentioned, like divine authority, inspiration, apostolicity, orthodoxy, wide acceptance and established usage.[16]

Based on these observations, one might say that one of the principal functions of the Christian canon is to preserve and give access to a certain segment of history. As opposed to this, Prof. Davidson's contribution points to the central notion of *mantra* with which the canon is intertwined in tantric Buddhism. It is certainly the case that some elements of the Christian scriptures can be and were used in a way that resembles *mantra* or more generally "magical" practices in the broadest sense of the term, for instance in liturgical contexts, meditation, exorcism, or apotropaic rites. However, the concept of *mantra* or

---

various ways: the canon strongly focuses on the Buddha Siddharta Gautama; the *sutras* of the Buddha and the Bodhisattvas are given preeminence; conflicting teachings are systematized, i. a., according to the Buddha's biography; based on the perception of differences in the status of *dharma* in different historical periods, different means of aspiring to *nirvana* are thought to be applicable. Cf. Reginald A. Ray, *Buddhist Saints in India*, New York: Oxford University Press, 1994, 491ff.

[15] Hence, Gamble's opposition between the gospels as historical records and the gospels as scripture is misleading (see Gamble, *Christianity* 42).

[16] Cf. F. F. Bruce, *The Canon of Scripture*, Downers Grove: InterVarsity Press, 1988, 266.278.283. Whether the judgments of the early fathers and institutional bodies on the historical value of the competing documents were correct, is another question. In addition, it must be stressed that "closest possible witness" cannot simply be identified with "earliest witness". James D. G. Dunn rightly points to the fact that there were other early writings which were not included in the canon of the New Testament; see Dunn, "Has the Canon a Continuing Function?", in: L. M. McDonald/J. A. Sanders, *The Canon Debate: On the Origins and Formation of the Bible*, Peabody: Hendrickson Publishers, 2002, 558–579, here 566–567. For an elaborated list and discussion of generally agreed upon criteria of canonicity see, e. g., Bruce, *The Canon* 255–269; Gamble, *Christianity* 47–48.

a functional equivalent of it was hardly officially accepted as a central element of Christian belief, and certainly it was never related to the process of canonization of texts by identifying them as *mantra*-like or assigning them a *mantra*-like function and choosing them to be included in the canon based on such a function.

Furthermore, usages of texts of the Christian canon corresponding to the use of *mantras* in the Buddhist tradition would always be limited to a narrow range of passages, whereas the "transactive mode"of using texts in the Buddhist tradition,[17] that is, "the reception of texts specifically *for the purpose of* taking some kind of action or establishing some kind of relationship,"[18] extends potentially to most of the texts in the various Buddhist canons. Instead, it was always, with respect both to the canon of the Old and the New Testament, the quality of these texts as witnesses to history that was the underlying criterion for the acknowledgment of their canonical status, and a possible transactive use of certain texts was only a secondary development in the function of these texts that surfaced predominantly in the aftermath of their inclusion in the canon. The diversity and historical variety of the canonical writings themselves suggested clearly that the proper use of these writings was their constant re-application and re-interpretation, not their simple repetition.[19]

[17] More or less in all its important branches, not just in tantric Buddhism.

[18] Levering, *Scripture* 72. Specific purposes mentioned by Levering are obtaining protection or powers; creating merit; bringing benefits to others, enacting confession or repentance; making vows; offering devotion and praise; expressing and bringing into effect relationships between members of the community living and dead, and between those members and transhuman agents (see Levering, *Scripture* 72; these purposes are elaborated in some detail in Levering, *Scripture* 73–81). Levering rightly states: "Almost all of the world's sacred texts contain material which is ... useful in bringing about an action or a transaction of some kind. What is striking in the Buddhist case is the degree to which all interactions with all texts, all receptions, are understood to be actions and transactions" (*Scripture* 81).

[19] Cf. also Dunn, *Has the Canon* 571. He speaks of the words of the New Testament as "icons" that must not be turned into "idols". With the shift in some important segments of Christianity from the perception of the biblical texts as witnesses to God's revelation in history to an understanding of the biblical texts as a substantial part of God's revelation in themselves (see Gamble, *Christianity* 50), the way to a more transactive and certainly less history-oriented use of biblical texts was opened. The Buddhist understanding that "words do not merely express truth", but "are the living presence of true and powerful reality" (Levering, *Scripture* 63) and that texts containing the word of Buddha are "the means by which he transforms the world through transforming the mind of sentient beings" (Levering, *Scripture* 64) could therefore find analogous counterparts in the Christian understanding of their canonical texts. On the other hand, various phenomena of re-application and re-interpretation going beyond

There is another aspect related to the presence or absence of the notions of history or *mantra* in the concept of canon: While in the Christian tradition, the canonical writings are testimonies of God's dealings in history, or – at a later stage – God's words spoken in history but with eternal meaning, in some branches of the Buddhist tradition canonical writings symbolize or represent Buddha or *dharma*.[20] The texts themselves stand for the ultimate truth and its power. This again ties in with the "magical" quality of texts mentioned above.[21]

The difference with regard to the importance of history in the Christian and Buddhist notion of canon is related to a difference in the perception of the origins of the respective sacred texts: a divine being intimately connected with history in the Christian case, eternal transcending Truth (or "nature of things"), lying beyond the concrete notion of a theistic deity, in the Buddhist case.[22]

There is yet another way in which history plays a role in the Christian concept of canon that has no counterpart in the Buddhist tradition: It is only in historical retrospection that certain writings can be acknowledged as canonical, because of the authority these writings have exercised in large parts of the Church.[23] As opposed to this, in the Buddhist tradition a canonical text can be produced *ad hoc* and imme-

the simple repetition of traditional texts or the production of new canonical texts can also be found in Buddhism.

[20] See Levering, *Scripture* 85. She elaborates this further under the heading of "The Symbolic Mode" (see Levering, *Scripture* 86–90). The Islamic doctrine of the eternal divine character of the Qur'an comes close to such a view. It is not correct that "belief in the notion of a 'heavenly book'" is an element that connects Judaism, Christianity, and Islam, as asserted repeatedly in the discussion (see, e. g., McDonald/Sanders, *Introduction* 8). The Bible mentions heavenly documents, but the concept of the Bible itself as a "heavenly book" is entertained only in minority circles within the Christian tradition.

[21] As analogous phenomena in the Christian tradition, Levering identifies "the way the presence of the divine is understood in Western Christian sacraments or in Eastern Orthodox Christian icons" (*Scripture* 88), but not the way canonical texts themselves are understood.

[22] Cf. Frederick M. Denny/Rodney L. Taylor, "Introduction", in: F. M. Denny/R. L. Taylor (eds.), *The Holy Book in Comparative Perspective,* Columbia: University of South Carolina Press, 1985, 1–9, here 3. The Christian concept is closely related to the Jewish and the Muslim concepts, though the Muslim understanding of the Qur'an as a verbatim record of Allah's revelation is not matched in the biblical realm. The Buddhist concept finds a close analogon in Hinduism (cf. Lester, *Hinduism* 127).

[23] See Eugene Ulrich, "The Notion and Definition of Canon", in: L. M. McDonald/J. A. Sanders, *The Canon Debate: On the Origins and Formation of the Bible,* Peabody: Hendrickson Publishers, 2002, 21–35, here 32; cf. McDonald/Sanders, *Introduction* 10–11.

diately be recognized as such by an enlightened official representative of this religious tradition.

4. *The Christian Canon as "Testament"*

Prof. Davidson points to the connection between the Semitic concept of canon and the notion of election in his paper. In fact, the Christian canon is directly related not only to the notion of salvation history, but more specifically to the concepts of election and treaty as particular parts of salvation history, culminating in the words and deeds of Christ. The other world-religions do generally not show a combination of these phenomena, with the exception of Islam where the giving of the Qur'an is also linked to a kind of election. A considerable difference remains nevertheless even in this case, in that the historical frame of the combination of election and canon is intermittent in the case of Islam, as opposed to Christianity, where the canon is related to a long historical period in which the election is asserted to take place.

The Christian canon consists of two "testaments", literally, according to the Greek word *diatheke*, "covenants".[24] The use of the term "testament" to designate the Christian canon(s) is rooted, i. a., in Heb. 9:18–20, a passage that refers to the covenant described in Exod. 24:4–8 as "the first covenant". This phrase is used in contrast with the "new covenant" promised in Jer. 31:31–34. Similar language is also found in 2 Cor. 3:14. According to the authors of the New Testament, this new covenant has been established by the blood of Christ (see, e. g., 1 Cor. 11:25: "This cup is the new covenant in my blood"). "It was not until the end of the second century AD that the two collections began to be described, briefly, as the Old Covenant (or Testament) and the New Covenant (or Testament)".[25]

5. *The Christian Canon as a Closed Canon*

The Christian canon after being fixed can be described on the one hand both as closed and as relatively coherent in its delimitations with respect to the numerous groups that constitute Christianity, as opposed to the situation in Buddhism, where the canon is open ("in

---

[24] See Bruce, *The Canon* 19–22.
[25] Bruce, *The Canon* 21.

some measure")[26] and subject to substantial divergences among different subgroups.[27]

The closed nature of the Christian canon is intimately related to its aforementioned function as a close description of divine revelation in history, because the orthodox view of the Church has it that this revelation in its special, foundational aspects was completed with the preaching of the apostles. On the other hand, the Buddhist concept of a (semi-)open canon is related to the timeless nature of the Truth (or nature of things) to which the texts testify,[28] and it is made manageable on both a practical and a dogmatical level by a principle of incorporation of different traditions in a system of graded reflections of the Truth or relatively valued positions.[29]

The opposition of a closed versus an open canon can perhaps be identified as the single most fundamental difference between the Christian and the Buddhist canons.

Whether an open canon such as we find it in Buddhism, really is a canon *stricto sensu* is a matter of debate.[30] In fact the differences

---

[26] To use a formulation by Ronald M. Davidson which he employs in the first sentence of the revised version of his paper.

[27] See, e.g., Denny/Taylor, *Introduction* 5. To some extent this verdict also applies to Hinduism (cf. Lester, *Hinduism*).

[28] Cf. Ray, *Buddhism* 150–151. Prof. Davidson has decided to tone down the description of the Buddhist notion of canon from "open" to "semi-open" in the revised version of his paper after the discussion of the paper at the conference. This certainly helps to clarify that the openness of the Buddhist canon(s) is not to be misunderstood in any absolute sense. However, since "open" does not have to be interpreted in a strict way excluding notions of semi-openness, and in order not to blur the substantial distinctions between any (semi-)open and close concept of canon, it may be semantically legitimate to stick to the broader term "open".

[29] See Ray, *Buddhism* 173–174.

[30] Cf. Ulrich, *The Notion* 21. Ulrich speaks about the "confusion" currently surrounding the term; he observes: "Some scholars think that canon is a theological *terminus technicus* with a clear meaning, a specific denotation, and a long history of discussion, while others think that the term may be used more broadly to fit any of several aspects related to the collections of authoritative sacred texts of Judaism or Christianity" (*The Notion* 21). Ulrich notes the fact that in theological dictionaries of both Jewish and Christian provenance the term "canon" implies the notion of a comprehensive list which is closed (*The Notion* 26–28). He strongly advocates a position which states that in order to prevent confusion, the term "canon" should only be used if what is meant is "the final, fixed, and closed list of the books of scripture that are officially and permanently accepted as supremely authoritative by a faith tradition" (*The Notion* 31); clearly, an open canon as endorsed by the Buddhist tradition would not qualify for the term. For a similar position see McDonald/Sanders, *Introduction* 11. Ulrich concludes: "[T]alk of an open canon is confusing and counterproductive; it seems more appropriate to speak of a growing collection of books considered as sacred scripture" (*The Notion* 34). Another element that in Ulrich's view is a necessary part of the concept of "canon" is

between the notion of an open and the notion of a closed canon are so big that the question arises as to whether the use of the same term "canon" provides more help or perhaps rather more confusion in trying to understand the respective phenomena.

Historically, the term "canon" as applied to the field of religion, developed within the Judaeo-Christian tradition, first referring to the *regula fidei*, the norm of the Christian faith, and ultimately, in the second half of the fourth century CE, to describe the list of scriptures or books that were thought to contain the essentials of this faith.[31]

One could argue that because of the rooting of the term "canon" with reference to a certain type of scripture in the Jewish and Christian traditions, it is probably advisable to let the use of the term in these traditions decide to what degree the use of the term "canon" with respect to related phenomena in other religious traditions can be judged as adequate or not.[32]

The term "canon" in the religious field as understood originally, that is, in the Judaeo-Christian tradition,[33] does not only imply selection, but more specifically the selection of a limited amount of specific texts out of a larger number of texts belonging to the same religious tradi-

---

the retrospective judgment made by a group about books which have been exercising authority in the past (see Ulrich, *The Notion* 32). As mentioned above, this element is lacking in the Buddhist tradition as well, where a canonical text can be produced *ad hoc* and immediately recognized as such by an enlightened official representative of this religious tradition.

[31] See, e.g., Bruce, *The Canon* 17–18; David G. Dunbar, "The Biblical Canon", in: D. A. Carson/J. D. Woodbridge (eds.), *Hermeneutics, Authority, and Canon*, Grand Rapids: Zondervan, 1986, 299–360, here 300; Gamble, *Christianity* 43–44; McDonald/Sanders, *Introduction* 12–13; Ulrich, *The Notion* 22.28. The earliest extant list of acknowledged and authoritative books showing full agreement with the New Testament canon of historic Christianity was the one composed by the Alexandrinian bishop Athanasius, dating back to the year 367. "Other lists of the same or closely similar scope were set forth by various local or regional ecclesiastical councils of the late fourth century, so that by the early fifth century there had emerged a widespread unanimity about the extent of Christian scripture" (Gamble, Christianity 44). It is, however, clear that at least in the mid-second century CE, in the context of Marcion's proposal of a canon consisting only of Luke and Paul, the Church had to address the question of canon in a conscious way. The earliest known list of books that were approved to be read in the churches was already drawn up at the end of the second century CE, the probable date of the so-called Muratorian Canon.

[32] In the present writer's view, however, such an argument is not compelling, because a semantic broadening of the term "canon" cannot a priori be classified as illegitimate. The question is, how useful such a broadening is. What must be demanded is a clear and coherent use of the term "canon" by scholars participating in the debate.

[33] In the sense of "canon II" according to Gerald Sheppard's definition of canon, in: *The Encyclopedia of Religion* 3:62–69; New York, Macmillan, 1987, here 62–63.

tion.[34] This is what we find in the case of the Christian canon, with the acceptance, for example, of the Acts of the Apostles, and the parallel rejection of the so-called Acts of Paul, or with the acceptance of the letter of Jude, and the parallel non-adoption of the letter of Clement, though those texts that were not adopted into the canon clearly share the same spirit and belong to the same religious tradition as those that were accepted, a phenomenon that finds no parallel in the Buddhist canons.[35]

One could further argue that in a sense the concept of an open canon could be called a *contradictio in adiecto*, much the same as "open borders" or "an open marriage": A border is there to limit and control somehow free movement, otherwise, it is no longer a border; and a marriage in most cultures is meant to be an exclusive commitment in some very central respects, otherwise it is no longer a real marriage, but a broken one, and one could name other examples.

Described from another angle, we might say the concept of canon in its strict version of a closed canon regards the definition of the *foundation* of faith, in an exhaustive and sufficient way, versus simple *expression* of that faith, which in fact can be found in many more inspired texts, that in turn are likely to be included in the canon in the Buddhist tradition or other models of an open canon.[36]

The closed nature of the Christian canon means that it can function as a *norma normans*, which in turn opens the way for self-criticism and renewal – two phenomena closely interconnected more often than not.[37] Is it too daring to say that these consequences of a closed canon are in fact more tangible in the history of the Christian tradition than in the history of, for example, the Buddhist tradition?

On the other hand, the opposition of the Christian and the Buddhist canons with regard to closeness and openness is not as complete as might appear at first glance. There are many elements that keep the formally closed Christian canon flexible to a certain extent. One element is the ongoing editing of texts during the process of the for-

---

[34] Interestingly, the same applies for the canon of Greek classics developed in Alexandria in the third century BCE (see, e.g., Smith, *Scripture* 40).

[35] Nor, for example, in the Hindu canon.

[36] Bruce uses a distinction similar to the one proposed here, stating with respect to the New Testament canon: "It is not an anthology of inspired or inspiring literature", but a corpus of literature whose „chief concern is to get as close as possible to the source of the Christian faith" (Bruce, *The Canon* 283).

[37] For similar observations see Dunn, *Has the Canon* 574f.

mation of the canon, as can perhaps most clearly be seen from the differences between the Septuagint and the Masoretic text as regards the Old Testament. We may also point to the near canonical status of texts interpreting the canonical documents, a phenomenon which can be observed even in the Protestant tradition with the high esteem given to creeds and confessions in several denominations at least some centuries ago, but sometimes even today.[38] Interestingly, Christian, especially Protestant, and Jewish traditions are not fully identical in this respect, for no interpretation of the canonical texts in Protestantism would achieve such a high quasi-canonical position as the Mishnah and the Talmudim in Judaism.[39] Generally speaking, the most important strategy to keep the formally closed Christian canon relevant in ever changing contexts was (and is) to constantly reinterpret it by means of varying hermeneutic rules.[40]

On another level, the Christian canon is perhaps in itself much more open than the Buddhist, or any other, canon, by virtue of its eccentric and diverse nature described above. It not only fully embraces the canon of another religious tradition, Judaism, but it is also remarkable that from a Western or European perspective not only the Old Testament, but also the majority of the New Testament scriptures to a high degree are Semitic in the specific Judaic version of Semitism, which means that the Church, although a gradually Westernized institution, still embraced as its roots a corpus of canonical texts that were part of a foreign cultural environment. Thus openness is here defined as openness towards a distinct other, whereas in the Buddhist canons it is rather an openness that embraces the continued acceptance of new texts of the same, own tradition. The openness of the Christian canon consists also in the fact that it enshrines not only one single form of Christianity as the only possible realization of the Christian faith, but rather a number of various forms. As mentioned earlier, this precludes

---

[38] Another, pre-Protestant example would be the glosses in the mediaeval *pagina sacra*.

[39] According to some scholars, the Mishnah and the Talmudim as well as some other works have to be considered as part of an ever-growing, and thus open, canon in the Jewish tradition; see., e.g., Rosenbaum, *Judaism* 10.24–25.31. It is, however, not clear, whether all Orthodox Jews would fully agree with such a view. What is clear is that there is a graded level of authority and holiness ascribed to different writings, with the Pentateuch being ascribed the highest level (cf., e.g., Rosenbaum, *Judaism* 26).

[40] See, e.g., James A. Sanders, "The Issue of Closure in the Canonical Process", in: L.M. McDonald/J.A. Sanders, *The Canon Debate: On the Origins and Formation of the Bible*, Peabody: Hendrickson Publishers, 2002, 252–263, here 259.

a simple *mantra*-like repetition of Biblical texts or their one-to-one enshrinment in a Sharia-like law corpus as the main mode of their application, and calls rather for a constant re-interpretation in accordance with the constantly changing historical situations.

The distinction between a closed Christian canon and open Buddhist canons can be related to the distinction between Canon I and Canon II as proposed by Kendall W. Folkert. Canon I denotes a collection of normative texts present in a certain religious tradition principally by the force of a vector such as ritual activity, whereas Canon II refers to a collection of normative texts that are more independently present in a certain religious tradition and which themselves often function as vectors, that is, carriers of religious activity.[41] However, whereas it may be acknowledged that there is in fact a high degree of congruence between the Canon I model and the Buddhist notion of canon, the Canon II model is not generally applicable to Christian notions of canon, but in its fuller sense only to Protestant notions of canon and their precursors in earlier church history.

The distinction between Canon I and Canon II has some parallels with Sam Gill's distinction between the "informative" and the "performative" function of canonical texts, though the two models do not fully overlap. In the informative vs. performative dichotomy, the Christian concept of canon leans more toward the informative side, while the Buddhist concept of canon leans somewhat more toward the performative side; however, the conceptual and doctrinal content is not totally marginalized.[42]

---

[41] For details see Kendall W. Folkert, "The 'Canons' of 'Scripture'", in: M. Levering (ed.), *Rethinking Scripture*, New York: State University of New York Press, 1989, 170–179, here 173–179.

[42] Cf. Denny/Taylor, *Introduction* 7–8, with a slightly different assessment. They mention Hinduism, Judaism, Islam, and Zoroastrism as those traditions "which place heavy emphasis on ritual performance of recitation ... which involves much more than the conceptual, mental, literal levels associated with mere reading and study for information, knowledge, and guidance" (Denny/Taylor, *Introduction* 8). For the case of Hinduism see Lester, *Hinduism*, especially 128–129; for the case of Islam see Frederick M. Denny, "Islam", in: F. M. Denny/R. L. Taylor (eds.), *The Holy Book in Comparative Perspective*, Columbia: University of South Carolina Press, 1985, 84–108; for the case of Zoroastrism see James W. Boyd, "Zoroastrianism", in: F. M. Denny/R. L. Taylor (eds.), *The Holy Book in Comparative Perspective*, Columbia: University of South Carolina Press, 1985, 109–125.

6. *The Combination of Unity and Diversity in the Christian Canon and its Manageable Size*

The Christian canon comprises texts that were written over a long period of time, approximately over one thousand years, by many different authors and with a broad range of cultural and even theological diversity, as opposed most clearly, in this respect, to the situation we find in Islam. At the same time, the shared focus on what can be called salvation history with a high degree of common ground in terms of theological outlook serves as a unifying bond holding the diverse documents[43] together.

Bringing these two aspects together, we can speak of a combination of pluriformity or diversity and unity which is typical of the Christian canon as opposed to the canons of the other large world religions, with the Islamic canon leaning towards unity and the Buddhist and Hindu canons leaning towards the opposite side of pluriformity.[44]

The Christian canon is large enough, as can be seen to this very day, to stimulate ongoing research and new insights in each new generation, and yet is quantitatively manageable. Pluriformous and diverse material of religious tradition is bundled up and channelled into unity, in a way that has been experienced to be meaningful and powerful, able to give spiritual orientation at a personal level and shape life at the community level. And indeed one can claim that Europe under the dominance of the Christian canon formed a culturally and spiritually coherent entity – long before and in many ways much deeper than what has been achieved by the modern construct of the European Union in our own time.[45]

---

[43] And in fact in many cases diverse layers within one and the same document.

[44] This is not to claim that the Buddhist and Hindu canons lack unifying elements. The distinction between *neyartha* (provisional teaching) and *nitartha* (ultimate or direct teaching) in Buddhism provides a rather effective instrument to hold diverse and even apparently conflicting traditions together as expressions of the same *dharma* (see Ray, *Buddhism* 172–174; cf. Levering, *Scripture* 65). A characterisation of the Christian canon (with a specific view on the New Testament) as a combination of unity and diversity is also found, and further developed, in Dunn, *Has the Canon*. Among other insightful observations, the following deserves to be mentioned: "To recognize the canon of the New Testament is to affirm the diversity of Christianity" (Dunn, *Has the Canon* 563). The combination of unity and diversity in the New Testament canon is described by Bruce as follows: "With all the diversity of their witness, it is witness to one Lord and one gospel" (Bruce, *The Canon* 277).

[45] See, e. g., Manfred Fuhrmann, *Bildung – Europas kulturelle Identität*, Stuttgart: Reclam, 2002, 13–16.25.34.39–40.48.55.94.100–101.

The quantitatively manageable size together with the relatively low level of technicality of the content of the Christian canon means that a single non-expert person can – at least under favourable conditions – have a reasonably informed overview over the whole canon. This is obviously not the case with the Buddhist canons where standard printed editions are 50+ volumes large and where a considerable part of the canonized texts are understandable only for the initiated, enlightened person. Similar problems are also typical of the Hindu canon. The consequences of the situation prevailing in Buddhism is the necessity to develop specialised groups of experts like monks and nuns or charismatic preceptors and the fact that a layperson will never be able to have insight into more than a small percentage of the canonical texts.[46] On the Christian side, the manageable size and the non-technicality of the canon not only precludes a necessary clear cut distinction between largely unknowledgeable laypersons and scriptural experts, but also provides every member of the community bound to this canon with spiritual orientation which he or she can incorporate in a meaningful sense into his or her personal life. The Christian canon thus offers a real basis for the spiritual life of the majority of the members of the faith community and for the concept of the priesthood of all believers; it has a potentially democratic effect and precludes the inevitability of a sweeping dominance of experts.[47]

7. *The Adaptability of the Canonical Writings to New Environments*

Departing from the track followed so far of focusing mainly on differences, it is important to mention one aspect of canon formation and canon function where close similarities between the Christian and the Buddhist canons can be detected: Prof. Davidson points out that Buddhist textual production was highly adaptive, by adopting local

[46] See, e. g., Levering, *Scripture* 69.

[47] This is of course not to claim that all this potential has been realized and fully developed in all parts of the history of Christianity. The preordinance of tradition against scripture in the Catholic (and Orthodox) branch(es) of Christianity in particular and the concomitant claim that the correct interpretation of the canonical writings can only be achieved by the officially ordained interpreters representing the Church have acted as major obstacles to the practical realization of this potential (cf. Gamble, *Christianity* 54). The aspect of the canonization of the *development* of the Christian faith within the Christian canon is also mentioned and further eloborated by Dunn (see *Has the Canon* 568–572).

genres, absorbing indigenous intellectual particularities, and generally preserving an "Indian perspective" while at the same time adjusting it to new socio-cultural environments, even across ethnic and linguistic borders. Similar remarks can undoubtedly be made with respect to the New Testament canon, with its linguistic and sometimes conceptual adaptation of a Semitic tradition to the categories of a Hellenistic world. A "fusion of two horizons" clearly takes place in the New Testament scriptures as much as in many Buddhist texts. Related to this feature is the fact that the Christian canon enshrines different stages – at different places over a certain period of time – in the development of the Christian faith as reflected in the different writings contained in it.[48] Along the same lines we may observe that like in the Buddhist tradition, there is no insistence in the Christian tradition on a sacred language as the necessary means to get access to the canonical texts.[49]

With respect to the aspect of adaptability outlined in this paragraph, the question would be why both in the case of the Christian and the Buddhist canon such an adaptive mode was able to develop, to what degree we might find it in other traditions as well, and where the results prove to be negative how this can be explained.

8. *The Bipolar Integration of the Christian Canon in Western Culture*

Another characteristic trait typical of the Christian canon, hinted at in passing in Prof. Assmann's paper, is its combination during much of European history with another canon, the canon of the classical texts of Greek and Roman literature, a canon whose own origins are completely independent of the religious canon of the Bible.[50] Of course, more precisely speaking this bipolar integration is not a characteristic of the biblical canon itself, but rather of Western culture which combined the biblical and the humanistic canons; but this phenomenon must certainly have some relation to the character of the biblical

[48] The statement is valid both with a view to the Old and the New Testament, though with respect to the Old Testament its relation to the Christian faith is of course "secondary".

[49] As opposed to Christianity and Buddhism, Hinduism, Judaism, Islam, and Zoroastrism all follow the concept of a sacred language. Cf. Denny/Taylor, *Introduction* 5.

[50] Roughly from late Antiquity until the era of Enlightenment as the dominating feature of European culture. A detailed discussion of this phenomenon can be found in Fuhrmann, *Bildung* 9–53. The canon of the Greek and Roman classics was of a more flexible nature than the biblical canon.

canon itself, which obviously allows for such a bipolar organization of culture. As far as I can see, there is no fully parallel phenomenon identifiable in the other main religious traditions. If this observation is correct, we should ask why this dual focus emerged in Christian Europe and not in other religious and cultural contexts.

9. *The Lasting Character of the Christian Canon's Texts for the Life of the Individual*

Whereas in certain currents of Buddhism the canons of the sacred texts constitute – at least from a specific perspective – "an aid that must be abandoned by each individual at a certain point on his journey to the Buddhist goal of enlightenment",[51] no such limitation of the foundational meaning and binding character of the canon exists in the Christian concept of canon. Also the notion found not exclusively, but in its most pronounced form in Zen-Buddhism, according to which it is the intuitive wisdom behind the text that has to be discovered, whereas attachment to the words and concepts of the canonical texts on the purely literal level would be misleading,[52] ascribes to the *sensus litteralis* of the canonical texts a potentially reduced status that finds no equivalent in the Christian notion of canon.

[51] Ray, *Buddhism* 148. He also speaks of "the relativity of external tradition", "based on the notion that each individual has the potentiality of enlightenment" which makes "the individual ... the final resting place of authority" (152). Similarly, Levering observes "what we might call an anti-authoritarian position with respect to the word" (Levering, *Scripture* 60); "the ultimate truth to which the Buddha was enlightened, is beyond the grasp of words, ... and its apprehension requires leaving words behind" (Levering, *Scripture* 63). Not all scholars would agree with such a sharp description of this aspect of the Buddhist concept of canon, because even those Buddhist teachers advocating a path that goes beyond the texts still justify their view by referring to texts. In any case, it is, somehow paradoxically, balanced by the high veneration given to the sacred texts and to the role of authentic tradition embodied both in texts and in communal institutions (see Ray, *Buddhism* 148.153–154; cf. Levering, *Scripture* 61). This balance can be described in terms of the "interaction of personal/internal and traditional/external factors" (Ray, *Buddhism* 153); in this interaction, the "literal text may not be an end in itself, but it is the necessary and revered means without which the end cannot be attained"" (Ray, *Buddhism* 165). Similarly, Ray states: "In fact, ultimately in every Buddhist's training, there comes a time when the supports and means of the tradition must be left behind. But according to Buddhist tradition, this best happens through the agency of the (relative) methodologies of the tradition, at the heart of which is the sacred text" (Ray, *Buddhism* 167). Remarkably, this paradoxical attitude of Buddhism toward its sacred texts is not mentioned in Davidson's paper.

[52] See Levering, *Scripture* 65.

10. *Problems Related to Variations in the Exact Delimitation of the Christian Canon*

At the end of this short *tour d'horizon* we must turn our attention to an open question related to the Christian canon that is of much more than purely scholarly interest. As is well known, different subgroups within the Buddhist tradition have highly different canons. In fact, there are also differences in canon delimitation between different denominational groups in the Christian tradition, though they are marginal compared to those found in Buddhism.

The main – though not the only – difference in the definition of the Christian canon in the Western world concerns the inclusion or exclusion of some apocryphal texts in the canon of the Old Testament.[53] The Catholic canon includes Tobit, Judith, 1 and 2 Maccabees, Wisdom of Solomon, Ben Sirach, and Baruch in addition to the books included in the Jewish and Protestant canons of the Old Testament.[54]

For various reasons, some Protestant scholars have suggested that in fact all or some of the writings found in the Septuagint should be added to the Old Testament canon in accordance with the Catholic tradition, and others have suggested removing Esther from the canon.[55] The main reason for the first suggestion is that the inclusion of texts like Ben Sirach or the Wisdom of Solomon would match the Septuagint which held a dominant position in the early Christian church; the main reasons for the second suggestion are that the canonical position of the Esther scroll was long disputed in the Jewish community, that it is the only book of the later Jewish canon not to appear in Qumran, that it is absent from New Testament citations and from the canon of Melito and some of the later Fathers, and finally that the nationalistic outlook of the book is theologically embarrassing.

A historical case for the traditional Jewish-Protestant canon can be made by pointing to the fact that many of the early church fathers sup-

---

[53] There are also differences with respect to the correct sequence of books within the New Testament; in addition, the Syrian church's canon as manifest in the Peshitta lacks 2 Peter, 2 and 3 John, Jude, and Revelation. The Gustavus Adolphus Bible of 1618, inspired by Martin Luther, classifies Hebrews, James, Jude, and Revelation as apocryphal writings.

[54] The Orthodox canon resembles the Catholic canon; in addition to the latter, the books of 2 Esdras, 3 Maccabees, and the Epistle of Jeremiah are also included.

[55] See, e.g., Maier, "Der Abschluss des jüdischen Kanons und das Lehrhaus von Jabne", in: G. Maier (ed.), *Der Kanon der Bibel*, Giessen: Brunnen Verlag, 1990, 1–24, here 4.

port it; among the Greek fathers: Melito of Sardis (perhaps), Origen, Athanasius, Cyril of Jerusalem, Epiphanius,[56] Gregory of Nazianzus, and Amphilochius; among the Latin fathers: Hilary of Poitiers, Jerome, and Rufinus. The fact that later a broader canon was accepted in the Church can be explained by developments that need not be given the status of binding decisions, such as an increasing ignorance among Gentile Christians of Jewish views on the subject, related to the ever widening gap between Church and Synagogue, and the introduction of the codex which probably was combined with an inclusion of non-canonical but highly-esteemed texts for reasons of convenience, texts that were subsequently misinterpreted as belonging to the canon as well because of their inclusion in the codex.[57]

At any rate, what kind of canon one follows *does* make a difference. It is, for example, likely that the inclusion or the exclusion of the following paragraph in one's canon will have some consequences:

> All wickedness is but little to the wickedness of a woman: let the portion of a sinner fall upon her.
>
> As the climbing up a sandy way is to the feet of the aged, so is a wife full of words to a quiet man.

These words are found in Ben Sirach 25:19–20,[58] a text that is part of the Catholic (and Orthodox) canon, but not of the Protestant canon. And this is just a randomly chosen example to show what kind of implications varying canon limitations may have.

[56] He gives both 22 and 27 as the total.
[57] See Dunbar, *The Biblical Canon* 310.
[58] Verse counting and translation follow the King James version.

THE CHRISTIAN-MUSLIM ENCOUNTERS ON THE QUESTION OF JIHAD

Muhammad Aslam Syed

1.

The Islamic concept of Jihad has been one of the most debated in the polemical as well as academic discourses between Muslims and Christians. It has been perceived as the obligatory holy war that Muslims are required to wage against the non-Muslims. Like so many other ideas that permeate political relations between these two religious communities, both sides have frequently used and abused the notion of Jihad during military confrontations; Muslims to sanctify fighting against the Christians and the latter to remind the former of the violent nature of their faith. In South Asia, Jihad was invoked against the British during the Uprising of 1857 in which, curiously enough, Hindus also participated. What is even more curious is that the British justified massacres and all forms of torture and cruelty after their victory and frequently quoted the Bible. Nicholson, for example, who was hailed as the hero of the war and the one "who has been the hero-god of our boyhood dreams, who more than any other man has been the prototype of the 'strong, silent, God's Englishman' of our fiction", wrote: "We are told in the Bible that stripes shall be meted out according to faults, and if hanging is sufficient punishment for such wretches (murderers), it is too severe for ordinary mutineers. If I had them in my power today, and knew that I were to die tomorrow, I would inflict the most excruciating tortures I could think of on them with a perfectly easy conscience."[1]

Many British officers claimed to have received divine support in this war. Robert Montgomery, who succeeded Lawrence as Lieutenant-Governor of Punjab, was known for his advocacy of propagating Christianity in India. He was confident that "it was not policy, or sol-

[1] Quoted in Edward Thompson, *The Other Side of the Medal*, Westport: Greenwood Press, 1926, 45.

diers, or officers that saved the Indian Empire to England. The Lord our God, He it was."[2] Frederick Cooper wrote: "wisdom and that heroism are still but mere dross before the manifest and wondrous interposition of Almighty God in the cause of Christianity." And "To those fond of reading signs, we would point to the solitary golden cross still gleaming aloft on the summit of the Christian church in Delhi, whole and untouched; though the ball on which it rests is riddled with shots deliberately fired by the infidel populace. The cross symbolically triumphant over a shattered globe."[3] Thus it was not just Muslims who sought God's help against their enemies; Christians did the same and used the Biblical hyperbole in their confrontations against the Muslims. However, some Christians could always point out that such acts of butchery and barbarism were not in keeping with the teachings of Christ who had asked his followers to 'render unto Caesar the things that are Caesar's; and unto God the things that are God's'. They would confront the Muslims with the argument that the Prophet of Islam led the battles against the non-believers and bequeathed the idea of Jihad as a living legacy for his followers to engage in wars with the non-Muslims.

The second half of the nineteenth century witnessed an intense debate between Muslims and Christians over the question whether Islam was a peaceful religion or it promoted aggression and violence. This brief note is devoted to the question of jihad that was raised after the Uprising of 1857 by various missionaries and scholars in different journals and books. The arguments advanced in these works were met with different responses by Muslim scholars belonging to different schools of thought. Within this limited frame of reference, I have chosen to discuss the views of Maulvi Chiragh Ali (1844–1895), author of many books in Urdu and English.

Chiragh Ali was born in 1844 and after receiving the traditional Islamic education, he started working in the office of Judicial Commissioner at Lakhnow. In addition to Arabic and Persian, he also knew English and Hebrew. During this period, public debates between Muslims and Christians were held almost on a regular basis. He started developing an interest in these debates at an early age. His intellectual outlook on Islam was profoundly influenced by the writings of Sir

[2] *Letter to Lord Lawrence* "Rulers of India" Series, 114, quoted in Thompson, *The Other Side*, 66.

[3] Frederick Cooper, *The Crisis in Punjab*, quoted in Thompson, *The Other Side*, 64.

Syed Ahmad Khan (1817–1898), one of greatest pioneers of Islamic Modernism in South Asia. After spending some time at Aligarh in 1876, he joined the civil service in Hyderabad Deccan. Chiragh Ali is remembered as a pillar of the Aligarh Movement.

The Aligarh Movement began after the East India Company's rule was replaced by the British Crown in 1858. Its aim was to provide modern education to Muslims on scientific lines as well as to point out the prejudices and misperceptions of Islam in the British polemics. It seems relevant here to briefly mention how the War of 1857 had assumed a religious colour. The causes of this war are embedded in the policies of the East India Company which were gradually becoming aggressive, exploitative, and insensitive to South Asian religions, social norms, and economic interests. The British traders had become rulers with huge standing army mostly composed of the native soldiers. What triggered the crisis was the introduction of new greased cartridges for the 1853 Enfield rifle. To load this rifle, the soldiers had to bite the cartridge open. Soon rumour had it that these cartridges were greased with lard which was forbidden for Muslims and beef tallow that was regarded as an anathema to Hindus. Both these communities, therefore, thought that these cartridges were deliberately introduced to defile their respective faiths. As stated earlier, it took on a religious colour to which the British, especially after their victory, responded religiously. It was not a national uprising in the contemporary sense yet an overwhelming majority of Indians participated in it. The British, however, singled out the Muslims as the main culprits. In addition to the untold brutalities inflicted upon them, Muslims had to encounter negative critiques of their faith and the Prophet. The Prophet's battles and the concept of Jihad occupied many administrators and missionaries who were relentless in their criticism of Islam.

William Hunter's book, *The Indian Musulmans: Are They Bound in Conscience to rebel against the Queen*?, created a strong resentment amongst the Muslims. He was commissioned to investigate the question of whether Indian Muslims were bound by their religion to rebel against the Queen. Basing his assertions on the evidence collected from various state trials, he concluded that there was a close causal connection between the Wahabi activities and the perennially disturbed state of the North-Western Frontier. The underground movement was skilfully organized, and its leaders were spreading disaffection and carefully indoctrinating the youth in the rural areas with extensive literature on the duty of waging war against the British. Circulation of such ideas did not help those Muslim leaders who were trying to promote cordial relations between the British rulers and their Muslim subjects. Syed Ahmad Khan wrote a rejoinder to Hunter's thesis and encouraged other like-minded Muslim scholars to initiate such studies on Islam that could lead to a better understanding of their faith. As stated earlier, his mission was not just to counter the negative perceptions of Islam but also to persuade Muslims to change their religious outlook. After the war, many Muslim clerics believed that India had ceased to be *Dar al-Islam* (Land of Peace), therefore, Muslims have only two choices: either to leave India and seek refuge in a Muslim land or fight against the British in this *Dar al-Harb* (Land of War). Syed Ahmad Khan did not regard India as the land of war. He insisted that even though it was not under Muslim rule, it was to be regarded as the land of peace, because Muslims were free to exercise their religion. The Christian missionaries, however, believed that the Quran did not endorse the idea of land of peace for a country where Muslims were subjected to a Christian rule. Malcolm MacColl, for example, believed that the Quran had indeed divided the world into the House of Peace and the House of War. As a prominent missionary with connections to the Downing Street, MacColl's assertions had to be taken seriously.

Chiragh Ali was familiar with his writings on Islam. His first encounter with MacColl was on the issue of the possibility of reforms in Muslim society especially in the Ottoman Empire. His book, *The Proposed Political, Legal, and social Reforms in the Ottoman Empire and Other Muhammadan States* (1883) was a response to MacColl's contention that political, legal, and social institutions of the Ottoman Empire needed radical reforms. Islam, however, did not allow any change in these institutions.[4] Chiragh Ali's study of Jihad is based on the Quran. He places the relevant verses in the context of their revelation and demonstrates how the Christian writers had quoted them with dubious purposes. This paper is based on his book, *A Critical Exposition of the Popular 'Jihad' Showing that all the Wars of Mohammad Were Defensive; and that Aggressive War, or Compulsory Conversion, is not Allowed in The Koran.*[5]

As the title suggests, Chiragh Ali's work is apologetic as well as critical. His contention is that the Quran does not endorse aggressive wars and that the battles that the Prophet led were defensive. The Christian

[4] *The Contemporary Review, London*, August 1881.
[5] This book was published by Thacker, Spink and Company from Calcutta in 1885.

writers were either ignorant of the proper historical context in which the commandments for fighting were revealed or they deliberately misquoted them to tarnish Islam and its founder. The book is written in a dialogue form where a quotation from a Christian writer is followed by his answer. I have retained that form in this paper in order to show the contours of the late nineteenth century encounters between Muslims and Christians.

Rev. Malcolm MacColl:

> The Koran divides the earth into parts: Dar-ul-Islam, or the House of Islam; and Dar-ul-Harb, or the House of the enemy. All who are not of Islam are thus against it, and it is accordingly the duty of the True Believers to fight against the infidels till they accept Islam, or are destroyed. This is called the Djihad or Holy War, which can only end with the conversion or death of the last infidel on earth. It is thus the sacred duty of the Commander of the Faithful to make war on the non-Mussulman world as occasion may offer. But Dar-ul-Harb or the non-Mussulman world, is subdivided into Idolaters and Ketabi, or 'People of the Book,' *i. e.*, people who possess divinely inspired Scriptures, namely, Jews, Samaritans, and Christians. All the inhabitants of Dar-ul-Harb are infidels, and consequently outside the pale of Salvation. But the Ketabi are entitled to certain privileges in this world, if they submit to the conditions which Islam imposes. Other infidels must make their choice between one of two alternatives – Islam or the sword. The Ketabi are allowed a third alternative, namely, submission and the payment of tribute. But if they refuse to submit, and presume to fight against the True Believers, they lapse at once into the condition of the rest of Dar-ul-Harb and may be summarily put to death or sold as slaves.[6]

Chiragh Ali:

> I am very sorry the Rev. Gentleman is altogether wrong in his assertions against the Koran. There is neither such a division of the world in the Koran, nor such words as 'Dar-ul-Islam' and 'Dar-ul-Harb' are to be found anywhere in it. There is no injunction in the Koran to the True Believers to fight against the infidels till they accept Islam, failing which they are to be put to death. The words 'Dar-ul-Islam' and 'Dar-ul-Harb' are only to be found in the Mohammadan Common Law, and are only used in the question of jurisdiction. No Moslem magistrate will pass a sentence in a criminal case against a criminal who had committed an offence in a foreign country. The same is the case in civil courts. All the inhabitants of Dar-ul-Harb are not necessarily infidels. Mohammadans, either permanently or temporarily by obtaining permission from the

[6] Rev. Malcolm MacColl, *The Nineteenth Century*, London 1877.

sovereign of the foreign land, can be the inhabitants of a Dar-ul-Harb, a country out of the Moslem jurisdiction, or at war with it.[7]

Rev. T. P. Hughes:

Jihád (lit. 'an effort') is a religious war against the infidels, as enjoined by Muhammad in the Qurán.

Fight therefore for the religion of God. (VI)

God hath indeed promised Paradise to everyone. But God hath preferred those who *fight for the faith.* (IV, 97)

Those who *fight in the defence of God's true religion*, God will not suffer their works to perish. (XLVII, 5)[8]

Chiragh Ali:

The first verse quoted by Mr. Hughes appertains to the war of defence. The verse in itself has express indications of its relating to the war of defence, but Mr. Hughes was not inclined, perhaps, to copy it in full. He merely quotes half a sentence, and shuts his eyes from other words and phrases of the same verse. It is as follows:

"Fight then on the path of God: lay not burdens on any but thyself; and stir up the faithful. The powers of the infidels, God will haply restrain; for God is stronger in prowess, and stronger to punish." (IV, 86)

The severe persecution, the intense torture and mighty aggression of the Meccans and their allies is referred to in the original word *Báss*, rendered *prowess* into English … which shows that the war herein enjoined was to restrain the aggressions of the enemy and to repel force by force. It is very unfair on the part of the Revd. T. P. Hughes to twist or dislocate half a sentence from a verse and put it forth to demonstrate and prove a certain object of his.[9]

Reverend E. M. Wherry:

The Prophet of Islam had taken Moses as his model, at least in terms of fighting against the infidels; however, "there is no comparison between them whatever so far as warring against infidels is concerned. The Israelites were commanded to slay the Canaanites as divinely ordained instruments of *destruction;* but Muhammad inaugurated war as a means of proselytism. The Israelite was not permitted to proselytize from among

[7] Chiragh Ali, *A Critical Examination of the Popular Jihad*, Calcutta: Thacker, Spink and Company, 1885, 158.

[8] T. P. Hughes, M. R. A. S., C. M. S., *Missionary to the Afghans, Notes on Mohammedanism: Being outline of the Religious System in Islam* (1877), 206, quoted in Ali, *A Critical Examination of the Popular Jihad.*

[9] Ali, *A Critical Examination of the Popular Jihad.*

the Canaanites, (Exod. XXIII. 27–33), but Muslims are required to proselytize by sword-power."[10]

Chiragh Ali:

> Mohammad never had said that he did follow the footsteps of Moses in giving the command of fighting in self-defence, and in repelling force by force. There could be no comparison whatsoever between the wars of Moses, which were merely wars of conquest, aggression, extermination, and expatriation, and those of Mohammad waged only in self-defence. Mohammad did not inaugurate his career by prosecuting war as a means of proselytism, and never did proselytize any one by the sheer strength of the sword. On the contrary, according to T. H. Horne, who wrote regarding the extirpation of the Canaanites, Moses was involved in compulsory conversion: 'After the time of God's forbearance was expired, they had still the alternative, either to flee elsewhere, as in fact, many of them did, or to surrender themselves, renounce their idolatries, and serve the God of Israel.' This was certainly compulsory conversion and proselytizing at the point of the sword.[11]

Robert Durie Osborne:

> "The Doctrine of Jehad" was introduced by the Prophet of Islam as "means of livelihood congenial to the Arab mind, and carrying with it no stain of disgrace or immorality. This was robbery. Why should not the faithful eke out their scanty means by adopting this lucrative and honourable profession, which was open to everyone who had a sword and knew how to use it? Surely, to despoil these infidels and employ their property to feed the hungry and clothe the naked among the people of God would be a work well pleasing in His sight … And thus was the first advance made in the conversion of the religion of Islam with the religion of the sword." Striving in the way of God [Jihad] was meant to follow "a mandate of universal war" with the result that "the Arab, with the Koran in one hand and the sword in the other, spreading his creed amid the glare of burning cities, and the shrieks of violated homes, and the Apostles of Christ working in the moral darkness of the Roman world with the gentle but irresistible power of light, laying anew the foundations of society, and cleansing at their source the polluted springs of domestic and national life"[12]

---

[10] E. M. Wherry, *A Comprehensive Commentary on the Quran*, London: Trubner & Co., 1882, 220.

[11] Thomas Hartwell Horne, *An Introduction to the Critical Study and Knowledge of the Holy Scripture* Vol. II, London: T. Cadell, 1828, 524, quoted in Wherry, *A Comprehensive Commentary on the Quran.*

[12] Robert Durie Osborne, *Islam under the Arabs*, London: Longmans, Green & Co., 1876, 46–47.

Chiragh Ali:

> He [Osborne] errs in two points: First, he makes the wars as wars of conquest, compulsion, and aggression, whereas they were all undertaken in the defence of the civil and religious rights of the early Moslems, who were, as I have said before, persecuted, harassed, and tormented at Mecca for their religion, and after a long period of persecution with occasional fresh and vigorous measures, were condemned to severer and harder sufferings, were expelled from their homes, leaving their dear relations, and religious brethren to endure the calamities of the persecution, and while taking refuge at Medina were attacked upon by superior numbers, several of the surrounding tribes of Arabs and Jews joining the aggressive Koreish, making ruinous inroads and threatening the Moslems with still greater and heavier miseries. From this statement it will appear that these wars were neither of conquest nor of compulsory conversion. The second great mistake under which Major Osborn seems to labour is that he takes the injunctions of war against the Meccans or other aggressors as a general obligation to wage war against all unbelievers in the Moslem faith. In fact, these injunctions were only against those aggressors who had actually committed great encroachments on the rights and liberties of the early Moslems, and had inflicted very disastrous injuries on them. These injunctions had and have nothing to do with the future guidance of the Moslem world.[13]

These encounters revealed the semantic problems in understanding the meaning of Jihad. Moreover, since the Christian missionaries had not given any consideration to the proper context of the relevant verses, they understood that all references to Jihad in the Quran were meant as commandments to fight against the infidels. Even those 'Jihad verses' that were revealed in Mecca were used to substantiate the violent nature of Islam when Muslims were actually persecuted and were hardly in a position to defend themselves. Chiragh Ali also pointed out that some writers had deliberately dislocated verses from their context or they had simply cited "disjointed portion of a verse" to formulate the theory of Jihad.

2.

The Quran was revealed to the Prophet over a period of about twenty three years. It was not compiled in a chronological order with the result that the verses revealed in Mecca were quite often placed after

[13] Ali, *A Critical Examination of the Popular Jihad,* 53–54.

those that were revealed in Medina. However, the place of revelation is mentioned in the beginning of the each chapter of the Quran. Some editions also contain information on the special circumstances *(Asbab al-Nazul)* surrounding the revelation. But the foremost task before our author was to explain the meanings of the word, Jihad. He elaborated that the root word for Jihad was "*Jáhada* [meaning] that a person strove, laboured or toiled; exerted himself or his power or efforts or endeavours or ability, employed himself vigorously, diligently, studiously, earnestly or with energy; was diligent or studious, took pains or extraordinary pains· For example, the term *Jáhada fil-amr* signifies that a person did his utmost or used his utmost powers or efforts or endeavours or ability in prosecuting an affair. The infinitive noun *Jihádan* also means difficulty or embarrassment, distress, affliction, trouble, inconvenience, fatigue, or weariness. Jauhari, a lexicologist of great repute, whose work is confined to classical terms and their significations, says in his Siháh that "*Jáhada fi Sabeelillah*" or *Mojáhadatan* and *Jihádan* and also "*Ajtahada*" and *Tajáhada* mean expending power and effort. Fayoomee, author of *Misbahel Moneer*, which contains a very large collection of classical words and phrases of frequent occurrence, also says that "*Jáhada fi Sabeelillah*" and *Ajtahada fil Amr* mean he expended his utmost efforts and power in seeking to attain an object.[14]

Chiragh Ali identified nine verses that were revealed in Mecca when the Prophet and his followers had to go through such a harrowing experience that they were constantly reminded to hold fast to their faith by 'striving inwardly'. It was doing Jihad with their inner feelings of insult and injury because they were not in a position to fight against the powerful tribes of Mecca. He points out that in one of the oldest of the Meccan revelations, believers are asked to be kind to their parents and obey them except when they strive *(Jahadaka)* to lead them to polytheism. Here "*Jáhadá*" means "if they (parents) task or toil thee, or make efforts and endeavour (that thou shouldst associate any god with God)," and none of the translators and commentators take the word to mean the making of war or hostilities or fighting.[15] In another

[14] The sources quoted here are: The Sihah of Jouhari (died 398 AH), the Asas of Zamakhshari (467–538 AH), Lisan al-Arab of Ibn Mokarram (630–711 AH), and Qamus of Fayrozabadi (729–816 AH), *vide* Lane's Arabic-English Lexicon, Book I, part II, 437.

[15] Chapter xxxi-15 of the Quran, Chiragh Ali, op. cit.

verse, believers are asked not to "obey the unbelievers, but by means of this *(Jáhid)* exert with them with a *(Jihadan kabirá)* strenuous exertion (or labour with great labour)."[16] Other citations are:

> And ('*Jáhidoo*') make efforts in God, as *(Jihádehi)* your making efforts is His due, He hath elected you, and hath not laid on you any hardship in religion, the Faith of your father Abraham. He hath named you the Muslims.[17]
>
> To those also who after their trials fled their country, then *(Jáhadoo)* toiled and endured with patience. Verily, thy Lord will afterwards be forgiving, gracious.[18]
>
> And whoso *('Jáhada')* labours *('Yojáhido')* toils for his own good only. Verily God is independent of all the worlds.[19]
>
> Moreover, We have enjoined on man to show kindness to parents, but if they *(Jáhadá)* strive with thee in order that thou join that with Me of which thou hast no knowledge, then obey them not. To Me do ye return, and I will tell you of your doings.[20]
>
> And those who *(Jâhadoo)* made efforts for Us, in our path will we surely guide; for verily God is with those who do righteous deeds.[21]
>
> And they swear by God with their *(Jahd)* utmost oaths that 'God will never raise him who once is dead.' Nay; but on Him is a promise binding though most men know it not.[22]
>
> They swore by God with their *(Jahd)* utmost oath that should a preacher come to them they would yield to guidance more than any people: but when the preacher came to them, it only increased in them their estrangement.[23]

Chiragh Ali postulated that it was unfair to translate the word Jihad as fighting whereas in fact it has been used for strong resolve, oath, and inner struggle. Furthermore, "none of the commentators take the word *Jâhadâ* in these passages to mean fighting or crusade, and it is difficult, therefore, to understand why the word should have been distorted from its proper literal and classical meaning in other places of the same book."[24]

---

[16] The Quran xxv–52.
[17] The Quran xxii–78.
[18] The Quran xvi–110.
[19] The Quran xxix–6.
[20] The Quran xxix–8.
[21] The Quran xxix–69.
[22] The Quran xvi–38.
[23] The Quran xxxv–42.
[24] Ali, *A Critical Examination of the Popular Jihad,* 149.

Turning to the Jihad verses revealed at Medina, Chiragh Ali discovered the same spirit in their contents except that even after the Prophet and his followers had been "expelled from their houses", they were "invaded upon and warred against"; and it was to repel incursions and to gain the liberty of conscience and the security of his followers' lives and the freedom of their religion, he and they waged defensive wars, encountered superior numbers, made defensive treaties, securing the main object of the war, *i. e.*, the freedom of their living unmolested at Mecca and Medina, and of having a free intercourse to the Sacred Mosque, and a free exercise of their religion: all these are questions quite separate and irrelevant, and have nothing to do with the subject in hand, *i. e.*, the popular *Jihad*, or the crusade for the purpose of proselytizing, exacting tribute, and exterminating the idolaters, said to be one of the tenets of Islam."[25]

The list of the verses revealed at Medina is long. We would include only those which, according to Chiragh Ali, have been misinterpreted.

> But they who believe, and who leave their country, and *(Jahadoo)* exert their utmost in the way of God, may hope for God's mercy, and God is Gracious and Merciful.[26]
>
> Do ye think that ye could enter Paradise without God taking knowledge of those among you who *(Jáhadoo)* have toiled and of those who steadfastly endured.[27]
>
> Verily, they who believe and have fled their homes and *(Jáhadoo)* toiled with their substance and themselves in the way of God, and they who have taken in and have helped, shall be near of kin the one to the other. And they who have believed, but have not fled their homes, shall have no rights of kindred with you at all, *until* they too fly their country. Yet if they seek aid from you, on account of the faith, your part is to give them aid, except against a people between whom and yourself there may be a treaty. And God beholdeth your actions.[28]
>
> Those believers who sit at home free from trouble and those who (1, *Mojáhidoona*) toil in the way of God with their substance and their persons shall not be treated alike. God has assigned to those who (2, *Majáhadoona*) strive with their persons and with their substance a rank above those who sit at home. Goodly promises hath He made to all; but God hath assigned to those (3, *Mojáhadína*) who make efforts a rich recompense above those who sit at home.[29]

[25] Ali, *A Critical Examination of the Popular Jihad*, ibid.
[26] The Quran ii–218.
[27] The Quran iii–142.
[28] The Quran viii–72.
[29] The Quran iv–97.

> O Ye believers! Take not my foe and your foe for friends: ye show them kindness although they believe not that truth which hath come to you: they drive forth the Apostle and yourself because ye believe in God your Lord! If ye have come forth *(Jihádan)* labouring in my cause, and from a desire to please Me, ye show them kindness in private, then I well know what ye conceal and what ye discover![30]

Chiragh Ali comments that it is wrong to translate *in kun tum kharajtum Jihadan fi Sabili*, as "if ye go forth to fight in defence of my religion," or "if ye go forth to fight on my path," or "if ye go forth fighting strenuously in my cause." It simply means, "if you have come out striving in my cause," and the sentence is a complement or correlative of the verse, meaning, if you have come out of Mecca, striving, or to strive, in my cause, suffering from exile and undergoing the afflictions and distresses of living homeless, leaving your family and property unprotected, and all these pains *(Jihád)* you have taken to please me, then you should not make friends with my foes and your foes, who do not believe in the truth which has come to you, and have driven out the Prophet and yourselves (from Mecca, your home) only for the reason that you believe in God your Lord.[31]

After quoting all these verses which contain the word Jahd or any of its derivatives, Chiragh Ali concludes that the word

> *Jahd* or *Jihád* in the classical Arabic and as used in the Koran does not mean waging war or fighting, but only to do one's utmost and to exert, labour or toil. The meaning which has come to be ascribed to the word is undoubtedly a conventional one, and is one that has been applied to it at a period much less recent than the revelation of the various chapters of the Koran.[32]

He, however, contends that this explanation should not mean that the Quran does not contain injunctions to fight or wage war. There are many verses enjoining the Prophet's followers to prosecute a defensive war, but not one of aggression.

> The popular word 'Jihád' or *Jihd*, occurring in several passages of the Koran, and generally construed by Christians and Moslems alike as meaning hostility or the waging of war against infidels, does not classically or literally signify war, warfare, hostility or fighting, and is never

---

[30] The Quran lx–2.
[31] Ali, *A Critical Examination of the Popular Jihad*, 149.
[32] Ali, *A Critical Examination of the Popular Jihad*, ibid.

> used in such a sense in the Koran. The Arabic terms for warfare or fighting are *Harab* and *Kitál*.[33]

But he is amazed to see that "almost all the common Mohammadan and European writers think that a religious war of aggression is one of the tenets of Islam, and prescribed by the Koran for the purpose of proselytizing or exacting tribute. But I do not find any such doctrine enjoined in the Koran, or taught, or preached by Mohammad. His mission was not to wage wars, or to make converts at the point of the sword, or to exact tribute or exterminate those who did not believe his religion. His sole mission was to enlighten the Arabs to the true worship of the one God, to recommend virtue and denounce vice, which he truly fulfilled."[34] Through these encounters with the Christian writers, Chiragh Ali realized that even Muslims believed that Jihad was obligatory and that it implied almost the same meaning that the missionaries had alluded to. How did this concept change from striving hard to fighting!

3.

Tracing the transformation of the concept of Jihad, Chiragh Ali discusses the views of prominent Muslim jurists. He affirms that Ata, a learned jurist of Mecca, who flourished at the end of the first century of the Hegira, and held a high rank there as a jurist-consultant, believed that Jihad was only incumbent on the Companions of the Prophet, and was not binding on any one else after them.[35] He emphasizes that all the fighting injunctions in the Quran are,

> in the first place, only in self-defence, and none of them has any reference to make warfare offensively. In the second place, it is to be particularly noted that they were transitory in their nature, and are not to be considered positive injunctions for future observance or religious precepts for coming generations. They were only temporary measures to meet the emergency of the aggressive circumstances. The Mohammadan Common Law is wrong on this point, where it allows unbelievers to be attacked without provocation.[36]

---

[33] Ali, *A Critical Examination of the Popular Jihad*, 190.
[34] Ali, *A Critical Examination of the Popular Jihad*, ibid.
[35] He refers to Tafsir Majma-ulBayan by Tabrasee, Para 112 under Surah II–212.
[36] Ali, *A Critical Examination of the Popular Jihad*, 116.

However, if the Jihad is waged in self-defence, it is incumbent on every believer. But attacking unbelievers without any provocation, or offensively, is not incumbent on every believer. The Mohammadan Common Law makes the fighting only a positive injunction

> where there is a *general summons*, (that is, where the infidels invade a *Mussulman* territory, and the *Imâm* for the time being issues a general proclamation, requiring all persons to stand forth to fight) for in this case war becomes a positive injunction with respect to the whole of the inhabitants-this is sanctioned by the Law of Nations and the Law of Nature.[37]

He criticizes the author of *al-Hidaya*, a compendium of the Hanafi Law compiled in the 12th century, for allowing the aggressive wars and terming them as Jihad. He declares them against the teachings of the Quran. After mentioning numerous sources that hold the original meanings of Jihad as striving, he brings to our attention how the jurists corrupted its meaning. Even they accept that it still means to toil and labour but only in technical terms, actually, it means fighting against the infidels. He quotes the author of Durr al-Mukhtár, a commentary on Tanviral Absár, by Sheikh Muhammad bin Abdullah Tamartashi (died 1004), who says in the chapter on *Jihád*, that "in the classical language it is the infinitive noun of *Jáhada fi Sabil-Allah*, and in the language of the law it means inviting the infidels to the true faith and fighting with him who does not accept it."[38]

In summation, Chiragh Ali is disturbed not just at the audacity of the Christian writers who read in Jihad what was not meant but also the way Muslim jurists have, over a period of time, changed its context. He blames the corruption of the classical Arabic because of contact with a host of foreign cultures and languages as well as holding the jurists in such high esteem as not to challenge their time and space bound interpretations. He finds the opinions of Muslim jurists not only wrong but inspired by other sources than the Quran. They justified Muslim conquests by committing "the unpardonable blunder of citing isolated parts of solitary verses of the Koran, which are neither expressive enough nor are in general terms. In doing so, they avoid the many other conditional and more explicit verses on the same

[37] Ali, *A Critical Examination of the Popular Jihad,* 117.
[38] Ali, *A Critical Examination of the Popular Jihad,* 118.

subject."[39] After going through the Muslim interpretation of Jihad, he arrived at the same judgment that he had given about the Christian writers. He concludes:

> I fully admit that in the post-classical language of the Arabs *i. e.*, that in use subsequent to the time of Mohammad, when the language was rapidly corrupted, the word "Jihad" was used to signify "warfare" or fighting, but this was in a military sense. Since that period the word has come to be used as meaning the waging of a war or a crusade only in military tactics, and more recently it found its way in the same sense into the Mohammadan law-books and lexicons of later dates. But the subsequent corrupt or post-classical language cannot be accepted as a final or even a satisfactory authority upon the point.[40]

[39] Ali, *A Critical Examination of the Popular Jihad,* 120.
[40] Ali, *A Critical Examination of the Popular Jihad,* 129.

PART FOUR

RELIGION IN THE AGE OF GLOBALIZATION

SHRINKING WORLD, EXPANDING RELIGION? THE DYNAMICS OF RELIGIOUS INTERACTION IN THE TIMES OF COLONIALISM AND GLOBALIZATION

Marion Eggert

1. *Collecting the Silent Undercurrents of Interreligious Dynamics*

In Heinrich Böll's well-known satirical story "Dr. Murkes gesammeltes Schweigen" (Dr. Murke's Collected Silence, 1958), set in Germany in the 1950's, an influential cultural figure called Bur-Malottke, whose talks are regularly broadcast on the radio, is suddenly beset by qualms about the frequent use he had made of the word "god" in his speeches since his conversion during the period of "religious enthusiasm (religiöse Begeisterung)" in 1945.[1] Now feeling "personally responsible" for the "preeminence of religion in public broadcast", he demands that the word "god" be replaced, in every instance of his recorded speech, with the phrase "that higher being which we revere". The young radio journalist Dr. Murke who is entrusted with the task of making the replacements in Bur-Malottke's most recent talk and who is deeply antagonized by the vanities of broadcast culture in general and of Bur-Malottke in particular, is allowed by the storyteller to vent his frustrations in two ways: by attaching a small devotional picture his pious mother had sent him to a wall in the broadcast company's building, a piece of "kitsch" in a self-consciously "cultured" environment, and by collecting (and eventually listening to) the brief phases of silence that he has to cut out of broadcast materials. In the story's final scene, another broadcast

[1] Immediately after the end of World War II, Germans turned in large numbers to the churches, which not only offered orientation but also assumed administrative and political functions in an otherwise chaotic society, as the allied forces accepted church representatives as negotiation partners. This short post-war period therefore gained the epithet "the hour of the church". See e. g. Kurt Jürgensen, Die Stunde der Kirche. Die Evangelisch-Lutherische Landeskirche Schleswig-Holsteins in den ersten Jahren nach dem Zweiten Weltkrieg, Neumünster: Wachholtz 1976. A similar, also short-term growth of the influence of the churches could be witnessed in Eastern Europe after the break-down of Socialism, see Detlef Pollack, *Rückkehr des Religiösen? Studien zum religiösen Wandel in Deutschland und Europa 2,* Tübingen: Mohr, 2009, 105–108.

journalist feels that he has to amend a radio drama about an atheist who stands in an empty church and asks skeptical questions by filling the silence in between the questions; the technician who had helped Dr. Murke to cut "god" from Bur-Malottke's speech offers him these snippets of "god" in exchange for the "silence" – a present to Dr. Murke.

While the main target of the story's satire probably is the empty verbosity with which post-war German intellectuals covered up their silence on Nazi crimes, it also offers a panoramic view of religious tensions in Western modernity. Movements of secularization, of strengthening of religion and of re-secularization are shown to follow on one another's heels, and to be intimately related to fashions of political and cultural proprium. While "lived religion" in the form of the unquestioning, habitual devotion of an old woman proves its resilience, the intellectual's unease with the falsehoods of both professed religion and professed a-religiosity can be answered only by "silence", with implicit references to meditation, spirituality and interiorized religion.[2]

Thus, the main elements of the narratives of modern religious studies are more or less assembled in this story. However, it does not contain any traces of awareness of the spatial and temporal extension of this situation, nor of the global interdependencies that, like the unseen mechanisms in a clock, were instrumental in setting in motion what met Böll the observer's eye. Indeed, the religious formations as depicted in the story appear to be fully and conclusively accounted for by the political and cultural situation of post-war Germany. Although the onslaught of globalization, with massive migration movements and a conspicuous pluralization of the religious scene, has brought more inclusive narratives to the fore and academia is experiencing a high tide of globalized perspectives in all major disciplines of the humanities, the ostensible plausibility of such self-contained historical frameworks as implied in Böll's story still poses challenges to our understanding of modern religious history. In other words, while we have learned to regard narratives that foreground interaction and plurality as superior in making our present world comprehensible, much needs to be done still to unearth these undercurrents of entangled histories that have formed and continue to form the world we live in. Research field 4 of our consortium attempts to rise to these challenges by studying the modern and contemporary religious situation

[2] Heinrich Böll, who had grown up a deeply religious Catholic, left his church in protest against Catholic conservatism in 1976.

in diverse regions and cultures of Eurasia from the perspective of the dynamics caused by greatly increased interreligious contacts, by the tensions due to imports of temporarily hegemonic cultural items, by the interaction and mutual observation of religious groups leading to appropriations and re-appropriations of elements of religious life across the Eurasian continent, as well as by the global expansion of scientific observation of "religion" as an object of academic study. In the following sections, I will give a few brief hints at how we intend to break down this vast research agenda into more concrete questions.

2. *The Age of Colonialism and the Ambivalent Western Model of Religion in the Nation State: The East Asian Example*

Ever since its beginnings in the 15th century, European economic and military expansion had been accompanied by the (attempted or actual) spread of Christianity and by confrontations with non-monotheistic creeds – encounters which were a decisive factor behind the rise of the term "religion" as a concept with (perceived) universal applicability. As part of this very same process, religion became a functionally differentiated part of social life in Europe, rather than its uncontested base. Indeed, as argued by José Casanova in his contribution to this volume, the whole "modern civilizing process" of the West in general was a contact phenomenon; in particular, enlightenment movements of setting limits to the power of religion – in other words, the seeds of secularization – would hardly have been conceivable without reference to non-Christian, especially Confucian societies.[3] These, in turn, received certain impulses concerning, among other fields of knowledge, political ideas like the awareness of the possibility of a non-sinocentric world, religiously relevant ideas like that of the superior moral persuasiveness of deistic beliefs,[4] and perhaps even before the 19th century a certain impulse to make use of the ordering power of organized religion in alliance with the state.[5]

[3] A text-based demonstration of these interrelations was recently delivered by Heiner Roetz, "The Influence of Foreign Knowledge on Eighteenth Century European Secularism", presentation at the conference "Reconfigurations of the religious field: Secularization, Re-sacralization and related processes in historical and intercultural perspective", Bochum, Dec. 1–3, 2009.

[4] Cf. the contribution by Eun-jeung Lee in this volume.

[5] The Manchu rulers of the Chinese Qing empire (1644–1911) had a very differentiated system of religious policy for their multi-ethnic state. While they certainly had

During the high tide of imperialism, these processes only gained in speed and incisiveness. In Europe, the model of the secular state that co-opted religion but held the latter's power in check prevailed. Communities in all of Asia, while certainly not surrendering to the onslaught of a "superior" Western civilization (as used to be construed in the West), still observed and analyzed with great alacrity the factors that were behind the obvious power imbalance in favor of the imperialist states, and depending on their specific domestic religious and political situation, came to their own respective conclusions as to what comprised the key to Western success.

Quite naturally, in each case those elements were chosen, at least initially, that appeared more "foreign" to the prevailing tradition. To observers in the Islamic world, secularism, equated not only with a certain circumscribed position of religion in society but also as the precondition for science and technology to reign supreme, appeared as the obvious explanans for the strength of Western states. Modernization movements thus usually had strong secularist tendencies, Kemalism being one of the obvious examples. In East Asia, quite to the contrary, especially in China and Korea where Protestant missions shaped the cultural image of the West during the later 19th century, intellectuals tended to believe that organized religion was one of the major factors behind Western power demonstrated by imperialist expansion. Of course, these initial responses were soon answered by counter-currents in the form of religious revivals in Islamic cultures and of strong secular movements, like socialism, in Confucian cultures.[6] The varying re-configurations of the religious field that were instigated by the respective cultural interpretations or social constructions of the "religious" and the "secular", and the tensions between the two, are therefore among the main research interests of Research Field 4. In the remainder of this chapter, I will give a few hints on the perspectives on the East Asian situation that we have developed so far.

During the 19th and early 20th century, confrontation with the Western form of religion in East Asia led to two phenomena that were

found some precedence in the Mongol rule, there may be some room for speculation about the role the Jesuits may have played, who worked at the Manchu court right from the beginning of their reign. Also, the Christian convert Fan Shouyi, who had sojourned in Rome between 1697 and 1719, then returned to China, may have brought some first-hand information about the workings of the Vatican.

[6] The vocabulary used here to signify the different cultural realms should not be understood as an expression of essentialism, but rather as shorthand.

quite different in appearance, but intimately related in their motivation: the emergence of New Religions, and attempts to reform existing religions, or whatever might qualify as such. In both cases, Christianity as perceived by the respective actors played a decisive role as model or inspiration.

Some of the New Religions were heavily indebted to Christian religious ideas, myths and iconography, like the Taiping movement in mid-19th century China which led to an extremely bloody rebellion.[7] Others, like the Tonghak movement in Korea a few years later,[8] ostensibly opposed or counterpoised Christianity but were clearly influenced structurally and ideologically by the encounter with the latter – even the name of *tonghak* or "Eastern Learning" was chosen in contradistinction to *sŏhak* or "Western Learning" (which comprised both secular and religious knowledge that had come from the West) in order to clear the Tonghak followers of the suspicion of believing in Christianity, which was still banned, and sometimes severely persecuted, at the time of the development of the Tonghak creed. Whatever guise they took, these new religions can be seen as a mimetic reaction to Christian phenomenology, combined with an understanding of the relationship between religion and politics, rather untainted by the Western secular model, that regarded political legitimation as intimately linked to religious authority.

The more intellectual reaction, which we can consider religious reform movements to be, must be seen in context with the spread of the Western concept of "religion" and reflections on its implications. In the Korean case, to which I will stick here, first reverberations of such a reflection can be sensed in the world geography *Chigu chŏnyo* prepared by the private scholar Ch'oe Han'gi (1803–1875, an avid reader of Western works in Chinese translation) in 1857. His chapter on the history of Western religions starts with deliberations on the relationship between religion (literally "teaching and learning", chin. *jiaoxue*/kor. *kyohak*) and politics (chin. *zhengzhi*/kor. *chŏngch'i*) from the per-

[7] The new religion behind this movement is sometimes understood as a Christian "sect". One online commentator on Jonathan Spence's influential book on the Taiping rebellion, *God's Chinese Son: the Taiping Heavenly Kingdom of Hong Xiuquan*, New York: Norton 1997, dryly remarked: "Who knew so many people were killed in China over a bad translation of the Christian bible?" (http://www.goodreads.com/book/show/281062.God_s_Chinese_Son_The_Taiping_Heavenly_Kingdom_of_Hong_Xiuquan).

[8] Tonghak also came to be connected to a rebellion, a large peasant uprising in 1894 which ultimately led to the Sino-Japanese war and domination of Korea by Japan.

spective of a theory of progress: religion needs to be rooted in politics, and to progress together with politics in harmony with a presumed general progress of human knowledge.[9] While seemingly expressing a basic Confucian notion of "teaching", and definitely privileging the Confucian idea of the relationship between "religious" orientation and politics, the wording reflects a new kind of historicized and differentiated understanding of "religion": Although Ch'oe Han'gi argues for the common horizon of both knowledge and political action, he avoids the term *dao* (kor. *to*), the Confucian "way", that would encompass both components (besides cult and morality). His example thus serves to show how re-configurations of the semantic field of religion-related terms were set in motion by intensified contact with Western religions even before the neologism "religion" (chin. *zongjiao*/kor. *chonggyo*) was introduced. The appearance of the new term at the turn of the 20th century signaled the end rather than the beginning of a conceptual battle between differentiated "religion" and encompassing "*dao*". With "religion" winning the day, both Confucian and Buddhist communities embarked on movements to adapt to the model of "religion" as presented by Christianity. The elements that needed to be enforced, in the opinion of the leading figures, usually included social service, missionary efforts, and a clarification of doctrines.

Of course, these movements were not just meant to enable competition on the new religious market-place and thus the establishment of a new or the perseverance of a traditional form of belief;[10] rather, they were intrinsically motivated by the search for some kind spiritual power or force of social cohesiveness that might enable the survival of state and, especially, nation. Thus, Confucian reform movements had their hey-day in the times of crisis around the establishment of modern state-hood, both in China and in Korea. In Japan, the belief in the usefulness of a national religion led to the establishment of State Shinto, while Christianity was deemed unpatriotic and experienced some decline. Perhaps this was exactly one of the reasons why Christianity was accepted comparatively readily in Korea after colonization, in the sense of befriending the foe of one's foe. Ch'ŏndogyo, the new religion

[9] Ch'oe, Han'gi, *Myŏngnamnu ch'ongsŏ* [Collected works of Ch'oe Han'gi], 5 vols., Seoul: Taedong munhwa yŏn'guwŏn 2003, kw.12, 23a.

[10] Using the market place metaphor for a situation of religious plurality and choice is not equivalent to subscribing to Rational Choice models for explaining religious behaviors in such a situation.

that had taken shape based on the anti-Japanese Tonghak movement, certainly owed some of its popularity to the same sentiments. The tags that were affixed to both religions in those days read "modern, anti-colonial" for Christianity, and "nationalist" for Ch'ŏndogyo, and they are effective to this very day in general Korean perceptions.

These examples only underline what Ian Reader argues in his "Comments and Responses": that East Asia can hardly serve without qualification as evidence to counter the secularization thesis. Not only can changes of observational focus trick us into believing in changes in the object of our observation, we (and this includes scholars of any background) also may be led astray by insufficient ability to decipher our present observations in the light of their historically grown significance. Our research field pays tribute to this insight by paying a great deal of attention to the historical foundations of the present situation, especially to the decades around 1900. For if, as has been suggested, we now have a global system of religion in which religious groups are characterized by heightened mutual awareness and mutual labeling, and are in turn observed and labeled by academic religious studies, its beginnings are to be sought in that period.

3. *The Age of Globalization and Localization*

Whether such a global system does in fact exist, or in other words, whether speaking of such a system helps us in understanding global religious currents and local peculiarities, is one of the research questions that form the horizon for the activities of Research Field 4 in regard to the immediate past and the present period. As some important arguments for such an assumption and the major themes that are relevant in and beyond this regard are outlined beautifully in the papers by José Casanova and Peter Beyer below, all I can do here is to assemble a few remarks on those of these issues that our research field is, at the present, most interested in.

First, we focus on observing the ongoing negotiations of the relationship between religion and politics. The local formations of the religious field grow out of more or less specific political and social circumstances, even as they respond to global currents. A fundamentalist movement like Hamas is certainly part of a world-wide current of Islamic resistance to a modern world order and global culture seemingly dictated by the West, but it is even more, as one on-going project elaborates, a mirror image of the equally fundamentalist Gush Emunim, and both would not work as they do without their counterpart. Such phenomena have lead to increased identification of religion as a politically inspired and in turn politically instrumentalized rallying point; but not every guiding ideology that people rally behind is religion, as Peter Schalk's contribution to this volume exemplifies through a discussion of the Tamil movement. A very different case studied in our consortium from which we can learn similar lessons is the rise of religious groups as agents of the welfare state in Germany due to certain support structures that privilege religious over other forms of migrant organizations. The way religion is observed and conceptionalized obviously may contribute much to the degree of visibility and indeed the degree of organization of religions. In this sense, the *mutual* observation of religions may also be an important factor that has to be taken into account.

A second topic that has emerged as deserving our attention is the phenomenon of "spiritualization" of religion, which we find as a trend within organized religion as well as the hallmark of individualized religious behavior. In both forms, spiritualization literally feeds off inter-religious contact. Yoga exercises in the basements of Christian churches, breathing practices in the Korean nationalist religion Taejonggyo, meditation lessons assembling hopeful practitioners of whatever personal conviction are testimony to this. While thus marked by strategies of absorption and a highly integrative rhetoric, spiritualization within organized religion is probably best conceptualized as an outcome of a competitive situation. In studying spiritualization in the modern age, we aim to bring together analyses of such processes resulting from both intra- and interreligious contacts and contests from the whole of the Eurasian continent, in order to account for the interrelations, similarities and specificities of these phenomena.

Finally, a topic that may be of future importance to our research field is the question of folklorization of religious customs. To the extent that the devotional picture sent to Dr. Murke by his mother is a complete misfit on the walls of the broadcast company, religious behavior is a statement of cultural identity, and as such may eventually lose religious as compared to cultural significance. In Korea, this is most visibly the case with the shaman ritual called *kut*, which had – after repression during forced modernization in the 60s and 70s – been rediscovered as a mode of expressing hopes and anxieties by protesting students and since made its way onto different kinds of stages, both avant-garde theatrical and state-sponsored performances with domestic and foreign tourists in mind.[11] A comparable, though different, phenomenon is probably some of the apparitions of the Blessed Virgin, e. g., those that have "happened" in the remote German village of Marpingen since 1983 (with a precedence in 1876/77),[12] and which, while carrying ideological messages (e. g., anti-abortion), have been well groomed for the tourist industry. Even if these phenomena look very local at first glance, the German apparitions of the Virgin Mary would not be conceivable without the global recurrence of such events, nor could shamanism possibly be used for cultural identity management, in spite of the uncanniness the ceremonies still hold for their participants, if not for the awareness of both local and global tags on the various religions.

While the contemporary religious situation – other than the parochial Germany experienced by "Dr. Murke" – is so obviously pluralistic that little additional effort to prove this point seems called for, this very fact by necessity creates movements of closure. Tracing the multiple ways in which religious communities, even while trying to demarcate their own spaces and identities, do so in awareness and partly in mimicry of each other may help not only to understand these movements better, but also to better integrate such movements into local and global society, and ultimately perhaps even to mitigate conflict situations that arise from the unending tensions between integration and disintegration.

---

[11] For an overview of recent trends of kut performances, see Maria Kongju Seo, "Kut in Sacred and Secular Contexts. Focussing on Musical Practices of Ritual Performances", in: *Han'guk musokhak* 3 (2001), 5–29.

[12] For the 19th century event, see David Blackbourn, *Marpingen: Apparitions of the Virgin Mary in 19th century Germany*, Oxford: Clarendon Press, 1993.

ON RESILIENCE AND DEFIANCE OF THE ĪḺAMTAMIḺ RESISTANCE MOVEMENT IN A TRANSNATIONAL DIASPORA

Peter Schalk

1. *Background*

As a reaction to the Christian mission in Ceylon/Īḻam/Laṃkā[1] in the 19th century both Tamiḻ speakers and Siṃhala speakers organised themselves in religious resistance movements, the former into a Caiva[2] and the latter into a Bauddha movement.[3] In the early 20th century this Caiva movement transformed mainly into a territorial movement that could unite all Tamiḻ speakers on the basis of territorial demands, whether Caiva, Vaiṇava, Christian, Muslim or Atheist. Religion was suspended in the self-presentation of this movement, but the connection between language and territory was strengthened. These territorial demands for a homeland – not yet a state – by the Tamiḻ movement, that also implied strong economic interests, were mainly directed not against the colonial administration, but against growing expansive territorial demands of Buddhist Siṃhala speakers who saw the whole island as an island of and for Buddhists only. These demands by Siṃhala Buddhists were directed against both colonial Christian administrators and against ethnic minorities on the island who were classified as "latecomers" to the island. This close connection

---

[1] Īḻam is Tamiḻ and Laṃkā is Sanskrit and Pali. Both have the same referent, the island as a whole. Īḻam is not Tamiḻīḻam which is a part of Īḻam. The expression "Īḻamtamiḻs" is now frequent. It has the same referent as "Lankatamiḻs". Ealam or Eelam are anglicised forms of Īḻam. For the history of the word Īḻam see Schalk, Peter, Īḻam <*sīhaḷa*. An Assesment of an Argument. *Acta Universitatits Upsaliensis. Historia Religionum 25*, Uppsala: AUU, 2004. "Ceylon" is a colonial, corrupted form of Siṃhala being here a toponym.

[2] Schalk, Peter, "Sustaining the Pre-Colonial Past: Caiva Defiance against Christian Rule in the 19th Century in Jaffna", in: Michael Bergunder/Heiko Frese/Ulrike Schröder (eds.), *Ritual, Caste, and Religion in Colonial South India*, Halle: Verlag der Fanckeschen Stiftungen [Forthcoming in 2010c].

[3] Schalk, Peter, "Semantic Transformations of the Concept of Dhammadīpa", in: Mahinda Deegalle (ed.), *Buddhism, Conflict and Violence in Modern sri Lanka*, London: Routledge 2006c, 86–92.

between Buddhism and language (Siṃhala) and territory ("island of the dhamma") became a characteristic the majority, the Siṃhala Buddhists, continually shared whilst the Tamil̲ Caiva movement changed into a territorial movement that intended to embrace all Tamil̲ speakers in the North and East. It became "secular" in a specific sense (see below). The colonial conflict generated an internal conflict between the majority and minorities within the integrated administrative system of the state created by the British in 1833.

The conflict between Tamil̲ and Siṃhala speakers on the island Īl̲am started with a war of words in the early 1920s. The concept of a Tamil̲ *tāyakam* 'motherland', sometimes rendered as 'homeland', was created as a cultural region of and for Tamil̲ speakers in the North and East. It became clear to the Tamil̲ speakers concerned that on a coming day of Independence from colonial administration, the majority of Siṃhala speakers would take over the role of the British colonial administrators and introduce majority rule. This became true in 1972 sometime after Independence in 1948.

The verbal conflict that started in the 1920s developed into militant, but non-martial demonstrations in the 1950s and 1960s and subsequently into rural and urban guerrilla wars in the 1970s. They then were to turn into conventional wars, four in total, from July 1983 up to May 2009 and into an economic embargo of LTTE controlled areas from the 1970s onwards. The LTTE responded by setting up parallel institutions in areas under its control: the Tamil Ealam Administrative Service, the Tamil Ealam Economic Development Organization, the Tamil Ealam Police, Tamil Ealam Judicial Service, the Tamil Ealam Health Service and the Tamil Ealam Educational Service.[4] In this process of institution building, which of course was hampered by the Sri Lankan Armed Forces (SLAF), the ideology of Tamil nationalism, including the LTTE concept of martyrdom, became an expression of the LTTE's resistance and resilience.[5]

[4] Stokke, Kristian, "State Formation and Political Change in LTTE-Controlled Areas in Sri Lanka", in: *Envisioning New Trajectories for Peace in Sri Lanka. International Seminar 7–9 April 2006, Zurich, Switzerland*, Zurich: Centre for Just Peace and Democracy, 2006, 139–146.

[5] Schalk, Peter, "Die Lehre des heutigen tamilischen Widerstandes in Īl̲am/Laṃkā vom Freitod als Martyrium", in: *Zeitschrift für Religionswissenschaft* 09/1 (2009b) 71–99; Schalk, Peter (ed.), *Die Lehre der Befreiungstiger Tamil̲īl̲ams von der Selbstvernichtung durch göttliche Askese: Vorlage der Quelle ÜBERLEGUNGEN DES ANFÜHRERS*, Uppsala: Uppsala University 2007 [E-book, http://uu.diva-portal.org/smash/record.jsf?pid =diva 2:173420]; Schalk, Peter, "Beyond Hindu Festivals: The Celebration of

The fighters of the Liberation Tigers of Tamil Ealam (LTTE) had been defeated many times in the battlefields resisting the Sri Lankan Armed Forces (SLAF), but they rose again in defiance to defend its basic and inalienable political interest in exercising the right of self-determination it had claimed for the Tamiḻ speakers on the island Īḻam. May 2009 was, however, the end of the military resistance, when the SLAF, with some 250 000 soldiers, quashed the LTTE armed resistance killing around 20 000 fighters.[6] The SLAF had re-conquered the territory in the North and East that the LTTE had controlled for more than 20 years. After the military defeat of the LTTE in May 2009 all these LTTE institutions were eradicated, but immediately new organisations were formed in the Diaspora including a provisional transnational Government of Tamiḻīḻam to become active in 2010 after democratic elections in the Diaspora among Tamiḻ speakers (see below).

In spite of this military defeat, parts of the worldwide Tamiḻ exile community were ready to continue to cultivate this interest and to transfer it to a second and third generation with the help of methods that are practicable and appropriate in the Diaspora. The Executive Committee of the LTTE therefore wrote on 21 July – when the defeat was unquestionable, and Vēluppiḷḷai Pirapākaraṉ had been dead since 16 or 17 May:

> Against the backdrop of Sri Lanka's boastful propaganda that the Liberation Tigers of Tamiḻ Eelam have been annihilated and destroyed, it is our historic duty to rise up and fight for our legitimate rights – a duty that has been left in our hands by our peerless leader and those martyred heroes and civilians who have given their lives in defending our soil.[7]

This transmitted political interest is what enables the Tamiḻ Resistance Movement to act and to reverse the situation of defeat into a final victory, but not into a military victory. It now has a victory through diplomatic means in mind. It comprises all who support the three "Ts"(see below), but there is no formal control. Even non-Tamiḻs like Siṃhala speakers or Westerners can be part of the Movement.

Great Heroes' Day by the Liberation Tigers of Tamil Ealam (LTTE) in Europe", in: *Tempel und Tamilen in zweiter Heimat. Hindus aus Sri Lanka im deutschsprachigen und skandinavischen Raum*, Würzburg: Ergon Verlag 2003, 391–421.

[6] For more reasons for the defeat see Schalk, Peter, "Der Kampf geht weiter", in: *Sydasien* 29. Jahrgang 3 (2009), 41–46.

[7] Anon. (2009a), *LTTE Officially Announces Restructure Process: Selvarasa Pathmanathan heads the Organisation*. Headquarters. LTTE 21 July 2009. http://ltteir.org/?p= 132. Accession: 22 July 2009.

There are Tamil̲ speakers in the following countries in the Diaspora, roughly one million, from Īl̲am, in India, Canada, UK, France, Germany, Switzerland, USA, Australia, Norway, South Africa, Italy, Sweden/Denmark/Finland, New Zealand, Singapore, Malaysia, Ireland, Middle East, Belgium, Netherlands, Luxemburg, Iceland, Fiji and Mauritius. During the whole period, and even after the military defeat of the LTTE in May 2009, defiance is cultivated intensively by the LTTE, on the island and in the Diaspora scene, not least through obligate grief and mourning, and in the form of militant and determined verbal resistance. We face a type of grief that does not incapacitate individuals in a state of melancholy, but transforms them into resistant and resilient re-actors against the Government of the island. In the Diaspora, their grief is transformed into wrath and expressed verbally in litanies of grievances and in slogans like *urimaip pōr* 'struggle for the right of ownership', *urimaik kural* 'voice for the right of ownership', and *cāvilum vāl̲vōm* 'though dying, we shall live'.[8] What is remarkable is the involvement of a second and third generation, also of young women at the forefront in the Diaspora, where traditional discriminatory gender relations are only partly eradicated. Many of the present activists were born in the Diaspora.

Elsewhere, I have described the different militant, not military, methods of resistance after the military defeat of the LTTE in May 2009[9] which were and are performed today in accordance with a well-known saying by the late leader of The LTTE, Vēluppiḷḷai Pirapākaran̲ (1954–2009): "Methods may change, the aim not".[10] He himself adhered systematically to the concept of a separate state as *punita ilaṭciyam*, a 'holy aim', but in his closest surroundings, other interpretations of Tamil̲īl̲am appeared, looking not only for alternatives to military methods, but also discussing the nature of the ultimate aim.

The background to the intensive commitment in the Diaspora is also the situation of Tamil̲ speakers on the island. In October 2009, the Lankan Government still held 280 000 Tamil̲ civilians captured allegedly as "hostages" in "concentration camps" – the terms are those of the Tamil̲ Resistance Movement – and an unknown number of LTTE-

[8] For this slogan see Schalk, Peter, *Cāvilum vāl̲vōm. 'Auch im Angesicht des Todes werden wir leben. Īl̲amtamile sein im Krieg und in der Fremde'*, Dortmund: Internationaler Verein Emigrierter Tamilischer Schriftsteller e. V. 2006b.

[9] Schalk 2009a, 41–45.

[10] Schalk (ed.) 2007, *Die Lehre*, No 12:1.

fighters for "questioning". The government describes these camps as "welfare villages."[11] However, detainees are not permitted to move in or out of their camps, which are surrounded by barbed wire fences and guarded by heavily armed soldiers. Relatives are allowed to see inmates only after the type of rigorous screening found in high security prisons.

Those inside are civilians – young and old, men and women – who lived in former LTTE-held territory and were simply herded into the camps. They had already suffered months of military blockade, with many starved, dehydrated, wounded and sick. Many had lost family and friends as a result of the army's indiscriminate shelling. Conditions inside the camps are appalling. There is inadequate food, sanitation, medical care, sufficient water or even space to sleep. Moreover, the military, which runs the camps, maintains an internal regime of terror and intimidation. Despite heavy media censorship, cases have filtered out involving the sexual abuse of women, the shooting of protesting prisoners and "disappearances".

Military intelligence personnel systematically interrogate young men and women. More than 10,000 have been branded as "LTTE suspects" and dragged off to "rehabilitation centres", which are notorious for abuse and torture. President Mahinda Rājapakṣa insists that forced detention is necessary to weed out "terrorists", but none of those held in the detention camps or the rehabilitation centres have been charged, let alone convicted, of any crime. In reality, the government is engaged in the collective punishment of a quarter of a million people solely because they are Tamiḻ speakers. In 2009, this holding of prisoners effectively prevented verbal militancy in the Diaspora from transforming again into organised martial militancy on the island; the prisoners in "the welfare camps" would be vicariously punished.

---

[11] For children and women in the camps see Schalk, Peter, "'Lest we forget'. On Women and Children under the Military Might of the Lankan Armed Forces". Committee for the Formation of a Provisional Transnational Government of Tamil Eelam. 25.01.10. http://govtamileelam.org/gov/index.php/press-release/component/content/arti-cle/45-press-release-english/154-lest-we-forget-on-women-and-children-under-the-mili-tary-might-of-the-lankan-armed-forces-?Itemid=107. Accession: 26 January 2010a. The following section on the camps is based on a report by the Socialist Party from 7 October 2009 by Anon. (2009b), "Demand the Release of Tamil detainees in Sri Lanka", http://www.wsws.org/articles/2009/oct2009/sril-o07.shtml. Accession: 1 November 2009. It is in accordance with other reports from international human rights organisations.

2. *Aṭaṅkāppaṟṟu*

In this section of my paper I will focus on the emotional side of the commitment for Tamiḻīḻam as condensed in the concept *aṭaṅkāppaṟṟu* which is an emic term. It consists of the morphemes *aṭaṅkā* and *p-paṟṟu*. The former is a negation and means in this case 'non-submissive'. The latter is a noun and means 'attachment'. The whole concept means 'non-submissive attachment' and refers to the bond that a Tamiḻ speaker in the Diaspora should develop and cultivate towards Tamiḻīḻam. We could paraphrase this meaning by the expression "total commitment", which also appears as connotation in every armed fighter's oath of allegiance to Tamiḻīḻam.

The concept *aṭaṅkāppaṟṟu* appeared on posters and flyers used in demonstrations by Tamiḻ speakers in the Diaspora and on the Internet worldwide in April 2009, at a time when there was a justified fear that the LTTE would be defeated. *Aṭaṅkāppaṟṟu* is not a substitute for Hinduism, Christianity, Islam or Buddhism, but is a basic nationalist sentiment of solidarity beyond religion among combatants. It shall unite all. No combatant is forced to abandon his inherited religion or even to marginalise it, still less to criticise it. In communication among combatants vertically or horizontally what counts is *aṭaṅkāppaṟṟu* whose visible icon is the Tiger flag.

One poster is of special interest for us. It was used in a demonstration at the Trocadéro in Paris on 25 April 2009. The poster's headline is *aṭaṅkāppaṟṟu* and it shows an imitation of the famous Iwo Jima incident when American soldiers, after heavy losses, conquered the island Iwo Jima from the Japanese in February/March 1945 and hoisted the American flag on the top of the island. This flag is replaced here by the *tēciyak koṭi* 'national flag (of Tamiḻīḻam)' (that is slightly different from the *pulik koṭi*, 'tiger flag' that is used only by the armed forces of the LTTE).

In April 2009 it was clear that the LTTE would be defeated. The poster[12] expressed hope against hope that would, however, only some weeks later prove to be a vain hope.

[12] *Aṭaṅkāppaṟṟu* 2009. Paris: Organisation des jeunes tamouls de France. [=poster, May 2009].

Fig. 1: Poster of the post-war Tamiḻ Resistance Movement encouraging *aṭaṅkāppaṟṟu* 'non-submissive attachment' to Tamilīlam.

The poster contains once more the concept *aṭaṅkāppaṟṟu* in the locative form *aṭaṅkāppaṟṟil* in the text on the left, second line. In this case we have to imply the reference to "region" which is the Vaṉṉi. This region showed a non-submissive attachment. It was the heart of the Tamiḻ Resistance Movement till the final end with Kiḷinocci as the centre and with a long legendary history of resistance as far back as the pre-colonial period. This application of the concept to a region had already been applied by the professor of mathematics and MP C. Cuntaraliṅkam (1895–1985) who also called himself *aṭaṅkāttamiḻaṉ* 'non-submissive Tamiḻ' and who founded a party called *aṭankāttamiḻar munnaṉi* 'front of non-submissive Tamiḻs'.[13] He is one of the ideological founders of Tamiḻīḻam as a separate state.

I shall now examine the concept *paṟṟu* isolated from *aṭaṅkāppaṟṟu* in the language use of Vēluppiḷḷai Pirapākaraṉ as documented in the book *talaivarin cintanaikaḷ* ['Reflections of the Leader'] from 1995 and

[13] I thank professor Āḷvāpiḷḷai Vēluppiḷḷai for this information.

2005, published by me in Tamiḻ and with translations into English, German, and Swedish with an added translation into Siṃhala in 2007.[14]

Paṟṟu is both a verb and noun ('attach' and 'attachment'). In *talaivarin cintanaikaḷ* it appears four times,[15] twice as attachment to the ultimate aim Tamiḻīḻam (36:6), once as attachment to the language Tamiḻ (47:2) and once as attachment to gaining liberation (51:3). It never appears in connection with religion.

In common Tamiḻ we find the word in compounds that all express some kind of attachment, like *paṟṟākkai* which refers to a cord for tying. We find *paṟṟukoḷḷa* which refers to being attached in the mind to worldly things, and *paṟṟukoṇṭāṭa* which also refers to a being attached to objects of sense. *paṟṟuvīṭu* refers to a relinquishment of earthly attachments. The counterpart is *paṟṟivi* which refers to a person who is free from sensual attachment. The word appears also in common Tamiḻ in a compound that interests us here, in *tēca-p-paṟṟu-āḷar*, 'person-attachment-land', a person who is attached to the land, which is lexically summarised by 'patriot'. This designation has been used by the LTTE as a honorific title for non-armed fighters who have contributed in civilian life to bringing the ultimate aim closer. In August 2008 the LTTE published a summary list of selected people it considered *tēca-p-paṟṟu-āḷar.*[16] All this brings us to the conclusion that the LTTE uses forms of *paṟṟu* within the context of its Tamiḻ this-worldly nationalism which is a kind of *akappaṟṟu*, attachment to 'the home' or 'the inside', to the *tāy-akam*, 'motherland'. This sentimental term in Tamiḻ became politicised into 'homeland' in English by the Movement.

The common and LTTE use of forms of *paṟṟu* is directed towards worldly matters. For the LTTE, it is an attachment to Tamiḻīḻam, but how to conceptualise Tamiḻīḻam? All those in the Tamil Resistance Movement agree that Tamiḻīḻam can be described by the three "Ts" – see below – which all belong to this world. *Paṟṟu* is "innerworldly" to use a term by Max Weber, and has no relation to a known religion or to religious thinking of ontological transcendence.

There are some scholars who have noticed this attachment, which also shines through in English texts by the LTTE. One does not need

[14] Schalk (ed.) 2007, *Die Lehre*, No 12:1.

[15] Loc. cit.

[16] 27.11.1982 toṭakkam 31.07.2008 varai vīraccāvait taḻuvikkoṇṭamāvīrarkaḷiṉ tokuppu. [2008]. tamiḻīḻam tamiḻīḻa māvīrar paṇimaṇai araciyalturai. [No pagination, LTTE statistics].

to know Tamiḻ to tap into this strong sentiment cultivated all over by the Tamiḻ Resistance Movement, like, for example, in the LTTE Executive Committee's statement in English on 21 July about the dead Vēluppiḷḷai Pirapākaraṉ.[17]

Observing this sentiment starts a process of reflection in the mind of some scholars, ending usually in a eureka-experience. After thinking associatively, not knowing Tamiḻ, they come to the conclusion that this attachment is an expression of religious *bhakti,* Tamiḻ *pakti* or *patti,* that belongs to a long Tamiḻ Vaiṇava and Caiva tradition. They conclude that the ultimate aim of the LTTE is a religious state and that the god to which this attachment or devotion is directed is Vēluppiḷḷai Pirapākaraṉ.

Another interpretation by scholars is that wherever there is an ultimate concern, there is religion. *Aṭaṅkāppaṟṟu* expresses an ultimate concern, indeed, but the final decision as to whether a person thinks religiously lies with that person's understanding of religion. LTTE combatants will always say that their ideology is beyond religion. The contradicting interpretations by scholars are not only ascriptive, but also based on the historical-philogically wrong statement that the oath of allegiance is directed towards Vēluppiḷḷai Pirapākaraṉ. It is directed towards Tamilīlam (under the guidance of Vēluppiḷḷai Pirapākaraṉ), and is also without an appeal to any divine power. Not even the known concluding phrase "So help me God" is included in the oath. Tamiḻīḻam shall be achieved by the combatants' own force. The ritual system of the dead heroes is also constructed beyond Hinduism and other known religions.[18]

True, there is a strong emotion that connects the combatant with his followers, but it is not described in terms of *pakti* or *paṟṟu.* Usually kinship terms are used to express the affection of his supporters towards him.

Bhakti according to these scholars means 'devotion' which is wrong. It connotes devotion, indeed, but it does not mean 'devotion'. *Bhakti* means 'share' and refers to the godly share within a human being which makes him devote and dedicate his life to find his ultimate goal in a god. *Bhakti, patti(pakti)* on one side and *paṟṟu* on the other do not mean the same thing, they mean 'share' and 'attachment', but they connote similar sentiments, a kind of attachment or devotion, which

[17] Anon. 2009a.
[18] Schalk 2003.

however is directed towards different objects, to a god in the case of *bhakti* or to objects of the senses in the case of *paṟṟu*. My observation is that these scholars have never heard of *paṟṟu*.[19] They foist on the LTTE the concept of *bhakti* which is just not found in the writings of Vēluppiḷḷai Pirapākaraṉ as an alternating concept for *paṟṟu* in a non-religious sense and in a wider context of a non-religious Tamiḻ nationalism. Non-religious should not be understood here as anti-religious, but as being beyond religion. There is simply no need for religion during the process of achievement of the ultimate aim.

I am aware that *paṟṟu* sometimes also appears in a religious context which however has no relation to the LTTE concept and is outside the LTTE concept. The verbal noun *paṟṟutal* especially, which can be translated here by 'devotion/attachment (to a god), alternates with *pakti*, 'share', *nampikai* 'trust', and *anpu* 'love' as relational terms to a god in Tamiḻ Caivam and Vaiṇavam. This has, however, not been taken into account by these scholars. In the end, the context as a whole determines the character of the part. Only by means of intellectual violence can *bhakti* be imposed on the LTTE concept of nationalism.

Moreover, *bhakti* has been used by Christians among Tamiḻ speakers. Scholars should therefore consider not only imposing a Caiva/Vaiṇava, but also a Christian label on Vēluppiḷḷai Pirapākaraṉ. I have already explained elsewhere that I am against such imposed labels.[20]

3. *The Three "Ts"*

Now we come back to *aṭaṅkāppaṟṟu* 'non-submissive attachment' as used by the Diaspora in 2009. It is directed towards the three "Ts" that many old and young Tamiḻ speakers in the Diaspora know by heart. These three are the objects of the attachment.

There is the concept *tāyakam* 'motherland' which is an emotional expression of the historical origin and descent of a given territory, in this case of Tamiḻīḻam. There is *tēciyam* which is conventionally translated into English by 'nationhood'. *tēciyam* is derived from *tēcam*, 'territory', 'land', 'country'. It is nationhood, not without, but with

[19] Schalk, Peter, "Historisation of the Martial Ideology of the Liberation Tigers of Tamil Ealam (LTTE)", in: *South Asia. Journal of South Asian Studies* 20 (1997), 68–72.

[20] Loc. cit.; Schalk, Peter, "War of Words – An Obstacle to Peace", in: *Envisioning New Trajectories for Peace in Sri Lanka. International Seminar 7–9 April 2006, Zurich, Switzerland,* Zurich: Centre for Just Peace and Democracy 2006a, 163–170.

land, with a well-defined territory. Finally there is *tannāṭciyurimai* 'right of self-determination', which implies theoretically, in the given context, the possibility of the integration into the formation of a new unitary multiethnic state, a federal state, a confederal state or a separate state. We can classify the three "Ts" as ideas which express a total dependence on an intense political interest, the creation of Tamiḻīḻam. Together we have the impression of a constructed, formative and normative Tamiḻ non-racial, cultural nationalism on the threshold to state formation. In spite of the difference in time and space, we can find similarities with Johann Gottfried Herder's (1744–1803) construction of a non-racial, cultural nationalism.[21]

The LTTE represented by Vēluppiḷḷai Pirapākaraṉ had chosen to conceptualise Tamiḻīḻam as a future separate state as its ultimate aim and so have different leading groups in the Diaspora after the military defeat of the LTTE in May 2009. I refer especially to members in some LTTE offices worldwide who point out that the LTTE has never surrendered and handed over arms (like the IRA) and who also deny that Vēluppiḷḷai Pirapākaraṉ is dead.

Other Tamiḻ speakers have interpreted the right of self-determination as a right to choose integration into the Sri Lankan unitary state that is expected to change into a confederal or federal state. This change was demanded by the former Federal Party and its successor, the Tamiḻ United Liberation Front (TULF). This was also the political program of Western countries lead by Norway as facilitator in theory and mediator in practice from 2002 onwards.

A third group supports some degree of devolution of power as prescribed in the 13th amendment of the Constitution, like the Eelam People's Revolutionary Liberation Front (EPRLF) and the People's Liberation Organisation of Tamiḻ Eelam (PLOTE) and the Tamiḻ Eelam Liberation Organisation (TELO).

A fourth group promotes total integration of the area of Tamiḻ speakers into the unitary state, like a part of the Tamiḻ Makkaḷ Viṭutalaippulikaḷ (TMVP) whose members have sought membership in the now dominating SLFP. This group does of course not request self-determination for Tamiḻ speakers as a people.

In short, there is no unitary front of Tamiḻ speakers in the Diaspora, nor on the island, where an attempt to unite all in the Tamiḻ National

[21] More about this in Schalk 2006b, 54–59.

Alliance (TNA) has failed. There is, however, in both the island's political underground and in the Diaspora a dominating demand for the three "Ts" – in English 'nationhood', 'homeland', and 'right of self-determination' – but the interpretation of these three is left to parties, organisations and individuals, and the result is diversity.

As all MPs on the island have to take an oath on the Constitution that prescribes a unitary state and as there is a sixth amendment to the Constitution that criminalises even the peaceful formation of opinion for a separate state it is impossible to advance the concept of a separate state in Parliament or through governmental and non-governmental institutions, organisations or parties on the island. The governmental administration and the leadership of the Buddhist *saṃgha* also consequently avoid all references to federalism because it interprets federalism as a step towards a separate state. Some extremist and totalitarian groups like the present Maoist Janatā Vimukti Peramuṇa (JVP) and the political Buddhist Jātika Hela Urumaya (JHU) interpret even the vague concept of devolution of power as a step towards the division of the country. This division would contradict the Buddhist prediction of the future according to which the island as a whole shall become the island of the *dhamma* for Sinhala speakers. This prediction is one of the sources of the dynamic behind the Government's political program. Because of the 6th amendment of the Constitution that criminalises even peaceful agitation for Tamiḻīḻam, the Diaspora of Tamiḻ speakers has become very important as a refuge for those who insist on the three "Ts". They are interpreted in a way which challenges the concept of becoming a unitary totalitarian Buddhist state of the Government of Sri Lanka.

It must be mentioned here that the Tamiḻ Resistance Movement does not argue religiously for Tamiḻīḻam. It is not classified as a Caiva/Vaiṇava state, or as *civappūmi* 'the land of Civan' as the whole island was known in the pre-colonial period among Tamiḻ *paṇṭitar*. The late 19th century attempt to assemble all Caivas against the Christian mission was also rendered obsolete.

The Movement under the leadership of the LTTE argued by referring to the Convention of Human Rights that recognises the right of self-determination to "peoples". The Movement also referred to the past when in the 13th–16th centuries a kingdom existed in Yāḻppāṇam, that, however, was eradicated by the colonial powers and an integrated state modelled after a nation-state was established by the British in 1833. The Movement's this-worldly-political line of argumentation is asymmetrical in relation to the Buddhist *saṃgha*'s religious line of argumentation. Media's and scholars' concept of the conflict as a conflict by Buddhists and by Hindus is on the emic level only a partial truth, valid only for Buddhist Siṃhala speakers. If the concept of a religious dynamic is actualised it fits for the party of Siṃhala speakers only. The other party's dynamic is based on a secular-political interest.

When I say that neither *paṟṟu* or "the three Ts" connote religious dimensions from the viewpoint of the actors I do not imply that scholars, especially those educated in a Durkheimian tradition, are also devoid of such connotations, but the object of study here is the perception of the actors in the Movement. The scholars themselves should distinguish between their perception and that of their objects. Furthermore, even if these actors of the Movement are trained to think in secular terms about their own ideology they are aware that this ideology is situation-specific: It is limited to the context of the struggle for Tamiḻīḻam. In other situations, for example in private life, they cultivate their inherited religions. It is often the case that a combatant visits a Catholic priest the night before a battle to get the sacrament. Furthermore, the Movement has a policy of religion with regard to its relation to the state. In this projected state of Tamiḻīḻam, the historical religions of old prevail de facto, Caivam, Vaiṇavam, Buddhism, Christianity and Islam. Yes, Buddhism as well, but of course not political Sinhala Buddhism which is regarded as a cover for Siṃhala expansion into the territories of Tamiḻ speakers, but "Tamiḻ Buddhism" that is compatible with Tamiḻ culture.[22] I shall come to this policy in the following section.

4. *A Provisional, Transnational Government for Tamiḻīḻam in the Making*

After the military defeat of the LTTE, many supporters within the Tamiḻ Resistance Movement realised that the military course for achieving a separate state had failed and that the death of more than 21 000 LTTE fighters[23] cannot be honoured by sending more young women and men to the battles against the Government Forces. Only

[22] For the concept of "Tamil Buddhism" see Schalk, Peter et al. (ed.), *Buddhism Among Tamils in Pre-Colonial Tamilakam and Ilam* (Acta Universitatis Upsaliensis), Uppsala University: Part 1–2, 2002.

[23] *27.11.1982 toṭakkam 31.07.2008.*

by trying by other means to achieve the three "Ts" for which they died can the ultimate aim be achieved. These means are mainly diplomacy and lobbying to exercise pressure on the Lankan Governments and make it accept the right of self-determination of Tamil̲ speakers. These means cannot be stopped with by armed force by the Lankan Government. The Movement's co-operation with the international community implies an acceptance of the rules of communication in inter-state relations which excludes the use of violence and totalitarianism of opinion-formation in a civil society that is no more a society at war. These two fundamental values have been adopted as pillars by a new organisation in the Diaspora called the Provisional Transnational Government of Tamil̲ Ealam (PTGTE). It strives for recognition as a Government from other Governments. It was called into existence by Kumaran̲ (Celvarācan) Patmanātan̲ soon after the death of Vēluppiḷḷai Pirapākaran̲ in May 2009. Kumaran̲ Patmanātan̲, also known as "KP", is a long-time collaborator with the LTTE and was appointed by Vēluppiḷḷai Pirapākaran̲ in January 2009 to organise the international relations of the LTTE.

Kumaran̲ Patmanātan̲'s role as organiser of the LTTE in the Diaspora became important after the defeat of the LTTE. He made it clear that the military approach to reaching the ultimate aim, the separate state, was a failure. He suggested instead forming the resistance of the Tamil̲ movement in the Diaspora in the form of a provisional transnational Government that worked in interstate relations (for the realisation of the three "Ts").

"Provisonal" indicates that a transition is expected towards a final Government established on the island and that its territory of administration will be called Tamil̲īl̲am (Tamil̲ Ealam).

"Transnational" indicates a common basis of interests shared by Tamil̲ speakers in the Diaspora that transcends the national interests of Tamil̲ speakers in the UK, France and the USA etc. It refers also to a type of organisation that goes beyond national structures. The transnational interests are the three "Ts" which are the ideological foundation of this transnational Government. It is no contradiction to form a provisional transnational Government whose ideology is nationalistic as illustrated by the three "Ts". It is possible to create a transnational solidarity network that responds for example to the West Papuan resistance or the Väddō on the island. Different groups may interact transnationally to improve the situation in West Papua or for the Väddō on the island. In the same way, the transnational Government of Tamiḻīḻam can be seen as a transnational solidarity network with the aim of creating a homeland for the island's Tamiḻ speakers. We face, in this case, a transnational inclusive nationalism that embraces all Tamiḻ speakers including Muslims and also Tamiḻ-friendly groups among Siṃhala speakers. They are not rare. The formation of this transnational network as a Government is of course unique. Internal discussions have distinguished between Government and governance and have suggested Council instead of Government. "Government" has, however, remained in place together with the traditional name of the ultimate aim, Tamiḻīḻam.

This transnational Government does not construct own national structures in the different countries of the Diaspora, but uses already established national structures like the British Tamiḻ Forum, The German Tamiḻ Forum, The Swedish Tamiḻ Forum, The French Tamiḻ Forum, etc., but also non-Tamiḻ national and national branches of international organizations like the Red Cross, Save the Children, etc.

The transnational Government is not an exile Government that has gone into exile from an original country to return after the ending of a conflict. An exile Government is national, located for a period in exile, and is therefore not a transnational Government. The transnational Government has no fixed place but has its members all around the world connected by the Internet. There may be a secretariat located in Geneva, but this secretariat is not a Swiss national secretariat. Meetings have been organised regularly in Zurich, Oslo and London by and for selected members of an Advisory Committee of the transnational Government in the making.

In October 2009, the formation of this Government had advanced. A programme was formulated by the Advisory Committee consisting of specialists, of Tamiḻ and non-Tamiḻ speakers from all parts of the world, for organising an election of members by popular vote in the Diaspora to this transnational Government. Its members will be democratically elected among Tamiḻ speakers in the Diaspora. The electorate vote for candidates that meet their expectations in direct personal elections in each country. The outcome will not necessarily promote a separate state as the ultimate aim. Again, the sixth Amendment of the Constitution and the terrorist phobia of the Lankan Government[24] make it impossible to work democratically on the island for the transnational Government's representatives and to elect members from there.

Kumaraṉ Patmanātaṉ disappeared from the political stage on 7 August 2009. He had been abducted and taken prisoner in Malaysia by agents of the Lankan Government and he is now in prison on the island awaiting trial. His role was taken over by Vicuvanātan Rutrakumaran, a lawyer in New York, who had served the LTTE as an advisor for many years.

It is evident then that there is continuity from Vēluppiḷḷai Pirapākaraṉ to Kumaraṉ Patmanātaṉ and to Vicuvanātan Rutrakumaran through their personal history and of course through the three "Ts". This continuity is important because it creates legitimacy through descent, which is important in the Tamiḻ Resistance Movement that is loyal to Vēluppiḷḷai Pirapākaraṉ. At the same time this continuity is fully exploited by media loyal to the Lankan Government to classify this transnational Government a derivation of the LTTE that is internationally labelled as a terrorist movement. Therefore, the Advisory Committee to the transnational Government also emphasises discontinuity. This is evident in the promotion of the two values mentioned above, i. e. the promotion of the exclusively non-armed form of the struggle and the creation of a democratic civil society in a future Tamiḻīḻam. The latter implies that the voters decide how the three "Ts" should be interpreted. There is no predetermined interpretation of them.

This tension between being loyal in one aspect and disloyal at the same time in another aspect to the past is crystallized in the discussion on whether the flag of the LTTE, the national flag with the tiger, should be used in public appearances of the transnational Government.

Another sensitive topic is how the famous Vaṭṭukōṭṭai resolution from 1976 should be interpreted. It has been the basis of the Tamiḻ Resistance Movement under the leadership of the LTTE. It has a normative history of interpretation that says that separatism (or external self-determination) is the only solution. It uses the concept of a sovereign state:

[24] For this phobia see Schalk, Peter, "Pax Americana, the EU, and the Tamiḻ Resistance Movement (TRM)". *TamilNet* 01 April 2008. http://www.tamilnet.com/img/publish/2008/04/Peter_Schalk.pdf. Accession: 2 April 2008.

> This Convention resolves that restoration and reconstitution of the Free, Sovereign, Secular, Socialist State of Tamil Eelam, based on the right of self-determination inherent to every nation, has become inevitable in order to safeguard the very existence of the Tamil Nation in this country.[25]

Furthermore it says:

> This Convention calls upon the Tamil Nation in general and the Tamil youth in particular to come forward to throw themselves fully into the sacred fight for freedom and to flinch not till the goal of a Sovereign State of Tamil Eelam is reached.[26]

The resolution also mentions that a federal solution has been rejected by the Government of the island.[27] There is then little room for another interpretation that goes in the direction of internal self-determination as already explained by Vicuvanātan Rutrakumaran in 1996:

> Self-determination may be realised in a variety of forms. According to the Declaration on Friendly Relations, the establishment of a sovereign independent state or the emergence into any other political state as freely determined by a people constitutes the mode of implementing the right to self-determination. The concept of any other political status suggests that the right to self-determination may be realised in a way short of secession. This is known as 'internal self-determination.[28]

Internal self-determination is not what the Vaṭṭukōṭṭai resolution teaches. It teaches external self-determination. It is therefore difficult for the Advisory Committee to refer to this resolution as the only base or as *the* ideological base for the construction of a transnational Government. In the press release issued in his name by the Advisory Committee from 31 August, the reference to this resolution is missing for the first time,[29] but it returned in January 2010 (see below). Now the focus is on the concept of self-determination only and leaves its interpretation to the voters. This unavoidably creates discontinuity

---

[25] Anon. (1976), *The Vattukottai Resolution*. tamilunitedfront.com, http://www.tail unitedfront.org/articles/Vattukottai.html. Accession: 1 December, 2009.

[26] Loc. cit.

[27] Loc. cit.

[28] Rudrakumaran, Visvanathan. 1996. *The Tamils' Right of Self-determination*. Tamilnation.org. http://www.tamilnation.org/conferences/tamil_eelam/96_australia/Rudra.html. Accession: 12 December 2010.

[29] rutrakumaraṉ, vicuvanātaṉ (= Rudrakumaran, Visvanathan), *nāṭu katanta tamiḻīḻa aracu amaippata ṟkā ṉa ceya ṟkuḻu*, 31 August, 2009.http://www.govtamileelam.org. Accession: 31 August, 2009.

in relation to Vēluppiḷḷai Pirapākaraṉ who certainly was flexible with regards to methods, but not to the ultimate aim understood by him as external self-determination.

Insisting on discontinuity in relation to the ideology of Vēluppiḷḷai Pirapākaraṉ has provoked opposition among some members in the LTTE offices in the Diaspora. Holding on to the belief that Vēluppiḷḷai Pirapākaraṉ is still alive is an indirect way of saying that his ideology is still alive. Those working for the emergence of the transnational Government try to meet this opposition in daily confrontations. In spite of all the diversity within the Tamiḻ Resistance Movement, there is a common consensus about the three "Ts".

On January 14, 2010, the Provisional, Transnational Government for Tamiḻīḻam issued a long statement called *Provisional, Transnational Government for Tamiḻīḻam. Report based on the study by the Advisory Committee 14 January.* It starts on page 1 with a declaration of loyalty towards the Vaṭṭukōṭṭai Resolution quoting its demand for a sovereign independent state. Evidently, internal self-determination has been replaced by external self-determination under the pressure of the majority in the Tamiḻ Diaspora. In the same period, elections in Norway, France, Netherlands, Switzerland and Germany had taken place to test the loyalty of the Diaspora with regard to the Vaṭṭukōṭṭai Resolution and the result gave an absolute majority.[30]

The report also has a section on page 17 on religion which is nothing but a revival of the policy of the state towards religion as documented in the Vaṭṭukōṭṭai resolution. It is summarised in a guiding principle.

> 2. Secularism
>
> It was resolved as part of the Vaddukoddai Resolution that Tamil Eelam shall be a secular state giving equal protection and assistance to all religions to which the people of the state may belong. This position was inspired by the Indian Constitution, adopted by the TULF and the LTTE. Therefore, it has a strong position and a background in modern Tamil culture and it is quite different from French and American secularism. The question about secularism has been a burning one in many sections of Tamil society for decades.

[30] Anon. 2010a., "Tamils of Switzerland, Germany, Holland vote on independence this weekend." *TamilNet*, 22 January, 2010. http://www.tamilnet.com/art.html?catid=13&artid=31035. Accession: 22 January 2010; Anon. 2010b., "Referendum conducted in exemplary way in Switzerland". *TamilNet* 25.01.10. http://www.tamilnet.com/art.html? catid=13&artid=31056. Accession: 25 January 2010; Anon. 2010c., "Overwhelming turnout of voters in Germany, 99% mandate Tamil Eelam". *TamilNet* 24.01.10. http://www.tamilnet.com/art.html?catid=13&artid=31054. Accesion: 24 January 2010.

GUIDING PRINCIPLE TWO
The State of Tamil Eelam will be a secular state. No religion shall be given the foremost place.

Here secularism is understood in the tradition of the Indian Constitution, not as a separation between state and religions like in France, but as an engagement of the state in *all* religions, but again not in the way the Lankan state is doing by giving preference to one religion among all religions, to Buddhism, or as the Indian Constitution does by giving preference to a cluster of religions of Indian origin only (Hinduism, Buddhism, Jainism and Sikhism), but to be equal in support and protection to all religions.

The concluding guiding principle is taken from the formulation of the Interim Self-Governing Authority (ISGA), section 5, from 2003 which was an LTTE-attempt to achieve a negotiated peace with the Lankan Government. It failed.

To sum up, secularism as a polity of the state toward religions is understood as pluralism that also includes the non-religious ideology of the Movement striving for Tamiḻīḻam. This ideology has put traditional religions in brackets, but has not replaced or annihilated them when it comes to striving specifically for Tamiḻīḻam. This ideology does not compete with an other-worldly Paradise. Tamiḻīḻam is worldly.

This "bracketing" of religion is motivated by the realisation that the collective effort of the Movement to reach Tamiḻīḻam just does not need religion, and that the absence of religions prevents a split on a religious basis when a strong unity is needed. We have a similar case in *La Legion Etrangère* that has banned all public religious signs to prevent a split in the organisation, but does not demand from its combatants to give up their religions.

This state policy of consequent pluralism of the future state of Tamiḻīḻam also aims to avoid a split like that in India between Indian and non-Indian religions, especially between Hinduism and Islam, and on Īḻam between Buddhism and the other religions. This state policy of religious pluralism is of course quite different from a Leninist-Stalinist-Maoist-Fascist state that strives for a complete replacement of all religions by its own ideology. Tamiḻīḻam has never been conceptualised as a totalitarian state. It is another matter that the LTTE in its internal and external relations has been totalitarian in many cases, like so many other resistance movements in a situation of war.

5. *Conclusion*

In January 2010, the time-frame for achieving the ultimate aim conceptualised as external or internal self-determination, is envisaged as lying one or two generations ahead by Tamil̲ speakers in the worldwide Diaspora. In some circles within the Movement a kind of Tamil̲ worldly Zionism is developed not very far from Theodor Herzl's. This Diaspora, guided by a provisional transnational Government or another form of self-chosen governance, sees itself as a resilient, highly motivated, self-confident and defiant resistance movement with a nonsubmissive attachment to the three "Ts". The long period of grieving does not incapacitate; it opens up the past and present as a time of continuous grievances that generates questions about justice and motivates followers to take action for change. In the eyes of government-loyal, Lankan media, however, the Tamil̲ Resistance Movement was and remains a terrorist organisation. The new transnational Government struggles for recognition in global interstate relations and is receiving unexpected help – from the Lankan Government.

The Lankan Government's interstate relations to the USA, UN and EU have deteriorated during 2009 due of its violations of human rights. On January 16, 2010, the People's Permanent Tribunal in Dublin came to the conclusion that the Lankan Government is guilty of war crimes and crimes against humanity.[31] Recommendations by the Tamil̲ Resistance Movement to boycott goods from, to stop development aid and tourism to the island, to reduce bilateral relations to humanitarian aid, and to put violators of human rights among Government officials on trial have been considered by some Western Governments and been partially applied. Facing mainly haughtiness from representatives of the Lankan Government, these Governments' humanitarian concern gradually turned in 2009 into a political concern that indicates discontent and sends threats of possible economic and political isolation to the present Lankan Government. The Tamil̲ Resistance Movement has learned how to behave in the community of states by channelling its defiance into a new form of lobbying internationalism.

When it comes to the concept of dynamics, we can say that these are generated by the defiance-creating, non-religious ideology of "the

---

[31] Permanent People's Tribunal on Sri Lanka 14–16 January 2010. Dublin: Irish Forum for Peace in Sri Lanka. http://www.internazionaleleliobasso.it/index.php?newsid=459. Accession: 10 January 2010.

three Ts" of the Movement which is incompatible with the religiously (Buddhist) motivated ideology of the Sri Lankan unitary state that is developing its own dynamics. The two forces are asymmetrical when it comes to religion, but also when it comes to political status. The Movement was classified as a terrorist movement and the Government as an ideal fighter against terrorism in the conceptualisation of the *pax americana* of the Bush administration that was adopted by the EU.

It is not so that two religions confront each other. The case is that a non-religious resistance movement confronts a religious (political Buddhist) state ideology. We should abandon the worldwide media image of Hindus fighting Buddhists in the conflict on the island.

The struggle goes on. The Government has gained a military victory, but no peace, that can only be achieved in negotiations by parties with equal political and diplomatic status.

OBSERVING RELIGION IN A GLOBALIZED WORLD: LATE TWENTIETH-CENTURY TRANSFORMATIONS

Peter Beyer

1. *Introduction: Inventing, Transforming, and Observing Religion in a Globalizing Context*

The basic hypothesis informing my presentation is that there exists a consonance between two strictly related historical developments: that of globalization and that of religion formation. The latter has in fact been and still is an integral dimension of the former, so much so that, for instance, any historical periodization of the one will likely parallel that of the other. Three important qualifications of this hypothesis are, however, necessary. First, both globalization and religion are categories of observation. They are interpretive and analytic/synthetic and therefore contingent: one could observe otherwise. Nonetheless, in so far as the terms and their meanings enter the normative vocabulary of a society, they help construct the reality to which they refer quite as much as they reflect it. Seeing it that way is already half way to making it that way, and thus institutionalized, the terms reflect and contribute to the reproduction of power relations in their societies. Second, the meaning of globalization and religion, which is to say the observation of globalization and religion, arises historically and changes over time. It is also constitutively subject to contestation. It is important not only to be aware of such arising and changes, but also to understand the socio-historical transformations that such emergence and changes reflect. Third, and flowing from the first two, just because globalization and religion are thus terms of observation, are invented and transform, does not mean that they are somehow inherently flawed or illusory. Concepts are our only way of seizing reality socially; one can and perhaps should deconstruct globalization and religion, but that very operation would only create replacement concepts that are equally as contingent.

Globalization is a relatively recent neologism in any language. Religion is a slightly less recent neologism in many languages, but even in those where the word has a long history, the meaning of the term has undergone significant transformations, especially but not solely beginning in about the European 16th century. There and around that time we witness the gradual crystallization of the idea, first, that religion refers to a differentiable and systematic domain and, second, that this domain manifests itself as a plurality of distinct religions. This understanding itself may not have been entirely original in western history at the time; there were perhaps both Jewish/Christian and Islamic precedents. But these did not become solidly institutionalized in the societies in which they arose, whereas that is precisely what happened among the Europeans. Here cannot be the place to even outline this argument properly[1], but suffice it to say that critical among the socio-structural correlates of this semantic development was the concomitant rise of differentiated institutional domains in politics, economy, and science especially, domains that structured themselves according to institutional rationalities increasingly decoupled from expressly religious determinations. The more this happened, the more difficult it became to think of religion and to institutionalize religion as *anything but* a differentiated category and domain. In combination with the religious wars of the 16th and 17th centuries, which solidified in quite bloody terms that religion was a sphere of difference; and in the context of accelerating expansion of European influence to more and more parts of the globe, this conceptualization became more or less self-evident for Europeans – at least their elites – and then, beginning in the late 18th century, for first a tiny and then an ever increasing number of people in all other parts of the world, albeit with significant variable particularization.[2] This development has never been uncontested, uniform, let alone inevitable or complete. But it has happened and our reflections here at this conference would be more or less incomprehensible without it.

2. *World Religions, Scientific Disciplines, and Secularizing Modernity*

The 19th and 20th centuries witnessed greatly accelerated development in the conceptualization and the institutionalization of religion and

[1] See Beyer, Peter, *Religions in Global Society*, London: Routledge 2006.

[2] Beyer, Peter, "Globalization and the Institutional Modeling of Religion", in: Beyer, Peter/Beaman, Lori (eds.), *Religion, Globalization, and Culture*, Leiden: Brill Academic Publishers 2007b, 167–186.

religions; and this as part of historical processes of increasingly worldwide integration that we now often call globalization. In the earlier decades of the 19th century, elite European observers, in the context of the increasing global expansion of their influence, supplemented their inherited list of observed religions with ones that they "discovered" in other parts of the world, notably Confucianism, Hinduism, and Buddhism to add to the older catalogue of Christianity, Judaism, Islam, and Paganism. European imperial expansion and these discoveries were strictly related.[3] At roughly the same time, however, began a reverse or complementary observational process: the participation in the (re)imagining of these religions by segments of the elites who were supposedly their carriers, and the founding of religious movements of reform or reconstruction as attempts to institutionalize such new visions. This aspect of the historical developments were again far from uniform or uncontested; and it was really only toward the end of the 19th and the beginning of the 20th century that the whole process, both among Western and non-Western observers, reached what one might call a take-off phase, again strictly reflective and consonant with globalization more broadly.[4] On the non-Western side, varied examples could be cited, ranging from Dharmapala's Buddhist movement in Sri Lanka and Dayananda Saraswati's Arya Samaj in India, to the Singh Sabha movement in Punjab, Kang Yuwei's abortive attempt to institutionalize Confucianism, and the explicit counter-direction expressed in the promulgation of Jinja Shinto in Japan. Parallel conceptual and institutional developments in Christian, Judaic, and Muslim realms could easily be added to this list.

In conjunction with these and other developments in the religious domain, the 19th and 20th centuries also saw the foundation of scientific disciplines, again beginning in the West, that made it their task to observe and understand this by then taken-for-granted conceptual and institutional religion. In particular what we today call religious studies (or history of religions, comparative religions, etc.) and the social scientific disciplines of anthropology and sociology trace their self-described origins to this period. Somewhat ironically, however, these

[3] Cf. Masuzawa, Tomoko, *The Invention of World Religions*, Chicago: University of Chicago Press 2005.

[4] Robertson, Roland, *Globalization: Social Theory and Global Culture*, London: Sage 1992; Campbell, George Van Pelt, "Religion and Phases of Globalization", in: Beyer, Peter/Beaman, Lori (eds.), *Religion, Globalization, and Culture*, Leiden: Brill Academic Publishers 2007, 281–302.

scientific endeavours arose in the context of the progressive and relative marginalization of religion as public power in the same regions. That is, even though the 19th and early 20th centuries were arguably periods of significant institutional religious revival in the West as in many sectors of the non-West, the public power of other institutional spheres – or what I, using Luhmannian language, would call function systems[5] – including the scientific, the political, the legal, and the economic, increased in comparatively greater proportion, giving rise progressively to the idea, that at least modern Western society was a characteristically secularizing society in which institutional religion especially had, would have, or should have a less and less important place. The scientific disciplines, arising as they did in this context, came to be very much informed by this orientation, whether directly through the development of secularization-oriented theories, or indirectly through the assumption that, in effect, real or the best religion was "traditional"; it was a reflection of the past.

During the first half of the 20th century, in particular after the end of the First World War, this conjunction of institutional and scientific observational elements continued. The idea that modern society was inherently secularizing because it was modern took increasing hold as the power of religion and religions receded or was deemed to recede. Not only in Western countries, but among the modernizing elites in the non-West, the notion became widespread that religion was antithetical to "modernization" and "development". From China and Japan, to India, Latin America as well as Western Europe, North America, and Australasia, each in their own particular way, secularist ideologies became dominant and religious powers more and more marginalized; which is not to say that the institutional expressions of what was meant by religion either disappeared or even lessened all that much in their societal presence. The scientific observation of religion, as I discuss in greater detail below, fell in lock step with these developments, becoming a similarly marginal enterprise among scientific observers as it had become among those with different kinds of institutional power.

[5] Beyer 2006.

3. *Reorienting the Observation of Religion in the Late Twentieth Century*

The late 20th century has seen a significant change in these respects, both in the institutional realities of religion and religions around the world, but even more so in terms of the scientific, official, and popular observation of religion. Here I continue to concentrate only on the scientific sort. In effect, the secularization orientation has ceased to be the dominant orientation, and this in light of a series of very specific worldwide developments that altered the context of observation in significant ways. These broader transformations have been captured in the idea of globalization.

One could point to quite a number of representative events and developments in this regard, but three are seminal in terms of their consequences for the perception and understanding of religion. These are the opening during the 1960s of Western countries to permanent migration from all over the world, thus facilitating and accelerating a "reverse flow" of people, ideas, and a multiplicity of religions that had been more restricted before; the rise of powerful political movements, inspired by various religions in various quarters of the world during the late 1970s and 1980s; and, in the early 1990s, the definitive end of the Cold War era, including the collapse of the Soviet Union and the victory of the "capitalist roaders" in post-Mao China.

In terms of the scientific literature on religion during this era, we see a clear reflection of these events. Included is, first, a strong focus on "new religions"; then, as of 1979, on religio-political movements, often dubbed "fundamentalisms". The same period saw ever increasing attention to non-institutionalized religious expressions, this under various headings like spirituality and, more recently, lived religion. Then, since roughly the late 1980s, the religions of immigrant and other minority groups, especially in Western countries, begins to increase. And finally, contextualizing all these empirical foci, one witnesses a serious reconsideration of the very idea of religion, including questioning and rejecting the notion that modern societies are necessarily secularizing societies, unpacking the concept of religion and of "world religions" in particular, and searching for alternative conceptualizations that better capture the exceedingly diverse phenomena that seem to fall under the heading of "religious". In fact, if there is a successor to the dominance of the secularization orientation, then it is *diversity or plurality* of the religious and religion in various dimensions – empirically, conceptually, geographically, and politically. A brief look at these several dimensions of religious plurality will serve to clarify how this reorientation of the observation of religion in the direction of religious plurality has taken place and how it makes sense in the context of contemporary processes of globalization.

4. *From Religious Marginality to Religious Diversity in Global Context*

4.1. *New Religious Movements*

In the immediate postwar decades after 1945, religion did receive a certain amount of scholarly attention, but it was a comparatively low-key affair operating under a double assumption: that religion was either of marginal importance or important mostly for the marginalized of society; and that religious diversity was relatively unproblematic[6] or actually contributed to the decreasing importance of religion.[7] Towards the end of the 1960s that situation began to change with the advent of what came to be known as "new religious movements", often popularly known under the pejorative title of "cults". The earlier attention was actually focussed not on Western countries – where most (social) scientific scholars were based – but on Japan. Here, the postwar era had seen both the revival of prewar religious movements, but also the rise of an increasing number of new ones. From Soka Gakkai and Rissho Koseikai to Kofuku no Kagaku and Aum Shinrikyo, new religions grew in number, visibility and variety, and continued to do so; the sheer diversity along with the fact of religious revival were what seemed so noteworthy, a combination nicely reflected in the title of McFarland's book, *The Rush Hour of the Gods*.[8] More critically for the topic at hand, this was not a temporary phenomenon. Since the 1960s, the category of "new religions" *(shinshukyo)* has in a real sense become the category of choice for scholarly attention to religion in Japan: the inherently diverse and constantly renewing character of

[6] See e.g. Herberg, Will, *Protestant, Catholic, Jew: An Essay in American Religious Sociology*, Garden City, NY: Anchor Books 1960.

[7] See e.g. Berger, Peter, *The Sacred Canopy: Elements of a Sociological Theory of Religion*, New York: Doubleday Anchor 1967.

[8] McFarland, H. Neill, *The Rush Hour of the Gods: A Study of New Religious Movements in Japan*, New York: Macmillan 1967.

religious groups is in an important sense what religion is deemed to be all about in Japan.[9]

In Western countries, the concerted attention to what was in those regions the seemingly sudden popularity of new religious movements began slightly later and has abated somewhat since the late 1980s, but its preoccupations have been similar: surprise that this should be happening at all, that there should be signs of religious revival in modern, industrialized, and presumably secularizing societies; and fascination with the sheer "strangeness" and variety of these movements.[10] Many if not most of these new manifestations were in fact the product of "non-Western" religious figures, founders and leaders who migrated to the West under new, more open immigration policies and attracted local followers, predominantly from among the youth of the dominant classes and far less from among the marginalized. Among the more prominent were, for instance, Swami Prabhupada of ISKCON, Sun Myung Moon of the Unification Church, Guru Maharaj Ji of the Divine Light Mission, and Maharishi Mahesh Yogi of Transcendental Meditation. In that context, the new religious movements also became highly controversial. To many observers they seemed positively dangerous; as a category of phenomena, they were not only unexpected, but an aberration. Hence the pejorative term, "cult", with its parallel in other world languages, to describe them.[11] The most visible factor in this negative assessment has been that some of these movements, like the Peoples Temple of Jonestown, the Order of the Solar Temple, and the already mentioned Aum Shinrikyo, did turn out to be violent and deadly. Yet the controversy began well before these developments,

[9] See Reader, Ian, *Religion in Contemporary Japan*, Honolulu: University of Hawaii Press 1991; Kisala, Robert, *Prophets of Peace: Pacifism and Cultural Identity in Japan's New Religions*, Honolulu: University of Hawaii Press 1999; Inoue, Nobutaka, *Contemporary Japanese Religion*, 25, Tokyo: Foreign Press Center/Japan 2000; Shimazono, Susumu, *From Salvation to Spirituality: Popular Religious Movements in Japan*, Honolulu: Trans Pacific Press 2004; Inoue, Nobutaka, "How Are the Concepts of 'New Religion' and 'NRM' Related", in: *International Association for the History of Religions*, Tokyo, Japan 2005.

[10] See, from a vast earlier literature, Glock, Charles Y./Bellah, Robert N. (eds.), *The New Religious Consciousness*, Berkeley, CA: University of California Press 1976; Needleman, Jacob/Baker, George (eds.), *Understanding the New Religions*, New York: Seabury Press 1978; Barker, Eileen (ed.), *Of Gods and Men: New Religious Movements in the West*, Macon, GA: Mercer University Press 1983.

[11] Lofland, John, *Doomsday Cult: A Study of Conversion, Proselytization, and Maintenance of Faith*, Englewood Cliffs, NJ: Prentice Hall 1966; Robbins, Thomas, *Cults, Converts, and Charisma: The Sociology of New Religious Movements*, London/Newbury Park, CA: Sage Publications 1988.

showing that the larger and more subtle issue has been the, for the observer, problematic nature of their existence: that they were new, different, and multiplying. Symptomatic of this assessment is that for a great many of those outside the narrow confines of the subgroup of scholars studying them (and even some of these), these movements should not even count as religions: as "dangerous cults", they were illegitimate to the point of requiring suppression. This negative attitude and even fear of new religious movements continues into the 21st century and is moreover not confined to Japan and Western countries. Rather it appears to have become worldwide. Irrespective of the fact that almost all of these movements actually attract very few followers, many people and governments continue to see this manifestation of religious diversity to be highly problematic.[12]

4.2. *Religio-Political "Fundamentalisms"*

If the new religious movements were one development of the post-war era to make religion appear in a different light, as more diverse, more visible, and *thereby* more controversial, even more important was what followed from about the late 1970s on. Beginning with the rise of what was then called the "New" Christian Right in the United States and the Islamic revolution in Iran, both in 1979, a series of highly-visible, sometimes violent, and often successful religio-political movements arose, not just in the United States and Iran, but in a variety of countries as diverse as Nicaragua, Poland, India, Israel, and Sri Lanka. Many of these were cases of longer standing movements or trends rising to renewed or unprecedented prominence, and not entirely new movements. What attracted so much attention was rather the combination of their seemingly sudden success, the fact that most observers, just as in the case of the new religious movements, had not expected them, and that they arose in various corners of the world and from different religions. At play was the assumption, shared by most scholars and other elite observers, that in a modern secularizing world such an assertion of religious power should at best be an exception and, where it occurred, it had to be a protest of the marginalized, a reactionary response to the encroachment of modern structures

[12] See Richardson, James T. (ed.), *Regulating Religion: Case Studies from around the Globe,* New York: Kluwer Academic/Penum 2004.

like the secular nation-state, capitalist economy, and modern science.[13] Accordingly, parallel to the term "cult" to refer to the similarly unexpected new religious movements, the word "fundamentalism" became the label of choice to describe these religio-political movements. Its dominant meaning is instructive. Rather than referring simply to religious movements that enter the political arena, fundamentalism denotes something both militant and defensive, hearkening to the past, in that sense "traditional" in its outlook, concerned with reinforcing threatened boundaries and above all combatting secular institutions.[14] The presumed opposition is to supposedly secular modernity, not to a different way of doing modernity. Accordingly, religio-political movements that take, for instance, a "socialist" option, like the liberation theological directions manifest during the same decades across the globe from Nicaragua to Korea; these are not deemed to be fundamentalist. Yet the Iranian revolution and India's Hindu nationalism are lumped with the Lubavitcher Hassidim and Italy's Communione e Liberazione, the latter two not in any sense political movements like the former.[15] Clearly, for many scholarly observers, manifestations of "strong" religion,[16] as contrasted with presumably "weak" religion that accords with secular modernity, needed special explanation. In that context, a large part of the question requiring answers was that virtually every "world religion" – from Christianity, Islam, and Judaism to Hinduism, Sikhism, and Buddhism – was producing these fundamentalisms, and this in every corner of the world.[17] As with the new religious movements, religious strength and global diversity are at much at issue when discussing these religio-political movements as their unprecedented nature during the postwar period.

---

[13] Cf. Juergensmeyer, Mark, *The New Cold War? Religious Nationalism Confronts the Secular State,* Berkeley, CA: University of California Press 1993.

[14] See Almond, Gabriel A./Appleby, R. Scott/Sivan, Emmanuel (eds.), *Strong Religion: The Rise of Fundamentalisms around the World,* Chicago: University of Chicago Press 2000, 17.

[15] Cf. Kepel, Gilles, *The Revenge of God,* Oxford: Blackwell 1994.

[16] Thus Almond, Appleby et al. 2000.

[17] See esp. Marty, Martin E./Appleby, R. Scott (eds.), *The Fundamentalism Project,* 5 vols. Chicago: University of Chicago Press 1991–1995; but also the series, Hadden, Jeffrey K./Shupe, Anson (eds.), *Prophetic Religion and Politics,* New York: Paragon House 1986; Shupe, Anson/Hadden, Jeffrey K. (eds.), *The Politics of Religion and Social Change,* New York: Paragon House 1988; Hadden, Jeffrey K./Shupe, Anson (eds.), *Secularization and Fundamentalism Reconsidered,* New York: Paragon House 1989; Robertson, Roland/Garrett, William R. (eds.), *Religion and Global Order,* New York: Paragon House 1991.

4.3. *Transnational Migration and Global Religions*

The migration of peoples more or less permanently from one part of the world to another is, of course, not new to the modern centuries, and even then the late 20th century has not been unprecedented in this regard. The specific character of post-World War II migration, in particular that which occurred after about the mid-1960s, is, however, highly significant in the present context. The relation between this migration and the flowering of new religious movements in the West has already been noted. More broadly, the opening up of the most powerful Western countries to migration, not just from Europe, but from virtually all around the world during these decades greatly enhanced the presence of religions that had hitherto had but a tiny presence in these regions, but also increased the awareness of this new diversity among both scholarly and non-scholarly observers.

Initially, it was Western European countries that experienced an influx of new residents from their erstwhile colonial territories or that solved the labour shortages of a booming economy by allowing in non-European guest workers. Up until the 1980s, the elites and dominant populations in most of these countries managed to ignore the implications of these developments, often by continuing to believe that the situation was temporary and that most of these people would eventually "go home". The European colonization states of North America and Australasia opened their doors to truly global migration only beginning in the 1960s; but then the influx of non-Europeans, complete with their often very different religions and different versions of the historically dominant Christianity, took on increasingly serious proportions. Although correspondingly serious attention to the religious implications of this new diversity was already noticeable in the 1980s,[18] as with the idea of globalization itself, the take-off period dates

[18] See, as examples, Kurian, George/Srivastava, Ram P. (eds.), *Overseas Indians: A Study in Adaptation*, New Delhi: Vikas 1983; Waugh, Earle H./Abu-Laban, Baha/Qureshi, Regula B., *The Muslim Community in North America*, Edmonton: University of Alberta Press 1983; Bhachu, Parminder, *Twice Migrants: East African Sikh Settlers in Britain*, London: Tavistock 1985; Burghart, Richard (ed.), *Hinduism in Great Britain: The Perpetuation of Religion in an Alien Cultural Milieu*, London: Tavistock 1987; Israel, Milton (ed.), *The South Asian Diaspora in Canada: Six Essays*, Toronto: Multicultural History Society of Ontario & Centre for South Asian Studies 1987; Charon, Milly, *Between Two Worlds: The Canadian Immigrant Experience*, Revised Edition, Montreal: Nu-Age Editions 1988; Williams, Raymond Brady, *Religions of Immigrants from India and Pakistan: New Threads in the American Tapestry*, New York: Cambridge University Press 1988.

only from the later 1990s. Since then, the religion of immigrants, in all its diversity has become a major scholarly preoccupation in Western countries, just as the migration patterns that brought it about continue virtually unabated into the 21st century. Unlike the case of new religious movements and religio-political movements, however, most of the literature on this kind of new religious diversity has not seen it to be nearly as problematic, symptomatic of which is the absence in this case of a new term, like cult or fundamentalism, to speak about it. Much of the literature is even celebratory of the new diversity. Nonetheless, to the extent that this migration is seen in conjunction with the religio-political movements – especially the Islamic ones and these especially in the wake of the September 11, 2001 attacks – there is a certain amount of concern that the migration will help establish those movements in the Western countries. And observers in Europe especially have been absorbed with the question of how the marginalization of many of these immigrant populations and their succeeding generations has created a persistent social and economic problem. Overall, however, the main questions that scholars have asked of the religious diversity thus introduced or enhanced is about how the religions of the migrants will change and adapt in the new "diaspora" environments, how they will add to the internal diversity of the religions in question as well as the religious diversity of the recipient countries[19] and how

[19] From a vast literature, see Deen, Hanifa, *Caravanserai: Journey among Australian Muslims,* St. Leonards, NSW, Australia: Allen & Unwin 1995; Khosrokhavar, Farhad, *L'islam des jeunes*, Paris: Flammarion 1997; Saint-Blancat, Chantal, *L'islam de la diaspora,* Paris: Bayard 1997; Haddad, Yvonne Yazbeck/Esposito, John L. (eds.), *Muslims on the Americanization Path?,* Atlanta, GA: Scholars Press 1998; Vertovec, Steven/Rogers, Alisdair (eds.), *Muslim European Youth: Reproducing Ethnicity, Religion, Cutlure,* Aldershot, UK: Ashgate 1998; Warner, Stephen/Wittner, Judith G. (eds.), *Gatherings in Diaspora: Religious Communities and the New Immigration*, Philadelphia: Temple University Press 1998; McLellan, Janet, *Many Petals of the Lotus: Five Asian Buddhist Communities in Toronto,* Toronto: University of Toronto Press 1999; Roy, Olivier, *Vers un islam européen,* Paris: Éditions Esprit 1999; Baumann, Martin, *Migration – Religion – Integration: Buddhistische Vietnamesen und hinduistische Tamilen in Deutschland,* Marburg: Diagonal Verlag 2000; Ebaugh, Helen Rose/Saltzman Chafetz, Janet (eds.), *Religion and the New Immigrants: Continuities and Adaptations in Immigrant Congregations,* Walnut Creek, CA: AltaMira 2000; Jonker, Gerdien, *Eine Wellenlänge zu Gott: Der "Verband der Islamischen Kulturzentren" in Europa,* Bielelfeld, Germany: Transcript 2002; Carnes, Tony/Yang, Fenggang (eds.), *Asian American Religions: The Making and Remaking of Borders and Boundaries,* New York: New York University Press 2004; Nayar, Kamala Elizabeth, *The Sikh Diaspora in Vancouver: Three Generations amid Tradition, Modernity, and Multiculturalism,* Toronto: University of Toronto Press 2004; Kurien, Prema A., *A Place at the Multicultural Table: The Development of an American Hinduism,* New Brunswick, NJ: Rutgers University Press 2007.

the already dominant religion, almost always Christianity, is changing as migrants bring with them their own variants and become increasingly important in the demographic makeup of this religion.[20] It is the transformation of religion through the spread and pluralization of its existing forms that is most at issue, less so how that new diversification represents a radically new, let alone threatening, global social reality. That theme of sheer plurality is especially evident in another growing focus of the last few decades, the possible transformations in the form of religion and religiousness itself.

4.4. *Spirituality and Lived Religion*

New religious movements, religio-political movements, and the religion of global migrants have captured attention to a large extent because they represent historically new, if not unprecedented, developments. Their effect has also, however, been to help change the ways that scholars and others look at religion more generally in the current globalizing context. A prime example of this shift in observation concerns what can generally be called "non-institutionalized" religious expression, or what Meredith McGuire has called "non-official" religion.[21] Already in such designations one can see that a key identifying feature of this sort of religiousness is that it contrasts with something else, whether institutional or official religion. The positive terms used to talk about it carry the same, but implicit, difference. Two such terms are increasingly common: *spirituality* now generally refers to a highly

---

[20] See, as examples, Ter Haar, Gerrie, "Ritual as Communication: A Study of African Christian Communities in the Bijlmer District of Amsterdam", in: Platvoet, Jan/van der Toorn, Karel, *Pluralism and Identity: Studies in Ritual Behaviour*, Leiden: E. J. Brill 1995, 115–142; Williams, Raymond Brady, *Christian Pluralism in the United States: The Indian Experience*, New York: Cambridge University Press 1996; Lawson, Ronald, "When Immigrants Take Over: The Impact of Immigrant Growth on American Seventh-day Adventism's Trajectory from Sect to Denomination", *Journal for the Scientific Study of Religion* 38 (1999), 83–102; Yang, Fenggang, *Chinese Christians in America: Conversion, Assimilation, and Adhesive Identities*, University Park, PA: University of Pennsylvania Press 1999; Adogame, Afe, "The Quest for Space in the Global Spiritual Marketplace: African Religions in Europe", *International Review of Mission* 89 (2000), 409; Vásquez, Manuel A./Marquardt, Marie Friedmann, *Globalizing the Sacred: Religion across the Americas*, New Brunswick, NJ: Rutgers University Press 2003; Wilkinson, Michael, *The Spirit Said Go: Pentecostal Immigrants in Canada*, New York: Peter Lang 2006; Jenkins, Philip, *The Next Christendom: The Coming of Global Christianity*, New York and Oxford: Oxford University Press 2007.

[21] McGuire, Meredith, *Religion: The Social Context*, 5th. Belmont, CA: Wadsworth 2002.

variable sort of religious belief and practice that is characterized by its great stress on individual experience and individual construction and authenticity. It contrasts consistently and often explicitly with religion, by which is meant collectively authoritative, institutionalized religion.[22] The much greater diversity or variability of spirituality versus the relative concentration into a few religions is evident in this opposition. A second term, *lived religion*, follows suite: it is the religion actually practised on a daily basis in the lives of usually non-elite individuals, which is not necessarily that ideally set forth in the dictates and institutional prescriptions of religious authorities.[23] In this context, the idea has resonances with a third, much older, term, popular religion, which contrasts even more clearly with "elite" religion, this latter referring not just or even primarily to the religion of elites, but again to the religion controlled and set forth by religious elites. In the absence of that authoritative control, lived religion and *popular religion* are automatically variable, even fluid and unpredictable in their directions and developments.

The concrete reference of these terms is correspondingly highly diverse. So-called "New Age" religion, itself a rather imprecise term with indeterminate range and variation, falls under the heading of spirituality especially; as arguably do the "new new religions" in Japan, cyberspace religion more generally, the religious expressions and traditions of indigenous peoples, certain developments in Sufi Islam, and quite often religious movements like neo-Paganism/Wicca that eschew or attempt to avoid clear institutionalization.[24] Lived religion,

---

[22] Roof, Wade Clark, *Spiritual Marketplace: Baby Boomers and the Remaking of American Religion*, Princeton, NJ: Princeton University Press 1999; Rothstein, Mikael (ed.), *New Age Religion and Globalization*, Aarhus: Aarhus University Press 2001; Shimazono, Susumu, *From Salvation to Spirituality: Popular Religious Movements in Japan*, Honolulu: Trans Pacific Press 2004; Heelas, Paul/Woodhead, Linda/Seel, Benjamin/Szerszyinski, Bronislaw/Tusting, Karin, *The Spiritual Revolution: Why Religion is Giving Way to Spirituality*, Oxford: Blackwell 2005; Bouma, Gary D., *Australian Soul: Religion and Spirituality in the 21st Century*, New York: Cambridge University Press 2007.

[23] See Hall, David D. (ed.), *Lived Religion in America: Toward a History of Practice*, Princeton, NJ: Princeton University Press 1997; McGuire, Meredith, *Lived Religion: Faith and Practice in Everyday Life*, New York: Oxford University Press 2008.

[24] See e. g. Lewis, James R. (ed.), *Magical Religion and Modern Witchcraft*, Albany, NY: State University of New York Press 1996; Inoue 2000; Rothstein 2001; Carozzi, Maria Julia, "Ready to Move Along: The Sacralization of Disembedding in the New Age Movement and the Alternative Circuit in Buenos Aires", *Civilisations: Revue internationale d'anthropologie et de sciences humaines* 51 (2004), 139–154; Ackerman, Susan E., "Falun Dafa and the New Age Movement in Malaysia: Signs of Health,

like its older parallel, popular religion, more often than not focuses on the religion of the marginalized and powerless in society, although now very frequently urban as opposed to rural people. More ambiguously included appears to be a range of more clearly institutionalized religious movements such as New World African religions like Candomblé, Voudon, Santería, or even Rastafarianism; and above all Christian Pentecostalism, especially the non-North American versions.[25] The diversity of phenomena included is characteristic.

The key question in the present context is the reasons for the rise of these terms and their greatly varied referents. To what extent is this attention a reflection of the fact that the religious manifestations in question are new, growing, and thereby difficult to ignore? To what extent is this more a matter of increased observation, a new appreciation, of what was already there? While clearly the answer to such questions will always be "both", in this case it is at least arguable that the balance favours the latter. Most of the movements and trends in question have indeed been growing, especially Pentecostalism in regions like Africa and Latin America. Yet in most cases we are also dealing with religious phenomena that are not particularly new – the main exception is those forms that involve cyberspace – or in many cases all that widespread. The presence of those things designated as spirituality may be growing, but not to the extent that one can really talk about a "spiritual revolution"[26] if by that is meant a replacement of the institutionally religious with spirituality manifestations. The categories of spirituality and lived religion are much more clearly a reflection of shifting attention, declarations on the part of the observers that we ought to revise our way of looking at religion and religious phenomena.[27] It is therefore arguable that the difference in the case of these

---

Symbols of Salvation", *Social Compass* 52 (2005), 495–511; Højsgaard, Morten T./Warburg, Margit (eds.), *Religion and Cyberspace,* New York: Routledge 2005; Howell, Julia Day, "Modernity and the Borderlands of Islamic Spirituality in Indonesia's New Sufi Networks", in: van Bruinessen, Martin/Day Howell, Julia, *Sufism and the 'Modern' in Indonesian Islam*, London: I. B. Tauris 2007, 217–240.

[25] Cox, Harvey, *Fire from Heaven: The Rise of Pentecostal Spirituality and the Reshaping of Religion in the Twenty-First Century,* Reading, MA: Perseus Books 1995; Clarke, Peter B. (ed.), *New Trends and Developments in African Religions,* Westport, CT: Greenwood 1998; Corten, André/Marshall-Fratani, Ruth (eds.), *Between Babel and Pentecost: Transnational Pentecostalism in Africa and Latin America,* Bloomington, IN: Indiana University Press 2001.

[26] Cf. Heelas/Woodhead et al. 2005.

[27] See, e. g. Parker, Cristian, *Popular Religion and Modernization in Latin America: A Different Logic*, translated by Robert R. Barr, Maryknoll, NY: Orbis Books 1996.

categories is that, in contrast to those of new religious movements and "diaspora" religions, where it is usually the rest of the world that has arrived to impinge upon the view of the (often Western) observer in his or her own backyard, spirituality and lived religion, like the religio-political movements, involve the globalization of the observer's attention to the rest of the world, the taking seriously of what so many people both "here" and in the rest of the world are doing. The simultaneous arising of all these conceptual developments, in fact, points to more general transformations in the observation of religion, especially in the scientific disciplines most concerned with this observation.

5. *The Observation of Religious Diversity in Global Context*

5.1. *Secularization and the "Return of the Sacred" in the Social Sciences*

The two social scientific disciplines that have historically paid the most attention to religion are sociology and anthropology. Until recently, these closely related disciplines have worked very much in the shadow of the secularization assumptions discussed above, albeit in somewhat different ways. For anthropology until about the 1970s and 1980s, the analysis of religion as an integral aspect of societies presented no difficulty, but the societies that dominated anthropologists' attention were small-scale, so-called "tribal", societies in the marginalized regions of the world system. These, according to the prevailing conception, were not "modern", but rather "traditional"; and therefore religion logically informed them because religion was something unmodern, belonging more to traditional societies. Sociology, the discipline primarily concerned with modern societies, again until relatively recently, isolated its study of religion into a rather marginal subdiscipline of the sociology of religion, reflecting the presumed marginal status of religion in modern societies; and even the sociology of religion was preoccupied with issues of religious decline and the "exceptional" cases of non-decline.[28] In both cases, the latter decades of the 20th century ushered in significant changes in this regard: anthropologists abandoned their implicit distinction between modern and traditional societies, focussing on religious phenomena in virtually all areas of the world, includ-

[28] Beckford, James A., *Religion and Advanced Industrial Society*, London: Unwin Hyman 1989.

ing in the backyards of the anthropologists who are still mostly people working in "developed", usually Western countries. In sociology, the subdiscipline has begun to move much more into the mainstream of the larger discipline, and within the subdiscipline itself, the secularization thesis has, not so much been abandoned, as removed from its formerly central position as the dominant assumption: now secularized cases, rather than cases of religious strength or resurgence, call for special explanation and are treated more and more as the exception.[29]

Looking at the case of the sociology of religion more closely, the recent transformations in theories, concepts, and orientations reflect and parallel rather precisely the empirical developments just discussed. The prominent focus on new religious movements during the 1970s and early 1980s already resulted in speculation that we were witnessing a "return of the sacred"[30], but this did not bring about a change in orientation: the secularization assumption still prevailed; new religious movements were minor enough that they could still be considered aberrations. On first flush, it also seemed that the rise of religio-political movements, so-called "fundamentalisms", could also be digested as protest and reaction to prevailing modern and secularizing trends, not as cause to rethink the sociology of religion. With hindsight, however we can see that the situation was changing specifically with the rise of globalization theories, such as that of Roland Robertson, to a certain degree formed in the context of these movements[31] and with the rise of religious economy theories, prominently those of Rodney Stark and his close collaborators.[32] The former had the effect of insisting that the primary unit of sociological analysis had to be the entire world with all its religious diversity along several dimensions, including internal variety, variation in form, content, strength, and degree

---

[29] See e.g. Davie, Grace, *Europe: The Exceptional Case: Parameters of Faith in the Modern World*, London: Darton, Longman & Todd 2003.

[30] Bell, Daniel, "The Return of the Sacred?", *British Journal of Sociology* 28 (1977), 4; Wilson, Bryan, "The Return of the Sacred", *Journal for the Scientific Study of Religion* 18 (1979), 268–280.

[31] Robertson, Roland/Chirico, JoAnn, "Humanity, Globalization, Worldwide Religious Resurgence: A Theoretical Exploration", *Sociological Analysis* 46 (1985), 219–242; see also Beyer, Peter, *Religion and Globalization*, London: Sage 1994.

[32] See Stark, Rodney/Bainbridge, William S., *The Future of Religion: Secularization, Revival, and Cult Formation*, Berkeley, CA: University of California Press 1985; Stark, Rodney/Iannaccone, Laurence, "A Supply-Side Reinterpretation of the 'Secularization' of Europe", *Journal for the Scientific Study of Religion* 33 (1994), 230–252; Stark, Rodney/Finke, Roger, *Acts of Faith: Explaining the Human Side of Religion*, Berkeley, CA: University of California Press 2000.

of institutionalization. As an indicator of paradigm change, the second encouraged the negation of the secularization thesis, but more importantly sought to reverse the value polarity of two central and inherited concepts with respect to religion: both the differentiation of religion as a separate social sphere and religious diversity, rather than being seen as prime symptoms or causes of the marginalization of religion in modern society, were henceforth to be regarded as prime conditions for the strength and "vitality" of religion. It is in the context of these and other parallel theoretical and conceptual changes, that one must understand the current dominance in the contemporary subdiscipline of the great amount of attention that is being paid to religion precisely in its diversity: diversity through transnational migration; diversity in form as lived religion, spirituality, or institutionalized religion; diversity in strength of religion; diversity in relations between religion and the non-religious domains of modern societies.[33]

5.2. *Religious Studies and World Religions*

The study of religion as a distinct enterprise, more or less distinct from Christian theology, had its origins in the 19th century in the context of both Christian missionary and European imperial expansion all around the world. It was during that era that both the idea and the names of the non-Western religions were invented, first by Westerners but then increasingly taken up and developed by non-Westerners.[34] The academic discipline that developed out of this crucible, going by various names, came to structure itself around the study of these "world religions" and therefore in one sense had a global orientation from its beginnings. Yet, in parallel with the social sciences, this globalism was in subtle ways muted by the implicit assumption that the most authentic manifestations of that religion and the world religions lay mostly in the past. Peculiarly modern developments in religion were correspondingly suspect, as was the discipline most concerned with modern society, sociology.[35] This mirror image of the secularization thesis also reflected itself in dominance within this scholarly domain

[33] Cf. Beckford 2003; Beyer, Peter, "Globalization and Glocalization", in: Beckford, James A./Demerath, N. Jay III, *The Sage Handbook of the Sociology of Religion*, London: Sage 2007a, 98–117.

[34] See Smith, Wilfred Cantwell, *The Meaning and End of Religion,* Minneapolis, MN: Fortress Press 1991; Beyer 2006.

[35] Cf. Sharpe, Eric J., *Comparative Religion: A History*, 2nd edition, La Salle, IL: Open Court 1986.

of historical methods, most notably the analysis of "core" religious texts as the privileged location and standard for genuine religion. The attempt of the mid-twentieth century to develop phenomenological method as one peculiar to religious studies went in the same direction, eschewing or at least underplaying the value of studying religion in the present. To the extent that such present study occurred, it was largely "anthropological", focussing on the small scale and the traditional setting deemed relatively untouched by the corrosive influence of the modern.

As in the social scientific disciplines, these prevailing orientations in religious studies began to change roughly during the 1980s. One sign of a fundamental rethinking has been an increasingly serious questioning of the idea of religion as such, and the "world religions" especially. Another is a greater emphasis on religion in the contemporary world, on present religion and religion around the globe, including as regards the relation between religion and other, "secular" domains of society. As regards the first, there has been an increasing preoccupation with the degree to which the idea of religion as a distinct domain of endeavour, as a reality *sui generis*,[36] is not only a recently invented notion, but one that uses Christianity as the standard by which to judge all religion.[37] Thus, according to this critical trend, religion is a Western invention, an ideology whose function is as part of an imperialist strategy to impose Western ways on the rest of the world. Therefore, not only is the idea of the world religions a prime example of such illegitimate invention, religious studies as a whole has been an ideological enterprise more than it has been a scientific one.[38] The second development is far less concentrated in a specific literature, but strong indicators are the reassessment of sociology – the discipline of the modern – as an appropriate discipline for understanding religious phenomena,[39] and a sharp increase in the sheer number of studies of

[36] McCutcheon, Russell T., *Manufacturing Religion: The Discourse on Sui Generis Religion and the Politics of Nostalgia*, Oxford: Oxford Univeristy Press 1997.

[37] Peterson, Derek/Walhof, Darren (eds.), *The Invention of Religion: Rethinking Belief in Politics and History*, New Brunswick, NJ: Rutgers University Press 2002; Masuzawa 2005.

[38] Smith, Jonathan Z., "'Religion' and 'Religious Studies': No Difference at All", *Soundings* 71 (1988), 231–244; Fitzgerald, Timothy, *The Ideology of Religious Studies*, New York: Oxford University Press 2000.

[39] Cf. Sharpe 1986; Crossley, James G., *Why Christianity Happened: A Socio-historical Account of Christian Origins (26–50 CE)*, Louisville, KY: Westminster John Knox Press 2006.

contemporary religion, including especially the religion of transnational migrants and the "lived" religion of non-elites all around the world.[40] In both cases, the critical reassessment of religion and the focus on religion in the modern present, the prime criteria are what is actually happening in the world, here including the entire world; and the great diversity of phenomena that such a study must then include. Above all, it is precisely the singularity of religion that has been put in question and, as in the social sciences, the diversity of (contemporary) religion that is becoming the increasingly dominant focus.

6. *Conclusion: The Paradigm of Religious Plurality*

Like early modern and modern phases of globalization, the more contemporary era – which corresponds to the invention of the term – has manifested itself both in terms of the forms that religion and the religious have taken and the observation of those forms, the two being to some extent of necessity interrelated. The early portions of this history saw the transformation of the prevailing understanding of religion among European observers to mean a distinct domain of human endeavour that became concrete in social and personal life as religions to which one adhered or not. Over the centuries that idea institutionalized itself to a large extent not just in Western regions of increasingly global society, but also in various non-Western ones; this latter in particularized form, haltingly, incompletely, and with a high degree of contestation, just as it was doing in the West. Over time, this also meant that Western observation and institutionalization, centred very much on Christian models, became more and

[40] See e. g. Babb, Lawrence, *Redemptive Encounters: Three Modern Styles in the Hindu Tradition*, Berkeley, CA: University of California Press 1986; Kumar, Pratap, *Hindus in South Africa: Their Traditions and Beliefs*, Durban, SA: University of Durban-Westville 2000; Eck, Diana L., *A New Religious America: How a "Christian Country" Has Now Become the World's Most Religiously Diverse Nation*, New York: Harper San Francisco 2001; Prebish, Charles S./Baumann, Martin (eds.), *Westward Dharma: Buddhism beyond Asia*, Berkeley, CA: University of California Press 2002; Waghorne, Joanne Punzo, *Diaspora of the Gods: Modern Hindu Temples in an Urban Middle-Class World*, New York: Oxford University Press 2004; Orsi, Robert A., *Between Heaven and Earth: The Religious Worlds People Make and the Scholars Who Study Them*, Princeton, NJ: Princeton University Press 2005; Baumann, Martin/Salentin, Kurt, "Migrant Religiousness and Social Incorporation: Tamil Hindus from Sri Lanka in Germany", *Journal of Contemporary Religion* 21 (2006), 297–323; Matthews, Bruce (ed.), *Buddhism in Canada*, New York: Routledge 2006.

more contested and challenged through other particularizations, even though it is arguable that the former still dominates on a global scale. The upshot is that the scientific and other observation of religion took on a fundamentally comparative aspect since, even if Christian versions dominated in various senses, these were never unequivocal, challenged as they were both in social reality and in observation by the models increasingly presented by other religions – notable world religions – and by in internal variety of the Christian domain itself, both geographical and in terms of organized "confessions".

The 19th and much of the 20th centuries were the period of the clear development, institutionalization, and ascendancy of this situation. Yet it was also a time of comparative religious marginalization, institutionally in the form of the more powerful development of non-religious (and in that sense "secular") institutional domains, especially the political, scientific, and economic; and observationally in the form of basic secularization assumptions about the dominant shape of the modern and globalizing world. That development reached its apogee toward the middle of the 20th century, and has since been largely succeeded by another institutional and observational combination.

The late 20th century has witnessed a double development: on the one hand, the decline in secularization assumptions with the weakening of secularist ideologies; on the other hand, the advent of some newly visible and newly powerful religious manifestations. These together have undermined, if not the evidence for secularization, then certainly the self-evidence of this basic assumption, and this more or less worldwide. The result has been the renewed visibility of religion, both in new developments – which, by the way, are constantly occurring, whether outside observers pay them much heed or not – and transformations in forms with an already long and checkered history. It is an open question whether there have really been all that many new developments, if religion, as it were, has experienced or is experiencing a resurgence in our world. What is certain is that this religion is gaining more observational attention. Under that renewed and often new gaze, what becomes remarkable or noteworthy is not just religion and religiosity as such, but the plethora of forms that this differentiated quality takes. Sometimes, in tune with the character of some recent developments, but probably also as the remnants of old secularization assumptions, this diversity itself comes to be observed as problematic as it is incontrovertible; a tendency witnessed in worried discussions about religion from Japan, China, and, more recently,

Korea, to India, Europe, and North America. At other times, the same diversity appears just as fundamental and self-evident, but the evaluation is more positive. Then the task becomes a combination of documenting that variety – sometimes even celebrating it – and engaging in the sort of comparison that characteristically does not seek the unifying essence of the phenomena, but rather examines the essential construction of the diversity: how it has come about; how boundaries are created, maintain, and transformed; how interaction – which must assume prior agents that can interact – generates both hybridizations and new purities. What is perhaps most characteristic is that the old search for unity in matters religious is almost entirely gone, and that, if anything the diversity becomes so self-evident as to dissolve the object of inquiry. This, in a nutshell, is the situation in which I think we now find ourselves.

RELIGION IN A GLOBALISED WORLD: COMMENTS AND RESPONSES

Ian Reader

1. *Introduction*

While the contributions presented in this volume until now have, for the large part, focused on historical and terminological issues, the article by Peter Beyer and my response move us on from studies centred primarily around the history of religion towards those centred on the contemporary era and on social scientific methods of study. In this process, the focus of what is studied as 'religion' moves from being primarily centred around canon, text, doctrine, specific traditions, institutions, and historical contexts, to that which is observed, practiced and engaged in – whether in 'religious' institutions or in other areas of life. It also moves from a predominant focus on 'traditions' (often referred to as 'world religions') that are treated primarily as discrete entities, to one in which such self-contained boundaries are set aside, and we find ourselves talking in 'global' terms, not just in the context of 'globalisation' as a process, but in terms of looking at topics and flows that have (or are claimed to have) some global presence, and at seeming patterns and practices that can be discerned across cultures and traditions.

This development has linked studies of religion to those of wider social, cultural, historical and political processes, thereby breaking down the notion of religions as self-contained entities based predominantly around texts and doctrines, and has enabled us to understand more about how religion is deeply embedded in and part of such wider social and other processes – an understanding that has fed back into and enriched historical and textual studies of religion. The new avenues of enquiry that have thus opened up have been shaped by the different methodologies that social science offers, aligned with changing circumstances in the world around us. Modernity, widely recognised as a factor in shaping and impacting upon the dynamics of religion and of religious change in the contemporary world, has also facilitated the ways in which we study the subject area, by enabling new approaches helped by easier travel and increased accessibility of fieldwork. Equally, the social sciences, in focusing on people and patterns of behaviour, have brought an immediacy to studies of religion via interviews with practitioners and participants, and via observations of what people do coupled with questions that seek to clarify why they act in certain ways, what meanings they ascribe to their actions, and so on. While we cannot interrogate those who wrote the texts upon whose study much of the history of religions has been based, we can talk to those who are involved in shaping the texts, practices and phenomena of the present. Through that process we can also gain understandings of how such processes might operate – understandings that can also be applied to and used to deepen our understandings of the past as well as the present.

While this can widen the scope of the study of religion greatly, it can also make it more complex and messy. Here I would note that when one uses interviews and when one draws opinions from participants and practitioners, one may well get a far less clear-cut picture of what may be going on in religious contexts, than if one operates predominantly through studies of seemingly "authoritative" forms such as texts. Social science methods, in effect, provide us with access to a multiplicity of voices and participant actors, and hence may alert us to the complexity of practices and of interpretations thereof – a point I was made strikingly aware of early in my fieldwork career in Japan in the 1980s while trying to make sense of and analyse a particular Shinto ritual I had observed at a prominent shrine. To this end I interviewed three priests – one junior, one middle-ranking, the other the most senior priest at the shrine. Each individually provided me with a different analysis of the meanings of the component parts of the ritual – and each individually commented on the misunderstandings of his fellow priests who, each knew, had alternative interpretations. The point here is that the more one engages in such methods and deals directly with people who engage in religious events and activities, the more one is likely to hear multiple voices; modern methods and modes of access to various religious phenomena and practices around the globe not only provide us with more examples and sets of data upon which to base our analyses but more complexities in their study. As my comments above on the tendency of participants to offer multiple analyses of events and practices indicate, the capacity to examine topics that go across the boundaries of particular traditions or that are found in a multiplicity of contexts, raises problems in terms of how we can keep such things within a viable framework of interpretation. One could cite the study of pilgrimage as a prime example here. This is a subject of academic study that, since the publication of Victor Turner's seminal works[1] has grown exponentially in terms of studies in recent decades. The increasing numbers of case studies that has resulted have, however, served to erode the various theories (notably Turner's theory of communitas) that in earlier periods appeared to have provided reliable parameters for interpretation and analysis of the practice. They have also made it increasingly hard, if not impossible, for any meta-narratives to hold sway – a point now recognised by theorists who had spent plentiful time working on the search for meta-narratives.[2]

2. *The Expansion of the Field, Global Flows and 'What is Actually Happening'*

The use of social science-based methods of study has not replaced textual and doctrinal studies, and may not have radically changed the centre of gravity of the study of religion, but it has added new dimensions to it that are of immense importance and need to be taken on board by all who are involved in the study of religion. In particular, besides the identification of what one can be argued to be global flows and patterns in religion in the modern world (a key theme of Peter Beyer's paper), this has led to an increased focus away from what might be called the 'high religion'[3] of priests, monks, monastic institutions, texts and doctrines, to what has variously been termed 'non-institutional religion', 'lived religion'[4], or 'common religion'.[5] This notion of 'lived'

[1] E. g. Turner, Victor, *Dramas, Fields and Metaphors*, Ithaca, NY: Cornell University Press 1974; Turner, Victor/Turner, Edith, *Image and Pilgrimage in Christian Culture*, Oxford: Blackwell 1978.

[2] See Eade, John, "New Introduction", in: Eade, John/Sallnow, Michael, *Contesting the Sacred: The Anthropology of Christian Pilgrimage,* Urbana, Ill: Illinois University Press 2000, ix–xxvii.

[3] Ortner, Sherry B., *High Religion: A Cultural and Political History of Sherpa Buddhism*, Princeton, NJ: Princeton University Press 1989.

[4] See above the article in this volume Beyer, p. 413 and passim, and also Hall, David D. (ed.), *Lived Religion in America: Toward a History of Practice,* Princeton, NJ: Princeton University Press 1997; Sullivan, Winnifred Fallers, *The Impossibility of Religious Freedom,* Princeton, NJ: Princeton University Press 2005, 138–146.

[5] Reader, Ian/Tanabe, George J. Jr., *Practically Religious: Worldly Benefits and the Common Religion of Japan*, Honolulu: University of Hawaii Press 1998.

or common religion refers to those activities and modes of behaviour – from buying charms, and putting statues of Jesus on the front lawn, to engaging in pilgrimages and bringing home bottles of Lourdes water – that are not grounded specifically in the institutionalised structures and doctrinal formulations of organised religions, but that are found across just about every culture. (To that degree, indeed, one could well argue that it is in such areas that one might be able to discern some degree of universalism to religious behaviour, far more than it is in terms of doctrines and the activities often seen as belonging to 'high religion'). While these areas have been discussed in the past, they have mainly been consigned to the rubric of 'folk religion', marginalised and often treated as if they were not really parts of bona fide religion.[6] Likewise they have tended to have been far less represented in departments focused on the study of religion, which have traditionally largely employed people who work on what are often referred to as 'world religions' such as Christianity, Judaism, Islam, Buddhist, Hinduism and so on. It is primarily with the advent of modern social science approaches that subjects that span boundaries and that are not immediately pigeon-holed under one 'world religion' banner or other have been recognised as central foci in the study of religion.

This development has turned attention more thoroughly to 'what is actually happening in the world' (to use Beyer's phrase) in terms of religion and religious phenomena and has led to an increasing awareness and understanding of the diversity and plurality that are key themes of Beyer's paper. This focus on diversity and plurality is based in a wholly global perspective in which, for example, studies of pilgrimage draw together examples of pilgrimage practice from across the globe, and in which studies of new religions movements – one of the themes Beyer identifies as an example of growth in the modern world – are unbounded by geographical constraints and by being limited to particular religious traditions. This emphasis on global flows, diversity and plurality, coupled with an emphasis on empirical research based in observation, has also called 'the singularity of religion' into question while making it clear that attention has to be paid to religion's diversity.[7] It has also emphasised the reality of 'religion' as a topic of study – a point emphasised by Beyer's comments on the links between what he calls 'religion formation' and the processes of globalisation, and

[6] On this point see Sullivan, 2005, 140–141.

[7] See above the article in this volume Beyer, p. 431.

his assertion that these form a reality. Thus, although terms such as 'religion' and 'globalisation' require critical examination, they should be seen as realities worthy of attention. While we may recognise that terms and concepts such as 'religion' and, indeed, 'globalisation' may well be invented categories and the products of particular times and modes of thought, this does not mean that they should summarily be dismissed as illusory. As Beyer notes, the emergence of terms such as 'religion' occurred at similar period and in conjunction with the rise of "differentiated institutional domains in politics, economy, and science"– and, as he points out, the 'more this happened, the more difficult it became to think of religion and to institutionalize religion as *anything but* a differentiated category and domain'. Hence, in a real sense, claims and debates over whether 'religion' is a constructed category (or a viable one in non-Western contexts) is something of a red herring in terms of the realities of how we consider religion as a field of human activity.

Crucially, too, while concepts such as religion and globalisation may be socially constructed by particular interest groups in ways that reflect particular modes of authority, they are nonetheless concepts that provide a way of 'seizing reality socially'.[8] And, while I am not so sure of Beyer's claim that concepts are our 'only way' of doing this, I fully concur with his view that the conceptual frameworks that we engage in through using such terms as 'religion' (and the varieties of conceptual discussions we arrange around them) are a verifiable and viable means through which we can work out ways of understanding the social contexts and realities within which we live, through which we can think about the behaviour of others and of other societies (and they of us) and can work out ways of analysing behaviours and practices across boundaries. That, in essence, is a sound enough starting point for me to reiterate that terms such as 'religion' remain useful terms for developing an understanding of the world and of the multiple forms in which people operate.

The emergence of such perspectives is another feature of a globalising process through which we have come not only to recognise the plurality of forms that one might associate with 'religion' but also the impossibility, as Beyer notes, of claiming a 'unifying essence of the phenomena' as Western hegemonies have been eroded and the paradigms

[8] See above the acrticle in this volume Beyer, p. 413.

that shaped much of the study of 'religion' (i.e., Christian/colonial) have been eroded. As our studies and perspectives have become more global, and as social scientific paradigms (which tend towards themselves creating or positing universal models) have become increasingly central to the field, a key shift has also been away from the study of religion as a study of named traditions, and towards the study of a variety of perceived phenomena, flows and processes that are considered to exist across the modern world.

In this globalising process, too, it is important to point out that we have seen the emergence of academies outside the Western world (even if part of the stimulus towards their formation came, as with the formation of modern Japanese universities and academic structures, through interaction with the West and with Japanese processes of modernity). This has led to the emergence of academic traditions of the study of 'religion' that have moved on from older Western, colonial-based, constructs of 'religion' and that have (while continuing to use that word or neologisms related to it in their own languages) themselves transformed the notion of 'religion' as a field of study, and by implication, the things studied under that rubric, in line with the understandings of the cultures in which they occur.[9] George Tanabe and I have noted this point elsewhere, commenting on how, for example, the Japanese academic use of the term *shûkyô* – a term with Buddhist origins and that existed in pre-modern times but adopted in the nineteenth century as a Japanese translation for the term 'religion' – has moved on beyond its narrower nineteenth century theological and textual focus. Via its usage by Japanese scholars whose interests lie more in the social scientific and folk fields, it has come to be closely akin in academic usage to the aforementioned concept of 'lived religion or, as George Tanabe and I called it, 'common religion'.[10]

[9] For further discussions of this issue, see Isomae (Isomae Jun'ichi, *Kindai Nihon no Shûkyô Gensetsu to Sono Keifu: Shûkyô, Kokka, Shintô*, Tokyo: Iwanami Shôten 2003), which discusses how Japanese Religious Studies developed, and indicates the extent to which it was based in 19th century Western theological notions and constructs of 'religion'; see also my review essay of Isomae's work (Reader, Ian, "Of Religion, Nationalism and Ideology: Analysing the Development of Religious Studies in Japan", in: *Social Science of Japan Journal* 8/1 [2005], 119–124), which shows how Isomae, while emphasising the how Japanese Religious Studies was grounded initially in such Western concepts, has overlooked later developments in that field and has paid less attention to how it has produced its own parameters and gone on beyond its initial Western-centric basis.

[10] Reader/Tanabe, 1998, passim but especially 4–6.

This widening of the scope of who studies religion (not just textual scholars, theologians and historians, but also social scientists, and not just those based in Western cultural milieus) has begun to have, and will in the future have even more, impact on the dynamics of the field of the study of religion. In this context, for example, one could point to the critiques of Weberian theories related to modernity, religious decline, magic and morality, that emerged from the 1970s onwards based in empirical studies done in Japan by Japanese scholars. These serve as one indication of how the expansion of the field and the growth of non-Western academic cultures, began to challenge the hegemony of Western-based theories, and helped to stimulate alternative viewpoints.[11] Such dynamics will continue to present fresh challenges to previously held Western assumptions as these fields develop further, and especially as and when (for example) Western scholars study with and absorb ideas from counterparts elsewhere; my own perspectives have, as I have written elsewhere, been greatly shaped by what I learned from working in Japan with Japanese scholars of religion.[12] As more and more younger scholars spend extended periods in countries such as Japan, China and India, studying and working with scholars there, this will further impact on and (re)shape the field, and will further challenge the previously Western-centric bias that has been embedded in the field of Religious Studies historically and in terms of its foci of study.

3. *Renewed Visibility, New Global Phenomena, and Problems of Definition*

Social scientific methods of study that revolve around observation of what is happening have produced what Beyer calls a 'renewed visibility

[11] On this point see, for example: Shimazono, Susumu, *Gendai kyûsai shûkyôron*, Tokyo: Seiyûsha 1992, and my review article (Reader, Ian, "Recent Japanese publications on the new religions: the work of Shimazono Susumu [review article]", in: *Japanese Journal of Religious Studies* 20/2–3 [1993], 101–120), which provides a detailed outline of the issues discussed here.

[12] Reader, Ian, *Religion in Contemporary Japan*, Basingstoke, UK, and Honolulu, US: Macmillans and University of Hawaii Press 1991, Preface; one should also note how prominent Japanese scholars such as Yanagida Seizan (working on Zen and Ch'an history and texts) and Shimazono Susumu (contemporary religions) have influenced generations of Western scholars who have studied with them in Kyoto and Tokyo respectively.

of religion', one that contrasts with earlier presumptions in the social sciences that religion was dying as modernity eroded its foundations and reduced it to a restricted area in the realms of the private (the so-called 'secularisation thesis'). While Beyer notes that this perception of renewed visibility might be primarily because more observation and fieldwork are being done, he also appears to affirm that such renewed visibility is a result of religious growth, by discussing four areas that he identifies as areas or factors leading to such growth and hence greater religious visibility. I am not so convinced that this intellectual leap (from claiming that because we now can observe these phenomena, therefore religion must be on the rise) is necessarily sound and, without conclusive empirical evidence to the contrary, am more inclined to think that such increased visibility is more likely to be because of the increasing amounts of observation going on, perhaps motivated by underlying wishes to emphasise the current widely held view that secularisation itself is dead, than it is because of any real religious growth. To this extent I would draw attention to a possibly similar situation in Japan during the 1970s, when secularisation theories were pushed aside in favour of the concept of a 'religious boom' or revival. In that period Japanese sociologists of religion, like their colleagues in the West, having keenly talked about secularisation during the 1960s and early 1970s as if it were a given fact, changed their tunes significantly from the mid-1970s as they became concerned that secularisation theories were too Western-centric and not suitable to Japanese contexts. This change of thinking led them to start looking beyond the formal structures of organised religion and to 'discover' a lot of 'lived religion' out, as it were, in the streets, ranging from high levels of visits to shamans and diviners, to high levels of acquisition of amulets and participation in religious festivals and calendar events at Buddhist temples and Shinto shrines. Their discoveries became interpreted as a form of 'religious boom' that was used to argue against the applicability of secularisation theories in Japan. Whether, however, this was really a case of 'boom' rather than an instance of making more visible what was already going while interpreting the available data via a new set of overarching assumptions, is a moot point; my view[13] is that it

[13] See Reader, Ian, "Returning to Respectability: A Religious Revival in Japan?", in: *Japan Forum* 2/1 (1990), 57–68. Where I briefly discuss such debates and the factors that led to reinterpretations of religious statistics in line with prevailing theories and

was more a heightened focus on what was already there but previously barely focused upon, than anything else.

Beyer, in drawing attention to a series of phenomena that he identifies as having a certain global presence, suggests that secularisation, once highly in vogue among sociologists and formerly a major paradigm in the study of religion, has lost its lustre in academic terms. Now we are, it is suggested, in a period of growth that can be primarily identified in four thematic areas. I shall briefly outline these as they are set out by Beyer along with a few comments on each.

The first theme Beyer mentions (although he does not suggest these are in any order of importance) is the global rise of new religious movements – a phenomenon that certainly does introduce notions of globalisation as a multivalent process. As Beyer notes, many of the new religions that have flourished in the West have come from Asia, thereby indicating that globalisation itself is not (as is sometimes erroneously portrayed) merely a 'from the West to the rest' process. New religions as a category are interesting scholastically, one might add, because (as Beyer notes) studies of Japan were at the vanguard in identifying 'new religious movements' as a particular form of religion and as a valuable area of academic analysis. Although Beyer does not develop this theme it is one that is indicative of the point I made earlier, about the potential influence of academic cultures beyond the West to help shape and lead the field.[14]

A second theme Beyer focuses on is the rise of what he calls religious and political fundamentalism(s) that are opposed to (but in effect stimulated by) secular modernity. Here he rightly warns us of a recurrent problem in the 'globalising' of religious analysis and in the use of grand categories, in which the tendency to make sweeping categorisations, such as the notion of 'religious/political fundamentalism(s)' as a grand theme of late twentieth century religion and globalisation, can lead to an almost indecent lumping together of disparate movements and trends that scarcely merit being treated as parts of the same phenomenon or that barely resemble each other. This point, however, is not just one limited to fundamentalisms, but to pretty much all the

---

trends in the Japanese sociology of religion, including the jettisoning of the 'secularisation thesis' and the development of the idea of a 'religious revival'.

[14] Indeed, the very use of the terms 'new religions' and 'new religious movements' may well have developed in Japan – in the late 1950s and early 1960s – well before their emergence (from around 1968 it would appear) in Western contexts.

categories Beyer mentions, although he does not make this point. After all, if, as he indicates, it is problematic to include all so-called 'fundamentalisms' together under one rubric, why is it valid (as he appears to thin) to use the collective term 'new religious movements' (above) as if they were as one entity, when the differences between (say) Hare Krishna, the Church Universal and Triumphant and Soka Gakkai – to name three groups commonly labelled as new religions but that come from different traditions and have very different hues – are so evident?

His third area of focus relates to migration patterns that have led in the modern world to increasing religious diversification, especially as immigrant groups have imported their faith and practices into various countries which, previously, had been more closely associated with notions of religious decline. Such movements of populations have (although Beyer does not go into particular cases) helped regenerate established religions; an example here would be how Roman Catholic churches in many areas of England (especially London and the South-East) have been revitalised in recent years by an influx of Polish immigrants, leading to the need to conduct services in Polish, and to import Polish priests. For Beyer, this aspect of growth has generally been seen as less problematic than the rise of new religions or of fundamentalisms, and he justifies this comment by stating much of the literature is rather celebratory of this new diversity and by commenting on the absence new and pejorative terms (such as 'cult' or 'fundamentalism') to label the phenomenon in the media and elsewhere. I am not sure that this assertion holds up especially well in Western Europe and specifically in the UK. Not only has the influx of new migrant groups with differing customs led to concern and disquiet in some quarters (even if Polish immigrants have boosted Catholic church attendance this has not always excited older British Catholics), but it has also led to disquiet about perceived 'threats' to cultural identity (as well, most recently, to a rise in the representation of unpleasant nationalist political parties). From early unease among Christian groups in the UK when immigrant religious communities have sought to purchase defunct chapels and churches and turn them into their own religious places (whether Hindu temples or Muslim mosques or Sikh gurudwaras) to more recent concerns among government agencies and in the media, that the rise in the numbers of Muslim immigrants poses a possible threat in the context of the so-called 'war on terror' that, to all intents and purposes is a 'war' associated with a particular brand of religious extremism, migration has not always enjoyed a positive reception as a source of religious diversity. Indeed, it has become a major political issue across Europe, from French concerns about Muslim symbols such as the headscarf, to the widespread use of the term and concept of 'radicalisation', a term now widely in vogue in the UK (and also, I believe, in the US). In contemporary parlance, 'radicalisation' – which I would argue has become precisely the sort of problematic term that Beyer assumes does not exist in this context – has become used to indicate the fear that some people within immigrant communities are 'deviating' from mainstream 'peaceful' practices and are becoming extremists. This notion assumes that 'real' or 'true' religion is peaceful, tolerant and 'middle of the road', and is a manifestation of public concern and governmental worry that Muslim communities across Europe may pose a threat to the liberal values of modern societies if disaffected young Muslims are 'radicalised' and become involved in extreme 'fundamentalist' forms of Islam. In such ways 'radicalisation' has become implicitly pejorative, suggesting both that pernicious influences are 'perverting' Islam and luring young people down a path of dangerous extremism, and that there is a 'true' Islam that is pleasantly accommodating to the West and that should be encouraged and publicised as the only true form of the faith. Behind terms such as 'radicalisation', then, we can perceive some interesting attempts to control and define particular forms of religion in ways that suit Western government agendas.

Beyer's fourth theme relates to what he terms 'spirituality' and 'lived religion'. The two appear different – spirituality being used to refer to a form of religious engagement based in individual experience while 'lived religion', about which I have commented earlier, relates more clearly to folk practices and behaviours. Spirituality, by contrast is an invented term used by its exponents to posit a clear difference between what they do, and what occurs in organised, institutionalised religion, and it has a wide array of associations, ranging from engaging in so-called New Age activities such as channelling, to the practice of yoga and other 'spiritual' acts on an individual basis. Thus, although Beyer has used the two terms ('lived religion' and 'spirituality') together as if they represent one common phenomenon, I would suggest that they need to be considered somewhat differently, and that it muddies the waters to lump them together. 'Lived religion' is, especially in its usages by scholars such as Sullivan and Robert Orsi[15] quite clearly associated with 'folk' manifestations of (and/or practices carried out by) people who have some formal or nominal association with organised traditions. Thus the 'lived religion' that Sullivan[16] discusses in terms of paraphernalia placed on graves in a Florida cemetery, reflects the traditions (Catholic, Jewish and Protestant) that the people who placed them there, considered themselves to be part of. This is very akin to the 'common religion' that Tanabe and I have discussed in Japan, and which, we show, is in essence found at and associated with, mainstream religious traditions, even as it cuts across religious boundaries.[17] This is rather different from 'spirituality' with its rather explicit denial and critique of a common folk institutional dimension and its emphasis on individual search and experience.

An additional problem here is that the term 'spirituality' itself remains remarkably unclear even as it has become adopted widely both by practitioners seeking to put across a point of view, and by scholars who have, rather too readily it appears to me, adopted it as a term of reference without, or before appropriately, interrogating its validity as a term of description and reference. This is an important issue; the field in recent years has rightly debated the use of terms such as 'religion' and has drawn attention to the cultural underpinnings and associations of such terms[18] and of categories widely assumed in the academy such as 'world religions'.[19] Yet it would appear that with 'spirituality' we are in the midst of creating, or rather accepting without any questioning, another overarching and culturally bound term with inherent nuances and biases. The term itself requires urgent interrogation now – rather than, as has happened with 'religion' so far down the line that any discussion is, in effect, too late. Thus far, while we have seen some attempts to provide a contextual basis for the rise of the term (such as Van der Veer's[20] discussion tying the adoption of the

---

[15] See Sullivan, 2005, 140–143.

[16] Sullivan, 2005.

[17] Reader/Tanabe, 1998.

[18] E. g. McCutcheon, Russell T., *Manufacturing Religion: The Discourse on Sui Generis Religion and the Politics of Nostalgia*, New York and Oxford: Oxford University Press 1997.

[19] E. g. Masuzawa, Tomoko, *The Invention of World Religions: Or, How European Universalism was Preserved in the Language of Pluralism and Diversity*, Chicago: University of Chicago Press 2005.

[20] Van der Veer, Peter, "Global breathing: Religious utopias in India and China", in: *Anthropological Theory* 7 (2007), 315.

term 'spirituality' to people such as Vivekananda and to the politics of cultural nationalism in India and China), there has been little critical analysis of the term, the implicit meanings it contains, and the ways in which it has been in effect created and promoted by particular interest groups that want to claim the title for themselves. Indeed, scholars studying such phenomena have all too readily appeared to have gone along with this process without giving it the analysis it needs. This failure to properly interrogate the term while so readily using it in academic contexts, is a methodological and theoretical failing that needs to be addressed.

4. *The Death of Secularisation – or a Methodological Problem of Focus?*

Beyer's focus on the above themes and on diversity and visibility certainly suggests that the predominant theme in religion today is growth not decline, and that this is a global trend. This, it seems to me, is a predominant view in contemporary studies of religion, and in many respects this overarching perspective provides us with an early twenty-first century reverse image of the assumptions about secularisation some decades back. It also illustrates the problems of thinking in overarching (globalising?) terms and contexts when perhaps the story on the ground may be rather different. And just as the narrative of secularisation began to look theoretically frail once people began to look more closely at what was happening in more localised detail, as the examples of Japan in the 1970s and of studies of 'lived religion' mentioned earlier, have indicated, I think the same might be so of the seeming growth of religion and spirituality today. My observations in Japan (and the results of recent surveys[21]) indicate that there has been quite a profound decline in support levels for all organised forms of religion since the mid-1990s, when the Aum Affair tarnished the image of religion, leading to large numbers of people stating, in surveys, that religion is 'dangerous'. Just about every organised religious group I have had contact with in recent years – from Buddhist temples to new religions (generally assumed to be areas of religious growth) – has informed me that they are losing members and support. Even in supposed growth areas such as pilgrimage the picture sug-

[21] E. g. Ishii, Kenji, *Gendai nihonjin no shûkyô deetaabukku*, Tokyo: Shinyôsha, 2007.

gests that, while the Shikoku pilgrimage has seen growth in the past few years, most others have experienced declining pilgrim numbers.[22] While some Japanese scholars have claimed that there has been a turn to 'spirituality' which is in effect replacing 'religion' (e.g. Shimazono[23], which seeks to discuss this issue both in Japan and globally) the empirical evidence thus far offered to justify this claim has been scant. And while it is certainly the case that one hears the term 'spirituality' (rendered as a foreign loan word in Japanese) increasingly when talking to people, it would appear to me that this more of a terminological trend than concrete evidence of an actual rise in 'spirituality' as a new alternative that is replacing or replenishing religion. Thus far, certainly, I have not seen concrete evidence that the decline in established religions, the falling numbers of adherents of new religions, and the increasing numbers who state in surveys that they dislike and shy away from 'religion', are being in any matched by a rise in 'spirituality' or 'spiritual movements', however one defines them. One can hardly say with any confidence that religion is flourishing in Japan. It would be more likely to say the reverse. I make this point to indicate that one cannot necessarily talk in global terms or flows, and to suggest that, in some contexts at least, it might as valid to think about whether some new secularising process is going on in Japan.

A major problem here is that social scientific studies of religion have tended to focus on the new and on phenomena that appear to be growing in strength; by contrast, rather little attention has been paid, at least since secularisation theories fell out of fashion, to areas of decline. The focus on the new (as in new religions or 'new' phenomena such a 'spirituality' coming up to replace 'religion', in apparently

---

[22] I have discussed the popularity of the Shikoku pilgrimage in recent years and shown how mass media attention and publicity have helped turn it into a highly visible cultural institution (e.g. Reader, Ian, "Pilgrimage growth in the modern world: meanings and implications", in: *Religion* 37 [2007a], 210–229; Reader, Ian, "Positively promoting pilgrimages: Media representations of pilgrimage in Japan", in: *Nova Religio* 10/3 [2007b], 13–31), but in my most recent fieldwork in March 2007 and March-April 2008 I found that most other significant pilgrimage routes – such as the Saikoku, Sasaguri and Shôdoshima pilgrimages – have suffered some decline in pilgrim numbers. In the case of the latter two, along with many other regional pilgrimages, the decline has been quite sharp, while even in Shikoku, temple authorities have expressed serious concern that the popularity of their pilgrimage may be on the wane, and are trying to get the route declared a UNESCO World Heritage Site to redress this possibility.

[23] Shimazono, Susumu, *Supirichuariti no kôryû: shin reiseibunka to sono sh*ûhen, Tokyo: Iwanami Shoten 2007; Shimazono, Susumu, *Seishisekai no yukue: gendaisekai to shin reisei undo*, Tokyo: Tôkyôdô Shuppan 1996.

newly emergent 'fundamentalisms' and so on), all seem to indicate areas of growth. By paying attention to such areas, studies of contemporary religion have contributed to the renewed visibility of religion today and have thus formulated an image of modern religious resurgence. Yet what is lacking is any serious attention to the other side of the coin – the declining fortunes of many institutions and groups. This is an area that needs to be studied, not just to gain a more balanced picture of religion in the modern globalising world, but in order to gain proper insights into the dynamics of the study of religion. Growth and dynamism are attractive subjects to study, and it is no wonder that so much of the contemporary study of religion focuses on such things. But to gain a more nuanced picture of the subject (and also to gain perspectives on the dynamics of growth) one also needs to pay attention to, examine and analyse decline – and that is a topic that, despite the widespread writings on spiritual revolutions and contemporary religious growth, is an issue that every bit as much visible today if one were to look, as are the diverse and plural patterns of growth Beyer draws our attention to.

5. *Concluding Remarks*

I will end with four points, in no particular order. The first is that I have noted how the field has witnessed a methodological development in the dynamics of the study of religion through the advent of social science methods, leading to an increasing emphasis on observation of what is happening, to an identification of broad patterns and flows in global contexts, allied to processes of globalisation, and to an emphasis on practice and to 'lived' (or common) religion. In many places – such as the United Kingdom, where much emphasis now has been placed on securing research grants and where much funding for academic activities is centred around the seemingly 'relevant' (whatever that means) matters that might be of use to public policy[24] – it is fair to say that the pendulum, once so strongly oriented to the historical and textual, has swung very much towards contemporary social

[24] While I have no statistics on this point, anecdotal evidence from colleagues in the UK suggests that, when posts do come up in the field of Religious Studies, the pressure from senior management is invariably towards appointments in the modern day and with the potential for research that might impact on policy and that is seen as more likely to attract grants.

science based studies. Yet this focus on the contemporary should be seen not as a replacement for historical and textual approaches, but as a complement to them. The social science emphasis on the contemporary provides a means of studying and analysing processes as they occur – and such insights can be useful to those working in historical contexts, and seeking to understand texts and the formation of religions in earlier periods. Likewise, the historical insights and methods of textual and doctrinal studies are valuable complements to a social science approach, to provide historical awareness and contextualisation. The future dynamics of the study of religion require the utilisation of these various modes and means of study rather than a parallel development; certainly one of the most important and rewarding aspects of my academic life was when I, grounded in social science and contemporary approaches, worked with a historian used to working on medieval Japanese Buddhism and on Buddhist texts.[25] My concern is that the dynamics of the study of religion should not trapped along temporal lines in which the historical becomes set as the established and centred on 'world religions', texts and doctrines, and the study of the contemporary does not get grounded only in 'lived religion', social science approaches and global flows.

The second is that, as the field has expanded, new perceptions of the field of study are impacting on us especially from academic cultures in Asia, and these need to be considered as significant elements within the wider field. It is no longer just the case that old Western hegemonic approaches centred on text, doctrine and assumptions about world religions, have been challenged by modern social science approaches, but that these very approaches may be called into question as scholars elsewhere in the world view the theories that have evolved out of Western studies and are challenging them in the light of their own cultural understandings.

The third point is simply to reiterate my concern at the tendency of social science studies to get caught up in overarching trends that fit with what is theoretically fashionable at any one time. The tendency, for example, to focus on the new and what is growing, while neglecting to study what is declining, is an example of this – and is in part at least a product of countervailing arguments designed to counter the notion of secularisation. Secularisation, after all, was itself a fashionable the-

[25] Reader/Tanabe, 1998.

ory in earlier decades, and a key item in the social science agenda on religion. The turn away from secularisation as an overarching theory has been understandable in the context of various empirical studies that identify a diversity of religious phenomena seemingly on the rise in the modern world – themes Peter Beyer has drawn attention to. Yet we should be cautious about seeing this as evidence that 'religion' somehow is clearly 'on the increase', that something else (currently labelled 'spirituality') is coming along to replace it, or that 'secularisation is dead'. As I have suggested above, that may be too partial a picture to paint and may be overly related to the continuing tendency to focus only on the visible and growing. What is in decline is every bit as critical– and it tells us, in my view, that secularisation is not as dead an issue as many social science-based scholars of religion like to think.

My fourth point is that we should not permit the mistakes of the past to be repeated by allowing new notions and labels to appear without first properly interrogating and defining them (or putting them into an appropriate context). Studies of the ways in which the term and notion 'religion' was constructed in Western-centric colonial terms from the nineteenth century onwards have provided salutary warnings to us about the inherent orientations of our field, and about the need for proper critical understandings of the concepts we use. They remind us of the problems of accepting terms that emerge from particular ideological standpoints, and then applying them as concrete universal categories. The term 'spirituality' is a term that has emerged into widespread usage without any accompanying analytical and critical assessment of its meanings, and of why it has come about and been so readily adopted and trumpeted by its proponents as a label – one with implicit ideological implications for, and inherent criticisms of – the term and notion of 'religion'. It is surely a key challenge for those interested in the study of religion in the modern day and in the ways in which the disciplinary field develops, to ensure that its language, terms and concepts are as appropriately critiqued and queried as have (in retrospect) terms such as 'religion'.

RELIGION, SECULARIZATION, AND SACRALIZATION

José Casanova

Much of the difficulty in analyzing processes of secularization, religious transformation and sacralization in our global age derives from the tendency to use the dichotomous analytical categories sacred/profane, transcendent/immanent, and religious/secular, as if they would be synonymous and interchangeable, when in fact they correspond to historically distinctive, somewhat overlapping but not synonymous or equivalent social systems of classification. The sacred tends to be immanent in pre-axial societies, transcendence is not necessarily religious in some axial civilizations, and obviously some secular reality (the nation, citizenship, the individual, inalienable rights to life and freedom) can be sacred in the modern secular age.

Sacred and profane, following Durkheim, should be viewed as a general dichotomous classificatory scheme of all reality, characteristic of all pre-axial human societies, encompassing within one single order what later will be distinguished as three separate realms: the cosmic, the social and the moral. All reality, what we later will learn to distinguish as the gods or spirits, nature and cosmic forces, humans and other animal species, and the political, social, and moral orders are integrated into a single order of things according precisely to the dichotomous classificatory system of sacred and profane. The entire system, moreover, is an immanent "this worldly" one, if one is allowed to use anachronistically another dichotomous category that will only emerge precisely with the axial revolutions.

What defines the axial revolutions is precisely the introduction of a new classificatory scheme that results from the emergence of "transcendence", of an order, principle, or being, beyond this worldly reality, which now can serve as a transcendent principle to evaluate, regulate, and possibly transform this worldly reality. As in the case of the Platonic world of "ideas", or the Confucian reformulation of the Chinese *tao*, transcendence is not necessarily "religious," nor does all "religion" need to become transcendent, if we are allowed once again to use anachronistically another dichotomous classificatory category, "religious/secular" that will first emerge within Medieval Christendom and will later expand into a central dynamic of secular modernity.

All axial revolutions introduce some form of transcendent path, individual and collective, of salvation, redemption, or moral perfection "beyond human flourishing". However, not all axial paths entail some kind of refashioning or transformation of the world or the social order. In some cases, as in Buddhism, this transcendent path may entail a radical devaluation and rejection of all reality and a flight from this world, as analyzed by Max Weber. But, according to Charles Taylor's analysis, all of them entail some refashioning of "the self", who is now "called" to live (or precisely to deny herself) according to some transcendent norm beyond human flourishing. In the case of the radical transcendent monotheism introduced by the prophets in Ancient Israel, the axial revolution entails a de-sacralization of all cosmic, natural, and social reality, of all creatures, gods and idols for the sake of the exclusive sacralization of Yahweh, the transcendent creator God.

1. *Western Christian Secularization*

Within this perspective, the religious/secular dichotomy is a particular medieval Christian version of the more general axial dichotomous classification of transcendent and immanent orders of reality. Unique to the medieval system of Latin Christendom is the institutionalization of an ecclesiastical-sacramental system of mediation, the Church, between the transcendent *Civitas Dei* and the immanent *Civitas hominis*, St. Agustin's well-known radical formulation of the irremediable chasm between two worlds that is common to most axial civilizations. The church can play this mediating role precisely because it partakes of both realities. As *Ecclesia invisibilis*, "the communion of the saints", the Christian church is an "spiritual" reality, part of the eternal transcendent City of God. As *Ecclesia visibilis*, the Christian church is in the *saeculum*, a "temporal" reality and thus part of the immanent city of man.

The modern Western process of secularization is a particular historical dynamic that only makes sense as a response and reaction to this particular medieval Latin Christian system of classification of all reality into "spiritual" and "temporal", "religious" and "secular." The term secularization, in this respect, derives from a unique Western Christian theological category, that of the *saeculum*, which has no equivalent term not only in other world religions, but even in Eastern Christianity.

As Charles Taylor has clearly shown, the historical process of modern secularization begins as a process of internal secular reform within Latin Christendom, as an attempt to "spiritualize" the temporal and to bring the religious life of perfection out of the monasteries into the *saeculum*, thus literally, as an attempt to secularize the religious. The process of spiritualization of temporal-secular reality entails also a process of interiorization of religion, and thus a certain de-ritualization, de-sacralization or de-magicization of religion, which in the particular case of Christianity takes naturally the form of de-sacramentalization and de-ecclesialization of religion. The repeated attempts at Christian reform of the *saeculum* began with the papal revolution and continued with the emergence of the spiritual orders of mendicant and preaching friars bent on Christianizing the growing medieval towns and cities and with the emergence of lay Christian communities of brothers and sisters, committed to a life of Christian perfection in the *saeculum*, in the world. These medieval movements of Christian reform already established the basic patterns of secularization which will be later radicalized by the accumulative processes of secularization brought first by the Protestant Reformation and then, from the French Revolution on, by all subsequent modern civilizing and reform processes.

It is important to realize, therefore, that the historical process of Western secularization begins as a process of internal religious reform within Medieval Christianity. But this historical process of secularization becomes radicalized later, first by the Protestant Reformation and then by the French Revolution. The process of religious reform of the Protestant Reformation, as well as the processes of secular/laicist reform initiated by the French Revolution, both are explicitly directed against Catholicism and against the ecclesiastical structures of mediation between transcendent and immanent, spiritual and secular/temporal reality, which the Catholic Church claimed as its exclusive institutional monopoly. In different ways both paths lead to an overcoming of the medieval Catholic dualism by a positive affirmation and revaluation of the *saeculum*, that is, of the secular age and the secular world, imbuing the *saeculum* with a quasi-transcendent meaning as the place for human flourishing.

The Protestant path, which will attain its paradigmatic manifestation in the Anglo-Saxon Calvinist cultural area, particularly in the United States, is characterized by a blurring of the boundaries and by a mutual reciprocal infusion of the religious and the secular, in a sense making the religious secular and the secular religious. It takes also a form of radical de-sacramentalization which will assume an extreme form with the radical sects in their attempt to dismantle all ecclesiastical institutions and to turn the *ecclesia* into a merely secular association of visible "saints". This Anglo-Saxon pattern of secularization does not entail necessarily the decline of religion. On the contrary, as the history of the United States clearly shows, from the American Revolution till the present processes of radical social change and secular modernization have often been accompanied by "great awakenings" and by religious growth.

The French-Latin-Catholic path, by contrast, will take the form of laicization, and is basically marked by a civil-ecclesiastical, and laic-clerical antagonistic dynamic. This explains the central role of anti-clericalism in the Catholic pattern. Unlike in the Protestant pattern, here the boundaries between the religious and the secular are rigidly maintained, but those boundaries are pushed into the margins, aiming to contain, privatize and marginalize everything religious, while excluding it from any visible presence in the secular public sphere. When the secularization of monasteries takes place first during the French Revolution and later in subsequent liberal revolutions, the explicit purpose of breaking the monastery walls, is not to bring the religious life into the secular world, but rather to laicize those religious places, dissolving and emptying their religious content and making the religious persons, monks and nuns, civil and laic before forcing them into the world, now conceived as merely a secular place emptied of religious symbols and religious meanings. This could well serve as the basic metaphor of all subtraction narratives of secular modernity, built upon secularist prejudices which tend to understand the secular as merely the space left behind when this-worldly reality is emptied of religion or to view unbelief as resulting simply from the progress of science and rational inquiry.

Even within Western secular modernity one can find, therefore, two very different patterns of secularization, one could even say two different types of secular modernity. This would be the basic underlying reality behind the different European and American patterns of secularization. But both can be viewed as pattern variables within the same basic post-Christian pattern of Western secularization. Moreover, using Taylor's analytical framework, both are embedded within a common immanent frame and within the same secular age.

2. *Global Secularizations*

It just happened, of course, as we are becoming increasingly aware, that this particular historical pattern of Western Christian secularization became globalized through the no less particular historical process of European colonial expansion. As a result the immanent frame became in a certain sense globalized, at least certain crucial aspects of the cosmic order through the globalization of science and technology, certain crucial aspects of the institutional social order of state, market and public sphere, and certain crucial aspects of the moral order through the globalization of individual human rights. But the process of European colonial expansion encountered other post-axial civilizations with very different social imaginaries, which often had their own established patterns of reform in accordance with their own particular axial civilizational principles and norms. The outcomes that will result form these long historical dynamics of inter-civilizational encounters, conflicts, borrowings, accommodations and *aggiornamentos* are likely to change from place to place, from time to time, and from civilization to civilization.

Moreover, one could argue following Peter van der Veer that the very pattern of Western secularization cannot be fully understood if one ignores the crucial significance of the colonial encounter in European developments. Indeed the best of post-colonial analysis has shown how every master reform narrative and every genealogical account of Western secular modernity, needs to take account those colonial and inter-civilizational encounters. Any comprehensive narrative of the modern civilizing process must take into account the Western European encounter with other civilizations. The very category of civilization in the singular only emerges out of these inter-civilizational encounters.

This becomes even clearer the moment one attempts a genealogical reconstruction of the unique modern secular category of "religion", which has now also become globalized. The modern secular invention of the "world religions" and the disciplinary institutionalization of the scientific study of religion are intimately connected with this globalization of religion. But one should be careful and avoid turning an essentialized secular modernity into the dynamic causal force of everything, including religion. One must simply recognize that there are no bounded histories within nation states, within civilizations or within religions. Even much of the master reform process of medieval

Christianity, as well as the renaissance and recovery of the memory of Greek and Roman antiquity, which have now become an integral part of the collective European past, are not fully intelligible without taking into account the Christian-European encounter with Islam and the many civilizational borrowings it acquired through such encounter.

Furthermore, Christian missions always accompanied European colonialism. Even in the case of French Republican colonialism, *l'Etat laïque* and *l'Eglise Catolique,* which were constantly at loggerheads at home, worked hand in hand in *la mission civilatrice* in the French colonies, whether in Muslim Algier, in pre-axial Madagascar, or in Buddhist Vietnam. In any case, even without looking at any particular outcome of the colonial encounter between Western, Christian and post-Christian, secular modernity and other civilizations, one can confidently say that generally the outcome is unlikely to have been simply the emptying of the non-Western and the superimposition of modern Western secular patterns and social imaginaries. Nor was it possible to simply reject the colonial encounter and preserve one's own civilizational patterns and social imaginaries unaffected by Western secular modernity. The modern secular immanent frame may become globalized, but this will always happen as an interactive dynamic interlocking, transforming and refashioning of pre-existing non-Western civilizational patterns and social imaginaries with Western modern secular ones. Moreover, in the same way as "our" modern secular age is fundamentally and inevitably post-Christian. The emerging multiple modernities in the different post-axial civilizational areas are likely to be post-Hindu, or post-Confucian, or post-Muslim, that is, they will also be a modern refashioning and transformation of already existing civilizational patterns and social imaginaries.

From this perspective and now adopting a necessarily fictitious global point of view, one can observe three different, parallel, yet inter-related global processes which are in tension and often come in open conflict with one another.

There is, firstly, a global process of secularization which can best be characterized as the global expansion of what Charles Taylor has characterized as "the secular immanent frame", which is constituted by the structural interlocking constellation of the cosmic, social and moral modern secular orders.

The cosmic order is configured as a disenchanted, impersonal, vast and unfathomable, yet scientifically discoverable and explainable, as well as technologically manipulable universe, which is nevertheless paradoxically open to all kinds of moral meanings, can evoke in us the numinous experience of a *mysterium tremendum* and *fascinosum* as well as a mystical sense of a profound unity of our inner nature with outer Nature and the entire cosmic universe.

The social order is comprehended as a self-constituted and socially constructed impersonal and instrumentally rational order of mutual benefit of individuals coming together to meet their needs and fulfill their ends. In the process those individual agents establish collectively new specifically modern forms of sociation, the most prominent of which are the market economy, the public sphere and the citizenship "democratic" state, all being characterized in principle by immediate, direct and equal access.

The moral order is built around the image of the "buffered" self, a disengaged and disciplined rational agent equally impervious to external animated sources and in control of its own inner passions and desires, ruled either by utilitarian calculus in the pursuit of individual happiness or by universalistic maxims inspired and empowered to beneficence not only by a rational impartial view of things but by the discovery of human dignity, sympathy and solidarity. All three orders are understood as purely immanent secular orders, devoid of transcendence, and thus functioning *etsi Deus non daretur*. It is this phenomenological experience that, according to Taylor, constitutes our age paradigmatically as a secular one, irrespective of the extent to which people living in this age may still hold religious or theistic beliefs.

But as the ongoing debates between the European and American paradigms and the discourse of American and European "exceptionalisms" make clear, this process of secularization within the very same immanent frame may entail very different "religious" dynamics.

3. *Global Religious Denominationalism*

Parallel to this process, which started as a historical process of internal secularization within Western Christendom, but was later globalized through the European colonial expansion, there is a process of constitution of a global system of "religions" which can best be understood as a process of global religious denominationalism, whereby all the so-called "world religions" are redefined and transformed in contraposition to "the secular" through interrelated reciprocal processes of particularistic differentiation, universalistic claims and mutual recognition.

4. *Global Sacralizations*

But the modern "secular" is by no means synonymous with the "profane" nor is the "religious" synonymous with the modern "sacred". Only "the social as religious" is synonymous with the sacred in Durkheimian terms. In this respect, modern secularization entails a certain profanation of religion through its privatization and individualization and a certain sacralization of the secular spheres of politics (sacred nation, sacred citizenship, sacred constitution), science (temples of knowledge), and economics (through commodity fetishism). But the truly modern sacralization, which constitutes the global civil religion in Durkheim's terms, is the cult of the individual and the sacralization of humanity through the globalization of human rights.

It is an open empirical question, which should be the central focus of a comparative-historical sociology of religion, how these three ongoing global processes of secularization, sacralization, and religious denominationalism are mutually interrelated in different civilizations, sometimes symbiotically as in the fusions of religious nationalisms, or in the religious defense of human rights, but often antagonistically as in the violent conflicts between the sacred secular immanent norms (of individual life and freedom) and transcendent theistic norms.

MULTI-MEDIA PERFORMANCE

REFLECTING RELIGIOUS DYNAMICS. ECHOES FROM ANCIENT EAST-WEST ENCOUNTERS

Heinz Georg Held

The following text is the slightly modified script of a performance given at the start of the conference, entitled "An audio-visual Journey through the Parthian Age". The thematic focus on what appears to be a marginal episode within the long and wide-ranging history of Euro-Asian East-West encounters is intended as an example. On the one hand, the Parthian Age, stretching from the third pre-Christian up until the third post-Christian century, and in which the cultural driving forces of the preceding Achaemenid and the subsequent Sassanid era culminate[1], offers a significantly broad spectrum of religious contacts, conflicts and transfers and thus varied forms of transmission, condensation, hybridization, differentiation and suppression of religious ideas and cult practices. On the other hand, the historiographic tradition represents a negative imagology[2] developed insistently since antiquity and whose terminology and vocabulary have also become milestones in a permanent East-West demarcation. Far beyond the contemporary context, the Hellenic-Persian concepts of the enemy which consolidate in the Roman-Parthian Age and communicate themselves in their intensified Byzantine-Sassanid form in the Islamic Age, have inscribed their reciprocal identifications into the collective imaginations of both

---

[1] Josef Wiesehöfer, *The Arsacid Empire: Sources and Documentation*, Stuttgart: Franz Steiner 1998; Rémy Boucharlat, ed., *Les Parthes*, Dijon: Remy Faton 2002; Hans Wilhelm Haussig, *Die Geschichte Zentralasiens und der Seidenstraße in vorislamischer Zeit,* 2nd reviewed and extended edition, Darmstadt: Wissenschaftliche Buchgesellschaft 1992, 185–241.

[2] Tonio Hölscher, (ed.), *Gegenwelten zu den Kulturen Griechenlands und Roms in der Antike*, München/Leipzig: Saur 2000, in particular the contributions by Hans-Joachim Gehrke, "Gegenbild und Selbstbild: Das europäische Iran-Bild zwischen Griechen und Mullahs", 85–109; Renate Schlesier, "Menschen und Götter unterwegs: Rituale und Reise in der griechischen Antike", 129–157; Alain Schnapp, "Pourquois les Barbares n'ont-ils point d'images?", 205–216; Tonio Hölscher, "Feindwelten – Glückswelten: Perser, Kentauren und Amazonen", 287–320; further A. Kuhrt, *'Greek' and 'Greece' in Mesopotamian and Persian Perspectives*, Oxford: Head Press 2002; Wiesehöfer, Josef and Huyse, Philip (eds.), *Eran und Aneran. Studien zu ost-westlichen Kulturkontakten in sasanidischer Zeit*, Stuttgart: Franz Steiner 2006.

civilizations. In the course of a continued political mythologization, "Europe" and "Asia" were condensed into monolithic blocks for religious reasons too. The oriental influence on "Europe" and the occidental influence on the "Middle East" did not just shape the history of the "world religions", but equally the way in which they are regarded in the history of religions.

Current research is exploring a scientific approach which is able to escape from the bias of these century-old constructions. As is well known, one of the characteristics of political mythology is that constructors and deconstructors work on it hand in hand.[3] The successful establishment of national, cultural and religious identities is based on a dense network of relationships that can only be untangled if the interdependence of differrent components – the materials, the collective driving forces, the narrative, out of which it is woven – become identifiable.[4] In all of this, the understanding of the different discursive and media techniques and their respective individual semiotic dynamics play a key role. In fact it is not hard to prove that political as well as religious constructs often return to similar figurations of the 'imaginaire collective' over and beyond long periods of time. What is more difficult to explain is how these patterns – democracy and tyranny, the realm of the evil and world of decadence, religious and secular society – always enjoy new appeal, why, instead of losing suggestive power, they can actually increase their efficiency through semantic recycling, through a religiously or politically charged 'remploi'.[5] Perhaps, by mediologically expanding the historical and sociological analysis to systematically include written, visual and sound media we could learn more.[6] Maybe accordingly correlative studies of the media "transmissions" – the representations, translocations, memorizations – particularly in areas of dynamic religious contacts could help to shed light on the far-reaching and reality-defining symboliza-

[3] Jean-Jacques Wunenburger, "Mytho-phorie. Formes et transformations du mythe", *Reliologiques* 10 (1994): 49–70; Christopher G. Flood, *Political Myth. A Theoretical Introduction*, New York/London: Garland 1996, 3–12.

[4] Bruno Latour, *Nous n'avons jamais été modernes. Essai d'anthropologie symétrique*, Paris La Découverte 1991, 9–18.

[5] Salvatore Settis, *Les remplois, Patrimoine, temps, espace*, Paris: Francois Furet (ed.), 1996, 67–86.

[6] Jean-Jacques Wunenburger, *La vie des images*, Strasbourg: Presses Universitaires de Grenoble 1995; Regis Debray, *Introduction à la Médiologie*, Paris: Presses Universitaires de France 2000, 12–31; Hans Belting, *Bild-Anthropologie. Entwürfe für eine Bildwissenschaft*, München: Fink 2001, 11–55.

tion processes which have become sedimented in the key terms of the major narratives – such as "Asia" and "Europe".

The performance aims to express conditions for and possibilities of mediological perception through the interplay and reciprocal impact of different media visually on stage. As it is not possible to include visual or audio material in this publication, the following text has had to limit itself to brief stage directions. In line with the essay-style form, apart from rudimentary source references, there is no critical analysis of the research literature or bibliographic references.

1. *Parthia*

At the front end of the hall there is a slightly raised, elongated podium, above it a screen (more screens on the side wall of the hall), in the corner a lectern and technical equipment too. Before and during the first sequence the actor has gone back and forth several times between the rear part of the hall and the podium, has had to push his way through the members of the audience as they come into the hall, has carried various books, folders, documents etc. to the podium and put them down on the table. Goes back and forth between the podium and the lectern, checks the equipment. Keeps looking at the screen as he does so. Finally, he sits down at the table on the podium, adjusts the note-book into the right position, watches the monitor until the end of the first sequence. The first sequence (in the form of a museum "slide show") has now been shown twice and then one more time half-way through.

MUSIC: KRECH, IMPROVISATIONS, THROUGHOUT THE ENTIRE SEQUENCE

SLIDES: ARCHITECTURES, RELIGIOUS SYMBOLS, COINS FROM THE PARTHIAN AGE

Show intertitle: PARTHIA

Show intertitle: WHY PARTHIA?

The Parthians, originally a nomadic people from what is now Turkmenistan and that reigned over a world empire between the Hindu Kush and Palestine from 230 B.C. to 224 A.D., have not been particularly popular in either Eastern or Western historiography. Politically and culturally, after the Achaemenid Persians and the Seleucid intermezzo, the Parthians came into the legacy of the Mesopotamian Empires, which has stood the test of time through the subsequent Sassanid Age and into the period of Islam. In their multicultural empire, alongside the trade languages of Aramaic and Greek and the administrative language Parthian, Persian, Sogdian, Choresmian, Bactrian, Babylonian and Armenian have equal status; people use a variety of scripts and writing systems to communicate.

After artists from Greece and Asia Minor left traces of their activities as far back as the 5th and 4th centuries, a range of syncretistic forms develops – notably in the urban centres: Edessa, Dura-Europos, Hatra, Ctesiphon-Seleucia, Susa, Persepolis, Nisa, Bactria, Samarkand – which fall back on Babylonian, Egyptian, Indian, Scythian and Hellenistic traditions. The Old Persian myths are first written down by the Parthians, and thereby transmitted to classical Persian literature and thanks to Arabic translations to European medieval literature. However, later Persian historiography portrayed the Parthians as usurpers whilst Roman sources see them as uncivilized barbarians.

Show intertitle: Why Parthian Age?

What appears as the "Middle East" from a European – and American – perspective is characterized at this time by dense religious networks: Ancestor worship joins with philosophical-rational notions of God; archaic cults, monotheistic trends of varying origin all meet in a cosmopolitan polytheistic pantheon. Shamanism, mystery and revealed religions interconnect in the ruler cult to become an overarching political theology. New religious ideas developed here out of archaic traditions, new religious sects emigrated from here to the far west and the far east. The later "world religions" – as they are known – Judaism, Zoroastrianism and Buddhism were modified here by mutual encounter and interconnection, Christianity and Manichaeism formed during this time through reciprocal confrontation, adaptation and disassociation. This religious interference corresponds with a long, continuing coexistence and cooperation between different cultures within the Parthian Empire: On the broad fertile planes, in the barren steppes, in the oases of the unending deserts, in the impassable high mountain regions, on the coasts of the seas, the rivers and lakes, ethnicities and communities with extremely different ways of life have crossed paths since time immemorial. They compliment one another economically, even if not without conflicts: nomads, semi-nomadic livestock producers and settled arable farmers, urban populations with a high degree of division of labour, merchants, who communicate with their immediate neighbours but also with the farthest regions, mercenaries and priests from local and cross-regional groups.

The region is a prime example of a permanent conflict situation, in which insistent concepts of the enemy are produced as weapons for an ideological "arms race" and which condense into a sustained East-West opposition, seeking affirmation in religious identities; however it is also a prime example of synchronic and diachronic religious exchange, of reciprocal integration, renewal, expansion, reflection and self-reflection amongst religious beliefs, in short of dynamics in the history of religions.

2. *Dynamics*

Actor has gone to the lectern to switch off the "slide show", now appears on all screens. Goes back to the podium and sits down, looks at the monitor of the note-book. Dissatisfied, unconvinced:

So that was "Parthian Age"... *Clicks the keyboard.* God knows why these Parthians were so unpopular. *Continues clicking, then suddenly stands up, goes to the lectern, walks back, sits back down, somewhat bewildered.* But why "dynamics"? *Clicks again, then suddenly snaps the lid of the notebook shut.* What do "dynamics" actually mean? *Grabs one of the books in front of him, reads briefly, puts it back down takes another, quotes* "Dynamics ...": Relating to the existence or action of forces; applied esp. to a theory that accounts for matter, or for mind, as being merely the action of forces: see "dynamism 1". Let's see ... dynamism 1, dynamism 1. Here we are. *Quotes:* Dynamic theory of Kant, a theory according to which matter was conceived to be constituted by two antagonistic principles of attraction and repulsion ... Aha ... *Reads again, paraphrases:* Friction generates heat, heat energy, then that leads to eruptions, then every thing goes quiet again. *Short pause.* Yes, we know that ... *Takes another book.* "Psychodynamics"... Dynamik – unbewußte Triebdynamik: ökonomische und topographische Gesichtspunkte ... "Rücksicht auf Darstellbarkeit"... "Rücksicht auf Darstellbarkeit"– yes, that's the problem. *Continous reading. Pause.* But that's too long to quote. *Opens the lid of the note-book again, types in something, waits a moment, stands up to pick up a folder lying on the edge of the table, walks with it to the lectern. With a slightly raised voice, as if starting a speech:* "Dynamics in the history of religion" ... *Stops, goes back to the podium, looks at the monitor, sits down. Starts again* "Dynamics in the history of religion between Asia and Europe" ... *Slowly, contemplative, considering* "Encounters, Notions, and Comparative Perspectives" ... *Interrupts his train of thought, nervous:* What does it mean, "Dynamics" – Dynamics – Dynamics? ... Religious dynamics in history or the historical dynamics of the religious, no: just "of religions". Dynamics of religions. Are there any without historical dynamics? Ok, those "between Asia and Europe" definitely have history, otherwise there wouldn't be a "between". But what's the point here? – Historical dynamics which influence the development of these religions? Or rather … *Leafs through the folder* "mutual dependency", "inter-religious contacts", that's good: so in the mutually dependent development, "religious interference", in the overarching and interlocking networks … maybe a bit simpler … *Makes a note of something, stops and thinks a moment.* By the way, where exactly is the frontier between … *takes another book* … and since when we distinguish … *still another book* … and what does it mean, "Asia", "Europe" … *read:* Agenor, son of Lybia, went from Egypt to Canaan … Zeus, Crete, Minoan culture … that's curious: Europe comes from Asia … Maybe you can't actually separate the two. *Pause, then reads on in the folder* "religious identities" as constructs … constructed by whom? *Reads on* By oneself and by others: "interconnections of self-perception and perception by the other" … the other, the Other … *to himself* Ok, and who are we in this "religious interference" ? – the others – or the completely other Others? *Reads on* "hermeneutics oriented mutual understanding". That's good. *Pause* Mutual understanding … *not sarcastic, more confused* who's really supposed to understand? *Reads on* "Reflection and self-reflection of religious ideas"… *Repeats it to himself in German* "Reflexion und Selbstreflexion religiöser Vorstellungen". Vorstellung: idea, imagination, projection, performance … *Reflects for a moment himself, then puts the folder down on the table, slightly unnerved.* A problem with translation, a problem with transmission … transmission means: representation, translocation, memorisation … All right, let's have a look … *Types something short into the notebook, goes to the lectern, operates the equipment. The film starts.*

3. *Apotheosis*

MUSIC: HOLST, SATURN

SLIDES: MAP, ARIAL IMAGES, LANDSCAPES, CYLINDER SEAL ETANA

Show intertitle: APOTHEOSIS

It is from Mesopotamia that we have the oldest known description to date of an ascension into heaven. Etana, whom Ištar, the Goddess of Fertility, and Enlil, the God of the Atmosphere appointed King over the city of Kish and "shepherd" of their people remained without an heir, despite his prayers and sacrifices.

Quote (archaic, rhythmic; not modernised):

> Etana kept on beseeching Shamash day after day.
> O Shamash, you have dined from my fattest sheep!
> O Netherworld, you have drunk of the blood of my sacrificed lambs!
> O Lord, give the command!
> Grant me the plant of birth!
> Reveal to me the plant of birth!
> Relieve me of my burden, grant me an heir!

Shamash made ready to speak and said to Etana:

> Find a pit, look inside,
> An eagle is cast within it.
> He will reveal to you the plant of birth.

Etana went his way.

> He found the pit, he looked inside
> The eagle was cast within it
> There he was for him to bring up!

In his search for the plant of birth, Etana leaves the earthly sphere and ascends into heaven with the help of the eagle.

Quote:

> Great indeed was the burden upon him.
> When he bore him aloft one league,
> The eagle said to him, to Etana:
> "Look, my friend, how the land is now
> Examine the sea, look for its boundaries
> The land is hills …
> The sea has become a stream".
> When he had borne him aloft a second league,
> The eagle said to him, said to Etana,
> "Look, my friend, how the land is now!
> The land is a hill".
> When he had borne him aloft a third league,
> The eagle said to him, said to Etana,
> "Look, my friend, how the land is now!"
> "The sea has become a gardener's ditch".

Ascending higher and higher, they both arrive at the gates of heaven.

Quote:

> After they had ascended to the heaven of Anu,
> They passed through the gates of Anu, Enlil and Ea,
> The eagle and Etana did obeisance together …[7]

and after having happily gone through them the fragment ends abruptly. From the text itself, we do not know whether the King's transcendental journey of discovery was successful or not. The history of religions does at least ascribe him an abundant offspring. In the area around the Euphrates and Tigris, which from a bird's eye view stretches from the Persian Gulf across the Syrian desert to Lebanon, religious beliefs from the Sumerian, Arcadian, Elamite, Assyrian, Babylonian and Hittite civilizations partly replaced, overlapped, added to and modified each other over a period of several millennia, and condensated into lasting traditions. What most certainly dates back even further is the idea that the mystery of life only reveals itself in the other world, and that whoever wishes to learn the truth must prepare carefully and undergo several tests to find the way there – and above all: in order to be able to return afterwards. Typical of the development and changes in religious practice are the measures taken to prepare for the encounter with the Other: the mental preparation, the intoxicants, incantations, images, rhythms and sounds which mark the process. The dynamic of crossing over has a meditative inward and an ecstatic outward focus. It plunges downwards into the depths, to the origins and perpetual strength of the forefathers and also upwards into the heights, to the celestial whose interstellar network determines present and future.

MUSIC: HOLST, NEPTUNE

SLIDES: MAP, VANTH, HELIOS, CHARIOT OF THE SUN

In the far west, in an outer district of the Greek hemisphere, which stages a virtually "classical" clash of cultures in the course of its intense war preparations around 500 years before Christ, another equally as perilous and momentous ascension is possible with the help of other "flying companions" who now point to the Sun God.

Quote (like epic song):

[7] Etana fragment, tablet II, IV.

> The mares which carry me, as far as ever my heart may desire,
> Were escorting me, when they brought and placed me on the resounding road
> Of the goddess, which carries through all places the man who knows.
> On it I was carried; for on it the well-discerning horses
> Were straining the chariot and the maidens were leading the way.
>
> There are the gates [separating] the ways of day and night
> And they are enclosed by a lintel and a threshold of stone;
> And the aetherial gates themselves are covered with big wing-doors,
> Of which Dike, whose vengeance is stern, possesses the rewarding keys.
> The maidens appeased her with gentle words.
>
> And the goddess received me gladly and took in her hand my right hand
> And addressed to me the following words:
> 'O young man coming to our abode joined with immortal charioteers
> With the horses which carry you,
> Welcome! since it is by no means an evil lot that sent you forth to travel
> On this road (for it is far away from the wandering of men),
> But right and justice. It is necessary that you shall learn all things,
> As well the unshaken heart of well-rounded truth
> As the opinions of mortals in which there is no true belief.'[8]

At this point, the Parmenides' account also comes to an abrupt end. Pity. Later philosophers and historians of religion have attempted to reconstruct the revelation of the nameless goddess out of different fragments. Some believe that this is where Western logic was invented, thinking in binary structures, which gives the political mythology of right and wrong, good and evil an appearance of rationality.

MUSIC: HELLAWELL, ON BLACK AND WHITE

SLIDES: AHURAMAZDA, RELIEF DARIOS, HERACLES

Centuries before – we don't know exactly – far away in the East, right at the edge of the regions which were soon to become the Persian Empire, another philosophical-religious author had meditated on the same opposites constructing the system of a fundamental dualism encompassing the entire cosmos.

Quote (with existentialistic pathos):

> This I ask Thee, tell me plainly, O Ahura:
> Who is through His begetting the primal father of Truth?
> Who assigned the course of the sun and of the stars (its proper place)?

[8] Parmenides, fragment B1, 1–30.

> Who (is He) through whom the moon (now) waxes, now wanes?
> These (are) the very (things) I wish to know, and other (things), O Wise One.
> This I ask Thee, tell me plainly, O Ahura:
> Which artist assigned both, light and darkness?
> This I ask Thee, tell me plainly, O Ahura:
> That religion which is the best (among the religions) of those who exist (and) which, in agreement with truth, might promote my herds.
> When the two warring hosts will confront each other
> because of those rules which Thou wishest to establish, O Wise One,
> to which side of the two (sides), to whom wilt Thou assign the victory?[9]

The fully good god Ahura Mazdā, who is depicted in Persian-Parthian iconography as a winged sun, stands opposite the fully evil demon of lies Angra Mainyu, often depicted with monstrous tongues, who leads humans to orgiastic rituals and bloody animal sacrifices during worship and to mistakes and erroneous decisions in social and political life. The incessant battle between the two principles develops a historical dynamic, which strives for a universal final judgement. At the end of all time, the evil people and powers will be burned by a holy fire; and the good will have eternal life. In the history of religions this is a revolutionary thought that the "shepherd of the peoples" must accommodate in one way or another.

Quote:

> I am Darius, the great king, king of kings, king in Persia, king of the countries, the son of Hystaspes, the grandson of Arsames, an Achaemenid.
>
> Proclaims Darius, the king: By the favour of Auramazdā I am king; upon me Auramazdā bestowed the kingship.
>
> Proclaims Darius, the king: Auramazdā bestowed this kingship upon me; Auramazdā brought me aid, until I had held together this kingdom. By the favour of Auramazdā I hold this kingdom.[10]

Music: Mesomedes of Crete, Hymnos to Phoebos

With this reasoning the ruler is not just the representative of a divine order in the specific present, but also the temporal incarnation of a providential history. His actions and accomplishments – set in stone, celebrated in hymns, recorded in writings – are measured against his role in the fight against Evil by the Gods and posterity.

[9] The Gathas of Zarathustra, IX, 5, 6, 10, 15.
[10] Inscription DNa, Nagash-e Rostam.

SLIDES: ANCIENT ALEXANDER ICONOGRAPHY, MODERN ADAPTATIONS

Alexander, the Macedonian, whom ancient history gave the dubious epithet "The Great" – in Zoroastrian literature he is given the title "the cursed Greek" – Alexander's success story is a very mixed one. His record is terrific when you look at his global performance as a reflection of the social imaginary. For culture history his campaign is certainly of less importance than later "orientalists" are wont to claim, he did not bring about a "hellenistic turn", first and foremost, as his contemporaries and the generations immediately after him report, he was a humanitarian catastrophe. Even the successor Diadoch kingdoms have remained a relatively insignificant episode from a long term historico-cultural perspective. Hellenistic trends left their mark before, alongside and independently of the mercenary armies, veteran settlements and the residences of the military dictators in various amalgamations. Of far greater significance was a cult transfer from east to west: the iconography of rulers based on a rather archaic but certainly forward-looking political theology. Alexander was at great pains to prove that he was of divine descent. As early as in ancient historiography, his detour to Egypt is interpreted as a political maneuver intended to bring about his apotheosis even before the world domination he planned materialized and thus to prepare the success of his campaign in advance through propaganda.

Quote (journalistic):

> Then Alexander went to the temple of Jupiter Ammon, to consult the oracle about the event of his future proceedings, and his own parentage. For his mother Olympias had confessed to her husband Philip, that "she had conceived Alexander, not by him, but by a serpent of extraordinary size." Philip, too, towards the end of his life, had publicly declared that "Alexander was not his son;" and he accordingly divorced Olympias, as having been guilty of adultery. Alexander, therefore, anxious to obtain the honour of divine paternity, and to clear his mother from infamy, instructed the priests, by messengers whom he sent before him, what answers he wished to receive. The priests, as soon as he entered the temple, saluted him as the son of Ammon. Alexander, pleased with the god's adoption of him, directed that he should be regarded as his son. He was told that "success in all his wars, and dominion over the world, was granted him." A response was also given by the oracle to his attendants, that "they should reverence Alexander as a god, and not as a king."[11]

[11] Iustin, XI, 11.

By transferring the sacral consecrations of a political reign intended to serve the deities and a superhuman order principle onto the real person, the human role-fulfiller and dignitary, his body doubles in size, which now functions as a thrice-fold figure: as a physically real human being, as a symbolical institutional being, and as an spiritually immortal being. His real presence becomes an epiphany which transcends the symbolic order of the temple and the palace and consequently should constantly renew and consolidate his real power. His political agenda becomes a divine mission which can and must find its legitimacy through religious punctuation alone: For the archaic festival of the New Year, the festival of the old gods governed by Ahuramazdā, the envoys of the subjugated nations bring symbolic gifts to the King of Kings and the representative of the divine world order.

Quote (in the tone of a government declaration):

> Proclaims Dareios, the king: this which I have done, by the favour of Auramazdā in one and the same year I have done it.
>
> You, whosoever shall read this inscription hereafter, let what has been done by me convince you, lest you should esteem Falsehood.
>
> You, whosoever hereafter shall look at this inscription which I have written down, or these sculptures, do not destroy them; as long as you shall be vigorous, thus care for them![12]

In the Roman sphere, the apotheosis of the Ceasers goes hand in hand with persuasive programmes of images, which in the fora, in the topographical heart of the public political stage demonstrate their successes in order to justify them being culturally revered. The ruler cult is not a religion in its own right, but a trans-religious system that is compatible with a whole range of different beliefs and ritual traditions. Thanks to its politically stabilizing function, it is in a position to integrate the most differing cults, even conflicting religious trends simultaneously or one after the other.

MUSIC: CHARPENTIER, TE DEUM

SLIDES: AURATIC IMAGES OF RULERS FROM BYZANTINE EMPERORS TO NAPOLEON AND KAISER WILHELM II

The idea of the sacral monarch survived in Europe through the Roman Emperor iconography and the medieval renovatio romana up until the French Revolution and in some European ethnicities even into the 20th century. Religious forms of expression can develop their

[12] Inscription DNb, Naqash-e Rostam.

own dynamic, they can say something more and something other than dogmatics or political context allow. Symbols are exchanged, accentuated in a new way, semantically modified, put into a new context, without losing anything of their charismatic or persuasive effect, to the contrary: iconographic recycling pools and updates the semiotic dynamic even of the forgotten, repressed cultic layers of meaning and transports them into other religious or secularized networks.

SLIDES: EXAMPLES OF THE ADORATION OF THE THREE MAGI

The Oriental-Hellenistic ruler cult thus shaped the Christological iconography in statu nascendi. And of course, they did not miss the opportunity to have the Zoroastrian Magi appear as the original representative of a competing monotheism in the form of a subjugated, tributary ruler. On the other hand it's no coincidence that the first miracle of the "coming God" was to turn water into wine.

SLIDES: EARLY CHRISTIAN SARCOPHAGI WITH DIONYSIAN ICONOGRAPHY, REPRESENTATION OF EUCHARIST

Show subtitle: I AM THE TRUE WINE ..., YE ARE THE BRANCHES: HE THAT ABIDETH IN ME AND IN HIM, THE SAME BRINGETH FORTH MUCH FRUIT: FOR WITHOUT ME YE CAN DO NOTHING (JOHN XV 5)

The Canaanite hypostases of Dionysus and Demeter are definitely excluded.

Show subtitle: WOMAN, WHAT HAVE I TO DO WITH THEE? MINE HOUR IS NOT YET COME. (JOHN II 4)

And at the same time the local and cross-regional mysteries of vegetable fertility are literally incorporated:

Show subtitle: JESUS TOOK BREAD, AND BLESSED IT, AND BRAKE IT, AND GAVE IT TO THE DISCIPLES, AND SAID, TAKE, EAT; THIS IS MY BODY. AND HE TOOK THE CUP, AND GAVE THANKS, AND GAVE IT TO THEM, SAYING, DRINK YE ALL OF IT; FOR THIS IS MY BLOOD OF THE NEW TESTAMENT (MATTHEW XXVI 26–28)

MUSIC: Limenios, 2nd Delphic Hymn to Phoebus

4. *Dionysos*

SLIDES: ANCIENT ICONOGRAPHY OF DIONYSOS, CHRISTIAN AND MODERN ADAPTATIONS

Show intertitle: DIONYSOS

Quote (elegiac):

> Come, blessed Dionysos, bull-faced god conceived in fire,
> Bassareus and Bacchos, many-named master of all.
> You delight in bloody swords and in the holy Maenads,
> as you howl throughout Olympus, O roaring and frenzied Bacchos.
> Armed with thyrsus and wrathful in the extreme, you are honored
> by all the gods and by all the men who dwell upon the earth.
> Come, blessed and leaping god, and bring much joy to all.[13]

The "primeval, two-natured, thrice-born, Bacchic lord", as Dionysos is called by an orphic hymn, is a newcomer on Mount Olympus with archaic features. Animal-like domination by one's physical urges, ecstatic mating calls and screams of terror, bestial tearing apart and consumption of sacrificial animals and orgiastic states of intoxication are attributed to his cult practices as is the binding of the same destructive energies in the civilized ritual feast designed to generate a sense of community in a peace celebration to reconcile gods and humans. However adaptable the god proves to be on his travels, he does however brutally punish anyone who resists his cult: In the tragedy by Euripides the enlightened King Pentheus, who forbids the ecstatic goings on and arrests the god without further ado, is torn to pieces by the Maenads, lead by his own mother. In later Orphism the god himself appears in the role of the victim that is torn to pieces and eaten and then comes back to life in his previous form.

Dionysos demonstrates in exemplary fashion the process of religious dynamics, far beyond his own cultic context, as an attempt to join forces with those numinous, superhuman urges and constantly renew this alliance, to contain their menacing, destructive energies in temples: to bind them by shaping them into language, images, sounds and thus to incorporate their divine energy into oneself and the religious community. As god of media metamorphosis, Dionysos has been able to establish himself in the cultures of both the East and the West, he is fused together with the sun god and bringer of light in both the Seleucid and Ptolemaic ruler cult and served as a model for the Christian belief in the "resurrection of the body". The god appears to have been particularly well received – at least from a Hellenistic perspective – amongst the Persians, whose particularly high regard for unmixed wine however was also judged a sign of decadence. In Hellenistic thought, the "two-shaped" "savage", "warlike" god has colonial

[13] Orphei Hymni, Quandt, 30.

features; his migration eastwards is seen as an exemplary symbol of the civilization of barbaric peoples.

Quote (in the tone of a narrator, animated to fast):

> The Indians were originally nomads who wandering in their wagons inhabit now one and now another part; not dwelling in cities and not reverencing any temples of the gods; but were clothed with the skins of animals slain in the chase. They also used as food what game they had captured, eating it raw, before, at least, Dionysus came into India. But when Dionysus had come, and become master of India, he founded cities, and gave laws for these cities, and became to the Indians the bestower of wine, as to the Greeks, and taught them to sow their land, giving them seed. Further, Dionysus taught them to reverence other gods, but especially, of course, himself, with clashings of cymbals and beating of drums and dancing in the Satyric fashion, the dance called among Greeks the 'cordax'; and taught them to wear long hair in honour of the god, and instructed them in the wearing of the conical cap and the anointings with perfumes; so that the Indians came out even against Alexander to battle with the sound of cymbals and drums.[14]

Music: Mozart, Entführung aus dem Serail, Overture

As a sign of respect for his divine half-brother, once Alexander reaches the Indian city of Nisa on his military expedition, he decides not to destroy it.

Quote (as above):

> Alexander wished that the legend about the wandering of Dionysus should be believed, as well as that Nysa owed its foundation to that deity, since he had himself reached the place where Dionysus came, and had even advanced beyond the limits of the latter's march. He was now seized with a strong desire of seeing the place where the Nysaeans boasted to have certain memorials of Dionysus. So he went to Mount Merus with the Companion cava lry and the foot guard, and saw the mountain, which was quite covered with ivy and laurel and groves thickly shaded with all sorts of timber, and on it were chases of all kinds of wild animals. The Macedonians made garlands, and crowned themselves with ivy, as they were, singing hymns in honour of Dionysus, and invoking the deity by his various names. Alexander there offered sacrifice to Dionysus, and feasted in company with his companions. Many distinguished Macedonians in attendance upon him, having crowned themselves with ivy, while they were engaged in the invocation of the

[14] Arrian, *Indike* 7, 2–8.

> deity, were seized with the inspiration of Dionysus, uttered cries of Evoi in honour of the god, and acted as Bacchanals[15]

Perhaps his most momentous institution is the theatre, the stage on which the sacrifice is transformed into word and song, simulated as a story and reflected upon as an ethical event.

Music: Euripides, Orestes, Stasimon

Slides: Theatre Architecture, Scenography, Masks Antiquity, Baroque, Present day

Show subtitle: I groan, I groan, thinking of the Blood of your Mother, the Blood that drives you mad.

Good Fortune has no Stability among Mortals: Like the Sail of a speeding Boat, a god Rocks it and Engulfs it in horrible Misfortune, fatal, voracious as the Waves of the Sea.

(Euripides, Orestes, 339–343)

Starting from Athens, the Dionysian "goat song" follows in the tracks of the god westwards and eastwards, and is integrated into existing temples and places of worship in many places and became part of various institutions in later times.

Music: Falkenbach fortissimo

Actor gets up, looks around for help though not at all in panic, seems more amused than anything else, goes to the lectern, fiddles with something, music stops. Short pause.

The theater has never completely left behind its religious dimension, right up to its postmodern derivatives.

Music: Verdi, Otello, Jago's drinking Song

Slights: Ruins of the Theatre of Antiochia

The ambivalent God, in the name of whom the separation of sacrifice and tragedy was completed, has also remained present in the performances that followed subsequently and is constantly poised to convert the symbolic game into reality. Even the political media spectacles of today point to a long Dionysian tradition. In his exemplary biography of Crassus, Plutarch tells,

Quote (the whole next section of narrative charged with tension):

> O Crassus, hair will grow there before thou shalt see Seleucia.[16]
>
> of how the ambitious Roman senator, driven by a thirst for material gain,

[15] Arrian, *Anabasis*, V, 2, 1–7.

[16] Plutarch, *Bioi paralleloi*, Crassus, XVIII, 2.

Quote:

> ... and spent many days weighing exactly the treasures of the goddess in Hierapolis ...[17]

and without sufficient knowledge

Quote:

> the first warning sign came to him from this very goddess, whom some call Venus, others Juno, while others still regard her as the natural cause which supplies from moisture the beginnings and seeds of everything, and points out to mankind the source of all blessings[18]

decides on military intervention against the Parthian Empire. His catastrophic defeat

Quote:

> Crassus was killed by a Parthian named Promaxathres ... In the whole campaign, twenty thousand are said to have been killed, and ten thousand to have been taken alive.[19]

culminates in a kind of reality show, in which the defeated commander plays the leading role.

Quote:

> While this was going on, it happened that Hyrodes was at last reconciled with Artavasdes the Armenia, and there were reciprocal banquets and drinking bouts, at which many Greek compositions were introduced. For Hyrodes was well acquainted both with the Greek language and literature, and Artavasdes actually composed tragedies, and wrote orations and histories, some of which are preserved. Now when the head of Crassus was brought to the king´s door, the tables had been removed, and a tragic actor, Jason by name, of Tralles, was singing that part of the "Bacchae" of Euripides where Agave is about to appear. While he was receiving his applause, Sillaces stood at the door of the banqueting-hall, and after a low obeisance, cast the head of Crassus into the centre of the company. The Parthians lifted it up with clapping of hands and shouts of joy, and at the king's bidding his servants gave Sillaces a seat at the banquet. Then Jason handed his costume of Pentheus to one of the chorus, seized the head of Crassus, and assuming the role of the frenzied Agave, sang these verses through as if inspired:

[17] Plutarch, *Bioi paralleloi*, Crassus, XVIII, 5.
[18] Plutarch, *Bioi paralleloi*, Crassus, XVII, 6.
[19] Plutarch, *Bioi paralleloi*, Crassus, XXXI, 5–7.

We bring from the mountain
A tendril fresh-cut to the palace,
A wonderful prey

This delighted everybody, but when the following dialogue with the chorus was chanted:
(Chorus): Who slew him.
(Agaue): Mine is the honour
Promaxathres, who happened to be one of the banqueters, sprang up and laid hold of the head, feeling that it was more appropriate for him to say this than for Jason. The king was delighted, and bestowed on Promaxathres the customary gifts, while to Jason he gave a talent. With such a farce as this the expedition of Crassus is said to have closed, just like a tragedy.[20]

5. *Mission*

MUSIC: CHRISTIAN HYMN FROM OXYRHYNCHOS

Show intertitle: MISSION

Another great invention, if it happens not to be true, is the tale that – centuries later and now under the banner of Christian condemnation of the Dionysian theatrical spectacle – when the Persians captured Antioch, the Pagan inhabitants, (wrongly) believing themselves to be in security, were watching a theatre performance, whilst the Christians they had been oppressing supported the invaders' attack.

Hostility towards a perceived enemy on both sides, concepts of the enemy which are built up into diametric opposites, are consolidated by more and more new projections and thus unleash a historical dynamic:

Good fighting evil, light against darkness, truth against falsity. Freedom against despotism.

Show intertitle: WHO IS WHO?

The construct "Asia" developed out of ancient orientalisms: as a categorical collective name for numerous "imagined communities", which sought to protect their borders, their identity in the face of another imagined community, notably Europe.

In Antiquity as today an incessant transculturation process circumvents the militant rhetoric – and practice – of the clashes of cultures with constantly new cultural interferences, through a permanent

[20] Plutarch, *Bioi paralleloi*, Crassus, XXXIII, 1–4.

exchange of goods, ideas and experiences forming religious networks which prove to be more durable than the "ore of weapons".

MUSIC: CHRISTIAN HYMN FROM OXYRHYNCHOS

SLIDES: DIFFERENT TYPES OF COINS WITH RELIGIOUS SYMBOLS

Show subtitle: MONUMENTUM EXEGI AERE PERENNIUS

Between the 7th and 4th century wide-ranging communication systems develop which connect the entire Mediterranean area and the Black Sea, Egypt, Palestine and the Arabian peninsular to the "land of 1000 cities", to Bactria and Choresmia, to the Indus, to the Central Asian Steppe, to China.

For long-distance trade the money economy is an important prerequisite. As early as under the Achaemenids, monetarisation of taxes, temple duties, in particular temple prostitution and army salaries takes shape.

Money is not just a practical tool for the trade in goods, as Aristotle notes, but also a form of symbolic communication across wide geographical and cultural distances.

Show subtitle: SHEW ME A PENNY. WHOSE IMAGE AND SUPERSCRIPTION HATH IT? ... RENDER THEREFORE UNTO CAESAR THE THINGS WHICH BE CAESAR'S, AND UNTO GOD THE THINGS WHICH BE GOD'S.

(MATTHEW XXII 15)

BUT SORRY MASTER – WHAT HAPPENS WHEN WE TURN THE COIN OVER? (APOCRYPHAL)

The notion of the transformative power of money is deeply shaped by religious features. The emblematics of the coins indicate the cooperating human and divine authorities, which legitimate the genesis and transformation of the money.

The religious ideas circulate at the same time as the money and with a similar dynamic on the major trading routes, they circulate in urban centres, the reshipment sites for mercantile and cultural goods, they accumulate in the residences of power.

During the Parthian age Shamanism, ancestor worship, local fertility cults all join cross-regional traditions to form hybrid entities. The "Kings of Kings" themselves state their allegiance, like the Achaemenid Dynasty before, and the Sassanide Dynasty after them, to Zoroastrianism: a religion which, after its reformer, is leaning towards monotheism. But the "ruler" of all Gods, Ahuramazda, who is equated with the Babylonian Marduk, the Egyptian Re or the Jewish sky god tolerates and integrates polytheistic diversity during this period. Whilst in the east of their Empire, Zoroastrian, Hindu and Greco-Roman deities are seen alongside Buddha statues in one and the same shrine, in the west an interpretatio greca-iranica develops which reciprocally classifies the names of the gods of the Babylonian and Hellenistic pantheon according to functions and competences.

The statue originating from Mesene of the god Heracles, whose worship was directly linked to the ruler cult in both the Parthian and Roman Empire, is identified in the bilingual inscription on the thighs as the Iranian deity Vahram or Verethraghua, who in turn in Mesene corresponds to the underworld God Nergal.

Slide: Statue of Heracles from Messene, bilingual Inscription

Quote (in the tone of political propaganda):

> Arsaces
> Vologeses, King of Kings
> son of King Mithridates, fought
> In Maishan against king Mithridates
> son of Pakoros, King of Kings. Mithridates
> the king, he expelled from the land. All
> Maishan he conquered. This statue
> of the god Verthraghna, which he
> carried away from Maishan, he installs as an
> offerin in the temple of Tiri.[21]

The piece is part of the spoils from a military campaign and is finally exhibited in Seleucia on the Tigris in front of the shrine of the Greek Apollo or the Parthian Tir and – like Nergal – is entrusted with apotropaic tasks, notably to guard the nearby city gates, at the same time – as Heracles – he is meant to serve as a reminder of the political context and the cultic presence of the "King of Kings" chosen by God.

Slides: Early Christian Iconography

Instead Christianity advanced as the Roman state religion in the 4th century: as a product of an unrelenting conflict between various groups, preachers and sect leaders, who argue bitterly over the true teachings of Christ and who – for only: "I am the way and the truth and the life" – call each others right to exist into question.

The new religion gains its characteristic profile thanks to an innovative double bind rhetoric.

---

[21] Acording to the reading of D. S. Potter, "The Inscriptions on the bronze Herakles from Messene": Zeitschrift für Papyrologie und Epigraphik 88 (1991), 279.

Show subtitle: CERTUM EST QUIA ABSURDUM.
(TERTULLIAN, DE CARNE CHRISTI, 5)
Its cult is conveyed by the persuasive and charismatic word.
Quote (not a sermon, anecdotal narrative, emphasizing the punchline at the end):

> And when the day of Pentecost was fully come … there came a sound from heaven as of a rushing mighty wind, and it filled all the house where they were sitting.
> And there appeared unto them cloven tongues like as of fire, and it sat upon each of them.
> And … the Spirit gave them utterance.
> … the multitude came together, and were confounded, because that every man heard them speak in his own language …:
> Parthians, and Medes, and Elamites, and the dwellers in Mesopotamia, and in Judaea, and Cappadocia, in Pontus, and Asia, Phrygia, and Pamphylia, in Egypt, and in the parts of Libya about Cyrene, and strangers of Rome, Jews and proselytes, Cretes and Arabians … .
> And they were all amazed, and were in doubt, saying one to another, What meaneth this?
> Others mocking said, These men are full of new wine.[22]

MUSIC: MELCHITE SACRED CHANT
Christianity joins its salvific history dynamic of the *metanoia*, a complete reorientation, with geographical expansion: for only then will the end of all time be reached, when its mission has reached all peoples all over the world.
Quote (not overly dramatic, almost everyday language):

> Go ye therefore, and teach all nations, … and, lo, I am with you always, unto the end of the world.

In the meantime, the actor has sat down in the audience, watches the animation with interest. During the quote, his mobile phone rings several times, noisily. The actor remains completely calm, as if there were no performance, no audience. As if he has all the time in the world, he checks which jacket or trouser pockets the phone might be in. Finally he finds it. He answers it, but it's already too late. No one there. He puts the phone away again. He gets up, walks a few paces up and down at the edge of the room. Finally he returns to the podium, sits down and looks attentively at the screen of the note-book.

---

[22] *Acta* II, 1–13.

Under the reign of the Parthians, different Christian congregations are able to establish themselves east of the Roman borders and later develop further independently of the Roman state church: Melchites, Monophysites, Mandaeans, or "Saint Thomas Christians" propagate their beliefs across the entire mideast to India and China. The Nestorian Church, rejected by Rome as heretical and which first settled in Seleucia-Ctesiphon, expanded as far as into the "Middle Kingdom".

SLIDE: NESTORIAN TABLET, INSCRIPTION

Show subtitle: NESTORIAN TABLET, CH'ING-TSING, 781 A.D.

Quote (factually, almost official language):

> Behold the unchangeably true and invisible, who existed through all eternity without origin; the far-seeing perfect intelligence, whose mysterious existence is everlasting; operating on primordial substance he created the universe, being more excellent than all holy intelligences. … The illustrious and honorable Messiah, veiling his true dignity, appeared in the world as a man; angelic powers promulgated the glad tidings, a virgin gave birth to the Holy One in Syria; a bright star announced the felicitous event, and Persians observing the splendor came to present tribute; … he laid down great principles for the government of families and kingdoms; he established the new religion of the silent operation of the pure spirit of the Triune; he rendered virtue subservient to direct faith; … he suspended the bright sun to invade the chambers of darkness, and the falsehoods of the devil were thereupon defeated …

~ *music fades*

SLIDES: ROMAN TRIUMPHAL ARCHS, PERSIAN RELIEFS

From the beginning of Sassanid rule in the mid 3rd century, this politico-religious network is constantly peppered with new tensions.

Just like the Demon of Darkness Ahriman, who is robbed of his power by Ahuramazda, the last Parthian king is depicted under the horse of the victorious Sassanid Ardaschir.

If the ruler chosen by God is eo ipso the incarnation of a good and just world order, then his adversaries must logically represent evil. The initially tolerant religious policy of the Sassanids becomes increasingly rigid towards the end of the century. As Christianity becomes the state religion of Rome, which now itself oppresses other cults, the many Christian sects in the Persian empire are viewed as political enemies and persecuted. In both the east and the west, new identity patterns of an aggressive dualist nature arise.

The Persian victories over the Romans are deliberately rendered in the iconography of Roman triumphal arches:

Quote:

> And when I first became ruler in the empire, Emperor Gordian drew Romans, Goths and Teutons from across the entire empire together into an army and came to Mesopotamia against the Eran empire and US. … And Emperor Gordian met his death and WE destroyed the Roman army … then Emperor Valerian advances on US … and WE captured Emperor Valerian with our own hands.[23]

Similarly to „Ērān"; the land of the Aryans, who proclaim their faith in Zoroastrianism, the term „Anērān" is coined; the land of the non-Aryans, of the Romans, Goths, Teutons: western "rogue states" in which the dēwān, the demonic opponent is up mischief.

In the West, the traditional enemy concept of the weak and devious Persian is updated: the hybrid bastard of the Zoroastrian priesthood and Babylon the whore becomes a direct servant of Satan himself. The military clashes take on the character of religious wars. In 614 the Cross of Christ, pointedly rediscovered by Helena, the mother of Constantine, is dragged off to Cteseiphon by the Persians, ten years later Roman troops destroy the Zoroastrian shrine in Gandzak.

The battle of the two world powers finally turns into self-destruction. In the same century the entire Iranian and large parts of the Byzantine Empire are conquered by the Arabs.

Immediately, the traditional conceptions of the enemy are adapted to the changed geopolitical context; and they gain new religious dynamics which extends into the present day.

6. *Apocalypse*

SLIDES: RECENT ARIAL VIEWS OF MESOPOTAMIA, RUINS

MUSIC: VERDI, REQUIEM, DIES IRAE

Show intertitle: APOCALYPSE

The dynamics of Christian salvific history end in an orgiastic frenzy of destruction. What was limited in time and place in the Dionysian excesses by ritual framing appears at the end of all time as a universal spectacle of death.

~ *music continues, piano*

Quote (with emphasis and insistence):

[23] Inscription ŠNR m 6, Nagash-e Rostam.

After this I looked, and, behold, a door [was] opened in heaven: and the first voice which I heard [was] as it were of a trumpet talking with me; which said, Come up hither, and I will shew thee things which must be hereafter.

And I saw another angel fly in the midst of heaven, having the everlasting gospel to preach unto them that dwell on the earth, and to every nation, and kindred, and tongue, and people,

Saying with a loud voice, Fear God, and give glory to him; for the hour of his judgment is come: and worship him that made heaven, and earth, and the sea, and the fountains of waters.

And there came one of the seven angels which had the seven vials, and talked with me, saying unto me, Come hither; I will shew unto thee the judgment of the great whore that sitteth upon many waters:

With whom the kings of the earth have committed fornication, and the inhabitants of the earth have been made drunk with the wine of her fornication.

And a mighty angel took up a stone like a great millstone, and cast [it] into the sea, saying, Thus with violence shall that great city Babylon be thrown down, and shall be found no more at all.

And the voice of harpers, and musicians, and of pipers, and trumpeters, shall be heard no more at all in thee; and no craftsman, of whatsoever craft [he be], shall be found any more in thee; and the sound of a millstone shall be heard no more at all in thee;

And the light of a candle shall shine no more at all in thee; and the voice of the bridegroom and of the bride shall be heard no more at all in thee: for thy merchants were the great men of the earth; for by thy sorceries were all nations deceived.

And there followed another angel, saying, Babylon is fallen, is fallen, that great city, because she made all nations drink of the wine of the wrath of her fornication.[24]

Show subtitle: APOCALYPSE NOW – OR LATER?

The Christian apocalypse expectation has not come true.

The mission has not been accomplished.

Not yet.

SLIDES: NECROPOLIS, BURIAL GROUNDS

MUSIC: SAMUEL BARBER, ADAGIO FOR STRINGS

The historical self-perception of this and several other "world religions" tends towards the dissolution of history: to a return to the original state of the universe, from which all the forces of evil which constantly disrupted the divine harmony will be banished, and because of this have actually not ceased to produce history. Considered dynam-

[24] *Apocalypsis*, IV, 1; XIV, 6–7; XVI, 1–2; XVIII, 21–23; XVI, 8.

ically, history of salvation collapses in an entropy of the unendingly good.

The last judgement will – posthumously and post-mortally – deliver the final verdict on Good and Evil, will destroy impure networks, dissolve hybrid constructs, condemn the syncretisms in order to return to pure identities: true or false, yes or no, dead or alive, blessed or damned.

It will also want to have the final say on history.

Show subtitle: WHAT IS AND TO WHAT END DO WE STUDY UNIVERSAL HISTORY?

(FRIEDRICH SCHILLER)

BUT – PLEASE DON'T FORGET THE HISTORY OF RELIGIONS, FRITZ!

(VOLKHARD KRECH)

Even the secular sciences of history have repeatedly attempted to play the role if not of a jury member then that of the court clerk on judgement day, in order to give their own cultural identities, norms, values, laws an objective signature from this elevated vantage point.

SLIDE: GRAFFITI IMMORAL IS IMMORTAL

But this perspective has never been without contradiction: What, for example, if one doesn't see the (pseudo-)identities, but rather the networks as the starting point of history and historiography? Networks the historians, who are themselves networkers, are part of. Can we better read the traces of history on the basis of this premise? Or is it perhaps completely different traces that come to light as a result?

SLIDE: PAUL KLEE, ANGELUS NOVUS

MUSIC: VOLKHARD KRECH, IMPROVISATIONS

Quote (factual description, not poetry):

> There is an angel looking as though he is about to move away from something he is fixedly contemplating. His eyes are staring, his mouth is open, his wings are spread. This is how one pictures the angel of history. His face is turned toward the past. Where we perceive a chain of events, he sees one single catastrophe which keeps piling wreckage and hurls it in front of his feet. The angel would like to stay, awaken the dead, and make whole what has been smashed. But a storm is blowing in from Paradise; it has got caught in his wings with such a violence that the angel can no longer close them. The storm irresistibly propels him into

> the future to which his back is turned, while the pile of debris before him grows skyward. This storm is what we call progress.[25]

The question is:

to be – part of a progressive (or regressive) history of religion
or not to be – part of it.

Are we shareholders in a global religious company, which constantly seeks to sell new ideas, products, inventions, although it is under constant threat of bankruptcy (and therefore pins all hopes on a celestial chairman who gives us unlimited credit)?

Or are we distanced spectators of a more or less interestingly staged history play, a multi-media show with longue durée passages, with a few crucial events und special reality effects, but which basically doesn't have anything to do with our present secular (whatever that means) life (whatever that means …)?

~ *music stops*

Show intertitle: TERTIUM DATUR?
Show subtitle: MORE PARTICIPATION FOR THE DEAD!
MUSIC: SEIKILOS
Show subtitle (while the music plays):
I AM AN IMAGE IN STONE
SEIKILOS PUT ME HERE, WHERE I AM FOREVER, THE SYMBOL OF ETERNAL REMEMBRANCE. AS LONG AS YOU LIVE, SHINE; AFFLICT YOURSELF WITH NOTHING BEYOND MEASURE; YOUR LIFE IS OF BRIEF DURATION; TIME CLAIMS ITS TRIBUTE.
Show intertitle: EPITAPH OF SEIKLLOS

7. *Epilog*

Actor has returned to the lectern. When he comes back onto the screen at the end of the animation, he's busy taking notes. Takes out his phone, dials, pinches it between his ear and shoulder, continues with his notes. No-one seems to reply. Picks up the phone again looks at it indignantly, checks the number, shrugs his shoulders, puts it to one side. Keeps writing, reads half out-loud.

"More participation for the dead"

Looks at the audience, ponders.

[25] Walter Benjamin, *Über den Begriff der Geschichte*, IX.

"Unsere Mängel sind unsere Hoffnungen"

Laughs.

Mängel: What is "Mängel" in English?

Looks at the audience

Audience: poverty, necessity, requirement, lack, meaning

Actor: Well I think that will do.

Gets up, puts mobile phone away, notes, sheets, folder etc. Shuts notebook. To the audience:

Enjoy the conference.

Leaves the podium.

BIBLIOGRAPHY

Abd Allah Suhaylī, *al-Rawḍ al-unuf*, 'Abd al-Raḥmān al-Wakīl (ed.), 7 vols., IV, Cairo: Dār al-Kutub al-Ḥadītha 1387/1967–1390/1970.

'Abd al-Razzāq, *Muṣannaf*, Ḥabīb al-Raḥmān al-A'ẓamī (ed.), 11 vols., V, Beirut: al-Majlis al-'Ilmī 1390/1970–1392/1972.

Abū l-Fidā' Ismā'īl ibn 'Umar Ibn Kathīr, *al-Bidāya wa-l-nihāya*, 8 vols., VII, Beirut: Dar Iḥyā' al-Turāth al-'Arabī 1412/1992–1413/1993.

Ackerman, Susan E., "Falun Dafa and the New Age Movement in Malaysia: Signs of Health, Symbols of Salvation", in: *Social Compass* 52 (2005), 495–511.

Adikaram, Edward Winifred, *Early History of Buddhism in Ceylon*, Migoda: D.S. Puswella 1953 (reprint Dehiwala, Sri Lanka: Buddhist Cultural Centre 1994).

Adogame, Afe, "The Quest for Space in the Global Spiritual Marketplace: African Religions in Europe", in: *International Review of Mission* 89 (2000), 400–409.

Aihanzhe (i.e. 'Philosinensis', Karl F.A. Gützlaff) (ed.), *Dong-Xiyang kao meiyue tongjizhuan* 1984.3., 48; as reprinted in Beijing: Zhonghua shuju 1997.

Albrecht, Michael, *Einleitung zu Wolffs Oratio de Sinarum philosophia practica (1721)*, Hamburg: Meiner Felix Verlag 1985.

Ali, Chiragh, *A Critical Examination of the Popular Jihad*, Calcutta: Thacker, Spink and Company 1885.

Almond, Gabriel A./Appleby, R. Scott/Sivan, Emmanuel (eds.), *Strong Religion: The Rise of Fundamentalisms around the World*, Chicago: University of Chicago Press 2000.

Anderson, Benedict, *Imagined Communities: Reflections on the Origin and Spread of Nationalism*, 2nd ed., London: Versa 1991.

Anon. (1976), *The Vattukottai Resolution*. tamilunitedfront.com, http://www.tail unitedfront.org/articles/Vattukottai.html, accession: 1 December 2009.

—— (2009a), *LTTE Officially Announces Restructure Process: Selvarasa Pathmanathan heads the Organisation*, Headquarters, LTTE 21 July 2009, http://ltteir.org/?p= 132, accession: 22 July 2009.

—— (2009b), "Demand the Release of Tamil detainees in Sri Lanka", http://www.wsws.org/articles/2009/oct2009/sril-o07.shtml, accession: 1 November 2009.

—— (2010a), "Tamils of Switzerland, Germany, Holland vote on independence this weekend", *TamilNet*, 22 January 2010, http://www.tamilnet.com/art.html?catid =13&artid=31035, accession: 22 January 2010.

—— (2010b), "Referendum conducted in exemplary way in Switzerland", *TamilNet* 25 January 2010, http://www.tamilnet.com/art.html? catid=13&artid=31056, accession: 25 January 2010.

—— (2010c), "Overwhelming turnout of voters in Germany, 99% mandate Tamil Eelam", *TamilNet* 24 January 2010, http://www.tamilnet.com/art.html?catid=13&artid=31054, accession: 24 January 2010.

Argyriou, Astérios, "Éléments biographiques concernant le prophète Muḥammad dans la littérature grecque des trois premiers siècles de l'Hégire", in: Fahd, Toufic (ed.), *La vie du prophète Mahomet: Colloque de Strasbourg (octobre 1980)*, Paris 1983, 160–182.

Ariyapala, M. B., *Society in Medieval Ceylon*, Colombo: K. V. G. deSilva 1997.

Armstrong, Karen, *Die Achsenzeit. Vom Ursprung der Weltreligionen*, Berlin: Siedler 2006.

——, *The Great Transformation: The Beginning of Our Religious Traditions*, New York, NY: Knopf 2006.

Arnason, Johann P./Eisenstadt, Shmuel N./Wittrock, Björn (eds.), *Axial Civilizations and World History*, Jerusalem Studies in Religion and Culture 4, Leiden/Köln: Brill 2005.

Asad, Talal, *Genealogies of Religion: Discipline and Reasons of Power in Christianity and Islam*, Baltimore, MD: John Hopkins University Press 1993.

——, "The Construction of Religion as an Anthropological Category", in: Lambek, Michael (ed.), *A Reader in the Anthropology of Religion*, Malden: Wiley-Blackwell 2001, 114–132.

Assmann, Aleida, "Jaspers, Achsenzeit, oder: Schwierigkeiten mit der Zentralperspektive in der Geschichte", in: Harth, Dietrich (ed.), *Karl Jaspers – Denken zwischen Wissenschaft, Politik und Philosophie*, Stuttgart: Metzler 1988, 187–205.

——, "Schriftliche Folklore. Zur Entstehung und Funktion eines Überlieferungstyps", in: Assmann, Aleida/Assmann, Jan/Hardmeier, Christof (eds.), *Schrift und Gedächtnis*, Archäologie der literarischen Kommunikation I, München: Fink 1983, 175–193.

Assmann, Aleida/Assmann, Jan (eds.), *Kanon und Zensur*, München: Fink 1987.

Assmann, Jan, "Axial 'Breakthroughs and Semantic 'Relocations in Ancient Egypt and Israel", in: Arnason, Johann P./Eisenstadt, Shmuel N./Wittrock, Björn (eds.), *Axial Civilizations and World History*, Jerusalem Studies in Religion and Culture 4, Leiden/Köln: Brill 2005, 133–156.

——, *Das kulturelle Gedächtnis*, München: Beck 1992.

——, *Die Mosaische Unterscheidung oder Der Preis des Monotheismus*, München: Carl Hanser 2003.

——, "Literatur und Einsamkeit im alten Ägypten", in: Assmann, Aleida/Assmann, Jan (eds.), *Einsamkeit*, Archäologie der literarischen Kommunikation VI, München: Beck 2000, 97–112.

——, *Ma'at. Gerechtigkeit und Unsterblichkeit im Alten Ägypten*, München: Beck 1990.

——, *Monotheismus als politische Theologie*, unpublished manuscript, Heidelberg 2001.

——, "Schrift, Tod und Identität. Das Grab als Vorschule der Literatur im alten Ägypten", in: Assmann, Aleida/Assmann, Jan/Hardmeier, Christof, *Schrift und Gedächtnis*, Archäologie der literarischen Kommunikation I, München: Fink 1983, 64–93.

——, *Stein und Zeit. Mensch und Gesellschaft im Alten Ägypten*, München: Fink 1991.

Assmann, Jan/Gladigow, Burghard (eds.), *Text und Kommentar*, München: Fink 1995.

Auffarth, Christoph, "Religio Migrans: Die 'Orientalischen Religionen' im Kontext antiker Religion. Ein theoretisches Modell", in: *Mediterranea* IV (2007), 333–363.

——, "'Weltreligion' als ein Leitbegriff der Religionswissenschaft im Imperialismus, in Mission und Macht im Wandel politischer Orientierungen: Europäische Missionsgesellschaften in politischen Spannungsfeldern in Afrika und Asien zwischen 1800 und 1945", in: *Missionsgeschichtliches Archiv* X (2007), 17–36.

Babb, Lawrence, *Redemptive Encounters: Three Modern Styles in the Hindu Tradition*, Berkeley, CA: University of California Press 1986.

Baḥrānī, Yūsuf al-, *al-Ḥadā'iq al-nāḍira fī aḥkām al-'itra al-ṭāhira*, 26 vols., XXIII, Beirut: Dār al-Aḍwā' 1405/1985–1414/1993.

Balādhurī, Ahmad ibn Yahya al-, *Ansāb al-ashrāf*, Ramzi Baalbaki (ed.), VII, i, Beirut: al-Sharika Muttaḥida li-l-Tawzī' 1417/1997.

—, *Futūḥ al-buldān*, Michael Jan de Goeje (ed.), Leiden: Brill 1863–1866.

Bareau, André, "Les sectes bouddhiques du Petit Véhicule et leur Abhidharmapiṭaka", in: *Bulletin de l'École française d'Extrême-Orient* 44.1 (1951), 1–11.

Barker, Eileen (ed.), *Of Gods and Men: New Religious Movements in the West*, Macon, GA: Mercer University Press 1983.

Barrett, Tim H., "'Kill the Patriarchs!'", in: Skorupski, Tadeusz (ed.), *The Buddhist Forum*, I, London: SOAS 1990, 87–97.

Barrett, Tim H., "Tominaga our Contemporary", in: *Journal of the Royal Asiatic Society*, series 3, 3.1 (1993), 245–252.

Barton, John, "Marcion Revisited", in: McDonald, Lee Martin/Sanders, James A. (eds.), *The Canon Debate*, Peabody, MA: Hendrickson Publishers 2002, 341–354.

Basham, Arthur L., *History and Doctrines of the Ājīvikas*, London: Luzac 1951.

Baumann, Gerd/Gingrich, Andre (eds.), *Grammars of Identity/Alterity: A Structural Approach*, The EASA series 3, New York, NY: Berghahn Books 2004.

Baumann, Martin, *Migration - Religion - Integration: Buddhistische Vietnamesen und hinduistische Tamilen in Deutschland*, Marburg: Diagonal Verlag 2000.

Baumann, Martin/Salentin, Kurt, "Migrant Religiousness and Social Incorporation: Tamil Hindus from Sri Lanka in Germany", in: *Journal of Contemporary Religion* 21 (2006), 297–323.

Baur, Ferdinand Christian, *Geschichte der christlichen Kirche*, vol. 1: Kirchengeschichte der drei ersten Jahrhunderte, 3rd ed., Tübingen: L. Fr. Fues 1863 (reprint Leipzig 1969).

Beatty, John, "Classes and Cladists", in: *Systematic Zoology* 31.1 (1982), 25–34.

Bechert, Heinz, *Buddhismus, Staat und Gesellschaft in den Ländern des Theravāda-Buddhismus. 1: Grundlagen, Ceylon (Sri Lanka)*, 2nd ed., Schriften des Instituts für Asienkunde in Hamburg 5, Frankfurt a. M.: Alfred Metzner Verlag 1966.

—, "Zum Ursprung der Geschichtsschreibung im indischen Kulturbereich", in: *Nachrichten der Akademie der Wissenschaften in Göttingen, philologisch-historische Klasse* 1.2 (1969), 35–58.

Beckford, James A., *Religion and Advanced Industrial Society*, London: Unwin Hyman 1989.

Bell, Daniel, "The Return of the Sacred?", in: *British Journal of Sociology* 28 (1977), 419–449.

Belting, Hans, *Bild-Anthropologie. Entwürfe für eine Bildwissenschaft*, München: Fink 2001.

Benjamin, Walter, „Über den Begriff der Geschichte" in: Gesammelte Schriften, vol. I, 2, Frankfurt a. M.: Suhrkamp 1980, 691-714.

Berger, Peter, *The Sacred Canopy: Elements of a Sociological Theory of Religion*, New York, NY: Doubleday Anchor 1967.

Berkwitz, Stephen C., *Buddhist History in the Vernacular: The Power of the Past in Late Medieval Sri Lanka*, Leiden: Brill 2004.

Berner, Ulrich, *Untersuchungen zur Verwendung des Synkretismus-Begriffes*, Göttinger Orientforschungen: Reihe Grundlagen und Ergebnisse, vol. 2, Wiesbaden: Harrassowitz 1982.
Beyer, Peter, "Globalization and Glocalization", in: Beckford, James A./Demerath, N. Jay III, *The Sage Handbook of the Sociology of Religion*, London: Sage 2007a, 98–117.
——, "Globalization and the Institutional Modeling of Religion", in: Beyer, Peter/Beaman, Lori (eds.), *Religion, Globalization, and Culture*, Leiden: Brill 2007b, 167–186.
——, *Religion and Globalization*, London: Sage 1994.
——, *Religions in Global Society*, London, New York, NY: Routledge 2006.
Bhachu, Parminder, *Twice Migrants: East African Sikh Settlers in Britain*, London: Tavistock 1985.
Bianchi, Ugo (ed.), *The Notion of 'Religion' in Comparative Research: Selected Proceedings of the XVIth Congress of the International Association of the History of Religions*, Rome: L'Erma di Bretschneider 1994.
Biardeau, Madeleine, *Le Mahābhārata: Un récit fondateur du brahmanisme et son interprétation*, Paris: Seuil 2002.
Blackbourn, David, *Marpingen: Apparitions of the Virgin Mary in 19th century Germany*, Oxford: Clarendon Press 1993.
Blenkinsopp, Joseph, *Prophecy and Canon: a Contribution to the Study of Jewish Origins*, Notre Dame, IN: University of Notre Dame Press 1977.
Blumenberg, Hans, *Die Legitimität der Neuzeit*, part 4: Aspekte der Epochenschwelle: Cusaner und Nolaner, Frankfurt a. M.: Suhrkamp 1976.
Boltz, William G., "The Religious and Philosophical Significance of the 'Hsiang Erh' *Lao tzu* in the Light of the *Ma-wang-tui* Silk Manuscripts", in: *Bulletin of the School of Oriental and African Studies* 45 (1982), 95–117.
Boucharlat, Rémy (ed.), *Les Parthes*, Dijon: Remy Faton 2002.
Bouma, Gary D., *Australian Soul: Religion and Spirituality in the 21st Century*, New York, NY: Cambridge University Press 2007.
Bourdieu, Pierre, *Das religiöse Feld: Texte zur Ökonomie des Heilsgeschehens*, Konstanz: Universitätsverlag Konstanz 2000 (tr. from French by Andreas Pfeuffer).
Boyarin, Daniel, *Border Lines: The Partition of Judaeo-Christianity*, Philadelphia, PA: University of Pennsylvania Press 2004.
Boyce, Mary, *A History of Zoroastrianism*. Vol. 1: The Early Period, Leiden/Köln: Brill 1975.
——, *A History of Zoroastrianism*. Vol. 2: Under the Achaemenians, Leiden/Köln: Brill 1982.
——, *Zoroastrians: Their Religious Beliefs and Practices*, London: Routledge and Kegan 1979.
Boyce, Mary/Grenet, Frantz, *A History of Zoroastrianism*. Vol. 3: Zoroastrianism under Macedonian and Roman Rule, Leiden/Köln: Brill 1991.
Boyd, James W., "Zoroastrianism", in: Denny, Frederick M./Taylor, Rodney L. (eds.), *The Holy Book in Comparative Perspective*, Columbia: University of South Carolina Press 1985, 109–125.
Bödeker, Hans Erich (ed.), *Begriffsgeschichte, Diskursgeschichte, Metapherngeschichte*, Göttingen: Wallstein 2002.
Brague, Rémi, *Europa, eine exzentrische Identität*, Frankfurt a. M.: Campus Verlag 1993.

Brereton, Joel, "*Dhárman* in the *Ṛgveda*", in: Olivelle, Patrick, *Manu's Code of Law: A Critical Edition and Translation of the Mānava-Dharmaśāstra*, New York, NY: Oxford University Press 2005, 27–67.
Bretfeld, Sven, "Zur Institutionalisierung des Buddhismus und der Suspendierung der ethischen Norm der Gewaltlosigkeit in Sri Lanka", in: *Zeitschrift für Religionswissenschaft* 11 (2003), 149–165.
Bronkhorst, Johannes, *Greater Magadha. Studies in the Culture of Early India*, Leiden, Boston, MA: Brill 2007.
Broughton, Jeff, "Tsung-mi's *Zen Prolegomenon:* Introduction to an Exemplary Zen Canon", in: Heine, Steven/Wright, Dale (eds.), *The Zen Canon: Understanding the Classic Texts*, New York, NY: Oxford University Press 2004, 11–51.
Bruce, Frederick Fyvie, *The Canon of Scripture*, Downers Grove: InterVarsity Press 1988.
Brunner, Otto/Conze, Werner/Koselleck, Reinhart (eds.), *Geschichtliche Grundbegriffe. Historisches Lexikon zur politisch-sozialen Sprache in Deutschland*, 8 vols., Stuttgart: Klett 1972–1998.
Burghart, Richard (ed.), *Hinduism in Great Britain: The Perpetuation of Religion in an Alien Cultural Milieu*, London: Tavistock 1987.
Burkert, Walter, *Antike Mysterien: Funktionen und Gehalt*, München: Beck 1990.
Burnett, D. Graham, *Trying Leviathan: The Nineteenth-Century New York Court Case That Put the Whale on Trial and Challenged the Order of Nature*, Princeton, NJ: Princeton University Press 2007.
Buswell, Robert, *The Collected Works of Chinul*, Honolulu: University of Hawai'i Press 1983.
Buswell, Robert/Gimello, Robert, *Paths of Liberation. The Marga and its Transformations in Buddhist Thought*, Studies in East Asian Buddism series, 7, Honolulu: University of Hawaii Press 1992.

Cahen, Claude, "Note sur l'accueil des chrétiens d'Orient à l'Islam", in: *Revue de l'histoire des religions* 166 (1964), 51–58.
Campany, Robert Ford, *Making Transcendents: Ascetics and Social Memory in Early Medieval China*, Honolulu: University of Hawaii Press 2009.
——, "On the Very Idea of Religions (in the Modern West and in Early Medieval China)", in: *History of Religions* 42 (2003).
——, *Strange Writing: Anomaly Accounts in Early Medieval China*, Albany: SUNY Press 1996.
——, "'Survivals' as Interpretive Strategy: A Sino-Western Comparative Case Study", in: *Method and Theory in the Study of Religion* 2 (1990), 1–26.
——, "Two Religious Thinkers of the Early Eastern Jin: Gan Bao and Ge Hong in Multiple Contexts", in: *Asia Major* 3rd ser. 18 (2005), 175–224.
——, "Xunzi and Durkheim as Theorists of Ritual Practice," in: Reynolds, Frank/Tracy, David (eds.), *Discourse and Practice*, Albany: SUNY Press 1992, 197–231.
Campbell, George Van Pelt, "Religion and Phases of Globalization", in: Beyer, Peter/Beaman, Lori (eds.), *Religion, Globalization, and Culture*, Leiden: Brill 2007, 281–302.
Carnes, Tony/Yang, Fenggang (eds.), *Asian American Religions: The Making and Remaking of Borders and Boundaries*, New York, NY: New York University Press 2004.

Caroli, Robert De, *Haunting the Buddha: Indian Popular Religions and the Formation of Buddhism*, Oxford: Oxford University Press 2004.
Carozzi, Maria Julia, "Ready to Move Along: The Sacralization of Disembedding in the New Age Movement and the Alternative Circuit in Buenos Aires", in: *Civilisations: Revue internationale d'anthropologie et de sciences humaines* 51 (2004), 139–154.
Carrithers, Michael, *The Forest Monks of Sri Lanka: An Anthropological and Historical Study*, Delhi: Oxford University Press 1983.
Ch'a, Sŏng-hwan, *Kŭllobŏl sidae Chŏng Yag-yong segyegwan-ŭi kanŭngsŏng-gwa han'gye* (Global Age and the Thought of Chŏng Yag-yong. Potentials and Limitations), Seoul: Chimmundang 2002.
Chakravarti, Uma, *The Social Dimension of Early Buddhism*, Delhi/Oxford: Oxford University Press 1987.
Chang, Eileen, *The Chinese Essay*, London: Hurst and Company 2000.
Chang, Hsüan 張瑄, *Zhongwen changyong san qian zi xing yi shi* 中文常用三千字形義釋 (The Etymologies of 3,000 Chinese Characters in Common Use [original English title: Explanation of the Shapes and Sounds of 3,000 Commonly Used Chinese Characters]), Hong Kong: Hong Kong University Press 1968.
Chang, Kwang-chih, *Shang Civilization*, New Haven/London: Yale University Press 1980.
Chang, Tsung-tung, *Der Kult der Shang-Dynastie im Spiegel der Orakelinschriften: Eine paläographische Studie zur Religion im archaischen China*, Wiesbaden: Otto Harrassowitz 1970.
——, "Indo-European Vocabulary in Old Chinese: A New Thesis on the Emergence of Chinese Language and Civilization in the Late Neolithic Age", in: *Sino-Platonic Papers* 7 (1988), 35–39.
Charon, Milly, *Between Two Worlds: The Canadian Immigrant Experience*, Revised Edition, Montreal: Nu-Age Editions 1988.
Chattopadhyaya, Brajadulal, *The Making of Early Medieval India*, New Delhi: Oxford University Press 1994, 183–222.
Chen, Guying 陳鼓應 (ed. and tr.), *Zhuang Zi jin zhu jin yi* 莊子今注今譯 (A Modern Annotation and Translation of the Chuang Zi), Beijing: Zhonghua 1983.
Chen, Jidong, *Shin-matsu Bukkyô no kenkyû*, Tokyo: Sankibô 2003.
Chen, Mengjia 陳夢家, "Shang dai de shenhua yu wushu" 商代的神話與巫術 (Myths and witchcraft during the Shang period [original English title: Myths and Magianism of the Shang Period]), in: *Yanjing xuebao* 燕京學報 (Yenching Journal of Chinese Studies) 20 (1936), 533–544.
——, *Yinxu buci zongshu* 殷虛卜辭綜述 (Summary of Oracle Inscriptions from the Wastes of Yin), Beijing: Kexue Chubanshe 1956.
Chi, Li, *Anyang*, Seattle: University of Washington Press 1977.
Chidester, David, *Savage Systems: Colonialism and Comparative Religion in Southern Africa*, Charlottesville: University of Virginia Press 1996.
Ching, Julia/Oxtoby, Willard G., *Moral Enlightenment: Leibniz and Wolff on China*, Nettetal: Steyler 1992.
Ch'oe, Han'gi, *Myŏngnamnu ch'ongsŏ* [Collected works of Ch'oe Han'gi], 5 vols., Seoul: Taedong munhwa yŏn'guwŏn 2003.
Chou, Fa-Kao 周法高 (chief ed.), 漢字古今音彙 (A Pronouncing Dictionary of Chinese Characters in Archaic & Ancient Chinese, Mandarin & Cantonese), Hong Kong: The Chinese University of Hong Kong 1973.

Chŏng, Yag-yong, *Yŏyudang chŏnsŏ* (Collected writings of Yŏyudang), Seoul: Minjok munhwa ch'ujinhoe 2001.
Clarke, Peter B. (ed.), *New Trends and Developments in African Religions*, Westport, CT: Greenwood 1998.
Collins, Steven, "On the Very Idea of the Pali Canon", in: *Journal of the Pali Text Society* 15 (1990), 89–126.
Commercial Press English and Chinese Dictionary, Shanghai: Commercial Press 1903.
Committee of the Educational Association of China (eds.), *Technical Terms English and Chinese*, Shanghai: Methodist Publishing House 1910.
Cook, Francis H., *Hua-yen Buddhism: The Jewel Net of Indra*, University Park: The Pennsylvania State University Press 1977.
Cornelius, Friedrich, *Indogermanische Religionsgeschichte*, München: Reinhardt 1942.
Corten, André/Marshall-Fratani, Ruth (eds.), *Between Babel and Pentecost: Transnational Pentecostalism in Africa and Latin America*, Bloomington, IN: Indiana University Press 2001.
Cox, Harvey, *Fire from Heaven: The Rise of Pentecostal Spirituality and the Reshaping of Religion in the Twenty-First Century*, Reading, MA: Perseus Books 1995.
Creel, Herrlee G., *Confucius, the Man and the Myth*, Seoul: Hangilsa 1949 (Korean Edition from 1983).
Crossley, James G., *Why Christianity Happened: A Socio-historical Account of Christian Origins (26–50 CE)*, Louisville, KY: Westminster John Knox Press 2006.
Csikszentmihàlyi, Mark/Nylan, Michael, "Constructing Lineages and Inventing Traditions Through Exemplary Figures in Early China", in: *T'oung-pao* 89 (2003), 59–99.

Damascus, John of, *Liber de haeresibus*, in: Kotter, P. Bonifatius (ed.), *Die Schriften des Johannes von Damaskos*, 5 vols., Berlin: de Gruyter 1969–1981, vol. 4 (engl. Daniel Sahas, *John of Damascus on Islam: The "Heresy of the Ishmaelites"*, Leiden: Brill 1972).
Davidson, Ronald M., "An Introduction to the Standards of Scriptural Authenticity in Indian Buddhism", in: Buswell, Robert (ed.), *Chinese Buddhist Apocrypha*, Honolulu: University of Hawai'i Press 1990, 291–325.
——, "*Gsar ma* Apocrypha: The Creation of Orthodoxy, Gray Texts, and the New Revelation", in: Eimer, Helmut/Germano, David (eds.), *The Many Canons of Tibetan Buddhism*, Leiden: Brill 2002, 203–224.
——, *Indian Esoteric Buddhism: A Social History of the Tantric Movement*, New York, NY: Columbia University Press 2002.
——, "Studies in Dhāraṇī Literature I: Revisiting the Meaning of the Term *Dhāraṇī*", in: *Journal of Indian Philosophy* 37.2 (2009), 97–147.
——, "The Place of *Abhi .seka* Visualization in the Yogalehrbuch and Related Texts", in: Franco, Eli/Zin, Monik (eds.), *From Turfan to Ajanta: A Festschrift for Dieter Schlingloff on the Occasion of his Eightieth Birthday*, 1, Lumbini, Nepal: Lumbini International Research Institute 2010, 185–198.
——, *Tibetan Renaissance. Tantric Buddhism in the Rebirth of Tibetan Culture and the Rise of Sakya*, New York, NY: Columbia University Press 2005.
Davie, Grace, *Europe: The Exceptional Case: Parameters of Faith in the Modern World*, London: Darton, Longman & Todd 2003.
Dawson, Christopher, *Religion and culture*, London: Ams Pr. Inc. 1936.
Debray, Regis, *Introduction à la Médiologie*, Paris: Presses Universitaires de France 2000.

DeCaroli, Robert, *Haunting the Buddha. Indian Popular Religions and the Formation of Buddhism*, Oxford: Oxford University Press 2004.

Deen, Hanifa, *Caravanserai: Journey among Australian Muslims*, St. Leonards, NSW, Australia: Allen & Unwin 1995.

Deissmann, Adolf, *Licht vom Osten*, Tübingen: J.C.B. Mohr 1923.

Denny, Frederick M., "Islam", in: Denny, Frederick M./Taylor, Rodney L. (eds.), *The Holy Book in Comparative Perspective*, Columbia: University of South Carolina Press 1985, 84–108.

Denny, Frederick M./Taylor, Rodney L., "Introduction", in: Denny, Frederick M./Taylor, Rodney L. (eds.), *The Holy Book in Comparative Perspective*, Columbia: University of South Carolina Press 1985, 1–9.

Deshpande, Madhav M., "What to do with the *Anāryas*: Dharmic Discourses of Inclusion and Exclusion", in: Bronkhorst, Johannes/Deshpande, Madhav M. (eds.), *Aryan and Non-Aryan in South Asia: Evidence, Interpretation and Ideology*, Cambridge, MA: Harvard Oriental Series 1999, 107–127.

Despland, Michel, *La religion en occident. Évolution des idées et du vécu*, Montréal: Fides 1979.

Didier, John C., *In and Outside the Square: The Sky and the Power of Belief in Ancient China and the World, c. 4500 BC – AD 200*, 3 vols., Sino-Platonic Papers 192 (2010).

Dodin, Thierry/Räther, Heinz (eds.), *Mythos Tibet. Wahrnehmungen, Projektionen, Phantasien*, Köln: DuMont 1997.

Donner, Fred McGraw, *The Early Islamic Conquests*, Princeton, NJ: Princeton University Press 1981.

Drake, Fred W., *China Charts the World: Hsü Chi-yü and his Geography of 1848*, Cambridge, MA: Harvard University Press 1975.

Dreyfus, George, *The Sound of Two Hands Clapping: the Education of a Tibetan Buddhist Monk*, Berkeley, CA: University of California Press 2003.

Ducellier, Alain, *Chrétiens d'Orient et Islam au Moyen Age*, Paris: Armand Colin 1996.

Dumont, Louis, *Homo Hierarchicus: The Caste System and Its Implications* (revised edition), Chicago: University of Chicago Press 1980 (1966).

Dunbar, David G., "The Biblical Canon", in: Carson, Donald Arthur/Woodbridge, John D. (eds.), *Hermeneutics, Authority, and Canon*, Grand Rapids: Zondervan 1986, 299–360.

Dunlop, Douglas, "Hafs' ibn Albar, the Last of the Goths?", in: *Journal of the Royal Asiatic Society* (1954), 136–151.

——, "Sobre af ibn Albar al-Qûtî Al-Qurtubî," in: *Al-Andalus* 20 (1955), 211–213.

Dunn, James D.G., "Diversity in Paul", in: Cohn-Sherbok, Dan/Court, John M. (eds.), *Religious Diversity in the Graeco-Roman World*, BiSe 79, Sheffield: Sheffield Academic Press 2001, 107–123.

——, "Has the Canon a Continuing Function?", in: McDonald, Lee Martin/Sanders, James A., *The Canon Debate: On the Origins and Formation of the Bible*, Peabody: Hendrickson Publishers 2002, 558–579.

Eade, John, "New Introduction", in: Eade, John/Sallnow, Michael, *Contesting the Sacred: The Anthropology of Christian Pilgrimage*, Urbana, IL: Illinois University Press 2000, ix–xxvii.

Ebaugh, Helen Rose/Saltzman Chafetz, Janet (eds.), *Religion and the New Immigrants: Continuities and Adaptations in Immigrant Congregations*, Walnut Creek, CA: AltaMira 2000.

Ebertz, Michael N./Schultheis, Franz, "Einleitung: populare Religiosität", in: *Volksfrömmigkeit in Europa: Beiträge zur Soziologie popularer Religiosität aus 14 Ländern*, München: Chr. Kaiser 1986, 11–52.

Eck, Diana L., *A New Religious America: How a "Christian Country" Has Now Become the World's Most Religiously Diverse Nation*, New York, NY: Harper San Francisco 2001.

Eisenstadt, Shmuel N. (ed.), *The Origin and Diversity of Axial Civilizations*, Albany: SUNY Press 1986.

——, *Kulturen der Achsenzeit. Ihre Ursprünge und ihre Vielfalt*, 2 vols., Frankfurt a. M.: Suhrkamp 1987.

——, *Kulturen der Achsenzeit II. Ihre institutionelle und kulturelle Dynamik*, 3 vols., Frankfurt a. M.: Suhrkamp 1992.

Eliade, Mircea, *The Forge and the Crucible*, New York, NY: Harper and Row 1971 (2nd ed., University of Chicago Press 1978).

Engberg-Pedersen, Troels (ed.), *Paul beyond the Judaism/Hellenism divide*, Louisville, KY: Westminster John Knox 2001.

Eno, Robert, "Shang State Religion and the Pantheon of the Oracle Texts", in: Lagerwey, John/Kalinowski, Marc (eds.), *Early Chinese Religion. Part One: Shang through Han (1250 BC - 220 AD)*, Leiden: Brill 2008, 41–102.

Erdosy, George, "The Prelude to Urbanisation: Ethnicity and the Rise of Late Vedic Chiefdoms", in: Allchin, Frank Raymond (ed.), *The Archealogy of Early Historic South Asia. The Emergence of Cities and States*, Cambridge, MA: Cambridge University Press 1995, 75–98.

Ess, Josef van, "Die Pest von Emmaus: Theologie und Geschichte in der Frühzeit des Islams", in: *Oriens* 36 (2001), 248–267.

Falk, Harry, *Aśokan Sites and Artefacts: A Source-Book with Bibliography*, Mainz: Philipp von Zabern 2006.

Faure, "Space and Place in Chinese Religious Traditions", in: *History of Religions* 26.4 (1987), 337–356.

Feil, Ernst, *Religio. Die Geschichte eines neuzeitlichen Grundbegriffs vom Frühchristentum bis zur Reformation*, 4 vols., Göttingen: Vandenhoeck & Ruprecht 1986–2007.

Ferguson, Everett, "Factors Leading to the Selection and Closure of the New Testament Canon: A Survey of Some Recent Studies", in: McDonald, Lee Martin/Sanders, James A. (eds.), *The Canon Debate*, Peabody, MA: Hendrickson Publishers 2002, 295–320.

Feuchtwang, Stephan/Wang Ming-ming, "The Politics of Culture or a Contest of Histories: Representation of Chinese Popular Religion", in: *Dialectical Anthropology* 16 (1991), 251–272.

Fishbane, Michael, *Biblical Interpretation in Ancient Israel*, Oxford: Clarendon 1986.

Fiskesjö, Magnus/Xingcan, Chen, *China Before China: Johan Gunnar Andersson, Ding Wenjiang, and the Discovery of China's Prehistory*, Stockholm: Museum of Far Eastern Antiquities 2004.

Fitzgerald, James, *The Mahābhārata: 11. The Book of the Women, 12. The Book of Peace*, Chicago: University of Chicago Press 2004.

Fitzgerald, Timothy, *The Ideology of Religious Studies*, New York, NY: Oxford University Press 2000.

Flavius, Josephus, *Contra Apionem*, cap. 22 (William Warburton, tr.), *The Divine Legation of Moses*, London: F. Gyles 1738–41.

Flood, Christopher G., *Political Myth. A Theoretical Introduction*, New York, London: Garland 1996.

Fohrer, Georg, *Geschichte der israelitischen Religion*, Berlin: de Gruyter 1969.

Folkert, Kendall W., "The 'Canons' of 'Scripture'", in: Levering, Miriam (ed.), *Rethinking Scripture*, New York, NY: State University of New York Press 1989, 170–179.

Foltz, Richard C., *Religions of the Silk Road: Overland Trade and Cultural Exchange from Antiquity to the Fifteenth Century*, New York, NY: St. Martin's 1999.

Francisco J. Martinez (ed. and tr.), *Apocalypse of Pseudo-Methodius*, in: *Eastern Christian Apocalyptic in the Early Muslim Period: Pseudo-Methodius and Pseudo-Athanasius*, Dissertation, Washington, DC: Catholic University of America 1985, 58–201.

Dīghanikāya, *Das Buch der Langen Texte des Buddhistischen Kanons. In Auswahl übersetzt* (Otto Franke, tr.), Göttingen: Vandenhoeck & Ruprecht 1913.

Freeden, Michael, *Ideologies and Political Theory – A Conceptual Approach*, Oxford: Oxford University Press 1998.

Friedrich-Silber, Ilana, *Virtuosity, charisma, and social order: a comparative sociological study of monasticism in Theravada Buddhism and medieval Catholicism*, Cambridge, MA: Cambridge University Press 1995.

Fritz, Kurt von, "Review of J. A. Philip: Pythagoras and Early Pythagoreanism, Toronto 1966", in: *Gnomon* 40 (1968), 6–13.

Frühauf, Tina, *Orgeln und Orgelmusik in deutsch-jüdischer Kultur*, Netiva: Wege deutsch-jüdischer Geschichte und Kultur 6, Hildesheim: Georg Olms 2005 [*The organ and its music in German-Jewish culture*, New York, NY: Oxford University Press 2008].

Fuhrmann, Manfred, *Bildung – Europas kulturelle Identität*, Stuttgart: Reclam 2002.

Gallie, Walter Bryce, "Essentially Contested Concepts", in: *Proceedings of the Aristotelian Society* 56 (1956), 167–198.

Gamble, Harry Y., "Christianity", in: Denny, Frederick M./Taylor, Rodney L. (eds.), *The Holy Book in Comparative Perspective*, Columbia: University of South Carolina Press 1985, 36–62.

Gehrke, Hans-Joachim, "Gegenbild und Selbstbild: Das europäische Iran-Bild zwischen Griechen und Mullahs", in: Hölscher, Tonio (ed.), *Gegenwelten zu den Kulturen Griechenlands und Roms in der Antike*, München/Leipzig: Saur 2000, 85–109.

Giebel, Rolf W., "The *Chin-kang-ting ching yü-ch'ieh shih-pa-hui chih-kuei*: An Annotated Translation", in: *Naritasan Bukkyō Kenkyū kiyō* (Journal of Naritasan Institute for Buddhist Studies) 18 (1995), 107–201.

Gil, Moshe, *A History of Palestine, 634–1099*, Cambridge, MA: Cambridge University Press 1992.

Glob, Peter Vilhelm, *The Mound People: Danish Bronze-Age Man Preserved*, Ithaca: Cornell University Press 1974.

Glock, Charles Y./Bellah, Robert N. (eds.), *The New Religious Consciousness*, Berkeley, CA: University of California Press 1976.

Gnuse, Robert, *The Authority of the Bible: Theories of Inspiration, Revelation and the Canon of Scripture*, New York, NY: Paulist Press 1985, 95–101.

Godakumbura, C. E., *Sinhalese Literature*, Colombo: The Colombo Apothecaries 1955.

Gong, Zizhen, *Gong Zizhen quanji*, Part 6, Shanghai: Shanghai renmin chubanshe 1975.

Goossaert, Vincent, "1898: The Beginning of the End for Chinese Religion?", in: *The Journal of Asian Studies* 65.2 (2006), 307–336.

—, "The Concept of Religion in China and the West", in: *Diogenes* 52 (2005), 13–20.

—, *The Taoists of Peking, 1800–1949: A Social History of Urban Clerics*, Cambridge, MA: Harvard University Asia Center 2007.

Gopin, Marc, *To make the earth whole*, Lanham. MD: Rowman & Littlefield Publishers 2009.

Gregory, Andrew F./Tuckett, Christopher M. (eds.), *The Reception of the New Testament in the Apostolic Fathers*, Oxford/New York, NY: Oxford University Press 2005.

Gregory, Peter N., "Tsung-mi and the Sinification of Buddhism", in: *Studies in East Asian Buddhism* 16 (2002), 93–114.

Gregory, Peter N., *Tsung-mi and the Sinification of Buddhism*, Princeton, NJ: Princeton University Press 1991.

Griffiths, Paul J., "The Very Idea of Religion", in: *First Things* 103 (2000), 30–35.

Griffith, Sydney, "Faith and Reason in Christian Kalâm: Theodore Abû Qurrah on Discerning the True Religion", in: Samir, Samir Khalil/Nielsen, Jørgen S. (eds.), *Christian Arabic Apologetics during the Abbasid Period (750–1258)*, Leiden: Brill 1994, 1–43.

—, "Theodore Abû Qurrah's Arabic Tract on the Christian Practice of Venerating Images", in: *Journal of the American Oriental Society* 105 (1985), 53–73.

Gunawardana, R. A. L. H., *Robe and Plough: Monasticism and Economic Interest in Early Medieval Sri Lanka*, Tucson: University of Arizona Press 1979.

Guo, Moruo 郭沫若, *Nuli zhi shidai* 奴隷制時代 (The Age of Slavery), Shanghai: Xin Wenyi Chubanshe 1952.

Haddad, Yvonne Yazbeck/Esposito, John L. (eds.), *Muslims on the Americanization Path?*, Atlanta, GA: Scholars Press 1998.

Hadden, Jeffrey K./Shupe, Anson (eds.), *Prophetic Religion and Politics*, New York, NY: Paragon House 1986.

—/— (eds.), *Secularization and Fundamentalism Reconsidered*, New York, NY: Paragon House 1989.

Hafs' Ibn Albar, *Le Psautier mozarabe de Hafs le Goth* (Marie-Thérèse Urvoy, ed. and tr.), Toulouse: Presses Universitaires du Mirail 1994.

Hall, David D. (ed.), *Lived Religion in America: Toward a History of Practice*, Princeton, NJ: Princeton University Press 1997.

Ḥamawī, Yāqūt al-, *Muʿjam al-buldān*, 5 vols., I, Beirut: Dār Ṣādir-Dār Bayrūt 1957.

Harris, Ian, *Cambodian Buddhism: History and Practice*, Honolulu: University of Hawai'i Press 2005.

Hartmann, Jens-Uwe, "Further Remarks on the New Manuscript of the Dīrghāgama", in: *Journal of the International College for Advanced Buddhist Studies* 5 (2002), 133-150.

Hasson, Isaac, "Le chef judhāmite Rawḥ ibn Zinbāʿ", in: *Studia Islamica* 77 (1993), 95–122.

Haußig, Hans Wilhelm, *Die Geschichte Zentralasiens und der Seidenstraße in vorislamischer Zeit*, 2nd reviewed and extended edition, Darmstadt: Wissenschaftliche Buchgesellschaft 1992.

—, *Der Religionsbegriff in den Religionen. Studien zum Selbst- und Religionsverständnis in Hinduismus, Buddhismus, Judentum und Islam*, Berlin: Philo 1999.

Havelock, Eric A., *A Preface to Plato*, Oxford: Blackwell 1963.

Heelas, Paul/Woodhead, Linda/Seel, Benjamin/Szerszyinski, Bronislaw/Tusting, Karin, *The Spiritual Revolution: Why Religion is Giving Way to Spirituality*, Oxford: Blackwell 2005.

Heissig, Walther, "Die Religionen der Mongolei", in: Tucci, Giuseppe/Heissig, Walther (eds.), *Die Religionen Tibets und der Mongolei*, Stuttgart et al.: Kohlhammer 1970, 296–427.

Herberg, Will, *Protestant, Catholic, Jew: An Essay in American Religious Sociology*, Garden City, NY: Anchor Books 1960.

Herbers, Klaus/Jaspert, Nikolas (eds.), *Eigenes und Fremdes in den deutsch-spanischen Beziehungen des späten Mittelalters*, Geschichte und Kultur der Iberischen Welt 1, Münster/Berlin: Lit Verlag 2004.

——/—— (eds.), *Grenzräume und Grenzüberschreitungen im Vergleich. Der Osten und der Westen des mittelalterlichen Lateineuropa*, Europa im Mittelalter, Abhandlungen und Beiträge zur historischen Komparatistik 9, Berlin: Akademie-Verlag 2007.

Herrmann-Pfandt, Adelheid, *Die lHan kar ma: Ein Früher Katalog der ins Tibetische übersetzten buddhistischen Texte*, Wien: Verlag der Österreichischen Akademie der Wissenschaften 2008.

——, *Ḍākinīs: Zur Stellung und Symbolik des Weiblichen im tantrischen Buddhismus*, Bonn: Indica et Tibetica 1992.

Hey, Jody, *Genes, Categories, and Species: The Evolutionary and Cognitive Causes of the Species Problem*, Oxford/New York, NY: Oxford University Press 2001.

Hildebrandt, Mathias/Brocker, Manfred (eds.), *Der Begriff der Religion. Interdisziplinäre Perspektiven*, Wiesbaden: VS Verlag 2008.

Hiltebeitel, Alf, *Rethinking the Mahābhārata: A Reader's Guide to the Education of the Dharma King*, Chicago: University of Chicago Press 2001.

Højsgaard, Morten T./Warburg, Margit (eds.), *Religion and Cyberspace*, New York, NY: Routledge 2005.

Hölscher, Lucian, "Industrie", in: Brunner, Otto/Conze, Werner/Koselleck, Reinhart (eds.), *Geschichtliche Grundbegriffe*, vol. 3, Stuttgart: Klett 1982, 296–297.

——, *Neue Annalistik. Umrisse einer Theorie der Geschichte*, Göttingen: Wallstein 2003.

——, "Religion im Wandel. Von Begriffen des religiösen Wandels zum Wandel religiöser Begriffe", in: Gräb, Wilhelm (ed.), *Religion als Thema der Theologie. Geschichte, Standpunkte und Perspektiven theologischer Religionskritik und Religionsbegründung*, Gütersloh: Gütersloher Verlagshaus 1999, 45–62.

——, "The Concept of Conceptual History (Begriffsgeschichte) and the 'Geschichtliche Grundbegriffe'", in: Hallym Academy of Sciences (ed.), *Concept and Communication*, vol. 1, no. 2, Seoul: Hallym University Press 2008, 179–198.

——, "The New Annalistic. A Sketch of a Theory of History", in: *History and Theory* 36 (1997), 317–335.

Hölscher, Tonio (ed.), *Gegenwelten zu den Kulturen Griechenlands und Roms in der Antike*, München/Leipzig: Saur 2000.

——, "Feindwelten – Glückswelten: Perser, Kentauren und Amazonen", in: Hölscher, Tonio (ed.), *Gegenwelten zu den Kulturen Griechenlands und Roms in der Antike*, München/Leipzig: Saur 2000, 287–320.

Holt, John Clifford, *Buddha in the Crown: Avalokiteśvara in the Buddhist Traditions of Sri Lanka*, Oxford: Oxford University Press 1991.

Holzman, Donald, "A Dialogue with the Ancients: Tao Qian's Interrogation of Confucius", in: Pearce, Scott/Spiro, Audrey/Ebrey, Patricia (eds.), *Culture and Power in the Reconstitution of the Chinese Realm, 200–600*, Cambridge, MA: Harvard University Press 2001, 75–98.
Honneth, Axel, *Kampf um Anerkennung: zur moralischen Grammatik sozialer Konflikte*, Frankfurt a. M.: Suhrkamp 1992.
—, *Verdinglichung: eine anerkennungstheoretische Studie*, Frankfurt a. M.: Suhrkamp 2005.
Hori, Ichiro, "On the Concept of Hijiri (Holy Man)", in: Williams, Paul (ed.), *Buddhism: Critical Concepts in Religious Studies*, New York, NY: Routledge 2005, 184–235.
Horne, Thomas Hartwell, *An Introduction to the Critical Study and Knowledge of the Holy Scripture*, Vol. II, London: T. Cadell 1828.
Horsch, Paul, "From Creation Myth to World Law: The Early History of *Dharma*", in: Olivelle, Patrick (ed.), *Dharma: Studies in Its Semantic, Cultural, and Religious History*, Delhi: Motilal Banarsidass 2005, 1–26.
Howell, Julia Day, "Modernity and the Borderlands of Islamic Spirituality in Indonesia's New Sufi Networks", in: Bruinessen, Martin van/Howell, Julia Day, *Sufism and the 'Modern' in Indonesian Islam*, London: I.B. Tauris 2007, 217–240.
Hoyland, Robert G., *Seeing Islam as Others Saw it: A Survey and Evaluation of Christian, Jewish, and Zoroastrian Writings on Early Islam*, Princeton, NJ: Darwin Press 1997.
Hughes, Thomas Patrick, *Missionary to the Afghans. Notes on Mohammedanism: being Outline of the Religious System of Islam*, rev. ed. London: Wm. H. Allen & Co. 1877.
Huizinga, Johan, *Homo Ludens: A Study of the Play-Element in Culture*, Boston, MA: Beacon 1955 (tr. from the German ed. of 1944).
Hurvitz, Leon, "'Render unto Caesar' in Early Chinese Buddhism: Hui-yüan's Treatise on the Exemption of the Buddhist Clergy from the Requirements of Civil Etiquette", in: Roy, Kshitis (ed.), *Liebenthal Festschrift*, Santiniketan: Santiniketan Press 1957, 80–114.

Ibn Abī Dāwūd al-Sijistānī, *Kitāb al-maṣāhif*, Arthur Jeffery (ed.), Leiden: Brill 1937.
Ibn Abī Ḥātim al-Rāzī, *Tafsīr*, ed. Aḥmad Fatḥī ʿAbd al-Raḥmān Ḥijāzī, 7 vols., I, Beirut: Dār al-Kutub al-ʿIlmiyya 1427/2006.
Ibn ʿAsākir, *Taʾrīkh madīnat Dimashq*, al-ʿAmrawī (ed.), 80 vols., XXI, Beirut: Dār al-Fikr 1415/1995–1419/1998.
Ibn Ḥajar al-ʿAsqalānī, *al-Maṭālib al-ʿāliya bi-zawāʾid al-masānīd al-thamāniya*, Ḥabīb al-Raḥmān al-Aʿẓamī (ed.), 5 vols., IV, Beirut: Dār al-Maʿrifa 1407/1987.
Ibn Ḥanbal, Aḥmad, *Musnad*, 6 vols., II, Cairo: al-Maṭbaʿa al-Maymaniyya 1313/1895, reprint Beirut.
Ibn Qutayba, *al-Maʿārif*, Tharwat ʿUkāsha (ed.), Cairo: Dār al-Maʿārif 1969.
Ibn Saʿd, *al-Ṭabaqāt al-kubrā*, 8 vols., II, Beirut: Dār Ṣādir-Dār Bayrūt 1380/1960–1388/1968.
Ibn Shabba, ʿUmar, *Akhbār al-Madīna*, Dandal and Bayān (ed.), 2 vols., I, Beirut: Dār al-Kutub al-ʿIlmiyya 1417/1996.
Ibn Yūsuf al-Janadī, Muḥammad, *al-Sulūk fī ṭabaqāt al-ʿulamāʾ wa-l-mulūk*, Muḥammad ibn ʿAlī ibn al-Ḥusayn al-Akwaʿ al-Ḥiwālī (ed.), 2 vols., I, Ṣanʿāʾ: Maktabat al-Irshād 1414/1993–1416/1995.

Inoue, Nobutaka, *Contemporary Japanese Religion*, 25, Tokyo: Foreign Press Center/ Japan 2000.

——, "How Are the Concepts of 'New Religion' and 'NRM' Related", in: Bocking, Brian (ed.), IAHR World Congress Proceedings Tokyo 2005. Religion and Society: an Agenda for the 21st Century. Cambridge: Roots and Branches, 2010, 115-135.

Ishihama, Yumiko, "On the Dissemination of the Belief in the Dalai Lama as a Manifestation of the Bodhisattva Avalokiteœvara", in: *Acta Asiatica* 64 (1993), 38–56.

Ishii, Kenji, *Gendai nihonjin no shûkyô deetaabukku*, Tokyo: Shinyôsha 2007.

Isomae, Jun'ichi, *Kindai Nihon no Shûkyô Gensetsu to Sono Keifu: Shûkyô, Kokka, Shintô*, Tokyo: Iwanami Shôten 2003.

Israel, Milton (ed.), *The South Asian Diaspora in Canada: Six Essays*, Toronto: Multicultural History Society of Ontario & Centre for South Asian Studies 1987.

Jaeger, Friedrich/Rüsen, Jörn, *Geschichte des Historismus*, München: Beck 1992.

Jao Tsung-i, "Questions on the Origins of Writing Raised by the Silk Road", in: *Sino-Platonic Papers* 26 (1991), 1–10.

Jaspers, Karl, *Vom Ursprung und Ziel der Geschichte*, München: Piper 1949, München/ Zürich: Artemis-Verlag 1949.

Jayawickrama, N.A. (ed. and trans.), *The Inception of Discipline and the Vinaya Nidāna*, London: Pali Text Society 1986, 55–64.

Jenkins, Philip, *The Next Christendom: The Coming of Global Christianity*, New York, NY/Oxford: Oxford University Press 2007.

Joas, Hans, "Die Kontingenz der Säkularisierung – Überlegungen zum Problem der Säkularisierung im Werk Reinhart Kosellecks", in: Joas, Hans/Vogt, Peter (eds.), *Begriffene Geschichte. Beiträge zum Werk Reinhart Kosellecks*, Frankfurt a. M.: Suhrkamp 2010, 309–338.

John Lamoreaux (tr.), "Early Eastern Christian Responses to Islam", in: Tolan, John (ed.), *Medieval Christian Perceptions of Islam: A Book of Essays*, New York, NY: Garland 1996, 3–31.

Jonker, Gerdien, *Eine Wellenlänge zu Gott: Der "Verband der Islamischen Kulturzentren" in Europa*, Bielelfeld, Germany: Transcript 2002.

Juergensmeyer, Mark, *The New Cold War? Religious Nationalism Confronts the Secular State*, Berkeley, CA: University of California Press 1993.

Jürgensen, Kurt, *Die Stunde der Kirche. Die Evangelisch-Lutherische Landeskirche Schleswig-Holsteins in den ersten Jahren nach dem Zweiten Weltkrieg*, Neumünster: Wachholtz 1976.

Kalin, Everett R., "The New Testament Canon of Eusebius", in: McDonald, Lee Martin/Sanders, James A. (eds.), *The Canon Debate*, Peabody, MA: Hendrickson Publishers 2002, 386–404.

Kamata, Shigeo, *Kegongaku kenkyû shiryô shûsei*, Tokyo: Tokyo daigaku Tôyô bunka kenkyûjo 1983.

Kao, Karl S.Y. (ed.), *Classical Chinese Tales of the Supernatural and the Fantastic*, Bloomington: Indiana University Press 1985.

Karlgren, Bernhard, *Grammata Serica Recensa*, Stockholm: Museum of Far Eastern Antiquities 1972.

Kawagoe, Eishin (ed.), *dKar chag 'Phang thang ma*, Sendai: Tohoku Society for Indo-Tibetan Studies 2005.

Kawerau, Peter, *Das Christentum des Ostens*, Stuttgart: Kohlhammer 1972.

Keightley, David N., "The Religious Commitment: Shang Theology and the Genesis of Chinese Political Culture", in: *History of Religions* 17.3–4 (1978), 211–225.
——, "The Shang: China's First Historical Dynasty", in: Loewe, Michael/Shaughnessy, Edward L. (eds.), *The Cambridge History of Ancient China: From the Origins of Civilization to 221 BC*, Cambridge, MA: Cambridge University Press 1999, 232–291.
Kepel, Gilles, *The Revenge of God*, Oxford: Blackwell 1994.
Kern, Otto, *Die Religion der Griechen*, vol. 1, Berlin: Weidmann 1926.
Keyes, Charles F., *The Golden Peninsula: Culture and Adaptation in Mainland Southeast Asia* (reprint), Honolulu: University of Hawaii Press 1995.
Khare, Ravindra S., *Culture and Reality: Essays on the Hindu System of Managing Foods*, Simla: Indian Institute of Advanced Study 1976.
—— (ed.), *The Eternal Food: Gastronomic Ideas and Experiences of Hindus and Buddhists*, Albany: State University of New York Press 1992.
——, *The Hindu Hearth and Home: Culinary Systems Old and New in North India*, Delhi: Vikas Publishing House 1976.
Khosrokhavar, Farhad, *L'islam des jeunes*, Paris: Flammarion 1997.
Kieschnick, John, *The Impact of Buddhism on Chinese Material Culture*, Princeton, NJ: University Press 2003.
Kippenberg, Hans G./Rüpke, Jörg/Stuckrad, Kocku von (eds.), *Europäische Religionsgeschichte. Ein mehrfacher Pluralismus*, Göttingen: Vandenhoeck & Ruprecht 2009.
Kippenberg, Hans G./Stuckrad, Kocku von, *Einführung in die Religionswissenschaft: Gegenstände und Begriffe*, München: Beck 2003.
Kisala, Robert, *Prophets of Peace: Pacifism and Cultural Identity in Japan's New Religions*, Honolulu: University of Hawaii Press 1999.
Kister, Meir Jacob, "The battle of the Ḥarra", in: Rosen-Ayalon, Myriam (ed.), *Studies in Memory of Gaston Wiet*, Jerusalem: Institute of Asian and African Studies 1977, 33–49.
——, "The social and political implications of three traditions in the Kitab al-Kharādj of Yahya b. Adam", in: *Journal of the Economic and Social History of the Orient* 3 (1960), 326–334.
Klauck, Hans-Josef, *Apocryphal Gospels: An Introduction*, London, New York, NY: T & T Clark International 2003.
Klein, Thoralf/Zöllner, Reinhard (eds.), *Karl Gützlaff (1803–1851) und das Christentum in Ostasien: Ein Missionar zwischen den Kulturen*, Nettetal: Institut Monumenta Serica, Sankt Augustin, Steyler Verlag 2005.
Kollmar-Paulenz, Karénina, *Zur Ausdifferenzierung eines autonomen Bereichs Religion in asiatischen Gesellschaften des 17. und 18. Jahrhunderts: Das Beispiel der Mongolen*, Akademievorträge, no. XVI, Bern 2007.
Komazawa Daijiten Hensanjo (ed.), *Zengaku daijiten*, Tokyo: Taishûkan 1978.
Kongju Seo, Maria, "Kut in Sacred and Secular Contexts. Focussing on Musical Practices of Ritual Performances", in: *Han'guk musokhak* 3 (2001), 5–29.
Koningsveld, Pieter Sjoerd van, "Christian Arabic Literature from Medieval Spain: an Attempt at Periodization", in: Samir, Samir Khalil/Nielsen, Jørgen S. (eds.), *Christian Arabic Apologetics during the Abbasid Period (750–1258)*, Leiden: Brill 1994, 203–224.
Korzybski, Alfred, *Science and Sanity: An Introduction to Non-Aristotelian Systems and General Semantics*, Lakeville, CT: International Non-Aristotelian Library Pub. Co. 1933.
Koselleck, Reinhart, *Begriffsgeschichten*, Frankfurt a. M.: Suhrkamp 2006.

Krämer, Hans Martin/Oesterle, Jenny/Vordermark, Ulrike (eds.), *Labeling the Religious Self and Others: Reciprocal Perceptions of Christians, Muslims, Hindus, Buddhists, and Confucians in Medieval and Early Modern Times*, Special Edition of Comparativ - Zeitschrift für Globalgeschichte und vergleichende Gesellschaftsforschung 4.20 (2010).

Kuhn, Dieter/Stahl, Helga (eds.), *Die Gegenwart des Altertums. Formen und Funktionen des Altertumsbezugs in den Hochkulturen der Alten Welt*, Heidelberg: edition forum 2001.

Kuhrt, Amélie, *'Greek' and 'Greece' in Mesopotamian and Persian Perspectives*, Oxford: Head Press 2002.

Kumar, Pratap, *Hindus in South Africa: Their Traditions and Beliefs*, Durban, SA: University of Durban-Westville 2000.

Kurian, George/Srivastava, Ram P. (eds.), *Overseas Indians: A Study in Adaptation*, New Delhi: Vikas 1983.

Kurien, Prema A., *A Place at the Multicultural Table: The Development of an American Hinduism*, New Brunswick, NJ: Rutgers University Press 2007.

Kuzmina, Elena E., *The Origin of the Indo-Iranians*, Mallory, James Patrick (ed.), Leiden: Brill 2007.

Kuzmina, Elena E., *The Prehistory of the Silk Road*, in: Mair, Victor H. (ed.), Philadelphia, PA: University of Pennsylvania Press 2008.

Kŭm, Chang-t'ae, *Chosŏn hugi sŏgyo-wa sŏhak* (Western Religion and Western Science in late Chosŏn), Seoul: Seoul National University Press 2005.

Lamotte, Étienne, *History of Indian Buddhism. From the Origins to the Śaka Era*, Louvain-la-Neuve: Peeters press 1988 [*Histoire du Bouddhisme Indien*, Louvain 1958].

——, "La critique d'interpretation dans le bouddhism", in: *Annuaire de l'Institut de Philologie et d'Histoire Orientales et Slaves* IX (1949), 341–361.

Lancaster, Lewis (ed.), *The Korean Buddhist Canon: A Descriptive Catalogue*, Berkeley, CA: University of California Press 1979.

Lanczkowski, Günter, *Begegnung und Wandel der Religionen*, Düsseldorf: Diederichs 1971.

——, *Einführung in die Religionswissenschaft*, Darmstadt: Wissenschaftliche Buchgesellschaft 1980.

Lang, Bernhard "The 'Writings': A Hellenistic Literary Canon in the Hebrew Bible", in: Kooij, Arie van der/Toorn, Karel van der (eds.), *Canonization and Decanonization*, Leiden: Brill 1998, 41–66.

Latour, Bruno, *Nous n'avons jamais été modernes. Essai d'anthropologie symétrique*, Paris: La Découverte 1991.

Lau, D.C./Chen, Fong Ching (eds.), *A Concordance to the Liji*, Chinese University of Hong Kong, Institute for Chinese Studies, The Ancient Chinese Text Concordance Series, Hong Kong: Commercial Press 1992.

Lau, Ulrich, "Vom Schaf zur Gerechtigkeit" [From the sheep to justice], in: Hammer, Christiane/Führer, Bernhard (eds.), *Tradition und Moderne. Religion, Philosophie und Literatur in China*, Dortmund: project 1997, 37–48.

Lawson, Ronald, "When Immigrants Take Over: The Impact of Immigrant Growth on American Seventh-day Adventism's Trajectory from Sect to Denomination", in: *Journal for the Scientific Study of Religion* 38 (1999), 83–102.

Lecker, Michael, "Biographical notes on Abū 'Ubayda Ma'mar b. al-Muthannā", in: *Studia Islamica* 81 (1995), 71–100.

——, "Judaism among Kinda and the *ridda* of Kinda", in: *Journal of the American Oriental Society* 115 (1995), 635–650.
——, *The 'Constitution of Medina': Muḥammad's First Legal Document*, Princeton, NJ: Darwin Press 2004.
——, "Zayd b. Thābit, 'a Jew with two sidelocks': Judaism and literacy in pre-Islamic Medina (Yathrib)", in: *Journal of Near Eastern Studies* 56 (1997), 259–273.
Leder, Stefan, "The attitude of the population, especially the Jews, towards the Arab-Islamic conquest of Bilād al-Shām and the question of their role therein", in: *Die Welt des Orients* 18 (1987), 64–71.
Lee, Eun-jeung, *"Anti-Europa". Die Geschichte der Rezeption von Konfuzianismus und der konfuzianischen Gesellschaft in Europa seit der frühen Aufklärung*, Münster: Lit Verlag 2003.
Lehmann, Hartmut, *Säkularisierung. Der europäische Sonderweg in Sachen Religion*, Göttingen: Wallstein 2004.
Leonard, Jane Kate, *Wei Yuan and China's Rediscovery of the Maritime World*, Cambridge, MA: Harvard University Press 1984.
Lepenies, Wolf, *Das Ende der Naturgeschichte: Wandel kultureller Selbstverständlichkeiten in den Wissenschaften des 18. und 19. Jahrhunderts*, Frankfurt a. M.: Hanser 1978.
Lester, Robert C., "Hinduism", in: Denny, Frederick M./Taylor, Rodney L. (eds.), *The Holy Book in Comparative Perspective*, Columbia: University of South Carolina Press 1985, 126–147.
Leuba, James H., *A Psychological Study of Religion: Its Origin, Function, and Future*, New York, NY: The MacMillan Co. 1912.
Levering, Miriam, "Scripture and Its Reception: A Buddhist Case", in: Levering, Miriam (ed.), *Rethinking Scripture*, New York, NY: State University of New York Press 1989, 58–101.
Lewis, Bernard, "An apocalyptic vision of Islamic history", in: *Bulletin of the School of Oriental and African Studies* 13 (1950), 308–338.
Lewis, James R. (ed.), *Magical Religion and Modern Witchcraft*, Albany, NY: State University of New York Press 1996.
Lieu, Samuel N. C., *Manichaeism in Central Asia and China*, Leiden: E. J. Brill 1998.
Lightstone, Jack N., "The Rabbis' Bible: The Canon of the Hebrew Bible and the Early Rabbinic Guild", in: McDonald, Lee Martin/Sanders, James A. (eds.), *The Canon Debate*, Peabody, MA: Hendrickson Publishers 2002, 163–184.
Lincoln, Bruce, "Theses on Method", in: *Method and Theory in the Study of Religion* 8 (1996), 225–227.
Liu, Li, *The Chinese Neolithic: Trajectories to Early States*, Cambridge, MA: Cambridge University Press 2004.
Lofland, John, *Doomsday Cult: A Study of Conversion, Proselytization, and Maintenance of Faith*, Englewood Cliffs, NJ: Prentice Hall 1966.
Lopez, Donald S. Jr., *Buddhism and Science. A Guide for the Perplexed*, Chicago: University of Chicago Press 2008.
——, *Prisoners of Shangri-la. Tibetan Buddhism and the West*, Chicago: University of Chicago Press 1999.
Lorenz, Edward N., *The Essence of Chaos*, Seattle: CRC Press 2005.
Luhmann, Niklas, "Die Ausdifferenzierung der Religion", in: Luhmann, Niklas, *Gesellschaftsstruktur und Semantik: Studien zur Wissenssoziologie der modernen Gesellschaft*, vol. 3, Frankfurt a. M.: Suhrkamp 1993, 259–357.

——, *Die Religion der Gesellschaft*, Frankfurt a. M.: Suhrkamp 2000.

Lutz, Jessie, "Karl F.A. Gützlaff, Missionary Entrepreneur", in: Fairbank, John K./ Barnett, Suzanne Wilson (eds.), *Christianity in China: Early Protestant Writings*, Cambridge, MA: Harvard University Press 1985, 61–87.

MacColl, Malcolm, *The Nineteenth Century*, London: Longmans, Green and Co. 1877.

McCutcheon, Russell T., *Manufacturing Religion: The Discourse on Sui Generis Religion and the Politics of Nostalgia*, New York, NY/Oxford: Oxford University Press 1997.

——, *Studying Religion: An Introduction*, London et al.: Equinox Publishing 2007.

McDonald, Lee Martin/Sanders, James A., "Introduction", in: McDonald, Lee Martin/ Sanders, James A., *The Canon Debate: On the Origins and Formation of the Bible*, Peabody: Hendrickson Publishers 2002, 3–17.

——/——, *The Canon Debate: On the Origins and Formation of the Bible*, Peabody: Hendrickson Publishers 2002.

McFarland, H. Neill, *The Rush Hour of the Gods: A Study of New Religious Movements in Japan*, New York, NY: Macmillan 1967.

McGuire, Meredith, *Lived Religion: Faith and Practice in Everyday Life*, New York, NY: Oxford University Press 2008.

——, *Religion: The Social Context*, 5th ed., Belmont, CA: Wadsworth 2002.

McLellan, Janet, *Many Petals of the Lotus: Five Asian Buddhist Communities in Toronto*, Toronto: University of Toronto Press 1999.

Maier, Gerhard, "Der Abschluss des jüdischen Kanons und das Lehrhaus von Jabne", in: Maier, Gerhard (ed.), *Der Kanon der Bibel*, Giessen: Brunnen Verlag 1990, 1–24.

Mair, Victor H., "Horse Sacrifices and Sacred Groves among the North(west)ern Peoples of East Asia", in: *Ouya xuekan* 欧亚学刊 (Eurasian Studies) 6 (2007), 22–53.

——, "Kinesis versus Stasis, Interaction versus Independent Invention", in: Mair, Victor H. (ed.), *Contact and Exchange in the Ancient World*, Honolulu: University of Hawai'i Press 2006b, 1–2.

——, "Old Sinitic **myag*, Old Persian *maguš*, and English 'Magician'", in: *Early China* 15 (1990a), 27–47.

——, "*Soldierly Methods*: Vade Mecum for an Iconoclastic Translation of *Sun Zi bingfa*", with a complete transcription and word-for-word glosses of the Manchu translation by H. T. Toh, in: *Sino-Platonic Papers* 178 2008, i–xvi, 1–195, web publication.

——, "Southern Bottle-Gourd (*hu-lu* 葫蘆) Myths in China and Their Appropriation by Taoism", in: *Zhongguo shenhua yu chuanshuo xueshu yantaohui lunwen ji* 中國神話與傳說學術研究討會論文集 (Proceedings of the Conference on Chinese Myth and Legend); Hanxue yanjiu zhongxin congkan 漢學研j究中心叢刊 (Center for Chinese Studies Research Series), No. 5, Taipei: Hanxue yanjiu zhongxin 1996.

—— (tr. and intro.), *Tao Te Ching: The Classic Book of Integrity and the Way*, New York, NY: Bantam 1990b.

—— (tr. and intro.), *The Art of War: Sun Zi's Military Methods*, Columbia: Columbia University Press 2007a.

——, "The Beginnings of Sino-Indian Cultural Contact", in: *Journal of Asian History* 38.2 (2004), 81–95.

——, *The Columbia Anthology of Traditional Chinese Literature*, New York, NY: Columbia University Press 1994.

——, "The Horse in Late Prehistoric China: Wresting Culture and Control from the 'Barbarians'", in: Levine, Marsha/Renfrew, Colin/Boyle, Katie (eds.), *Prehistoric steppe adaptation and the horse*, McDonald Institute Monographs, Cambridge, MA: McDonald Institute for Archaeological Research 2003, 163–187.
——, "The North(west)ern Peoples and the Recurrent Origins of the 'Chinese' State", in: Fogel, Joshua A. (ed.), *The Teleology of the Modern Nation-State: Japan and China*, Philadelphia, PA: University of Pennsylvania Press 2005, 46–84, 205–217.
——, "The Rediscovery and Complete Excavation of Ördek's Necropolis", in: *The Journal of Indo-European Studies* 34.3–4 (2006a), 275–318.
—— (tr. and intro.), *Wandering on the Way. Early Taoist Tales and Parables of Chuang Tzu*, New York, NY: Bantam 1994, Honolulu: University of Hawaii Press 1998.
Mallory, James Patrick/Adams, D. Q. (eds.), *Encyclopedia of Indo-European Culture*, London and Chicago: Fitzroy Dearborn 1997.
Mallory, James Patrick/Mair, Victor H., *The Tarim Mummies: Ancient China and the Mystery of the Earliest Peoples from the West*, London: Thames and Hudson 2000.
Mango, Cyril/Scott, Roger, *The Chonicle of Theophanes the Confessor*, Oxford: Clarendon Press 1997.
Marriott, McKim, *India through Hindu Categories*, Contributions to Indian Sociology, Occasional Studies 5, New Delhi/Newbury Park, CA: Sage Publications 1990.
Marty, Martin E./Appleby, R. Scott (eds.), *The Fundamentalism Project*, 5 vols., Chicago: University of Chicago Press 1991–1995.
Masini, Federico, *The Formation of Modern Chinese Lexicon and its Evolution Towards a National Language: The Period from 1840 to 1898*, Journal of Chinese Linguistics Monograph Series no. 6, Berkeley, CA: University of California 1993.
Mason, Steve, "Josephus and His twenty-Two Book Canon", in: McDonald, Lee Martin/Sanders, James A. (eds.), *The Canon Debate*, Peabody, MA: Hendrickson Publishers 2002, 110–127.
Masuzawa, Tomoko, *The Invention of World Religions: Or, How European Universalism was Preserved in the Language of Pluralism and Diversity*, Chicago: University of Chicago Press 2005.
Mateer, Ada Haven, *New Terms for New Ideas: A Study of the Chinese Newspaper*, Shanghai: Presbyterian Mission Press 1917.
Matthews, Bruce (ed.), *Buddhism in Canada*, New York, NY: Routledge 2006.
Meicun, Lin, "Qilian and Kunlun – The Earliest Tokharian Loan-words in Ancient Chinese", in: Mair, Victor H. (ed.), *The Bronze Age and Early Iron Age Peoples of Eastern Central Asia*, 2 vols., vol. 1, Washington, DC: The Institute for the Study of Man; Philadelphia, PA: The University of Pennsylvania Museum Publications 1998, 476–482.
Mendelssohn, Moses, "Jerusalem oder Über religiöse Macht und Judentum", in: Thom, Martina (ed.), *Schriften über Religion und Aufklärung*, Berlin: Union Verlag 1989, 422–423.
Meserve, Ruth I., "History in the Search for Precedent: 'Animal Judgments'", in: *Altaica* (Moscow) 5 (2001), 90–97.

Meserve, Ruth I., "Public Ridicule", in: Sárközi, Alice/Rákos, Attila (eds.), *Altaica Budapestinensia, MMII*, Proceedings of the 45th Permanent International Altaistic Conference (PIAC), Budapest, Hungary, June 23–28, 2002, Budapest: Research Group for Altaic Studies, Hungarian Academy of Sciences; Department of Inner Asian Studies, Eötvös Loránd University 2003, 225–233.
Metzger, Bruce M., *The Canon of the New Testament: Its Origin, Development, and Significance*, Oxford: Clarendon Press 1987.
Miles, Jack, *God: A Biography*, New York, NY: Vintage Books 1996.
Mills, Martin A., *Identity, Ritual and State in Tibetan Buddhism: the Foundations of Authority in Gelukpa Monasticism*, New York, NY: RoutledgeCurzon 2003.
Mochizuki Shinkô, *Bukkyô Daijiten*, Tokyo: Sekai seiten kankô kyôkai 1957–68.
Moerman, Michael, *Being Lue: Uses and Abuses of Ethnic Identification*, Reprint No. 275, Proceedings of the 1967 Spring Meeting of the American Ethnological Society, Berkeley, CA: Center for Southeast Asia 1968.
——, "Ethnic Identity in a Complex Civilization: Who Are the Lue?", in: American Anthropologist 67 (1965), 1215–1230.
Moraw, Peter, *Über König und Reich. Aufsätze zur deutschen Verfassungsgeschichte des späten Mittelalters*, Sigmaringen: Jan Thorbecke 1995.
Mozi, *Zhuzi jicheng*, edition, vol. 4, Hongkong: Zhonghua 1978.
Müller, Dietmar, *Staatsbürger auf Widerruf: Juden und Muslime als Alteritätspartner im rumänischen und serbischen Nationscode: Ethnonationale Staatsbürgerschaftskonzepte 1878–1941*, Wiesbaden: Harrasowitz 2005.

Nakamoto, Tominaga, *Emerging from Meditation*, London: Duckworth 1990.
Nakamura, Hajime, *Bukkyôgo daijiten*, Tokyo: Tokyo shoseki 1975.
Nattier, Jan, *A Guide to the Earliest Chinese Buddhist Translations: Texts from the Eastern Han* 東漢 *and Three Kingdoms* 三國 *Periods*, Tokyo: The International Research Institute for Advanced Buddhology, Soka University 2008.
Nayar, Kamala Elizabeth, *The Sikh Diaspora in Vancouver: Three Generations amid Tradition, Modernity, and Multiculturalism*, Toronto: University of Toronto Press 2004.
Nedostup, Rebecca, *Superstitious Regimes, Religion and the Politics of Chinese Modernity*, Cambridge, MA: Harvard University Press 2010.
Needleman, Jacob/Baker, George (eds.), *Understanding the New Religions*, New York, NY: Seabury Press 1978.
Neelis, Jason, *Early Buddhist Transmission and Trade Networks: Mobility and Exchange within and beyound the Nortwestern Borderlands of South Asia*, Leiden, Boston, MA: Brill 2011.
Niewöhner, Friedrich, *Veritas sive Varietas: Lessings Toleranzparabel und das Buch von den drei Betrügern*, Heidelberg: Schneider 1888.
Norman, Kenneth Roy, *The Group of Discourses (Sutta-Nipâta)*, vol. I, London, Boston, MA: Pali Text Society 1984.

Oldenberg, Hermann, *Die Lehre der Upanishaden und die Anfänge des Buddhismus*, Göttingen: Vandenhoek & Ruprecht 1915.
—— (ed.), *The Vinaya Piṭakaṃ*, vol. 1, Oxford: Pali Text Society 1997.
Olivelle, Patrick, "Caste and Purity: A Study in the Language of the Dharma Literature", in: *Contributions to Indian Sociology* 32 (1998), 190–216.

——, "Explorations in the Early History of Dharmaśāstra", in: Olivelle, Patrick (ed.), *Between the Empires: Society in India 300 BCE to 400 CE*, New York, NY: Oxford University Press 2006, 169–190.

——, "Food in India: A Review Essay", in: *Journal of Indian Philosophy* 23 (1995), 367–380.

——, *Manu's Code of Law: A Critical Edition and Translation of the Mānava-Dharmaśāstra*, New York, NY: Oxford University Press 2005.

——, "Power of Words: The Ascetic Appropriation and the Semantic Evolution of dharma", in: Olivelle, Patrick, *Language, Texts, and Society: Explorations in Ancient Indian Culture and Religion*, Florence: University of Florence Press 2006.

——, "The Semantic History of Dharma. The Middle and Late Vedic Periods", in: Olivelle, Patrick (ed.), *Dharma: Studies in Its Semantic, Cultural, and Religious History*, Special issue of Journal of Indian Philosophy 32 (2004), 491–511.

Ong, Walter J., "Writing is a Technology that Restructures Thought", in: Baumann, Gerd (ed.), *The Written Word: Literacy in Transition*, Oxford: Clarendon Press 1986, 23–50.

Oppenheim, Leo, *Ancient Mesopotamia: Portrait of a Dead Civilization*, Chicago: University of Chicago Press 1968.

Orsi, Robert A., *Between Heaven and Earth: The Religious Worlds People Make and the Scholars Who Study Them*, Princeton, NJ: Princeton University Press 2005.

Ortner, Sherry B., *High Religion: A Cultural and Political History of Sherpa Buddhism*, Princeton, NJ: Princeton University Press 1989.

Osborne, Robert Durie, *Islam under the Arabs*, London: Longmans, Green & Co. 1876.

Paper, Jordan, *The Spirits are Drunk: Comparative Approaches to Chinese Religion*, Albany: SUNY Press 1995.

Parker, Cristian, *Popular Religion and Modernization in Latin America: A Different Logic* (Robert R. Barr, tr.), Maryknoll, NY: Orbis Books 1996.

Patzia, Arthur G., *The Making of the New Testament: Origin, Collection, Text & Canon*, Downers Grove, IL: InterVarsity Press 1995.

Perera, Lakshman S., *The Institutions of Ancient Ceylon From Inscriptions*, vol. 1, Kandy: International Centre for Ethnic Studies 2001.

Permanent People's Tribunal on Sri Lanka 14–16 January 2010. Dublin: Irish Forum for Peace in Sri Lanka, http://www.internazionaleleliobas-so.it/index.php?newsid=459, accession: 10 January 2010.

Peters, Francis E., *The Monotheists: Jews, Christians, and Muslims in Conflict and Competition*, 2 vols., Princeton, London: Princeton University Press 2003.

Peterson, Derek/Walhof, Darren (eds.), *The Invention of Religion: Rethinking Belief in Politics and History*, New Brunswick, NJ: Rutgers University Press 2002.

Pollack, Detlef, *Rückkehr des Religiösen? Studien zum religiösen Wandel in Deutschland und Europa 2*, Tübingen: Mohr 2009.

Pollock, Sheldon, *The Language of the Gods in the World of Men: Sanskrit, Culture, and Power in Premodern India*, Berkeley, CA: University of California Press 2006.

Poltermann, Andreas (ed.), *Literaturkanon – Medienereignis – Kultureller Text. Formen interkultureller Kommunikation und Übersetzung*, Berlin: Erich Schmidt 1995.

Pommaret, Françoise (ed.), *Lhasa in the 17th Century. The Capital of the Dalai Lamas*, Brill's Tibetan Studies Library, 3, Leiden: Brill 2003.

Potter, David S., "The Inscriptions on the bronze Herakles from Messene", in: *Zeitschrift für Papyrologie und Epigraphik* 88 (1991), 277–290.

Power, Daniel/Standen, Naomi (eds.), *Frontiers in question: Eurasian borderlands 700–1700*, Basingstoke: Macmillan Press 1999.
Prebish, Charles S./Baumann, Martin (eds.), *Westward Dharma: Buddhism beyond Asia*, Berkeley, CA: University of California Press 2002.
Proudfoot, Anne, "The Sources of Theophanes for the Heraclian Period", in: *Byzantion* 44 (1974), 367–439.
Pye, Michael, "What is 'Religion' in East Asia?", in: Bianchi, Ugo (ed.), *The Notion of 'Religion' in Comparative Research: Selected Proceedings of the XVIth Congress of the International Association of the History of Religions*, Rome: L'Erma di Bretschneider 1994, 115–122.

Qāsim ibn Sallām, Abū 'Ubayd al-, *al-Nāsikh wa-l-mansūkh fī l-qur'ān al-'azīz*, Muḥammad ibn Ṣāliḥ al-Mudayfir (ed.), Riyadh: Maktabat al-Rushd 1411/1990.
Qudāma ibn Ja'far, *Kitāb al-kharāj wa-ṣinā'at al-kitāba*, Muḥammad Ḥusayn al-Zabīdī (ed.), Baghdad: Dār al-Rashīd 1981.
Qu Xutong 瞿旭彤, "Gu Hanyu wu *(*myag)*, Gu Bosiyu *Maguš* he Yingyu *Magician*" 古汉语巫*(*myag)*, 古波斯语 *Maguš*, 和英语*Magician*", in: Xia Hanyi 夏含夷 (ed.), *Yuanfang de shixi <Gudai Zhongguo> jingxuan ji* 远方的时习《古代中国》精选集, Shanghai: Shanghai Guji Chubanshe 2008, 55–86.

Ray, Reginald A., "Buddhism", in: Denny, Frederick M./Taylor, Rodney L. (eds.), *The Holy Book in Comparative Perspective*, Columbia: University of South Carolina Press 1985, 148–180.
——, *Buddhist Saints in India*, New York, NY: Oxford University Press 1994.
Reader, Ian, "Of Religion, Nationalism and Ideology: Analysing the Development of Religious Studies in Japan", in: *Social Science of Japan Journal* 8.1 (2005), 119–124).
——, "Pilgrimage growth in the modern world: meanings and implications", in: *Religion* 37 (2007a), 210–229.
——, "Positively promoting pilgrimages: Media representations of pilgrimage in Japan", in: *Nova Religio* 10.3 (2007b), 13–31.
——, "Recent Japanese publications on the new religions: the work of Shimazono Susumu (review article)", in: *Japanese Journal of Religious Studies* 20.2–3 (1993), 101–120.
——, *Religion in Contemporary Japan*, Basingstoke: Macmillan 1991, Honolulu: University of Hawaii Press 1991.
——, "Returning to Respectability: A Religious Revival in Japan?", in: *Japan Forum* 2.1 (1990), 57–68.
Reader, Ian/Tanabe, George J. Jr., *Practically Religious: Worldly Benefits and the Common Religion of Japan*, Honolulu: University of Hawaii Press 1998.
Reinink, Gemit J., "Pseudo-Methodius: A Concept of History in Response to the Rise of Islam", in: Cameron, Averil/Conrad, Lawrence (eds.), *The Byzantine and Early Islamic Near East 1*, Princeton, NJ: Princeton University Press 1992, 149–187.
Rhoton, Jared Douglas (tr.), *A Clear Differentiation of the Three Codes. Essential Distinctions among the Individual Liberation, Great Vehicle, and Tantric Systems. The sDom gsum rab dbye and Six Letters*, Suny Series in Buddhist Studies, New York, NY: State University of New York Press 2002.
Ricci, Matteo, *Ch'ŏnju sillŭi* (Tianzhu shiyi – Die wahre Bedeutung des Herrn des Himmels), Seoul: Seoul National University Press 1999.
——, *Tienzhu shiyi*, Seoul et al.: Seoul National University Press 2006.

Richardson, James T. (ed.), *Regulating Religion: Case Studies from around the Globe*, New York, NY: Kluwer Academic/Penum 2004.

Riesner, Rainer, "Ansätze zur Kanonbildung innerhalb des Neuen Testaments", in: Maier, Gerhard (ed.), *Der Kanon der Bibel*, Giessen: Brunnen Verlag 1990, 153–164.

Ro, T'ae-hwan, "Chŏngjo sidae sŏgi suyong nonŭi-wa sŏhak chŏngch'aek" (Debate on the Reception of Western Technique and on Policies toward Western science during the reign of of King Chŏngjo), in: Chŏng, Ok-cha, et al. (eds.): *Chŏngjo sidae sasang-gwa munhwa* (Philosphy and Culture during the Reign of King Chŏngjo), Seoul: Tolbaegae 1999, 201–245.

Robbins, Thomas, *Cults, Converts, and Charisma: The Sociology of New Religious Movements*, London/Newbury Park, CA: Sage Publications 1988.

Robertson, Roland, *Globalization: Social Theory and Global Culture*, London: Sage 1992.

Robertson, Roland/Chirico, JoAnn, "Humanity, Globalization, Worldwide Religious Resurgence: A Theoretical Exploration", in: *Sociological Analysis* 46 (1985), 219–242.

Robertson, Roland/Garrett, William R. (eds.), *Religion and Global Order*, New York, NY: Paragon House 1991.

Rocher, Ludo, *Orality and Textuality in the Indian Context*, Sino-Platonic Papers 49, Philadelphia, PA: University of Pennsylvania, Department of East Asian Languages and Civilizations 1994.

Roetz, Heiner, *Konfuzius*, 3rd rev. ed., München: Beck 2006.

Roof, Wade Clark, *Spiritual Marketplace: Baby Boomers and the Remaking of American Religion*, Princeton, NJ: Princeton University Press 1999.

Rosch, Eleanor, "Cognitive Representations of Semantic Categories", in: *Journal of Experimental Psychology: General* 104.3 (1975), 192–233.

Rosenbaum, Jonathan, "Judaism", in: Denny, Frederick M./Taylor, Rodney L. (eds.), *The Holy Book in Comparative Perspective*, Columbia: University of South Carolina Press 1985, 10–35.

Roth, Norman, *Jews, Visigoths and Muslims in Medieval Spain*, Leiden: Brill 1994.

——, "The Jews and the Muslim conquest of Spain", in: *Jewish Social Studies* 38 (1976), 145–158.

Rothstein, Mikael (ed.), *New Age Religion and Globalization*, Aarhus: Aarhus University Press 2001.

Rotter, Ekkehart, *Abendland und Sarazenen: das okzidentale Araberbild und seine Entstehung im Frühmittelalter*, Berlin: de Gruyter 1986.

Roy, Olivier, *Vers un islam européen*, Paris: Éditions Esprit 1999.

Rubin, Uri, "Qur'ān and poetry: more data concerning the Qur'ānic *jizya* verse *('an yadin)*", in: *Jerusalem Studies in Arabic and Islam* 31 (2006), 139–146.

Rüdiger, Axel, *Staatslehre und Staatsbildung*, Tübingen: Niemeyer 2005.

Rudrakumaran, Visvanathan, *nāṭu katanta tamiḻīḻa aracu amaippataṟkāṉa ceyaṟkuḻu*, 31 August 2009, http://www.govtamileelam.org, accession: 31 August 2009.

Rudrakumaran, Visvanathan, *The Tamils' Right of Self-determination*, Tamilnation.org, 1996, http://www.tamilnation.org/conferences/tamil_eelam/96_australia/Rudra. html, accession: 12 December 2010.

Ruegg, David Seyfort, *The Symbiosis of Buddhism with Brahmanism, Hinduism in South Asia and of Buddhism with 'Local Cults' in Tibet and the Himalayan Region*, Wien: Verlag der Österreichischen Akademie der Wissenschaften 2008.

Saage, Richard, *Politische Utopie der Neuzeit*, Darmstadt: Wissenschaftliche Buchgesellschaft 1990.

Saint-Blancat, Chantal, *L'islam de la diaspora*, Paris: Bayard 1997.

Samhūdī, Ali bin Ahmad al-, *Wafā' al-wafā*, Qāsim al-Sāmarrā'ī (ed.), 5 vols., London-Jedda: al-Fur-qān 1422/2001.

Samir, Samir Khalil, "The Earliest Arab Apology for Christianity (c. 750)", in: Samir, Samir Khalil/Nielsen, Jørgen S. (eds.), *Christian Arabic Apologetics during the Abbasid Period (750–1258)*, Leiden: Brill 1994, 57–114.

Sanders, James A., "The Issue of Closure in the Canonical Process", in: McDonald, Lee Martin/Sanders, James A., *The Canon Debate: On the Origins and Formation of the Bible*, Peabody: Hendrickson Publishers 2002, 252–263.

Sanders, James A., "Canon as ambiguous", in: McDonald, Lee Martin/Sanders, James A., *The Canon Debate*, Peabody, MA: Hendrickson Publishers 2002, 252–266.

Schäfer, Peter, *Mirror of His Beauty. Feminine Images of God from the Bible to the Early Kabbala*, Princeton, NJ: Princeton University Press 2002.

Schalk, Peter, "Beyond Hindu Festivals: The Celebration of Great Heroes' Day by the Liberation Tigers of Tamil Ealam (LTTE) in Europe", in: *Tempel und Tamilen in zweiter Heimat. Hindus aus Sri Lanka im deutschsprachigen und skandinavischen Raum*, Würzburg: Ergon Verlag 2003, 391–421.

——, *Cāvilum vālvōm. 'Auch im Angesicht des Todes werden wir leben. Īlamtamile sein im Krieg und in der Fremde'*, Dortmund: Internationaler Verein Emigrierter Tamilischer Schriftsteller e.V. 2006b.

——, "Der Kampf geht weiter", in: *Sydasien* 29.3 (2009), 41–46.

——, "Die Lehre des heutigen tamilischen Widerstandes in Īḻam/Laṃkā vom Freitod als Martyrium", in: *Zeitschrift für Religionswissenschaft* 9.1 (2009b), 71–99.

—— (ed.), *Die Lehre der Befreiungstiger Tamilīlams von der Selbstvernichtung durch göttliche Askese: Vorlage der Quelle ÜBERLEGUNGEN DES ANFÜHRERS*, Uppsala: Uppsala University 2007 [E-book, http://uu.diva-portal.org/smash/record.jsf?pid =diva 2:173420].

——, "Historisation of the Martial Ideology of the Liberation Tigers of Tamil Ealam (LTTE)", in: *South Asia. Journal of South Asian Studies* 20 (1997), 68–72.

——, *Īlam* <sīhaḷa. *An Assesment of an Argument*, Acta Universitatits Upsaliensis, Historia Religionum 25, Uppsala: AUU 2004.

——, "'Lest we forget'. On Women and Children under the Military Might of the Lankan Armed Forces", Committee for the Formation of a Provisional Transnational Government of Tamil Eelam, 25 January 2010, http://govtamileelam.org/gov/index.php/press-release/component/content/arti-cle/45-press-release-english/154-lest-we-forget-on-women-and-children-under-the-mili-tary-might-of-the-lankan-armed-forces-?Itemid=107, accession: 26 January 2010a.

——, "Pax Americana, the EU, and the Tamiḻ Resistance Movement (TRM)", *TamilNet*, 01 April 2008, http://www.tamilnet.com/img/publish/2008/04/Peter_Schalk.pdf, accession: 2 April 2008.

——, "Semantic Transformations of the Concept of Dhammadīpa", in: Deegalle, Mahinda (ed.), *Buddhism, Conflict and Violence in Modern sri Lanka*, London: Routledge 2006c, 86–92.

——, "Sustaining the Pre-Colonial Past: Caiva Defiance against Christian Rule in the 19th Century in Jaffna", in: Bergunder, Michael/Frese, Heiko/Schröder, Ulrike (eds.), *Ritual, Caste, and Religion in Colonial South India*, Halle: Verlag der Franckeschen Stiftungen [forthcoming in 2010c].

——, “War of Words - An Obstacle to Peace”, in: *Envisioning New Trajectories for Peace in Sri Lanka. International Seminar 7–9 April 2006, Zurich, Switzerland*, Zürich: Centre for Just Peace and Democracy 2006a, 163–170.

Schalk, Peter/Veluppiḷḷai, Āḷvāpiḷḷai/Nakacami, Ira (ed.), *Buddhism Among Tamils in Pre-Colonial Tamilakam and Ilam*, Acta Universitatis Upsaliensis, Part 1–2, Uppsala: Uppsala University 2002.

Schieder, Wolfgang, “Kommunismus”, in: Brunner, Otto/Conze, Werner/Koselleck, Reinhart (eds.), *Geschichtliche Grundbegriffe*, vol. 3, Stuttgart: Klett 1982, 455–457.

——, “Religion in der Sozialgeschichte”, in: Schieder, Wolfgang/Sellin, Volker (eds.), *Sozialgeschichte in Deutschland. Entwicklungen und Perspektiven im internationalen Zusammenhang*, vol. III: Soziales Verhalten und soziale Aktionsformen in der Geschichte, Göttingen: Vandenhoeck & Ruprecht 1987, 9–31.

Schlesier, Renate, “Menschen und Götter unterwegs: Rituale und Reise in der griechischen Antike”, in: Hölscher, Tonio (ed.), *Gegenwelten zu den Kulturen Griechenlands und Roms in der Antike*, München/Leipzig: Saur 2000, 129–157.

Schluchter, Wolfgang, *Religion und Lebensführung*, 2 vols., Frankfurt a. M.: Suhrkamp 1988.

Schmidt, Ernst A., “Historische Typologie der Orientierungsfunktionen von Kanon in der griechischen und römischen Literatur”, in: Assmann, Aleida/Assmann, Jan (eds.), *Kanon und Zensur*, München: Fink 1987, 246–258.

Schnapp, Alain, “Pourquois les Barbares n’ont-ils point d’images?”, in: Hölscher, Tonio (ed.), *Gegenwelten zu den Kulturen Griechenlands und Roms in der Antike*, München/Leipzig: Saur 2000, 205–216.

Schnädelbach, Herbert, *Philosophie in Deutschland 1831–1933*, Frankfurt a. M.: Suhrkamp 1983.

Schönborn, Christoph von, *Sophrone* de Jerusalem: vie monastique et confession dogmatique, Paris: Beauchesne 1972.

Schröder, Winfried, *Ursprünge des Atheismus. Untersuchungen zur Metaphysik- und Religionskritik des 17. und 18. Jahrhunderts*, Stuttgart/Bad Cannstatt: Fromman Holzboog 1998.

Schuessler, Axel, *ABC Etymological Dictionary of Old Chinese*, Honolulu: University of Hawai’i Press 2007.

Schüssler Fiorenza, Francis, “Religion: A Contested Site in Theology and the Study of Religion”, in: *Harvard Theological Review* 93 (2000), 7–34.

Schwartz, Benjamin I., “The Age of Transcendence”, in: Schwartz, Benjamin I. (ed.), *Wisdom, Revelation, and Doubt: Daedalus*, spring 1975, 1–7.

Schweitzer, Albert, *Indian Thought and its Development*, New York, NY: Beacon Press 1960 (1936).

Seneviratne, H. L., *The Work of Kings: The New Buddhism in Sri Lanka*, Chicago: University of Chicago Press 1999.

Settis, Salvatore, “Les remplois”, in: Furet, François (ed.), *Patrimoine, temps, espace*, Paris: Fayard 1996, 67–86.

Sharpe, Eric J., *Comparative Religion: A History*, 2nd edition, La Salle, IL: Open Court 1986.

Shaughnessy, Edward L., “Western Cultural Innovations in China, 1200 B. C.”, in: *Sino-Platonic Papers* 11 (1989), 1–8.

Sherratt, Andrew G., “The Secondary Exploitation of Animals in the Old World”, in: *World Archaeology* 15.1 (1983), 90–104.

Shih, Heng-ching, *The Syncretism of Ch'an and Pure Land Buddhism*, New York, NY: P. Lang 1992.
Shils, Edward, *Tradition*, Chicago: University of Chicago Press 1981.
Shimazono, Susumu, *From Salvation to Spirituality: Popular Religious Movements in Japan*, Honolulu: Trans Pacific Press 2004.
——, *Gendai kyûsai shûkyôron*, Tokyo: Seiyûsha 1992.
——, *Seishisekai no yukue: gendaisekai to shin reisei undo*, Tokyo: Tôkyôdô Shuppan 1996.
——, *Supirichuariti no kôryû: shin reiseibunka to sono shûhen*, Tokyo: Iwanami Shoten 2007.
Shupe, Anson/Hadden, Jeffrey K. (eds.), *The Politics of Religion and Social Change*, New York, NY: Paragon House 1988.
Simonsen, Jørgen Bæk, "Mecca and Medina. Arab city-states or Arab caravan-cities", in: Hansen, Mogens Herman (ed.), *A Comparative Study of Thirty City-State Cultures: An Investigation*, Copenhagen: Kgl. Danske Videnskabernes Selskab 2000, 241–250.
——, "Muhammad's letters", in: Folsach, Kjeld von, et al. (eds.), *From Handaxe to Khan: Essays Presented to Peder Mortensen on the Occasion of his 70th Birthday*, Aarhus: Aarhus Univesity Press 2004, 215–223.
——, *Studies in the Genesis and Early Development of the Caliphal Taxation System*, Copenhagen: Akademisk Forlag 1988.
Skilling, Peter, *Mahāsūtras: Great Discourses of the Buddha*, vol. II, parts 1 & 2, Oxford: Pali Text Society 1997.
——, "The Advent of Theravāda Buddhism to Mainland Southeast Asia", in: *Journal of the International Association of Buddhist Studies* 20 (1997), 87–112.
Smith, Brian K., "Eaters, Food, and Social Hierarchy in Ancient India: A Dietary Guide to a Revolution in Values", in: *Journal of the American Academy of Religion* 58 (1990), 177–205.
Smith, D. Howard, "Chinese Religion in the Shang Dynasty", in: *Numen* 8.2 (1961), 142–150.
Smith, Jonathan Z., *Map is not territory: studies in the history of religions*, Leiden: Brill 1978.
——, "'Religion' and 'Religious Studies': No Difference at All", in: *Soundings* 71 (1988), 231–244.
Smith, Wilfred Cantwell, *Faith and Belief*, Princeton, NJ: Princeton University Press 1979.
——, "Scripture as Form and Concept: Their Emergence for the Western World", in: Levering, Miriam (ed.), *Rethinking Scripture*, New York, NY: State University of New York Press 1989, 29–57.
——, *The Faith of Other Men*, New York, NY: Harper and Row 1963.
——, *The Meaning and End of Religion*, Minneapolis, MN: Fortress Press 1991.
——, *Towards a World Theology: Faith and the Comparative History of Religion*, London: Macmillan 1981.
——, "Traditions in contact and change: towards a history of religion in the singular", in: Slater, Peter J. B./Wiebe, Donald (eds.), *Traditions in Contact and Change: Selected Proceedings of the XIVth Congress of the International Association for the History of Religions*, Waterloo (Ontario): International Association for the History of Religions 1983, 1–23.
Snellgrove, David L., *Indo-Tibetan Buddhism*, London: Shambhala 1987.

——, "Note on the *Adhyāśayasaṃcodanasūtra*", in: *Bulletin of the School of Oriental and African Studies* 21 (1958), 620–623.

Snow, Justine T., "The Spider's Web. Goddesses of Light and Loom: Examining the Evidence for the Indo-European Origins of Two Ancient Chinese Deities", in: *Sino-Platonic Papers* 118 (2002), 1–75.

Sobisch, Jan-Ulrich, *Three Vow Theories in Tibetan Buddhism. A Comparative Study of Major Traditions from the Twelfth through Nineteenth Centuries.* Contributions to Tibetan Studies, 1, Wiesbaden: Dr. Ludwig Reichert Verlag 2002.

Sommerville, Charles John, *The Secularization of Early Modern England: From Religious Culture to Religious Faith*, New York, NY/Oxford: Oxford University Press 1992.

Song Si-yŏl, *Songjadaejŏn* (Collected writings of Song), Seoul: Minjok munhwa ch'ujinhoe 1993.

Soothill, William Edward, *The Three Religions of China*, Oxford: Oxford University Press 1923.

Sophronius, *Christmas Sermon* (Walter Kaegi, tr.), "Initial Byzantine Reactions to the Arab Conquest", in: *Church History* 38 (1969), 139–149.

Spence, Jonathan, *God's Chinese Son: the Taiping Heavenly Kingdom of Hong Xiuquan*, New York, NY: Norton 1997.

Stark, Rodney/Bainbridge, William S., *The Future of Religion: Secularization, Revival, and Cult Formation*, Berkeley, CA: University of California Press 1985.

Stark, Rodney/Finke, Roger, *Acts of Faith: Explaining the Human Side of Religion*, Berkeley, CA: University of California Press 2000.

Stark, Rodney/Iannaccone, Laurence, "A Supply-Side Reinterpretation of the 'Secularization' of Europe", in: *Journal for the Scientific Study of Religion* 33 (1994), 230–252.

Stäheli, Urs, "Die Nachträglichkeit der Semantik – Zum Verhältnis von Sozialstruktur und Semantik", in: *Soziale Systeme* 4.2 (1998), 315–340.

Steiner, George, *Von realer Gegenwart: Hat unser Sprechen Inhalt?*, München et al.: Hanser 1990.

Sterckx, Roel, *The Animal and the Daemon in Early China*, Albany: State University of New York Press 2002.

Stillman, Norman A., *The Jews of Arab Lands: a History and Source Book*, Philadelphia, PA: Jewish Publication Society of America 1979.

Stokke, Kristian, "State Formation and Political Change in LTTE-Controlled Areas in Sri Lanka", in: *Envisioning New Trajectories for Peace in Sri Lanka. International Seminar 7–9 April 2006, Zurich, Switzerland*, Zürich: Centre for Just Peace and Democracy 2006, 139–146.

Storch, Tanya, "The Past Explains the Present: State Control over Religious Communities in Medieval China", in: *The Medieval History Journal* 3 (2000), 311–335.

Stroumsa, Guy G., *A new science: The Discovery of Religion in the Age of Reason*, Cambridge, MA: Harvard University Press 2010.

——, *The End of Sacrifice: Religious Transformations of Late Antiquity*, Chicago: Chicago University Press 2009. [*La fin du sacrifice: les mutations religieuses de l'antiquité tardive*, Paris: Odile Jacob 2005].

Stroumsa, Sarah, *Maimonides in his World: Portrait of a Mediterranean Thinker*, Princeton, NJ: Princeton University Press 2009.

——, "On Jewish intellectual converts to Islam in the early middle ages", in: *Peamim* 42 (1990), 61–75.

——, "On Jewish intellectuals who converted in the early middle ages", in: Frank, Daniel (ed.), *The Jews of Medieval Islam: Community, Society and Identity: Proceedings of an International Conference held by the Institute of Jewish Studies*, London: University College 1992, Leiden: Brill 1995, 179–197.

——, "The Muslim Context of Medieval Jewish Philosophy", in: Nadler, Steven M./ Rudavsky, Tamar (eds.), *The Cambridge History of Jewish Philosophy: From Antiquity throught the Seventeenth Century*, Cambridge, MA: Cambridge University Press 2009, 39–59.

Sugimoto, Masayoshi/Swain, David L., *Science and Culture in Traditional Japan*, Rutland, VT/Tokyo: Charles E. Tuttle 1989.

Sullivan, Winnifred Fallers, *The Impossibility of Religious Freedom*, Princeton, NJ: Princeton University Press 2005.

Suzuki, Norihisa, *Meiji shûkyô shichô no kenkyû*, Tokyo: Daigaku shuppansha 1979.

Swearer, Donald K., "Buddhism: Buddhism in Southeast Asia", in: Jones, Lindsey (ed.), *Encyclopedia of Religion*, vol. 2, 2nd ed., Detroit: Macmillan Reference USA 2005, 1136–1138.

Swidler, Ann, *Talk of Love: How Culture Matters*, Chicago: University of Chicago Press 2001.

Ṭabarī, Muhammad bin Jarir al-, *The History of al-Ṭabarī*, XIV (G. Rex-Smith, tr.), New York, NY: State University of New York Press 1994.

——, *Ta'rīkh al-rusul wa-l-mulūk*, Michael Jan de Goeje et al. (eds.), 15 vols., I, Leiden: Brill 1879–1901.

Tamari, Ben, *Conservation and Symmetry Laws and Stabilization Programs in Economics*, Jerusalem: ecometry 1997.

Tambiah, Stanley J., *The Buddhist Saints of the Forest and the Cult of Amulets*, Cambridge, MA: Cambridge University Press 1984.

——, *World Conqueror and World Renouncer: A Study of Buddhism and Polity in Thailand against a Historical Backdrop*, Cambridge, MA: Cambridge University Press 1976.

Tarocco, Francesca, *The Cultural Practices of Modern Chinese Buddhism: Attuning the Dharma*, London: Routledge 2007.

——, "The Making of Religion in Modern China", in: Green, Nile/Chatterjie, Mary Searle (eds.), *Religion, Language and Power*, New York, NY: Routledge 2008, 42–56.

Taylor, Jim L. *Forest monks and the nation-state: an anthropological and historical study in northeast Thailand*, Singapore: Institute of Southeast Asian Studies 1993.

Taylor, Philip, *Goddess on the Rise: Pilgrimage and Popular Religion in Vietnam*, Honolulu: University of Hawai'i Press 2004.

Ter Haar, Gerrie, "Ritual as Communication: A Study of African Christian Communities in the Bijlmer District of Amsterdam", in: Platvoet, Jan/Toorn, Karel van der, *Pluralism and Identity: Studies in Ritual Behaviour*, Leiden: E.J. Brill 1995, 115–142.

Thapar, Romila, *A History of India*, vol. 1, Baltimore, MD: Penguin Books 1966.

The Oxford English Dictionary, vol. 7, Oxford: Oxford University Press 1961.

Thompson, Edward, *The Other Side of the Medal*, Westport: Greenwood Press 1926.

Tiyavanich, Kamala, *Forest Recollections: Wandering Monks in Twentieth-century Thailand*, Honolulu: University of Hawai'i Press 1997.

——, *The Buddha in the Jungle*, Honolulu: University of Hawai'i Press 2003.

Tokuno, Kyoko, "The Evaluation of Indigenous Scriptures in Chinese Buddhist Bibliographical Catalogues", in: Buswell, Robert (ed.), *Chinese Buddhist Apocrypha*, Honolulu: University of Hawai'i Press 1990, 31–74.

Tolan, John, *Saracens: Islam in the Medieval European Imagination*, New York, NY: Columbia University Press 2002.

——, *Sons of Ishmael: Muslims through European Eyes in the Middle Ages*, Gainesville: University Press of Florida 2008.

Toorn, Karel van der, *Scribal Culture and the Making of the Hebrew Bible*, Cambridge, MA: Harvard University Press 2007.

Tov, Emanuel, "The Status of the Masoretic Text in Modern Text Editions of the Hebrew Bible: The Relevance of Canon", in: McDonald, Lee Martin/Sanders, James A. (eds.), *The Canon Debate*, Peabody, MA: Hendrickson Publishers 2002, 234–251.

Travis, John, "Trail of Mare's Milk Leads To First Tamed Horese", *Science* 322 (2008), 368.

Tsuchida, Ryutaro, "Die Genealogie des Buddha und seiner Vorfahren", in: Bechert, Heinz (ed.), *The Dating of the Historical Buddha 1*, Göttingen: Vandenhoek & Ruprecht 1991, 108–131.

Tsukamoto, Zenryū, *A History of Early Chinese Buddhism: From its Introduction to the Death of Hui-yüan*, 2 vol. continuously paginated, Tokyo: Kodansha 1985.

Turner, Victor, *Dramas, Fields and Metaphors*, Ithaca, NY: Cornell University Press 1974.

Turner, Victor/Turner, Edith, *Image and Pilgrimage in Christian Culture*, Oxford: Blackwell 1978.

Ulf, Christoph, "Rethinking Cultural Contacts", in: *Ancient West & East* 8 (2009), 81–132.

Ulrich, Eugene, "The Notion and Definition of Canon", in: McDonald, Lee Martin/Sanders, James A., *The Canon Debate: On the Origins and Formation of the Bible*, Peabody: Hendrickson Publishers 2002, 21–35.

Veer, Peter van der, "Global breathing: Religious utopias in India and China", in: *Anthropological Theory* 7 (2007), 315–328.

Veluppiḷḷai, Āḷvāpiḷḷai, "History of Tamil Buddhism in Śri Lankā", in: Murthy, R.S./Nagarajan, M.S. (eds.), *Buddhism in Tamil Nadu: Collected Papers*, Chennai: Institute of Asian Studies 1998, 46–47.

Vertovec, Steven/Rogers, Alisdair (eds.), *Muslim European Youth: Reproducing Ethnicity, Religion, Cutlure*, Aldershot, UK: Ashgate 1998.

Vetter, Tilmann, *The Ideas and Meditative Practices of Early Buddhism*, Leiden, New York, NY: Brill 1988.

Voegelin, Eric, *Order and History I, Israel and Revelation*, Baton Rouge, LA: University Press 1956.

Vrijhof, Pieter H./Waardenburg, Jean Jacques (eds.), *Official and Popular Religion: Analysis of a Theme for Religious Studies*, The Hague: de Gruyter 1979.

Vásquez, Manuel A., "Studying Religion in Motion: A Networks Approach", in: *Method and Theory in the Study of Religion* 20 (2008), 151–184.

Vásquez, Manuel A./Marquardt, Marie Friedmann, *Globalizing the Sacred: Religion across the Americas*, New Brunswick, NJ: Rutgers University Press 2003.

Waghorne, Joanne Punzo, *Diaspora of the Gods: Modern Hindu Temples in an Urban Middle-Class World*, New York, NY: Oxford University Press 2004.
Wagner, Andreas (ed.), *Primäre und sekundäre Religion als Kategorie der Religionsgeschichte des Alten Testaments*, Berlin, New York, NY: de Gruyter 2006.
Wagner, Falk, *Was ist Religion? Studien zu ihrem Begriff und Thema in Geschichte und Gegenwart*, Gütersloh: G. Mohn 1986.
Waley, Arthur, "The heavenly horses of Ferghana: a new view", in: *History Today* 5 (1955), 95–103.
Wang Chong, *Lunheng, Zhuzi jicheng* edition, vol. 7, Hongkong: Zhonghua 1978.
Warner, Stephen/Wittner, Judith G. (eds.), *Gatherings in Diaspora: Religious Communities and the New Immigration*, Philadelphia, PA: Temple University Press 1998.
Wataru, Masuda, *Japan and China: Mutual Representations in the Modern Era* (Joshua Fogel, tr.), Richmond/Surrey: Curzon 2000.
Watt, James C. (ed.), *China: Dawn of a Golden Age, 200–750 AD*, New York, NY: The Metropolitan Museum of Art; New Haven and London: Yale University Press 2004.
Waugh, Earle H./Abu-Laban, Baha/Qureshi, Regula B., *The Muslim Community in North America*, Edmonton: University of Alberta Press 1983.
Weber, Alfred, *Kultursoziologie*, Amsterdam: A.W. Sijthoff 1935.
Weber, Max, *Gesammelte Aufsätze zur Religionssoziologie*, vol. 1, MWG I/19, Tübingen: Mohr Siebeck 1920.
——, *The Sociology of Religion*, Talcott Parsons (intro.), Boston, MA: Beacon Press (1922) 1993.
Weinstein, Stanley, *Buddhism Under the T'ang*, Cambridge, MA: Cambridge University Press 1987.
Wei Yuan, *Wei Yuan ji*, Beijing: Zhonghua shuju 1976.
Welch, Holmes, *The Buddhist Revival in China*, Cambridge, MA: Harvard University Press 1968.
Wernle, Paul, *Renaissance und Reformation*, Tübingen: J.C.B. Mohr 1912.
West, Andrew C., *Catalogue of the Morrison Collection*, London: School of Oriental and African Studies 1998.
Wherry, Elwood Morris, *A Comprehensive Commentary on the Quran*, London: Trubner & Co. 1882.
Widmaier, Rita, "Nachwort zum Buch", Widmaier, Rita (ed.): *Leibniz korrespondiert mit China. Der Briefwechsel mit den Jesuitenmissionaren (1689–1714)*, Frankfurt a.M.: Klostermann 1990, 271–305.
Wiesehöfer, Josef, *The Arsacid Empire: Sources and Documentation*, Stuttgart: Franz Steiner 1998.
Wiesehöfer, Josef/Huyse, Philip (eds.), *Eran und Aneran. Studien zu ost-westlichen Kulturkontakten in sasanidischer Zeit*, Stuttgart: Franz Steiner 2006.
Wiesinger, Liselotte, "Die Anfänge der Jesuitenmission und die Anpassungsmethode des Matteo Ricci", in: *China und Europa*. Catalogue for the exhibition from 16.9. to 11.11.1973 in Schloß Charlottenburg, Berlin: Verwaltung der Staatlichen Schlösser und Gärten 1973, 12–17.
Wildung, Dietrich, *Imhotep und Amenhotep*, München: Deutscher Kunstverlag 1977, 25–27.
Wilkinson, Endymion, *Chinese History: A Manual*. Harvard-Yenching Institute Monograph Series 52, Cambridge, MA: Harvard University Asia Center 2000.
Wilkinson, Michael, *The Spirit Said Go: Pentecostal Immigrants in Canada*, New York, NY: Peter Lang 2006.

Williams, Raymond Brady, *Christian Pluralism in the United States: The Indian Experience*, New York, NY: Cambridge University Press 1996.
——, *Religions of Immigrants from India and Pakistan: New Threads in the American Tapestry*, New York, NY: Cambridge University Press 1988.
Wilson, Bryan, "The Return of the Sacred", in: *Journal for the Scientific Study of Religion* 18 (1979), 268–280.
Wolff, Christian, "De Rege philosophante et Philosopho regnante", in: Wolff, Christian, *Gesammelte Werke*, II. p. vol. 34.2, Hildesheim/New York/Zürich: Georg Olms Verlag 1983, 563–632.
——, "Oeconomica Methodo Scientifica Pertractata", in: Wolff, Christian, *Gesammelte Werke*, II. p. vol. 27, Hildesheim/New York, NY: Georg Olms Verlag 1972.
——, *Oratio de Sinarum philosophia practica. Rede über die praktische Philosophie der Chinesen*, Hamburg: Meiner 1985.
Wunenburger, Jean-Jacques, *La vie des images*, Strasbourg: Presses Universitaires de Grenoble 1995.
——, "Mytho-phorie. Formes et transformations du mythe", in: *Reliologiques* 10 (1994), 49–70.

Xu Jiyu, *Yinghan zhilue* 6.25a, in: Beijing: Zhongguo quanguo tushuguan wenxian suowei fuzhi chongxin, 2000, reprint of 1861 Japanese edition.
Xu Shen, *Shuowen jiezi* 10a, Hong Kong: Zhonghua 1977.

Yamazaki, Hiroshi 山崎宏, *Shina chūsei Bukkyō no tenkai* 支那中世佛教の展開, Tokyo: Shimizu Shoten, Shōwa 1942.
Yan Fu, *An Inquiry into the Nature and Causes of the Wealth of Nations* by Adam Smith (*Yuan Fu*, 1901–1902, reprint Shangwu Yinshuguan, Beijing 1981, 2 vols.).
Yang, Fenggang, *Chinese Christians in America: Conversion, Assimilation, and Adhesive Identities*, University Park, PA: University of Pennsylvania Press 1999.
Yi Yik, "Chŏnjubalŭisilmun", in: Ricci, Matteo, *Tienzhu shiyi* (Song Yŏng-bae, tr.), Seoul et al.: Seoul National University Press 2006, 435–448.
Yoshizawa, Satoru, et al. (eds.), *Tenba – Shiriku Rodo o kakeru yume no uma/Pegasus and the Heavenly Horses: Thundering Hoofs of the Silk Road*, Nara: Nara National Museum 2008.
Yu, Anthony C., *State and Religion in China: Historical and Textual Perspectives*, Chicago: Open Court 2005.

Zevit, Ziony, "The Second-Third Century Canonization of the Hebrew Bible and its Influence on Christian Canonizing", in: Kooij, Arie van der/Toorn, Karel van der (eds.) *Canonization and Decanonization*, Leiden: Brill 1998, 133–160.
Zhao, Xiaohuan, *Classical Chinese Supernatural Fiction: A Morphological History*, Lewiston: Edwin Mellen Press 2005.
Zhengzhang Shangfang 郑张尚芳, *Shanggu yinxi* 上古音系 (Old Chinese Phonology), Shanghai: Shanghai Jiaoyu Chubanshe 2003.
Zhou Jixu, "Old Chinese '*tees' and Proto-Indo-European '*deus': Similarity in Religious Ideas and a Common Source in Linguistics", in: *Sino-Platonic Papers* 167 (2005), 1–17.
Zhu Xi, *Chujadaejŏn* (Zhuzi daquan – Collected Works of Zhu Xi), Seoul: Kyŏngmunsa 1977.
Zumthor, Paul, *Introduction à la poesie orale*, Paris: Éd. du seuil 1983.

Zürcher, Erik: "Buddhism Across Boundaries: The Foreign Input", in: McRae, John/ Nattier, Jan (eds.), *Buddhism Across Boundaries - Chinese Buddhism and the Western Regions: Collection of Essays 1993*, Tapei: Foguang Cultural Enterprise 1999, 1-59.

—, "Han Buddhism and the Western Region", in: Idema, Wilt L./Zürcher, Erik (eds.), *Thought and law in Qin and Han China: Studies dedicated to Anthony Hulsewé on the Occasion of his Eightieth Birthday*, Leiden: Brill 1990, 158–182.

—, *The Buddhist Conquest of China*, Leiden: E. J. Brill 1972.

—, *The Buddhist Conquest of China: The Spread and Adaptation of Buddhism in Early Medieval China*, 3rd ed., Sinica Leidensia 11, Leiden: Brill 2007.

INDEX